VOLUME ONE

Has been presented to the

Learning Resource Centre

Douglas College

in the interest of a better understanding of Canadian political history

BY

The Hon. Donald Fleming

AND

McClelland and Stewart Limited

The Canadian Publishers

DECEMBER 1986

So Very Near

So Very Near

THE POLITICAL MEMOIRS OF THE HONOURABLE DONALD M. FLEMING

VOLUME ONE

THE RISING YEARS

McClelland and Stewart

McClelland and Stewart Limited
The Canadian Publishers
25 Hollinger Road
Toronto, Ontario
M4B 3G2

Canadian Cataloguing in Publication Data

Fleming, Donald M. (Donald Methuen), 1905-
 So very near : the political memoirs of the
Hon. Donald M. Fleming.

Includes indexes.
Contents: v. 1. The rising years — v. 2. The
summit years.
ISBN 0-7710-3155-6 (v. 1). 0-7710-3157-2 (v. 2)

1. Fleming, Donald M. (Donald Methuen), 1905-
2. Politicians – Canada – Biography.   3. Cabinet
ministers – Canada – Biography.   4. Canada –
Politics and government – 1935-1957.*   5. Canada –
Politics and government – 1957-1963.*   I. Title.

FC616.F58A3 1985   354.7104′092′4   C85-098005-4
F1034.3F58A3 1985

Printed and Bound in Canada by
John Deyell Company

Table of Contents

To Alice
the mainstay of my life.

Preface

"There is properly no History, only biography," wrote Ralph Waldo Emerson. "Every man is a volume if you know how to read him," wrote William Channing. Having had a part in the making of political and parliamentary history in Canada, I was at last persuaded that I was under a compelling duty to record it in autobiographical form. "The end of writing," quoth the great Dr. Samuel Johnson, "is to instruct." Perhaps I have rather sought to preserve before it becomes too late to do so.

In a notable speech in the House of Commons on October 20, 1949, John Diefenbaker drew attention to the failure of most Canadian political leaders of the past to leave a personal historical record. He said:

"All of us who read extensively on this subject must be impressed by the fact that our great leaders in parliament have not left personal records of the history of their time as it came within the ambit of their public life and experience. One can go into the library and read the records of the steps in the development of our nationhood, but except for Pope's 'Life of Macdonald' and Skelton's 'Life of Laurier,' which involve in part a reference to state papers, our national leaders other than Sir Robert Borden have failed to leave an intimate record of day-to-day experience as it has come to them during their period of office. I hope that the former Prime Minister of this country, Mr. Mackenzie King, will proceed with his memoirs and thereby give to posterity a record of one of the most challenging periods in our constitutional history. I hope, too, that Mr. Arthur Meighen, whose contribution to parliamentary government was, I believe, among the greatest in this country, will not only prepare a book containing his speeches, but will also give to posterity a record of the great developments that took place during his period of office, and particularly during the days of the first great war. These things animate peoples. The records of our great leaders become the history of this country. These are of the things of which the national spirit is built."

Since that time Mackenzie King, Mike Pearson and Diefenbaker himself have left memoirs or personal records which, though often-times slanted, have given the public and students of history an insight into the thoughts and experience of these leaders in the setting of their times. Unfortunately, Mr. St. Laurent did not do so, nor did C.D. Howe. I think most Canadians will regret that they did not leave us first-hand accounts of their years in public life.

Twenty years have passed since I withdrew from the Ottawa scene. The public memory is notoriously short. Whether sufficient interest remains in the period or its public figures to justify the labour of compiling these memoirs or the expense of publishing them is yet to be determined.

I confess I undertook the task with some reluctance. I was urged by many to do so at the time I departed from public life. It would have been much easier to do so then than now. Everything then was fresh and recent, and the interest of the public was at a high pitch. I rejected the idea at that time, both because I was busy endeavouring to re-establish myself in private life and legal practice, and also because I was loath to say anything which might hurt or reflect on men who were still serving in public life. Moreover, there was no use, I thought, writing memoirs that would be merely bland. So I deferred action. In April 1964, I made a speech to those good friends who had been my election workers in Eglinton. I referred to the subject of memoirs, and my words were reported in the press. Within ten days I received letters from nine Canadian publishers, all not merely offering, but asking to publish my memoirs. The nine included the then three Toronto daily newspapers who wished to publish them in serial form. I was flattered by this quite unexpected response. I thanked each of them, but said I had not yet commenced to write nor had I even decided to write memoirs. I still remained unconvinced. Entering the service of a bank and moving to the Bahamas in the course of that service seemed to make any remaining possibility of writing memoirs very remote indeed.

But some very close friends would not allow the idea to die. To their persistence I owe the ultimate decision to undertake the task. I single out in particular my dear friends Sydney Hermant of Toronto, the Honourable Richard A. Bell and Professor Jack Firestone, both of Ottawa. Year after year they impressed upon me the thought that I owed a duty to my country to put down in writing the history of a very important period in Canadian political and parliamentary history on which I had had unique opportunities for observation. There was also the consideration that such accounts of the period as had been written by others, both professionals and participants, had not always been balanced and fair or complete.

My service with the Bank of Nova Scotia ended on my 75th birthday, May 23, 1980. I was then free of the restrictions on utterance which bankers are expected to observe, and for the first time in my life I had the necessary time available. Enough of my former associates had departed from the public scene that I felt free to write without fear of hurting anyone.

I should add that throughout these years I have been besought by a steady parade of university professors and post-graduate students to supply information and comment on events and policies of the years I spent in public life. I have supplied not a little comment, but thus far have withheld all access to my papers. These I placed in the National Archives in 1963 at the insistent and kind invitation of Dr. Kaye Lamb, the National Archivist.

Two results have flowed from the postponement of this task, one good and one bad. The first is that I now enjoy the advantage of a longer perspective in appraising events and policies. These stand against an ever-enlarging background. The other result is that the publication of these memoirs unhappily coincides with a most severe recession which has had the inevitable effect of aggravating the normal problems of publication.

I finally commenced writing in January 1981, and completed the initial manuscript on October 14, 1982. I had always reckoned that it would require a year and a half of full-time effort. The estimate proved surprisingly accurate. The writing has at the same time proved to be for me an intensely interesting task. Indeed, it has enabled me in a very real sense to relive my life. Unfortunately, this being history and not fiction, it had to be recorded exactly as that life was, without benefit of amendment or reform in the tempting light of afterthought, hindsight, regret or genuine repentance. "Paint me, warts and all" was the command of Oliver Cromwell to his portrait painter. I have told it as it was.

The writing was all done in Nassau, in very casual attire and at a small desk in my library. Every word of the text, numbering about 600,000, was written in longhand. My chair often felt hard, but I was driven by the thought that I was writing history, Canadian history. I have endeavoured to approach my task with meticulous accuracy. I have sought to avoid mere self-justification. I did not write for that purpose.

The research was extensive. I did it all myself. I spent long weeks on it in Ottawa in 1981, dividing my time between my own papers in the National Archives and the Cabinet records in the Privy Council Office covering the period I was a Minister. I thank the officials of both these efficient government offices and in particular Dr. Margaret Matson of Archives, for the valued help they so generously gave me. I reviewed over 200 cartons of my own papers and more than 10,000 pages of Cabinet minutes and records. The minutes covered 826 meetings for which minutes were kept. This latter source alone yielded about 1,500 pages of notes. I also reviewed 120 volumes of Hansard, the official record of the debates of the House of Commons. My review covered 125,000 printed, double-column pages. I also made full use of the diaries I wrote on my travels and the bulky scrapbooks which I kept throughout the years in government. Most of all I have drawn on a responsive memory.

A friend who was an official of the Department of Finance throughout my years as its Minister and who now holds a position of international importance, in welcoming completion of my memoirs, wrote me on January 19, 1983, as follows:

"I often thought that you should write a book about your public years and I am, therefore, particularly glad that this is now done. Of all Cabinet Ministers I met during that fateful era (and before that, and since) you stand out in dedication, integrity and quiet wisdom. You were also patient and kind, and these human qualities, together with a willingness to hear the opinions of others, endeared you to your staff in Finance.

"If I mention all this it is only to underline that it is important, I think, that the general public be allowed to see the man and that the author has not been too modest in hiding behind the events he describes. How different the history of Canada would have been to this day had you not lost the leadership Convention."

I thank the Social Sciences and Humanities Research Council of Canada and the Ontario Arts Council for their grants toward the cost of producing these memoirs.

In the production of the typescript I have received invaluable assistance from Mrs. Hilda Barrett, Mrs. Patricia Fowler and Mrs. Cyprianna Fleischer, all of Nassau, and my daughter-in-law Barbara, of Toronto. I am deeply grateful to them.

I also warmly thank many friends for their encouragement and advice. I needed both. The advice of my old friend Douglas J. McLeod has been most helpful.

Finally, I express the hope that those who read these memoirs may find as much interest in reading them as I found in writing them.

Donald M. Fleming

Nassau, Bahamas
July 18, 1984

Prologue

It was one of those hot August days. The sun beat down mercilessly, and the air was heavy with humidity. The old street-car rumbled west along College Street and stopped at McCaul Street in front of the University of Toronto campus. Two passengers alighted and after looking about to identify their objective began walking north toward the campus. They needed to be certain of their bearings for they had never been there before. To be sure, they had visited Toronto before; indeed, every year in late August they came to attend the Canadian National Exhibition and to see the Maple Leaf team of the International Baseball League play in the old stadium at Hanlan's Point.

The campus was deserted, but that only served to make the buildings stand out. There stood University College before them, with its solid Romanesque architecture, its stone walls breathing strength and stability, almost permanence, and its imposing front door with its majestic carving. The sight created a sense of awe in the minds of the two persons as they approached it. It was their first view of any university, so why should they not be filled with awe in the presence of these symbols of higher learning, and was not this one of the most famous buildings in all of Canada? The excitement of this new experience grew as the two figures entered the portals of the august seat of learning.

There was a marked resemblance between the two. The one was a lady of forty-seven years of age, with a pretty face, brown eyes and a kindly mouth set over a strong jaw. Beside her walked a youth of a mere sixteen years of age, wearing his first suit of long trousers and a flat sailor straw hat, as was the fashion in those days. He presented a rather short, sturdy appearance. His eyes were blue, his hair dark, his jaw firm. The movements of both figures bespoke strength of purpose even in the novel and awesome surroundings. This was obviously a very important occasion for both of them.

In those days the university registrar had his offices in University College, just east of the front door. A pleasant-looking lady clerk standing behind a high counter greeted the two visitors. No doubt she had seen many a mother and son before come to register the son, and, sensing the strangeness of the scene for them, sought to put them at ease. The youth opened the conversation: "My name is Donald Fleming. This lady is my mother. I have attended the Galt Collegiate Institute and have just received the results of the Scholarship Matriculation exams. I should like to inquire about registration." He handed a slip of paper to the clerk – a very important slip, for it was the official certificate of passing some very important examinations with honours. The clerk read the paper, excused herself and went back into the private office of the registrar. A moment later a distinguished-looking man with white hair came out with the slip of paper in his hand. It was none other than Dr. James Brebner, the eminent Registrar of the University of Toronto. He nodded politely to the lady, then turned to the youth and with a smile uttered these never-to-be-forgotten words, "So very near, but just not quite." They were simple words, referring to the narrow margin by which the young man had missed winning one of the Edward Blake scholarships in competition with Fifth Form students over the entire province of Ontario. But the words were more than that. They were prophetic of the narrow margins by which he was in later years to be denied attainment of some cherished goals, among them the prime ministership of Canada.

That was in 1921. Little did I realize – for that eager young man was I – the future that lay in store. There have been disappointments, admittedly; but there have also been many privileges and compensations. What follows is the record of those great opportunities and of my years spent in the service of Canada.

CHAPTER ONE

Early Boyhood

Goose Hollow may not be the most famous place on earth, but whenever I think of my boyhood in Galt it springs to mind. No one has yet seen fit to build upon its steep sides, though houses now stand on the summit fronting on Rose Street. But the path I climbed so many times on my way to Victoria School, now long gone, still winds its way up the steep face of Goose Hollow. The hill was also a playground for active children. In the fashioning of young character it became a symbol of both duty and play.

Although more than sixty years have passed since I left Galt I have always thought of the city as home. My parents and my brother Bob lie buried there. I trace to it the origins of many of the elements which shaped the course of my life. I was fortunate to grow up there while it was still a small city typical of the industry and integrity of western Ontario. It has expanded since, and there have been many changes. It is no longer populated, as it was in my youth, chiefly by people of Scottish descent. In those days it was said that 75 per cent of the inhabitants were of Scottish descent, and the other 25 per cent wished they were. But in the last twenty-five years there has been a large influx of thrifty and industrious Portuguese. The ownership of many of the factories and businesses, owned in my boyhood by sturdy Galtonians, has passed into American hands. A few years ago the provincial government, in its zeal for uniting municipalities into larger units without regard for history and local sentiment, consolidated Galt with Preston and Hespeler to form the city of Cambridge. It remains Galt to me. That name is part of my heritage, and it will take more than a statute of the Legislature of Ontario or an order of the Department of Municipal Affairs to change that. Named after the famous Scottish colonizer John Galt in honour of his visit in 1827, it is part of Canadian history, which we forget at our peril.

However, Galt did not become home to the Fleming family until 1910. My maternal grandparents, John Wright, born in 1822, and Hannah Bradford, born in 1827, came from County Down in Northern Ireland. They were married on March 11, 1848, and emigrated to Canada soon after. The voyage took six weeks. as was usual in those days, and on the voyage they must have been very homesick and very seasick. I am told that my grandfather was given a choice of a grant of land in what is now Toronto or in Durham County, and he chose the latter, settling near the village of Garden Hill. How different life might have been for his children and grandchildren had he not made that choice! They faced all the rigours of early pioneer life. They raised a family of eleven children without benefit of social services or pensions, and they depended upon themselves and God. The Wrights were Presbyterian and Conservative. I have been told that on the first Sunday in the new land my grandfather, keeping the custom of his native land, drove to church at Garden Hill three miles away wearing a Prince Albert coat. He found he was the only man in the congregation so formally garbed.

John Wright prospered on his 250-acre farm and bought a second just to the north to provide more opportunity for his sons. In my time these farms were owned and worked respectively by my Uncle Bill and Uncle Bob. My mother, Maud Margaret, was born on the family homestead in 1874. Although the youngest of the family, she was never spoiled. Indeed, her upbringing was almost painfully strict. She learned to do without many of the things that children nowadays take for granted. I once heard my father, standing beside my maternal grandfather's grave outside Port Hope, say: "There lies the straightest man I ever met."

My father's background was quite different. His father, David Flamand, was French-Canadian. He was born in 1840 at St. Patrice in the County of Lotbinière in the eastern part of Quebec south of the St. Lawrence River. He was raised a Roman Catholic and spoke no English until the age of twenty. A carpenter by trade, he came up to Northumberland County in Ontario in search of employment in 1860 and anglicized his name to Fleming. He was a fiery Liberal, brown-eyed and ever ready for a political argument. He proudly told me that one of our ancestors had fought under Montcalm at the Battle of the Plains of Abraham.

My grandmother was born Elizabeth Plews in Northumberland County near Bewdley, where her father James Plews had taken a grant of land after emigrating from his native Yorkshire. His wife was a Laing, from Aberdeen. Descendants of both the

Plews and Laing families are still to be found in the vicinity of Baileyborough and Peterborough. My grandmother was a very calm, kindly, strong, fearless and intelligent woman. She had pale blue eyes, drew her hair back tight with a roll at the back. I remember her well; whenever she went out she wore a black bonnet tied under the chin, in the fashion of those days. With the benefit of the higher education of today she would have gone far. She wrote a history of Bewdley and the countryside which she had privately printed in Oshawa and which I prize highly. It gives an authentic picture of early pioneer life in eastern Ontario. In it she tells of going to sleep at nights as a little girl hearing the wolves howl.

My grandparents married in 1862 and settled in Harwood, on the shores of Rice Lake, where they raised a family of twelve, seven boys and five girls. It was at Harwood that my father Louis Charles was born, the sixth child, in 1871. The family were Methodists and were all intensely devoted to each other. None of them ever became rich, but all were upright honourable citizens respected in their communities.

In his youth my father was "farmed out" to a neighbour of my mother. His declared ambition was to be "a school-teacher and a fiddler." By dint of hard work and strict thrift he put himself through Port Hope Collegiate and the old School of Pedagogy in Toronto, where one of his classmates was one Arthur Meighen. He went back and taught in the country school north of Garden Hill, which had been attended by the Wright family and taught earlier by one of them, my Aunt Jane.

My father was earning an annual salary of $250 when he and my mother married in 1895. They settled in Millbrook where my brother Robert (called both Robbie and Bob) was born in 1899, and moved thence to Goderich where my brother Gordon was born in 1903. The family then moved to Exeter, where my father was the principal of the Continuation School, a combination of primary and junior high school. The school is gone, having given way to a modern edifice, but the house in which I was born, half a block away, remains. It was a trim little red brick house with a garden. I was born on May 23, 1905, and weighed in at 12 lbs. 9 ozs., enormous by today's standards. Although she already had two sons my mother had hoped for a third son, rather than a daughter. I was never to have a sister. Mother gave her sons strong Scottish first names. My second name, Methuen, was inspired by Lord Methuen, a general who led the British forces into the Orange Free State in the South African War. He was no relative – Mother just liked the name.

I have no remembrance of life in Exeter. When I was two we moved to Clinton, another town in Huron County, where for two and a half years my father took leave of the teaching profession to serve as Secretary to the local YMCA. We occupied half of a white brick double house on Vinegar Hill with what seemed to me at the time an enormous side-yard until I visited it in 1960 and found it to be relatively small.

When I was four we moved to Galt. My father had decided to go back to teaching and was appointed junior mathematics master at the Galt Collegiate Institute. He preceded us to our new home. We followed, travelling by railway from Clinton to Kitchener, where my father met us. The rest of the journey was made by electric railway – my first ride in this new, clean, swift mode of conveyance.

The move to Galt was very exciting. We stayed a few days at the old Iroquois Hotel in which a caged parrot, able and always willing to say, "Polly wants a cracker," fascinated us young boys. My father then rented a house on Rose Street, within convenient walking distance of the Collegiate and Victoria Public School, which we boys attended. Our first telephone was installed there. When I first used it to telephone a friend, I was so overcome by the sheer novelty of this strange device that I could not say a word to him. We also had the luxury of indoor plumbing. It had been installed some years after the house was built, and to use it it was necessary to walk through the bedroom which we boys shared. We brats maintained a vigilant watch on the passing traffic.

A year later we moved downtown to Colborne Street into a brand new red brick house on a corner. My father rented it for two years. It has since disappeared in favour of a widened traffic artery. We were within two blocks of the Grand River, which regularly overflowed its banks when the ice went out every spring. One year the flood was accompanied by heavy rain and our cellar filled with water to the ceiling. The furnace was quickly drowned, and my mother's preserves in jars went floating into the furnace-room.

I spent three years at Victoria School, and several incidents still stand out in my memory. The first day in kindergarten I mistook the recess for dismissal of the class, and went home. I was quickly hustled back. The schoolyard was rough and stony. One day at recess two years later I aimlessly threw a stone over the fence and out of the yard and was petrified when I heard the sound of shattering glass. The irate proprietor of the house standing just outside the fence quickly descended on the principal, who made a tour of the classes with him inviting the culprit to identify himself. I do not know for certain whether the stone which I threw broke the window. However, the circumstantial evidence was very strong. I therefore identified myself at once and said I would pay for the pane. That was rather big talk for a penniless seven-year-old. However, Mother came to the rescue with 40 cents, and I was spared punishment.

In the same year, in a reading lesson the teacher threatened to strap any pupil who did not keep his head down over his book. She suddenly summoned me to the front of the class for a strapping. This offended my sense of justice for I had been keeping my eyes on my book. I walked to the front of the class, brushed right past her, walked out of the room and went home. I returned the next day. Before I was permitted to take my place, however, she insisted that I make an apology to her in front of the class. I found it very difficult to bring myself to that. I stood there silent for a long time before finally mumbling a reluctant and scarcely audible apology. I never received any other punishment in that school, but I always resented that injustice.

In 1913 we moved across town to Ramore Street, where we were to spend the next nine years, and I left Victoria School. The rent for the new house was $20 per month, and one of my errands on the first day of the month was to take the money to the landlord. The house had a cellar kitchen, which was a convenient place for the older boys to stage Wild West dramas for the edification of the younger children on the street. My role was to coerce the audience to remain until the end of the entertainment, employing strong-arm methods if necessary – and they often were.

At the rear stood a large hen house, neatly divided into four pens. Here my father kept approximately forty laying hens. I assisted him daily in feeding and watering the fowl, cleaning the roost-boards, and collecting and tabulating the eggs. We kept incubators where we incubated and sold hundreds of baby chicks every spring.

There were many errands to be run and chores to be done. I regularly assisted my father in jobs about the place, such as building fences, digging, hoeing and tending the garden, shovelling the snow. He was accustomed to say gratefully of me: "That boy is worth a whole carload of boys."

Money was scarce. My father's starting salary at the collegiate was $1,500 per annum, reaching the handsome sum of $1,700 under the inflationary pressures of the First World War. Every cent was needed and was accounted for. My mother was a very competent manager. She could make a dollar go further than anyone I have ever known. We children never lacked any necessity, but there was not a cent for luxuries. The trousers of my father and brothers after suitable wear were reduced and handed down to me. I was given an Ingersoll watch, which cost one dollar and kept excellent time. Mother put me on an allowance of 5¢ a week when I was about eight. It was increased by 5¢ a week annually until it reached the sum of 35¢ before I left home to attend university. This allowance, which came out of Mother's housekeeping funds, was supplemented at times by running errands for the corner grocery. I owned a small wagon which was useful for this purpose, and I was paid 5¢ for each delivery, working after school in the afternoons. My brother Gordon had a paper route, and I helped him with it. The *Galt Reporter* was and is still the only newspaper published in Galt. We had approximately one hundred papers to deliver each day, and the route extended over several miles. Profit was about 60¢ per week. The tips at Christmas were handsome, averaging between 5 and 10 cents per customer. The experience was tiresome and an interference with fun and sports, but it was beneficial. We learned the value of money and that it had to be earned.

After the move to Ramore Street I attended the nearby and very old Dickson School. A year later I was fortunate to be transferred to the newly constructed St. Andrew's School. Along the way I skipped two grades, graduating into the collegiate (Grade 9) in 1917 at twelve years of age. Homework was regularly assigned and never neglected. My brother Bob had completed the nine years of public school grades in six, graduating just before his eleventh birthday. That set a mark for the other members of the family to live up to.

The distractions of radio and television were unknown in our youthful lives. On the other hand, we had the moving picture shows – silent, of course. The Saturday afternoon matinee at Scott's Opera House at 5 cents admission was good value and was regularly patronized. The movies were invariably of the Wild West variety, with the good cowboys always overcoming the bad Indians in the end. In imitation we youngsters took upon ourselves such famous names as "Buffalo Bill" and "Bronco Bill." One of the Hollywood masterpieces of those days was "The Last Fight at Grizzly Gulch." The drummer in the orchestra used to have some kind of hard sofa which he pounded with a drumstick to simulate rifle fire.

We attended Knox Presbyterian Church. It was one of the largest churches in western Ontario with a seating capacity of more than one thousand. The galleries were spacious, and our pew for years was the front row of the north gallery just above the pulpit. This necessitated a high degree of decorum. Mother's eye was ever on us, and she could convey her meaning with a look of strong disapproval and an eloquent shaking of her head. Anything else was bound to be observed by my father, who sang in the choir and sat facing us. The minister, the Reverend R.E. Knowles, a man of towering eloquence, was a very close friend of my parents. In later life he turned to journalism and wrote a daily column for the *Toronto Daily Star*. My father taught the adult Bible class, and I well recall the ceremony of his induction as an elder. That was a proud day for the family. The Sunday School was large and well organized. Our attendance was regular throughout the twelve months of the year.

The Galt YMCA when I was very young completed a fine new building downtown with excellent facilities. Here I learned calisthenics, gymnastics, basketball and swimming. I excelled at wrestling, basketball, swimming and running. I was not a good jumper. My legs and arms were rather shorter than average, and did not propel me as well in jumping as in sprinting.

Galt is bisected by the Grand River, which had been dammed and was crossed by a series of bridges. When the ice broke up and the flood followed at the end of winter the river became a raging torrent, damaging the bridges and making them impassable for several days. As we lived west of the river and the Galt Collegiate stood to the east, attendance at school for those few days each year in March was usually impossible. Above the dam the river widened, permitting swimming and canoeing in the summer and skating in the winter until the snow became too deep. Crossing the river on the ice was sometimes dangerous. A friend of mine once barely escaped drowning when the ice broke beneath him.

In the summer the river became quite shallow and the current diminished, exposing many pretty views along its banks. Several miles north of Galt on the river stood the village of Doon. Its most famous citizen was the painter Homer Watson, whose canvasses are still highly valued by collectors. He used to station himself on the river banks near the bridges to paint scenes in oils. My brother Gordon and I were fascinated to look over his shoulder at the scenes which were taking shape under his brush. We were careful to be silent and to do nothing to disturb the painter's intense concentration.

"He must have been a very pugnacious little boy," commented Marjorie to her husband, my friend Jim Macdonnell, MP, after hearing some of my early speeches in the House of Commons. "I guess I was," was my unhesitating response. My father used to say that when he first saw me soon after birth my fist was clenched and that this gesture was prophetic. At school I was frequently involved in fights; I was ready with or without provocation to take on anybody anywhere near my size or age, and I was never bested. But I never was a bully. Indeed, I had a strong dislike for bullies and enjoyed taking them on. But I must confess I revelled in rough games with plenty of physical contact. And I was always ready for a bit of mischief.

Hallowe'en gave greater scope for mischief in those days than now. Until they passed into history, outhouses were regularly overturned by the bigger boys. In 1912 I woke up the morning after Hallowe'en to observe our neighbour's favourite rocking-chair perched on top of his barn. When I was ten I discovered I was sufficiently strong to pull a picket off the picket fence around the property at the nearest corner. Having made that thrilling discovery I was not content until I had pulled off all the pickets. Unfortunately this heroic operation was observed by one of the elderly spinsters who lived there, and she lost no time in reporting to my mother. Hallowe'en came to an end with my restoring the wretched pickets to the fence and concluding that it wasn't such a cheerful occasion after all.

All of us in the Fleming family had a keen sense of humour. We had fun, particularly around the dining-room table, and employed the gift of mimicry to create laughter and enjoyment. It was said of us boys that we were "born mimics." My parents were both good at it, too. In spite of the strict discipline my parents believed necessary to bring up three high-spirited boys, ours was a happy family. Christmas in particular was a joyous season in our family. There were no coloured lights in those days; our house was decorated with bright, though cheap, paper bells. Even with their limited means, our parents always managed to find presents for all of us children, and these presents would always include a book. Our parents were constantly making sacrifices for our sake.

CHAPTER TWO

Home Life

My parents were godly people; that is to say, they lived as in the sight of God, believing in His promises and obedient to His commandments. Their aim was to bring up their children in the nurture and admonition of the Lord. Life was always a struggle; my father never made more than $3,500 in any year in his life. They invested their lives and efforts in seeking the best for their children. My debt to them is immeasurable. I do not believe there ever existed a closer or stronger bond between any mother and son than the one that bound my mother and me to each other. She was as strong as a rock, physically, mentally and morally. I admired and loved her. Her house was ever spotless. Her cooking knew no equal. She zealously guarded her family's health.

My father was a small man, just over 5' 6" in height and weighing 127 pounds. He was light on his feet and quick in his movements. From his mother he inherited pale blue eyes and a very open countenance, from his father a quick temper, a balding pate, a high forehead and a leaning toward the Liberal party. In the course of time this predilection happily gave way in the face of solid presentation of the merits of the Conservative party by Mother and me and also, and perhaps even more influentially, a strong distaste for Mackenzie King. My father's health was always uncertain and a cause of feelings of insecurity in the family. He was plagued by what we would identify today as migraine headaches of overpowering intensity; then they were known merely as "headaches." He was highly sensitive. Mother mastered or hid her feelings; his were always close to the surface. I have often seen him shed tears, Mother hardly ever. With more toughness in his nature he would have achieved greater material success in life. He was highly intelligent, an excellent teacher, and an accomplished speaker, always at home on a platform, whether engaged in singing or delivering a speech. Of these I most admired his ability to make a speech. Had he had the educational opportunities that he provided for me he would have gone far in life. Even as a young boy I had an intense admiration for eloquence and the art of oratory, hoping that some day I might attain this talent. My affection for my father survived the stern discipline of my growing years, and deepened and mellowed as the years passed. I would have done anything within my power to show my love and gratitude to him. "Daddy" of earlier years became "Wee Da" to his grown sons.

My father enjoyed high respect in the community, and we children were well aware of it. We were also kept aware that such respect was won and kept only by strict honesty and honourable conduct. He was a gentleman in his manners and conduct. I never heard him take the name of God in vain. There was no alcohol in any form in our home. In middle life my father smoked a pipe and cigars, but cigarettes were taboo. I early resolved never to drink or smoke. I have never had cause to regret that decision.

Life was always a financial struggle, but to my parents the formation of character in their sons took first place in their goals over the hope of affluence or ease or even security. Robbie was high-spirited and gifted. He was athletic, musical, handsome, popular, possessed of a brilliant mind and nimble wit. Gordon was different from both Robbie and me. He was gentle, diffident, handsome, musical and artistic. He was neither a leader nor a businessman.

Music played a dominant role in the activities of the family. My father had a strong, true bass voice, and he loved to sing. Both during and after the years he sang in the church choir he was the bass in the Manchester Male Quartette of Galt and later the Galt Maple Leaf Quartette. Both were eminent musical organizations and toured the smaller towns of Ontario providing concerts. My father was known as "the little man with the big voice," a title of which he was rather proud. I inherited my voice and platform presence from him.

Mother played no musical instrument and her singing was confined to the hymns at church, but she loved music and did everything in her power to develop the musical talents of her three sons. Bob and Gordon both developed into accomplished pianists, and Gordon became a professional pianist and later an organist. My father used to say that when we came in at noon from school Gordon made straightway for the piano and I for the *Globe* (now the *Globe and Mail*). It was never necessary to tell

26

Gordon to practise. I had two years of lessons on the violin, but when the teacher from the Hamilton Conservatory of Music ceased coming to Galt I put away my violin and never again exhumed it. I loved music, but amid my other activities I was just not sufficiently interested to continue. I did, however, reach the dizzy heights of playing "Humoresque" at the annual Sunday School Christmas entertainment accompanied by Robbie at the piano. I played leading roles in some Sunday School plays and musicals, but I came to look down on singing as an effeminate pastime, suitable for girls, but quite unfit for young boys. I even stopped singing in church and did not resume it until attending university. Such musical talents as I possessed were not developed until a later stage in life.

My Aunt Sarah, an older sister of my mother, made her home with us for many years. A spinster, she had a sweet disposition, and we boys loved her very much. She paid the fees to give me dancing lessons in a mixed class. I soon concluded that this pastime also was too effeminate for me, and I ungratefully quit. I was determined not to be a sissy.

One morning Aunt Sarah delivered a timely lecture to me. I had been taking too much time reaching the breakfast table in the mornings. Auntie said, "If the prize was given for the slowest you would win it, but the prize is never given for the slowest. It is given for the fastest." This was a sound admonition. I confess that to this day I do not like to be hurried in the mornings before breakfast. I reserve bursts of speed for later periods of the day.

Discipline at home was strict; indeed, compared with the looser standards prevailing in 1984 it was very strict. Disobedience and disrespect were not tolerated. Children knew their "place"; they must treat adults with due respect. Parents always knew where their children were. Children were held to strict accountability for their time, their actions and the use made of their opportunities. The biblical precept, "Spare the rod and spoil the child," was applied as a religious duty, with excellent results. But truth to tell, I never reacted well to punishment. Mother used to say, "There was no use punishing Donald. It never did any good. I could always accomplish more by talking to him. You could always talk to Donald and reason with him." As time passed I became a severely self-disciplined man. Indeed, a friend of wide experience told me when in my seventies that I was the most disciplined man he had ever met. I never learned, however, even in the army, to take kindly to the external application of discipline by others. If I were convinced of the rightness or necessity of doing or refraining from doing something I did not need anybody to order me to do it. I sought advice and welcomed instruction; I cordially disliked receiving commands.

Most of our evenings were spent at homework and reading. Good books were always at hand. Saturdays were devoted to play, but not after supper time. That evening was set aside for baths, washing hair, polishing shoes and preparing our lessons and memorizing our verses for Sunday School the next morning. The Lord's Day was not for work or play, but for more serious pursuits. I spent Sunday afternoon and evening reading. I was never happier than with a book and a dish of apples. It did not deter me one whit when I became known at school as a "bookworm." I was happy in the thought that I was cramming my mind with information that would be valuable to me in years to come, when it would be a tremendous asset to know good literature and possess a full command of the English language. Besides, I was balancing off the hours of reading with vigorous sport and organized games and calisthenics at the YMCA, as well as such pastimes as baseball (scrub), wrestling and other games on the street and lawns in our neighbourhood.

One indignity I bore with open resentment. Mother had bought Gordon and me white sailor suits which we were made to wear to Sunday School and on other special occasions. Gordon wore his without protest, but I loathed mine, and said so. I thought it made me look like a sissy, and anything that did that to me was intolerable. I had to pass the home of the Barber family on the way to Sunday School, and I could always depend upon it that all the boys and girls of that household would turn out to make fun of me and shout "Sailor! Sailor!" as I passed their abode. One Sunday morning after being subjected to their catcalls I turned back home and informed Mother that I refused to wear that wretched outfit to Sunday School any longer. Mother thought otherwise, however, and quickly directed my course back to Sunday School. I went back with a heavy heart and a crushing sense of self-pity.

We developed strong loyalties. One principal loyalty was to Galt. It was large enough (14,000 souls) that we had a representative team in such sports as hockey, baseball, rugby in competition with other towns and small cities like Guelph, Kitchener, and Preston. We regularly turned out to cheer for the home team. Youngsters growing up in large cities do not have the advantage of such intimate local loyalties. Our athletes were heroes to us, and they were not remote from us.

Loyalty to Canada, to the King, to the church (the Presbyterian Church, of course) was inculcated and took strong root.

The Scottish predilection for jokes and stories about the Scots, and particularly about their parsimony, held sway. Most of the jokes I learned in my boyhood had to be at the expense of the Scots to be recognized as worth a laugh.

At an early stage of life I became aware, mostly from children, of the fact that people were divided into Catholics and Protestants, and that we were Protestants. I am glad to say that I learned little of this from my parents. One day a group of us six-year-olds proceeded to razz some young neighbours with cat-calls of "Catholic! Catholic!" The particular object of this abuse informed us, however, that his family were English Catholics, not Roman Catholics. This to me was a mysterious differentiation, but it seemed to make everything right, and so we brats stopped our abusive agitation.

One day at school when I was all of seven years of age I was asked to join a group of boys who were to accompany our leading fist-fighter, Ivan Rayner, who was going to seek a fight on the way home from school with the champion fighter of the Roman Catholic Separate School in the vicinity. This seemed to be a good means of settling the feud between Catholics and Protestants, so I joined the group. We met the Separate School champion, who must have been alerted, for he was accompanied by several supporters. I took one look at these boys, saw nothing about any of them to dislike, wondered why we should not be friends, and recoiled from the idea of the fight. Fortunately, a man came by, prevented the scrap, and sent us all on our way with some very sound advice on the subject of being friends.

That little incident long ago taught me lessons I have never forgotten. My life was to bring me into close association with a host of Catholics, into warm friendship with many of them, including cardinals, bishops and priests, and into the presence of two popes in private audiences and a third at a reception. I think that, while recognizing differences which exist and the reasons behind them, I have learned to look upon Roman Catholics with Christian love and growing understanding.

As well as unswerving loyalty to the church, the overriding claims of duty and the sacred imperative of courage in its performance were lessons driven home sternly and constantly in my boyhood. They were inculcated even before the Great War gave them painful urgency. One of the favourite hymns we sang in Sunday School, and which to my regret appears to have gone out of use since, was,

Dare to be a Daniel;
Dare to stand alone;

Dare to have a purpose firm;
Dare to make it known.
With conviction we sang from another hymn:
Where duty calls or danger,
Be never wanting there.
These were lessons I never forgot. They helped to mould my
character. Years later in many an issue in public life I sought to
emulate Daniel.

CHAPTER THREE

The Great War and High School

I was only nine years old when the First World War burst upon us, but the event made an indelible impression on my mind. We youngsters of the neighbourhood gathered in front of our house gravely to discuss the outbreak of hostilities. We concluded, of course, that we would win and the war would be glorious. It was only a question of how soon and who would be our victorious allies.

One morning several days later I stood beside Scott's Opera House where about twenty-five soldiers in uniform had fallen in. They were Galt's first contribution to the Canadian Expeditionary Force and were en route to London, the seat of Military District No. 1, to join the Second Battalion. I was aglow with pride until I heard a quavering female voice behind me say, "I wonder how many of them will ever come back." In a state of shock I turned around to see an elderly lady standing there with tears flowing down her cheeks. For me she had in one short poignant sentence destroyed all the glory of war. Misery, grief and pride were to be our mingled portion.

After their training at Valcartier Camp those men were in the front lines in France by April, and there withstood the onslaught of German military might and the first poison gas attack at St. Julien in that fateful phase of the Second Battle of Ypres. The Canadians suffered heavy casualties, but our men held the line. Our pride knew no bounds. Canadians had attained a new dimension, but the cost in lives was grievous.

From that point on men from Galt and the vicinity were called to fill the ranks of the 34th, 71st, 122nd battalions and other units. All of them included friends of ours. I can still see the 122nd, made up almost entirely of local men, on a Sunday afternoon in 1916 march with fixed bayonets out of the Armouries down Main Street, and up Water Street to the CPR station on their way overseas. We cheered them to the echo. We were proud of them, every man, but we were gripped with sadness. Emotions were running deep.

We children in public school marched into classes singing patriotic songs, such as "Keep the Home Fires Burning," "Tipperary," "Three Cheers for the Red, White and Blue." I joined my classmates in giving up recess, learning to knit, and producing knitted face-cloths which were sometimes mistaken by the recipients overseas for scarves. We enlarged our garden and raised more vegetables. The war effort was paramount. One of my teachers, the gallant Captain Frank Welland, went overseas and was killed at the bloody Battle of Paschendale in 1917. His death was a heartbreak to his pupils.

The war also came to our own family. My brother Bob left school in 1914 when he was fifteen and joined the Union Bank. In 1916 he enlisted in the Canadian Army Service Corps, adding a year to his age to meet the required minimum age of eighteen for recruits. There was no holding him back. Three of his friends joined up with him. I well recall what good spirits they were in the night Mother invited them all to dinner. But it was a different mood when the time came a few days later for them to entrain for overseas. It was February 1917 and the war was not going well for us. I shall never forget the final evening as the clock relentlessly ticked away the last minutes before Robbie's appointed departure at 9 p.m. Mother served her best dinner, then we moved into the living-room. The conversation lagged. Finally Robbie rose, and embraced first me, then Gordon, then Mother, then Da. My father followed him to the front door and stood there as Robbie walked up Ramore Street through the falling snowflakes and disappeared into the night. It was not necessary for any of us to say a word. We all knew the thought that was on the minds of all: would we ever see him again?

Robbie wrote some letters of fascinating interest from France and Belgium, where he was engaged in driving transport vehicles up to the front lines and removing the wounded. Mother retained all his letters. She and I wrote letters to him every Sunday afternoon. I fear mine followed a rather stereotyped form, but at least we sought to support his morale with news and love from home.

The end of the war came on a Monday morning, November 11. The air was filled with rumours of a German surrender. On the previous Thursday afternoon a premature report of an armistice circulated, and I remember Dr. Harry Mackendrick, our family physician, standing on his upper balcony firing rifle shots into the air. I hope he was using blank cartridges. By Sunday everyone was keyed up to receive the news momentarily, and the churches were crowded. Monday morning we were roused early by the ringing of church bells and the blast of factory whistles. The war was over! It was incredible. A victory parade was hastily organized. As many of the cadets from the Galt Collegiate as could be organized were mustered, and I marched with the Bugle Band at the head of that parade. For three days people went wild. The sense of relief was overwhelming, but ours was tempered by the news that Bob Weir, a neighbour, had been killed in action at Mons only several hours before the armistice took effect.

Nineteen-nineteen was a year of excitement when "the boys" came home from France. Mother and I, lacking any word of Robbie's troopship, were spending a day in Toronto at the beginning of September. There on the street by the strangest of chances we met a soldier friend just arrived that day, who told us he thought Robbie would reach Galt that very afternoon. On our arrival at the Galt station that evening Robbie was there to meet us. It was a joyous reunion. He had come on the afternoon train, walked home unannounced and had overtaken my father on the street also walking home. It was one of the happiest surprises of Da's life.

So the war ended, but the consequences and the memories had left an imperishable mark on all of us. Canada had become a nation. At Versailles in 1919 the peace treaty was signed for Canada by her Prime Minister, Sir Robert Borden. It was the first time that Canada had signed a treaty in her own right, and it marked the recognition of Canada as an independent and sovereign state among the nations of the world. Sir Robert's eyes are known to have filled with tears as he put his signature to the historic document, and he said afterward that he felt that he was signing in the blood of sixty thousand young Canadians who had made the supreme sacrifice.

While my brother had gone off to the war in 1917, I had graduated from public school to the Galt Collegiate Institute. The collegiate had the reputation of being one of the leading secondary schools in Ontario, and I was the youngest pupil in my class. When I joined the Cadet Corps I was thought to be too small and too young to carry a full-size Ross rifle, so I was issued a .22 instead. I avoided this embarrassment, however, by transferring to the Bugle Band and learning to blow a bugle. I was initially the smallest and youngest member of the band.

For the first time I found myself one of my father's pupils. It is not an ideal relationship for either father or son. In my first year he taught me arithmetic, algebra and writing. He was obviously embarrassed when I scored a mark of 99 on our first arithmetic examination. No doubt he feared that all other members of the class would suspect I had seen the examination paper beforehand at home. He was at some pains to review my answers before the class, evidently to demonstrate that the marking was honest and impartial.

My standing in the first year was marred by the inclusion of art in my course. I loathed it and had no aptitude for it. Rid of it in the second year I began to take off, and was allowed at its end to jump to Fourth Form (now Grade 12). I was steadily pulling to the top of the class, though two or three years younger than the average. The homework was growing much heavier; by the fourth year I was spending as much as four hours a night.

It must not be thought, however, that those four years at collegiate were all spent in the classroom or study. I played rugby and soccer at the school and other games at the YMCA. The school boasted a gymnasium with one shower, which would have made a Spartan whimper. The water did not run from it, it merely trickled, and it was always ice-cold. One towel at most served the whole team.

The Bugle Band also claimed a high place in my interest. I was promoted one stripe each year, becoming the bugle sergeant in Grade 12. The leader of the Galt Kilty Band had come to offer instruction to us. After hearing me play he announced that I could play the bugle as well as he could. My brother Gordon, who had dropped out of school for a year and had fallen behind me, was drum sergeant. The selection of drum major in my final year had to be between the two of us. The choice fell on me. I felt keenly sorry over it for Gordon's sake, for he was an excellent drummer. That year the band did well, and it was an honour to be "leader of the band."

I also had time for extracurricular activities. In conjunction with Sunday School was a Tuxis program for teen-age boys operated under the auspices of the Ontario Boys Work Council. I became praetor (president) of our group. This led me into debating in the Inter-Sunday School League with success. I participated in debates under school and other auspices as well, and gained increasing confidence in my efforts to master the techniques of the art.

Even at the age of ten I had decided I wished to become a lawyer. My parents commended my ambition, but they must have wondered where the money required for so much education would be found. Throughout the four years in collegiate I never wavered from this goal. No Fleming had ever attended university before, and only one Wright. My aim was set on the University of Toronto, the nearest and most prestigious of all Canadian universities.

When I was just half-way through collegiate my father was compelled by ill health to retire from his profession. This created very serious questions for all of us. He entered the life insurance business and soon found his efforts better rewarded. This helped to overcome our worries over the gnawing problem of insecurity. He received a handsome pension of $27 per month after teaching for a quarter of a century.

Nevertheless, the strictest economy was still necessary. The collegiate was three miles from home, so I saved my money and bought an excellent bicycle. Except during the winter months I rode it to and from school, even to come home for lunch. In the winter months I walked to and from school, crossing the frozen Grand River as a short cut. Only in foul weather were we permitted the luxury of riding the street-car.

My first job was summer employment with the Dominion Tack and Nail Company in 1918 after my first year at collegiate. The job commanded a salary of $9.13 per week for 55 hours. My work was to feed steel laths into machines which bit off pieces and made tacks of them. I had six machines to tend, and I had to hustle to keep up with them. Those were the longest days I had ever experienced. I had the misfortune to be under the clock, which I had to face every time I went down the line of machines. The hands moved with painful slowness.

One day I was told that another boy, older and bigger than I, was determined to lick me and would be waiting for me at the door at six o'clock. I had no quarrel with him, but I was not backing away from any such challenge. Sure enough, at six o'clock he was standing by the door waiting for me. I do not know what possessed me to do it, but as I approached him I broke into a run with my arms stretched forward. We collided and he went back head over heels under the machines. He was too dazed to stand up. The encounter was watched not only by the boys but the men also at the factory. I did not receive any more challenges.

The influenza epidemic closed the schools that autumn. I was fortunate to obtain a job with a building contractor for three weeks. I worked 59 hours per week, at 30 cents per hour. The duties included excavation by pick and shovel, carrying hods of bricks, building and scraping cribbing, and unloading carloads of brick. We began in the dark at 7 a.m. and finished in the dark at 6 p.m.

The next summer (1919) I was fourteen, but jobs were less plentiful. The contractor took me on as a hoist operator, but at a reduced wage of 25 cents per hour. I operated a hoist with two platforms moving in opposite directions, powered by a gasoline motor. One day we nearly had a serious accident. When an old workman with a clay pipe in his mouth stepped on the platform at the top it began to drop swiftly. I heard a shout, saw the old man dropping fast, then observed the cable spinning off the drum. I must have failed to engage the brake tightly. I grasped and applied it so firmly that the platform stopped its descent with such force that the old man was nearly thrown off. He bit off the stem of his pipe. It was a very frightening experience for both of us.

Jobs were even scarcer the next summer. For a while I had a job behind the counter in a tobacco shop. An infection in my right foot laid me up for most of the summer. I sat in the garden with my foot exposed to the sun and read some big books. I came close to losing my great toe.

By the summer of 1921 there were no steady jobs to be had. I helped my father, driving him on business to nearby towns and villages. He had bought a car that spring – a new Gray-Dort open touring car, but never learned to drive it. There was no licensing of drivers in those days, so at sixteen I took up driving. I felt very grand roaring up Main Street or the Preston Highway at 15 miles an hour. The springs squeaked constantly. It was one of my jobs to crawl under the car and "paint" them with oil.

Unfortunately, I stopped growing at sixteen. I wished to be tall, but reached only 5′ 7½″. Even at that I managed to pass my father and Robbie by a fraction, and that was some satisfaction, but I have always remained conscious of being short. Perhaps that added to a natural combativeness. But my build was sturdy, my health robust, and my stamina and physical strength extraordinary.

I express my gratitude to the teaching staff of the Galt Collegiate Institute during my four years there, 1917 to 1921. There was no better staff in any collegiate in Ontario. To me the outstanding teachers were Dr. Thomas Carscadden, who taught English and history, Mr. Robert Hamilton, who taught science, and Miss Janet Carter, who taught French and German. They were known to the students respectively as "Timmy," "Bobby" and "Mammy." In his late years Dr. Carscadden said in my hearing, "All my life I have made a point of forgetting the unpleasant things that have happened. Consequently, looking back all my memories are pleasant." What a healthy attitude toward life! I owe a heavy debt to all my teachers. They were all ladies and gentlemen, held in the highest respect.

I have one unforgettable memory of the principal, A.P. Gundry. We fifth formers were returning to the classroom from a PT period out on the campus. I was feeling somewhat playful, and came stamping down the hall and into the classroom making a thunderous noise with my heels. The principal was not expected in the vicinity, but as soon as I entered the classroom I came face to face with him. He delivered the following admonition which I have never forgotten: "You don't measure a man's importance by the noise he makes. If you did the men outside the midway sideshows would be the most important people in the world, and they aren't." I recommend it to all politicians and hopeful aspirants.

By my fourth year at the collegiate I had jumped to the top of the fifth form and held that coveted position throughout the year. Hard work was yielding its reward. Early in that year I was prevailed upon by the staff to commence German in the hope of qualifying for one of the Carter scholarships for the County of Waterloo, as they were awarded on the basis of aggregate marks. This meant doing five years' work in German in one year, in addition to eleven other subjects. It was no small task. I devoted every Saturday to learning German. Once I gave it up as impossible, but then felt ashamed of myself for admitting failure and resumed it three weeks later. The loss of those three precious weeks itself proved a severe setback. Then in the spring I was asked by the staff to prime myself for the University of Toronto Edward Blake scholarships, which were open to competition over the whole province. Other Galt students seeking these scholarships had invariably taken two years in fifth form. I was quite determined to take my chances with one year. I wrote thirteen papers, twelve of which went very well. Mathematics had always been among my best subjects, but after doing well with the algebra and trigonometry papers I stumbled on the analytical geometry. I knew the book work well, but encountered trouble with the problems on the examination paper that unhappy morning. My heart sank when I left the examination hall after handing in my paper. When the results were published I had scored First Class Honours in all other subjects, including the two German papers, but slipped to Third in the maths. I won the first Carter Scholarship for Waterloo County, defeating a Kitchener student who had spent two years in fifth form and had written more papers than I had. That one wretched geometry paper, however, had denied me the Edward Blake Scholarship for which I had worked very hard and sacrificed much. I realized that by waiting another year and spending two years in the fifth form, a scholarship would have been a virtual certainty. But it had not seemed to me worth a whole year of my life; ever very impatient, I sought to press on. It seemed at that time so important to complete my preparation to enter the full stream of life and earn my own way as soon as possible. But that episode left a scar on my memory.

CHAPTER FOUR

University

The four years which I spent at the University of Toronto were among the most important and formative of my whole life. They exerted a powerful influence on my character, my attitudes, my outlook, and expanded my knowledge enormously. For this experience I shall always be grateful; for the opportunity I owe much to my parents.

I looked forward to my university course with high excitement. It was to be so new and different. True, it meant leaving home, emerging from its protective influence, and facing life on my own to a far greater degree than ever before. It meant growing maturity. It also meant hard work.

I had turned sixteen the previous May, but I was conscious of assuming a great responsibility. I was the first Fleming to attend a university. On the Wright side of the family I was the second, having been preceded by my cousin, Dr. Stewart Wright, a distinguished orthopaedic surgeon practising in Toronto. I was the recipient of much very sound advice, mostly from my mother, but also from my father, the YMCA secretary, teachers and friends. I absorbed it all very seriously. Some very wise and helpful advice had been given to me by Dr. Brebner, the Registrar, at our meeting. Looking at my record and noting that I intended to enter the honours course in political science in preparation for the practice of law, he said: "The first year in political science is too easy for you. I think you should take a harder course, say, English and history, in the first year. At the end of it you could transfer to political science, which is hard enough in the second year." I followed his advice and have never regretted doing so. The first year of the English and history course fully measured up to his prediction. It was hard, and the competition was keen. It was made harder by my choice of Latin as one of my honours language options, along with French. The

German would have been much easier, but I have never regretted that year of university Latin. I completed the year with First Class Honours (the only student with the Latin option in the course to do so) and then transferred to the political science course. James Brebner ranks high in my grateful memory.

Money as usual was a critical problem. Da and I had a heart-to-heart talk about it. There were two aspects: the first, my immediate requirements; the second, ultimate accountability. We readily agreed that as I was being given an opportunity not enjoyed by my brothers, I should one day repay every cent my father advanced to me. There were no university loans provided by the government in those days, and I had no affluent sponsor. I was dependent on my father and on my own efforts. I well knew that every dollar he lent me meant a sacrifice by him and Mother. I resolved that I would live as frugally as possible. I did. In the end I repaid him every cent and with 5 per cent interest, which I insisted on paying, but it took me some years to do it. The result was that from the age of sixteen I was on my own, and I became very self-reliant and independent. It was part of my nature to be very careful in the use of money; my brothers called me a "tightwad." Part of that characteristic was ingrained by necessity.

The preparations for my departure seemed very elaborate. The shopping included the purchase of a strong steamer-trunk, a new suit and a dressing-gown, as well as various accessories. The new suit was a salt-and-pepper beauty. The dressing-gown was the first of its kind in our family. I felt that I had grown up overnight.

Sunday, September 25, 1921, was my last night at home. Mother presented me with a wrist-watch, my first, and a final round of sound advice. Next morning we loaded my new steamer trunk and bags and books aboard the Gray-Dort, and we were off to Toronto, a three-hour drive. There, after enrolling in my various courses at University College, I said good-bye to my parents and Gordon and suddenly realized I was on my own. I did not permit my heart to sink or my spirit to quail; I made myself busy.

I was fortunate enough to be admitted to the University Residence on Hoskin Avenue, now known as Devonshire House. Here I was one of fifty men drawn from all faculties. The rooms were very simple and furnished in green; the furniture was hard and durable; the floors in the rooms and the halls had warped and squeaked. There were no rugs or cushions. Indeed, there was no trace of luxury or comfort. We inmates appropriately called the residence "the barracks." There were three "houses," North, East and South. I was assigned to South House. The three houses faced inwards over a tennis court with a filthy cinder top. Each house had its own resident housemaster, and ours was Dr. George Duff. Eddie Dowler, my friend and classmate in Galt, also located in South House, and I had the benefit of his companionship, which meant a great deal to me, particularly in the first lonely days. He had proposed that we share a double suite, but I opted for a single room in deference to my study habits.

The term opened with Convocation the next afternoon. For the first time I saw freshmen being "passed up." Those who had the temerity to enter on the ground floor were hoisted up manually to the upper tiers. I escaped this vigorous welcome. We were addressed by the president, Sir Robert Falconer, who spoke with a rich, mellow voice, and by the new warden of Hart House, J. Burgon Bickersteth. He and I were destined to become close friends.

The meals at Hart House were plain, monotonous and unappetizing. Breakfast cost 20 cents, lunch and dinner 35 cents. A glass of milk was 5 cents extra. I soon tired of them all. With the aid of an old toaster donated by a cousin, a tiny teapot and a few dishes, I set myself up in business for breakfast and, for a short time, supper also. This latter became monotonous, but I continued to make my own breakfast for four years. For lunch and dinner we gravitated to such splendid Chinese restaurants in the College and Spadina area as the Red Rose, the White Rose, and later the Goblin. There we could obtain a meal for 30 cents, so we students saved 5 cents by walking a mile and wore out shoe-leather. The best joke prevalent at campus entertainments was the exclamation of a student pretending to be on the point of starvation, "I'm so hungry I could eat at the Red Rose."

It had been agreed that I should come home every third weekend. This meant a trip by CPR, which provided an excellent service. The first trip home could never be forgotten. I never enjoyed Mother's incomparable cooking more. She did my laundry over the weekend, and packed me off on Sunday evening loaded with eggs and jars of preserves for my breakfasts. In the course of time the trips were stretched to six weeks apart, but Mother never failed me. She wrote me a letter every week, and I wrote her every Sunday afternoon. It became my first chore after lunch, and nothing was permitted to interfere.

A service of worship was conducted every Sunday morning at Convocation Hall. I attended it on the first Sunday morning, but never again. It was too cold and geared to the intellect. Like so

41

many other students I took to attending Bloor Street Presbyterian Church, where the minister, the Reverend Dr. George C. Pidgeon, was destined to become a revered friend to me and to exert an enormous influence on my life and thought.

My lectures, with a few exceptions, were of absorbing interest. I took copious notes and pored over them in the evenings. Spaces between lectures were spent at the library, or studying in my room. My first examination led to thrilling results. It was in French, and Professor Cameron, who lectured us in French grammar, decided that we should be tested early in the year. The exam was set for a Saturday morning. I worked so hard and was so excited over my first university exam that I scarcely slept the night before. The next week when the results were announced he singled out my paper as the best in the class, gave me a mark of 95 and announced that I was really ready for second-year honours French.

There were many activities and organizations which claimed the attention of students. I could have immersed myself quite pleasantly in them, but I rigorously subordinated them to my studies. I devoted the evenings until 11 p.m. to reading and study. It was often hard to remain awake, but I fought off sleep by washing my hands and face in cold water when necessary.

My other activities were physical and social. I took the physical training classes at Hart House, and kept up my exercise with walking, skating at Varsity Rink in the winter, and swimming. In my first year I took part in the formation of the University Conservative Club and became its secretary. It was not, however, a very active organization. In later years I took part in the Hart House debates.

In my last three years I played rugby for University College in the interfaculty series. I began on the line but quickly moved to quarterback. In my third and fourth years I was quarterback for the Senior Arts team when it was known as "The Scoreless Wonders." We lived up to our reputation most of the time, but one day I spoiled it all. Seeing an opening I ran the ball myself up to scoring position, and on the next down I kicked it not only over the touch-line, but for good measure right over the fence into the property of the women's residence, Annesley Hall. I won my College colours for rugby.

I probably should have joined the wrestling classes, but feared involving myself deeply in a competitive sport at which I had done so well in the Galt YMCA. Time was limited, and studies came first. Indeed, concern began to be expressed that I was working too hard. The Reverend R.E. Knowles once said to me,

"Do you realize that your name has become synonymous with hard work?" I felt flattered. I asked lots of questions in class and groups where that was permitted. We read Latin authors with Professor E.A. Dale in the first year. When I did not return to the Latin classes in the second year he was interested enough to ask about me, and was told that I had transferred to the political science course. He was kind enough to express his regret, and to comment of me, "He is a very earnest seeker after knowledge." It was true.

Meeting fellow students and professors is one of the most valuable opportunities afforded by university. Although I did not go out of my way to be popular or to seek friends I had the good fortune to make many. There were the other inmates of South House. One of them was R.P. Vivian, who later became Ontario's Minister of Health, and still later sat in the House of Commons. Ron Perry, later headmaster of Ashbury College, Ottawa, lived across the road at Wycliffe College and became a very close friend. Through him I became a friend of the popular Joe McCully, later headmaster of Pickering College and still later warden of Hart House. In my group on Greek and Roman history I met a very friendly and soft-spoken student with a handsome face and pale blue eyes. His name was Ewart ("Grub") Fockler, and he came from Newmarket. He later moved into South House, and we became inseparable companions. He developed into a consulting geologist of wide experience. We have remained the closest of friends. I was best man at his wedding in 1932, and he was my best man a year later.

My cousin Jack Wright from Garden Hill entered medicine in 1923. He and I were more like brothers. Years later I was best man at his wedding, and he head usher at mine. Harold Brown, one of the janitors at South House, and I became lifelong friends. In 1984 we are still exchanging greetings and good wishes. Also in South House were two brothers, studying medicine, who were destined to achieve fame. They were Evan and Wilfred Shute, who located in London and developed the uses of Vitamin E. In my last year Evan occupied the room immediately above mine. Sunday mornings at an early hour he chose to practise on his violin. He was both intercollegiate heavyweight boxing and wrestling champion, so I was obliged to endure his violin without challenge. Wilfred scrupulously respected the Sabbath. When necessary he would begin studying Sunday nights at one minute after midnight.

I followed the Varsity teams loyally and faithfully. I allowed myself to watch the rugby games on Saturday afternoons in the autumn with unfailing regularity. Those were great days in intercollegiate rugby. Queen's was dominant with the great Batstone-Leadley-McKelvey combination. In later years I came to know Fred Veale and Dunc McIntosh of that outstanding team. For Varsity we had Warren Snyder, Sandy Somerville, Jack Sinclair and other stars. In the Big Four I watched with something approaching awe Lionel Conacher, "the big train" of Argonauts, mowing down the opposed. Joe Breen, later president of Canada Cement Company, was a star for Parkdale. Dr. Smirlie Lawson, a former Varsity great, was starring for Argos. Those three men all became friends of mine in later years.

I joined the Student Christian Movement, and along with some classmates in Latin who were destined for the ministry, I attended a group for one hour per week. In the first year Professor Dale led us through the Epistle to the Romans; in subsequent years the great Dr. J.R.P. Sclater, later to become the Moderator of the United Church of Canada, led us through some fascinating studies of religious poetry.

I had neither time nor funds for much entertainment. In my first year I went to one movie; in later years I attended the plays in the Hart House Theatre. Some of them were excellent, some, written by students, were something less. I attended the "Year dances," arranged by our Year Executive. They were inexpensive, and afforded an opportunity to meet our lady classmates. Nearly all of them I addressed formally and respectfully as "Miss"; they were all older than I.

Sundays after mid-afternoon were a problem at the outset, but that was overcome by mastering the art of "spearing meals," as it was known. Some of the inmates of South House were very proficient at it. I had three married Wright cousins and some friends of Mother in town, so I made it my business to go the rounds of visiting them on Sunday afternoons and remaining for supper. They had no difficulty in divining the purpose of a telephone call from me toward the end of any week. They were very kind to me. My cousin Jack Wright joined me in these attentions to our relatives. It did me good to escape from the university environment for half a day each week. To rest my mind and eyes on the Sabbath I refrained from reading or studying that day.

I practised rigid economy from the beginning to the end. I was determined to resort to my father's aid as little as possible. One thing I keenly regret having done: I sold off most of my textbooks at the end of each term to make ends meet. I have often wished since that I still had them. In this way and with the money I earned in the summers and in scholarships I succeeded in holding my net expenditure each year to below $500. It was a triumph of thrift. I look back on it with some pride.

In the autumn of 1922 Da bought a house on the other side of town in Galt, at 11 Cameron Street, and we left 11 Ramore Street after nine eventful years there. Our new home was not a recent structure, but it was a fine house standing on a corner set off by a spacious lawn. The furnace was not too effective. When I was home for the Christmas vacations I did my studying in the kitchen as close as possible to the stove. My father died in that house in 1940.

Summer work was a necessity, to supplement the money my father was able to provide. In the summer of 1922 I was employed by the Galt Machine Screw Company. I worked at a lathe and also ground spindles for parts for Ford cars. I often went home with a black face. In the summer of 1923 I was employed at an office job by the Canadian Pacific Express Company. I liked the work. By the summer of 1924 jobs were very scarce, and I was compelled to turn to farm labour. I worked half the summer for Mr. Elliott, the Progressive MP for South Waterloo, at $2.50 per day, and the working day lasted from 5 a.m. till dark. I was not happy there. I was refused an egg for breakfast, although there were lots of hens and lots of eggs. The cold stewed mutton just had to be eaten for breakfast. When a visiting Progressive MP arrived for a visit I was naturally evicted from my bed to make way for him and his family, and slept with the other hired man. He was a fine fellow, but he wore the same shirt day and night. By the end of that experience I was not too well disposed toward Progressive MPs.

The farm was located three miles out of Galt and my period of labour there coincided with the haying season. The loading was tolerable; I was driving the horses and building the loads on the hayracks. But the mowing was torture. Being the junior labourer I was assigned this worst of all jobs, distributing the hay evenly as it was dropped from slings at the top of the mow, while endeavouring to stay on top. The dust was unpleasant, and the temperature high in the mow under the metal roof resembled a furnace. As if that was not enough I had to suffer the MP's father, Andrew. He was a bossy and antiquated old Scot. He had not been a farmer, but a government agricultural representative, and was now retired. He did no work, but just stood there issuing staccato commands to me which never stopped. He eventually goaded me to the breaking-point. One morning, unable to take any more, I raised my pitchfork, pointed it right at him and roared, "One more word out of you and I'll run this fork right through you."

Not another word did he utter. I had convinced him that I meant exactly what I said. I quit the job soon after that incident.

At the beginning of August I went to Garden Hill and was given another job as farm labourer by my Uncle Bill Wright at $40 per month. After the milking each morning for the first week I went to the same twenty-acre wheat field to stook sheaves all by myself. It was a long and lonely week. Sunday morning I fainted, evidently the result of sunstroke. That put an end to my promising career as a farm labourer. A cousin summed it up: "I guess, Donald, you were meant to be a gentleman." The balance of the summer was spent loafing and reading economics textbooks. That marked the end of the jobs en route to my profession. None of them was lucrative, but I learned much from the experience. I could understand the feelings of labouring men.

I loved my course. Just as I was sorry to drop German on entering it I was even more sorry to drop French at the end of the first year. There was no place for it with so much economics, constitutional history, constitutional law, political theory, English and actuarial science. I had derived so much benefit and sheer enjoyment from my class in conversational French with Professor ("Papa") Deschamps, a Frenchman with a magnificent black spade beard, that I sought his permission to continue to attend his classes. Even that was crowded out by prescribed subjects. Another French professor I was very sorry to leave was Professor Arch Jeanneret, destined to become chancellor of the university, and a very warm friend of mine.

In my final year one of my subjects was world history, which included the history of art, in the course of which I took some lectures at the Royal Ontario Museum and others at the Ontario College of Art. Our lecturer at the latter was Arthur Lismer, a member of the renowned Group of Seven. It was a privilege to have been one of his students.

One morning in September 1923, the class was assembled for the opening lecture on English constitutional history of the seventeenth century. In walked the new young lecturer, looking, apart from his gown, more like a student than a professor. He proved to be an entertaining lecturer, apart from a slight lisp, and became popular with the class. His name was Mike Pearson, and he had just returned from Oxford. Our paths were destined to cross in later years. He was soon coaching the Varsity junior rugby team. In Parliament I often complimented him on his lecturing and said he should have stayed with it.

I revelled in the English lectures and texts, conscious of a developing command of the language. In my second year I wrote an essay in which I quoted freely from an essay by the head of the department, Professor Alexander. The professor (a lady) who marked the essay was critical only of these quotations. She commented, "You could have said it better yourself." She was evidently unaware of the source of the quotations! My first essay in fourth-year English was on Carlyle. It pleased the professor (also a lady) so much that she gave me a mark of 95 and excused me from writing any more essays for the year.

At the end of my third year the course was changed and divided into two courses – economics, and politics and law. I opted, of course, for the latter.

While I thoroughly enjoyed the course I could not say as much for the examinations. Lectures ceased by mid-April at the latest, and from then till May 23rd I was preparing for or writing examinations. It was a severe strain, protracted for six long weeks. Somehow I was always the last resident of South House to finish exams. The place became steadily more deserted and depressing. In 1923 I had a special problem. A year earlier I had made the mistake of having my eyes examined. The optometrist pronounced my eyes "a little tired" and prescribed glasses. I foolishly wore these for reading during the next year. In April, when I needed my eyes most, they gave out. Finally, with a little rest they saw me through the exams successfully, but I decided I would never wear glasses again. I rested my eyes during the summer, and they never again gave me trouble. The next time I resorted to glasses for reading was in 1970.

On two occasions when the mental and nervous strain seemed almost overpowering I derived needed assistance. On one Saturday I was persuaded to see a Harold Lloyd comedy film. I nearly split my sides over it. I left all the strain behind at the theatre and came away totally relaxed. I had the pleasure of meeting Harold Lloyd personally at a Shrine Convention in Toronto in 1962.

The other incident occurred on a Sunday afternoon when the strain was at its height. I was at the home of a cousin and casually picked up a hymn book. My eyes landed on two famous lines, "Look ever to Jesus, He will carry you through." I should not have needed this timely reminder. I have never forgotten it since, and I have never followed it in vain.

Examinations were a torture to me all through university. As I have mentioned, I completed the first year with First Class Honours, the only student in the English and history course taking the onerous Latin option to do so. The second-year results gave me one of the greatest thrills of my university days: I headed the political science course, was the only student in it to win First

Class Honours and was awarded the First Alexander Mackenzie Scholarship, worth $75, which looked like a fortune. In the third year I again headed the course with First Class Honours, but this time Wishart Spence tied with me. Again I was awarded the First Alexander Mackenzie Scholarship.

The fourth year was my greatest challenge. I was prevailed upon by one of the assistant registrars of the college to compete for the Governor General's Gold Medal, the highest award in the faculty of arts and open for competition to fourth-year students in the four arts colleges. This necessitated taking an additional and heavy course in English and writing an extra exam. The subject that year was Elizabethan drama. I enjoyed the course throughout, and hoped that the extra subject would not hurt my standing in the political science subjects.

I wrote my last examination on the morning of my twentieth birthday, and went home to Galt to rest and anxiously await the results. Those of the course were published in the *Globe* on June 3. I raced downtown in Galt that morning for a copy. I could scarcely believe my eyes: once again I stood first in my course with First Class Honours. The special awards were published two days later. Again I rushed downtown early in the morning for the paper. My heart leaped at what I saw: I had won the coveted Governor General's Gold Medal, and had also been awarded the Breuls Gold Medal for Political Science, a new prize. My joy knew no bounds. I rushed home with the news to share it with two proud and joyous parents.

Convocation Day, June 5, 1925, must rank as one of the most outstanding days of my life. In the presence of my parents I walked across the campus from University College to Convocation Hall in the traditional procession and was showered with congratulations at Convocation and the garden party which followed. Angus Macmurchy, QC, president of the U.C. Alumni Association, sent for me to thank me for bringing the Governor General's Gold Medal back to University College. The *Telegram* carried my photograph on the front page. Never before had there been such a day in my life. It was rounded off with a dance at Hart House, which continued till past midnight. As we drove back to Galt in the early hours of the morning I was still excited and thrilled.

I registered for my M.A. and took some lectures in 1925-26, but my work at Osgoode Hall compelled me to discontinue. After two years of extramural study and writing a thesis I received my LL.B. degree in November 1930.

The study habits I learned in collegiate and refined in university have stood me in good stead throughout life. Concentration is of the essence of study and absorption. All distractions must be avoided. A hard chair and comfortable mode of dress greatly aid concentration. I chose to work in slippers and dressing gown, free of collar and tie, with a celluloid green eye-shade eliminating from view all else but my book. I never found studying boring or unpleasant; frankly, I loved it.

Soon after I graduated from university I took on a new status: I became an in-law. In 1926 Gordon married Hilda Lee, a Galt girl. They took up residence first in St. Thomas, then Windsor. In 1928 Robbie, who had gone to live in Detroit, married Ethel Phillips, a Detroit school teacher. These were major events in my life. Both brothers are long since gone, but in 1984 Hilda and Ethel are both alive and well. I have always been closely and lovingly attached to both of them and their children. Robbie and Ethel had two children, Jeanne and Bob. Gordon had four children, Bruce, Margaret and twin sons Gordon and Paul. Another generation has followed them. The family bonds remain strong and enduring. From being the youngest I have become the last survivor of the original family and the head of an enlarged brood.

CHAPTER FIVE

The Law

When I became an articled student-at-law in June 1925, I was committed finally to a career on which I had first set my heart in public school. That spring, however, I had felt a strong tug to turn to the ministry of the church. For a short time I considered offering myself for a student mission summer appointment on the prairies, thinking that would aid me in making the final choice of callings. Dr. Gandier, principal of Knox College, offered me such an appointment, but insisted I should leave before Convocation to take it up. This I was unwilling to do. Instead, I proceeded to follow the law. I have never doubted since that I made the right choice and entered the profession to which I was best suited.

In those days Osgoode Hall Law School was the only institution in Ontario to train students for admission to the bar. Some universities, Toronto for example, had a law faculty, but only to lead students to the bachelor of laws degree, and not to the practice of the law. Osgoode Hall Law School, attached physically to the famous building containing the highest courts in Ontario, was operated by the Law Society of Upper Canada, and was not affiliated with any university. Admission was limited to students serving a solicitor under articles filed with the Law Society. Graduates of a recognized university formed the majority of the students enrolling in the Law School; the remainder were those with honour matriculation standing who had served two years under articles. Among the latter was my cousin Stuart Fleming from Peterborough. He and I were classmates for the next three years.

It was necessary to find a law firm willing to accept a student's articles, and some competition developed among the Varsity graduates for places with the best firms. At this point the advantages of influence and position became very apparent. I had no one with influence to aid me, but obtained an introduction to a small firm through the husband of a friend of my parents. The firm was Mercer, Bradford & Company, with offices at 217 Bay Street. In June I was articled to Jacob Henry Greenberg, a young and enterprising lawyer in the firm.

While composed of only three lawyers the firm was well known. Its founder was General Mercer, who led the Queen's Own Rifles out of the University Avenue Armouries in 1914 and was killed in the costly Battle of Sanctuary Wood two years later. When his division was ordered to attack against hopeless odds I have been told that General Mercer said, "If my boys must go over the top I'm going with them." He perished with them. Samuel Bradford, KC, was the head of the firm when I joined. He wore a goatee, and was regarded as a very senior and respected member of the inner bar. His son Dalton and Jake Greenberg completed the firm. I was the only student, and this was to my advantage, as all the student work came to me. The practice carried on by the firm was quite general in scope. This also was an advantage to me as it brought me into contact with more branches of practice than would have been possible in a more highly specialized office. Specialization in the law should come later, not at the outset.

At first I felt suddenly thrust out into a cold world. Gone were the summers at home; there would never be a return to them. I was committed to Toronto. In my four years at Varsity I had led, as I now soon learned, a sheltered, almost isolated, life. Now I had no place to live, no place to eat, no place to study, no place to play tennis or swim. After all the excitement of graduation I felt utterly lost in Toronto, removed from the protection of my alma mater. I moved to a room on Yorkville Avenue, near Avenue Road, in the home of Mrs. Lamb, who kept three other roomers, including two friends of mine from Hespeler. Happily, she provided breakfast. For all this I paid $5 per week. A year later we all moved to Chicora Avenue, also close to Avenue Road. Thus I was placed within walking distance of both Osgoode Hall Law School and the office, the former thirty minutes, the latter forty. I walked it both ways every day.

I keenly missed the dining and sports facilities of Hart House. The meals there had greatly improved over the standard of 1921. Although I was earning a handsome salary of $5 per week I did not think I could afford the annual graduate membership fee of $15 until a couple of years later. After that I stopped eating dinner in restaurants downtown and enjoyed the privilege of taking that meal in the graduates' dining room at Hart House. It made a convenient stopping place in walking home from downtown.

Lunch was very austere. Some days I lunched on shredded wheat, toast and milk at Bowles' Lunch for 20 cents, some days at Bingham's lunch counter where a sandwich, a cinnamon roll with a daub of whipped cream and a glass of milk cost 25 cents. I remained healthy.

Lectures at the Law School commenced in September. The system was quite different from university. At Osgoode each student was assigned a particular seat, and attendance was recorded. There were two one-hour lectures per day, from 9 to 11 a.m., and the balance of the day was available for work in the office. The evenings were spent in study at home. The year was divided into two terms, ending respectively at Christmas and the end of May. No subject was carried over from one term to the other. Final examinations, usually four in number, were written in December, and five or six in May. Thus the agony of writing final exams was visited upon us twice a year, but it lasted only half as long as at Varsity. I liked this sytem better.

The lecturing staff consisted of three full-time and several part-time lecturers. The three were the Dean, John D. Falconbridge, QC, and Dr. Donald Macrae and Sidney Smith. The last two were newly arrived from Dalhousie. They were destined to become warm friends of mine, and Sid's path and mine were to cross in later years. Among the part-time lecturers was my chief, Mr. Bradford. My arrival at Osgoode happened to coincide with the adoption of a new teaching method, the case system, borrowed from the Harvard Law School. The lecturer operates less from textbooks and more from actual cases reported in the official law reports. This meant that the student needed ready access to a law library for his materials. There were no photocopying machines in those days, and I found myself carrying home as many big volumes of law reports as my bag could contain.

We began with a class of about 120, of whom only three were ladies. A total of 111 survived to the end of the three-year course. We met for our two lectures each morning, and then dispersed. There were few organized student activities and scarcely any teams. A student parliament was organized at one point, and I took part in its political debates, but, generally speaking, we were increasingly becoming individualistic. Professionally we were being more and more shaped by the offices in which we were serving. Most members of the class were serious, ambitious and concerned for their futures in the profession. Numerous members also began to exhibit political interest and loyalties.

The prevailing spirit was friendly, and I had the good fortune to enjoy the friendship of many of my classmates. Some of them were of particular interest. Morley Callaghan, from St. Michael's College, parallelled attendance at lectures while serving as a reporter for the *Toronto Daily Star*. Paul Martin also came from St. Michael's, and Lionel Chevrier from the University of Ottawa. Paul in particular was clearly headed for politics; he never missed an opportunity to make a speech about Sir Wilfrid Laurier. Francis ("Red") Flaherty was also a newspaper reporter while at the Law School. Bill Bate, commonly known as "Master" Bate, was quite a character. He was an ardent Conservative, while his closest friend Wishart Spence was an equally ardent Liberal. Wishart and I continued at the Law School a rivalry which began in the political science course at Varsity. Our backgrounds were quite different, but we were always good friends. He later was appointed to the Trial Bench of the Supreme Court of Ontario and finally to the Supreme Court of Canada. By comparison with others, the class of 1928 achieved unusual distinction in practice, in politics, and in the judiciary. Among the other judges were Neil Fraser, George Elliot, Ben Grossberg, Ian Munro.

At this period I was made conscious of an unfortunate mannerism. When my two brothers were singing in the choir of Knox Church and faced me in the congregation they pictured me sitting through the sermons with my arms folded and looking very cross. No doubt some of the monotonous sermons preached by the Reverend J. Keir Fraser were partly responsible for this regrettable facial expression. My father, who was no admirer of Dr. Fraser, used to say that he had one hundred sermons, and he just kept repeating them year after year. We came to know some of them so well that I could tell even what sentences were coming next. Mother kept a record of the dates on which he preached on various texts. Some verses in her Bible had as many as seven dates in the margin.

I think the facial expression was more attributable to concentration. At any rate, Dean Falconbridge observed to Mr. Bradford one day that I looked at him in class "as cross as cross." This was unfortunate. The Dean was always polite, even though a trifle vague at times in his lectures, and I never dared consciously to direct a cross look in his direction. I admittedly took life seriously, but this was no excuse for looking unpleasant. The mannerism was harder to cope with because I was unaware of it.

Wishart Spence outside class one day made a very penetrating observation to me on a characteristic which seemed to be developing out of my sense of independence, "My God, Fleming, you do hate to be in a majority."

In their offices in those days students were often used as messenger boys. I did my share of these boring tasks, consoling myself with the thought that I was mastering the geography of downtown Toronto and acquainting myself with the offices of the leading law firms. I served writs, notices and pleadings, did the filing chores at Osgoode Hall, protested cheques, and spent much of my time in the City Registry Office, the County Registry Office and the Land Titles Office searching titles to land. I had very little opportunity to sit in courtrooms to hear cases. I excelled, in Mr. Bradford's frequently expressed opinion, in reading law and preparing memoranda for his court cases and opinions. For this type of work it is necessary to have a grasp of the issues and to know where to find the sources of the applicable law. It is very exacting work. Mr. Bradford thought I showed a special aptitude for it. This opened up an unusual opportunity for me. Mr. Bradford and Mr. Greenberg were recognized as leaders in the field of bankruptcy law, and they had been asked to write an annotation of the Bankruptcy Act, which was published as Volume VI of the *Bankruptcy Reports*. Even as a first-year student I was given several chapters to write, and this contribution to what became the accepted textbook on the subject was recognized in the introduction. It was my first published work of authorship, and I felt deeply gratified.

Mrs. Lamb was the daughter of Judge Barron of Stratford, who wrote a major textbook in 1925 on *The Canadian Law of Motor Vehicles*. I was given the task of compiling the subject index. The remuneration was not very grand, but the work was instructive.

My salary at the office responded handsomely to my progress and diligence. The second year it was raised to $8 a week and then to $12 for the third year. These figures were slightly above the prevailing average. Half-way through my final year when nearly all members of the class were worried about how and where they were to locate after graduation I received an offer from Lewis Duncan of a princely wage of $18 per week till graduation, $25 per week for three months, then $30 and the prospect of a partnership with one-third of the profits. Duncan had a small practice and was known to be unpopular, but he was able and exacting, and I could not afford to reject his financial terms. I left Mercer, Bradford & Company and joined Duncan at the end of January 1928. It was not the happiest of situations, but I think the experience was beneficial while it lasted.

The Law School offered little in the way of awards until graduation, but standing in the examinations was of high importance for professional recognition. Two misfortunes overtook me at different times, and I blame myself largely for them. In preparing for the Torts exam at Christmas 1925 I decided to conduct a last review of my notes, and in consequence left myself so little time that I bolted my lunch and had to run all the way to Osgoode. I had barely begun the paper when I became ill, and had to be excused for three-quarters of an hour out of the precious three hours. As a result I fell to ninth place in the class aggregate standings. My mark in Torts would have disentitled me to attain honours even with an overall average of 75 per cent or more. My petition in this respect was granted by the Law Society. I believe I could have obtained permission to write another exam in the subject, and should have, but I hoped at the spring examinations to overcome the setback. I did move up to second place in the combined standing for both Christmas and spring examinations, and achieved honours, but could not fully overcome the Torts disaster.

The second year results also left me short of my goal. Wishart and I outdistanced the class, but he again led at both Christmas and spring examinations. The great test came in the third year, when a gold medal and scholarship were at stake. I was determined to make my supreme effort, and did. We wrote four papers at Christmas, and I came out on top, but by only one mark. The result demonstrated that it could be done, but the rejoicing was perforce brief. In March I went to Wishart at his office and proposed that we should agree to leave our offices on the same day to prepare for the spring exams. He commended the fairness of the proposal, but said he thought no agreement was necessary, and that if I chose to leave my office at March 31 he would tell anybody that I had acted entirely fairly and had sought no advantage. In early April I plunged into the final preparations.

I was well prepared for the five subjects. I did as well as could have been expected in four. The issue was determined by one question in the fifth exam, which was on the subject of Trusts. Indeed, it was resolved by one sentence. The paper had been set by Sidney Smith, who had a habit of setting complicated questions. The particular problem was intended to illustrate what is known in the history of English law as "the hardening of Equity." I wrote a perfect answer, but was so appalled at the inequity of the result that I allowed myself to add one fatal sentence, "But Equity could not countenance so inequitable a result, and the decision of the Chancellor must be the opposite." What a pity I didn't run out of ink before penning that well-meant but technically wrong answer! It cost me the gold medal. In the marking I probably forfeited at least ten marks over that sentence. When the results were posted up a fortnight later, out of a possible total of 800 marks Wishart had 714, and I 712. It was small comfort that I had led in more subjects than he had, and that I had scored a respectable 89 per cent overall. Wishart took the gold medal and the Chancellor Van Koughnet Scholarship, worth $400. I was awarded the silver medal and the Christopher Robinson Memorial Scholarship, worth $100. That offending rider to my correct answer has haunted me ever since. I was deeply depressed over the results. As in 1921, I had once again come "so very near" to attaining a cherished goal.

The gold medalist in each of the two preceding years had proceeded to the Harvard Law School for a year of postgraduate studies. Had I won it I would have made a strong effort to borrow the money needed for a year at Harvard. As it was, Wishart went to Harvard and won his master of laws degree. I went into practice with a sad heart.

The call to the bar for about twenty of us came on June 21, 1928. Duly robed, we were admitted to Convocation of the Benchers of the Law Society, introduced and congratulated. We were then conducted to Weekly Court where before Mr. (later Chief) Justice Rose we were called to the Bar of Ontario and enrolled as solicitors of the Supreme Court of Ontario. My parents were present to witness the fulfilment of a dream.

The next week I was appointed a notary public in and for the province of Ontario. My qualifications for the practice of law were now complete. Along with my classmates I was turned loose on the unsuspecting people of Ontario for better or for worse.

I continued to work with Mr. Duncan. By September 1928 I was earning $30 a week and no longer needed my father's help. He had paid my bar admission fees of $165 and that was to be my last borrowing from him. After being a drain on his slender financial resources for seven years I was now self-supporting at last.

Lewis Duncan was a meticulous lawyer, and I learned much from him, particularly about litigation. He had, however, a bad habit of quarrelling personally with other solicitors. The office was too small to provide me with the scope I sought, and I therefore did not seek to exercise my right to partnership. My opportunity to move came in the spring of 1929 when I learned that Dyce Saunders, QC, was looking for a junior.

Mr. Saunders was head of the firm of Saunders, Kingsmill, Mills & Price. He was one of the most respected members of the legal profession, a Bencher of the Law Society, chancellor of the Anglican Diocese of Toronto, and a famous cricketer. There were three other partners: Walter B. Kingsmill, QC, a member of an old Toronto family, and commanding officer of the 123rd Battalion (Royal Grenadiers) in the Great War; Stanley S. Mills; and Vincent W. Price. All were honourable men adhering to the highest standards of the profession. By the standards of 1929 it was a medium-sized firm, with a variety of clients, of which the most important was the New York Central Railroad, lessee of the Michigan Central Railroad and sub-lessee of the Canada Southern Railway, crossing southern Ontario from Windsor to Buffalo. The firm had its office in the Federal Building, 85 Richmond Street West, and a branch office in St. Thomas handling the railway claims work. On April 29, 1929, I joined the firm and immediately felt the challenge of a much enlarged opportunity. I parted from Lewis Duncan on the best of terms. He was good enough to praise my work and to say that he had realized early in our association that "I would not be able to hold you long."

As the junior member of the firm I naturally fell heir to some of the less agreeable chores, including collections and real estate, but along with these I had the privilege of working personally with Mr. Saunders as his junior in some important pending cases in the courts. I not only appeared with him, but also shared the briefs with him and as junior counsel addressed the court. This brought me before the Court of Appeal for the first time. Mr. Saunders commended me on the manner in which I conducted myself. I was also introduced to the railway work, and assumed increasing responsibilities in that very interesting quarter. On top of all these blessings I was paid a salary of $40 per week with the prospect of admission to partnership.

A year later this happy relationship was harshly jolted by the death of Mr. Saunders in London. He had gone overseas on an appeal to the Privy Council; a bad cold contracted in Toronto had turned into mastoid, which proved fatal. I felt I had lost a warm friend and a valued sponsor whom I needed. His death left a major gap in the firm and some sense of insecurity for me. I found myself on my own to a greater degree. Agreeably, my salary was increased to $200 per month, plus half of the fees on any business I brought in and handled myself.

Then the Great Depression struck and the firm's earnings declined alarmingly. Many bright pictures and dreams faded, and the path ahead became rough. Farmers were selling eggs in Galt at 10 cents per dozen. My brother Bob lost his job in Detroit, and I sent him assistance for a time.

I welcomed opportunities to increase my income and expand my studies of the law. Dr. Macrae of the Law School staff had become editor of the *Canadian Encyclopaedic Digest*, a digest of all the Ontario case law, and he invited me to write for it. I was tried out cautiously at first with a brief subject, "Lis Pendens," which I dispatched in three months to the complete satisfaction of the editor and the publishers. That was followed by a larger assignment, "Malicious Prosecution." That went so well that I was offered one of the major subjects, "Negligence." I devoted every available moment for one year to that fascinating undertaking, working nights and Saturday afternoons and evenings in the firm's excellent library. I read and digested over 1,000 reported cases. My treatise won acclaim from the editor and the publishers. For this monumental work I was paid approximately $300. Other articles followed. Finally, on invitation, I wrote the portions on "Federal Taxation" and "Provincial Taxation" in the digest on "Taxation." This writing of legal texts became a useful guided course of studies.

Later I spent over a year writing a considerable portion of a new edition of Holmested's *Judicature Act*, the standard work on practice and procedure in the courts. Articles published in the *Canadian Bar Review* and in *Canadian Railway Cases* followed. All this writing was in addition to my office work and practice. It meant ceaseless work, but I think it was highly beneficial.

My practice was still varied, but I was leaning more toward litigation. The court work attracted me, and although it was hard and exacting it offered excitement and drama. I did take a few criminal cases, but definitely preferred the civil. For one thing they were more remunerative. Court cases themselves offered wide variety. I appeared in all the courts, including the Supreme Court of Canada. I regretted never having the opportunity to appear in London before the Judicial Committee of the Privy Council before Canadian appeals to it were abolished. I had the good fortune to appear in some important civil cases with recognized leaders of the bar, including W.N. Tilley, N.W. Rowell, I.F. Hellmuth, D.L. McCarthy, R.S. Robertson, Gersholm Mason and others. I was with Mr. Tilley as junior counsel in what I believe was his last big case.

One lesson must be learned early in a career before the

courts – the necessity of careful preparation. I never found that any time I devoted to preparation was wasted. It makes a vast difference to one's confidence, particularly for a young barrister, in appearing before the courts.

In the autumn of 1928 I enrolled at Varsity in the Faculty of Law. With credits for the subjects taken at Osgoode Hall Law School it became possible for me to take the course leading to the degree of bachelor of laws extramurally in two years. In the spring of 1929 I wrote five examinations successfully, without the assistance of lectures. The following year I wrote a thesis on the prescribed subject, "The Doctrine of Hot Pursuit in International Law." I received the degree of LL.B. at the autumn Convocation in 1930.

All this intensive work might seem to have left time for little else. In the summers of 1925 and 1926 I was a member of the old Toronto Canoe Club in Parkdale and played my tennis there. The club and clubhouse have disappeared long since, but the courts remain to this day. In the summer of 1926 I was introduced to Ward's Island and Centre Island by my cousin Margaret Boddy, who had a cottage on Ward's. This seemed such a pleasant place to spend summers which were hot and uncomfortable and dull in the city that my friend Bob Barber and I decided to give the island a trial the following summer. That marked the commencement of a new experience which continued for nineteen consecutive summers, and brought me great enjoyment.

Centre Island then was extensively built upon, with a summer population of some five thousand. Bob and I rented an apartment there in the summers of 1927 and 1928. We joined the Island Aquatic Association, and played tennis there. I also took up a new sport – racing paddling – and a new pastime – lying on the sandy beach on Sunday afternoons. There were dances at the club on Friday evenings, followed by romantic walks to Ward's Island two miles away and back. We made a whole new circle of friends, many of whom have remained among our dearest and closest to this day, among them Ken and Tori Bottoms.

Lake Ontario is six hundred feet deep and cold. It seldom warmed up enough to make the bathing comfortable before August. Yet we did swim. It was delightful at the end of a hot summer day downtown to cross by ferry to the island and to enjoy the cooler air there and the delightful informality of the place. It was great fun bicycling or walking from end to end. I served the IAA in several offices, and finally as commodore from 1933 to 1935. As commodore I accompanied our paddlers to the various club regattas through the summer and finally to the annual regatta of the Canadian Canoe Association at Gananoque in 1927. Our club, though small, had some very strong entries in these competitions.

On Centre Island I established a church connection which proved vital and enduring. St. Andrew's Church stood on Cherokee Avenue facing the beach and lake. Its status was that of a mission of St. James' Cathedral, but it really operated independently under a committee. While Anglican, it actually functioned on an interdenominational basis during the summer. The minister was usually a professor from either Wycliffe or Trinity College, and we were therefore favoured with a succession of eminent ministers. I had not attended the church more than once or twice before I was asked to sing in the choir, and just as quickly was appointed "recruiting sergeant" to the choir. My job was to round up my friends and others with voices, to stand in front of the church on Sunday mornings prior to the service and separate the sheep from the goats, making certain that none with voices slipped my net. We could usually muster up to a dozen on Sunday mornings. After two years I was elected treasurer and a year later chairman of the Church Committee, and held these offices for many years, the latter, indeed, until 1945. Those were happy days. We enjoyed harmony in the church. The experience was proof abundant that members of various denominations can work together and worship together. I developed a strong attachment to the Anglican Church and its form of worship.

Bob and I gave up our attempts at housekeeping after the first two summers. Then for the next four summers I boarded at the home of a friend, Miss May Kells, on St. Andrew's Avenue, with others. Those were happy days. The others have died long since, but two of the members of that congenial household, Ivy Sharpe and Mabel Henderson, to this day remain very close and dear friends to us. After Alice and I were married in May, 1933, we continued to spend half of each summer on the same street for six more summers in a rented cottage. Even after ceasing to rent the cottage we continued for another seven years to spend Sundays on the island. In all, I lived twelve summers on the island, six before and six after marriage, and the island connection lasted for a total of nineteen consecutive summers. I look back on it as one of the happiest periods of my life.

CHAPTER SIX

Marriage and Expanding Activities

Many young men make a pretence of wishing to remain bachelors throughout life. I never did. From my own experience I recognized the value and necessity of marriage to happiness and fulfilment. Similarly, I believed that the family is the bedrock of society. I never thought of myself as detached or detachable from my family, and I always missed my home when I was absent from it. Out of persistent loneliness emerged a strong desire for a home like the one in which I was nurtured.

I was not uninterested in female company. I "dated," to use a more modern idiom ("took out," as we said then), lots of girls. I was fond of dancing and good conversation. There is safety in numbers, and I learned to be cautious. Many young ladies of my acquaintance were attractive, but with none of them could I have thought of marriage. My friends accused me sceptically of carrying around with me a list of "qualifications" I sought to find in some young lady some day. Blessed with a mother like mine I was bound to be hard to please. I was certainly not searching for a career woman, but for a partner and homemaker. I found her, thank God!

In 1930 my friend Ewart Fockler had gone to the Arctic, exploring for precious metals. He left his fiancée Marjorie (Jorie) Forbes in my care. She set to work to find me the perfect but elusive young lady of my hopes. She began to tell me she had found her, and her name was Alice Mildred, daughter of Mr. and Mrs. William G. Watson. While I had never met Mr. Watson I knew him as a prominent and highly respected figure in the business world and general manager of the Toronto General Trusts Corporation. Both Alice and Jorie were dietitians, and I had a high respect for people in that calling. Both were then on the staff of the Sick Children's Hospital. Alice was in charge of the children's diets there. I expressed keen interest in meeting her. On September 25, 1930, an unforgettable day in my life, Jorie and Alice appeared at my office without an appointment. Alice innocently walked into the lion's den. She escaped from that den, but never from the lion. After several dates I was invited to the Watson home for supper one Sunday, and there I met the family: Alice's parents, her younger sister Margery, her older brother Hal (Lieutenant-Colonel W.H. Watson), his wife Aileen and children Phyllis, Hugh and Mary. Another brother, Hugh, had died of wounds while serving overseas in the Great War. It was a charming and impressively closely knit family. They gathered every Sunday afternoon at the home at 30 Dunvegan Road, and spent the balance of the day together. The family were pillars of Metropolitan Church. Alas! They were also strong Liberals!

My first meeting with Mr. Watson was brief, but not to be forgotten. I was calling to take Alice out for the evening. She very properly presented me to her father. He was sitting in the sun-room reading that well-known Liberal newspaper, the *Toronto Daily Star*. He greeted me warmly, and spoke of his high esteem for my law firm. His appearance and manner were impressive. He was not a big man – indeed, he was not as tall as I – but he had a large and unusually handsome face, set off by dark brown eyes, and a crown of thick grey hair parted in the middle. He was most urbane, courteous, and immaculately attired. I took an immediate liking to him.

Mrs. Watson was tall, dignified, immaculate, outspoken and motherly. She was completely devoted to her family. Alice was very dear to her, as she was also to Margery and Hal and her father.

Alice came up to Galt with me for a weekend to meet my family. It could not have been easy for her under the circumstances, but the meeting proved to be wonderfully happy on both sides. On January 25, 1931, four months after we first met I asked Alice to be my wife, and she accepted. We were sublimely happy. I lost no time in asking Mr. Watson's permission to marry his daughter, and he cheerfully gave it. He commended my sense of humour as a wholesome guarantee of a happy home. On her birthday, February 15, Alice accepted a diamond ring from me. That was 1931, over fifty years ago. It was a turning point in my life.

Engagements were long in those days, partly by custom, and partly by necessity. There were few working wives, and consequently young people in planning marriage could count on only one income. We were in the midst of the Great Depression, and economic conditions were steadily deteriorating. After two years of betrothal Alice and I decided we would wait no longer. I broke the news to Colonel Kingsmill, whose response gladdened my heart: "I think the time has come to admit you to partnership." So in May 1933, when the Depression had reached its worst, I entered into two partnerships. Both proved eminently successful.

Alice and I were married in Metropolitan Church on May 13, 1933, before more than four hundred guests. Mr. and Mrs. Watson spared nothing to give Alice a great wedding. She was a beautiful bride, as the photographs taken on the day attest. We were launched on our matrimonial voyage under the happiest auspices.

We honeymooned in Bermuda, in glorious weather. We navigated the island by bicycle and electric railway. Two weeks later we arrived back in Toronto; I had exactly 35 cents in my pocket, all of which I bestowed on a grateful porter in the old Union Station for carrying our six heavy bags. Fortunately, Margery met us with the car.

We rented a cottage on Centre Island for the summer. For the balance of the year we lived in North Toronto, at 24 Anderson Avenue, on the corner of Colin Avenue. We did not move into North Toronto by any design or in keeping with some far-reaching plan. The move, however, was destined to shape my political career. We made our home there from 1933 to 1958.

In the last year before being admitted to partnership in the firm my income was $2,912. In the first year of partnership it dropped to $2,400; then it began to pick up slowly. Partnership agreements normally last two years. With each renewal my percentage of the profits was raised modestly. We never lacked any necessity, but every dollar had to be watched. Alice never complained. By 1935, with Alice's concurrence, the last cent of my indebtedness to my father for my education was repaid.

Before our marriage Ewart Fockler said of Alice, "She will be a great homemaker." She was. Her father said of her, "She'll make a great mother." She did. Our three children were all born in the Private Patients Pavilion of the Toronto General Hospital. David arrived on the evening of Saturday, December 12, 1936, a healthy boy of nine pounds. Mary was born on August 24, 1939, just one week before the outbreak of war. Alice and I were so pleased to have a daughter, I the more so because I never had a sister. I had always hoped that one day I would have a daughter and that her name would be Mary. Donald was born on April 21, 1942. That completed our little family. We had two high-spirited boys and a quiet, poised, even-tempered daughter. There were not many dull moments ahead of us in rearing our beloved children. They were fortunate to have such a devoted mother and custodian of their health.

Alice and I have now been married over fifty years. Our marriage was the best thing that ever happened to me. Alice has been a tower of strength in my life. She possesses the great gift of common sense and a sense of humour. She has taught me sympathy for others. She has been unselfish, ever thoughtful of others, modest and uncomplaining. She has been my sternest and most reliable critic, a benign and restraining influence. She has been a lady of refinement under all circumstances. I have never lost a friend over anything she has ever done or said. My parents loved her, and she was always good to them. A devout Christian, she has lived up to her own high code of duty. She has served God loyally and been a true follower of His Son. She has ever been firm in the defence of her convictions. There is not a trace of vanity in her nor desire for vainglory. No one could ever question her sincerity nor her homespun, down-to-earth genuineness. She became for six years, in the official Table of Precedence, the fourth lady of the land. That did not change her one whit. Her feet were too firmly planted on the ground to allow success or social position to sway her attitudes. In the moulding of myself and the shaping of my career she has exercised an influence beyond praise. For all of this I am humbly and everlastingly grateful.

Admission to partnership in the firm gave me needed security and status. In 1935 the name was changed to Kingsmill, Mills, Price & Fleming, which it retained for the next twenty-five years. But now the time had come for me to become more widely known, to broaden and expand my activities and to serve worthy causes.

The church continued to claim first place in my interests and efforts. After singing for two years in the choir of Avenue Road United Church I had renewed regular attendance at Bloor Street Church in the autumn of 1929, and it was to remain spiritual home for nearly forty years. I was general superintendent of the Sunday School for six years. In 1937 I was ordained an elder. The ordination was for life. I served also as a member of the Board of Missions.

Other activities were closely allied to church. In 1927 I had commenced attending the weekly meetings of the Business Men's Noonday Bible Club, for the purpose of Bible study under the leadership of Toronto's best expositors. I took an active part in holding the club together when it was on the point of disintegrating during the Depression because many of our members could not afford to pay one dollar for the lunch at the King Edward Hotel. For my efforts I was elected president and held that office for twenty years. To this day, notwithstanding my removal from Toronto, I continue as the club's honorary president. As president I arranged the various series of Bible studies. This brought me into close or closer contact with some of the great Toronto preachers, such as Dr. Pidgeon, Dr. J.R.P. Sclater, Dr. John McNeill, Canon H.J. Cody, Archbishop Owen, Dr. Trevor Davies, Canon (later Bishop) F.H. Wilkinson, Dr. John Mc-Claurin, Principal McElheran, Professor Coggan (later Archbishop of Canterbury) and others. It was an inestimable privilege to be closely associated with such leaders.

In 1938 I was elected to the board of directors of the Upper Canada Bible Society, and remained a director for twelve years. After serving on various committees I was vice-president for four years, and finally president for three. It was an honour to have a part in the great worldwide work of the British and Foreign Bible Society through its auxiliary in central Ontario.

In 1935 I was asked to advise on the constitution of the Inter-varsity Christian Fellowship. This led to my election to the board of directors on which I served over a decade, including four years as vice-chairman, and five as chairman. The fellowship carried on active evangelical work on the university campuses throughout Canada, and through the Interschool Christian Fellowship in the secondary schools. This admirable work is still expanding in 1984. It has borne much fruit. As chairman of the Camp Committee I played an active role in the acquisition of property on Mary Lake in Muskoka and development thereon of the Pioneer Camps for boys and girls. This work has remained very close to my heart.

I joined Toronto's two outstanding luncheon forums, the Canadian Club and the Empire Club, and availed myself of the most valuable educational opportunities afforded by the speeches week by week on a wide variety of subjects of public interest. I served for a term each as second vice-president and first vice-president of the Canadian Club. The presidency awaited a much later stage of my career. I also served for a term on the executive committee of the Empire Club. I have now been a member of both the Canadian and the Empire Clubs for over half a century. They have performed an enormous service to Toronto and to Canada.

On April 7, 1937, I was initiated into Freemasonry in Ionic

Lodge. Thus commenced one of the most vital relationships of my life. This fraternal bond has enriched my entire life, and given me cause to admire the craft and its members throughout the world.

I joined the League of Nations Society in the early thirties, and gave strong support to its efforts to mobilize public opinion behind the causes of collective security, disarmament, world peace and international justice. I found myself in increasing demand as a speaker on these themes before many forums. Through this admirable organization my first active interest in international affairs was most constructively channelled. The world paid a tragic price for failing to support the League. Its weakness was exposed in 1935 when Mussolini attacked Ethiopia. Be it remembered that Canada dishonourably led the retreat from sanctions against the aggressor.

I joined the Canadian Bar Association immediately after being called to the bar in 1928, and attended its delightful and useful annual meetings when possible. Two of its meetings stand out in my memory, because I made them the occasion of lengthy travel. I was feeling acutely the need of knowing my own country at first hand, and knowing it well. Financial stringency had denied me earlier opportunity to indulge my longing to travel Canada from coast to coast. Until 1936 I had not set foot on the soil of Canada east of Quebec City, or further north than North Bay, or further west than Windsor. Our honeymoon in Bermuda, with visits to New York, Buffalo and Boston, had been my longest travel. In 1936 the Bar Association met in Halifax, and I attended. I went by train to Boston, then by overnight ferry to Yarmouth, thence by rail through the Annapolis valley and the Evangeline country to Halifax. On my way home I was able to see something of New Brunswick. That trip gave me great satisfaction; my horizon had been widened, and I experienced a sense of pride and uplift.

In 1938 the Bar Association met in Vancouver. This gave me the opportunity to cross the prairies and the mountains and view the Pacific. I made stops at Winnipeg, Saskatoon, Edmonton, Jasper Park, Prince Rupert, Vancouver, Victoria, Seattle, Sicomoos, Lake Louise, Banff, Calgary, Regina, Fort William, Port McNichol. I revelled in the beauty and the grandeur of my native land. I have returned to all of these places many times since, but the impact of that first contact was unique. I am glad that the first time I saw the Rockies I was on foot on the ground below gazing up at them in awe. Had I first seen them from above I would have missed the impression of my own utter insignificance and the ephemeral quality of human life in beholding these towering monuments of God's creation, reflecting His eternity. Travel has been one of the great sources of instruction, knowledge and enjoyment throughout my life.

Local travel remained a necessity. After several years of travel by street-car or by good fortune as the guests of friends who owned cars, in 1936 I bought his used car from my brother Gordon. It was a tall Chevrolet sedan with solid disc wheels. For years I had to be content with a used car; it was not until 1946 that I bought my first new car.

By 1939, 24 Anderson Avenue was becoming somewhat snug for us so we went house-hunting. We were incredibly fortunate to buy a fine home at 259 Glencairn Avenue and at a price we could afford. To add to our joy, it was in North Toronto, in Ward 9 and Eglinton riding. I could scarcely believe that I was now a home-owner, and possessed of a very imposing residence in one of the most desirable locations.

Mary was born on August 24 and the move to the new house was accomplished on August 31 while she and Alice were in the hospital. On Sunday morning, September 3, we heard Chamberlain's voice on the radio announce "We are at war." My heart sank.

CHAPTER SEVEN

War Again

The Second World War had its prelude and part of its cause in a series of events which Canada, like Great Britain, watched with inadequate concern: the rise of Hitler to power in 1934, the collapse of the Weimar Republic, Mussolini's successful defiance of the League of Nations in Ethiopia in 1935, the shameful Hoare-Laval treaty, Hitler's occupation of the Rhineland in 1936, his axis with Mussolini, the aloofness of the United States, pacifism and indecision in Britain, deafness of both government and people to the dire warnings of Churchill, Hitler's success in suppressing dissent and persecution of the Jews in Germany without even protest from, and inexcusably often without the knowledge of, the Western world. The march of events carried us inexorably to Munich in 1938.

I listened with feelings approaching despair to the radio reports from Germany and Czechoslovakia that fateful autumn of 1938, as Hitler whipped up the German people to a frenzy over the fictitious reports of persecution of their kinsmen in the Sudetenland as the calm and courageous Czechs prepared to defend their homeland from invasion. War seemed inevitable, and who could predict that it would not engulf Europe and even Canada? Chamberlain's proclamation of peace in our time on his return from Berchtesgaden and Munich and his waving of the piece of paper – "See! I have it on this piece of paper" – all seem so pathetic to us now in the light of subsequent events, but it must be confessed that most people in Britain and in Canada received the news at the time with inexpressible relief. Yet while sharing in the general sense of deliverance, I was among those who entertained feelings of disquiet, anxiety and doubt over the promise of "peace in our time." No one who had reached adult years at the time could ever forget those critical days in the autumn of 1938.

Hitler lost no time in betraying the confidence of his new friends and exposing his contempt for honour, truth and even his own plighted word. The occupation of Austria and then Czechoslovakia exposed the grim reality of Hitler's unprincipled plan to dominate and conquer. Canadians feebly began to ask, "Why did Mackenzie King, our Prime Minister, go to see Hitler in Berlin and praise what he had earlier accomplished in Germany?" Preparations at Ottawa to meet the holocaust which daily became closer and more threatening were slow, hesitant, half-hearted and pitifully inadequate.

On that fateful September morning, Chamberlain's words "We are at war" sounded like the pronouncement of doom. Everything in a moment of time had changed. All that had seemed secure and unshakeable became insecure and shaken to its roots. What was this to mean to Western civilization? What was it to mean to Canada? What was it to mean to my efforts to build a career, to my family, to our new home, to me?

I took David to the hospital that morning to see his mother and his new sister. University Avenue was already filled with squads of men from the Armouries drilling, some in uniform and some in mufti. Passing the Canadian National Exhibition grounds we saw more men at drill. On returning to our new house I wondered now how I would ever be able to pay for it. To have committed myself to such an obligation on the eve of war could spell only financial ruin. In the event, I worried unnecessarily. The real estate market did indeed sag for eight months, then slowly recovered. What appeared at the time to be a dismal blunder proved in the end to be one of the best deals I ever made.

Alice's brother Hal, a former commanding officer of the Toronto Scottish Regiment, was soon called up and served throughout the war at the Officers' Training School at St. Jean, Quebec. Her sister Margery's husband, Don Tow, was adjutant of the same regiment and went overseas with its First Battalion in the autumn of 1939, and later advanced to the rank of brigadier. The arrival in England of Canada's First Division boosted morale both in Canada and England. Two members of my law firm, D'Arcy Kingsmill and Nicol Kingsmill, went overseas. I was needed in the firm more than ever. I took over most of Nicol's work along with my own. These men had all had army experience and held commissions. I had had no military training or connections since I graduated from the Galt Collegiate Cadet Corps in 1921. What should I do? This question began to weigh heavily on my mind.

Poland was quickly overrun by the Wehrmacht, and the Russians occupied the eastern half of the country. The period of the "phoney war" in Western Europe ended suddenly in the spring of 1940 when the German army overran Norway, Denmark, Holland, Luxembourg and Belgium. The north end of the supposedly impregnable Maginot Line was turned, and the German attack divided the British and French armies. General Weygand was called in too late to take supreme command. His assessment of the position was given to the public and chilled our blood: "Militarily the situation is beyond repair." That evening I was cutting the grass in the front lawn, dazed at the thought of what the approaching debacle would mean for us and for our children. The words of Wordsworth ran through my mind,

> It is not to be thought of
> That the flood of British freedom,
> Which to the open sea of the world's praise
> From dark antiquity hath flowed
> With pomp of waters unwithstood,
> Should perish.

The words suddenly seemed so hollow. Was Britain, the bastion of our freedom, to be subjugated by a tyrant? Was freedom to perish from the earth? My mowing of the grass seemed so inconsequential. True, the grass was long, but what mattered grass, streets, homes, books if freedom was to disappear? What mattered a law practice, what mattered even the courts and our renowned rule of law, if we were to become slaves of the Nazis? The phone rang. I rushed in to answer it. On the line was my friend Harold Wright to discuss business pertaining to St. Andrew's Church, Centre Island. That too seemed inconsequential at that moment, and I wondered what was likely to be the fate of the church if our vaunted freedom of worship ended on a gibbet. Harold, who had been born in England, and I discussed the news from the battlefields. "God help England," he said with emotion.

My father died on March 11, 1940. Death was a merciful deliverance from the torture of his sufferings as the cancer spread in his bones and finally into his spine. For six months he had prayed each day that it might be his last. He had expressed to me his sorrow that he would not live to see the fulfilment of the promise of my career. Mother nursed him day and night to the end. She and I were with him at the end. With his passing I became responsible for whatever support Mother might require.

In June I joined the Queen's Own Rifles Regiment of Canada. I had not consulted Alice as directly as I might have, but I knew that in such a matter of conscience she would leave the decision to me. It was natural for Alice's family to wonder why I had not chosen the Toronto Scottish, but with two brothers-in-law and many friends among the senior officers of that unit I thought perhaps I should stand on my own feet elsewhere. The Queen's Own was Canada's second-oldest infantry regiment, and it had a long and honourable history. A friend of mine, Baptist Johnston, had just been appointed commanding officer of a new battalion, the Second, the First having been placed on active service and dispatched to Newfoundland and Bermuda on guard duty en route to England. I presented myself to Bap, and he immediately took me on strength – as a rifleman, the lowest rank in a rifle regiment. I had no assurance of a commission. Members of the new battalion joined for service in Canada. It was part of Canada's NPAM, Non-Permanent Active Militia.

I did not sleep that night. I was assailed by questions as to what would become of Alice, of David and Mary, and of my mother if I were called up for service overseas. If I remained a rifleman there was no possibility of maintaining my home on my army pay. I did not feel like a hero. Having taken the step, however, I was determined to put forward my best effort.

I was soon selected to attend the NCO school and a little later given a provisional commission. The battalion turned out for training on Monday and Wednesday evenings and numerous weekends. I attended the District Camp at Niagara-on-the-Lake for a fortnight in each of the summers, 1940, 1941 and 1942. As well, I attended the regimental school, passed the exams, completed my qualifications and was promoted to first lieutenant. The classrooms at Osgoode Hall were placed at the disposal of the regimental school. Thus, by the strangest coincidence after twelve years I found myself back sitting in the same seat in the same classroom as in my final year at the Law School.

For two years I commanded Platoon 9 in "A" Company, then was transferred to Headquarter Company, and placed in command of Platoons 2 and 3. I became a lecturer on poison gas, a suitable appointment, I suppose, for an aspiring politician, and on army organization. I became vice-president of the officers' mess, and chairman of the regimental canteen. It was not my choice of military war-winning responsibilities, checking on the supply and sales of chocolate bars and soft drinks.

In April 1942 the battalion was called up for overseas service, and about 40 per cent of the strength volunteered to go. I knew this choice was coming, and I faced a weighty decision. Donald had just been born; I was a month short of my thirty-seventh birthday. My responsibilities within my family and to the law firm were greater than ever before. I did not "step forward" on the parade floor. Later that evening in the mess I went to Dick Sankey, who had been appointed commanding officer of the new battalion, and asked, "Dick, where do I fit into your battalion?" He in turn asked, "How old are you?" I explained that I would be thirty-seven within a month. He said "I'm afraid there is no place for you. We're not taking platoon officers over twenty-seven years of age." Thus ended any thought of overseas service. Later I was offered a pen-pushing job at headquarters in Ottawa, but concluded that what I was doing was just as important as an office job in uniform in the capital. The appointment went to another first lieutenant, who remained in that rank until the end of the war. His experience did not confer great importance on the position.

I became acting second-in-command of Headquarter Company, and I enjoyed serving there under Major Barnum. My relations with Bap Johnston, however, became strained. I am convinced that it is often unwise for two friends in civil life to place themselves in the position of commander and subordinate in military life. I concluded that my best course was to transfer to the Corps Reserve of Officers. I regretted leaving my fellow officers and the men under my command, but it had become clear that the battalion would now play only a very limited training role for the balance of the war.

The war found me in a military sense at an awkward age. My role in the army was not altogether glorious, but I am glad that I did have even this limited part. I helped to train men who fought and died on the battlefields of northwestern Europe. A number of my younger fellow officers also gave their lives. I salute the Queen's Own Rifles of Canada, and I proudly echo the regimental slogan, "Once in the Queen's Own always in the Queen's Own."

CHAPTER EIGHT

Initiation into Politics –
Board of Education

Politics was in my blood. I can scarcely contemplate any possibility of having passed through life without having committed myself in full measure to the joys and sorrows of political life.

From early boyhood I became conscious of public affairs, governments and political parties, Liberal and Conservative. I had the advantage of being reared in a home where there were frequent discussions of political affairs. My mother was staunchly Conservative; my father Liberal. I had no difficulty in adopting Mother's side of the arguments. There were many of them. Sir Wilfrid Laurier was almost worshipped by Liberals. A photograph of his boasted "Cabinet of all the talents" adorned the home of my grandfather David Fleming in Cobourg. I well remember the Reciprocity Election of 1911, Laurier's fall, and the rise to power of Borden. Then came the war, and in 1917 the Union Government and its triumph on the conscription issue. The Conservatives under Sir Robert Borden had led Canada during the war, but by 1919 a strong reaction had set in against them both in Ottawa and in Ontario. That year the Conservatives in Ontario, led by Sir William Hearst, went down to defeat before a conglomeration of newcomers calling themselves variously United Farmers of Ontario and Labour. Then in the election of December 1921 the voters decisively rejected the federal Conservatives under Arthur Meighen and elected Mackenzie King and his Liberals. The Conservatives retained only fifty seats. It was not a popular time to be a Conservative, and it was destined not to be the last of such times.

No one is born with a ready-made political philosophy. It is developed out of thought, reading, discussion, study and experience. I do not quite know how or when my own philosophy reached the completion of its development; I do know, however, that relatively early in life I had formed a political philosophy and that it guided, and at times perhaps even dictated, my approach to political issues. A politician must be a pragmatist, but he dare not be a mere will-o'-the-wisp. I have always looked upon mere expediency as a treacherous and unworthy guide to political decisions. In serving the public a man must have principles and convictions and be loyal to them. How else can he hope to maintain his honesty and his self-respect?

Before I reached university or identified myself with the Conservative party or later took to the hustings or engaged in election organizing chores in my riding I had formed a view of Canadian politics and history. I looked upon Laurier as a respected Canadian who had, however, proven unequal to the great issues of 1911 and 1917. I saw Borden as a statesman. I considered Meighen a great parliamentarian and man of character who, though lacking the tactical cleverness of a Howard Ferguson, was made by lesser men to pay a dreadful price – indeed was politically crucified – for honest and necessary service to his country. Mackenzie King I came to regard as an adroit, shifty, often ruthless and unprincipled partisan manoeuverer to whom success alone mattered. My politics were not too theoretical; they were rather "applied" and practical in their approach.

I was intensely Canadian, but very conscious of our debt to the mother country, a firm believer in parliamentary democracy, the constitutional monarchy, the party system and the rule of law. I was profoundly interested in history and drew political instruction from it. But a man can possess these attributes and beliefs, yet deliberately abstain from involvement in any form of public life. I was well aware of the weaknesses of democracy, the short view, the brief memory and seeming ingratitude often exhibited by the sovereign electorate. I also understood the harsh demands of the public life, the sacrifices it imposes. How then did I come to sacrifice my family's interests, to prejudice my career at the bar, to forgo material gain for the illusory and phantom rewards of public service?

I was early taught to respect public duty. "The vocation of every man and woman," wrote Tolstoy, "is to serve the people." I had no intention of being an ungrateful freeloader enjoying the priceless benefits of citizenship and the franchise at the expense of others. I accepted without hesitation Edmund Burke's famous dictum, "All that is necessary for the triumph of evil is that good men do nothing." Appeals to a sense of public spirit and public duty were ever my Achilles' heel.

And with all the imperfections of democracy, I was bound to recognize that we Canadians are profoundly fortunate that we have inherited the best form of democratic government from England. We have been largely spared the struggles by which institutions, conventions and traditions were evolved over the centuries at Westminster to safeguard freedom. We have succeeded to a living and invaluable heritage. We are the heirs of Simon de Montfort, Pym, Hampden, Walpole, the Pitts, Burke, Fox, Russell, Disraeli, Gladstone and a host of men who fashioned the Mother of Parliaments. While our parliamentary institutions are thoroughly British in their origin, form, purpose and operation all Canadians can count ourselves blessed that our French-speaking compatriots proved themselves readily and totally adaptable to institutions that were essentially British. French-speaking Canadians took to British parliamentary institutions like ducks to water, and Canada has produced some outstanding French-speaking parliamentarians.

I was a lad of only fourteen when Sir Robert Borden led Canada to nationhood in 1919. Little did I dream that one day I would become the owner of his Hansard library, the gift of his nephew, my friend Henry Borden. Each volume contains the Borden coat of arms. Its motto is written in French, "Avauncez lentement" (advance slowly). It is a compendium of conservative philosophy. My approach was simple: let us by all means have change, but not merely for the sake of change. Before we tamper with what has been tried and proven let us be very sure that the proposed change will assure improvement. If it will, let us lose no time in making it. Our goal should be steady progress, not mere changes by fits and starts.

Confederation made it possible for Canada to become a great nation spanning half a continent. Both federal and provincial levels of government command the highest importance. No one who is committed to a public career or party activity in Canada dare ignore either of them. From the outset, however, my interest was devoted principally to the federal sphere. Somehow, to me it offered much more challenge.

My initiation into political activity began early. In the spring of 1926 the customs scandal brought Mackenzie King to the verge of defeat in the House. He avoided that fate by asking the Governor General, Lord Byng, for a dissolution. Byng declined on the ground that Arthur Meighen was entitled to an opportunity to form a government. King then resigned, Meighen formed a government which was defeated by several votes, and we were plunged into another general election campaign. King's dubious tactics had one consequence which he could not have foreseen: it brought me out on the hustings for the first time.

I was just twenty-one, and through the recommendation of Alex Edwards, our MP in Galt, I was given an opportunity to participate in the campaign. I was given $20 for travelling expenses, sent up to North Bruce to support Colonel Hugh Clark, and asked to report on Labour Day at Wiarton to Reeve Byers. There were two trains per day from Toronto to Wiarton. It did not dawn on me that there would be any political meetings on the holiday, so I played tennis and took the late train to Wiarton, arriving at 11 p.m. I was puzzled to find no one at the station to meet me, but made my way to the hotel carrying a heavy suitcase. The day had been hot, so I made the trip wearing my sailor straw hat and carrying no overcoat. I had scarcely arrived when the winds began to blow off Georgian Bay and the mercury dropped sharply. Bitterly cold weather pursued me all week.

I presented myself next morning to Reeve Byers, whose reception of me was as chilly as the weather. "Where were you yesterday?" he asked gruffly. "We held two meetings last night, and we had advertised you as speaker at both of them." I was appalled. I had let the party down. What a way to launch a career in politics!

It seemed a little presumptuous for a young law student who had never cast a vote himself to tell the mature farmers of North Bruce how they should vote, but there was no turning back. I had five more nights to redeem myself and there were one or two meetings each night scattered the length of the Bruce peninsula. At these I arrived in a topcoat borrowed from Reeve Byers and my straw hat. The coat reached to the ground. I must have presented a comical sight.

At most of our meetings I was billed as the principal speaker. I hewed to the party line, and I delivered it with conviction. One of the local speakers was a dentist, who was impressed by my oratorical efforts. The third evening we were together he sought to pay me a compliment in his speech, but he became slightly confused. What he said was, "I have heard Mr. Fleming speak these past two evenings, and I want to tell you that I've never yet seen such a young head on such old shoulders."

One evening we were addressed by George Spotton from Huron County. He was a great stump speaker. Some years later he was himself elected to Parliament. Another evening we arrived at the Orange Hall to find that the Liberals had also rented it for their meeting. The problem was resolved by uniting the two meetings and holding a debate. I think I did better than hold my own with the Liberal spokesman. On the final evening we covered several meetings, and the speakers leap-frogged. One of them was a newcomer who had just arrived from Toronto, to which he had recently moved from his native Nova Scotia. His name was Colonel J. Keiller McKay. He and I were destined to become close friends in the course of his very distinguished career at the bar, on the Bench and as Lieutenant-Governor of Ontario.

After our final meeting on Saturday night the local Liberal organizer drove me back to Toronto. Reeve Byers was quite disturbed about my accepting a lift from a Liberal. "Don't give him any of our secrets," he admonished. I assured him I would not, because I knew no secrets.

The Liberal organizer told me an interesting story about Mackenzie King's recent visit to the area. After the election meeting there was a dance. King was drinking after the meeting when he heard about the dance and wanted to go to it. The organizers thought he was in no fit condition to go, and endeavoured to dissuade him. Someone said, "It's only a square dance, Mr. King. You wouldn't like that." "Square dance?" replied King. "We'll damn soon take the corners off."

On election day I scrutineered in a poll on Queen Street for Colonel Reg Geary, Minister of Justice, our candidate in Trinity. When all the ballots were counted Geary had gone down to defeat, Hugh Clark had gone down to defeat, Meighen had gone down to defeat. My efforts had produced impressive, though not desirable, results.

I took no part in the provincial election in 1929 because I did not support the Conservative government's policy on the sale of liquor. I was given no part in the federal election of 1930, but exulted in the return of a Conservative government to office under R.B. Bennett – just in time, alas, to take the blame for the Great Depression. In the federal election of 1935 I again campaigned for the party, speaking at Stirling, Wolfe Island, and other small places. The Bennett government was defeated. My record remained consistent.

In the autumn of 1933 Alice and I moved into Eglinton riding, and I joined the Progressive Conservative Association. In the 1935 federal election I canvassed my district and acted as a scrutineer on polling day; in the 1937 provincial election I worked hard as a district organizer for our candidate, Leslie Blackwell, but we lost. By this time I was recognized in the riding organization as a veteran and active party worker. I was blissfully unaware, however, that events were shaping a stage for me.

My friend Grant Gordon, QC, and I had just completed our labours as joint organizers of the area west of Yonge Street and south of Eglinton Avenue in the provincial election in the autumn of 1937. One evening he said to me, "Don, have you ever considered municipal politics?" I flatly replied that I had never entertained any thought whatever of entering politics at the municipal level. He continued, "Dr. Spaulding, the senior of our two school trustees in Ward Nine, is retiring. You should run to fill the vacancy. You'd get a lot of support. Think it over."

I was dazed at the suggestion. I almost laughed it off. My father by this time was an alderman in Galt, but I simply had taken no part, or, indeed, interest in municipal politics in Toronto. I arrested my first negative inclination and proceeded to discuss the situation with Dr. Spaulding, Laurie Wallace, the other trustee, my father, and some of the leading party figures in the riding. Fortunately, Eglinton riding, provincial and federal, and Toronto Ward Nine were identical. From everyone I received encouragement to run. I consulted my partners and won a reluctant acquiescence on their part. The pressure began to build up. Some of the school principals and caretakers called me and urged me to announce my candidature. Party politics were taboo municipally, and I was definitely warned that the Conservative organization in the riding could take no official part in the campaign, but I was also told that I could count on the personal and active support of many of our party workers. Nowhere did the idea encounter opposition, but I still had difficulty making a decision. In the end the decision was made for me. On November 2, at the annual municipal night of the Eglinton Riding Women's Progressive Conservative Association, the chairman, on seeing me present, announced, "Our own candidate Donald Fleming is here. He is a candidate for the Board of Control." There was nothing left for me to do at that point but to go to the platform, announce firmly and definitely that I was a candidate for the Board of Education, not the Board of Control, and ask the support of each one of the ladies present. My campaign had begun.

It did not take me long to discover that it was a one-man campaign. There was no formal organization behind me. I had no funds, and I was a newcomer, largely unknown. I called on the editors of three newspapers, which were accustomed to publish slates of their recommendations for election. It was vitally important to win a place on their slates. I prepared a short

78

biographical memorandum and letters for friends to send to their friends and acquaintances in the riding. The response was amazing. Many friends, even those with no political connections, came forward to sign and send the letters. I visited all fourteen schools in the riding, always met the principal and the caretaker, and as many teachers as possible. In the cases of schools which had a Home and School Association I made contact with the association, and in some cases was permitted to address the executive. The campaign proceeded without a hitch. At one meeting another candidate complained that I was flooding the riding with letters. This was the best possible news, for it proved that my mail campaign was reaching the electors. Polling day was Monday, December 6. A week ahead of it the newspapers published their slates. To my delight I won endorsement on every slate. The *Globe and Mail* referred to me as "one of the most brilliant students ever to graduate from the University of Toronto," and said I had a great contribution to make to the Board of Education.

On December 6 I made the rounds of all the polls, and greeted the deputy returning officers and poll clerks. As I watched the voters flocking to the polls, particularly in the late afternoon, I began to have a sinking feeling. What could the great majority of these good people possibly know about me, and how could they be expected to vote for a man they did not know? As the returns came in that evening to my joy and shocked amazement I headed the poll by a large margin, and received the highest vote given to any candidate in any of the nine city wards. This gave me the right to break any tie vote in the Board of Education by casting a second vote in that event. The news was incredible. In the city of my adoption, Canada's second-largest city, I had suddenly sprung into prominence.

I soon found that I had become a marked man. Other school trustees telephoned me with congratulations and requests for my support for election to certain committees or chairmanships. I was literally inundated with messages of congratulation from supporters, friends and acquaintances. I saw to it that everyone who had assisted in my election in any way whatever received a prompt personal letter of thanks.

The inaugural meeting of the Board of Education was a full-dress affair. Like the other men I appeared in white tie and tails. The new members were introduced and welcomed. I was elected to the Administration Committee, which was my choice. The Board of Education had its own building on College Street. It was an excellent structure. The board members sat around a horseshoe table in an attractive-looking chamber with a public gallery. I was seated between John Weir, a Communist, and May Robinson, a new trustee and strong Conservative. She and I became very good friends. The board met in the evenings twice a month. Committee meetings were usually held at 4 p.m. I was able to keep my absences from the office under reasonable control, which was very necessary if my partners were not to become dissatisfied. I never missed a meeting of either the board or a committee on which I was serving.

There was no remuneration for trustees, but cars were provided for their use on board business. I never rode in a board car; indeed, I introduced a motion that this privilege be abolished. It was soundly defeated. Quite understandably, members liked to be driven to schools, board meetings and public functions by a chauffeur in an official car. But my motion at least established in the minds of the public and the press that I was economy-minded.

Another measure which I sponsored took on a controversial aspect. In a wave of pacifism some years earlier, cadet training in the Toronto schools had been abolished. In 1938 the Canadian Corps of Signals asked for permission to encourage male students in the senior grades to take training in wireless and line communications with the corps. It was a sensible constructive proposal, and I sponsored it. The pacifists immediately denounced it as the thin edge of the wedge for the return of cadet training. My motion was defeated, and some of the ladies in the Women Electors' Association expressed strong disapproval of my stand. A year later we were at war.

Much of the work of the Board of Education is of a routine nature. The content of education is determined by the provincial Department of Education; the board is concerned with the provision of facilities, the hiring of competent teachers and other staff, and the inevitable problem of meeting the cost. At that juncture in Depression days the teachers and caretakers were regarded as among the most fortunate groups in the community because they had security and their salary scales had never been reduced. The scales in my opinion were not unduly generous, nor were the annual increments, and I defended both. I always held in high regard the importance of the role of the teacher. In the eleven public schools and three secondary schools in North Toronto I considered we had teaching staffs and principals of very high quality and I did not hesitate to say so publicly.

The board had an inflexible rule that men must retire at sixty-five, and women at sixty-two from all teaching and administrative positions. I thought this discriminated against women, and I sponsored an amendment to allow women to continue at their option to sixty-five. This was opposed by the senior administrative officials and some principals, all of whom were men, and the motion was defeated. This did not alter my opinion that pensions were not sufficiently generous to alleviate a palpable injustice to women teachers.

Membership on the Board of Education provides an unexcelled opportunity for making contact with the public and for instruction in the essential art of public relations. Whenever invited I attended functions in the fourteen schools of North Toronto, whether of pupils, parents or Home and School Associations. The annual commencement exercises (graduation) in the three large secondary schools were major events in the community, attended by nearly a thousand parents, and I attended them with unfailing regularity, assisting in the presentation of diplomas and awards, and making congratulatory speeches. I always enjoyed these contacts with students, parents and teachers.

The term of municipal office at that time was one year. I look back with pleasure and satisfaction on that year of 1938, the first I spent in public office. I learned much from it, concerning what might be called the techniques of democracy, of public life, and of elections. I became conscious of growing facility and effectiveness in the art of debate and in the kindred art of delivering public speeches, and this fed an ambition of which I was becoming increasingly aware.

I never operated in a more pleasant medium of public life. It is true that I was at the beck and call of the public, and sometimes the telephone calls came at awkward times. There was, of course, the occasional irate parent complaining that his blameless child had been undeservingly punished. Happily, however, education still holds an exalted place in the public regard. In the contentious and controversial years which were to follow, I confess that there were times when I wished I had remained on the board. After another couple of years I might have hoped to become chairman. That I consider an office of great honour and distinction, which I would have been proud to serve.

I have clung to my connection with the schools. Throughout the next quarter of a century I continued to attend the annual commencement exercises of my three big secondary schools, North Toronto Collegiate, Northern Vocational School and Lawrence Park Collegiate, to take part in the presentation of diplomas and awards. I always looked forward to these events with zest. They brought me very close to parents, students and teachers. Whatever the occasion of a meeting in school premises I never failed to search out the caretaker and to greet him as a friend. Alice has often said that I was invariably the last person to leave the building after I had assisted the caretaker with his tidying-up duties.

Many a time since that happy year I have asked myself the question: why didn't I have sense enough to stay on the Board of Education?

CHAPTER NINE

Alderman

Circumstances often have an unexplainable way of determining decisions and events and the timing of them. In the autumn of 1938, I expected to be a candidate for re-election to the Board of Education. Ward Nine, like the other eight, had its quota of two aldermen, Bill Croft and Mr. Ellis. Croft was considered to be on his way up to the Board of Control in due time. Mr. Ellis was elderly; he had held his seat for many years. I had entertained no thought whatever of seeking election to the City Council. Little did I realize that I would soon be a candidate, and that I would be elected, not once only, but for six consecutive terms. How did it all come about?

In October Bill Croft announced he would run for Board of Control. A vacancy thus opened up. My friend Colonel H.O. Hollinrake called me and expressed his desire to run for election, but stated he would not do so if I ran for council. At that point I indicated I would be little interested, but added that I would give thought to the question. News travelled swiftly, and soon I was sitting uncomfortably on the horns of a dilemma. Calls came from school principals, teachers and others urging me not to forsake the Board of Education; on the other hand there were political workers urging me not to allow the opportunity for advancement to pass. If some new candidate were elected I might find it difficult to break in at a later date after he had become established and when there would be no vacancy. I had to make the decision. Finally I decided to run. Once again, my law partners reluctantly gave their consent. I had given up the security of the board, with the virtual certainty of being re-elected, to plunge into a contest with an uncertain outcome and offering a somewhat doubtful prize. To add to the uncertainty, I soon found that I was not the only person training an eye on the vacancy. John Innes, a popular Scot and retired builder, who had been defeated in a previous aldermanic contest, announced his candidature. There was no turning back. I set to work conducting exactly the same type of campaign that had produced such successful results the year before. Out came the letters, the biographical memoranda, the blotters and even several billboards. I called on the same friends for assistance, descended on the editors of the three newspapers seeking their endorsement, and made speeches at the municipal night of the same organizations as a year earlier.

This time there were two differences. First, all Separate School supporters were now included in the electorate I faced. Second, I encountered strong opposition from the Liberal editor of a little weekly newspaper, the *North Toronto Herald*. He had supported me the previous year, and he was strongly supporting Bill Croft. He hated anything related to the Conservative party. He imagined that the party was backing my candidature officially, and he ignored assurances from the president of our riding association that the party organization was taking no part in the campaign. He attacked me with anything that would serve his purpose, but particularly on the ground that I was not a homeowner. I was pictured as a kind of fly-by-night opportunist. He even seized on the fact I attended a church outside the riding to prove that I had no real attachment to Ward Nine. Besides, he was a Roman Catholic, and I was facing Roman Catholic electors for the first time. I did not know whether he had any following or influence among them, but I made it my business to make a personal call on the priests who were pastors of the two large Catholic parishes in the Ward. I was courteously received by them.

Election day had been moved to January 1, 1939. This lengthened the campaign by four weeks, and obliged candidates to spend the Christmas season campaigning. It also sent them into the New Year worn out by the campaign. The theory that electors would turn out in larger numbers to vote on the holiday proved to be a myth.

The publication of the newspaper slates gave me an enormous boost. I was picked for first place by all three. Equally important was the fact that they divided support for the other aldermanic post between the other two candidates. The weather on election day was inclement and the turnout of voters light. That evening the results came in by radio. I had headed the poll in Ward Nine by a comfortable margin, and among the eighteen elected candidates in the city's nine wards I had the second-largest vote. Only Ernie Bray, a popular alderman of some years' standing in Ward

Eight, had a higher vote, and that by a small margin. The sheer exhilaration of that victory had to be experienced to be understood.

I remained alderman for Ward Nine for six years. There were six elections in those six years. Victory is almost always thrilling, but none of the other five could match the first in excitement. As the years passed I could no longer submit myself as the promising young newcomer; I had to run on my record, and that is a less exciting position to be in. John Innes was my colleague throughout all six years, and we had no personal difficulties or differences. In 1940 I again headed the poll in a three-way contest. In 1941 he and I were given an acclamation. This was a welcome relief from the rigours of campaigning, but I lived to regret it. I never again succeeded in whipping up my workers to maximum effort. No matter how hard I had worked during the year they became lackadaisical through over-confidence. John Innes was elected in first place, and I in second, in 1942, 1943 and 1944.

I was urged to run for the Board of Control each year, but declined. It demanded almost full-time service, and I had stretched my partners' forbearance to the limit attending to my time-consuming aldermanic duties. Nathan Phillips, later mayor, told me repeatedly in later years that I should have remained at the City Hall until I had become mayor, and that I would then have gone to Ottawa with much more prestige. Of course, I would have regarded it as a high honour to be mayor of Toronto, but that would have meant giving up my place in the firm with such security as went with it, and I had a family to feed, clothe and educate. Economic necessity closed the doors of the Board of Control and the mayor's office to me.

The stipends paid at that time to members of council bore little resemblance to those of 1984. Aldermen received $1,200 per annum, controllers $5,000, and the mayor $11,500. Chairmen of committees received an extra $100 per annum and a preferred seat in the council chamber. For my six years' service, including the chairmanship of three standing committees, I received a total of $7,500. All of this went into the coffers of the firm. My appointed share of the firm's profits no doubt rose more slowly because of giving so much time and attention to my aldermanic responsibilities.

Council met regularly twice a month. Meetings began at 2 p.m., often did not end until past midnight. Committees met also in the afternoons, and there was an average of over one per week. The reading of lengthy agendas and reports occupied considerable time on alternate weekends. There were many phone calls, and numerous persons seeking an interview; an alderman is never far removed from his electors.

The atmosphere in council was much more contentious than in the Board of Education. For the last four years of my six Lewis Duncan was a member of the Board of Control. In his attitude toward his colleagues and the city officials he was venomous, often abusing his privileged position to make the most outrageous charges against them. All semblance of restraint in the conduct of city business disappeared with the arrival of Duncan on the scene. Our former friendship, always somewhat guarded, now disappeared.

In 1939 we had two Communists on the council, Stewart Smith and Joe Salsberg. They were both good speakers. Smith in particular was an excellent debater with an acid tongue. It was bound to be only a matter of time before he and I clashed. Joe, on the other hand, was most personable, with a ready wit and a keen sense of humour. Soon after the Russian attack on Poland in September 1939 the leading Communists all went underground. Evidently anticipating internment they simply disappeared for two years. Soon after the forging of our common cause with Russia following Hitler's attack on her, the Canadian Communists emerged from their hiding. As Russia stopped the Wehrmacht at Stalingrad and Leningrad the Communists became popular heroes in the eyes of some electors, and Smith and Salsberg returned to council, this time accompanied by two other Communists. They were able to make their presence felt in the debates. Their entire time appeared to be devoted to their aldermanic activities, and they often delayed committee meetings interminably. Nevertheless, and in spite of all differences, Stewart and Joe, on the one hand, and I on the other, retained a sincere respect and a personal liking for each other. To encounter Joe on the street-corner was always an occasion for a chat. After serving on the Board of Control Stewart broke with the Communist Party, as did Joe.

Every ward was represented by one alderman on each of the five standing committees of council. John Innes and I always reached harmonious agreement on the distribution. The Legislation Committee attracted the lawyers, of whom there were not a few, and I served on it for the full six years. The two heaviest committees were those on Works and Property. I sat on the Property Committee for two years, and became its chairman in 1940. I then sat on the Works Committee for the next four years, and was its chairman in 1942. That was the senior position in the council. In my last two years, 1943 and 1944, I also sat on the

Welfare Committee, and was its chairman in 1944. I never missed a meeting of either council or any committee of which I was a member in the entire six years.

I represented the council for several years on the Claims Commission, dealing with claims of all kinds against the city, and became its chairman. I also represented the Works Committee on the Traffic Conference and was its chairman for two years. It was composed of representatives of various organizations, led by the Board of Trade, and dealt with traffic problems and improvements. In 1942 I served as one of council's representatives on the board of directors of the Canadian National Exhibition. This I valued as an outstanding honour and experience. I have always been a strong supporter of the CNE, and I formed a very high opinion of the contribution to its success made by the businessmen and civic leaders who composed its board and committees. For six years I represented the council on the board of trustees of the Toronto General Hospital. In this responsibility I took a very keen interest. It was one of the best and best-run boards on which I have ever sat.

When war came in September 1939 council was immediately called into a special meeting. It was the most sombre meeting of council I ever attended. We could do little but pass resolutions affirming our loyalty and our unshakeable belief in the righteousness of our cause. The war naturally had the effect of progressively reducing the public's interest in municipal affairs.

Newspaper writers have said that I was one of the best speakers who ever sat on the Toronto City Council. I certainly took an active part in the debates, and enjoyed doing so. I never went to a council or committee meeting unprepared. I read the advance material thoroughly, decided what my stand ought to be on each of the scores of items, and selected one to be the subject of a speech. By not speaking too frequently and concentrating my oratory on one major subject I hoped to secure better publicity and a more attentive hearing.

Five major debates stand out in my memory. The first occurred in 1939 after I had first taken my seat, and it established me in the eyes of the council and the press as a formidable debater. The two Communists in the council were making great headway. Many members were becoming afraid to cross swords with Stewart Smith in debate. I had a call one day from General Dennis Draper, the chief of police, who wished to show me his department's file on Smith. It contained a record of Smith's Communist activities, particularly in earlier days in the Young Pioneers and his writings derisively lampooning Christian be-

liefs in a most offensive manner. I agreed with General Draper
that this record ought to be exposed, and that this should be done
in council. I prepared carefully and bided my time until the opportunity presented itself one Monday afternoon. I began quietly
and slowly, then opened up on Smith and the activities of the
Communists in Toronto. After forty minutes I sat down to thunderous applause. As a power in debate in council I was made. I
should add that Stewart Smith sat through the entire performance without any attempt at interruption. At the conclusion I
moved over to where he sat and assured him there was nothing
personal in what I had to say. He smiled, thanked me and generously congratulated me on my speech. Six months later the two
Communist aldermen went underground.

When the Nazis marched into Czechoslovakia I introduced a
motion that the city cease buying goods produced in Germany.
Mayor Ralph Day, an able man who spoiled many a good performance by truculence, immediately committed the blunder of ruling my motion out of order. I appealed his ruling, and it was sustained. As a result I drew front-page publicity, and Day hurt
himself severely. Six months later we were at war.

Welfare was always a knotty problem, and the administration
of the Welfare Department was a running source of contention.
Mrs. Adelaide Plumptre had tried repeatedly to convince council
to create a Standing Committee on Welfare, but the Board of
Control had fought like tigers to retain authority over administration of the department. I strongly supported Mrs. Plumptre in
what looked like a lost cause. When Lewis Duncan became a
member of the Board of Control he took a special delight in attacking and harassing Bert Laver, the Commissioner of Welfare.
One evening in council he opened up a ferocious attack on Laver,
accusing him of wrongdoing in relation to some shortages of
clothing and shoes in the department's stores. The other members of the Board of Control made a poor and half-hearted defence
of their oversight of the Department of Welfare and its administration. At 3 a.m. I saw my opportunity. I rose and moved the
appointment of a Standing Committee on Welfare. It carried by
an overwhelming majority. Duncan's teeth had been pulled, and
a major step forward in the civic administration had been taken.
Welfare ceased to be a political football, and Laver received fair
hearings and just treatment. I think I can claim the major credit
for lifting welfare out of the realm of political exploitation.

The next year another debate arose out of Duncan's oppor-
tunism and attempt to malign the city officials. The debate was
on the budget. Duncan accused two of the most respected offi-

88

cials, R.C. (Roly) Harris, Commissioner of Works, and George Weale, City Clerk, of embezzlement and falsification of figures. They were present and the gallery was full throughout this shameful tirade. The other members of the Board of Control were too weak or cowardly to answer Duncan, so I stepped into the breach. I rose to the defence of the officials, and answered every charge made by Duncan. My words that day bit like sharp teeth. Duncan's attack collapsed. Both Harris and Weale thanked me in tears. Roy Greenaway, veteran reporter of the *Toronto Daily Star*, said to me afterward, "I have heard many speeches. Never in all my life have I heard one man give another man such hell as you have given Duncan today, and do it in such a gentlemanly manner."

The last important debate occurred on the budget in my final year. The Board of Control was playing politics to appear to oppose an increase in taxes, while in effect opposing elimination or reduction of expenditure. As council could add or increase items only by a two-thirds majority the board put council to the sheer and stupid futility of meeting every morning for a week to accomplish nothing. After several days of this make-believe I had had enough. To the surprise of everyone, especially the controllers, I jumped to my feet, saying: "This farce has gone far enough." Then I laid the rod on the back of the Board of Control.

My most lasting contribution to civic government was in the field of town planning and housing. Desultory efforts had been made previously at various times to create planning organizations, but without enduring consequences. Backed by the Board of Trade I took up the cause in council. We already had a planning office at city hall with Tracy Lemay as commissioner, and numerous members of council were dubious about the whole new enterprise. Council in 1942 did give somewhat hesitant approval and appointed the City Planning Board of seven members, six from outside council and myself. I was to be the connecting link between the Planning Board and council, and spokesman for each to the other. The board set up its offices outside City Hall and recruited its own staff. After nearly two years of devoted effort it completed its master plan and a monumental report. It proposed many works which have since come into being, including the Yonge Street subway, the Gardiner Expressway, Highway 401 and a multitude of other programs which have proved of lasting benefit. It became my responsibility to win the support of council and also of the public. I made numerous public speeches explaining and defending the plan and the report, and acceptance had been won before I left council at the end of 1944. By that time many people were showing interest in long-term city planning, and the provincial government was supporting it. I was invited to take part in conferences called at that level. By this time I was becoming known as something of an authority on planning. On invitation I delivered a two-hour lecture at the University of Toronto on planning legislation.

The City Planning Board also included housing within the scope of its studies and its recommendations. We took trips to New York, Boston and other places in the course of our investigations. The board's report contained a sweeping recommendation in favour of redevelopment of the downtown area bounded by Parliament, Gerrard, River and Dundas streets as a beginning, and construction of public housing there. This monumental rehousing and planning effort was carried to completion in due time. The board built upon the pioneering studies conducted by the Bruce Commission of some years earlier. The value and the weaknesses of existing federal housing legislation were demonstrated by the board's efforts. Looking back I am very gratified to have played a role of leadership in relation to housing in Toronto, particularly in the struggle to eliminate slums and substandard housing.

Undoubtedly there was more excitement in council than on the Board of Education; there was also more personal rivalry among the members. The more publicity I attracted and the more deeply I became involved in civic affairs, the more concerned I became about the attitude of my law partners and the serious economic risks I was taking with my professional future. It seemed to many of my friends – and, I confess, even to myself at times – that I was imperilling my family's future for the uncertain rewards of serving the public.

The public can be a hard taskmaster, as every person serving it will learn. The phone calls came at all hours, and at times that were embarrassing both at the office and at home. People when they telephone their alderman do not like to be put off and told that he is too busy to come to the phone. Of all public servants the alderman in my experience is the closest to his electorate. He is never further away than the nearest telephone or doorbell. I began to wonder if there wasn't some other avenue through which I could serve the public.

The decision to seek the Conservative nomination in Eglinton riding was made in 1944. Six years' service was long enough as alderman, and it was obvious that if I was to remain at City Hall I must seek advancement to the mayor's chair. It was more than I could possibly afford to continue to give at that stage of my life and career. So I chose the federal arena, but it was a hard decision. I was appalled at the thought that I would be throwing away much of the expertise that I had toiled to gather on municipal affairs and city planning, and that others would reap where I had industriously sowed. While I was known to be a committed Conservative I had never allowed partisanship to enter into my public actions or my campaigns. I was now about to squander goodwill of my electors in order to plunge into party politics to the hilt. My decision led to wide expressions of regret that I was forsaking municipal service, not least of all from the senior city officials, for whom I entertained a very high regard, and who had seen many aldermen come and go.

My partners were divided on the question, but gave reluctant permission. Alice had become reconciled to my course; it had been hanging over her head for a long time. Family circumstances were not favourable. The children were seven, five and two years of age. Following my father's death my mother had moved from Galt to North Toronto to be near us. She was seventy years of age. I was thirty-nine, an age when I was ready for a major professional advance. With all these concerns and responsibilities I sometimes wonder to this day how I came to place my family and my career in jeopardy and to seek election to Parliament. At least if I had been satisfied with a career in provincial politics I would have been much closer to my family and my practice at all times, and the sessions of the legislature were appreciably shorter than those of Parliament. But I took the decision and never looked back.

I learned much from my municipal experience, which I was able to put to use in later years. Indeed, when I took my place in the House of Commons I soon concluded that the Toronto City Council had been excellent training ground for my new responsibilities. In those years nowhere better could have been found to learn the rules of order, the technique of debate, and the paramount duty of serving the public.

CHAPTER TEN

Conservative Party Activist

While I kept party politics out of my municipal service I did not keep them out of my life. On the contrary, in those seven years from 1938 to 1944 I was becoming increasingly active in the Conservative party, its organization, its affairs and its policies.

In 1935 the Bennett government had sustained a devastating defeat at the polls, and the Conservative party had gone into the wilderness of opposition from which it was not to emerge till 1957. Only thirty-nine Conservative members graced the opposition side of the House. Bennett struggled on for a while, then resigned as leader. Bob Manion emerged victorious at the national convention in 1938, defeating Murdo Macpherson in a close contest in which my sympathies were strongly with Murdo. The party was divided and in disarray.

In Ontario Mitch Hepburn, after administering a severe defeat to the provincial Conservatives in 1934, had repeated his success in 1937. The Conservative party was obliged to wait until 1943 for an opportunity to return to power. Eglinton went to the Liberals in both 1934 and 1937, Harold Kirby defeating Coulter Maclean and Les Blackwell in succession. I worked hard for Les in the 1937 contest. Even in Ontario the party was defeated, divided and in disarray. Earl Rowe had hopefully been elected the new leader over George Drew. But when Earl Rowe resigned the leadership to return to the federal arena, Drew was elected leader at the next provincial convention.

Then came the war. Hepburn began to assail the Liberal government at Ottawa, and gradually an informal truce in the Ontario Legislature ensued between Hepburn and Drew. In Ottawa in March 1940, Mackenzie King, having summoned Parliament to meet in the afternoon, had it dissolved on the same day, and a general election was precipitated for which the Conservatives appeared to be ill prepared. I took a very active part at the local level, but it was all in vain. The election was a disaster for the party. King triumphed, Manion was defeated in Fort William, and Eglinton went Liberal federally for the first time in its history. Fred Hoblitzel, a newcomer without any previous political experience, was elected to represent Eglinton in Parliament for what proved to be the duration of the war.

The Conservative party was almost shattered; its morale at Ottawa was destroyed. Manion resigned as leader, but no national convention was called to select his successor. Instead, the president of the Dominion Conservative Association, John R. Macnicol, MP, called a meeting of the association in Ottawa. There were no delegates, and the meeting could make no pretence of representing the rank and file of the party. It is seriously open to question whether it had any legal right to appoint or elect a leader. Dana Porter and I as secretary and president of the Conservative Business Men's Club of Toronto, respectively, decided that we would go to Ottawa and do our best to attend the meeting although we had no credentials.

On arrival we presented ourselves to Macnicol and requested permission to attend. He said he would do what he could for us. The halls of the Chateau Laurier were abuzz with lobbyists and others promoting ideas, the principal one being that Arthur Meighen, Leader of the Opposition in the Senate, should be offered the leadership. George McCullagh, publisher of the *Globe and Mail*, was active in supporting this proposition with all the heat, profanity and influence he could muster. When the meeting opened John Macnicol said there were present two young men from Toronto, who had paid their own expenses to come to Ottawa, and although they had no status and could not speak or vote he recommended that they be allowed to attend the closed meeting. This permission was readily given, and Dana and I were witnesses to another miscarriage at the hands of those in authority in the party. Dana and I did not think of ourselves as particularly "young" men, but we were only about half the age of most of those present.

Arthur Meighen made an opening and most effective speech. The meeting had not long been under way when the Honourable C.H. Cahan, an elderly and eminent lawyer from Montreal, proposed the election of Meighen as party leader. In spite of some resistance, a committee was appointed to weigh the question. Later in the day the committee issued a report in favour of the election of Senator Meighen, which the meeting adopted with enthusiasm. As Dana and I watched the proceedings the fateful decision was taken and Mr. Meighen was elected.

Dana and I returned to Toronto with heavy hearts. Meighen was undoubtedly the ablest man in the party, and the ablest parliamentarian in Canada. But there was no doubt that the meeting had made a grave mistake. In the first place, its action was of doubtful legality; secondly, the association was not able to interpret the feeling of the party, for it was not representative; finally, it was doubtful if Meighen was acceptable to the rank and file of the party.

Meighen as always acted honourably, unselfishly and forthrightly. He resigned his seat in the Senate and accepted the party's nomination in South York when Alan Cockeram resigned to create a vacancy. The rest is a matter of history. In the campaign Meighen took a forthright line of attack on the government and made no attempt to appeal for Liberal votes. Instead of according to a newly elected Opposition Leader the traditional clear path to the Commons, Mr. King treacherously threw Liberal support behind the CCF candidate, Joe Noseworthy, and he was elected. Meighen's defeat brought undisguised joy to the Liberals and cast the Conservative party into uttermost gloom. This was the lowest point in the history of the party. Nothing before or since has ever come close to it.

The Conservative Business Men's Club of Toronto was a most useful party organization. It had been established in 1921 to attract to the party business and professional men who did not care to become members of a riding organization and also to provide a leading forum for prominent figures in the party to address luncheon meetings. I joined it soon after being called to the bar and was elected president in 1940. I held the office for five consecutive annual terms. At the beginning of my tenure the club's membership and finances, like everything else in the party, were at the lowest ebb; when I left the position in 1945 the club had a greatly increased membership and its finances were so sound that it was able to help the party.

Between 1940 and 1945 I brought speakers such as Howard Green, John Bracken, Jim Macdonnell, John Diefenbaker and Ivan Sabourin to the club. During the war it was hard to interest businessmen in political activities. Many of them were too busy, and others were fearful of jeopardizing government contracts. The building of memberships proceeded slowly, but we worked at it. My activities as president of the club during those five years brought me recognition within the party.

The Conservative party had long been pictured as a collection of Anglo-Saxons. I set about changing that image. At one of the meetings I gathered at the head table recognized leaders of the various ethnic groups in Toronto and planned the program as a salute to New Canadians. My friend John Grudeff, a lawyer and an immigrant from Bulgaria, was the speaker. From the chair I hailed all our guests as Canadians and threw wide the party's doors to them. The meeting drew a strong response not only from the ethnic representatives but from our club members and party stalwarts as well. George Drew telephoned me to commend my imaginative efforts. At his request I continued the approach to the New Canadians by various means. George Drew always had a strong sympathy for them and they admired his forthright denunciation of communism.

By 1941 the executive of the club was giving thought to the need for revival of the party through examination of what it actually stood for. A committee was formed consisting of Jim Macdonnell, as chairman, Roly Michener, Dave Walker, Dana Porter and myself. Over a period of months we met about once a fortnight to study policy. We knew the party was in dire straits; we did not then know that far beyond our ken we were to be instruments of its regeneration. That would have been impossible without Jim. He was the leader. He was widely known and universally respected within the party, and he had the contacts which we badly needed. We set up correspondence with numerous leading Conservatives in all parts of Canada, and later added Fred Gardiner and Cecil Frost to our original committee. We took pains to keep in contact with R.B. Hanson, Leader of the Opposition at Ottawa, and George Drew in Ontario, to make certain that no jealousies or misunderstandings arose, and to assure them that our status was informal and we did not pretend to speak for the party. Both of them gave us their sympathy and blessing. One new MP at Ottawa was known to view our activities with suspicion, believing that we were just a springboard to boost Murdo Macpherson to the party leadership. His name was John Diefenbaker.

Out of the planning by this little group of strictly unofficial party thinkers emerged the famous Port Hope Conference over the Labour Day weekend in 1942. Here for three days 150 dedicated Conservatives from all parts of Canada, including Quebec, met together to hammer out a new and comprehensive statement of the party's philosophy. The conference succeeded far beyond even the most sanguine hopes. We had assembled some of the best brains in Canada from outside Parliament and the provincial legislatures. To one man – Sidney Smith – we owed the superb way in which the various committee reports were woven together into a comprehensive and coherent statement of philosophy. The conference and the report which it issued will always remain a credit to every person who played any part in it. It came at exactly the right time; it proved that the party was neither dead nor even dying, but rather that it had a well-defined political philosophy which it held strongly and was prepared to preach vigorously.

It remains only to add that Jim Macdonnell became a Member of Parliament and Minister without Portfolio. Roland Michener became a member of the Ontario legislature and Provincial Secretary in the Ontario cabinet, Member of Parliament, Speaker of the House of Commons, High Commissioner to India and Governor General of Canada. Dana Porter became a member of the Ontario legislature, Minister of Planning, Attorney General and Provincial Treasurer in succession, and Chief Justice of Ontario. Dave Walker became a Member of Parliament, Minister of Public Works and Senator.

The Port Hope Conference led straight to the national convention in Winnipeg in December 1942. Whether it would have been possible to hold a national convention at that time but for the Port Hope Conference is debatable; at least it would have been a very different convention but for Port Hope.

On the policy side the convention was modelled on Port Hope, and Port Hopers manned the committees to a large extent. I was again secretary of the Committee on Social Security and Housing. The work on policy went very smoothly, encountering only one major problem. That inevitably was over conscription. The Quebec delegates opposed conscription, and pleaded earnestly for support in the plenary session of the Resolutions Committee. Opinion was divided. The strongest speech was made by Leslie Blackwell, who had lost a leg in the Battle of Cambrai in the Great War. Les spoke eloquently against saddling the Conservative party with the responsibility for conscription again. He argued that conscription was not needed then and might not be later, and that its introduction would be counterproductive. He was loudly applauded by the Quebec delegates, and his speech carried the day. Our Quebec friends had found the sympathetic understanding for which they had pleaded.

I was assisting in weaving the reports of the subcommittees into a coherent whole when Gustave Monette, the silver-tongued orator from Quebec, came to me and urged that the report of the main committee contain the same statement in recognition of the contribution of French Canada to our national unity as had been written into the Port Hope report. I saw that this was done. This statement of principle was approved unanimously by the convention – a gratifying demonstration of the sympathetic understanding extended by the party to our French-speaking compatriots.

Nothing in the policy resolutions and statements adopted at Winnipeg was in the slightest degree at variance with the Port Hope report; indeed, it was treated almost as if sacrosanct. I remember my friend Horace Hanson, who had not been at Port Hope, at one point petulantly exclaiming, "I'm getting sick and tired of having Port Hope thrust down my throat." From Winnipeg the party emerged with the most comprehensive, progressive, forward-looking policy it had ever adopted. The party demonstrated that it had shaken off the demoralizing effects of defeat and rejection, and that it was still capable of fresh thinking and vigorous leadership of the Canadian people.

The spotlight quickly and dramatically turned to the election of a new leader. Howard Green and John Diefenbaker had declared themselves candidates. There were well-supported rumours that Meighen favoured going outside the party and inviting John Bracken, the Progressive premier of Manitoba for the last twenty years, to assume the leadership. This caused no little concern. Bracken was not known in eastern Canada, and his position on leading issues remained a question. Bracken chose that opportune time to deliver a series of public speeches which stated a coherent body of principles wholly in keeping with Conservative philosophy. I was supporting Sidney Smith, who had not totally committed himself. Sid was then president of the University of Manitoba. To make a good showing he considered it essential to his success that he have a solid base of support in the Manitoba delegation, and this would be impossible with John Bracken in the field. Murdo Macpherson had also not declared himself. In 1938 he had held back his entry into the race until it was too late for him to win. Would he repeat this mistake? Harry Stevens of Vancouver, who had led an insurrection against Mr. Bennett in 1934 and formed another party and split the Conservative vote in many ridings in the disastrous 1935 general election, was considering signalling his return to the fold by entering the race. The situation bristled with dramatic possibilities.

In the midst of seething speculation a delegation went to see John Bracken to invite him to run for the leadership. They found him "tough." He wanted assurance that the party was really serious in adopting its very progressive platform, and he wanted the party name altered to include the word "Progressive" if there was to be any hope of his bringing the survivors of the Progressive party in western Canada into union with the Conservative party. This position was duly reported to the convention and precipitated a sharp debate. This was the first national convention I had attended officially and at thirty-seven I was one of the youngest delegates. Before a gathering of several thousand persons I jumped into the debate. I said that the convention had several declared candidates; all must be treated alike and with scrupulous fairness; therefore no special terms could be made in advance for the benefit or at the behest of any particular candidate. The change of the party's name was a serious matter and required calm and unforced consideration. No other candidate was asking for the change, or for any other special terms and conditions; if John Bracken chose to be a candidate he was welcome to enter the contest, but if so he must submit to the same conditions as all the others. If following the election the new leader, whoever he might be, asked the convention to change the party's name or take any other action he would be free to do so, and the convention should consider the proposal, but on its merits and not under any compulsion. As a maiden effort it was somewhat courageous, and it won loud applause, and in the end my position was adopted.

Tension was steadily rising as delegates awaited the deadline of 8 p.m. for filing of papers by candidates.

Sid filed his papers at 7 p.m. John Bracken filed his at 7.45. Thereupon Sid withdrew. Murdo filed his. At 8 p.m. five candidates took their places on the platform with their sponsors. John Bracken entered first. A great cheer went up. This was notice to the convention that he had decided to take his chances with the other candidates and on precisely the same footing with them. His courage in doing so undoubtedly won him wide support. Bracken spoke first, followed by Harry Stevens; neither speech swept the convention. John Diefenbaker was next. He made a good speech, though perhaps with too many gestures. Howard Green had just nicely begun his speech and was doing well when he collapsed unconscious on the stage. Dr. Herbert A. Bruce rushed toward the stage, tripped on the top step and fell flat on his face; many thought he, too, had taken a heart attack. Pandemonium reigned. Finally Howard was assisted off the stage, and an attempt was made to resume the program. Murdo Macpherson endeavoured to speak, but the crowd was too upset to be attentive. With Sid Smith's withdrawal I was supporting Murdo. To the relief of all Howard recovered, and he completed his speech the next afternoon prior to the voting.

In the first ballot Bracken placed first, followed by Macpherson, Diefenbaker, Green and Stevens. It needed only the second ballot to give Bracken the necessary majority. Thereupon a motion was introduced and adopted to change the name of the party to "Progressive Conservative Party of Canada."

That same day also, George Drew, although he had declined to put himself forward as a candidate, was invited to address the convention. He made an excellent speech and a very favourable impression on the delegates. Many thought George should have been a candidate and that he might have won. I consider that he followed the right course. He had sought and had accepted the leadership of the party in Ontario. In the absence of any general election he had not yet fulfilled his mandate there. His turn to seek the national leadership would come. It did six years later.

The Winnipeg national convention of 1942 marked a turning-point in the life of the party. I had taken a prominent role at my first national convention, and was satisfied with it. However, like most other Conservatives, I had not even met the new leader. It was now necessary that he should meet the rank and file of the party on the widest scale.

I arranged for Mr. Bracken to address a meeting of the Business Men's Club. He made a good speech, but not any masterpiece. His sincerity stood out, however, and it was obvious that he was trying hard to fulfil his new and unaccustomed role. His wife was charming and intelligent, and a great help to her husband.

What Jim Macdonnell and others and I considered a grievous mistake was then made. It seriously hurt John Bracken, and we blamed his advisers at Ottawa. Instead of entering the House of Commons by the quickest by-election route possible and taking his place there as Leader of the Opposition, it was decided that he would remain out of the House until the next general election some two years or more away, and travel about the country studying its problems and meeting the people. Gordon Graydon would be House Leader. We were aghast at this decision; it denigrated Parliament, and was bound to be interpreted as cowardice.

CHAPTER ELEVEN

On to Ottawa

The spotlight now shifted to Ontario. Hepburn abandoned politics, there was a struggle over the succession, a general election followed, and the Liberals were annihilated. The Conservatives elected thirty-eight members, and the CCF 34. George Drew was called upon to form a government, and wisely decided that there would be no coalition, but that he would carry on as a minority government. After he became leader George Drew invited me to become the party's spokesman on municipal government in Ontario. I promised him assistance, but declined a provincial role, since for some reason provincial politics did not attract me nearly as much as federal.

Once I had resolved to stand for the federal nomination in Eglinton I communicated my decision to over a score of the officers and leading figures in the Men's and Women's Riding Associations. It occasioned no surprise, and nearly all received the announcement with enthusiastic approval. I had reckoned, however, without two other factors: the party high command, and another candidate for the nomination. After I had publicly and irretrievably committed myself I received a message from Charles P. McTague, national president, requesting me to stand aside in favour of Henry Borden. Had I received this request six months sooner I might have found it difficult to refuse; at this stage, however, I could only reply that Henry was my friend, that I held him in the highest esteem, but it was much too late for me to be asked to stand aside for him; I had already committed myself to my supporters and publicly. Charlie McTague's subsequent demeanour clearly showed that he was displeased by my refusal. It also came to light that my friend Tom (Doc) Deacon also had his eye on the nomination. He had been the official organizer in the riding in the 1940 general election, and was a party veteran with many years of service.

The nomination meeting was called for October 30, 1944. I was nominated by the presidents of the Men's and Women's Associations. Tom Deacon was nominated, made a short speech, then withdrew in my favour. My nomination was unanimous. In my acceptance speech I promised to wage a vigorous campaign, acknowledged all the help I had received from Alice, and appealed for a strong spirit of team-play.

The nominating convention had given me everything I could have asked for: a unanimous and enthusiastic nomination. I stood at the door and shook hands with everyone present. Once safely nominated, I immediately proceeded to set up my campaign organization, even though the election was some months away. Finance was a worrying problem, and I was enormously relieved when my friend Ardagh Scythes undertook to raise funds for me. The extent of the party's financial aid was quite uncertain, and was bound to be inadequate.

In November I was created a King's Counsel, a distinction I owed to Les Blackwell and for which I was most grateful. It meant that I would be permitted to address the court from within, not outside, the bar.

I did, of course, pay a price for my partisan plunge. The *Toronto Daily Star*, a Liberal supporter, had always given me strong support in my municipal campaigns. I now forfeited that support totally. Having served the Canadian Club as vice-president I knew I had forfeited any possibility of becoming president. On the other hand, two responses gave me special encouragement. Dick Bell, national secretary of the party, told me that I could become a national figure in seven years. Fred Hoblitzel, the sitting Liberal MP for Eglinton, fell out with his party, withdrew from the contest for the Liberal nomination and quietly promised me his support.

I set to work to create a young people's organization, the first in Eglinton. It was a conspicuous success. Out of the university and high school students who responded we drew in years to come some of our best material for office in the adult associations and in our election organization. The members proved to be enthusiastic and efficient workers.

Within a few days of my nomination the conscription crisis burst on Ottawa, and Colonel Ralston, the Minister of National Defence, resigned. Mackenzie King endeavoured to sidestep the issue, but did not entirely succeed. His compromise, to conscript for home defence, then apply pressure on the conscripts to "volunteer" for overseas service, alienated some in his cabinet and some of the electorate. In the famous by-election in Grey

101

North in February 1945, Mr. King's ace-in-the-hole, General McNaughton, the new Minister of National Defence, was defeated by Garfield Case, an impressive Conservative orator. The political fires were heating up.

In early 1945 the Progressive Conservative candidates were invited to Ottawa in batches to meet the leader and the party officials and to undergo instruction. There were about forty in my group. In the discussions and the questions I took a very active part. Harry Willis afterward gave me the encouraging assessment that John Bracken was much impressed with my performance.

The Drew government was defeated in the Ontario legislature by a combination of Liberals and CCF, and a provincial general election was called for Monday, June 11, 1945. King immediately called a federal election for the same day. It was an attempt to be adroit, but he was outfoxed; Drew promptly advanced the date of the provincial election to June 4. Battle was now joined at two levels. I had supposed that in Eglinton we would operate with one organization, share committee rooms, and thus reduce expense and make the best use of our workers. To my surprise and disappointment Les Blackwell would have none of this. The provincial organization of the party had concluded that it was much surer of success than the federal wing, so it insisted on conducting its own campaign rigidly separated from the federal candidates of the party. Fortunately, this embarrassment never occurred again.

George Drew won a resounding victory and Les was re-elected in Eglinton by a large majority. This augured well for my chances, especially since the provincial organization immediately swung right in behind the federal in that last torrid week. The public was not responding too well to public meetings, so we took the campaign into the homes with tea-parties for the ladies in the afternoons and house meetings in the evenings for men or mixed groups. We attempted as many as five in an evening, with Les and me leap-frogging, but found that two was the optimum number. Radio was beginning to play a leading role in the campaign, even at the local level. I found that my voice was well suited to this form of campaigning, and I made increasing use of this, to me, new medium.

A despicable effort was made at the last minute to paint me as anti-labour. I had appeared as counsel for one labour group in a case before the Ontario Labour Relations Board. The other group was AFL-CIO. One of the officers of my group defected to the AFL-CIO and attacked me. The *Toronto Daily Star* played up the slanderous attack with headlines, and called on Mr. Bracken to disown me. He was wise enough to take no notice of this canard.

The campaign ended Friday night. I had been going at top speed throughout a long campaign, and on the Saturday afternoon I suddenly and completely lost my voice. My overworked vocal organs had had enough, but our organization was in readiness for Monday.

The results exceeded my fondest expectations. They were: Fleming, 21,476; Rayfield (Liberal), 13,586; Gee (CCF), 4,435; Burrill (Social Credit), 369; and Varley (Lab. Prog.), 238. In all Canada my plurality (7,890) was exceeded by only one other Conservative candidate; Howard Green in Vancouver-Quadra had a few more. Victory was sweet. We held open house at 259 Glencairn Avenue. Such a crowd of workers and celebrants attended that they trampled all our precious flower beds. I was too elated to care.

Unhappily, the party did not do as well elsewhere as in Eglinton. Only sixty-nine Conservatives were elected, Mackenzie King had retained a bare majority, and the new House would include twenty-nine CCF members, mostly from western Canada. King would not be free of troubles, but he had pulled the rabbit out of the hat again. I saw Arthur Meighen at the Albany Club the next day. "You are lucky to be starting in the Opposition," he said. I was astonished, thinking he was trying to console me, but I was soon to learn that he was right. He imparted one piece of advice: "Never throw a bouquet across to the other side of the House unless there's a brick in it."

When the official tabulation of the voting by polling stations was published, it was clear that my support had been distributed over the entire riding. This was most gratifying, since it gave me a sense of strong mandate from the people I was chosen to represent. On one point I was quite firm: I had been elected to represent all the people of Eglinton, those who voted for me and those who did not, alike. I adhered to this principle throughout my entire public service. Anyone who needed my help had a right to call upon me to render it. If his cause was just I must do everything in my power to see that justice was done; if his claim was unjust he was entitled to an expression of my views and reasons.

In midsummer at my own expense I made a trip to Ottawa which proved to be very important. I presented myself to the Clerk of the House of Commons, the crusty Dr. Arthur Beauchesne, the greatest living authority on parliamentary procedure, and was sworn in as member for Eglinton. This gave me access to stationery and supplies. It also gave me two books which became close companions throughout all my years in Parliament: one contained the Standing Orders of the House of Commons; the other was Dr. Beauchesne's celebrated book on procedure in the House, which was to become a veritable Bible to me. I studied both books eagerly.

I presented myself to John Bracken at his office, and he kindly invited me back to his farm at Manotick, just outside the capital, for dinner. It was situated on a scenic spot overlooking the Rideau River. I found Mr. Bracken direct, straightforward and down-to-earth. It was a thoroughly delightful visit, and that evening together was the beginning of a very close friendship which I valued most highly. I learned to esteem both Mr. and Mrs. Bracken as very genuine persons, quite unspoiled by success and totally without guile.

I asked Mr. Bracken what importance he attached to mastery of procedure in Parliament. He answered that in his twenty years in the legislature of Manitoba he had been guided by common sense rather than technicalities, and that he had left it to others to master the rules. In the light of my own experience and what I came to see of the highly technical application of the rules in the Commons I am very glad that I then decided to master the rules myself.

A few days later I received information on the appointments made in our caucus. I had been assigned to three important committees, those on taxation, social security and justice, and had been named vice-chairman of the Committee on Social Security. Denton Massey had been named chairman of the committee, but he found himself unable to take on the responsibility, so I was appointed to fill it. This challenge exceeded all my expectations. It meant that on entering the House of Commons for the first time I would bear responsibility as the party's spokesman on all questions pertaining to social security, the Department of National Health and Welfare, and housing.

The Twentieth Parliament met on September 6, 1945. The first order of business, as usual in a new Parliament, was the election of a Speaker. On motion of the Prime Minister, seconded by the Leader of the Opposition, the House elected Dr. Gaspard Fauteux as Speaker. Gaspard Fauteux was a dental surgeon from Montreal. He came from a distinguished Quebec family and was a nephew of two former premiers of Quebec, Honoré Mercier and Sir Lomer Gouin. The appointment savoured somewhat of a "Family Compact" in Quebec. Fauteux, although he was not an outstanding Speaker, had a good sense of humour, and he and I became good friends. He once said that having spent much of his life telling his patients to open their mouths he now found some difficulty in telling members to close theirs. At first he pronounced my name as "Mister Fleeming," but in time that was corrected. His English was none too good, but it was better than Mackenzie King's French, which was hopelessly bad. He pronounced the Speaker's name as "Fotto."

It was a thrilling experience to take one's place in the House by right, to enter the opposition lobby and to pass through the door and curtain into the Chamber, and bow to the Speaker's chair before taking one's seat. The view of the House from a seat on the floor is very different from the view from any of the galleries, or at least it creates a different effect on the viewer. The rugs and curtains are green, and the woodwork of uniform medium hue. The Speaker's chair is elevated and dominates the House. The table of the House, which is a very official part of the furniture of the Chamber, is a handsome piece of woodwork. At its end sits the Clerk, and on the two sides the Assistant Clerks.

The members themselves are the most interesting part of the panorama. At the time I first entered Parliament the Liberals were all accommodated to the right of the Speaker. There sat Mackenzie King, with Louis St. Laurent as his desk-mate, Ian Mackenzie, the House Leader, on his left, and J.L. Ilsley, the Minister of Finance, to the right, C.D. Howe and Jimmy Gardiner to the left of Ian. In the hands of these men resided the ultimate power and authority in Canada. I studied the seating chart to acquaint myself with the members and their ridings. To the immediate right of the Speaker in the front row sat two men, both from Quebec, of fascinating interest to me. They were P.J.A. Cardin, a well-groomed, short man wearing a wing collar, and Chubby Power, ever popular and fearless. Both men had broken with King and resigned from the cabinet the previous year over his conscription policy.

The party whip, A.C. Casselman (known as "Cass"), was responsible for assigning the Conservative seats in the House. I was not among those few who were for various reasons given special seats, but was among those seated alphabetically in accordance with length of service in the House. My seat-mate was Davie Fulton, from Kamloops, B.C., just out of the army after distinguished overseas service, and at twenty-nine the youngest Conservative member. On my other side across an aisle was Julian Ferguson from Simcoe North. There are five rows of seats on each side of the House. Mine was in the fourth row, five seats from the top end of the Chamber. I would need to make full use of my voice in order to be heard at the far end. However, I was close to the Speaker, and that was an advantage.

Thrilled as I was to take my seat in Parliament, I was equally thrilled to look up at the members' gallery and to see both Alice and my mother there. I hoped they were proud of me, though I may not have looked very significant as a back-bencher in a House of 265 members. Their verdict was expressed by Alice in these words: "Donald has arrived where he has always wanted to be."

I attended my first caucus the following day. I soon came to recognize the importance and indispensability of this adjunct to Parliament. The members of each party can meet in private to discuss the business before the House or anything else they choose. A caucus of the opposition is untrammelled by any formal restrictions. John Bracken chose always to preside himself at caucus. We sat in three rows facing him. I soon discovered that the best position in which to address caucus was from one end of the room, and I occupied that same spot for years.

The first caucus took up the examination of the throne speech, and decided on the amendment to the address. One sentence in the speech puzzled the veteran members, namely, "You will be asked to approve a measure to extend certain specified emergency powers to meet emergency conditions in the period of reconstruction." They were all too familiar with the use during wartime of the extraordinary powers conferred on the cabinet by the War Measures Act to make laws by order-in-council, and could not understand what the government now intended. My first intervention in caucus related to this question. I said I thought that the government had become sensitive to our criticism of "government by order-in-council," that they had selected the particular orders-in-council which they considered necessary to continue, and that they had chosen to ask Parliament to give precise statutory effect to them, thus speeding the time when the War Measures Act could be declared to be no longer in effect. This set some members, such as Howard Green and John Diefenbaker, to examine the sentence in the address again. John rose to say he thought I was right. Indeed, that proved to be precisely the case. From that time caucus was always ready to listen to me. Of all my hundreds of interventions in caucus discussions, that first one was most significant in winning me the ear of caucus and giving me confidence in offering my views.

I had no thought, however, of making an early intervention in the debate in the House. I had been duly warned by well-meaning friends to "bide my time," and not to "rush in too soon." I quietly decided that I would wait three weeks. I had not reckoned with the party whip, however. On the Monday, leaders' day, he came to me and warned me to prepare my maiden speech. Tuesday afternoon he told me I would be "up" that very evening. That jolted me into action. My precious three weeks for preparation and to accustom myself to the mood and atmosphere of the House had suddenly vanished. I was on my feet at 8.45 p.m.

I have reread this maiden speech thirty-nine years later. To me it now reads like a mature parliamentary effort, completed just within the forty-minute time limit. It is modest, but determined; critical, but constructive. I began on a personal note, then proceeded to attack government abuse of orders-in-council. I dwelt on the need of housing and the government's confusion and ineffectiveness in coping with that serious problem, and the need for a more constructive and efficient administration of social security measures. If I were making the same speech in 1984 in the same circumstances I doubt if I would change it in form or content. The veteran Gordon Graydon told me that evening that it was the best maiden speech he had ever heard delivered in the Commons.

The speech was delivered too late in the day to receive the best treatment in the morning press next day, but the *Toronto Telegram* and other newspapers paid tribute to it and said the feature of the debate was the devastating attack on the government by new Conservative MPs like George Pearkes, Cec Merritt, and myself. The veteran members of the party delayed their participation in the debate to allow new members to deliver their maiden efforts. Diefenbaker did not speak until September 26. His speech was very effective, and the Prime Minister was in his place throughout. I observed that John was constantly looking up at the press gallery, evidently to judge reaction there.

I cast my first vote in the House on September 25. The Conservative amendment on the address was defeated on division by a vote of 163 to 57. It was the first time I had witnessed a vote by roll-call. The new Assistant Clerk of the House, Roy Graham, called every name correctly without reference to any list, and received an ovation from the House at the conclusion for a triumph of diligent memory work.

Following the debate on the address the House appointed its standing committees; I was fortunate to be appointed to the two most sought after, Banking and Commerce, and External Affairs. I was destined to be a member of these same committees for the entire twelve years I served in the opposition.

I busied myself asking questions in the House, both oral and written, and participated in discussions in Committee of the Whole.

Following my maiden speech, I plunged into debate in the House with growing confidence and enthusiasm. In this first session I made several major speeches, each one charting an area of policy on which I would be increasingly expert and associated with over the years. I spoke on the establishment of the United Nations, especially UNESCO, on October 18. A week later I was again on my feet with a thorough-going criticism of the government's housing policy on the occasion of the introduction of a bill to incorporate the Central Mortgage and Housing Corporation.

I also put up a spirited resistance to the government's bill to give statutory approval to the wartime orders-in-council. In this, the party was led by John Diefenbaker, who was at his best in matters concerning civil rights.

As time proceeded I began to be slightly wary of my relations with John Diefenbaker. Prior to the Winnipeg convention in December 1942, he had been very friendly to me. At my invitation he had twice addressed the Conservative Business Men's Club of Toronto, and had been a guest in my home on an occasion when I had invited a number of keen Eglinton Conservatives in to meet him. I did not support him for the leadership at the national convention. Several months later, when we were alone, he went out of his way to tell me how much he appreciated Dave Walker's support at the convention and that he would never forget it. He looked at the time so menacing that I concluded he was telling me he would never forget that I had not supported him. My relations with him in the House were thoroughly pleasant until marred by one incident. I was serving on his caucus committee on justice, and had been assigned two matters to discuss in the House on the Estimates of the Department of Justice. Davie Fulton, as secretary of the committee, and I went to him in the House to discuss when these might be expected to be heard in the House. Suddenly and without any warning he turned on me in blazing anger, and accused me of trying to take things out of his hands. There was simply no sense to his outburst, but it was obvious that I had aroused his ire in some way.

CHAPTER TWELVE

The New Member

The first session of the Twentieth Parliament ended on December 8, I had packed a great deal of activity into those few months and no little experience of parliamentary life.

One thing I had discovered was that public life was not exactly rewarding financially. The sessional indemnity for members was $4,000 – a sum that had not increased in years. With all-party support a measure to augment this meagre sum with a non-taxable expense allowance of $2,000 was passed. I welcomed this, even though the extra money, like the indemnity, went to the firm, not to me personally.

During those first months in Ottawa I became all too aware of the additional expense attached to my new way of life. I had begun commuting between Toronto and Ottawa, and that hard grind was to continue at least once each week for twelve long years. It is true that railway passes were issued to members, and these imparted a sense of privilege and affluence, but I was amazed as time went on at how little use I made of my pass except on parliamentary business. I left home on Sunday nights for Ottawa, and left Ottawa on Friday nights for Toronto. Had I been able to sleep normally on these overnight train trips my life would have been very different, but in my twelve years in opposition, during which I must have taken at least six hundred overnight train trips, I never had one unbroken night's sleep. The effect was always evident the next day. There were no free air flights for members, and I could afford to fly only for very special purposes. As time went on and the business of the House made it possible I endeavoured to take the Friday afternoon train home to escape the exactions of the night trip.

Saturdays at the office became a nightmare. The office was open until 1 p.m. I was attempting to do a week's work in one day, and it was very hard on my secretary as well as myself. In the course of time the firm adopted Saturday closing, but it did not affect my routine. Even with the assistance of a second secretary my day became longer. I regularly took my lunch to the office, and often did not leave there until 7 p.m. I might not see my partners for several weeks at a time, and this had unfortunate consequences. When it became necessary to see clients they were asked to come at an unpopular hour on a Saturday, and I always took work home to be completed before I returned to Ottawa on Sunday night. I saw less and less of my family, and the pleasure I normally derived from the practice of law began to fade. The periods between sessions of Parliament seemed like a picnic by comparison.

With one custom this wearing grind was never permitted to interfere. We never failed as a family to attend church on Sunday mornings. That included Sunday School for the children.

I hated leaving home on Sunday nights. The expectation of it had an unsettling effect all that day and I never became reconciled to this grim routine. I could with better grace and more resignation have left home on any other night than Sunday. I felt even more sorry for the members from the West and the Maritimes who had to spend the weekend in Ottawa away from home and family. My anxiety over my absence from home was already deepening. I reproached myself with the thought that the opportunities which I was missing to be with my children while they were growing up would never return.

After an initial period of search and experimentation I was fortunate to obtain excellent living accommodation in Ottawa at the home of Mrs. Henry G. Campbell at 196 Clemow Avenue. I shared the top floor of the house with George Burgess, a civil servant, and took breakfast there. This enabled me to walk the two miles to and from the Parliament Buildings each day. These walks, in all kinds of weather, helped to offset the physical effects of long hours of sitting. They were supplemented by a walk about Parliament Hill before dinner, and when possible by a very short quick one before the afternoon session in fine weather. Jim Macdonnell usually shared the walks with me.

Nowadays members enjoy private offices and individual secretaries, free air travel privileges, and relatively handsome remuneration. It was not so in 1945. New members were assigned two to an office, and each secretary served two members if they were new. For four long years Jim and I shared one office and for a long time one secretary. It is difficult now to conceive of anything so inconvenient. With one phone between us there was no semblance of either privacy or quiet. It became at times a kind

110

of bedlam. To make matters worse, Jim was president of the party's federal Association, and he endeavoured to hold frequent noon-hour executive meetings in the office. He was also chairman of the Board of Governors of Queen's University, and was constantly on the telephone over its business, so I was kept fully informed of all that was transpiring at Queen's and in the party's federal organization and finances. Jim revelled in the weekends when he had the office to himself, and he spread his papers over both his desk and mine, as well as the sofa and the telephone table. On my arrival on Monday mornings I found the office looking as though a cyclone had blown through it.

I quickly learned the importance of a thorough knowledge of the rules and procedures of the House. Here I found my years of experience in the Toronto City Council invaluable. I was also very conscious of the importance of the press gallery. It contained men of long experience such as Fred Mears; there were also young men seeking successful careers. As I began to establish a position for myself as a debater and an opponent to be reckoned with, I realized that the power of the press gallery should not be underestimated.

The second session of Parliament did not begin until March 14, and continued until August 31. The summer was unbearably hot. The Chamber was not equipped for long summer sittings in those days, and there was no air conditioning system. Members were prevented from enjoying any vacation with their families. The sheer misery of that experience could never be forgotten.

The session opened with a debate on the Gouzenko espionage case. Following the revelations of Igor Gouzenko, a cipher clerk in the Russian embassy, the government had appointed a royal commission to inquire into Russian espionage. Canadians in the public service and the Communist Member of Parliament for Montreal-Cartier, Fred Rose, were involved. The commission found it necessary to detain persons under warrant to interrogate them. This startling incident was bound to provoke debate in the Commons. Mr. King made a lengthy report to the House on March 18. The reply would have fallen within Diefenbaker's responsibility, but he was absent, and Art Smith replied for the opposition. In view of the serious revelations of espionage, violations of the Official Secrets Act and disloyalty, caucus was not disposed to be too critical of infringements of civil rights. When Dief returned to Ottawa he behaved like a raging bull. He thought caucus had taken the wrong line and that we should have attacked the government's actions without mercy. Numerous members thought he was chagrined that he had missed a golden opportunity to make a speech on one of his favourite themes and that Art Smith had replaced him at this critical juncture. History must be the judge.

I did not take part in the espionage debate, but in this session I did make three major speeches which carried me into new fields, and were to have enduring consequences. Before entering Parliament I had limited acquaintance with the legislative and administrative aspects of radio broadcasting in Canada. The act creating the Canadian Broadcasting Corporation was introduced by the Bennett government and enacted in 1932. Up to and including 1946 the House had appointed a committee to study the operation of the system and the annual report of the Corporation in nine of the fifteen years. It was never made a standing committee, and required a special resolution to be passed by the House each session. I had no experience of sitting on the committee or any claim to special information or interest in the subject. My faithful attendance at the meetings of the Standing Committee on Banking and Commerce and the Standing Committee on External Affairs had established me as a persistent cross-examiner and one who always came to the meetings prepared. When the Radio committee was appointed I was one of the Conservative appointees, along with Diefenbaker, Fulton, Hackett, Ross and Art Smith. The committee was obliged to work under pressure. It held twenty-eight meetings, of which I attended twenty-six. When I say I "attended," I do not mean that I cruised in and out of meetings as I chose, but that I remained at my place from beginning to end. Diefenbaker operated differently; he was not in my opinion a good committeeman. His attendance was irregular, and he never sat through an entire meeting. He had a way of finding out when some question of particular public interest was to arise, then attending, firing enough questions or expressing opinions sufficient to attract the attention of the press, then leaving. He had sat on the Radio committee in previous sessions, and knew the subject in its most contentious aspects well, but he had no thought of burdening himself with laborious committee work. He should have led the opposition members on the committee; instead, he did not even consult with his colleagues. Gradually the role of leader on the committee fell on my shoulders.

Radio broadcasting was at the crossroads. Was the CBC to operate as a monopoly without any real competition? Were the privately owned stations to be limited to weak power and to serve only small local communities? Was the CBC to continue to regulate these puny competitors, and to act as judge, jury and

112

sheriff without appeal? I decided that I must fight what I regarded as a dangerous monopoly, and to struggle for competition and for fair play to competitors. I set out to master the previous history of the subject, the reports of all the earlier committees, and the technical questions which were constantly arising. The House did not sit on Wednesday evenings; but, all through those hot months the light in my office burned to a late hour every Wednesday evening. The committee reported on August 16. In the debate on second reading of the government's bill to amend the act the following week I was chosen to lead off for the opposition. My speech on that occasion was thought to be one of the most comprehensive ever made in Parliament on the subject. For the eleven years we remained in opposition I was the party's parliamentary spokesman on radio broadcasting and later television.

Early in the 1945 session a few of us English-speaking opposition members and some of the new young Liberal members from Quebec sought opportunity for closer acquaintance. Meeting informally with us were René Beaudoin, later Speaker, Jean Lesage, later a Minister and Prime Minister of Quebec, Léon Raymond, later Clerk of the House, and Alcide Coté, later Postmaster General. I endeavoured to revive my French, which had lain dormant for twenty-three years, since it disappeared from my course at Varsity in 1922, and commenced conversing informally in French with some of my French-speaking colleagues. They were patient with my shortcomings and encouraged my efforts. I was far from ready, however, to attempt to speak even a few words in the House. That would call for strong courage. Yet I wished to do it, as a gesture of goodwill and understanding. I was on the point of making a decision which was to prove momentous in my life and to shape my political career as few resolves have ever done.

I was not then aware that Sir John A. Macdonald in 1856, in a private letter to Brown Chamberlin of the *Montreal Gazette*, had stated that a British Canadian who seeks political success "must make friends with the French, without sacrificing the status of his race or lineage, he must respect their nationality. Treat them as a nation, and they will act as a free people generally do – generously." Sir John had thus precisely defined ninety years earlier what became one of the major principles of my public life. French Canadians responded to my efforts exactly as Sir John had prophesied – generously; indeed, with overwhelming generosity. The course I chose enabled me to make a contribution to Canadian public life which at that time was unique and to set an example which has been so widely followed since that the party rejected unilingual aspirants to its leadership in June 1983 in favour of a bilingual candidate.

The Citizenship bill of 1946 seemed to offer the perfect vehicle. It was non-contentious, and its purpose was germane to mine. It created a Canadian citizenship for the first time, and was hailed as a recognition of a true Canadian identity and a lasting contribution to Canadian unity. I composed a few paragraphs in English, had them translated into French by a friend, and wrestled with the challenge. In those days no English-speaking member from outside Quebec ever spoke in French in the House, and very rarely did any English-speaking member from Quebec do so. There was no system of simultaneous translation in the House; its introduction had to wait for a Conservative government. With some trepidation I exposed my text to two close friends and sought their advice. Gordon Graydon commented: "I have thought at times of saying something myself in the House in French, but have always hesitated to attempt it for fear of offending somebody back home [i.e., in Peel County]. If I were you I wouldn't do it. Some of your electors in Eglinton might misunderstand and disapprove." John Hackett, who represented Stanstead in Quebec, was bilingual. He thought the content of my text was good, but hesitated to advise me to deliver it, not being sure of the reaction in Ontario. I put the text away for three months, then I decided I was going to take the fateful plunge. I would take my chances with any elector whose breadth of mind was unequal to this test.

I spoke on the afternoon of April 9. Already the debate had run for several days, the positions taken by all parties were known, there was no disagreement over the principle of the bill, and interest in the debate had begun to flag. I looked on faces and newspapers hiding faces while I spoke. After speaking twenty minutes in English I turned to French. I can never forget the sheer electricity of that moment: the Speaker sat bolt upright, the newspapers went down, faces appeared from behind them, the chamber was suddenly magnetized. I continued in French:

> Our Canadian citizenship links us together in bonds of unity and equality, from whatever province we come and whatever be the race or language of our fathers. . . . As Canadians we should constantly endeavour to emphasize those things that are common to all of us and that form our common heritage. It seems to me that we could strengthen our bonds of unity in Canada by avoiding the use of a hyphen when defining our citizenship. We should be proud and happy to call ourselves simply "Canadians." . . . Am I

114

a French-Canadian, a Scottish-Canadian, an English-Canadian, or an Irish-Canadian?. . . . The races I have just mentioned, as well as others, have made a splendid contribution to the building up of this country and to the enrichment of our national heritage. This heritage can surpass all others in richness owing to the diversity of our origins. Our citizenship will be all the more precious if we are ready to unite and work for Canada in a spirit of cooperation, mutual respect and equality.

I sat down to a storm of desk-pounding, not only from Quebec members, but English-speaking members as well. The Speaker nodded and smiled. I received many congratulations, and never a word of disapproval, whether within the chamber or elsewhere. I had just turned one of the most important corners in my life.

Another French speech still lay in store at that eventful 1946 session. It concerned redistribution. To remedy an injustice to Quebec, Manitoba and Saskatchewan and to give them increased representation in the House the government proposed an amendment to the British North America Act. Louis St. Laurent, the Minister of Justice, accordingly moved a resolution requesting the British Parliament to amend section 51. There had been no consultation whatever with the provincial governments. In fact, there had been a federal-provincial conference on other matters only a few days before, but the federal representatives had said not a word about the redistribution and the intended amendment. There was danger for a Conservative party in appearing to oppose a measure of increased representation for Quebec in the House of Commons. Nevertheless, we decided that we must take a strong stand in principle against attempts to amend the constitution without even consultation with, not to mention consent of, the provinces. Diefenbaker made one of his finest speeches on the issue. He examined statements by previous prime ministers – Bordon, Laurier, Meighen, Bennett – and by Ernest Lapointe, and Thomas Crerar, all of whom had been unanimous that there must be consultation with the provinces before Parliament may ask Westminster to amend the BNA Act. At the conclusion of an eloquent and learned speech he moved that "the Government be required to consult at once the several provinces and upon satisfactory conclusion of such consultations" be authorized to present the address.

I am not aware of any issue arising or argument employed in the major debates in the House of Commons on the constitution in 1980, 1981 and 1982 that was not raised in the 1946 debate. In my speech I intended to rely particularly on some important declarations on the subject made by Laurier and Lapointe. To give them added effect I used the French edition of the debates in which they were uttered. I was immeasurably assisted by St. Laurent, who immediately preceded me. Art Smith had asked him if Parliament without consulting the provinces could ask and obtain from Westminster an amendment of section 51 of the BNA Act why it could not without consulting the provinces obtain an amendment to repeal section 133 and thus abolish all guarantees of the French language in Parliament and Quebec. St. Laurent obligingly quoted section 133, and speaking of its repeal uttered these words: "Can that be dealt with without the consent of the provincial legislatures? Legally I say it can."

In that one sentence he had destroyed the constitution. He had placed the French language and its constitutional status at the mercy of a majority in Parliament. I was neither slow nor reluctant to step into this ready-made breach. I spoke in terms of solemn warning of the perils which would ensue from the precedent being set by the government. Then I launched into ten minutes of impassioned French:

> The British North America Act is not an ordinary statute to be amended at the whim of Parliament. It is our national constitution; it contains the pact entered into by the old Provinces at the time of Confederation, binding the Dominion and each Province, and it is the great charter of the rights of minorities, particularly of those of the French tongue and culture. Let no bold hand be lightly laid on this constitution to overturn its provisions without consultation with the Provinces.

I quoted Lapointe with great effect: "No change should be accepted without the consent of all those who were parties to it. It [the BNA Act] is a sacred treaty just as is any other treaty; it is no scrap of paper."

Many times this issue was to be renewed in my speeches in the province of Quebec. I alluded to St. Laurent's declaration as "La Doctrine St-Laurent." Against it I placed the position of the Progressive Conservative party: no amendment of the constitution without consultation with the provinces and their consent. I think St. Laurent's declaration, while honest, must be likened to Mr. King's famous and costly "five cent speech" in 1930.

My speech in that evening of climax was followed intently by an elderly, dignified member to the right of the Speaker. At my close he congratulated me on having delivered what he called one of the greatest speeches he had listened to in all his thirty-five years in Parliament. In the corridor later he added, "You are almost more eloquent in French than in English." It was the great P.J.A. Cardin. His own speech in the same debate was a classic of logic and eloquence. Said he, "I am in favour of unity, but I am against unification." Supporting the amendment on the necessity of consultation with the provinces, he declared,

> I am in accord with that view, and in that stand I remain in the family of the old Liberals among whom I have been brought up in my political life. I stand with Blake; I stand with Laurier; I stand with Lapointe, and on that constitutional issue I also agree with leaders of the Conservative party in the past. No, I am not alone. I am at present preaching the gospel they all have preached, the gospel I myself have been advocating in my province and in Canada as a whole for the last 35 years.

From that moment he was my friend and mentor. By his death on October 20 I lost a friend whose memory will ever be dear to me.

I was not aware that the Prime Minister had taken any personal notice of me in the House until one day, when I was chatting with René Beaudoin in the corridor, Mr. King walked by, stopped, addressed me by name and shook hands. He asked me if I was enjoying the House, to which I replied in the affirmative. He could not have been more pleasant. But he took no notice of René, who was almost agape at the personal interest shown by the Prime Minister. Said René ruefully: "He doesn't speak to his own members like that. He doesn't even know us."

CHAPTER THIRTEEN

Workhorse of the Party

A by-election in the riding of Pontiac in the autumn of 1946 drew me into campaigning in Quebec for the first time. In the week I spent there I did not find the task easy. The riding was close to the west border of the province, and the meetings were conducted in both languages. I learned something of campaign customs in Quebec. Unlike other provinces Quebec has always looked on Sunday as the principal day for campaign meetings, and in the French-speaking areas the "after-mass" meeting was an established custom. Indeed, such meetings often were held on the church premises. We had a team of young lawyers from Montreal taking part, and they planned our after-mass meeting as a matter of course. They hired a truck, and we planned to speak from its platform. Word of our plans must have reached the ears of the parish priest, who proved to be of Irish, not of French, extraction. It was reported to us that in his homily he had warned his parishioners that they were not to attend any political meeting, and he would not allow such a sin to be perpetrated on church property. We had just time to drive the truck out of sight and to remove ourselves from the scene before the end of the mass.

That was my only experience with after-mass meetings in Quebec. Unfortunately, all our campaign efforts were in vain; the Conservative candidate ran in third place. The Liberals, notwithstanding their appeals to racial and religious prejudice, lost the seat to a young Social Credit candidate by the name of Réal Caouette making his first run. He talked like a machine-gun in either language, and he would soon make himself heard in the House.

The 1947 session began with a cabinet reshuffle. St. Laurent went from Justice to External Affairs, Ilsley from Finance to Justice, Paul Martin to National Health and Welfare, and Doug

Abbott became Minister of Finance. These shifts were all of direct concern to my responsibilities in the House. Doug Abbott proved a staunch defender of his predecessor in Finance. When on March 28 I complained of the "uncompromising rigidity" exhibited by Ilsley in his attitudes and policies when Minister of Finance, Abbott rose to his defence.

As the session proceeded two changes became evident. My workload in the House increased, and ministers paid more attention to me. More and more asperity discoloured their remarks in the House to me and about me. Ian Mackenzie became nasty at times, and although I still had little to do with C.D. Howe's departments of Trade and Commerce and Reconstruction, that crusty minister managed to exhibit his capacity for making personal aspersions. Even the relatively restrained J.L. Ilsley allowed himself at times to become personal and caustic. These passages clearly indicated that my words were effectively hurting the government. I was in fact drawing the fire of senior ministers. It was no surprise to me to learn that in the House of Commons fire draws fire in response; if one is thin-skinned or fearful of wordy retaliation one should refrain from attack or make innocuous speeches. I had not been sent to Parliament for any such insipid purpose. I had no fear of any of the cabinet, and my duty as I conceived it was to oppose and attack wherever the circumstances warranted it.

A sound critical faculty is a powerful ally in any walk of life – it is invaluable in Parliament. I was well aware that I was developing such a faculty and using it in the House with increasing effect. Alice found at times that I was not confining the use of it to the House of Commons. "It is much easier to be critical than correct," said Disraeli once. I was determined to be both critical and correct. I was all too well aware of the dangers of exposing myself to shattering rebuttals if my criticisms were not fully supported by the facts. It was my purpose not to be caught "off base," and I don't believe I ever was.

My entry into the debate on the budget on May 22 had the effect of concentrating attention on the weaknesses of Doug Abbott's first budget. It was considered one of the most effective speeches in the long debate. I deplored the utter inadequacy of the token reductions in the income tax, attacked the weight and unfairness of many commodity taxes, exposed the pyramiding of the federal sales tax, drew attention to the growing plight of the gold mining industry, and for the first time discussed the worrying state of our foreign trade. That last sally brought me quite deliberately into C.D. Howe territory. Finally, I referred to the

119

strained state of relations between the federal and provincial governments, warned of the futility of the attempted coercion on the part of the federal government, and condemned them for their attempts to bully the provinces and particularly the premiers of Ontario (Drew) and Quebec (Duplessis).

I contributed to various debates during the session, including those on broadcasting and the CBC, and housing – which journalists were now calling my favourite subject. I also advocated a better method of scrutinizing the Estimates, claiming that the procedures of the House did not enable members to discharge their essential responsibility of controlling expenditure. It was the first salvo in what became a long war and led ultimately to the creation of an Estimates Committee.

But there was one subject which dominated the course of the 1947 session and drew opposition censure on the government for its weak, bureaucratic and inept handling. This was the retention by the government of the powers granted to it in wartime. A year and a half had passed since the conclusion of hostilities, yet most of the vast mass of legislation created during the war by orders-in-council passed under the authority of the War Measures Act still remained in force. It was a trespass on the authority of Parliament and an invasion in many respects of the jurisdiction of the provinces. The government was reluctant to yield up any of these vast powers, pleading the necessity of "orderly decontrol." Instead of selecting such measures as were really necessary for this purpose and asking Parliament to legislate for that purpose, the Liberals gathered up the whole volume of orders-in-council, numbering fifty-seven in all, and in a short bill asked Parliament to give them full statutory effect till March 31, 1948, reserving to the government the right to rescind any of them in whole or in part in the meantime. This was asking Parliament for a blank cheque and the enactment of the equivalent of an annual volume of statutes in one short bill. The bill was preceded by a resolution which Ilsley as Minister of Justice introduced on March 20. At the conclusion of Ilsley's lengthy introductory statement John Bracken spoke for two minutes, agreeing to the passage of the resolution and reserving comment until the bill had been introduced. Both the gravity of the subject and the political opportunity offered by the resolution were misjudged. The CCF and Social Credit, however, were not so naïve; they leaped into the vacuum left by the Conservative default. M.J. Coldwell for the CCF resisted any dismantling of the mechanism of the managed economy. At this point the House was taken by surprise by the entry of Chubby Power into the debate. This popular, respected veteran Liberal flayed the government for its attempt to introduce an omnibus measure under the resolution. His speech was a masterpiece of incisive logic and defence of the rights of Parliament. It shook Ilsley, but it did much more. It compelled the Conservatives to reverse their strategy and enter the debate at once.

How I came to be chosen on short notice to enter the breach and speak for the official opposition may well invite explanation. Both Diefenbaker and Howard Green had sat in the House throughout the war and had frequently attacked government by order-in-council. The subject was no part of my caucus responsibilities. Nevertheless, it was I who was given the task of replying. I did not mince words. I said that CCF support for the bill as necessary to its program of socialistic planning was enough to put the House on guard. I made a slashing assault on bureaucracy, government control of the economy, the centralization of all power in Ottawa, and socialism. Again, on second reading of the bill I denounced the measure as "the greatest hodge-podge of legislation ever presented to this House":

> The only principle that can be found in it, in the manner in which it has been presented to the House, is this, that a government which has grown accustomed during time of war to treat Parliament with something between tolerance and contempt, has decided that it will ask Parliament to give legislative sanction, willy-nilly and holus-bolus, to a whole volume of legislation, in a manner which absolutely precludes any detailed examination by Parliament of the language of the orders to which it is proposed that statutory effect shall be given. We are asked to swallow the measure on second reading – and in one swallow.

At the conclusion of my speech I introduced an amendment declaring that while willing to support properly drafted legislation dealing with certain named matters, "This House is unalterably opposed to the enactment of a measure to continue indiscriminately the sweeping powers of the presently existing boards outside the control of Parliament." Debate was allowed to continue on this amendment for two weeks before Mr. Ilsley challenged it on a point of order and the Speaker obligingly ruled it out of order. The bill continued on its thorny course, and eventually was passed. The debate was the longest, most challenging and fundamental in the issues it raised until the great debate on the pipeline in 1956. By my intervention I had recovered the initiative for the party after it had thoughtlessly cast it away, and had made two of the most timely speeches of my entire parliamentary career.

That, however, was not the end of new and unexpected responsibilities undertaken at the request of the leader and the whip. I had not previously been a member of the Standing Committee on Public Accounts. It had been quite inactive and nobody in our caucus had the industry to revive its usefulness. I was appointed to the committee in March 1947. The occasion was the introduction of a government bill respecting Trading with the Enemy and the Custodian of Enemy Property. Some of our members, such as Green and Diefenbaker who had sat in the House throughout the war, should have taken charge of this task. I knew precious little about the subject beforehand, but before I had finished I think I knew more about it than anyone else in the House, the Secretary of State included. I led off in the debate on second reading, and the bill was referred to the Public Accounts Committee. Having opened up the committee, the government could not close it, and I took full advantage of the opportunity to expose two areas of scandalous maladministration by the government.

When Japan entered the war with its attack on Pearl Harbor the Canadian government rounded up and interned for the duration of the war persons of Japanese ancestry, of whom there were about twenty-five thousand in British Columbia. Their property was taken into the custody of the Custodian of Enemy Property. It was in many cases broken into, vandalized and sold by the Custodian at prices far below true value. It was a blot on the honour of Canada. The government had chosen to ignore the complaints of these unfortunate people. Almost single-handed in that committee I ripped aside the veil cast over this sordid episode and exposed shocking maladministration and injustice. I made so strong a case that most of the Liberals on the committee felt obliged to support me. The bill was reported back to the House in greatly improved form, the government accepted our amendments, and it was adopted on May 9. But, more important, the committee recommended that a royal commission be appointed to review the claims of all Japanese who had been involved in the internment. The government acted on the recommendation and appointed Mr. Justice Bird to conduct the inquiry. This commission was to report in June of 1950, recommending payment of amounts totalling $1,222,829 to thirteen hundred Canadians of Japanese extraction. For my part in winning belated justice for these aggrieved people I take strong and abiding satisfaction.

I opened up another issue in the Public Accounts Committee – the scandalous mismanagement in the Veterans Land Act Administration. There had been numerous complaints by veterans over the way they had been flim-flammed into purchasing government housing through the VLA, but the Department of Veterans Affairs, headed by the wordy Ian Mackenzie, brushed them all aside. I persuaded the committee to look into VLA operations in Sarnia Township and to call the veterans concerned as witnesses. Their testimony revealed such shocking abuses that there was no possibility of stifling the scandal any longer. The director of VLA was Gordon Murchison. Normally I was sympathetic to civil servants, but Murchison made the mistake of trying to cover up the misdeeds of his department. The committee in its report to the House stated specifically that it "was not favourably impressed by the way evidence was given by Mr. Gordon Murchison." The sittings of the committee extended into July, and the Ottawa heat was searing, but we stayed with the task. The *Windsor Daily Star* carried full reports of the proceedings. It was the first to label me "The party's workhorse."

The VLA Estimate came before the House on July 16. Ian Mackenzie and Mr. Warren, a Liberal member, both became personally abusive of me in the debate. Ian had a habit of fortifying himself with spirits, and that may have accounted for his abusiveness on this occasion. He and Warren stoutly defended Murchison as a blameless victim of my ruthless interrogation employing "police court methods." They should not have been so rash. Within weeks the government relieved Murchison of his position. My exertions in the committee had won a hearing, vindication and remedy for the veterans. Moreover, the committee had been brought to life. I had a good working relationship with its very able Liberal chairman, Philippe Picard, and he had no intention of allowing the committee to become a rubber stamp for the government. In those days, unlike now, the chairman was a government supporter, not a member of the opposition.

The 1947 session was notable in other respects. The Prime Minister was absent for part of the winter as the result of illness and St. Laurent was Acting Prime Minister. Appearances pointed to him as the man chosen by Mr. King as his ultimate successor.

Outside the Commons Chamber, I found my parliamentary activities were expanding and drawing me into diverse interests. For example, the Commonwealth Parliamentary Association was becoming a source of very keen interest to me. Its general secretary, Sir Howard d'Egville, located in London, visited the Commonwealth branches from time to time, and when in Ottawa or Toronto never failed to see me. I fully subscribed to the purposes of the organization, of bringing closer together the countries of the Commonwealth and the members of their

Parliaments. Under its auspices I had in 1945 just after my election to Parliament met a British MP, also just elected, on a visit to Canada. His path and mine were destined to cross many times, and we became close friends. His name was Derick Heathcote-Amory. By 1947 my interest in the association had been noticed, and I was elected to the executive of the Canadian branch. I served on it for ten years.

At this time I inaugurated an annual parliamentary prize for each of the secondary schools in Eglinton riding – North Toronto Collegiate, Northern Vocational School and Lawrence Park Collegiate. The winner was to be a senior student selected by the staff on the basis of his ability to make intelligent observation of Parliament in action and report to the school assembly. They came to Ottawa on the Wednesday afternoon train and returned on Friday night. I saw to it that they met as many ministers and as many Liberal MPs, especially from Quebec, as possible. Louis St. Laurent was always very gracious about meeting the three boys in his office, and Paul Martin was always at his entertaining best at dinner with them. The Speaker also received them, and René Beaudoin when Speaker dined them in his chambers. They met the other leaders, of course; no one could ever say I endeavoured to influence them in a partisan way. I could not arrange the business of the House to assure maximum excitement, and there was always an element of luck in the business before the House during the visit. Sometimes the boys struck highlights, one year only Agriculture Estimates. Some outstanding young men developed out of the forty or so who came to Ottawa as my guests. I never met one who wasn't thrilled to be selected. I made a rule never to be present when one of them was reporting afterward to his school assembly. On my part I have been delighted to meet these young men years later.

My relations with John Bracken were becoming ever closer. He often asked me to join him at a sandwich lunch in his office, where we discussed current questions before Parliament and he dipped into his storehouse of experience to instruct his disciple. Billy McMaster, the member for High Park, once told a meeting of his constituents that a member observing Bracken and me in conversation remarked, "There's the party. That's where the decisions are made." The comment was based on a mistaken view, but it illustrates how close John Bracken and I were to each other. It is also an indication of how my hard work and devotion to principles, in a party whose members were becoming demoralized by long years in Opposition, were coming to be appreciated by the leader.

CHAPTER FOURTEEN

Budget by Radio

The lull between the 1947 and 1948 sessions was brief and disturbed. Four months after MPs had joyfully dispersed in July we were called back to confront a serious emergency. It was Mackenzie King's last session as Prime Minister, and it proved to be troubled and disputatious.

The deaths of two Liberal members led to by-elections in York-Sunbury and Halifax. The Liberals retained both. I campaigned in both constituencies, but to no avail. The Maritimes were not yet ready to support Conservative candidates, however impressive their personal merits. The season was dry, and the roads dusty. After a sixty-mile drive in Halifax County on a hot day in an open car I arrived at our meeting covered with a layer of dust to face an audience of just twenty persons. I asked myself, was all this effort worthwhile?

York-Sunbury had been a Conservative stronghold, represented by R.B. Hanson. It had been won in 1945 by Frank Bridges, who became Minister of Fisheries and was very popular in the House. On Frank's death Mr. King staged one of his coups. Milton Gregg, VC, former Sergeant-at-Arms of the House of Commons, had recently been appointed president of the University of New Brunswick. He was reputed to be a Conservative, but Mr. King coaxed him into politics and on September 2 appointed him Minister of Fisheries. Milton took the bait and held the seat. He was highly respected for his war record, and Conservative denunciations of him as a "turncoat" were unavailing. Always polite and pleasant, he never became involved in a wrangle.

The session began with the announcement by the government of a cabinet shuffle. Ian Mackenzie was appointed to the Senate, and was replaced as Minister of Veterans Affairs by Milton Gregg. C.D. Howe was appointed Minister of Trade and Commerce, while retaining his portfolio of Reconstruction and Supply. Ian Mackenzie's departure from the House removed a colourful figure. A very verbose and sometimes eloquent Scot, he acted as House Leader. He sat immediately to Mr. King's left, and was thought to be as close to being a personal friend of the Prime Minister as anyone was permitted to be. They often engaged in personal conversation in the House. One of the most amusing sights I ever witnessed in the House involved the two. Ian was in his seat when Mr. King took his own place. Ian, evidently having something confidential to impart, leaned toward the Prime Minister. Mr. King politely leaned toward Ian over the narrow aisle which separated the two desks. Ian had quite evidently been drinking, which was not unusual, and he kept leaning farther and farther to his right, while Mr. King politely followed Ian by leaning farther and farther to his own left. Soon they both actually disappeared from sight behind their desks. Those of us who saw all this from the opposite side roared with laughter. The two heads slowly reappeared from the low position to which they had gradually sunk.

Ian, who had been a life-long bachelor, married about this time, and Mr. King modestly sent the bride and groom a photograph of himself as a wedding present. He confided to me one day in the parliamentary dining room that Mr. King would be succeeded as prime minister by Louis St. Laurent, but that C.D. Howe undoubtedly could have the prime ministership if he wanted it. With the departure of Ian Mackenzie, Mr. King himself took over the duties of House Leader more actively than ever before in my time.

The Prime Minister announced on October 30 that Parliament would be recalled, ostensibly to ratify the General Agreement on Tariffs and Trade (GATT) that had been recently signed at Geneva. That proved, however, to be only a pretext. A crisis was developing, and Canada's reserves of foreign exchange were dwindling fast. On the evening of November 17 the Minister of Finance, Doug Abbott, in a radio speech announced measures being taken to meet the financial crisis. Under the powers of the Foreign Exchange Control Act, passed at the 1946 session, the government was now prohibiting the importation of many commodities, placing quotas or requiring special permits for other goods, and imposing foreign travel restrictions on Canadians. In addition, a 25 per cent excise tax was imposed on a wide range of imports. He had no authority to impose this tax. The announcement burst like thunder over the business community and the Conservative opposition. Parliament was summoned to meet on December 5. The scene was laid for a major political showdown.

When the Foreign Exchange Control bill was before Parliament in 1946 Ilsley, then Minister of Finance, had given this plain and unequivocal assurance: "We have no intention of using this exchange control legislation to restrict anything but certain types of capital movement." His successor had destroyed this solemn assurance. Only Parliament could levy taxes; therefore, in imposing the special excise tax, which, incidentally, could only hurt Canadian producers and consumers and not foreign sources, the government was acting unconstitutionally, and ordering the civil servants in the Department of National Revenue to act illegally to collect it. Both Abbott and Howe had recently delivered very optimistic forecasts of economic growth, giving not a hint of the approaching exchange crisis, which had been allowed to reach critical proportions before the government lifted a finger to meet it. It was small wonder that everyone was stunned at the disclosure reluctantly made by the ministers.

Parliament assembled on December 5 but the debate on Abbott's emergency measures to conserve foreign exchange did not open until December 16. Abbott led off with a speech lasting an hour and a half. He was followed by Jim Macdonnell as opposition financial critic. The next day Howe spoke, and I followed him. The drama was tense. Abbott was in a difficult corner. He pleaded the necessity of restricting U.S. imports, rationalized similar restrictions against imports from other countries in order to avoid discrimination against the United States, and justified the special excise taxes on Canadians in order to protect the position of U.S. exporters to the Canadian market. He stated that currency devaluation had been considered as an alternative and rejected on the ground that it would tend to raise the price level.

Jim Macdonnell's speech was one of the best he ever delivered. His denunciation was forceful: "This bill gives powers which have never been given before in peacetime, perhaps never even approached in wartime. . . . We who have struggled for generations to achieve the position of living under the rule of law are now to live, as far as business is concerned, to a very large extent under the arbitrary powers of one man. This is control – complete, final and absolute. . . ."

In reply Howe sought to be as disarming as possible, excusing his absolute powers over imports and disclaiming any intention of being unfair. Then it was my turn to enter the debate, and I welcomed the challenge of following Howe. I placed full responsibility for the crisis on the shoulders of the government, and accused them of treating Parliament with contempt, of reneging on Ilsley's assurance that the Exchange Control Act would not be used to restrict anything but certain types of capital movement, of imposing austerity on the Canadian people, and of misleading them. I thundered, "The Minister of Reconstruction holds the Canadian economy in the hollow of his hand" and no man "clothed with powers like these will ever be able . . . to divest himself completely of caprice and whim and favouritism and partisanship. . . . Gone are objective standards in the application of law to the citizens of the country, regardless of their walk of life or of their station. . . . The government has thrown business in this country into a welter of confusion, into utter turmoil. . . . The essence of this bill is dictation from above, the remaking of the Canadian economy." I challenged the government to call a general election on the issue. Howe sat silent through this arraignment, but I knew he was bursting with rage. I returned to the fight on February 12 and 16, denouncing this "priceless example of economic lunacy" and its "strangulation of our economy." On February 17, when I began speaking of the rights of Parliament and democracy, Howe called for the question to be put to terminate the debate. This gave me an opportunity to deliver him a lecture on democracy and his own starved failure to understand it. I knew his anger was rising day by day and it would at some point boil over. On February 20 while I had the floor he burst out: "Sit down, my boy." With encouragement from such a source another Liberal MP called out, "Sit down. You are too young." At forty-two years of age I considered myself quite mature enough to reply, "When the Minister of Reconstruction and Supply, Trade and Commerce and everything else, the jack of all trades in the Cabinet undertakes to make remarks intended to disparage those in the House who do not happen to have his years I want to say to him that I think references of that kind do not reflect any credit on him." I had no more interruptions from Howe that day, but I was well aware that his anger was still accumulating. The bill was finally carried on February 24.

Meanwhile, another crisis had arisen which claimed as much attention as that concerning our reserves of foreign exchange. Prices, wholesale and retail, were rising rapidly, and the cost of living had taken a major leap upwards. On January 26 John Bracken had endeavoured unsuccessfully to force a debate on the subject. Mr. King knew that he would be facing a running battle over the cost of living throughout the session, especially as the government was itself forcing up prices with its new excise taxes and its failure to encourage production. Craftily, on February 2 he brought forward a motion to appoint a committee of the

House to inquire into the causes of the recent rise in the cost of living, into prices which had been raised above levels justified by increased costs, and into price rises due to acquisition, accumulation or withholding from sales of goods beyond reasonable needs. No committee of the Commons was needed for such an inquiry: the Wartime Prices and Trade Board, the Tariff Board, the Combines Investigation Commissioner could all have done it. But the Prime Minister sought to make it appear that the government was doing something, and he wished to stifle the inevitable discussion of the subject in the House of Commons. A committee of the House would serve these purposes admirably; once the question was committed to it no further discussion on the subject would be permitted in the House under its rules. It was all a transparent trick, typical of the crafty Mr. King. The committee was given no power to make recommendations in its report; the Conservative attempt to amend the motion to permit such recommendations was ruled out of order. In my speech on February 5 I ridiculed the government for raising taxes on commodities and thus the cost of living and thereby making a mockery and a sham of the appointment of the committee. I called it the equivalent of sabotage and I dubbed it "Abbotage." I said action against increase in the cost of living should come from government. It was simply endeavouring to escape its responsibility and to stifle Parliament. I added, "The sky over Ottawa is black with the chickens coming home to roost on this government." The committee was appointed on February 10 by a vote of 119 to 80, with only the Social Credit supporting the Liberals on the motion.

The committee consisted of sixteen members. The government's nine appointees included Paul Martin, Minister of National Health and Welfare, and four parliamentary assistants. It was evident that the Liberals were "loading" the committee, and it was unusual to have a minister on a committee. Martin's election as chairman clearly exposed the government's partisan designs. Four Conservatives were appointed. The selection followed a familiar pattern. Green and Diefenbaker were asked to serve on it, but declined. When asked I could only agree. The others were Cec Merritt, Doug Harkness and Karl Homuth. John Bracken called us in and said I was to lead them. The committee met constantly during the four and a half months it was in operation, and held seventy-seven public meetings. In this way Mr. King was able to keep out of the House of Commons all questions concerning the cost of living, which continued to rise rapidly, from February 10 to June 25.

I will not forget the events of June 24, 1948. Parliament was to be prorogued in six days' time. The committee was called to meet that day in "executive session," which means behind closed doors. It had called and examined numerous witnesses, but had carried no part of its inquiry to finality. It had made no attempt to arrive at any findings, and, of course, it had been denied authority to make recommendations. At noon a voluminous draft report, extending to seventy pages, was placed before the members of the committee, who were told that they might discuss it and make observations and offer amendments, but unless these concerned merely the dotting of "i"s or the crossing of "t"s they would not pass. No amendment of substance would be tolerated. Many of the statements in the draft departed from the evidence or distorted it; others went beyond or outside the evidence. Clearly the draft was a barefaced vehicle of Liberal political propaganda, and it contained no recommendations. The committee remained in session on it past midnight. After an adjournment, the Liberal members returned in a group to the meeting room looking as though they had collectively laid an egg. Thereupon the chairman produced a new document containing numerous recommendations, many of which related to matters which had never been before the committee. At 1.30 a.m. on June 25 the report was adopted over my strong protests. I was the only Conservative present at the bitter end. The others had gone home to bed. The whole proceeding was a political farce and a barefaced travesty. Every Liberal who took part in it ought eternally to be ashamed of himself, not least the chairman.

The report was tabled June 25, and Paul Martin moved concurrence the next day. I led off in the debate, which continued for two and a half days. I lashed the Liberal majority on the committee, and I lashed the government. I was aroused by the sheer iniquity of those final proceedings and the transparent attempt of the government to hoodwink the electorate. It was, I believe, one of the most effective speeches I ever made in Parliament.

Jim Macdonnell in his speech on June 28 analysed Mr. King and his role with the Prices Committee in these words:

> I would have thought that this report was in the Prime Minister's best style, ear to the ground, ready to move any way, making the best of all worlds, facing both ways, the little brother of the rich and the big brother of the poor. If there is one thing that the Prime Minister has succeeded in doing it is to create the impression somehow or another that he has been championing the poor against the rich. How he has done it I do not know. It is one of the things for which we all give him credit, at any rate for his dexterity.

Personally I despise the misuse of parliamentary dexterity to fool the people.

While the work of the committee had been going on, the business of the House continued unabated, and I was expected to play an active role. For example, the Estimates of the Department of National Health and Welfare afforded me an opportunity on June 11 to renew my annual appeal for the appointment of a standing committee on public health, welfare, social security and housing. My motion to that effect had been standing on the Order Paper for four years and never reached. I urged more encouragement for research, observing that "research has been largely starved in Canada." I think I can claim that the estimates of no department of government received as thorough a review as did those of this department. The figures of expenditure and budget requirement for every item were submitted to careful scrutiny. At the same time I longed for the day when the House would establish a Standing Committee on Estimates to undertake this badly needed microscopic control of government expenditure.

A government bill to amend the National Housing Act gave me another opportunity to fire a cannonade at the government, and particularly Howe, for their failures to cope with acute housing needs across Canada. In the face of extravagant Liberal campaign promises in 1945 their record of performance was pathetic. They were shirking their responsibility, and seeking to throw their own proper duty onto the backs of the overburdened municipalities. I put the lash of my tongue to their backs.

In the normal course of events the government had an adequate majority on its own; it could also usually depend upon the CCF for voting support. Rarely did the three parties in opposition combine their votes to challenge the government. On one occasion, however, the government sustained a technical defeat. In the debate on a bill to amend the Canadian Wheat Board Act, the bill was being referred after second reading to the Committee on Agriculture. C.D. Howe, in charge of the bill, had agreed to the Conservative request that the committee be given power to divide it into two bills – one dealing with wheat and the other with oats and barley. True to his word, Howe introduced the necessary motion. To the surprise of the Conservatives, on the vote only Howe and a few Liberals joined the Conservatives in voting for the motion. Most of the Liberals present joined the CCF in opposing it, and it was defeated by 94 votes to 58. Whether it was just another Liberal trick and Howe regretted having made his promise, or whether Liberal back-benchers were irritated by Conservative words in the debate I know not, but it seemed that Howe had been left out on a limb by his own party. However, I lost not even a second in pointing out that the House had just defeated a government motion. I inquired if it was the intention of the government to take the honourable course and resign, or were they going to attempt to cling to power with the help of the CCF coalition? Howe grinned, but made no response.

This was not the first time I had thrown down the challenge to the government to resign. I think some of my Conservative colleagues were worried by these challenges, but I knew the government would never dare to call a general election on such issues and on such a record as theirs. From the point of view of our party it is a pity they didn't; we could not possibly have fared as badly as we did when the general election did come in 1949.

But if there was to be no general election at least the government could not avoid calling by-elections to fill three vacancies, two in British Columbia and one in Ontario, in June. Two of the seats had been held by Liberals, and one by us. The CCF won all three. This brought little comfort to us Progressive Conservatives. I recalled in the House the treachery of the Liberals in South York in 1942, when their collaboration with the CCF had engineered the defeat of Arthur Meighen. I told the Liberals that that was the springboard for the rise in the fortunes of the CCF, and they could thank themselves for nourishing this threat to their own security.

The rules of the House are highly technical and difficult to master. They demand long study, and few members really become authorities on them. Grote Stirling had been looked upon as the Conservative authority on the rules, but his resignation at the end of 1947 left a vacuum. I applied myself to the task, and found myself taking an ever-increasing role in the technical discussions of points of order. On January 30 the Prime Minister appointed a committee to meet with the Speaker to revise the rules and change the hours of sitting. I was appointed a member of this small and intimate committee. Its labours over two sessions were destined to bear fruit in modernizing some of the rules and particularly the burdensome hours of sitting.

The confidential nature of advice tendered by civil servants to ministers came under scrutiny during the session. On this occasion Diefenbaker put his foot in it. In speaking on the Continuation of Transitional Measures Act on December 11, 1947, he suggested that Dr. Clark, the Deputy Minister of Finance, Graham Towers, the governor of of the Bank of Canada, Louis Rasminsky, deputy governor, "and others of that group" be brought before a committee of the House and examined as to "whether they made the recommendation to the Government on November 17 prior thereto or whether it was the Government that suggested to them the means whereby they could utilize the Foreign Exchange Control Act for the purposes they had in view." For this proposal Dief was warmly rebuked by Abbott and Coldwell. Diefenbaker endeavoured to make a strategic retreat; there can be no doubt that he was quite wrong in his proposal.

Important changes were about to come over the face of the House of Commons. On December 17, 1947, Mr. King observed his seventy-third birthday, and numerous tributes were heaped upon him in the House. Before the end of the session we knew it would be his last as Prime Minister. A national convention of the Liberal party was called for the first week of August 1948. It was fully expected that the courtly Louis St. Laurent and the redoubtable scrapper Jimmy Gardiner would be the principal contestants for the succession. The highly respected J.L. Ilsely had earlier been regarded as a prime contender, but his claims had been steadily fading. This session also proved to be his last. In one of his last interventions in debate on February 5 he drew on his long experience as Minister of Finance to warn against the folly of paying subsidies out of the public purse. He said "it was extremely sound for the government to disentangle itself from that insidious subsidy system." It was, I think, his valedictory, though we did not realize it at the time. I share the wise sentiments he expressed. Later that year he resigned his seat, left public life and took up the practice of law in Montreal. I was sorry to see him leave the House of Commons. He was a very genuine man, even if somewhat pedestrian in thought and manner. Among so many Liberals whose purpose was to fool the public Ilsley's homespun honesty of purpose stood out.

December 17, 1947, also marked the thirtieth anniversary of Chubby Power's first election to Parliament. He and Mackenzie King vied for the honour of being dean of the House. Although King's first election preceded Chubby's by some years Chubby with his thirty years in the House had a slightly longer record of continuous service. In the good-natured banter which marked the occasion in the House, Chubby made a comment on the uncertainties of public office which I have never forgotten. He said:

> I should like to write a book about this Commons House of Canada. I perhaps would put it in the form of a homily, ashes to ashes and dust to dust, and I would entitle it "Back to Front and Back Again." I would tell of the long and painful progress down five rows of seats to the front benches, and I would tell also of the

short and rapid and sudden transition from a private car to an upper berth. I would perhaps dedicate it to the over-ambitious youth who inhabit the back benches and also to the over-pretentious elderly ones who inhabit the front benches. . . . I have spent half of my life as a member of this House. It has been a good half life. It has been joyous; it has been filled with comradeship and kindness. There are no moments of it which I regret. I say that with perfect sincerity. There are those who have the idea that politics is a mean kind of game, that it is filled with disappointments and delusions, but, so far as I am aware, and so far as I have been able to observe during all these years, politics is filled also with loyalties, with decencies, with honesties, with comradeship, with evidence of the helping hand and the sympathetic spirit.

In all my eighteen years in the Commons, Chubby Power was the most popular member of it. Perhaps that accounts for his uniquely happy career in it. It has been given to few others to draw such unalloyed satisfaction from their careers in it. In the course of his remarks that day he indulged in one dig at Mr. King: "As one of the few of us who are still continuing Liberals, I pray that he will return to the faith of his fathers." Chubby concluded a memorable speech with a peroration in French, and sat down to a storm of applause. Yet seven months later as a candidate for the party leadership he drew a scant fifty votes.

Perhaps it is time to pause and take stock of my position and progress in Parliament. I had now sat through four sessions. I had taken a more active role in the debates in the committees than any of the new members of the 1945 crop, indeed more active than almost any other private member. I had advanced beyond my expectations and even my hopes. I had perhaps incurred some lifting of eyebrows on the part of some senior members who disapproved of new members' moving up too soon and too fast, but I had at the same time won commendations from them for my zeal and indefatigable industry. Eager beavers are not always appreciated by the indolent. The latter could always be depended upon during the hot summer sittings to complain in caucus, "If some of you fellows would stop talking we could get out of here." I did my own research work, and plenty of it. It was said that I spent more time in the parliamentary library than any other member. As the result of my constant reading and study I was developing a filing system which enabled me to produce material for a speech on most subjects at short notice, and which many members came to inspect and admire.

I was handicapped by the location of my seat in the fourth row in the corner at the end of the chamber on the Speaker's left. I experienced no difficulty whatever in making myself heard anywhere in the Chamber; the problem was sometimes to catch the eye of the Speaker or chairman of the Committee of the Whole, and almost always to hear the interjections from the Treasury benches. Ministers were seated conveniently close to the Hansard reporter, and were wont to contribute wisecracks which appeared next day on the record, but were inaudible to me when on my feet speaking; the worst offender was Doug Abbott. In the debates I was moving more and more into the orbit of the redoubtable C.D. Howe, as well as Abbott, Ilsley and Martin, all leading ministers.

I was speaking in French with increasing frequency and ease. Moreover, I was supporting the positions taken by the governments of Quebec and Ontario in resisting the fiscal encroachments of the federal government. Premier Duplessis was not popular in Ontario at the time, but I thought he was right on the fiscal issue, and I was not afraid to say so. Little did I realize at the time that my advocacy of Quebec's rights, my outspoken opposition to centralization, and my use of the French tongue were winning me attention and favour in a new and unexpected quarter.

One half-critical judgment began to surface occasionally – that I was too serious. At a caucus dinner one evening Art Smith in a speech referred to "Don Fleming, who carries the worries of the whole world on his shoulders." I resented this aspersion. I was tempted to tell the popular and able Art that if he would pull more of the weight I would be pleased to be relieved of part of my excessive load, but I refrained. Nevertheless, his remark was indicative of the fact that my labours were less appreciated by some of my colleagues and that in the last analysis I must look to my own conscience for ultimate satisfaction and approval. I knew that I was taking neither advancement nor opportunity from anyone else; the job I was doing would not be done as well or not at all if I didn't do it. Moreover, I had won the full confidence and gratitude of my leader, John Bracken. Admittedly, some of the photographs taken at the time give me a very serious expression. I was determined not to take myself too seriously, but I was equally determined to take seriously the job I had been elected to do in Parliament and to excel at it if I could possibly do so. Diefenbaker was also smarting at the time because of gossip that he was a prima donna and a loner. At the same caucus dinner, to a request for further comment, he acidly replied, "Prima donnas do not give encores."

A look at the press comment at this point may be illuminating. On December 11, 1945, the *Globe and Mail* ran a serious-looking photograph of me in the parliamentary library with this caption, "Rated as the heaviest reader of any of the newer MPs in Ottawa is the Toronto-Eglinton Member, Donald Fleming, who, if not in the House or in his office, can nearly always be found in the Parliamentary Library." *Maclean's* magazine of April 1, 1947, carried a major article by Blair Fraser entitled "Who's the Opposition?" He selected John Bracken, Gordon Graydon, Jim Macdonnell, Ivan Sabourin, Howard Green, John Diefenbaker, Art Smith and myself. He concluded his treatment of me with these words:

> In Ottawa, Fleming channels all that energy into his work as a Member of Parliament. For instance, he improves his French by having lunch weekly with Liberal MPs from Quebec; he has on three occasions addressed the House in French. His specialty is housing and social security, and he has mastered details of Government policy to an extent that keeps civil servants hopping when he asks questions. All this activity has carried Fleming far beyond the station usual to his age and seniority. It has drawn upon him, too, the jealous glances of older and more indolent Members, who call Fleming an Eager Beaver. But at least one Liberal Minister describes him as "the most effective man the Opposition has in the House."

On July 26, 1947, Arthur Blakely, the seasoned and able representative of the *Montreal Gazette*, wrote in that journal: "Donald Fleming now rates with John Diefenbaker as an effective government critic within the ranks of the Official Opposition."

In the second of a series of articles on "Parliamentary Personalities," the *Windsor Daily Star* featured me on February 28, 1948, as "one of the main cogs in the Tory Opposition machine in the House of Commons." It said:

> He has been a party stalwart since 1945 and in that short time has stamped himself as an able debater and one tenacious as a bulldog after the facts. . . . Last July he carried the brunt of the examination into the construction of the veterans' homes in Sarnia and Windsor. For two solid weeks he conducted six hours of questioning every day to have put before the people of Canada the facts in the housing scandal. . . . Currently he is the Tory spokesman on the Martin Prices Enquiry Committee and is showing the same bulldogish determination to get the underlying facts concerning the rise of prices in Canada. . . . He is a man with a thunderous voice – one which commands attention and reaches every nook and cranny of the spacious Commons Chamber. The latter fact is

regarded as something phenomenal considering the poor acoustics of the Commons room.

Noticeably throughout the 1947-48 session the French-language press of Quebec was giving more space and more prominence to reports of my speeches in the House, whether in French or English. My increasing facility in French was also making an impression. Attention was being paid moreover to the support I voiced for Duplessis's position on federal-provincial fiscal relations.

It had been a long and gruelling session. I hailed prorogation on June 30 with relief. I could at last look forward to a delectable respite of seven months from parliamentary attendance. That I was to be back home with my family and my practice for so long a period of time seemed almost incredible. I also looked forward with zest to a new and thrilling experience. A Commonwealth Parliamentary Conference, always a notable event, was to be held in London in the autumn under the auspices of the Commonwealth Parliamentary Association, and our party had been accorded three places on the Canadian delegation. For these much-sought prizes Bracken had selected Senator Moraud, Art Smith and myself. It all seemed too good to be true. I had never crossed the Atlantic beyond Bermuda. The opportunity to visit Britain and Europe was dazzling; to participate with representatives of other parliaments in the Commonwealth in important discussions and debates at Westminster exceeded my dreams; and a grant toward the expenses of each delegate, while not covering his entire outlays, made it possible for me to go. I was profoundly grateful to John Bracken for giving me this opportunity. On July 1, I was back home in Toronto with the prospect of the summer there and the trip to London in the autumn. Little did I dream that a dark shadow was waiting to cross the political scene and that it would have a powerful influence on the course of my life.

CHAPTER FIFTEEN

Candidate for the Leadership, 1948

I have always maintained that if John Bracken had won office without having to serve as Leader of the Opposition he might have gone down in history as a great prime minister. He took a balanced view of all questions, and functioned as the captain of the team. He would have given scope and opportunity to the other members of the team. He was always considerate of the viewpoints of others, and he was a man of character and integrity.

Unfortunately, however, he did not adapt easily to the role of Leader of the Opposition. In his long and successful political experience in Manitoba he had been Premier for over twenty years, but had never sat in opposition. Staying out of Parliament for the three years after his election as party leader in 1942 was a tactical mistake of the first magnitude. Gordon Graydon served well as House Leader, but it was embarrassing to the party that its leader by his own choice remained outside Parliament. Whether he would have led the party effectively in the House from 1942 to 1945 will never be known. The Conservative opposition was very weak in numbers, and its role in the House in wartime was bound to be difficult. It became easy for the Liberals, however, to picture Bracken as afraid to face the Commons.

The result was that when John Bracken took his place in the House of Commons in 1945 he was entering that chamber, the arena of federal politics, for the first time, and he was seated in the opposition for the first time in his life. Around him were some very able men who possessed years of experience in the Commons and in the role of opposition; across the chamber sat shrewd men with years of experience in the Commons and a readiness to exploit for their own partisan advantage any misstep of a newcomer. Bracken's path in these circumstances was bound to be thorny. It was not easy to stop thinking of himself as head of the government, and to substitute the mixture of positive and negative thinking expected of a leader of the opposition. He never found himself at ease in the cut and thrust of debate in the House, or in the swift exchanges and repartee.

There had, of course, been criticisms of Bracken's performance in the House before 1948, but this was to be expected. There were rumblings of discontent in some party quarters during the session of that year, but nothing to prepare us for what was to happen that summer. I had been home less than a week when there came the announcement of Bracken's resignation as party leader. I was completely taken aback; I was also chagrined that I had not been taken into his confidence, nor given even the slightest hint as to his intention. It was evident that the resignation had been precipitated under some compelling circumstances not fully or long foreseen. Immediately there were cries from within the party for an explanation, which was never forthcoming. I was told later that it had become impossible as long as Bracken continued as leader to raise funds to keep the party organization alive, and that he reacted decisively when this was reported to him; but I never probed to verify this report.

I was profoundly disappointed in the events. I could not believe that I would ever be on such close terms with any other leader, and possibly I could not hope to enjoy the confidence of and receive encouragement from another leader to the same degree. But nothing stands still very long in politics, and another question insistently pushed these thoughts aside – who would be the new leader?

The party machinery was soon set in motion and a leadership convention called for September 30-October 2 in Ottawa. John Diefenbaker was the first to declare himself a candidate. That occasioned no surprise, as he was obviously a major contender. Howard Green decided against standing. Davie Fulton's name was mentioned, but at thirty-two he rightly concluded it would be too soon for him to seek the leadership. Murdo Macpherson was out of public life. At the provincial level there was only one man, George Drew. He was then the only Conservative provincial premier in Canada. He had been Premier of Ontario for five years and had given vigorous and courageous leadership to the government and the party. His minority victory at the polls in 1943 had been followed by smashing Conservative majorities in 1945 and 1948, but his most recent success had been marred by his personal defeat in High Park, largely over the issue of liquor sale. George's interest in federal issues had long been demonstrated, and he had assailed the Liberal government on many fronts, latterly Dominion-provincial fiscal relations.

There remained the possibility of my own candidacy. I was forty-three. King had been elected leader of the Liberal party at forty-two. I had served through four sessions in the Commons, and had undoubtedly attained recognition as a leading figure there. I was not, however, as widely known throughout the country as Diefenbaker or Drew. Had John Bracken's resignation come several years later I might have been in a far stronger position. In the developing circumstances there was no time for such idle speculation. My name was being widely mentioned as a possibility, and I was receiving numerous approaches. I had to make a decision. If I announced myself a candidate would I appear brash and presumptuous? Would my candidature be taken seriously across Canada? Would other and more likely candidates resent my running? Would my partners agree? Was it fair to Alice and the children for me to seek to assume the heavy burden of party leadership? Was I equal to the task in the remote chance of being elected leader? In good conscience I answered this last question affirmatively, and Alice gave her consent to my standing. My partners reluctantly concurred, probably thinking that I would not win, anyway.

I consulted my friend Joe Fisher of the *Toronto Telegram*. He had been in the press gallery at Ottawa in 1945 and 1946, but had then returned to Toronto. Joe brushed aside any questions concerning my fitness to be a candidate for the party leadership and told me I had every right and reason to enter the contest. His advice was timely and influential.

At this moment of acute indecision help came from a totally unexpected quarter. Up to this time I had never heard of Robert Rumilly. I had never met Camillien Houde, the colourful mayor of Montreal, and had no reason to believe he had ever heard of me. I was wrong. Robert Rumilly was a writer, a nationalist, living in Montreal to which he had emigrated from his native France. He came at his own request to meet me in Toronto; obviously he wished to size up the young Toronto Conservative who had demonstrated a sympathy for Quebec and who spoke in French in the Commons. He was in communication with Houde. Some time after the event (for the English-language press in the other provinces had totally missed it), I learned that Houde had made a powerful intervention in the Quebec provincial election campaign that year in support of the Duplessis government. He had strongly attacked St. Laurent over his declaration in the

House that Parliament by a majority of one, without consulting the provinces, could obtain an amendment of the British North America Act at Westminster, and thus destroy the constitutional safeguards of the French language. With masterly oratory he asked who rose in the Commons to repel this attack on the sacred rights of the provinces, and particularly Quebec's right to her language, culture and law. He mentioned various Quebec Liberals, and of each of these he asked and answered his own question, "Did he rise to defend our rights? No." After this telling enumeration he added, "It remained for a young Conservative Member from Toronto, English, Protestant, a Freemason, to rise in his place and speaking in excellent French, to defend our sacred rights. It was Mr. Donald Fleming." Only the French language on the eloquent lips of Camillien Houde could convey the full effect of this declaration. I am told that the crowd went wild. I had been made famous in Quebec. All this was missed by the press in the other provinces, and by myself.

Under arrangements made by Robert Rumilly I went to Montreal and met Camillien Houde. He was most genial, and we had an excellent talk. He was much interested in my family background. Inevitably we discussed his internment during the war. He thought St. Laurent had treated him very unjustly, and assured me that he was not the anti-war prodigal the English-language press had pictured him to be. While in his office a telephone call came from Mr. Begin, a member of the Duplessis government and organizer of the Union Nationale party. He expressed a wish to meet me. "That means Duplessis," said Houde with evident satisfaction.

The Canadian Bar Association was meeting in August in Montreal, and I made a point of being present. Premier Duplessis attended the opening session and I had a brief, formal meeting with him afterwards. After a day or two in Montreal I proceeded to Quebec City with my friend René Gobeil, who later took charge of my campaign in the province. René and I held an important meeting with Duplessis at the home of Gerry Martineau, a close personal friend and political confidant of the Premier. Present were Duplessis, our host and hostess, René and myself. We had a very uninhibited discussion. Duplessis made it abundantly clear that neither Drew nor Diefenbaker could generate any support for the Conservative party in Quebec. He showed he knew much more about me than I had ever supposed. He had been told that I was very serious, and urged me to cultivate a more easy and mirthful manner. I realized he was sizing me up, and I spoke very frankly. I was immensely attracted to him. He was bright, witty, highly intelligent. He gave me an insight into the French-Canadian political mind which has always remained with me. He was intensely opposed to the Liberal government at Ottawa and to St. Laurent, Mr. King's Quebec lieutenant and political heir apparent.

At the conclusion of the meeting I drove back to the Château Frontenac with Duplessis and he invited me into his suite to show me his remarkable collection of paintings. It was late when I took my leave and thanked him warmly for his kindness. I had the feeling that he would give me as much support as might prove possible without hurting himself or his party's interests in Quebec.

I was jolted the next morning to be informed by Gerry Martineau through René that I should not have driven back to the Château with the Premier as we might have been seen together, and I should have been sensitive to that possibility. He also criticized me for not wearing a hat. It had been a warm evening, but Gerry thought I should have been aware that political leaders in Quebec dress more formally, and never appear hatless. I expressed my regret, and assured him I was learning. We became very good friends from that time on. Actually the lobby at the Château was deserted when Duplessis, his detective and I entered after midnight. No one but the desk clerk and elevator operator had seen us.

I knew that the real test of the impression I had made would be the instructions given to René. It soon became clear that he was left free to carry on. He took complete charge of my campaign in Quebec, and handled it capably and enthusiastically. I made further forays into the province from time to time and met increasing numbers of party supporters.

To Camillien Houde I am indebted for another boost at this time. I had not previously heard of La Société du Bon Parler Français of Montreal. It was a society composed of intellectuals, teachers, professors and clergy, dedicated to the defence of the French language and the preservation of its purity. I received a letter from the society advising me that for my use and defence of the French tongue I had been elected a Chevalier of the society and was invited to receive this distinction at a dinner to be held in my honour in Montreal. I naturally accepted most gratefully. The dinner was a very challenging occasion. I outlined my education in French and my reasons for endeavouring to speak it in Parliament as a contribution to national unity and understanding. I praised the French language for its beauty and clarity and its contribution to the logic of the French mind. I urged them to

142

continue to work for the preservation of the French tongue in its strict purity: "S'il vaut parler français il vaut parler le français le plus pur." The reception accorded by this audience of savants to my speech was profoundly encouraging. I am sure I owed this entire flattering recognition to the good offices of Camillien Houde.

With this encouragement from Quebec I made my decision to run. The announcement of my candidature which I made in Toronto brought open support from some leading Young Progressive Conservatives. John Trimble, national secretary of the Young Progressive Conservative Association of Canada, and Allan Lawrence, president of the Progressive Conservative Student Federation, came out solidly for me, and pictured me as able to attract to the party the support of young voters. There were adverse developments, too. In the face of George Drew's announced candidature mine was pictured by the Ontario Liberal press as anti-Drew, which it was not. The whole party machine in Ontario was swung in behind George Drew. Les Blackwell and Ardagh Scythes and even some of the members of my own Eglinton riding executive informed me to my bitter disappointment that they must support George Drew. My close friends Jim Macdonnell, now national president, and Dick Bell, national secretary of the party, while prevented by their offices from openly engaging in the campaign, made it clear to me that they supported Drew. The West would give Diefenbaker strong support; the Maritimes were divided. Quebec was my only real base of political strength.

I can truthfully say that at no time did I expect to win, but I hoped to make a creditable showing. I was convinced also that my candidature was beneficial to the party. A straight contest between Drew and Diefenbaker might have had divisive and polarizing consequences and regional overtones. My campaign, without financial support, looked very thin alongside theirs. The only possibility of my winning rested on a stalemate developing between the two stronger candidates, and their supporters turning to me as an acceptable compromise. Shortly before the convention opened I spoke to Gordon Graydon, to whom in the past I had so often turned for candid advice. He shared my assessment of the situation, and urged me to stay in to the end.

Strong press support for my candidature developed in Quebec, but the English-language press in the other provinces was either unaware of it or largely ignored it. But John Bird, writing on September 25 in a series for Southam newspapers, faithfully reported: "Only the other day the nationalist newspaper *Le*

Devoir came out with a ringing statement that if the Conservative party wishes to survive it should elect Donald Fleming as leader forthwith." He added on his own: "Fleming is the workhorse of the Conservative party in the House of Commons. . . . He is . . . an able rough-and-tough fighting politician, . . . In any case, but particularly if he loosens up, learns to play a little more and presents a more human appearance to the world as he matures, Fleming may indeed become the hardest Conservative of them all to beat."

The French-language press gave me powerful endorsement. The eminent Lorenzo Paré in *L'Action Catholique* wrote a lengthy report which I still find flattering. He told of my family history, my understanding of Quebec, my breadth of view, my "Canadian" approach to problems, and what he called my talents, ambitions, convictions, and eloquence. He solemnly warned the Conservative party to select me as the only possible opponent for Louis St. Laurent, chosen that same month as the new leader of the Liberal party. He commended me to the delegates as "the dark horse" running. Jacques Bergeron writing in *Notre Temps* hailed me as a worker, fighter, the most effective debater in the Conservative ranks, and the best candidate in the circumstances, but thought my youth and limited experience might make my election doubtful. *Le Devoir* wrote a lengthy article in the same vein. It noted that Ivan Sabourin was lobbying Union Nationale members to support George Drew, but that Duplessis was avoiding any alliance with Drew. Robert Rumilly wrote a masterly article in *Le Devoir*. He based it on opinions expressed to him personally by the late P.J.A. Cardin in his last days. Cardin had stated that he was ashamed that the person most understanding of French Canadians was not to be found in the Liberal party, but was myself, and that he spoke with pride of the friendship which had grown up between us. Rumilly's article reviewed my speeches in French in the House, noted my defence of the constitution, my struggle against centralization, and concluded with this advice to the delegates: "You will get nowhere, neither you nor anyone else, without a certain support in the Province of Quebec; the only means offered to you at this moment is to carry Mr. Fleming to the leadership of your Party; and it is your last chance, if you do not wish the Party of Macdonald and Cartier to become a mere historical memory." But the Progressive Conservative party in 1948 outside Quebec was unaware of these words of advice. There were still those who thought the party could and should "win without Quebec." The party had still to learn a lesson that Sir John A. Macdonald knew well.

For the convention we rented some rooms near the main gate of the Exhibition grounds. René initially placed in charge of them two French-speaking girls who, unfortunately, did not speak English. Bill Smith arrived from Eglinton in time to take charge. We had buttons and ribbons to distribute, but nothing elaborate. As the delegates arrived I endeavoured to keep constantly in circulation. In the last two days I became more and more conscious of a swing to George Drew. The full weight of the Ontario delegation's support for him was becoming very evident.

Friday evening, October 1, was the highlight. No adequate instructions were issued to the candidates as to the manner or time of their entry into the vast auditorium. I had assumed we would all mount the stage together, as had been done in Winnipeg in 1942, but I was mistaken. Drew and Diefenbaker with their wives made their appearances at the rear of the huge auditorium and were cheered by their supporters in well-planned demonstrations. Alice and I walked up that long aisle virtually unnoticed until we mounted the platform. Both Dick Bell and Bill Smith apologized afterward for this costly oversight.

In the order of speeches I drew the second position, Drew first and Dief last. I was nominated by René's father, Samuel Gobeil, who had been one of the ministers in the cabinet of R.B. Bennett. My seconder was the youngest speaker, Al Lawrence. The speeches of the three candidates were all of a high order. I was assured that mine was fully the equal of the other two, and I was given a very warm reception by the huge audience. My French portion drew loud cheers. There was no radio or television broadcast. I sensed a rising sympathy for the underdog. The delegates seemed to welcome a new, young face in the contest. A curious mischance intervened at that moment.

Bill Brunt, an old classmate of mine from Varsity and Osgoode Hall days, was directing the Diefenbaker campaign. He confessed to me the next day a serious tactical error he made that evening. He knew Dief would win no Quebec votes. Those which eluded me would go to Drew. Bill had arranged a vociferous demonstration for Diefenbaker when he rose to speak. It was the loudest of the evening. We learned that many of the Quebec delegates were frightened by it into believing that Diefenbaker might win and that they then swung to Drew as the surer hope of defeating Dief. Bill became well aware of this fact, and he told me afterward that he wished he had told his rooters to give me a big cheer in order to convince the Quebec delegation that I had strong support outside Quebec.

Saturday morning was spent on resolutions and policy. The other two candidates circulated among the delegates milling around outside the auditorium. I spent most of the morning at my office in the Parliament Buildings putting my affairs and papers in shape for my departure for Europe the next day. I had given up all hope of being elected, but yielded finally to two frantic telephone calls from Bill Smith to return to the milling crowd.

There was only one ballot. Drew received 827 votes, Diefenbaker, 311, and I, 104. The announcement was received with wild acclaim by the delegates. Diefenbaker moved and I seconded the usual resolution that the election of the new leader be made unanimous. George Drew made an admirable speech, and his wife Fiorenza made a very graceful speech in French. Alice and I remained on the platform until the end. Diefenbaker and his wife made a conspicuous departure from the platform in very bad taste soon after the result of the balloting was announced.

I returned to our suite in the Château to thank my supporters. Most of those present were French-speaking, and some were in tears. I made a rousing speech, calling upon all, "À bas ces centralisateurs Liberaux." (Down with these Liberal centralizers!) One of our Quebec supporters at that point contributed $2,000 to our little campaign fund. In the end we managed to break even.

I was satisfied with the outcome. I did not win, but I had not expected to. My relations with the other two candidates suffered no strain. The same could not be said of relations between the other two. I was grateful for the support I had received, particularly from Quebec, Nova Scotia and the Young Progressive Conservatives. Mrs. Bracken had no vote, John Bracken refrained on principle from voting, but both supported me. My 104 votes compared not unfavourably with the fifty polled by Chubby Power in third place at the Liberal national convention a few weeks earlier. My position in the party had not suffered a setback; on the contrary, it had rather advanced. Nothing untoward during the campaign or at the convention had marred it, and that was something to be thankful for after an exposure to such risks. So far as the Canadian public was concerned, Dick Bell's prophecy that I would become a national figure within seven years of entering Parliament had been fulfilled in half the time.

Sunday was a beautiful autumn day. The sun shone brightly,

and the maples in the Ottawa Valley were a blaze of glorious colour. My sense of relaxation was complete. René Gobeil drove Alice and me to Montreal, Alice to return thence to Toronto and I to board the plane at Dorval for London on my first crossing of the Atlantic and my first visit to Britain and Europe. The convention lay behind me; its excitement had vanished. A great new and very different experience lay before me.

CHAPTER SIXTEEN

A New Dimension

For many years I had harboured a very strong desire to visit Britain and Europe. I had visited some of the principal cities of the United States – New York, Chicago, Detroit, Boston, Buffalo and others of less note – and Alice and I had spent our honeymoon in Bermuda in 1933, but that was the extent of my travel outside Canada until October 1948. I did not regard myself as fully educated without seeing Britain and northwestern Europe at first hand. The prospect of achieving that goal and at the same time flying the Atlantic for the first time dazzled me. Until my return on November 24 I was to enjoy such an experience as dreams are made of. It would include visits to no fewer than twelve countries, and meetings with many of the most famous monarchs, statesmen and leaders of their day. It would prove rugged and physically exacting; sleep and I would be strangers for long periods, but I believe I made the utmost use of all my fabulous opportunities. Fortunately, I kept a full diary of the entire trip. The writing of it proved to be a harsh master many an evening to a late hour, but I stayed with it to the very end. The result is that I have an invaluable record, which I find fascinating rereading even now, in 1984. It is no exaggeration to say that in those fifty-three days life for me took on a new dimension.

Transatlantic passenger aviation was then in its infancy. The North Star was a new aircraft, powerful, but noisy and suffering from extreme vibration. A stop had to be made at either Gander or Goose Bay for refuelling before setting out across the Atlantic. Our flight to London occupied more than sixteen hours, the return over twenty. Passenger planes then rarely cruised at altitudes over 8,000 feet, and cruising speed was an unbelievable 200 m.p.h.

I was a week late in arriving for the Commonwealth Parliamentary Conference. I caught up to the other delegates in Edin-

148

burgh the morning after my arrival. All the Canadian delegates, regardless of party, were hungry for news from Canada, particularly about the Conservative leadership convention. Art Smith, while he had supported George Drew, agreed that my candidature had been good for the party.

Although I had lost a precious week as a result of the convention the tours preceding the conference still included five days in Scotland, four in Northern Ireland, four in the English Midlands and a day in London to settle in at the Savoy Hotel before the opening of the conference. In Scotland, from Edinburgh we toured the Border country by bus, visiting Dalkeith, Little France, Lammermuir, Bemersyde, Dryburgh Abbey, Trimontium, Melrose Abbey, Abbotsford. We dined at Edinburgh Castle. I sat in John Knox's chair in his house in Edinburgh, and Sir Walter Scott's at Abbotsford. From Glasgow we sailed down the Clyde, and visited Clydebank, Loch Lomond and Loch Sloy. We concluded our visit to Scotland with a great dinner in the Glasgow City Chambers on a Saturday evening, with stimulating renditions of Harry Lauder's song, "I belong to Glasgow," and at the end joined hands and sang "Auld Lang Syne." This simply fascinated the delegates from India, Pakistan and Ceylon, who had never seen this touching Scottish custom before.

Our tour of Northern Ireland was fascinating. I detached myself for a day to visit Newry, a small city near the border where my maternal grandparents John Wright and Hannah Bradford grew up. One hundred years before they sailed from Londonderry to begin a new life in Durham County, Ontario.

At Ballygally Castle Hotel on Sunday morning I took matters into my own hands. The program made no provision for a service of worship. The Speaker of the Ontario legislature, the Rev. M. Cooke Davies, an Anglican clergyman, agreed at my urging to conduct a brief devotional service during our bus stop, and I obtained the necessary permission from the hotel manager and the tour guide. At first we were assigned to the bar, then more appropriately to a lunch room. The response of all delegates to the invitation I went about and extended was nearly complete. Padre Davies led us in prayers and we sang, "There is a Green Hill Far Away." At this point one of the Indian delegates, Mr. Thirumala Rao, a handsome Brahman, asked permission to offer a prayer. Rev. Davies readily assented. The prayer which Mr. Rao offered in English was a beautiful Hindu prayer for personal consecration. One could have heard a pin drop. These parliamentarians, from diverse countries and backgrounds and colours, had found a unity in prayer and worship. Of all the delegates on that rainy morning only our Roman Catholic brethren abstained. Had it occurred in 1984 instead of 1948 I believe they would have joined us. Ireland needs such an example.

In all three countries we visited we were received and entertained everywhere with the utmost hospitality. The fare was the very best available in those days of postwar austerity. Nothing was too good for the visitors from the overseas countries of the Commonwealth. We were eating five times per day (counting morning coffee and afternoon tea), and we listened to many speeches, from most of which I must say I derived much instruction. Oatmeal porridge being my favourite food I naturally looked for something very special in the Scottish breakfasts. Nowhere, however, was the porridge as good as my dear Alice makes me at home.

The tours afforded an unrivalled opportunity to become acquainted with other delegates as we travelled together, ate together, talked together. This fraternization offers great benefits of itself, but it is of special benefit preceding a conference. I made a special effort to avail myself of the opportunity to develop terms of friendship with the delegates from the more distant lands – Asia, the Antipodes and the Caribbean, and particularly those of different colour. I thought every delegate had a duty to show respect and friendship to the delegates from every country, and not least of all the newer and "emerging" countries. What country, I thought, could do that better than Canada?

I did not neglect my fellow-Canadian delegates. I never had a better opportunity to become acquainted with some, even from other parties, such as Speaker Fauteux, Senator Arthur Roebuck, Senator Thomas Vien, Senator Lucien Moraud, M.J. Coldwell, Premier Tommy Douglas of Saskatchewan, Social Credit leader Solon Low, Premier Johnson of British Columbia, "Padre" Davies, Art Smith. These close associations produced lasting friendships.

The day and a half back in London before the opening of the conference gave me a very welcome feeling of being "settled" after two weeks of constant movement. The Savoy Hotel was to be my home during the balance of my time in London, and I found it excellent. I also took advantage of every opportunity for sightseeing in London. I made my first call at Canada House, on Norman Robertson, our high commissioner. He and I were destined to become good friends and have many close contacts in years to come. He had a strong sense of duty, and was highly respected everywhere as a model civil servant. His private secretary was my dear cousin Eleanor Grundy. I spent as much

150

time with her and her husband John as opportunity permitted. They were very kind to me, and helped to show me about London.

Meeting in London at the same time were the prime ministers of the Commonwealth countries. The British government gave a reception in honour of them and of all delegates on the eve of the conference. There I met some very distinguished heads of government – Nehru of India, Aliquat Khan of Pakistan, Herbert Evatt, Deputy Prime Minister of Australia, Peter Fraser of New Zealand. Two days later I met Malcolm MacDonald, former British high commissioner to Canada, now Governor General in South-Eastern Asia. I enjoyed renewing acquaintance with him.

The conference opened at Westminster Hall on October 18. It was the first Commonwealth Parliamentary Conference since before the war, and it therefore drew special attention. All the self-governing nations of the Commonwealth and some of the colonies sent delegations representative of parliaments and not of governments. They included men of various local parties. There was only one female delegate from overseas, from India, but British MPs were free to attend sessions, and they included some women. The overseas delegates numbered 89; the British MPs brought the total to 160. The delegations were seated by countries, with Canada as the senior dominion in the senior position to the right of the chair. The first day was devoted to a discussion on "Migration and Movement of Population," which provoked some very warm debate, with the Asian and West Indies countries attacking racial discrimination in the immigration policies of other Commonwealth countries.

The subject for discussion the second day was "The Future of Parliamentary Government." An emergency was transformed into an unexpected opportunity and that in turn into a triumph. The delegate who was to speak for Canada failed to appear, and part way through the opening speech by a delegate from Ceylon Fauteux leaned over and asked me to fill in. I was not even told that I would be the next speaker. Fifteen minutes after Fauteux nudged me I was called on. For an important speech on such a principal theme before such a distinguished and critical audience I would have liked at least two days' notice. However, there are occasions when impromptu efforts seem more effective than prepared ones, and this proved to be one of those occasions. I must have been inspired by the audience, the surroundings, the theme and the challenge. I spoke for twenty minutes, not avoiding some critical aspects of the theme. I sat down to an ovation. I received very generous compliments from the Canadian delegates and numerous others; Senator Roebuck told me he thought I had a great future in Canadian politics, and I should stick to it.

The conference continued until October 27. I spoke once more, and under similar circumstances. The theme was "Defence." A.V. Alexander, the British Minister of Defence, led off. I was again asked to speak for Canada on fifteen minutes' notice, and my remarks were well received. There was just no use to expect adequate warning.

The program of entertainment was fantastic, and the hospitality overflowing. I could have visited London a dozen times and missed most of these privileges but for the auspices. The events included luncheon at the Baltic Mercantile and Shipping Exchange, dinner at Drapers' Hall as guest of the Master and Wardens of the Drapers' Company, a visit to the city, a formal dinner in the ancient Guildhall as guest of the Lord Mayor, a reception in the Speaker's chambers at Westminster by the Lord Chancellor as Speaker of the House of Lords and the Speaker of the Commons, a formal dinner at Vintners Hall tendered by the Council of Shipping, a formal dinner by the Council of the London Chamber of Commerce, a visit to the Tower of London, attendance at the first state opening of Parliament since the war, a day in Cambridge, a day in Oxford, and, greatest honour of all, a reception by the King and Queen at Buckingham Palace.

Trafalgar Day, October 21, provided a close-up view of an unforgettable spectacle – the unveiling of monuments to Admirals Jellicoe and Beatty, heroes of the Battle of Jutland, by the Duke of Gloucester in Trafalgar Square. I had a ringside seat at Eleanor's window on the second floor of Canada House just across the road. Over ten thousand people massed to see the Royal Navy stage the ceremony which went off like clockwork, without a hitch.

The visits to the two world-famous universities were a rare privilege. At Cambridge we met the renowned historian, Dr. G.M. Trevelyan, Master of Trinity College, inspected Cavendish Laboratory where we saw machines splitting the atom, and I was lost in wonder and awe at the beauty of King's Chapel in King's College. At Oxford I was privileged to be luncheon guest at Corpus Christi College, and to spend part of the afternoon with its Master, the famous Sir Richard Livingston. Everything about the college reeks of history, and it fascinated me. At Christ Church College I met an old friend, Rev. John Lowe, the dean, who had been our minister at St. Andrew's Church, Centre Island, Toronto, in the summer of 1936.

I was a guest at two private dinners, the one in the home of E.

Duvall Davies, whom I met at the Chamber of Commerce dinner, the other at the flat of Alex Spearman, MP, at which six young aspiring politicians were present. They included Harold Holt, later to become Prime Minister of Australia, Peter Thornycroft, later to become Chancellor of the Exchequer, John Hope from the United Kingdom, Harry Jackman and myself. Anyone who heard the exchange of ideas and experiences at that dinner table could never believe politics to be dull.

The spectacle preceding the state opening of Parliament on October 26 was fascinating. We were in our places in the royal gallery at 9.30 a.m. At 11 o'clock the procession past us commenced. The passageway down the middle of the royal gallery was flanked by Beefeaters in their brilliant uniforms dating from Tudor times, and bearing halberds. Twelve trumpeters in colourful costumes bearing the royal coat of arms led the way, followed by aides from the fighting services and an escort of senior officers from the Life Guards. Next came the King and Queen moving at a stately pace, and wearing the state crowns which normally repose in the Tower of London. His Majesty looked every inch a king in a long robe of scarlet and ermine. The Queen was dressed in pure white, and looked radiantly beautiful. Her luminous smile outshone even her diamonds. Next followed attendants, including the Earl of Athlone and Princess Alice. It was all a silent and profoundly moving spectacle. My instant feeling was, this is *my* King. After Their Majesties had retired and joined the procession to Westminster we could hear the crowds cheering from far away. Londoners do love a pageant, and they saw one that day that warmed their hearts.

The supreme event was the reception at Buckingham Palace by Their Majesties that afternoon at six o'clock. I recorded it in my diary as follows:

> We were received by the King and Queen in a medium-sized reception room, then passed through a second into a third where we were received by Queen Mary, and the Duke and Duchess of Gloucester. . . . When the receiving was completed the King and Queen took up positions in the large drawingroom where we were. From then until they retired at 7.30 they chatted with delegates who were presented. I record with grateful satisfaction that I had individual chats with the King, the Queen, Queen Mary, the Duke of Gloucester, Princess Alice (Countess of Athlone), and several peeresses. The King was much interested in the Canadian National Exhibition, asked about this year's attendance, and how it all started in the first place. I was able to recall the part his great-uncle, the Marquis of Lorne, played in helping the Exhibition get on its feet. When I referred admiringly to the state opening of

Parliament, His Majesty said to me with no attempt at reserve, "Attlee didn't want a state opening, but I insisted. I thought the people needed a lift." They got it, and so did I.

The Queen recalled her visit to Toronto and the reception in front of the City Hall, and commented on how well it was done. They were both exceedingly pleasant. They are the most natural people in the world. The King speaks with great readiness in conversation, and without any trace of stuttering. The Queen is beautiful beyond all description, and much of her beauty is in her expression. It is pleasant, sympathetic, and good.

I had quite a lengthy chat with Princess Alice about Canada. She told me she and the earl would have come to Toronto oftener, but there was no place to stay. She didn't think very highly of Premier Hepburn's closing of Government House. She also passed some stricture on the idea voiced by Eire and India that they can remain in the Commonwealth, and at the same time renounce any loyalty to the King. Incidentally, the Irish and Indian delegates lost no opportunities of talking to Their Majesties.

That evening the delegates met together for their farewell dinner. Only two speeches were allowed, and they were reduced to five minutes each. The delegates could take no more. They had been listening to speeches for a solid month. After dinner there was a great round of hand-shaking and good-byes. Real friendships had developed among the delegates, and there was sincere regret over the parting.

The conference had been a brilliant success. It had achieved its two purposes: to provide a forum for discussion of matters of import to the Commonwealth and its member nations, and to afford parliamentarians an opportunity for personal meeting with others of their own kind from all parliaments of the Commonwealth. Britain, still suffering from the deep wounds of war, had afforded us the warmest welcome and unforgettable hospitality; London, not yet able to mask the cruel scars left by the savage blitz, had opened her heart to us. We who are the heirs of the mother of Parliaments were consciously proud of our heritage. For my part I had entered into a new experience which permanently enriched my life.

I was thrilled by another opportunity. The Greek government had extended an invitation to four of the Canadian delegates to visit Greece after the conference, and Fauteux informed me that I was one of the four chosen. I could hardly believe my good fortune. The invitation sprang undoubtedly from a desire to give renewed expression through a group of Canadian parliamentarians to Greek gratitude to Canada for aid, particularly gifts of

154

food, arriving at a critical juncture in Greece's agony, and to expose to view the otherwise incredible actuality of Greek suffering at the hands of her Communist neighbours. We were a group of half-a-dozen, and we included two senior officers of the Canadian Aid-to-Greece Mission, Dr. William Birks and B.C. Salamis, both of Montreal. Before I left London I had arranged instead of returning directly to London to make a rather rapid visit to Italy, France, Belgium, Holland, Denmark, Norway, Sweden, and applied for a flight to Berlin. It made sense while I was in Europe to make such a tour, however hurried. I would, of course, no longer be travelling under favoured auspices as a delegate, but even though on my own and at my own expense assistance had been arranged by Canada House through our embassies in these countries. I thus had the benefit of official auspices, as well as an official passport.

On arrival at Hassani Airport we were given an impressive official welcome by representatives of the government, the mayor, the Red Cross Society, and the Canadian ambassador, General LaFleche. We were lodged at the Grande Bretagne, the leading hotel in Athens, then hurried off to the Canadian embassy, where we met a large group of guests, including leaders in the political, diplomatic and cultural life of the country. Following a fish supper at a seaside tavern as the guests of Mr. Georgkapoulos (president of the Greek Red Cross Society), Mr. Gyftakis (who had lived in Montreal for twenty-five years before the war), and Dr. Moraitis (who studied medicine at McGill), three gentlemen who very kindly devoted every attention to us during our visit, we were taken to visit the Parthenon at midnight. By order of the Minister of the Interior it was illuminated for our special benefit. For three-quarters of an hour we walked about this ancient wonder, the most exquisite survival of the architectural glory of ancient Greece. Under the eerie floodlighting we gazed in awe at the columned temple to the Greek goddess Athena. It has no straight lines; all are faintly curved.

Less impressive to the eye, but more significant in world history, is a nearby rock part way down the slope of the Acropolis, where St. Paul preached his first sermon on European soil, beginning with the immortal words, "Ye men of Athens, I perceive that in all things ye are too superstitious, for as I passed by and beheld your devotions I saw an altar bearing this inscription, 'To The Unknown God'. Whom therefore ye ignorantly worship Him declare I unto you." It is the Areopagus, and to behold that spot was a moving experience. I had been walking on clouds all evening sustained by such excitement as I have rarely experienced. October 27, 1948, remains an unforgettable day. When I finally climbed into bed at 2 a.m. I had been up for forty-three hours non-stop.

The next day, October 28, was a national day of thanksgiving, the anniversary of that day in 1940 when Greece said "No" (*Ochi*) to Mussolini's ultimatum. The Greeks fought Mussolini's invading forces to a standstill, and were only overcome when the Germans threw in superior forces. The crowds were gathering in the streets as we drove to the cathedral to attend the Te Deum service, led by Archbishop Damaskinos. The royal family and all the great of the land were present. The singing of the men's choir was superb. The service was followed by a military parade. The King took the salute in front of the Tomb of the Unknown Soldier.

Later we made official calls on the Prime Minister, the Speaker of the Chamber of Deputies, the Acting Minister of Foreign Affairs, and the mayor. Everywhere we were simply overwhelmed by expressions of gratitude to Canada for timely gifts of food which arrived when the country was on the verge of starvation. They described the seriousness of the war waged by the Communists in the north. The government forces had sustained heavy casualties, particularly among officer personnel.

We then were accorded the high honour of being received at the Palace by the King and Queen. They both spoke perfect English and they received us with great cordiality. They, like the ministers, expressed their thanks for Canadian help.

Our conversation began on a formal level, with all standing, and light refreshments were served, but soon we found ourselves in a very serious discussion of the war problems and the Queen's efforts to organize relief for the refugees who had been driven from their homes by the Communist guerillas. We all pulled up chairs in a circle and had a grippingly interesting talk, which lasted one and a quarter hours. We parted with the warmest feelings for these young monarchs, and profoundly moved by what we had been told. In my diary I recorded some of the details of our conversation:

> The population of Greece is less than 8,000,000. No fewer than 700,000 are homeless refugees as the result of the Communist terrorism. The bandits raid villages, kill the men, carry off the young women and all the children, and burn the houses after helping themselves to everything having any value. Already half the homes in the villages of Greece have been destroyed. Over 10,000 children have been stolen from their parents, and sent to Communist training centres in Yugoslavia and other countries where they

156

are indoctrinated with communism and hatred. Apart from the refugees altogether, it has become necessary to move large numbers of children south from their homes in the north, even though it has often meant separation from their parents. This is where the Queen stepped in to organize a fund for children's relief. It was raised from among the Greek people entirely, and none has been contributed from outside sources. She has raised $4,000,000. This has been used to set up children's centres in different parts of the country, and they are now housing and schooling 40,000 children. There are enough teachers, since most of the schools in the outlying areas have been closed as a result of guerilla raids.

The Queen sought the support of the labour unions. It was arranged that they would ask their members to work an extra day (Sunday, August 15), and contribute their earnings to the fund. The Communists denounced it, and sought by every means to defeat the attempt, telling the men that the Queen would steal their money. The response of the men was complete. All turned in their day's work and contributed $400,000 to the Fund. To understand how much this generosity means one must realize how very poor the average Greek is.

The Communist guerilla bands are in different parts of the country, and their strength and the mountainous terrain make it most difficult to deal with them. Some months ago they attempted an invasion in force from an Albanian base. A heavy battle resulted in the Grammos Mountains. After heavy casualties had been sustained on both sides the guerillas withdrew over the Albanian border, and thus eluded capture. Time and again such bands have been pursued by the Greek forces to the frontier of Albania, Yugoslavia and Bulgaria, to escape into safety there. These Communist countries are being used as bases for these operations which are terrorizing Greece. Over 3,000 of the guerillas are said to be in hospital in Albania recovering from wounds sustained in battle with the Greek forces. Yugoslavia is the biggest base of operations, but many raiders come from Albania. The guerilla bands receive their supplies at night. They are dropped from Russian aeroplanes. The King asked the U.S. for ten night fighter planes to fight them off, but none have been forthcoming.

A U.S. naval force visited Salonika recently. The King told us that the U.S. forces reported to him that they had seen a Russian submarine in the harbour, and were able to give a complete description of it.

A story which we had heard and which the Queen confirmed, demonstrates her devotion to her people. Several months ago when the fighting was heavy and the outlook dark, the King wished to visit his troops at the front, but went down with typhoid fever. The Queen volunteered to go in his place, and the King agreed. When the Ministers heard of it they opposed it strenuously, but the Queen went anyway. She arrived at the front in the midst of great danger accompanied by a convoy of only two jeeps. When the men in the outposts saw her they burst into tears, and the Queen did the same, and told them: "When a man is very sick he likes those he loves to be with him. The King must love you more than he loves me."

The Greeks are a very clean and tidy people and very temperate. There were many restrictions in effect. Hot water was available at our hotel only three days per week. Poverty and pride went hand in hand everywhere. Inflation was rampant. Before the war the drachma was quoted at 1,000 to the dollar, now it is 13,000 to the dollar. I changed $20 into drachmas for pocket money. My pocket bulged with over a quarter of a million drachmas. Never have I felt so wealthy with so little.

At a government dinner in our honour Speaker Fauteux replied in French and I in English. Everyone spoke French, and I found myself conversing almost exclusively in that language. The next morning was a round of well-planned and most interesting official engagements. At the University of Athens we were received by the president, Dr. Economos, and senior staff, and thanked for equipment sent by Canada; at the Chest Institute we saw equipment furnished by Canada being used to check the population for tuberculosis, which has always been a menace. At Eleusis near the ruins of the ancient Temple of Ceres we saw a medical and dental unit in operation for the benefit of mothers and children, using equipment donated by Canada. The Germans when they were driven out stripped the country bare of usable equipment.

The program of the remainder of the day I recorded in my diary as follows:

> We continued at a stiff pace, returning to Athens and driving thence to Piraeus to examine a section on which are erected hovels which still house those who were refugees driven out of Asia Minor by the Turks in 1922 after the disastrous defeat suffered there by Greece. Most of the hovels contain one or two rooms, usually about 10 feet square. There is barely head-room in them. Sometimes two families will occupy a two-room dwelling. In one such I entered seven people lived. They were all barefoot. I saw no sanitary convenience anywhere, but found no bad odours, and the places were kept clean. Tuberculosis is rampant in this poor section. As we passed along one street (or alleyway) I heard sounds of grief and lamentation which I traced to a one-room house where two women, presumably the mother and grandmother, were wailing and weeping over the body of a little 10-year old girl, surrounded by the women and children of the neighbourhood sitting around in silence. On inquiry I learned that she had just died of tuberculosis, and that she was one of ten children in the family,

and that the other nine are all tubercular. They could hardly fail to be infected when they are living in such close quarters. If it were not for the abundance of sunshine disease undoubtedly would be epidemic.

Some were at lunch while we were there. The lunch in most cases consisted of bread and olives. These people never see butter or meat. The children never wear shoes or stockings, and many of the mothers go about barefoot. The fathers are either working or dead. The older sons are in the army fighting. A boy offered to share his handful of olives with us.

At 3.00 p.m. our party proceeded to the Tomb of the Unknown Soldier, where Dr. Fauteux laid a wreath for us. A guard of honour in Evzone costume was present with a band, and a large crowd appeared from nowhere, and cheered us. There is no doubt that Canada is very popular here. We owe it to the help we have given to Greece. General LaFleche has done good work here, and is obviously popular. The Canadian flag on his car draws many cheers on the streets. After eight years of war these people have learned to appreciate friendship and help where they find it.

Our next visit was to the Anti-Cancer Institute in the city. It is an up-to-date hospital building. Before the war it was well equipped. The Germans carried off all their equipment and their radium. The Canadian Allied War Relief Fund replaced it all, and there is no limit to the gratitude to Canada which was expressed by Dr. Aristote Kousis, the head of the Institute, and his staff. A Canadian flag decorated the main hall, and the staff were all present to applaud our arrival. . . .

Our next engagement was one of the most important of our entire visit in Athens. We were received in the Chamber of Deputies, which was in session, and given a standing, cheering reception as we took our places on the bench reserved for government ministers. The House interrupted its business while the leaders of all parties made speeches welcoming us and paying tribute to Canada for her help to Greece. It was a thrilling experience.

After four hours' sleep we left early next morning for the north. What I saw that day I could never forget. Heart-rending as were the sights I witnessed, I would not have missed that day for anything. My diary tells the story:

We were met on arrival at Jannina by the commanding general and the Minister of Welfare. Jannina is an old city with a normal population of 22,000. It is located in the Province of Epirus, an agricultural area in the mountains from which traditionally come the best and most rugged fighting men in Greece. In the province today are no fewer than 126,000 refugees driven out of their homes by the Communist terrorists. Of these 53,500 are located around Jannina, 25,000 of them in the town also, so one can imagine the conditions there. Another 5,000 are living in tents, and many others without shelter under the trees. Thank God the weather has been bright and warm. What conditions will be like when the wet season and the winter come can only be conjectured with horror. . . .

The first refugees we saw were in tents about 30′ × 18′. In the first one I entered 55 people were living on the dirt floor. All were barefoot. All these people had to flee from their homes for their lives. Today they possess only what they were able to carry with them. An odd family had a goat, or a calf, or a sheep, or several hens. Most had only a few clothes and an odd blanket. They looked the picture of misery. The women were wizened and old before their time; the children looked sadly undernourished; few men had survived the wars. Many of these people are tubercular. They are living at the subsistence level. I saw some preparing a dinner of dried corn kernels, or boiled beans, or boiled onions. They use tiny fires to set pots on.

In the city we saw old buildings housing as many as seven people to a room. In the open spaces I saw huts where people had made a bed by laying an old blanket over a stone floor. I saw diseased children, including one poor little baby whose head was covered with scabs which it was trying to scratch, and crying bitterly over the irritation. The Minister of Welfare explained that as he had only 12,000 million drachmas for relief, and as the numbers of refugees had multiplied so greatly, it had been necessary to reduce the daily relief allowance per person from 12,000 drachmas (10 cents) to 7,000 drachmas (six cents) per day. The American Relief Administrator is insisting that these refugees return to their homes, but the Welfare Minister told me that the government is unwilling to force them back, for their homes are not safe, the people fear for their lives, and many of them have already gone back as many as four or five times, to rebuild their homes, only to have the Communists raid and destroy them again. . . .

By way of happy contrast are the camps of saved children which are operated under the Queen's Fund. We saw several of them. The children are adequately, though simply, housed, fed and schooled. They looked very happy and healthy. They are very good-looking and intelligent children.

The most moving experience of all was our visit to a girls' orphanage. This is a permanent institution, in which some refugee children have been added to those already there. They were lined along the driveway, clapping and cheering us. When our car stopped they sang for us, one girl presented Senator Vien, who was leading our party, with a bouquet of flowers, and a procession of little girls came up to present us all with individual flowers. The radiant faces of these children, so full of gratitude to Canada for what she has done for Greece, were a moving sight. Senator Vien was in tears. They lined the road again and cheered us as we left. Surely of such is the Kingdom of Heaven.

The strategy of military operations in this sector was vividly portrayed to us by the general at his office with the aid of a relief map. As long as the Communists are free to take refuge in Albania and Yugoslavia it becomes almost impossible to wipe them out. To close the border would require 300,000 men, and the country cannot undertake so large an operation without substantial help from the United States in material and money. The Greeks would naturally like some outright military help in men from the United States or Britain or the United Nations, for they feel they are fighting a battle not simply for themselves, but for all of Western civilization as well, and I agree that they are. In peacetime 80 battalions (80,000 men) kept the border closed. Today there is a war weariness in Greece. These poor people have been thwarted of the hopes of victory. The Communists seized control of the resistance movement during the war, and almost succeeded in seizing political power when the Germans moved out. They would have done so had not British troops, under General Scobie, taken control. As it was, there was much bloodshed and destruction of property in Athens and elsewhere.

While the people are grateful to Britain and the U.S.A. for all they have done, the leaders do not consider they are doing enough to help Greece now. We found traces of bitterness toward Britain over the destruction by British troops of large quantities of British war material at Crete after the war ended, when Greece needed it so badly. Today they estimate the Communists at 25,000. The difficulties of campaigning against them in the mountains are tremendous. Many of the guerillas are conscripts, taken from the villages by the raiders, and given their choice of serving or death. Women are among the guerillas too. They are said to be even more cruel than the men. I was told of one incident which was reported to the United Nations. Forty women fighters, who were mothers carrying babies on their backs, were in a party of raiders pursued by government forces. They strangled their babies to facilitate their own escape. The bodies of the forty infants were found.

Sometimes a Communist will leave his family, and disappear to join the guerillas. The government gives relief to the family as it does to the victims of the Communists.

The Communists carry off their wounded, if possible. Those they cannot carry to safety they shoot. Skirmishes go on every night, and Communist forces are known to be lying both east and west of the road between Athens and Jannina and might attempt to cut the road at any time. The position would be very insecure but for the aeroplanes.

I asked about the treatment of prisoners by the government forces. I was told the prisoners are sent to concentration camps in the Grecian islands. The King told us of a scheme he inaugurated to reclaim these enemies, feeling, as he told us, that they must be taught to live with us. Many of them have been taught useful occupations for the first time, and in some cases have enlisted in the King's forces, and have fought well.

At noon the Bishop of Epirus came to see us, and to thank us for Canada's help. He joined us at a luncheon given by the Minister of Welfare in a restaurant at Jannina. At it Senator Vien made a most moving speech in French. The wife of the Governor-General of the Province of Epirus was with us also. She was born in Paris, and speaks no English. Consequently, I spoke practically no English that day. Her son, her only child, was killed by the Communists. He was 25.

Our visit ended the next day, Sunday, with lunch in glorious sunshine beside the gorgeous blue waters of the Mediterranean and a visit to the Areopagus. I walked about the place, feeling I was treading on holy ground. It was easy to reconstruct the scene which unfolded before the eyes of St. Paul. Above him stood the Parthenon, dedicated to the worship of Athena; to the side he looked upon the area where the freemen of Athens were wont to gather in the days of her freedom, and where Pericles three hundred years before in his immortal funeral oration declared that freedom is the right only of those who have the courage to defend it. I came away on that Sunday evening with feelings of profound admiration for those courageous, grateful and kind-hearted Greek people, still maintaining their heroic struggle after the terrible sufferings of war and the cruelties of the German occupation. For me "The glory that was Greece" became "The glory that is Greece." Had Greece given up the resistance to the Communists the whole balance of power in southeastern Europe would have changed, to the critical detriment of the Free West. The world owes "For Greece a tear."

November 1st found me in Rome, sharing a sumptuous hotel suite with my friend Senator Moraud. I had planned three days in Rome, but as the result of trouble over air service my stay was extended to five, which were made infinitely enjoyable by the kindness of our Canadian ambassador, Jean Désy. We were received by the Prime Minister, Mr. de Gasperi. The mayor held a reception in our honour at the Capitol, the Red Cross Society held a luncheon in our honour, the president of the Senate and the president of the Chamber of Deputies received us and conducted us on tours of their chambers and buildings, and we combed the eternal and beautiful city and the countryside. We

162

could not have been in better hands, for Mr. Désy was an authority on art. We feasted our eyes and our senses on the treasures of art which abound in a profusion unequalled in any other centre in the world.

But the highlight of our visit to Rome was the privilege of a private audience with Pope Pius at his summer residence of Castel Gandalfo, about ten miles out of Rome. His Holiness received the five of us with great kindness. Senator Vien acted as spokesman. Most of the audience was conducted in French, the balance in English. When I was presented, the Pope said, "Oh, Mr. Fleming, I presume you are an English-speaking Canadian." I replied, "Yes, Your Holiness, but I also speak French." That was the week of the U.S. presidential election, and I obtained a new insight into papal infallibility. His Holiness said to us, "I suppose Mr. Dewey will be elected president." We all assured him with great confidence that Mr. Dewey would indeed be elected. The conversation then turned to the struggle against communism in Italy, and the influential role of the Pope's speech to an audience of 400,000 in St. Peter's Square in defeating the Communists that year in the general election. He obviously derived much satisfaction from his participation and the results. He presented us all with rosaries as souvenirs of our visit. We were deeply impressed by his kindness, wide knowledge, and serenity.

The sponsor of our audience was a French-Canadian priest, the Superior of the Canadian Pontifical College in Rome. He was destined to rise to great heights in the service of the church, and to gain fame as Cardinal Paul Emile Leger. He and I were destined also to become personal friends. He took keen interest in the fact that my son David, then twelve years old, collected stamps, and as long as he remained in Rome he sent David a package of stamps at regular intervals.

Within one week, one of the most eventful in my entire life, between Tuesday, October 26 and Monday, November 1, I had been privileged to be presented to my own King and Queen, to the King and Queen of Greece, to the head of the Greek Orthodox Church (who had also been Regent of Greece for a time), the Pope, and to enjoy their hospitality and conversation. My thoughts turned back to those days in Victoria Public School, Galt, when as a seven-year-old boy my copybook bore the scriptural text, "Seest thou a man diligent in his work, he shall stand before kings." I was and am grateful to God for the fulfilment of that prophecy.

Monsignor Leger was our host at dinner at the Canadian Pontifical College, where about forty-five young Canadian priests were studying. I chatted with a number of them, including two from Toronto. Our tour of the Vatican was conducted personally by Monsignor Leger. It lasted two hours, but I could have spent two weeks at it. Rarely have I been so fascinated. We visited the office buildings, the Loggia of Raphael, the Museum of Sculpture, the art gallery and the library. In its splendour, rich beauty, originality, vivid colours and prolific extent the art which adorns the Vatican is unique the world over.

Rome cast a spell over me. It is such a beautiful city. Its population, numbering over two million, was then approximately the same as in the first century of the Christian era. Any city that possesses its ancient history would be great; any city that possesses its subsequent history, most of which it owes to the church, would be great; any city that possesses its art treasures would be great; any city that possesses its buildings and ruins from the past would be great; any city that possesses its natural and man-made beauty would be great. Rome possesses all these title-deeds to greatness.

It had been arranged that I would fly into Berlin with the RAF on November 15. In the ten days at my disposal before then I was able to fit in a whirlwind tour of northern Europe. I paid brief visits to Paris, Brussels, The Hague, Copenhagen, Oslo and Stockholm. At The Hague I attended the opening session of the International Court of Justice on the famous Corfu Case. In all of these places I was assisted, briefed and entertained by our diplomatic representatives. These intensive briefing sessions added greatly to my enjoyment and to my understanding of the problems confronting these countries in the difficult postwar period, and of the ways in which Canada was helping in the reconstruction of the shattered European economies.

On November 13th I was back in London.

I formed a very high opinion of our diplomatic and trade representatives both personally and collectively. Pierre Dupuy in Brussells, Jean Désy in Rome, and General LaFleche in Athens were outstanding ambassadors in their grasp of conditions in the countries to which they were accredited and in the goodwill which they won for Canada. The trade representatives were vigilant, well-informed and devoted to Canada's best interests. I was much impressed by them. Wherever I went I made a point of conferring with our officials and inspecting our offices abroad. I found that they appreciated the interest I showed in them and their work. Some missions abroad rarely see a Canadian MP.

164

I had built up a lively interest in my trip to Berlin. The timing was opportune. The Russians were making utmost trouble for the Western Allies over the air corridor. The Allies, particularly Britain and the United States, responded with the hastily contrived airlift to maintain their foothold in Berlin and to supply the inhabitants of their sectors of the beleaguered city with food, fuel and materials. It was a dangerous situation which could easily have carried the nations concerned to the brink of war.

I reached Gatow airport in Berlin at 10 p.m. on November 15. I have never seen so much destruction in a city. Three and a half years after the war the rubble was still piled twenty feet high in the middle of the roads, and people were living in the basements of ruins. A greater weight of bombs was dropped on Berlin during the war than on the entire British Isles. There were no street lights except an occasional single light suspended over an intersection. Otherwise it was pitch dark by 4.30 p.m. An occasional store burned a candle, but the shelves of the shops were mostly bare. The airlift was a triumph of organization and determination with inadequate resources. The Russians permitted no one to carry food or fuel into the western sectors. The Allies were operating nine hundred cargo planes a day into the two airports to provision the two and a quarter million inhabitants in their sectors. It was a costly operation, but untold woe would have befallen the West and the cause of freedom in Europe had the Allies not stood their ground. The fuel allowance was fifty pounds per person for the entire winter, and I saw hard-pressed German families searching about for even sticks and twigs in the Grünwald.

I made two forays into the Russian sector. Mr. Molson of the Canadian Military Mission and I went to the City Hall to confer with Dr. Frederik Friedensburg, the acting Oberbürgermeister (mayor), who did not hesitate to denounce the Russians and their efforts to bolshevize Germany. Two blocks from the City Hall on our drive back we were stopped and interrogated by the Russian-controlled German police. Mr. Molson handled the situation, and we were allowed to proceed. The next morning we re-entered the Russian zone so that I might see the ruins of Hitler's Chancery and the location of the bunker in which he perished. On our way back, approaching the Brandenburg Gate, I saw an old man selling picture postcards. I asked that our car stop so that I might buy some. No one was in sight, but within seconds of our stepping onto the pavement we were surrounded by a dozen Russian soldiers with rifles at the ready. I had visions of spending the rest of my days in the salt mines of Siberia, wondering who would win the by-election in Eglinton. Not a word was spoken. We ignored the soldiers, completed our purchases and drove off. Captain O'Hagan's uniform had won us our escape.

Dr. Ernst Reuter, leader of the Social Democratic Party, the largest of Berlin's political parties, came to have lunch with us at the Mission. He had not been permitted by the Russians to take his seat. We had a fascinating discussion for two hours. We had been told by Dr. Friedensburg that after capturing the city the Russian soldiers embarked on a wild spree of pillage and rape. As far as plundering was concerned the British had the best record. He and Dr. Reuter shared the opinion that Communism was on the uprise. Dr. Reuter, who was sent to a concentration camp by Hitler and then was a political exile in Turkey from 1934 to 1946, blamed Britain and France for allowing Hitler to occupy the Rhineland. He could have been stopped then and there, and the German army expected to be prevented by the Allies.

We left Berlin in the evening by RAF plane after two of the most fascinating days of my life. We flew to Buckeburg, slept overnight at Minden, and were back at the Savoy in London at noon. The plane immediately behind us in the airlift crashed, and the pilot was killed. Freedom always exacts a price.

I stopped at the Savoy just long enough to unpack and repack for Dublin, to which I had been invited by the delegates from Eire at the Parliamentary Conference. My visit unfortunately was limited to twenty-four hours, but during that time I was able to meet many of the leading figures in Irish public life. The Dail was in session, and Senator Hayes gave a dinner in my honour there. I had an extended private conference with the Prime Minister, Mr. Costello, and one also with the famous Mr. de Valera, former Prime Minister and then Leader of the Opposition. Never had I expected to sit down with him for a friendly chat. He was interested to ask me how we handled the problem of divorce in Canada. My rides and walks around Dublin, including Trinity College and St. Patrick's Cathedral, where Dean Swift lies buried, and all the famous landmarks were delightful. Who could fail to be charmed by Dublin and its people? Senator Hayes was a perfect host, guide and ready source of information and history.

Back in London the next morning, November 20, I was away to Canterbury to spend a delightful day with my friend J. Burgon Bickersteth, Warden of Hart House in my student days at Varsity. We had a rollicking reunion and a tour of the cathedral and its precincts, steeped in history, of which Burgon had mastered every feature. We traversed the spot where Becket was mur-

166

dered, where Archbishop Stephen Langton, one of the fathers of Magna Carta, lies buried, St. Michael's Chapel and the shrine of the Buffs Regiment with which the Queen's Own Rifles Regiment of Canada is affiliated, the tomb of Edward, the Black Prince. We sat in the crypt, built in 1100, and listened to evensong from the chancel over our heads. In the meditation which this uplifting experience inspired I wrote in my diary: "The voices of the choir-boys and choristers raising God's praise to the lofty nave of the Cathedral reminded us that for long centuries first monks, then priests and laymen have lifted their praises heavenward in these sacred and stately precincts. Man with his three score years and ten is admonished to remember that as a flower of the field so he withereth, but the praise of our God shall live forever."

I was back in London in two hours, to have dinner and a happy evening with Eleanor and John in their flat near Regent's Park. Eleanor had gone to the trouble of baking a delicious-looking apple pie with the help of ready-mixed dough sent out from Canada to relieve the austerity of the British diet. We all licked our lips in contemplation, but after the first mouthful put down our forks and exchanged startled glances. It tasted of soap. Someone had evidently packed soap close to the dough in the package!

Sunday was to have been my last full day in London, so Eleanor and John took me sightseeing. We watched the changing of the Guard, took the train to Hampton Court, and listened to the soapbox orators in Hyde Park.

Fog over London prevented our taking off for Canada until Tuesday noon. Fog had also closed the airport at Montreal, so we continued on to Toronto. I crept upstairs at 4.30 a.m. Wednesday, November 24, the fifty-third day of my epic travels. The children were soon awake. The air at home was filled with excitement and joy. What a trip! What a homecoming! In one fantastic trip I had been to enough places and had met enough great men and women to have filled up a dozen trips. I had seen hunger, want, devastation and sorrow and joy and gratitude. With the help of all the meetings and discussions I had absorbed a wealth of valuable information. I revelled in the history I had actually beheld. I had inevitably gained an increased sense of confidence. I have had sand in my shoes ever since. More important, I had consciously matured as the result of this fabulous experience. I had proved to myself that I could make friends wherever I went and that in international gatherings I could hold my own with credit to Canada.

Three amusing incidents should conclude the narrative of my trip. One occurred in London, one in Berlin and one in Portrush. At the dinner tendered by the Council of the London Chamber of Commerce I found myself sitting between two of its members. The one had been a member of the council for ten years, the other two. They had never been introduced to each other, and consequently did not know or speak to each other. The junior knew who the senior was, but to the senior the junior was a total stranger. I introduced them, having come thirty-five hundred miles for such a purpose.

In Berlin there was no need for street-cleaners. Fertilizer was very scarce. Citizens with gardens competed for the opportunity to pick up whatever horses deigned to drop in the streets. Captain O'Hagan was telling me about seeing a well-dressed gentleman in a frock coat out one day with a shovel on the streets gathering horse droppings. Ten minutes later our car almost ran down a dignified-looking lady on a bicycle who had been pursuing a horse-drawn vehicle, and who stopped suddenly when the horse obliged, produced a paper bag from which she withdrew a little shovel and proceeded to scoop the droppings into her bag. Having completed the operation she resumed her dignity and proceeded on her way, no doubt rejoicing at her good fortune.

At Portrush one of the Canadian provincial delegates was replying to our hosts' toast on behalf of all the visitors. He waxed eloquent about Ireland, but when he came to reciting the well-known song he became a little confused. Instead of saying "And they sprinkled it with stardust" he said with a burst of oratory,

And they sprinkled it with sawdust,
And they called it Ireland.

CHAPTER SEVENTEEN

1949: Year of Disaster

George Drew moved with characteristic vigour to take up his task as the new leader. He resigned as Premier of Ontario and Leslie Frost, Leslie Blackwell, Dana Porter and Kelso Roberts contested the leadership. Frost won, and Les Blackwell soon after retired from public life and returned to his law practice. His seat in Eglinton was taken by Dr. W.J. Dunlop, the newly appointed Minister of Education. Les Blackwell and I had been congenial running mates in Eglinton, but I was fortunate now to have Dr. Dunlop in that role. We had for a long time been close friends. After supporting George Drew at the leadership convention Les Blackwell turned hostile toward him over the events which followed on the provincial stage.

Roly Michener had suffered the same fate as George Drew at the 1948 Ontario general election. In the midst of the Conservative triumph across the province he had been defeated in his own riding of St. David's. As provincial secretary it was known that George Drew relied heavily on him. He was now free, and George determined to make use of his valuable services and experience in a new federal role. Roly was enlisted to act as a kind of executive assistant to the leader and to organize the caucus for its duties in the House. The latter was totally unnecessary, for if there was one achievement to which John Bracken could lay claim it was that our caucus was highly and efficiently organized, and it was handed over intact to his successor. George had not yet fully acquainted himself with the internal affairs and the personnel of caucus. I advised Roly not to change the caucus organization or the allocation of duties already in effect. I also urged that George cultivate first-hand relationships as quickly as possible with the chairmen of caucus committees and as many of the other members as opportunity would permit. I was personally sorry to appear to narrow Roly's new role, but I was concerned over George's relations with a caucus to which he was a newcomer, and of which a large number of members had not supported him in the leadership race. I was alarmed when told that George proposed to appoint Roly as secretary of the caucus, for no person who was not a duly elected Member of Parliament or senator had been admitted to any session of it, and I feared that the proposal would give rise to strong opposition. Roly was wise, discreet and utterly unselfish, and I was able to speak frankly to him.

Russ Boucher generously resigned his safe seat in Carleton to make way for George, who was elected in a by-election in January 1949. He should have received an acclamation, but the CCF, playing the role of nuisance as usual, contested it by nominating my friend Eugene Forsey. The campaign proved stormy, but the CCF fell far short of repeating their success in South York in 1942, and George duly took his place in Parliament.

He immediately confirmed the existing caucus organization and all positions thereon. Thus I remained chairman of the Committee on Social Security and Housing, and continued as the Opposition critic on those subjects. However, he did request caucus to allow Roly to attend its sessions and to act as secretary, a suggestion caucus was strong enough to decline. Someone had to speak out in opposition to a proposal which was quite unacceptable, but no one wished to incur that embarrassment. I would have done it if necessary, but as a personal friend and admirer of Roly and a recent candidate for the leadership I was loath to do so. I was profoundly relieved, therefore, when John Hackett opposed the proposition. George quickly realized that John was expressing the general feeling and withdrew his request. George deserved great credit for accepting the will of caucus in rejecting his wish. In this first taste of defeat in caucus George demonstrated his stature. It was not to be the last time, however, that he would experience difficulty in carrying caucus with him.

The session opened on January 26, 1949. Some major changes had come over the face of the House of Commons since it had last met. Mr. King, now merely the member for Glengarry, had shifted to a seat on the right of the Treasury benches, and Mr. St. Laurent occupied the seat of Prime Minister, with C.D. Howe as his desk-mate. Mike Pearson, appointed Secretary of State for External Affairs on September 10, occupied a seat on the Front bench. Stuart Garson, Premier of Manitoba from 1942, had been appointed Minister of Justice, and C.D. Howe, while remaining Minister of Trade and Commerce, had given up the portfolio of

Reconstruction and Supply, and had been succeeded by my good friend Bob Winters, who now became responsible for housing. The Conservatives had been joined by George Nowlan, a major addition in both debating skill and political stature to the ranks of the opposition. He had won back the riding of Digby-Annapolis-King's in the by-election following Ilsley's resignation.

Mr. King made only one speech. On February 16 he spoke for the last time in a House he had first entered forty years before. He hailed the entry of Newfoundland into Confederation, and congratulated those who had negotiated it. Mike Pearson soon became popular in the House. He had the advantage of holding an uncontroversial portfolio. There were not a few Liberals in the House who would have liked to become Minister of Justice, but they were nearly all from eastern Canada, and Mr. St. Laurent in choosing Stuart Garson sought to win support in the West and at the same time find a spokesman from provincial ranks to defend the government's fiscal policies in relation to the provinces and to fend off or at least blunt the attacks which were expected from George Drew in that respect. It has been said that politics makes strange bedfellows; it also makes strange adversaries at times. Garson had been provincial Treasurer in John Bracken's cabinet in Manitoba, and had succeeded Bracken as Premier when John accepted the federal leadership of the Progressive Conservative party. I had known and liked Garson personally before he came to Ottawa. In one of his first interventions in the House he twitted George Drew in saying that if George wished to learn how to present a case he could learn from me. This bouquet with a brick inside did not go down very well. Stuart was lame and pleasant by nature. The shoes left by St. Laurent in the Department of Justice were just too large for him to fill, particularly when debates on the constitution and federal-provincial fiscal relations were absorbing the attention of Parliament more and more.

The stage was set for high drama on leaders' day, January 28. It was the acid test for the two new leaders. Mr. St. Laurent, after being kept waiting in limbo for four months while Mr. King clung to the coveted prime ministership, had finally assumed that office on November 15. George Drew sat across from him awaiting his long-sought opportunity to enter the federal fray. The two leaders amid general applause had greeted each other warmly and shaken hands in the middle of the chamber at the opening two days before. On this day, however, such pleasant amenities found no place.

George had served as an artillery officer in the Great War. He wheeled up all his big guns that day and pounded the enemy lines on the other side of no man's land. It was, after all, really his maiden speech in the House, and in that sense it was lacking in grace and modesty. He spoke for over two hours and devoted most of his time to an assault on the government's handling of federal-provincial fiscal relations. Much of the cannonade was directed personally at Mr. St. Laurent. In his tirade against bureaucracy George actually named Mr. St. Laurent as "the biggest bureaucrat in Canada." This was nonsense and in bad taste. The Liberals were enraged, the Conservatives embarrassed. The urbane and courtly Louis St. Laurent should not have been selected as a personal target, and, anyway, the essence of bureaucracy was that it functioned outside Parliament, not inside it. At this personal accusation the Prime Minister flushed, sat up straight, turned his head to the left and made a gesture with his mouth as if to say, "Phew!"

It was a brilliant but disastrous performance, and none knew that better than the Conservative back-benchers. George had been guilty of very bad judgment; his speech should have been reserved for some party rally where it would have drawn cheers. Every Liberal came to look on George as something of an avowed personal enemy. He brought every manner of attack from them on his own head. His personal relations with Liberal members never recovered from that opening and costly barrage. Of itself it predetermined the outcome of the next election, which was just around the corner.

The remainder of the session proceeded in a rather hostile atmosphere under the shadow of the approaching general election. I was in the debates early and late, at the beginning and at the end. I laboured without ceasing.

In the debate on the throne speech on February 3, I questioned the Prime Minister's avoidance of the subject of Dominion-provincial fiscal relations in his long reply to George Drew's attack, and lambasted the government over its position on the constitution and the failure of its housing policies – a subject I returned to in two other speeches during the session. Of its television policy I said, "I characterize it today as a dog-in-the-manger attitude, born out of the infernal paternalism which characterizes this government's attitude at all times. . . . They will not let private stations do anything; they will not let Canadians who are quite prepared to risk their money in developing this field go ahead and do so."

The entry of Newfoundland into Confederation was a major historical event. The Terms of Union had been signed in Ottawa on December 11. On February 7, Mr. St. Laurent moved approval, and George Drew made one of his finest speeches. It was a day of parliamentary eloquence. Only one member, an Independent, dissented. Later on the address stage the official opposition sought to force the government to consult the other provinces, but the government resisted, and the Conservative amendment was defeated 137 to 66. On April 1, 1949, Newfoundland became the tenth Canadian province, and Gordon Bradley representing it entered the cabinet as Secretary of State.

The extension of the Transitional Measures Act again provoked a battle royal. The fifty-seven wartime orders-in-council had shrunk to twelve, but the government insisted on giving these continued statutory effect for another year. They should have brought in a separate measure on rent control or any other specific measure needed instead of prolonging this holus-bolus monster. I played an active role in the debate on this measure and the similar one to extend the Agricultural Products Act. Both measures trespassed on provincial authority, and the government sought to justify this constitutional aberration on the ground of national emergency. The government was skating on very thin ice. Diefenbaker also made a very effective speech on the subject, and on the following day I denounced the government for its drive toward centralization of power. Garson was hardly a match for Drew, Diefenbaker and myself on that issue. Mr. St. Laurent chose not to come to his rescue. Perhaps it would have been embarrassing under the circumstances to do so.

Doug Abbott brought down his budget on March 22. He and other Liberals called it "the sunshine budget," since he introduced substantial tax reductions, particularly in the income tax. It was perfectly clear that the stage was now set for a general election. The budget debate was permitted to run only five days before it was snuffed out. The tax changes were put into effect on March 22 illegally by the same man who a year earlier had introduced tax changes by radio. I was one of the members denied the opportunity to speak on the budget by the government's decision to throttle discussion. This may have helped to shape the position I took in comparable circumstances in 1962.

The next question was how the government was going to pay the bills until the budget and the Estimates were adopted. There would be no possibility of a spring election if the government was to wait for their adoption; they therefore sought a vote of interim supply until September 30th, and obtained it, but not before I had denounced their demand for a blank cheque from Parliament without any review of their proposed expenditures. Ministers exhibited only cynicism. It was at an earlier point in the same session that Howe had cynically rejected the Conservative plea to save some money with his famous contemptuous reply, "What's a million dollars?" (which I heard him say, even though it may not have appeared in Hansard) and Mr. St. Laurent on November 6 had referred to $180 million as "peanuts." I flailed them both in my last speech of the session for their irresponsible attitude toward expenditure.

Just as the approaching dissolution was made the occasion for stopping debate on the budget and avoiding a responsible course of voting supply, so it was made the occasion for strangling the Public Accounts Committee. That body had held two meetings and had just embarked upon its tasks when it was snuffed out.

Dissolution came on April 30, and the election was called for June 27. In Eglinton we were well prepared, and our campaign organization, headed again by Bill Smith as organizer and Bill Murchie as official agent, set out to repeat or improve upon our 1945 success. Before leaving Ottawa every member had a photograph taken with George Drew, and these were enlarged to life-size for publicity use in the ridings. I sensed that, as in the Ontario general election of 1948, the Conservative campaign was about to be built to excess around George Drew personally.

I should comment here on my personal relations with George. After the happy and secure relations I had enjoyed with John Bracken his resignation from the leadership disturbed my feelings toward my parliamentary tasks. It would take a long time even in the best of circumstances to establish the same warm feelings and mutual confidence with the new leader. George was a man of convictions; he was also very confident of his own mastery of public affairs, not least in defence, Dominion-provincial fiscal relations and foreign affairs. Our caucus committee on External Affairs met for dinner every Tuesday evening, and George attended these meetings. One evening I expressed an opinion based on my recent observations on my trip to Europe. George brushed my remarks aside, and I was neither flattered nor pleased. It would take the chastening hand of adversity to teach George some hard lessons, one of which was to cultivate and encourage the human resources at his command in the caucus. When such lessons had been learned and George came to recognize and appreciate my loyalty we were destined to become very close friends. As it was, I carried out my duties in the House faithfully, if not altogether enjoyably. I sought and obtained the ever-reluctant consent of Alice and my partners to stand for election once again, and plunged into the campaign, both national and local, with all my vigour.

Increasingly I was called to speak in Quebec. The truth is that the party had no one else outside that province with any known command of French. It became difficult for me to keep up with the advertising given by the party to such facility in that tongue as I had attained. On a short speaking tour of the Eastern Townships I found posters hailing me as "Canada's Great Bilingual Orator." I struggled to live up to the billing, but I must confess that my speeches in French were largely confined to the subjects of the constitution and provincial and language rights. One experience in the 1949 campaign provided a very harsh and unexpected test.

Over the first weekend in June I was billed for three speeches in the eastern part of the province. On Friday evening we had a good outdoor meeting in Quebec City. It went well; I confined myself to my favourite themes. Saturday morning I left for Amqui with Onesime Gagnon, Quebec Minister of Finance. It was a long, hot eight-hour drive from Quebec City. About an hour before our arrival I thought it time to ask a question or two about our evening meeting, and indiscreetly inquired of Onesime as to what proportions of the expected audience would be English-speaking and French-speaking respectively. Onesime looked at me in utter astonishment. "Nobody at the meeting would understand a word of English. You must speak entirely in French." Then he proceeded to tell me that I was the principal speaker and that I would be expected to discuss a number of current issues. Up till that moment I had assumed that he and I would divide the speaking responsibilities and that I could confine myself to the constitution and provincial and language rights. Onesime was a graceful orator, and I had looked to him to cover all the other subjects. Suddenly I was faced with a very different task for which I was not prepared. I realized that if I failed I could damage my growing reputation in the province. We finally arrived at Amqui at six o'clock. There a large and enthusiastic reception awaited us and a banquet at which Onesime and I were to be the guests of honour. I was impaled on the horns of a dilemma: if I attended the banquet I would have not one minute to prepare my speech; to excuse myself would appear strange and would acutely disappoint my gracious hosts. I should have attended the banquet, but I felt compelled to excuse myself, go to my room and spend an hour frantically struggling to assemble the first speech I had ever attempted in French on old-age pensions, agriculture, social security and other themes. I clutched my precious notes as we arrived at the meeting in the evening. To my utter dismay I found that it was to be in the open air in a park, that I would be speaking from the bandshell and it was not sufficiently well lit for me to read anything. My notes had become useless. To add to my predicament both the mayor and Onesime in their remarks gave me a very flattering build-up and roused the crowd to expect much of me. Somehow I struggled through my speech, every word of it in French. I was not particularly pleased with my performance; it lacked the fire that speeches in French in Quebec should always possess.

On Sunday after a good night's rest we moved on to Rimouski, where in the afternoon to a much larger audience I delivered my same speech on diversified subjects and did far better. But the Amqui speech stands out in my memory as a source of embarrassment. Never again was I caught unprepared to make a speech in French on any subject of current political interest, and often off the cuff.

The campaign went well for a while, then it became evident that Drew's popularity did not match his stature. I encountered this strongly in the West, in Quebec, and in the Maritimes, for I had now become one of the party's national campaign speakers. I returned to Toronto realizing that Ontario must rally to the support of this outstanding native son if we were to win. What I encountered alarmed me. George had become so unpopular in Ontario that at the grassroots level he was being played down. My own Eglinton organizers had gone so far as to remove his photograph and name from my committee rooms. Those life-size photos of him and me together had disappeared. Even those of the riding executive who had supported George at the leadership convention against me a few months before concurred in this act of suppression. It dismayed me. Mr. St. Laurent's campaign was going smoothly; he was being well received everywhere. George was being denounced in the Liberal press in Ontario and the West as the friend of Duplessis and Houde, and as having shirked his unfinished provincial responsibilities. The tide was running against us everywhere. Both George himself and the Liberals had succeeded in making him the principal issue in the campaign. The outstandingly good work done by Conservative members in the House was thus overlooked. In its last issue before the election the *Toronto Daily Star* ran a scurrilous headline: "Keep Canada British. Destroy Drew's Houde. God Save the King."

On election night we sorrowfully saw nearly half of our sitting members go down to defeat. We were reduced from 70 to 41, back to where Bennett had sunk in 1940. The Liberals had won 190 seats, many more than they had ever elected under King. Some of our excellent MPs were defeated, never to return to Parliament. Unhappily, these included John Bracken. In Eglinton I obtained 19,853 votes, as against 16,426 for the Liberal candidate and 4,305 for the CCF. Yet despite my hard work and growing prominence in the House and in the country, my plurality had dropped from 8,000 in 1945 to 3,500. The Liberal vote had increased by 3,000, while mine had declined by 1,600. Even so, it looked enormous beside the vote of other Conservative candidates.

As I looked about there seemed not a ray of hope. We had not even held our ground. Clearly George Drew had become a burden to the party only months after he had been acclaimed as leader with a huge majority. The party, or what was left of it in the Commons, was shattered and in disarray. As I faced the grim road ahead I felt crushed and discouraged. With our reduced numbers I well knew I would be called upon to bear heavier burdens in the House and in the committees. The task all seemed so thankless, and so futile. My law partners were convinced I had dug myself into a deep hole.

Had Diefenbaker or myself been elected leader in 1948 would the party have done better in 1949? The answer must be yes. I once heard Diefenbaker say that had he been leader in 1949 he could have won the election, but he was not sure about 1953. I don't believe that either he or I could have won the 1949 election, but with either of us the party would have won considerably more seats than it did. I unexpectedly encountered Jack Pickersgill on York Street in Toronto one day while he was still secretary of the cabinet. He told me that C.D. Howe had said the Conservative party should have run the risk of electing me as the young man and given me the time and opportunity to build both myself and the party, but that the Conservative party would not take the long view. I, too, was to learn to my cost that the party would not take the long view; it is all too often looking for a shortcut to victory.

The federal and provincial spheres of politics and government in Canada are different. The longer a man stays in one of them the more difficult it becomes for him to make the transition to the other. The party's experience in choosing John Bracken, George Drew and later Bob Stanfield demonstrates how different and severe is the testing ground of the House of Commons.

The Twenty-First Parliament opened in September; it presented a very different appearance from the Twentieth. Of 262 members, 190 were Liberals. They not only occupied every seat to the right of the Speaker; they overflowed to his left as well. Those to the left became known as "Little Chicago." The Conservatives with 41, the CCF with only 13, the Social Credit with 10 barely outnumbered Little Chicago. More than one-third of all the members were new to Parliament, and they were nearly all Liberals. Gone were Mackenzie King, John Bracken, Cec Merritt, John Hackett, Art Smith, Jim Macdonnell and other stalwarts, though Jim re-entered the House in November after winning a by-election in Toronto-Greenwood. Roly Michener had been defeated in St. Paul's. Joe Noseworthy was back as the CCF member for South York. Two bright and personable young Conservatives had been elected in Quebec constituencies, Léon Balcer in Trois Rivières and Henri Courtemanche in Labelle. Newfoundland was represented for the first time. Of its seven members five were Liberals and two, both from the city of St. John's, Conservative. A new Speaker, the popular Ross Macdonald of Brantford, was in the chair, and René Beaudoin was deputy chairman of the Committee of the Whole.

In the presence of so many new members I felt like a seasoned veteran. To help that impression I had been advanced to the second row in the seating, although my seat was at the end of the row, farthest from the Speaker, and beside the CCF. I sat next to their whip, Stanley Knowles, and M.J. Coldwell was immediately in front of him. I admired them both, and we became closer friends there. More important, I was now assigned an office for my exclusive use. It was not a very good one, being located at the front of the building where my one window looked out on the masonry of the Peace Tower, and I consequently had little light. However, at least I had privacy and quiet at last.

What should be our attitude as the official opposition? The government had received from the electorate the strongest mandate ever given to a cabinet, leader and party. Should we submit to their program? On the other hand, we as individual members had been elected in opposition to the government. Many of the Liberals were cocky and arrogant after their sweeping success. We determined that we had a responsibility to try to keep the government true to the promises on which they had been elected, to resist any attempt to override Parliament, to oppose whenever we thought they were wrong, even though we knew we would never be able to defeat them. We conducted ourselves with vigour and confidence in debate, even though we were a scant minority, holding only 16 per cent of the seats in the House.

Much depended, of course, on George Drew's own attitude

and relations between him and the caucus. George conducted himself in the House with courage and ability. His position was exceedingly difficult, but he met the challenge. There had been speculation in the press that Diefenbaker and I might attempt to combine forces to overthrow George, but this was nonsense. Nevertheless, there were some in caucus who were convinced we could never succeed with George as leader. I resolved that I could do no less than give him my total support in the discouraging circumstances.

The budget of the previous session was reintroduced by Abbott on October 20 with some modifications, but interest in it had largely evaporated. Later I drew attention to the multiplying effect of sales taxes levied at the manufacturer's or producer's level in subsequent markups. This was a theme to which I would return in later sessions.

In this session rent control leapt onto the parliamentary stage. It was the last of the major wartime controls, and the pressures were becoming intense as the housing shortage grew more acute. The government sought to sidestep the issue by referring the control order to the Supreme Court of Canada to determine whether it was still valid. At the same time the government modified the controls by allowing increases up to 25 per cent across the board. This gave rise to a massive hue and cry from tenants across the whole country, and I launched a sustained attack on the government for thus legislating by executive decree while Parliament was in session.

Nearly five years after the end of the war the shortage of housing was steadily on the increase. I attacked the government's failure at every opportunity, and I must say their defence was very weak. Control was divided. Doug Abbott as Minister of Finance was responsible for rent control, and Bob Winters as Minister of Reconstruction and Supply was in charge of the administration of the National Housing Act. A government bill to amend the act and place large sums at its disposal gave me heaven-sent opportunities to make major speeches on the subject. On this subject I felt completely at home. I was confident I knew more about it than other members. I was pleased also when I could direct my fire at Howe. He made the mistake of being present when the bill was before the committee on November 29. I exacted from Winters a thorough explanation of every clause in the bill. At one point Howe so far lost his patience that on one of my questions he said quite audibly to Winters, "Don't answer that." I turned on Howe and acidly commented, "Perhaps the Minister of Trade and Commerce would assist by keeping quiet."

We heard no more from Howe, and I obtained the answers I sought. As a very senior minister he had belittled a young minister before the entire House. His wrath toward me was accumulating.

Later I was chosen to lead off for the opposition in the debate on the Estimates of Howe's department. Britain had been faced with a critical shortage of foreign exchange, and had devalued sterling by 30 per cent. It was obvious to anyone that this was coming, and that it would result in a severe curtailment of British purchases of Canadian exports, including wheat; but until the election was over Howe had continued to say publicly that our trade with the United Kingdom was normal. Either he did not know what was happening or he was misleading the Canadian public. On September 20 the government devalued the Canadian dollar by 10 per cent. My intervention on December 1 was my first major speech in the House on the subject of external trade. It was filled with figures and facts, the products of research. I concluded with this solemn warning: "The situation is fraught with the greatest danger. What is needed on the part of the government is a sense of realism, of candour, of honesty with the Canadian people, and, above all, a sense of pressing urgency." I had for the time being moved directly into the orbit of the all-powerful C.D. Howe, and he resented my criticisms.

Typical of the approach of the new Prime Minister were two bills of a constitutional nature, trumpeted as heralding the end of the two last "badges of colonialism." This claim was on the face of it sheer nonsense. The purpose of the one bill, introduced by Stuart Garson, was to abolish appeals to the Privy Council in London; the other, introduced by St. Laurent, was to ask the British Parliament to amend section 91 of the BNA Act to permit the Canadian Parliament to amend the act in federal matters. In both cases the government deliberately asserted its right to proceed without consent of the provinces. On both bills the Conservative opposition supported the principle of consultation with the provinces and counselled against haste. We urged that effort be made in cooperation with the provinces to find a formula for amendment in Canada of a patriated constitution, rather than complicate, prejudice and delay that larger project by the government's limited measure. I appealed for a conciliatory approach, a friendly discussion within the Canadian family, and a renewal of the spirit of Confederation. I delivered the last third of my speech in French, and concluded with these words (translation):

180

We in Canada must above all else seek harmony, understanding and agreement. We must strive to protect the rights of minorities and the rights we believe were guaranteed by the constitution. . . . We must approach those subjects in a spirit of conciliation. I urge upon the Prime Minister to refrain from hurting the feelings of many Canadians and from thus creating disagreement and disunion in the Canadian family. . . . I appeal to the spirit of understanding of each and everyone; I plead for a spirit of agreement; in short, I plead, on the part of all, for the spirit of the Fathers of Confederation.

I would have made the same plea in 1980 and 1981. The patriation of the constitution was for years delayed and thwarted by impatient and intolerant approaches and sometimes bluster instead of cooperatively and constructively seeking to find a formula for amendment. It remains the key to any constitutional problem. As I said on October 17 in one of the best speeches I ever made, "The formula by which a comprehensive amending procedure is to be achieved in Canada must be one that is acceptable to the provinces. It is the height of folly to proceed to carve up this subject."

A debate on external affairs, led off by Mike Pearson with an excellent comprehensive review, afforded me at long last an opportunity the next day to recount my trip to Europe the year before and the impressions I formed in the course of it. I opened my speech by telling the story of Professor Pearson arriving in my history class at Varsity in 1923 to commence a course on English constitutional history. I had waited a year for the opportunity to tell of my trip to Europe. I dwelt particularly on the plight of the Greek refugees and the heroic resistance to Communist invasion. I also emphasized the lessons to be drawn from opposing Russian machinations in Berlin. I concluded with these words: "As we survey the uneasy present and the dark past I think we can all take fresh heart when we remember that there is committed to us as one of the western nations the cause of freedom, the cause of the dignity of man, the cause of honour and fair dealing among nations." I later warned against allowing UNESCO funds to be used to educate captive Greek children held in Communist camps in Bulgaria, Romania, Yugoslavia and Albania.

After it had sat on the order paper for four sessions my motion to establish a Standing Committee on Health, Welfare, Social Security and Housing was finally reached on October 12. I made a strong plea for it, and won support from all the opposition parties. But the government now held a commanding majority in the House and it was determined to give no ground to ideas emanating from the opposition. My motion was defeated by the submissive Liberal majority.

I also renewed my plea for a Committee on Estimates, to save the time of the House and to assure a more thorough review of proposed expenditure. The Estimates of the Department of External Affairs were sent to the Standing Committee on External Affairs, where they were very thoroughly studied. On their return to the House they were passed in half an hour. I would have welcomed such a procedure for examining the Estimates of the Department of National Health and Welfare, for which I continued to be responsible.

Stuart Garson immersed himself in deep trouble late in the session and merited the pounding he took over it. The law plainly required that every report of the commissioner under the Combines Investigation Act be published within fifteen days of its receipt by the Minister of Justice. The commissioner had written a report on the flour milling industry which Garson did not publish for over ten months. When he was cornered over it he offered some very unconvincing excuses. He never denied George Drew's accusation that Howe, fearing the results of publication before the general election, would not allow the report to be published. I denounced him for deliberately breaking the law:

> What we have witnessed here . . . in this last and most trivial of all his excuses, this grasping at straws on the part of the Minister of Justice, has been an incredibly inept and desperate attempt to palliate, in a belated and blundering brainstorm, a deliberate, calculated and callous breach of the law.
>
> Whether his breach of the law was due to inexperience in obeying the law, or to weakness and impotence in the face of the behests of a blustering dictator in the cabinet, or a reprehensible attempt to cozen the votes of unsuspecting Canadians at the polls on June 27, the fact remains that the Minister of Justice, who should be the chief law enforcement officer of Canada, has become Canada's No. 1 lawbreaker.
>
> The Prime Minister . . . in the amazing statement which fell from his lips this morning, tore to shreds that fundamental principle of our democratic and parliamentary institutions, that all men, regardless of rank and quality, are equal before and under the law. No man, whether or not he is a Minister of the Crown, has any right to override the law. It binds him just as much as it binds the humblest citizen in any walk of life. The Prime Minister, along with the Minister of Justice, has torn that fundamental principle to shreds. Those who sit with him on the treasury benches, participating as they did with the Minister of Justice in this deliberate breach of the law, are equally guilty.

182

I was now gaining more confidence in the House, even in the face of such formidable Liberal strength, and my efforts were receiving attention from the press. The French-language press noted that I now felt free to speak French in the House without a text and that defeat in the contest for the party leadership and the defeat of the party in the general election had not lessened my effort to speak French. *Le Devoir*, in an article written by Pierre Vigeant in September, observed that the setbacks which I had suffered "have not in the least modified his sentiments nor cooled his zeal to master our language."

Wilfrid Eggleston, in *Saturday Night*, wrote that one of the principal factors that accounted for the new spirit in the House was "the way in which Diefenbaker and Fleming have matured as parliamentary debaters." The *Toronto Star*, ascribing the party defeat to George Drew's leadership, noted that two men had been re-elected "who might team into a combination that would rebuild the party into its former greatness. These men are John Diefenbaker, able and energetic Saskatchewan lawyer, and Donald Fleming, quiet, modest and sensible Toronto lawyer." Praise from the Liberal *Star* was rare indeed.

Fred Mears, veteran representative of the *Montreal Gazette* in the press gallery, wrote a lengthy article on me, hailing me as the "Apostle of Bonne Entente." He reviewed my background and declared views, and compared me with St. Laurent, both Irish on the maternal side and French on the paternal, and both seeking "a closer accord between the two principal racial components of the Canadian scene." He noted my wish to see women and young people taking a more active and influential role in shaping the policies and the thinking of the Progressive Conservative party.

CHAPTER EIGHTEEN

At the Half Century

The decade of the forties ended happily. It was a joy to be back at Glencairn Avenue, Toronto, with my family. Christmas was a happy day. My mother spent the full day with us, and all of Alice's family joined us for supper. David, Mary and Donald staged a puppet show, and we sang a few carols. It was a Christmas program that had become quite standardized over the years, but none the less enjoyable. But what would the decade of the fifties bring?

February 15 was Alice's birthday. We all celebrated it that evening, then I took the night train to Ottawa. I dreaded that train, partly because I knew I would not sleep, and partly because it meant the beginning of another five months of weekly commuting between Toronto and Ottawa and separation from my family for five days out of every week. The weekends were always short and lived under intense pressure. The challenge of parliamentary duty, however, was inescapable.

When the 1950 session opened on February 16 the economic climate was changing. Prices were rising, unemployment was increasing, our export markets were shrinking. We Conservatives had plenty of ammunition to expend on the government, though our efforts all seemed so futile as we looked upon a House of Commons dominated by 193 Liberals submissive to the will of the government. It was of very limited comfort to us that they had been elected with less than half of the popular vote. In Parliament it is the number of members that counts.

Tommy Church died the week before the session opened. He had been one of the most colourful and best loved members of the House. He was mayor of Toronto from 1915 to 1921 inclusive, longer than anyone else. He had been a Member of Parliament from 1921 to 1930 and from 1934 to his death. Although handicapped by deafness he spoke frequently in the House and he had a memory for names and faces which was the envy of every politician. Very feeling tributes were paid to Tommy's memory at the opening of the session. All emphasized his legion of acts of personal kindness. I thought the two most impressive tributes were those paid by two friends whose views were often poles apart from Tommy's, namely M.J. Coldwell and J.F. Pouliot.

Colin Gibson, Secretary of State, had been appointed to the Ontario Court of Appeal. I was sorry to see him leave the House; we were good friends, and I looked upon him as a man of character rather than a partisan. Thus two seats became open, Toronto-Broadview and Hamilton West. In Broadview the nomination was won by George Hees. In Hamilton West the Conservative nomination went to Ellen Fairclough, who had already won success in Hamilton's municipal life. Ellen and George won the two vacant seats and took their places in the House on May 25. Together with George Nowlan, these two were a formidable recruitment to our strength in the House and did much to restore our shaken party morale. We were admittedly thin in numbers, but we packed a powerful debating punch.

George Drew played a towering role in debate. He conducted himself with great courage and ability. In the face of discouragements which would have daunted lesser men he devoted all his energies and his impressive talents to his tasks. His private secretary, the able and astute Mel Jack, resigned to join the civil service. This upset some of his friends in our caucus. George appointed Derek Bedson, drawn from the Department of External Affairs, to fill the vacancy. Derek had abilities and experience which were most helpful to George. One of Derek's first acts on taking over his position was to examine my filing system and methods of gathering material on subjects for use in the debates. George also had the invaluable assistance of Rod Finlayson, a Winnipeg lawyer, who had been an assistant to R.B. Bennett when Prime Minister. He gathered material for George and aided in the preparation of his speeches. I esteemed him as a friend and a most competent aide to the leader.

The Liberals, both ministers and back-benchers, were still feeling very cocky over their triumph at the polls in 1949. Many were yielding to an attitude of "Why should we listen to you?" toward the opposition in the House. More and more they exhibited what Jim Macdonnell called "studied contempt" toward us, and it did not take us long to pick up the theme of their "treating Parliament with contempt," a running issue which was to reach its climax in 1956.

The government began by juggling the debate on the throne

speech. Instead of allowing it to take and complete its course they gave government business precedence, with the result that it became a debate by instalments and dragged on wearily from February 17 to March 16 before the address was adopted by a vote of 151 to 51. I spoke on February 22, following Mike Pearson. He had just conducted an admirable review of Canada's external relations, and I allowed myself in my opening paragraph to comment: "If in this country we must, unfortunately, it seems, for the next several years, have a Liberal administration, nevertheless we are very glad that in that Liberal administration the portfolio of External Affairs is in the very capable hands of Mike Pearson." This compliment was well deserved, but it drew much louder applause from Liberal than Conservative benches. Some of our members voiced their disapproval to me later. I had violated Arthur Meighen's admonition, "Never toss a bouquet to the other side of the House unless there's a brick in it." I had omitted the brick.

Two subjects rose above many others in the 1950 debates – Communist activities and old-age security. George Drew was never happier than when exposing and attacking communism, and the growing aggressiveness of the Kremlin around the world gave him a perfect target. George had visited Russia and the countries behind the Iron Curtain when it was rare to do so, and he knew more about the worldwide aggressive Russian strategy than anyone else in the House. On May 2, on a supply motion, he launched a powerful attack against communism, Soviet plans for world revolution, and Communist activities in Canada, and introduced the following amendment, "This House is of opinion that appropriate legislation should be introduced so that Communist and similar activities in Canada may be made an offence punishable under the Criminal Code." The terms of the amendment were somewhat amorphous, but it led to the best debate on communism in all my eighteen years in Parliament. In speaking the next day I was careful to stress that

> There is no suggestion in the amendment of penalizing people for their mere thoughts. There is no suggestion here of the suppression of unpopular ideas, if they remain nothing more than ideas, and do not result in overt acts which, in effect, strike at the security of the state or strike at human freedom. It is of the essence of freedom and our conception of it that no man should be subject to punishment for what he thinks, provided his thoughts do not issue in acts of the kind I have described. The acts at which this amendment is directed are acts which . . . strike at the security of the state and those which strike at the roots of our freedom. . . .

186

There is one further resource that we have which the Communists have not, and which in my humble opinion will yet prove to be the deciding factor in the outcome of this struggle. It is the fact that we are spiritual creatures. We believe that the issues in life are not to be determined by materialistic forces. We believe that the supreme forces in life are not the forces of materialism. It is my humble expression of opinion that that supreme resource, if we will but practise it and use it, will yet prove to be the deciding factor in this war of ideas.

The amendment was defeated by a vote of 147 to 32, but we had gained ground by taking a firm stand. We forced the government to bring in legislation to strengthen the Official Secrets Act, and we had unwittingly laid the groundwork for a strong Canadian reaction to Communist aggression in Korea which burst upon an unsuspecting world the next month.

The inadequacy of provision for old-age security had been a favourite ground of our attacks on the government. We had denounced the invidious means test, which penalized thrift. A pension of $40 a month could not pretend to be adequate for the needy in the face of rising prices, and seventy years as the minimum qualifying age left many persons in serious need after reaching sixty-five. The Conservative party was committed to a policy of a comprehensive contributory retirement pension payable to everyone at age sixty-five without a means test. This policy had two flaws: it would be enormously costly, and there were serious constitutional and financial obstacles in the way of making it contributory on an individual basis. On March 10 the government moved to establish a joint committee of both Houses to examine into the subject, but without specific power to make recommendations. I led for the opposition, attacking this further attempt by the government to evade its responsibility. I had in mind their scandalous misuse of the Committee on Prices in 1948, and suspected they were endeavouring to use the proposed committee to stifle debate. My speech was a lengthy and scorching indictment of the government for its reluctance to take action. Nevertheless, the motion was carried, and a clumsily large committee of thirty-seven was appointed, of whom six were Conservative members, including Diefenbaker and myself. Jean Lesage came to me privately and asked me to nominate him for the office of chairman, which I was pleased to do. The committee toiled long and arduously, and, I am pleased to say, constructively. The Conservative leadership on it gravitated almost immediately to me, and I was given first opportunity to question all the witnesses, one of whom was a civil servant from the

Department of Finance by the name of Mitchell Sharp. Diefenbaker attended occasionally and contributed nothing. Eventually we arrived at a unanimous and pragmatic solution: to propose payment of $40 a month at age seventy without a means test. This was not a final and complete remedy, but it had practicality and unanimity behind it. The committee thus performed an enormous service. Exposing the impracticability of numerous other approaches to the problem, it selected a universal pay-as-you-go program, based on the contributory principle and administered by the federal government. For persons aged sixty-five to sixty-nine and in need the committee recommended assistance, subject to an eligibility test.

The committee's report was tabled in late June only several days ahead of prorogation. I had the unanimous mandate of caucus to endorse the report. George Hees, recently arrived in the House, however, insisted on making a speech on June 29 criticizing the report, thus breaking the agreement reached among the members of the committee. Considering all the toil which I had expended and the fact that caucus had approved the report I was deeply disturbed over this breaking of ranks. I could have made the same criticisms of the committee's findings, but in view of the enormous cost of giving effect to more generous proposals I would have considered it irresponsible to do so.

Doug Abbott's budget, brought down on March 28, was an interesting contrast to his "sunshine" effort of a year earlier. Its tone was gloomy and sober, and it offered no tax reductions. It marked the end of his "cyclical" budgeting; the program had been tied to the political, rather than the economic cycle, anyway, as I acidly observed. I deplored the fatalistic attitude taken by the Minister toward high expenditure, and called for improved methods of reviewing the Estimates. One of the government's costly extravagances I attacked with relish: the Prime Minister's official residence. The House had given full approval to the idea of providing such a residence, and the government had expropriated a well-located property on Sussex Drive across the road from Government House. It should have demolished the old building and erected a new one. Instead, without any idea as to cost it plunged into reconstruction of the existing structure. The job was botched; the Minister of Public Works floundered; and the cost in the end reached staggering figures. I lashed the government for its ineptitude and extravagance.

Although five years had passed since the end of the war the government was back asking Parliament to extend the Transitional Measures Act to April 30, 1951, for the last time. Only rent control and the tidying up of odds and ends of price control were said to remain, but the government refused to put these into a proper bill. While supporting rent control under a proper measure we took strong objection to the government's course and to the excessively wide powers the government was still seeking to retain. George Drew took a creditable part in resisting the government's method.

On June 20 I found myself again leading the review of the Estimates of the Department of National Health and Welfare. I did not know then that it was for the last time. For six years I had given Paul Martin's Estimates the most meticulous scrutiny possible. We had fought many a battle over them, but always in the best of humour. On this occasion I roasted him over his ridiculous expenditures on publicity, and chided him for his long delay in introducing national health insurance. On one evening we had been battling away, hammer and tongs, trading harsh blows. After the adjournment we both moved to the middle of the chamber and began to chat. I was told afterwards that a couple of spectators in the gallery had lingered and watched this friendly meeting. They left disgusted, convinced that our earlier battle was a mere pretence, and muttering, "The whole thing is just a sham." In fact, it was anything but a pretence. It would be a pity, however, if parliamentarians of adverse parties denied themselves friendship and courtesy.

Far away from the pleasantries in the House dark shadows were gathering. On June 25 the armed forces of Communist North Korea, trained by the Russians, crossed the 38th parallel and commenced the invasion of South Korea. This unprovoked aggression gave rise to an immediate debate on the Estimates of the Department of National Defence, and in view of the approaching prorogation on the 30th, to a promise by the government to recall Parliament if the situation in Korea or elsewhere should deteriorate. In the event, Parliament was recalled on August 26 for two purposes: to deal with the national stoppage of rail transportation as the result of the strike called by unions representing non-operating employees of the CNR and CPR; and to grapple with the very serious military problem in South Korea. Parliament sat morning, afternoon and evening. It took only two days to pass legislation to compel resumption of rail service. The group of bills to meet the Korean emergency took much longer.

The general debate on the challenge of Communist aggression opened on August 31. The Defence Appropriation Bill was introduced, followed by a new budget with increases in various taxes. As usual there came a bill, entitled the Essential Materials Defence Act, to confer sweeping powers of control over the economy on C.D. Howe until July 31, 1952. I took a leading role in attacking the breadth of the emergency powers sought, particularly in the light of the government's reluctance to declare a state of national emergency.

Gene Tunney, former heavyweight boxing champion of the world, whom I had always admired, visited Ottawa at the time he joined the board of directors of the *Globe and Mail*, and I had the great pleasure of meeting him. He lived up to his reputation as a gentleman. He had the biggest hand I have ever seen. It appeared to be about twice the size of mine.

Before the opening of this emergency session, Mackenzie King died on July 22. An era had closed with his passing. I am thankful that I was privileged to have a share in that remarkable era, one of the most important in Canadian history.

CHAPTER NINETEEN

Christmas in the Trenches

Korea and the autumn session of 1950 mutilated my dreams of a half-year at home with my family and my legal practice. More and more I was becoming conscious of a bifurcation of my life between its public side and its private side, each competing for a larger share of my time and my interest. I was straddling two unruly steeds. The interval between sessions of Parliament was very precious in restoring a greater degree of normalcy to my existence as well as my outlook. The burden of parliamentary duty in 1951 was to tip the scales heavily toward the public side of life. Had I not enjoyed robust health and what was sometimes called "the constitution of an ox" it simply would not have been possible to maintain the pace.

It would have been impossible for me to maintain this crowded lifestyle for months on end without the unfailing help of Alice. She was always concerned as to how I could meet the demands of all kinds that were being made upon me by Parliament, the party, the public, my electors, my partners, my clients and my family. No one could have been more understanding and devotedly helpful.

It was not easy for the children to have a father away for five out of seven days each week and to be so preoccupied on the other two. I longed to be with them more. I was very unhappy to think that the opportunities which I was missing to be with them, to help them, and to demonstrate my affection for them would not return. By this time (early 1951) David was fourteen, Mary eleven and Donald eight. David was attending Lawrence Park Collegiate, and Mary and Donald were at John Ross Robertson Public School. I made it a rule to attend parents' functions in these schools and meetings of the Home and School Associations with Alice whenever possible.

During the sittings of Parliament I saw little of my partners, and this had regrettable consequences. While I was a partner I was absent often when I should have been readily available for consultation. They knew how hard I was working to do justice to my responsibilities to them and to our clients, but more and more they inevitably came to feel that I was detached from the firm and carrying on a separate practice. In the earlier days of my practice I was blessed with highly competent secretaries. Marriage in those days meant a total severance from further office employment, and so I lost Mary Simons and Muriel Hardcastle in turn to matrimony. Later I was fortunate to find Audrey Hanna, one of the most conscientious persons I have ever met. She placed duty before any personal interest. She never left the office at the end of the day without asking me if there was anything else I wished done. She was taking the night classes at the Toronto Bible College, of which I was a member of the board of governors. She wished to become a missionary, and decided to enrol for the full-time, three-year course. I lost her for most of that period, but on successful completion of her course her application for appointment with the Sudan Interior Mission was rejected on the grounds of health. This nearly broke her heart, but in time it brought her back to me.

One other friend deserves special mention. Emil Simonsen was my barber, but he was much more: he was an esteemed personal friend. Born in Denmark he had migrated to Canada and raised a Canadian family. At first he had his shop in the Federal Building, where the firm of Kingsmill, Mills, Price and Fleming was located. During the war he gave up barbering, but came to the office after hours to cut my hair in the library. Then he joined the barber shop at the Royal York Hotel, where he cut my hair on alternate Saturday afternoons for years until 1957. What happened then must be told later.

As I entered upon the year 1951 I had special reasons for hoping for a return to a single annual session lasting no more than six months at most. In December 1950, I was installed as the Worshipful Master of Ionic Lodge, A.F. and A.M. I had reached a senior office in the Scottish Rite. I still was president of the Business Men's Noonday Bible Club, meeting every Friday from mid-October until Easter. I arranged the meetings for the year with our various leaders, but was becoming worried over my irregular attendance. After serving the University of Toronto as a member of the Senate from 1944 to 1948, and the Upper Canada Bible Society as president from 1945 to 1947, and the Intervarsity Christian Fellowship as chairman from 1938 to 1943, I had been obliged to give up these challenging responsibilities which had

My mother, Maud Margaret (Wright) (1874-1955), in the year of my birth, 1905, at Exeter.

My father, Louis Charles Fleming (1871-1940), taken about 1915.

The three brothers in 1915: Robert (sixteen), Gordon (twelve), Donald (ten).

On graduation from the University of Toronto in 1925, Bachelor of Arts, Governor General's Gold Medallist, Breuls Gold Medallist, at age twenty.

Called to the Ontario bar, 1928, Silver Medallist and Christopher Robinson Memorial Scholar.

Member of Parliament for Toronto-Eglinton – in my first Session, 1945, studying in the Library of Parliament.

My wife, Alice Mildred (Watson), in 1948 during my first campaign for the Party leadership. (Photograph by Ashley & Crippen)

The children, David (eleven), Mary (nine), and Donald, Jr. (six), in 1948 with the candidate for the Party leadership. (Photograph by Norman James)

In Uganda, Africa, standing astride the equator, with a group of Canadian delegates to the Commonwealth Parliamentary Conference at Nairobi, Kenya, September 1954.

Minister of Finance, June 1957, the first photograph.

The Queen in an historic meeting with her Canadian cabinet, October 14, 1957, at Government House, accompanied by the newest member of Her Majesty's Privy Council for Canada, H.R.H. Prince Philip and Governor General Vincent Massey.

Royal reception at Government House, October 14, 1957, following the State Dinner.
(Ashley & Crippen)

As Minister in attendance on H.R.H. Princess Margaret on her visit to Ottawa, August 2-4, 1958. (Capital Press Service)

With Alice in Paris, December 1957, for the Heads of Government
meeting under NATO auspices.

"The Vision" lampooned by Macpherson in the Toronto Daily Star in the general election
campaign of 1958. (Reprinted with permission – the Toronto Star Syndicate)

A visit to Renfrew in the 1958 election campaign with Chief Big Flower, Princess Pheegee, Prince Running Deer, Chief White Eagle and Jim Baskin, MP.

Budget Night, June 17, 1958 – arriving at Parliament Buildings with Alice and Donald to deliver my first budget. (Dominion-Wide photographs)

At the Commonmwealth Trade and Economic Conference, September 1958, at Montreal, with three good friends, (l. to r.) Sir David Eccles, President of the Board of Trade, Derick Heathcote Amory, Chancellor of the Exchequer, and Morarji Desai, Minister of Finance of India.

With Prime Minister Diefenbaker and the Chancellor of the Exchequer, September 1958.

With Prime Minister Diefenbaker, 1959. (Canada Pictures Limited)

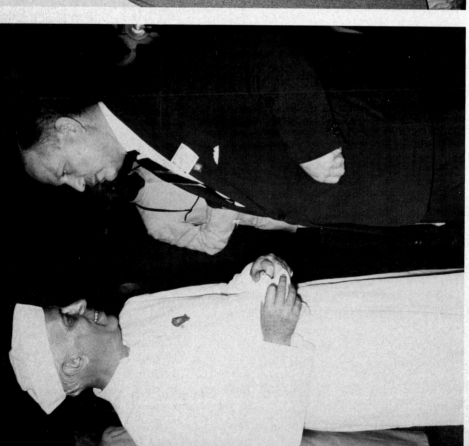

At New Delhi, India, October 10, 1958, with Prime Minister Nehru, at a reception at the President's Palace.

had a beneficial significance in my life. At Bloor Street Church I no longer served as general superintendent of the Sunday School, but I performed my duties as an elder faithfully.

Maintaining physical fitness always demands time and effort, and time was lacking. However, I carried out every morning a program of calisthenics and walked whenever possible. In the summer in Toronto I played tennis and lawn bowling in Lytton Park near home and was for many years a member of the North Toronto Tennis Club and the North Toronto Lawn Bowling Club. My attendance at meetings of the North Toronto Horticultural Society declined, but I worked hard to keep abreast of my gardening duties at 259 Glencairn Avenue. We had many flowers, but principally roses, peonies and Shasta daisies, and a large lawn to mow. The soil of North Toronto is a hard clay, and never easy to work. I still think of the delicious fruit produced by our peach tree in the back garden near the kitchen door.

I was always blessed with a hearty appetite, but I learned to control it. Selection in diet is of the highest importance. I have always had strong likes and dislikes in foods, fortunately leaning to plain foods, raw fruits and salads. I have always loved oatmeal porridge. A bowl of it is the right way to begin the day. I avoided alcohol totally, enjoying only milk and water at meals. I eschewed snacks between meals. I am thankful that with me good digestion waited on appetite, and health on both.

Back to Ottawa members trekked for the opening of Parliament on January 30, 1951. The session lasted five months. As Parliament had held two sessions in 1949 and again in 1950 members were confident there would be no more occasion for double sessions. Then one fine day St. Laurent announced Parliament would be called back in the autumn for another session. Personally, I was appalled. My heart sank, but back we went for a second session lasting from October 9 to December 29. Was there to be no let-up from these constant sittings?

There seemed no reason to expect the 1951 session to be other than lacklustre and routine in nature. But it proved to be quite otherwise: it produced some solid progress; it also saw some volcanic partisan battles. For me it also brought a new role in Parliament, a seat on the front bench, and an open difference with my party and leader.

Canada was not formally at war, but like other members of the United Nations she was engaged in hostilities in Korea. She had also been taught the need for massive rearmament in the face of Communist aggression in that country. The pitifully weak state into which the defences of the Western nations had been allowed to sink had been exposed, and the dangers confronting them in many areas, but most of all in Europe, were laid painfully bare. The speech from the throne on January 30 acknowledged "a further deterioration in the international situation." This, to put it mildly, was an understatement. The entry of Chinese forces into the fray in Korea opened up a new peril for the United Nations forces. Strategically and militarily the situation was very serious for our cause. Domestically the rearmament program, though just at its outset, was encountering or creating shortages of materials, and prices were rising rapidly. The government was failing in its task of giving the nation leadership. At times it was demanding extraordinary powers to cope with an emergency; at other times it was refusing to use them, and Mr. St. Laurent was declaring "we feel it is wise to proceed cautiously." George Drew chose to act as a spur upon a government which at times appeared hesitant and timid, and at others fully aware of the prevailing dangers.

The rearmament program meant a heavy increase in government expenditure, therefore more taxes. The declared objectives of the budget introduced on April 10 were "the pursuit of peace and the control of inflation." Defence costs were soaring. The budget proposed expenditure of $3.7 billion – $1.664 for defence and $2.036 for non-defence purposes. Taxes were increased all along the line, but the increases in the sales tax and commodity excise taxes were particularly unfortunate because they were certain to increase the cost of living. I roasted the government for their inaccurate budgeting, their failure to control non-defence expenditure, and the folly of their ill-timed and inflationary tax increases. The last of these criticisms was adopted by our members as a theme throughout the session in laying on the shoulders of the government much of the responsibility for the soaring cost of living.

Meanwhile at every opportunity the CCF was demanding the imposition of controls, particularly price controls. That was their solution for all domestic economic ills, and they lured George Drew and many Conservatives into a carefully laid trap, which for a time placed my links with my colleagues under a strain. At the conclusion of the throne speech debate George Drew proposed an amendment which deplored the failure of the government "to take effective measures to combat inflation and the rapidly rising cost of living."

The wording was purposely broad and general in scope. It left the Conservatives full latitude to put forward particular measures and policies to combat inflation, and the CCF was not slow to take advantage of this beckoning opportunity. Bert Herridge moved the addition of the following words: "such as the immediate reimposition of price controls, and the payment of subsidies where necessary, so as to protect the health and living standards of the Canadian people." We were trapped; we must vote either for or against price controls and subsidies. I made it quite clear in caucus that in my view we must vote against the CCF subamendment if we were to be consistent and true to the principles which we had proclaimed since the war, and I could not support the CCF now. But neither Drew nor the caucus was strong enough to follow the line of consistency and principle. On February 12 Drew made a speech of a specious nature, in which he pathetically tried to speak on both sides of the subject. I listened to his advocacy of selective and flexible controls with a heavy heart. It did not change my views in the least. Indeed, I viewed with something approaching scorn this departure from principle, and I refrained from participating in the debate. In my twelve years in the opposition it was the only time I ever did so.

The vote on the Herridge amendment was taken the next day. For the first time I deliberately absented myself on the vote. I went to my office and listened to the harsh grating ring of the division bell. When the phone rang in my office I did not answer it, expecting that it was the whip calling me to the House. To escape any more calls I betook myself to the washroom, where I found Rodney Adamson, who like myself was absenting himself from the vote and for the same reasons. The CCF subamendment was defeated on the division by a vote of 150 to 54, but it attracted the support of all the Progressive Conservative and Social Credit members in the House at the time. Incidentally, Diefenbaker also was absent, though I know not for what reasons. I did nothing to explain my absence, because I did not wish to embarrass George Drew or my other colleagues, but I was most unhappy. I hoped we had heard the last of the subject, but fate would not have it so. Worse lay in store and soon.

The government had available to it all the powers it might need in war or national emergency under the War Measures Act, but it was reluctant to proclaim that massive act, preferring a less drastic course. They therefore introduced a bill called the Emergency Powers Act, to confer extraordinary powers upon them, even at the cost of Parliament and the provinces, but powers more limited than those available under the War Measures Act. The bill none the less declared the existence of a national emergency. On February 20 on the resolution stage Drew faced

the issue that the time had come to apply wage and price controls or at least to set up a skeleton organization in anticipation thereof. He accepted as a fact that the imposition of controls was inevitable, sooner or later, and that Canada already had inflation by procrastination as the result of the government's failure to exercise the powers voted to it by Parliament in September 1950. It was a strong argument, but in my view it was not one that could properly come from a Conservative source. I had carefully considered my course and had concluded that honesty compelled me now to state my position openly. When the four leaders had spoken I rose, well realizing that I might be delivering my valedictory to my party. I warned the House not to expect too much from price controls. The fact that they had been successful during the war was no evidence that they would succeed now: in 1941 they began from a low price level, now they would be launched from a very high price level; in 1941 we were at war and the people were ready to support them, although even then their enforcement presented great difficulty; now they would not be successful without strong public support, and this would require a clarion call from the government, and no such clarion call was forthcoming; it was impossible to control prices without controlling wages and salaries, and to impose controls on wages and salaries would perpetuate existing injustices and anomalies. Having asserted my firm opposition to price control I turned positively and constructively to what could and should be done to grapple with runaway prices and outlined a needed five-point program of action:
– the Bank of Canada should use its power to restrict the credit extended by the chartered banks;
– stop the increase in the money supply;
– reduce government expenditure on non-defence items;
– adopt a pay-as-you-go policy, but avoid those forms of taxation that are directly inflationary; and
– seek nation-wide restraint on the part of the consumer and increased production.

I concluded by saying that in the face of the emergency, some powers of an extraordinary nature must be taken, but Parliament faced an inescapable duty to examine the powers sought, to scrutinize the legislation and to exercise utmost vigilance over the government's exercise of the powers it conferred.

I sat down confident that I had said what I ought to say, but prepared for a very adverse reaction. There was some hesitant applause from the Conservative benches, none from the CCF, and surprising applause from the Liberals. The bill was introduced without division, and after some debate, given second reading also without division. I took a parting shot at the bill at the committee stage, deploring this type of legislation, and asserting that I was not one of those who had been demanding that the government take and exercise wide powers, and that the rights of Parliament should be defended against trespass. The climax was reached on March 6, shortly before the bill finally passed. Stanley Knowles chided me for being one of the recipients of a flood of letters advocating price control. I corrected him sharply; I said I had received three letters on the subject during the past week. On the theme of inflation I repeated that anything the government could do under the bill would be less effective than measures they already could have taken outside it, and nothing said in the debate had convinced me that price controls would be effective:

> Short of all-out and total war you cannot make a system of this kind work, the kind of overall price controls advocated here, unless you have behind it an almost unanimous public support determined to see that it works effectively and that advantage is not taken of it by people who wish to enrich themselves by operating in the black market. . . . For myself I wish to make it as clear as I can that I am opposed to any freeze on wages and any freeze on salaries under present conditions or anything approaching present conditions.

I was listened to with close attention. At one point Jimmy Sinclair, parliamentary assistant to the Minister of Finance, interrupted to ask, "How did you vote on price control?" I replied, "You will not find my vote recorded on the CCF amendment." Sinclair persisted, and Doug Abbott swung around in his seat and shushed him. I decided to tell the whole story: "When the CCF brought in their amendment two weeks ago I did not vote. No vote of mine in this House has been given to any doctrinaire subscription to what I think to be a program which will not work under present conditions."

I had crossed the Rubicon. Jean François Pouliot congratulated me on my "courageous speech," and notes from the Liberal benches in similar vein came from Dave Croll, Léon J. Raymond and George Prudham. Lorenzo Paré, writing at length in *L'Action Catholique*, thought it "remarkable that one of the most brilliant members of the Opposition had stood true to his principles and fearlessly contradicted his leader's policy which was neither flesh nor fowl." He said that after my speech consternation reigned in the ranks of the Conservatives, who had been talking out of both sides of their mouths. He described my program for combatting inflation as a "masterly idea," then added this verdict: "An act of courage like Mr. Fleming's does not receive many popular plaudits, and last evening a very dim view was taken of it in his party. But the people always in the end recognize their true friends." The *Globe and Mail* the next morning concluded that my "stand seemed to vary considerably from that expressed by Mr. Drew." For this and the sense of having been true to my convictions and also true to the positions that for six years I had been authorized by the caucus to take on its behalf in the House I was prepared to pay a price.

Perhaps it was only my imagination, but I seemed to detect a coolness in the attitudes of my colleagues. I kept out of the way as far as possible, and I absented myself from a couple of meetings of caucus. I received no word of reproof from either George Drew or the whip, Clare Casselman. George was wise enough to ignore the whole episode. I dined one evening with René Beaudoin, who intimated to me that I would be welcomed into the ranks of the Liberals. I gave no encouragement to that thought, and nothing was ever heard of it again. After a couple of weeks I was back in the firing line, waging battle with the foe, and nothing was heard again of the episode over price control.

The next measure in the government program was a bill to establish the Department of Defence Production as "a separate Department to carry out the procurement functions needed for the defence program and to control essential materials." Howe cheerfully admitted that the bill conferred special, extensive powers. I suggested that the bill might have been introduced in briefer form, as follows, "The minister shall be and be deemed to be, to all intents and purposes whatever, omnipotent." Howe, of course, became minister of the new department.

This, perhaps, was behind a surprise visit I received in the middle of the session from Gordon Graydon, chairman of our caucus organization. He said that he and George were of opinion that Howe was "getting away with murder" in the House, that I was the one person in the ranks of the opposition who could stand up to him, therefore they wished me to give up social security and become opposition critic on trade and commerce, and defence production, indeed anything that was C.D. Howe's. I had been happy with my responsibility for social security and the Department of National Health and Welfare. I felt entirely at home with it and my relations with the minister, Paul Martin, were pleasant, though I maintained a strict vigil over him and his department. I suspected that trade and commerce and defence production would by comparison seem very impersonal. I was aware also that crossing swords constantly with Howe could become very unpleasant because of his violent temper. However, I could not reject this challenge, backed by George's request, so I accepted. It was also decided that along with my new role I would retain responsibility with respect to housing, radio broadcasting and old-age pensions. It was clear that my burden was not being lightened as the result of the change. One other unforeseen consequence followed from my disassociation with social security. In later years I came to be pictured as a "right wing" or orthodox Conservative. The media forgot that I began my career in Parliament as a specialist in and supporter of social security and welfare measures.

I made my first major speech on the subject of trade on May 21. It was in fact a keynote speech, and it set forth the basic lines of policy from which I never deviated in the remaining twelve years of my parliamentary career. The speech was made on a government motion to approve accession to the Torquay Agreements. The Geneva Agreements (General Agreement on Tariffs and Trade–GATT) had been negotiated by twenty-three countries in Geneva in 1947, the Annecy negotiations had been conducted by thirty-three countries at Annecy in 1949, and the Torquay negotiations by thirty-four countries at Torquay in 1951. The GATT and Annecy Agreements had never been approved by Parliament, although they had been examined in committee. The Torquay Agreements modifying both GATT and Annecy were referred to the Standing Committee on Banking and Commerce. The policies I endorsed in my speech, which was well received, might be very tersely put as follows:
– recognition of the vast importance to Canada of international trade;
– support for efforts to expand trade on a multilateral basis, and, therefore, endorsement of the GATT, Annecy and Torquay Agreements;
– support for the objective of freer trade, free trade being impracticable;
– promotion of a Trade and Economic Conference attended by the nations of the Commonwealth and dependent countries to restore lost markets;
– a better balance in our commodity trade with the United States, to avoid placing all our trading eggs in one basket.

The report of the Massey Commission on the Arts, Letters and Sciences, set up two years before, was tabled in the House on June 1. It had been eagerly awaited, particularly for solutions in two important fields – radio broadcasting and federal aid to education. It was too late in the first session to attempt a study of the report or to take action on its recommendations in general. However, the government deemed financial assistance to the CBC and the universities sufficiently urgent as to demand immediate action. In spite of the Conservative plea that the entire report should be studied as a whole and debated before any action was taken on its recommendations respecting broadcasting, the CBC in June was voted $1.5 million as a grant for general use and another $1.5 million to assist in the development of television. Later a Committee on Radiobroadcasting was set up, where the report was examined in detail, particularly as to finances and regulation. The Canadian Broadcasting Act was amended to provide CBC with annual grants of $6.25 million for five years. The government favoured the majority report as against the minority report of Dr. Arthur Surveyer, thus continuing regulation of all broadcasting by CBC, rather than by an independent regulatory body, which Dr. Surveyer and our party favoured. Television development was to be further delayed and no private TV broadcasting was to be permitted.

Federal grants to Canadian universities, recommended by the Massey Commission, stirred up a hornet's nest. Mr. St. Laurent proposed an interim grant, not to the provincial governments, but directly to the universities, to be divided among them on the basis of student registration. George Drew stepped in and warmly endorsed the proposal. A total grant of $7.1 million was voted for this purpose in ten minutes on June 30, minutes before prorogation. But all had acted without taking account of the views of Premier Duplessis, who made it abundantly clear that he considered this action an invasion of Quebec's dearly held autonomy in matters of education. Mr. St. Laurent endeavoured to defuse the bomb by disclaiming any intention ever to provide federal assistance to schools at levels below universities. In the end Duplessis forbade the universities of Quebec to accept the federal grants. This was one of the unsolved problems which I inherited six years later when I became Minister of Finance and of which I was able to achieve a solution in cooperation with the Quebec government, but it was after the redoubtable Maurice Duplessis had passed from the scene.

But the principal achievement of 1951 was the introduction of the old-age pension. It was the fruit of the admirable work done in 1950 by the Special Joint Committee of both Houses. The measure necessitated an amendment of the British North America Act, and this was accomplished by adding a new section 94A with the unanimous consent of all ten provinces. On June 4

Mr. St. Laurent announced that the government intended to proceed without delay with the required legislation and that an autumn session would be called for the purpose. George Drew urged that the government proceed at the present session, but evidently the government was not ready.

October 25, 1951, remains one of the great days in the history of the Parliament of Canada. Paul Martin that day introduced the resolution for the universal pension of $40 per month to all persons seventy years and over with residence qualifications; the necessary legislation had already been passed providing for a federal contribution up to 50 per cent of the cost of assistance up to $40 a month from age sixty-five to sixty-nine subject to a needs test. Doug Abbott followed with the financial proposals for establishing a fund to be built of individual contributions on a 2-2-2 formula, a 2 per cent sales tax, a 2 per cent personal income tax and a 2 per cent tax on corporate profits. I had the honour to lead for the official opposition. I gave the measure strong support and bestowed generous praise on the committee whose recommendations had been adopted almost intact. A remarkable spirit of unity, harmony, and common effort pervaded all the discussions, such as rarely occurs in Parliament. All parties, including the government, refrained from laying claim to credit for the achievement; credit was rather shared by all, and particularly the members of the 1950 committee. I was proud of the leading role I had played in that committee. Dave Croll, surveying the course followed, summed it all up in saying, "It was Parliament at its best." It was indeed. I think every member must have felt a glow of satisfaction and achievement. I certainly did.

Until April 6 I had never made a speech on gold. Alan Cockeram and Rodney Adamson, who had both had extensive experience in gold mining, were our accomplished spokesmen in the Twentieth Parliament. Alan's defeat in South York in 1949 was a severe loss to Parliament. Rodney was unable to be present on April 6 when George Prudham, Minister of Mines and Technical Surveys, introduced a bill to extend the Emergency Gold Mining Assistance Act for a year. The party workhorse was as usual summoned to fill the breach. I went to the heart and fundamentals of the problem faced by the Canadian gold mining industry, criticized the emergency, temporary, short-time, hand-to-mouth, stop-gap approach of the government, and complained that the burden of supporting the International Monetary Fund's policies was being laid to an unfair degree on Canada, and in turn on Canada's gold mines. I concluded on a strong note:

I say that the case, on balance, is overwhelming for a substantial movement at the present time in the direction of a freer market for Canadian gold . . . I do not think for one moment that we can any longer submit to a mere continuation of the present structure and policy of the International Monetary Fund. Unless there is some change in the price of gold at which we may sell our production in the markets of the world, then it seems to me that we must pound on the doors of the International Monetary Fund, and of those responsible for its administration. And, unless there is some change in their policy, then I think this Parliament must be prepared to take action.

The speech was years ahead of its time. George Prudham was taken by surprise, not having expected to see me taking part and not being ready to discuss IMF policy. On June 18 I made another lengthy speech in the debate on second reading. My command of this new subject was now established. It was destined to become an official responsibility of mine in later years, and the last reference I ever heard to the same statute came while I sat in an inconspicuous seat in the public gallery of Parliament and heard debate on "the Fleming formula" in the autumn of 1963.

The opening of the Prime Minister's official residence was not the only event that distinguished my birthday that year. The *Montreal Star* chose the afternoon of May 23 to announce my resignation, and to give it a headline, "Toronto M.P. Soon to Resign." There had been occasions and there were in future to be not a few times when a suitable opportunity to resign would have been welcome, but May 23, 1951, was not one of them. How the notion originated in the mind of a journalist at that time I know not. I immediately nipped the rumour in the bud, issuing the following terse statement: "I have heard with surprise that rumours are being circulated that I intend to resign my seat in the House of Commons at the conclusion of the present Session. I have neither expressed nor formed any such intention. I hope this statement will put a stop to the rumour." I heard no more of it.

Mr. St. Laurent had already shown himself capable of reversing himself in matters of policy. He now did a volte-face on the subject of petition of right. The crown could not be sued in the courts. They were the King's courts. So the claimant was obliged to petition the crown for leave to sue. The Canadian Bar Association and Diefenbaker had long urged the removal of this archaic survival. On December 13, 1945, I had asked St. Laurent, at that time Minister of Justice, when we might look for action to eliminate petitions of right in actions against the crown, to which he had flatly replied, "Not while I am Minister of Justice." Garson on May 28 introduced a bill the purpose of which he described as "to place the Crown in right of Canada in petition of right proceedings in the Exchequer Court in substantially the same position as an ordinary litigant." Naturally we welcomed Mr. St. Laurent's change of heart even though the bill did not go far enough to satisfy Diefenbaker and me.

Just before the conclusion of the first session four pending by-elections were called – in Winnipeg South Centre, Queen's (PEI), Waterloo South and Brandon. Only Waterloo South had previously been held by a Conservative. The news that we had won all four seats hit the House of Commons like a clap of thunder. Conservatives were elated, and not least of all George Drew, who had endured much in the two years since the general election. "One swallow doesn't make a summer," warned Coldwell rather disconsolately. We Conservatives held a victory celebration that evening in our offices. The by-elections brought not only a needed addition to our numbers in the House, but considerably augmented our debating power, and we were joined by Gordon Churchill, Angus MacLean, Howie Meeker and Walter Dinsdale. Three of the four were destined to become ministers.

Mr. St. Laurent's announcement of a second session in the autumn occasioned an immediate exchange of conflicting opinions. The new session would entitle members to an additional sessional indemnity, and this may have been the real reason for following this course. The Prime Minister may have been facing some restlessness among his members over the prospect of sitting eight or nine months out of twelve, or he may himself have genuinely thought one indemnity inadequate. At any rate, the press thought the payment of a second indemnity was the real purpose behind Mr. St. Laurent's announcement on June 4. George Drew was very critical of this action. However, Coldwell propounded the CCF view that membership in the House "can no longer be regarded as something in the nature of a sideline to a particular profession or business. Membership . . . today is a full-time position, and members must devote their entire time, sooner or later, to the business of the country." I could not allow this comment to pass unchallenged. It was acceptable enough to the financially secure or those members who could not earn outside Parliament as much as their indemnity, or those who were comfortably housed with their families in Ottawa or had no family responsibilities. I flatly took issue with Coldwell:

> If the time ever comes when the House accepts the view that membership is a full-time position you will thereby automatically

be closing the doors of public life, of public careers, to a great many people who cannot afford to take the risks and insecurity of public life. . . . Membership in the House of Commons will be open only to those who are fortunate enough to be so independent financially that they can give twelve months a year full time to their work as members of Parliament or to those who have no family responsibilities and can somehow get along on the somewhat meagre amount that is left out of the sessional indemnity after the expenses and cost of keeping up two establishments and the other financial burdens of public office are met. There is nothing that can be more anti-democratic in its conception than anything which will confine public life to people who are on the one hand possessed of independent means and are completely independent of any financial worries, or to those on the other hand who do not have the responsibilities that most of us have, and somehow can eke out an existence on what may be left out of the sessional indemnity. . . .

What we must do in shaping the course of parliamentary affairs and parliamentary work in the future is to try to see to it that the doors of public life are not closed to people who, having family responsibilities and responsibilities in other respects, are nevertheless capable of making a most valuable contribution to public life in the House of Commons. If you shut off from public service people bearing these responsibilities, then make no mistake about it, democracy will pay the price in Canada.

It has been said that the government determines when Parliament should be called to meet, but that the opposition determines when Parliament shall prorogue. It was one thing for Mr. St. Laurent to call a second session, commencing October 9; it was quite another matter for him to terminate it. In addition to the business which was the declared reason for sitting in the autumn the government through some brainstorm allowed an entirely new item to find its way into the program – the subject of resale price maintenance, in other words, the practice whereby manufacturers determined the price at which their goods should be retailed.

The origin of the government's interest in this long-standing business practice remains obscure. The MacQuarrie Royal Commission was at the time reviewing the Combines Investigation Act and its operations and the government asked its opinion of resale price maintenance. Without hearing any evidence on the subject the commission recommended its prohibition. The government seized on this interim report as something warranting legislative action at the autumn session. A joint committee of both Houses was appointed on November 6 to study the commission's interim report and appropriate legislation. The Conservative members from the House were Ellen Fairclough, Gordon Churchill, Davie Fulton, Doug Harkness, George Hees and, as usual, myself. Our members urged a widening of the scope of the committee's task; we suspected the purpose of setting it up was to distract public attention from the government's failure to cope with inflation and to make it appear that the Liberals were really doing something effective to fight high prices. Mr. St. Laurent seemed to have swept away the ground from under any such hope by acknowledging that the abolition of resale price maintenance would probably not have any effect on retail prices, but Liberal members made the claim anyway. Garson and Jimmy Sinclair headed the long list of Liberal appointees to the committee.

If in creating the old-age pension Parliament was at its best, most assuredly in dealing with resale price maintenance Parliament was at its worst. Sinclair was elected chairman of the committee, and quickly abandoned any pretence of impartiality. It swiftly became clear that the minds of the Liberal members were made up before the hearings began. The committee majority declined to hear witnesses, particularly from retail business, who wished to be heard, treated witnesses supporting resale price maintenance in a hostile manner, and closed off the hearings without hearing witnesses who had a right to be heard. The chairman permitted himself to apply the guillotine.

The committee sat from November 13 to December 7, when it simply closed down over the loud protests of the Conservative members and reported to the House in favour of the government's legislation to ban resale price maintenance. On December 17 the debate on the bill commenced. Garson presented the evidence in a very one-sided manner and quoted statistics which had been refused to the minority on the committee. He contended that the practice of resale price maintenance tended to result in the formation of combines and in higher prices to the public. Davie Fulton led off for us and reviewed the unfair way the committee's hearings had been conducted and argued that as important available evidence had not been heard the committee could not reach a proper conclusion. Moreover, the evidence indicated that the real culprit was the practice of loss-leadering. He moved that the bill be given a six months' hoist. Then Sinclair as chairman took the floor. He indulged in as partisan a performance as the Commons is ever likely to witness. Instead of endeavouring to be an objective chairman reporting fairly he was bitter, loud, prejudiced and wild in the charges he hurled at the Conservatives. It had been arranged that I would follow Sinclair whenever he spoke, as it seemed to us likely that he would behave as he did. When I spoke I pointed out that after Sinclair's performance it must now be obvious how utterly hopeless it was to obtain a fair hearing in the committee, and that the "great conglomeration of distorted references to evidence and abuse of witnesses" heard from Sinclair in the House were in keeping with what we had had to bear from him day in and day out in the committee. I denounced the MacQuarrie Interim report as, in the words of the Trades and Labour Congress, "a contrived argument to support a preconception." I concluded by reviewing the evidence and denouncing the government for trying to make a scapegoat of the small retailer. The House was in an uproar. The feelings which had been aroused were slow to subside.

The debate continued throughout December 18 and 19, with the CCF supporting the government. At the opening of the sitting on December 20 Stanley Knowles stunned the House by moving that the House continue to sit without recess and not adjourn at 10 p.m. This would mean a continuous sitting for twenty-four hours till 11 a.m. on the 21st. He piously announced that the purpose of the motion was to provide an opportunity for members who felt they had the right to be home with their families on Christmas Day to vote on the contentious issue under debate. The motion was intended to have the effect of exhausting Conservative members to the point where they would be unable to continue the debate. Everyone wished to be home for Christmas; that could be accomplished simply by adjourning the House for a week. Knowles's motion so completely suited the purposes of the government as to suggest collusion between them, but this was denied by him. He never adequately explained, however, why he came to the aid of the government.

The motion, however, was debatable, and I leaped to my feet. After the uproar had subsided I began to speak and continued long enough so that Drew and others could recover from the shock of surprise and decide tactically what to do. This held off a snap vote on the motion and made possible what followed. Mr. St. Laurent obliged by announcing that if the business of the House was not completed the next day he would give notice under the closure rule that it would be applied on December 27. The Liberals had stifled discussion in the committee; they were about to stifle debate in the House.

The motion and the ultimatum had remarkable results. The Conservatives, notwithstanding their limited numbers and the desire of everyone to head home for Christmas, courageously resolved to stand up and fight. With the aid of an amendment introduced by George Nowlan the debate was continued until 1.00 p.m., when the House under the rules automatically stood adjourned to 2.30. I had the floor and at 2.30 with the approval of the leader and caucus I offered a compromise – to extend the evening sitting by two hours. This proposal was made in the spirit of cooperation, but was ignored. At 4.00 p.m. the debate on the Nowlan amendment collapsed, and it met defeat by a vote of 101 to 27. Thereupon Ellen Fairclough moved another amendment, and the debate was still in progress at 6.15, when the House automatically stood adjourned until 8.00 p.m. It would still be possible to force an all-night sitting unless the motion was still under debate at 10 p.m. At 8.40 the debate on Ellen's amendment collapsed, and it was defeated by a vote of 91 to 24. Gordon Churchill then stepped in with another amendment, the debate on which was still continuing at 10 p.m., when the House automatically stood adjourned until the next day at 11 a.m. We Conservatives were jubilant. We had defeated an unworthy stratagem to deprive members of their rights. All that the government and CCF had accomplished was to waste a precious day.

The debate on the combines bill continued on the 21st. The Fulton amendment for a six months' hoist was defeated and the House adjourned until December 27. At that time the debate on the combines legislation was completed and the bill was adopted. The remaining business of the session was disposed of briefly, and prorogation was held on the 29th. Parliament Hill was quickly deserted. Many members, of course, did not return for the three days of sitting after Christmas. Those who had gone to more distant homes could be excused for not returning, but no member could be excused for not returning from Toronto. The whole episode threw a cloud over Christmas in the Fleming home. When New Year's Eve came I looked back on 1951 as the most difficult and the most exacting and in some ways the most unpleasant of the years I had spent since entering Parliament.

There were some redeeming features. My relations with George Drew were totally and happily restored, and I had made that known publicly. On June 8 one Liberal had been imprudent enough to say that George and I were in accord for the first time in that session. This gave me an opportunity to leap to my feet on a question of privilege and to say, "That is absolutely untrue. The Leader of the Opposition commands my confidence and my loyalty as my leader." This brought applause from the Conservative benches.

The arrogance of the government, supported by an enormous and submissive majority, was growing. Notwithstanding the efforts of the Liberal party's advertising agents to picture the Prime Minister as the kindly and courtly "Uncle Louis," we were finding him at times irascible and petulant. Jimmy Gardiner, anxious to nominate himself to a triumvirate with the Prime Minister and C.D. Howe, had modestly stated on March 20, "As long as the three of us remain where we are, I think it will be fairly generally agreed across the country that we have an exceedingly good government." But it remained for C.D. Howe as usual to put his foot in it on May 21 by taunting Howard Green, "If we wanted to get away with it who would stop us?"

CHAPTER TWENTY

Scant Respite

After barely a fortnight at home members returned to Ottawa, but not to resume battle in the Commons. It was for a much pleasanter purpose, to meet Winston Churchill, then on an official visit to Ottawa. Historically speaking it is a pity that Parliament at the time was not in session, so that the British Prime Minister might have addressed a joint session of both Houses. However, on January 14, 1952, he did address a dinner at the Château Laurier to which the Prime Minister invited all senators, MPs, and senior public servants.

It was the first time that I had met Churchill. It was all too obvious that he was tired. He did not stand in the receiving line, where all the guests had hoped to exchange a handshake with him, but soon after arrival made his way slowly to the nearest chair and remained seated until all moved in to dinner in the adjoining ballroom. All this was acutely disappointing to the guests, and two of them decided to do something about it. My friend Sarto Fournier and I, lending each other courage, presented ourselves to Churchill, and shook hands with him. He was a bit gruff at first, but asked Sarto what party he belonged to. On Sarto confessing that he was a Liberal, Churchill replied, "Humpf! I was one once, but I reformed."

At the dinner Churchill showed no signs of fatigue. Perhaps earlier he had been conserving his strength. His speech was rather intimate, and not too heavy. He spoke to us as a fellow parliamentarian. I recall vividly two passages. "Democracy," said he, "is a poor system of government. It is slow, inefficient, and often unjust, but this may be said of it, that all other forms of government are worse." At another point he described the unique value of the constitutional monarchy. "The best form of democracy," he quipped, "is the constitutional monarchy. In days of national victory the people turn out and cheer the King.

In days of national defeat they turn the government out." His sympathetic audience roared with laughter.

Twenty-three days later King George VI died. He had never sought or expected to be king, but he will be remembered as a courageous man who overcame the disability and embarrassment of a stammer, and became an understanding and deeply beloved monarch. Glowing tributes were paid in Parliament to his service to all his peoples while expressions of loyalty and sympathy to our new monarch, Queen Elizabeth II, were offered. George Drew, a loyal subject to the core, was eloquent. On this and other occasions where the royal family was involved, Mr. St. Laurent was superb. He was devoted to the constitutional monarchy; there was no creeping republicanism in the Liberal party in his day. That came later with the advent to power of a man of different outlook.

The term of office of Governor General Lord Alexander of Tunis came to an end, and he and Lady Alexander left Canada early in 1952. Alice and I had the honour of being their guests at dinner at Government House on December 5 and expressing our farewells to them then. They had discharged their onerous duties with distinction, honour and success. I had the privilege of meeting this hero, one of the greatest of the Second World War, several times later in both Britain and Canada.

There had been many an informal discussion as to whether to depart from past practice and appoint a Canadian governor general. As expected, Mr. St. Laurent followed the new course with the Queen's approval, and Vincent Massey was installed in the office on February 28, 1952, in a colourful ceremony in the Senate chamber. Some of our members were quite upset and declared they would boycott all functions at Government House. I took a very different view. I recognized that Britain had sent us some very distinguished governors general, and I hoped that the office would be regarded as important enough to justify the appointment to it of a member of the royal family. My choice was Elizabeth, the Queen Mother. Failing that, the appointment of a Canadian was inevitable in my view, particularly in the mood of the St. Laurent government. My concern was that the high position should not be cheapened or degraded by partisan political considerations. I had no doubt whatever that Vincent Massey, although he had actively engaged in politics at an earlier stage in life, was so devoted to the Crown and the Queen that he would strive always to serve them worthily. Jim Macdonnell, Vincent Massey's brother-in-law (though he always contended that the fact that they had married sisters did not make them brothers-in-law), went so far as to write Vincent a letter seriously urging him not to damage the office by accepting it. To this unusual missive he received no response. I took the position that Vincent Massey was the personal representative of the Queen, and we could not show disrespect for him without failing in our duty to her. He proved to be an excellent governor general, and in later years he and I became personal friends. The danger, however, remains that in the hands of a prime minister who is not fully and loyally attached to the monarchy the appointment may not be sufficiently detached from partisan influences.

Parliament met on February 28 and sat until July 4. This session proved to be a pleasant contrast to the interminable sittings of 1951. Moreover, the House met in a much more relaxed and pleasant mood than in the stormy Christmas season of 1951. Resale price maintenance had largely dropped from conversation, and the anger which the government's bill to prohibit the retail practice had fortunately subsided. Hostilities in Korea appeared to have come to a standstill. The parliamentary agenda outlined in the speech from the throne looked lighter than its predecessor. A severe outbreak of foot-and-mouth disease among the cattle in western Canada absorbed Parliament's attention. In the by-election occasioned by the death of Art Smith the Conservatives had retained Calgary West by a good margin, and the new member, Carl O. Nickle, took his seat at the opening. A leading authority on the oil and natural gas resources of western Canada and a competent speaker, Carl quickly made his mark on Parliament.

My first speech of the session was in the debate on the throne speech. My themes were not new. I made a plea for better organization of the business of the House and more extensive use of committees to assist the House in its work, particularly in reviewing the government's estimates. I urged that there be no more autumn sessions and advocated the appointment of women to government boards. Then I indicted the government for its loose guesswork in budgeting, its failure to cope with unemployment or to eliminate waste and extravagance, and demanded a reduction in taxes, particularly the removal of discriminatory taxes and those which added to the cost of living. In the face of a developing and unplanned budget surplus I quoted the great Philip Snowden who, when Chancellor of the Exchequer, declared that any government that takes so much as a sixpence more than it has budgeted is taking money under false pretences.

The budget presented a month later was evidence that the government was continuing on its spendthrift ways, and no amount of criticism from the opposition would deflect it.

Although combines legislation lay outside the scope of my caucus responsibilities, in view of the role I had played in resisting the government steamroller on resale price maintenance, I inherited another responsibility. This subject was part of Diefenbaker's responsibility, but he had left for the West at the time and missed the climax of the battle over resale price maintenance. The burden of leading the opposition on the government's bill to revise the Combines Investigation Act based on the report of the MacQuarrie Royal Commission was placed squarely on my shoulders. I carried the lead at all stages. Diefenbaker took no part in the proceedings at any stage.

Housing received some attention. For the first time the annual report of Central Mortgage and Housing Corporation was referred to the Banking and Commerce Committee, where I had a field day. Although the terms of reference to the committee prevented the calling of witnesses from the construction industry or others outside the corporation, Mr. Mansur, the president of CMHC, was a very competent and cooperative witness, and the hearings produced some timely and useful evidence. Mr. Mansur testified that in the six-year period from 1946 to 1951, net family formations in Canada reached 513,000, whereas new housing units completed totalled 495,887, showing a deficit of 17,113 units. In the postwar period, therefore, we were still falling behind current housing needs, and the backlog was growing. Moreover, the rate of new starts in 1952 was less than in 1951 even in the face of a plentiful supply of building materials of all kinds. The Estimates of the Department of Resources and Development afforded the first opportunity during the session for a debate in the House on housing, and I led with a review of conditions and the evidence heard by the committee. Regrettably, it was the second last day of the session, and the debate was too brief to do justice to the importance of the subject.

The part played by their political activities and party allegiance in appointment of barristers to the bench came under scrutiny in an excellent debate on May 29 on the Estimates of the Department of Justice. It was precipitated by an article on the subject written by General J.A. Clark, president of the Canadian Bar Association and a former Conservative MP. I stated my views on the subject and have never had cause to depart from them. I followed those views when I was Minister of Justice in 1962-63. Judges should be appointed on the basis of ability and character.

Political views should not be regarded as either a qualification or a disqualification.

Retirement pensions on a contributory basis for MPs were with the support of leaders of all parties studied by the Committee on Banking and Commerce. A favourable recommendation from that source was adopted by the House with only three dissenting votes, Fulton, Green and Churchill. Diefenbaker did not vote. I supported the proposal, believing it to be a sound method of helping to attract good men to enter and remain in public life. I qualified for a contributory pension of $300 per month after serving seventeen sessions in the House, payable on my departure from public life. Parliament has gone far since that time in reducing the length of service required. In increasing the pension substantially in 1970 former members like myself, already retired, were omitted. In April 1983 my pension is $760.28 per month, or $570.21 after income tax deduction.

It is unparliamentary to say that an honourable member is stupid, but it is not unparliamentary to say that what he has said is stupid. On June 30 Dr. McCann, Minister of National Revenue, thought he was being very smart in saying, "It is an entirely barren township. . . . I suggest that the name be changed to 'Fleming.' " At this flash of wit he laughed merrily. The chairman ruled there was no insult in the words. The next day in another connection I commented, "The Minister was too stupid to take it in." Dr. McCann was furious and demanded a withdrawal. After some angry discussion I said very quietly and with pretended contrition, "Mr. Chairman, I always like to make a contribution to peace and harmony in the House of Commons; and if it will assuage the injured feelings of the Minister of National Revenue, for what I said I will substitute the statement that the minister made a very stupid remark." McCann was so angry he could scarcely contain himself. The chairman ruled, however, that I had gone as far as the rules required. McCann was left muttering to himself and red in the face.

The most contentious issue of the session proved to be redistribution. The decennial census had shown that Saskatchewan had lost population and was over-represented in the House. It is not very pleasant for a province to suffer a reduction in the number of members to which it is entitled, and equally unpleasant for its members. To mitigate the loss the government proposed to amend the British North America Act, and to do so without consulting the other provinces. We were again faced with the same issue which had divided the House in 1946 and later years. I led for the party in the debate, and offered an amendment, to defer consideration until the principle of the bill "has been made the subject matter of consultation between the Dominion and the Provinces." It was defeated by a vote of 121 to 27. Diefenbaker courageously voted for the amendment even though the rights of his province, Saskatchewan, might have been hurt or delayed by it.

The process of redistribution then commenced. A special committee was appointed to revise riding boundaries in all provinces. As usual I was pushed onto the committee. The Liberal majority proceeded in the most barefaced way to gerrymander the ridings of a number of our leading Conservative members, Diefenbaker, Fulton, Nowlan, Charlton, Catherwood and others. On June 28 George Drew moved for the appointment of an independent commission to effect the redistribution, and to take it out of party politics. I spoke in strong terms in favour of the commission, basing my views on what had been happening in the committee. I concluded:

> While I did not come to this decision quickly or lightly I am satisfied, on the strength of an extremely unhappy and disappointing experience as a member of the Committee on Redistribution appointed by this House, that the present method can no longer be retained. It is no longer entitled to any respect on the part of the public or of this House. It is at best a piecemeal method. It is not a method that is based upon principle. It is a method that is based largely upon political expediency. I say the time has come to discard this method and at least give a fair trial to another method such as the alternative that has been found to work in an eminently satisfactory way in the United Kingdom and in our sister nations of the Commonwealth.

But the Liberals with their big majority were determined to have redistribution on their terms. So I opened up an attack on June 30 on what I variously described as the political surgery, the abortions, the distortions, the juggling, the gymnastics practised by the Liberals in their own party interests, and declared their conduct was devoid of principle. The House was in an uproar. The Liberals hurled abuse at me, and I denounced their sanctimonious pretensions of innocence. We lost the vote, but not without satisfaction. Some of our members assured me my performance was "fabulous." I spoke out of deep indignation.

Moreover, instead of respecting the strict independence of the chief electoral officer, the Liberals brought in legislation to authorize the government within certain limits to determine his salary. I denounced this measure affecting an officer of Parliament. That was the end of redistribution 1952 model, and a sordid story it was.

214

The session did not end without another encouraging success and reinforcement for our numbers and debating strength in the House. Six spring by-elections were held in Quebec, Ontario and New Brunswick. All six seats had been held by Liberals. They retained two and lost the other four to us. The CCF won nothing. We were jubilant. We had fared much better than we had dared to expect. On June 12 the six new members took their places, and we welcomed Gage Montgomery, Albany Robichand, Mike Starr and Paul Spence. Mike Starr was destined to become a minister. Albany Robichand proved himself an eloquent debater in the House. I took part in due time in his appointment to the Supreme Court of New Brunswick. No one, not even George Drew, could have been more pleased than I over these four resounding victories.

On July 4 instead of proroguing, the House adjourned to November 20. George Drew had opposed this course. I had spoken strongly against any resumption of sittings in the autumn having regard to the regrettable experience with the autumn session of 1951. St. Laurent answered that, the coronation having been set for June 2, 1953, and as many MPs would be attending it, the House should meet in the autumn and have the address in reply to the speech from the throne and the preliminaries completed so that immediately after the New Year the regular course of the normal business of the House could be proceeded with in an attempt to have Parliament prorogue by the end of April or early in May. This seemed to make sense, but the Prime Minister might have added that it would also give the government more latitude in selecting the date of the 1953 general election.

It was with feelings of relief that I packed my papers and effects and headed homeward. The children were already in summer camp for the month of July. I spent the month putting matters in good shape at the office. August we spent on Balsam Lake near Coboconk in a pleasant cottage. A tennis court guaranteed a daily match if the balls weren't lost in the poison ivy, and every afternoon I swam across the lake, accompanied with increasing frequency by David and Mary. Donald acted as boatman, as became the fisherman of the family.

In July my good friend Joe Fisher died in Toronto. He had been my closest friend in the press gallery when I entered Parliament. The *Telegram* moved him to Toronto two years later and I missed his presence and his advice keenly. He had been most helpful in advising me when I was considering seeking the party leadership in 1948.

Among the former colleagues who had been defeated in the general election of 1949 one whom I most missed was John T.

Hackett. At the close of the session I was delighted and grateful to receive a note from John: "Dear Donald. Just a word to tell of my keen appreciation of your excellent work during the Session. You are well-informed, aggressive and unafraid. The opponents like you because you are fearless and fear you because you work. It's unfair to be separated from wife and children, but such is the price of glory. Your friend, John T. Hackett."

The time had come for another Commonwealth Parliamentary Conference, and Canada was to be the host. I was still the Conservative member on the executive committee of the Canadian branch of the Commonwealth Party Association, and George Drew designated me as one of the two Conservative delegates to the conference, the other being Gordon Higgins. The conference was held in September. Elaborate tours across Canada were planned for the visiting delegates from all countries of the Commonwealth with the local provincial branch acting as host for the part of the tour in its province. At Ottawa I devoted my efforts to playing host to the visitors. A few, like Harold Holt of Australia, had attended the London conference in 1948, and I was delighted to see them again. Most, however, were attending their first conference, and the majority of these were visiting Canada for the first time. We Canadians were determined that nothing should be lacking in hospitality to our distinguished visitors, and we were equally anxious that the deliberations of the conference itself should measure up to the high standard set at the London conference. Just one discordant note jarred the atmosphere of the conference. A mistake had been made in inviting the Republic of Ireland to send delegates. They came apparently prepared to make utmost trouble. They objected to their seating, to the label "Eire" and to almost everything else. They were a very disagreeable delegation. The U.S. Congress sent delegates to the last two days' sittings. They acquitted themselves with great credit and in the most friendly manner.

Ottawa suffered a heat wave during the conference. The Senate Chamber and the rooms at the Château Laurier remained at a comfortable temperature, but the heat out-of-doors was almost too much for some of the delegates. It was surprising that those who appeared to feel the heat most were men who came from warm countries. Perhaps the humidity was a trying experience for them, but they mopped themselves constantly and declared they had never encountered such heat.

The discussions were profitable, but I think the greatest benefit afforded by the conference was the opportunity to establish terms of personal friendship with legislators from the other countries. This proved a most valuable privilege. Thirty years later I still exchange communications with some of the survivors.

Many delegates to the conference were returning home by charter flight to London at the beginning of October. Two seats were surplus, and I was given the opportunity to occupy one of them. I responded with alacrity. The delegates had all enjoyed their visit to Canada. I doubt if there has been a better Commonwealth Parliamentary Conference and tour than that of 1952. Gratitude to Canada was on every delegate's lips.

Steps were taken by party headquarters to draw attention to what was described as my "fact-finding mission." George Drew was already in London, and we were to confer on the economic problems of the United Kingdom and western Europe. I was to meet leading trade and economic authorities. The British United Press reported:

> The fact that the Progressive Conservative leader is enlarging his fact-finding mission to a two-man project is interpreted on Parliament Hill as significant indication that he believes the field on which he is working is one of major possibilities as well as of key importance.
>
> His selection of Fleming as his co-crusader in the issue is also looked upon as a clue to the direction in which Progressive Conservative trade and currency policies are veering. Fleming not only ranks as one of the most effective Parliamentarians in the P.C. group in the Commons; in addition, he is recognized as the leading exponent in it of the policy of close Commonwealth connection.

This build-up was very helpful to me. My trip was given a special status. The party derived great benefit from it, but did not contribute a cent to my expenses. I received, however, great assistance from Canada House and our diplomatic representatives in West Germany and France in making appointments and arranging program and travel. I doubt if one short fortnight was ever put to better use. I was privileged to confer with some of the leading figures on the European stage at the time and to come to grips with the problems besetting western Europe, many of them of Russian creation.

The formation of the North Atlantic Treaty Organization (NATO) was the great outstanding fact and achievement since my first visit to Europe in 1948. By 1952 General Matthew B. Ridgway was Supreme Commander Allied Forces in Europe, and General Ismay, Churchill's personal chief of staff throughout the war, had been persuaded by Churchill much against his own wishes to become secretary-general. The two men worked in close cooperation. "Pug" Ismay handled all government relations. I had extensive interviews with both Ismay and Ridgway in Paris. The infancy of NATO and the improvisation necessary in creating even temporary headquarters in Paris were well illustrated by the fact that while General Ismay and I conversed in his office, showers of dust fell upon us as the October wind blew the insulating material through the walls.

The other outstanding changes which had occurred since 1948 were the return of a Conservative government in Britain and the economic recovery on the continent, particularly in West Germany.

In London Parliament was in session, so I had an unrivalled opportunity to watch both Houses and to feel the pulse and the moods of the mother of Parliaments. I enjoyed the privilege of a conference with Anthony Eden and his assessment of the problems facing western Europe and Britain in particular. I had a good visit also with my friend Derick Heathcote-Amory, now Minister of Overseas Trade. Sir Arthur Beverley Baxter was an old friend of my wife's family, and I knew his mother and sister Grace well. They were neighbours of ours on Glencairn Avenue. Bax showed me great kindness. In his column in the *Financial Post* he wrote, "A welcome visitor to London last week was Donald Fleming, who sits for the Toronto riding of Eglinton at Ottawa. He saw Eden and other M.P.s and attended a debate. . . . He has a quiet humour and an alert mind which impressed the Britishers at Westminster."

I found the pace of public business at Westminster noticeably faster than at Ottawa. The daily question period in particular moved very swiftly. The Speaker, aided by the much smaller size of the chamber, recognized members with remarkable speed, and the members were ready and quick to put their supplementary questions. They were no more orderly than at Ottawa, and they could be quickly aroused to a chorus of dissent and disapproval. Speeches tended to be more matter-of-fact and less rhetorical. At one of the sittings Churchill entered carrying a long ear-horn, which on taking his seat he proceeded to use. I wasn't sure whether his purpose was to improve his hearing or to steal the show; whichever it was he certainly attracted the entire attention of the House, to the disconcerted annoyance of the Labour MP who was putting a question at the time.

Britain was faced with serious problems. She had borne a heavy share of the cost of defeating the Axis powers. Much of her industrial plant was obsolescent, and she was fighting hard to retain her markets. Her currency was losing value; it was proving unequal to the task imposed upon it at Bretton Woods as an international reserve currency. Her taxation was stifling. Yet my confidence in Britain was renewed. I knew that the world needed and would continue to need her leadership.

I flew from London to Düsseldorf, which was fast becoming the financial heart of West Germany. At Bonn, formerly a quiet university town, and now bulging at the seams as the chosen political capital, I attended meetings of the Bundestag and Bundesrat, the two houses of the German Parliament. I found Cologne of great interest, and I was fascinated by the twin-towered cathedral, which was still undergoing repair of war damage. We then drove two hundred miles through the pleasant German countryside to Hanover, where I spent an evening with Brigadier Geoffrey Walsh, Commander of the Canadian 27th Infantry Brigade, our first contribution to the NATO defence forces. Germany's recovery in the four previous years was unmistakable and impressive. True, American financial assistance had done much for the German economy, but the most important ingredient in the recovery was hard work on the part of the people. They were working long hours; and there were no labour troubles. The production of West Germany already exceeded that of prewar Germany in its entirety. The cities were brighter; food was ample, and the people well dressed and more cheerful. Production in the Ruhr exceeded its prewar production.

I wondered what changes would meet my eye in Berlin. I recalled the airlift of 1948 and the courage and determination of Britain and the United States in standing up to the Russians. I found tremendous progress had been made. Goods in the shops were plentiful, food was reasonably sufficient, fuel was far more plentiful, and substantial headway was being made with rebuilding. The principal streets were ablaze at night with lights. The national air lines of almost all countries in western Europe were operating into Templehof Airport. Unemployment was very high. The Russians, who controlled all means of access by land, permitted only nineteen trains per day to enter. All other cargo reached the city by costly air transport. I entered the Russian sector by car from the Canadian Military Mission, and experienced no trouble. At the border a sign greeted us in English, "You are now entering the democratic sector of Berlin." On departing there was another large sign, "End of the democratic sector of Berlin." Pictures of Stalin and red flags decorated the buildings everywhere. Apartment blocks were under construction on a large scale. I was struck by the youthfulness of the East German police. They were recruited at sixteen years of age.

219

There were many escapes to the Western Sector; the Berlin Wall had not yet been built. The Russian grip on East Berlin was everywhere to be seen. The comparison at close quarters between East and West was all favourable to the West. The contrast was stark.

The role filled by the 27th Infantry Brigade was unparalleled in Canadian history. Never before had a Canadian military force been sent into another country in time of peace in such circumstances, and it was difficult for the Germans at first to understand that new role. The quality of the Canadian brigade was best attested by the fact that every one of the British divisions in Germany, including the flower of the British armoured forces, asked that our brigade be attached to it. The Canadian troops looked fit and smart. I felt proud of them.

German rearmament had become one of the most important questions facing the world. No one would have thought of sponsoring German rearmament but for Russian aggression. It was the Russian menace which compelled the Allies to subordinate their fears of German rearmament. The British rightly asked themselves why they should bear the heavy burden of defending West Germany.

Three days in Paris gave me an excellent opportunity to study our NATO organization. The Canadian delegation was headed by my esteemed friend Arnold Heeney. He enjoyed ambassadorial rank and did everything possible to make my visit instructive. I was guest of General Vanier, Canadian ambassador to France, and Mme. Vanier at lunch on Sunday. That was the beginning of a relationship which was to ripen with the years and led me to admire them both keenly. I was one day to participate in his selection as Governor General of Canada.

France also had made impressive progress in four years. American financial aid through the Marshall Plan had helped her to recover from the enormous losses in men and material she had suffered during and since the war. She had not yet achieved political stability, and she was being bled white by the costly war in Indochina. I found an overpowering fear of war in France.

Back in Canada, I plunged back into work. Following my visit to Europe in 1948 I had been privileged to address the Empire Club of Canada on it, choosing as my title, "Where the Iron Curtain Falls." I was invited to address the Club on December 11, 1952, on my second trip. This time I chose the title, "The Pulse of Western Europe." I concluded my address with a tribute to the way the United Kingdom was meeting the challenges and problems of 1952, with these words: "She is going through great difficulties, she has immense problems, but I think she is going to surmount them with the same spirit of resolution and courage that has enabled her to triumph over so many trials in the past. Emerson truly said, 'The British always see most clearly in a fog'."

CHAPTER TWENTY-ONE

Horses on the Payroll

Apart from some reverberations over defence expenditures arising out of evidence gleaned by the Special Committee on Defence Expenditure at the previous session and the appointment of
George Currie to investigate some limited aspects thereof, there
appeared to be no reason to expect any extraordinary fireworks.
Everyone expected, of course, that it would be the final session of
the Twenty-First Parliament and that an election was certain to
come in 1953; so the government could be expected to offer some
tasty legislative morsels and a budget with tax reductions – all of
which had been previously advocated by the Conservatives – but
would not seek to rock the boat or face any unnecessary dis-
turbances. The opposition, on the other hand, would be looking
for any opportunity to expose ineptitude and incompetence on
the part of the government. No one could have foreseen in late
November that the House was launching into a tempestuous session which would wear thin its calm, its dignity and its patience.
I had learned by this time never to be surprised by any turn of
events in public life, but I little realized that I would be called
upon to wage battle almost ceaselessly for long months.

The session began on an uncontentious note. The appointment
of Mr. Mayhew as ambassador to Japan left a cabinet vacancy
for British Columbia. The choice lay between Jimmy Sinclair
and Ralph Campney. Sinclair, a Rhodes scholar, had incurred
the displeasure of Mackenzie King during the war and only
found opportunity for advancement with Mr. St. Laurent. He
was sharp-tongued, abrasive and very partisan. Campney was a
competent lawyer who enjoyed respect in the House and was
much less given to playing politics. The Prime Minister cut the
Gordian knot by awarding portfolios to both, appointing Sinclair
as Minister of Fisheries and Campney as Solicitor General.
Campney was also appointed Associate Minister of National

222

Defence on November 24, just in time to become innocently involved in the miseries which were about to overtake that department.

The annual debate on the motion to refer the Estimates of the Department of External Affairs to the Standing Committee on External Affairs gave me an opportunity to speak of my visit to Britain, West Germany, Berlin and France. I pointed to the Kremlin as the source of danger to the free world and reluctantly conceded the necessity and inevitability of German rearmament. The debate was on a high, non-partisan plane. Lester Pearson led off with a comprehensive review of Canada's external relations, followed by our spokesman Gordon Graydon. I enjoyed the work on the committee and took a very active part in its deliberations. Among members aspiring to appointment it was the most sought-after committee in the House.

The House was allowed to proceed with the debate on the speech from the throne without the interruptions which the government had imposed in the several previous sessions. It was thus concluded on December 17, just before the Christmas recess. I entered the debate early, on November 26, with a speech made with one eye cocked on the approaching general election. I asserted that "the problems facing this country are greater by far than they were in 1949. . . . These past three and a half years will go down in history as the wasted years." I lashed the government for over-taxation and over-expenditure, and predicted that they would eat their denials when the budget was brought down. I pointed to their purchase of 1,153,155 neckties in the cause of rearmament, followed by additional outlay of $32,638 on neckties in the first half of October. I noted also their purchase of 1,304,407 pairs of men's leather shoes in eleven months and 117,800 pairs of women's shoes in thirteen months and 15,000 raincoats for a strength of 900 in the Canadian Women's Army Corps. I commented: "There is no possible way of explaining or justifying expenditures on this scale except that they are being made now with a conscious view toward making friends for this Government." I added, "I tell you that there is shameful over-taxation, there is shameful extravagance in the way this Government is throwing around the hard-earned money of the Canadian taxpayer. . . . The Government spending machine has been running wild." I related their spending to the remaking of the constitution. In 1939 the federal government took 51 per cent of the Canadian tax dollar, in 1951, 77 per cent. The result of federal occupation of the field of direct taxation is that "there is nothing left even in the way of bare pickings for anybody else coming into these fields." The provinces and municipalities were suffering a severe shortage of revenues. The power to tax being the power to govern, it was clear that the federal government had been remaking the constitution without taking the trouble formally to amend it.

On December 15 the Currie Report was tabled in the House by the Prime Minister. Ottawa was rocked to its political foundations. In all my years in Parliament no document produced a devastating effect to equal it. The report immediately absorbed the attention of Parliament, producing consternation in the ranks of the government and setting the opposition afire. George Currie was ideally qualified for his task. One of the leading figures in the accountancy profession, he had served with distinction in the First World War and later as Deputy Minister of National Defence. He was a man of the highest integrity.

The Special Committee on Defence Expenditure had unearthed evidence of irregularities at Petawawa, but our members had not been permitted to investigate thefts there or include them in the committee's report. The chief auditor of the department had written seventeen reports to the department heads drawing attention to 153 irregularities since May 1949. No action followed. Brooke Claxton, the minister, admitted that he became aware of these reports in October 1951. Six months later he appointed Currie with a limited mandate, and later admitted that the irregularities then known to him were "grave." Currie was limited to an "investigation into the deficiencies and irregularities of the engineering detachment of the Army Works Services at Petawawa and elsewhere." Actually he reviewed only a fraction of 1 per cent of expenditures of the department.

When the report was tabled it was found that seven pages bore changes, some of a substantial nature, as compared with a copy which had mysteriously found its way previously into the hands of M.J. Coldwell. These discrepancies, when exposed, were acutely embarrassing to Mr. St. Laurent. Later it was learned that Coldwell's document was a copy of the draft report, and that the changes had been reluctantly made by Currie at the request of Bud Drury, the deputy minister of the department, who sought to vet the draft before the report was signed. The minister had refused to see the draft or any of the documents until the report had been signed, but later conceded that the idea of vetting the report was his, not his deputy's.

The report confirmed the 153 irregularities in every detail. It added, "These then represent the ascertained cases of irregularity at Petawawa. How many more there may have been will never be known. It was apparent from the beginning of the investigation that the accounting records were in a chaotic condition and would be of little use in determining the nature and extent of irregularities. . . . My view would be, however, that the generally lax administrative situation would give rise to waste and inefficiency far more costly in loss than that covered by actual dishonesty." He reported barefaced frauds such as the sale of 550 tons of serviceable army equipment as scrap, the ripping up and sale of a railway siding, and horses placed on the payroll. I quote the report,

> Horses were hired by army personnel and placed on the payroll. . . . A boat and several washing machines were obtained by putting through a false order for 1,000 bags of cement. Two freight carloads of pulpwood appear to have been stolen. . . . The overall shortage appeared to be 18,000 bags of cement. . . . There has been a general breakdown in the system of administration, supervision and accounting. . . . Internal warnings had not been lacking in the Department of National Defence. The Chief Auditor of the Department had performed his functions conscientiously. Time and again he had reported unsatisfactory conditions. The Deputy Minister, in each case, had directed the Quartermaster-General to investigate and report. Lack of adequate action at this point had, however, caused a progressive deterioration in the situation.

Currie substantiated his report in every particular. The report was tabled eight days after it was delivered to the department.

As a matter of fact, the whole investigation had been precipitated by an anonymous letter to the RCMP, and articles and inquiries which began to appear in the press. This led to prosecutions and convictions in the local court at Petawawa.

The theme of horses on the payroll had a unique place in all the publicity concerning the report, no doubt because of its quaint originality. It deeply disturbed Mr. St. Laurent personally. Three times in the House in succeeding months he denied there were horses on the payroll, but Currie stuck to his guns and repeated his statement that there were horses on the payroll under the names of non-existent labourers.

The ink was scarcely dry on the report before the government and its servile followers went to work to discredit it: the losses were insignificant; the malefactors had been prosecuted; the minister was such a busy man; we should be proud of the Canadian Army; Currie had exaggerated so much; trust the government to put everything back in applepie order; Coldwell had received stolen property – he would hear from the RCMP. The opposition, though few in numbers, was not to be cowed, but surely it could be frustrated by the right tactical use of the government's big and obedient majority. At least so they thought.

The battle opened within hours of the tabling of the report. General George Pearkes, our critic on defence matters, led off. The next day Douglas Harkness followed, then came George Drew with a powerful speech. Then I spoke, and placed the blame for the scandal squarely on the shoulders of the ministry, and made a slashing attack on the government for its shocking failure to do its duty and on its followers in the House for their servile support of the government. My speech was constructed on short notice, but I think it hit home. With all the experts we had in the Conservative ranks on national defence it was the first time I had allowed myself to enter a debate on the subject. I quoted with relish the words of Sir Joseph Porter to Captain Corcoran in *HMS Pinafore*, "Captain Corcoran, it is one of the happiest characteristics of this glorious country that official utterances are invariably regarded as unanswerable."

On January 13, 1953, Mr. St. Laurent introduced his motion to appoint a select committee "to continue the examination of all expenditure of public moneys for national defence and all commitments for expenditure for national defence since March 31, 1950, and to report from time to time their observations and opinions thereon." He did not speak, but left that to Claxton, who had been in Europe when the Currie Report was tabled, and was now fighting for his political life or at least the former promise of his career. He spoke for an hour and a half, for most of that time reading a detailed statement. At the conclusion he took the unprecedented course of moving an amendment to the Prime Minister's motion by inserting the words, "and initially to give priority in their examination to the expenditures and commitments of the Canadian Army Works Services as dealt with in the report of G.S. Currie." After hearing argument the Speaker ruled the amendment to be in order, and also ruled that Drew must not reflect upon the independence of thought of Liberal members. They had become demonstrably sensitive on that subject. I commented, "We must be becoming exceedingly thin-skinned around here if words like those cannot be used."

The Conservatives took the position that as far as the Currie Report was concerned the need was for action, not a review of a review, and that Currie should be asked to continue a similar investigation into all aspects of organization, accounting and administration of the department. On January 15 the Prime Minister spoke at length in defence of the government and the course it proposed. Diefenbaker in an excellent speech replied that the government's intention was to have the committee whitewash the report and that, being indicted, it was selecting a jury of its own to determine whether the judge came to the right conclusion. My turn to speak came that evening. I voiced this solemn warning to the government: "No amount of denial or propaganda or gainsaying or cajolery on the part of ministers or Government followers will ever minimize the importance of this report. It has, indeed, revealed the worst scandal in the affairs of government since the Beauharnois scandal was exposed twenty years ago. Make no mistake about it, it has shocked the Canadian people. It has shocked the Canadian conscience." Excellent speeches were also made by Doug Harkness, Jim Macdonnell and Davie Fulton. The debate was rousing strong feelings and only ended on the 22nd, when the Claxton amendment and the original motion were adopted.

The Conservatives were allotted six places on the committee out of twenty-six, the Liberals seventeen. In the committee the previous year our representatives were selected because of being experts on defence questions, and they had done excellent work. It now became advisable to add someone who was tough, a fighter, a lawyer with experience in cross-examination, a sense of tactics, and a knowledge of the rules. The need was tailored precisely to the specifications of John Diefenbaker, but John was not responsive where a tedious committee job was involved. I was asked to undertake it and agreed. I was under no illusions. I knew that it would be strenuous, contentious and unpleasant. The other Conservative members were Adamson, Fulton, Harkness, Macdonnell and Pearkes. It was a superb team. Pearkes and I were appointed to the steering committee. My friend the able Dave Croll was chairman.

The committee held twenty-seven meetings, devoting the first thirteen to the Currie Report. I attended every meeting and remained present throughout. Numerous witnesses were called, including Currie and senior officials from the department. At times the atmosphere was calm, at times tempestuous. I found myself in the midst of the battle, and usually leading it, on the latter occasions. The army representatives, and they were numerous, must have envied the bellicose spirit demonstrated at times by members of the committee. Of the nine subjects proposed in the steering committee only two were covered, viz., the Currie Report and construction. I pleaded for more meetings and in particular for investigation of aircraft production. Consistently we Conservatives urged an enlargement of the investigation to include the entire department. The Liberals voted solidly against the continuation of the inquiry. A battle royal ensued over the contents of the committee's report to the House, which was written in camera. The Liberals made it so innocuous as to invite my contemptuous charge that it was a whitewash. My attempt to extend the report by a lengthy review of the Currie Report and a solemn judgment on the department and the government for their delinquencies was defeated by the majority. The report was tabled in the House on May 5 by the chairman, whereupon though I was out of order I was quick to point out that it represented "the view of the majority of the Committee, but the Progressive Conservative Members strongly dissented from it." The report was never adopted; indeed, no motion for its adoption was ever proposed. Quite manifestly the government wanted no further discussion of the subject of defence expenditure or the Currie Report in the House; the committee had served its useful purpose by preventing discussion of these subjects in the House during the three months of its sittings and then writing a whitewash report. Only nine days of the session remained, and the House was bent upon hurrying toward prorogation. The stage was set for a quiet interment of the whole vexed subject of the Currie Report and scandal in the Department of National Defence. But the government reckoned without some astute tactical moves by the Conservatives.

The Estimates of the Department of Defence Production were placed before the Committee of Supply (the whole House) the next day. This was our only hope of opportunity to discuss the report of the Committee on Defence Expenditure, and under the rules it was but a faint hope. C.D. Howe led off with a statement carefully confined to the operations and activities of his department as the procurement agency for defence purchases. I led for the opposition, announcing our determination to see to it "that the public is receiving value for the huge amounts of money being expended." Then I launched into quantities and cost. Howe was evidently expecting this. He was up like a shot to tell the chairman that I was out of order, that his department had no responsibility whatever for quantities, but only for purchases according to requisitions received from the Department of National Defence. "If the services say they need a gold-plated piano it is our duty to buy it," quoth Howe in one of his famous declarations from Mount Olympus. I was reading from a return of the Department of Defence Production, and the chairman ruled me in order. I proceeded to read the quantities, which were astronomical – 2,338,479 pairs of footwear, 4,673,648 pairs of socks, 1,752,696 handkerchiefs and many others – while Howe's choler swiftly mounted. He made repeated appeals to the chairman to rule me out of order, but failed in his purpose. When I said to the chairman, "May I make an observation?" Howe retorted peremptorily, "No. Just let me say a word." I retorted, "Mr. Chairman, I was not asking the Minister's permission. I do not think we have reached the stage yet where any member speaks by permission of the Minister." And so I continued, speaking of purchases equivalent to 23 pairs of shoes per man in the Canadian armed forces in 21 months; 46 pairs of socks per man in 21 months; 17 handkerchiefs and 15 sets of winter underwear and 28 sets of summer underwear for every man. I innocently concurred in a reference Howe had made to the "dangers and expense of stockpiling." The department had placed orders between April 1, 1951, and December 31, 1952, amounting to $2,229,838,000. I then stirred up a hornet's nest by complaining over the concentration of these orders in the industrial provinces instead of distributing them more widely and fairly and aiding areas which needed industrialization. This can always be depended upon to be a sensitive issue with many members. Then I finally came to the report of the Defence Expenditure Committee and succeeded in reading into the record five of the eleven paragraphs in the long amendment I had introduced in the committee. Having succeeded that far I let loose this final paragraph, speaking at top speed before anyone could stop me as being out of order:

> The fact of the matter is that the Committee in this report has attempted to whitewash the government in this matter. The facts will not be hidden. It may be that a committee with a government majority of 17 as against 9 Opposition Members can carry a whitewashing report and defeat a Progressive Conservative amendment which stated the facts, but the committee in question is not the final court in this matter. It may be that this House with its overwhelming government majority will again seek to whitewash the Government's record in this regard of profligate expenditure, of waste, of extravagance and of shocking inefficiency, but even that will not end this matter. This matter will be carried, whenever the Government calls the time, to the people as the court of final appeal for an effective decision.

I had baited the hook. The committee, its report and our indictment of government waste had all been introduced into the debate, and our other members on the committee took up the theme in their speeches while Howe's exasperation mounted.

The next day, May 7, Liberal members on the committee decided they should answer the charge of whitewashing. Dickey, Croll, Applewhaite all swallowed the bait and spoke, contending that the report was non-political. I answered each of the Liberals who had spoken, or, rather, corrected their more serious errors, with reference to the manner in which the committee conducted itself, then I returned to the report and the Conservative amendment. Howe's temper was almost beyond control. He was bobbing up and down demanding what relationship my remarks had to the estimates of the Department of Defence Production. I innocently pointed out that three Liberal members had chosen to discuss the report of the committee, and had been permitted by the chair to do so, and all I was doing was replying to them. This was too hard a nut for the chairman to crack, and he allowed me to proceed. Howe asserted in white heat that I was spreading on the record the whole Conservative election campaign platform. He was right. I continued. Howe, red in the face, accused me of reading the Currie Report. I innocently denied this, pointing out that I was reading the amendment I had introduced in the committee which merely made certain references to the Currie Report. Howe's fury exploded. He rose, picked up the papers on his desk, raised them high above his head and slammed them down on the desk. Dr. McCann, evidently fearing Howe was in danger of apoplexy, moved over beside his colleague, but received no thanks for his pains. I completed the reading of every word of my lengthy amendment, and concluded that by the rulings of the chairman of the committee, supported by the majority of the committee, we had been denied access to essential information, and the committee had been prevented from conducting the kind of inquiry the country expected of us. The discussion continued until we were satisfied to conclude it. We had outwitted the Grits and achieved our debate on the committee's report.

In the Currie Report we Conservatives were confident that we had found an issue on which we could defeat the Liberals in the forthcoming general election. One evening in the lobby in the midst of the debate, Alphonse Fournier, Minister of Public Works, chided me. He said, "Why are you becoming so excited about the Currie Report?" I replied that we would win the election on that issue. Alphonse said, "Not a chance. By the time of the election the people will have forgotten about horses on the payroll." Unfortunately, he was right. The people did lose interest. The subject eventually became a source of amusement to many. The disappointing lesson drawn by many in government positions from this epilogue to the Currie Report is that the public just doesn't care.

My own role in the debates on the Currie Report expanded steadily into one of leading responsibility. Austin Cross, one of the ablest and most independent members of the press gallery, writing in the earlier stages of the debates, commented:

> On the elevator going down [to the House to take part in the debate] was the Lord High Executioner from Toronto, Don Fleming, M.P. for Toronto-Eglinton. He looked baby-faced and innocent when accosted with the Hatchet Man role. But what he had in his hands were not violets; they looked like a few notes that he would turn into torrential eloquence, which indeed he did. . . .
> Appointment of Don Fleming of the Progressive Conservatives as Lord High Executioner is a picturesque choice. The Jimmy Gardiner of the Tory Party, Don is like his counterpart, a hatchet man, a loud lunged, fast talking politician. He can develop an indignation as fast as you can say it. He can read the telephone book and get het up about it.
> Honest, sincere, head of the Bible Society in Toronto, he forges his Bible into the Sword of Gideon at times; and, with all the zeal of an Old Testament prophet, he goes after the evil Grits. He never lets Holy Writ interfere with raising hell.
> Not great of stature, he has a resourceful mind, a forceful way of speaking. But, above all, his political virtuosity lies in his ability to hack away with his tongue. Don can be tough.
> One thing against the high-minded, hard talking M.P. from Toronto Eglinton is that he is apt to be repetitive. He keeps his indignation at high pitch for too long, tends to beat a subject too hard too long. He would be twice as effective sometimes if he talked half as long.
> But he is a mighty man in getting his words into a headline, and the chances are that he will give the newspapers some live copy across Canada.
> The pint-sized prosecutor is on his way, and he should liven up the Commons this winter.

I was not in the least displeased to find that I could rile the Grits as no man in the opposition, with the possible exception of George Drew, could. I was readily disposed to sail into them with guns blazing, and their interjections and interruptions bothered me not at all. Rather, they were proof that my words were penetrating their tough hides and hurting them. I had absolutely no fear of any or all of them. As long as I made sure of my ground I had learned that I was a match for any of them on the floor of the House. It therefore continued to be of the highest importance that I be very carefully prepared at all times, and this meant digging, reading and hard work. There were no evenings off. I lived on a constant diet of work, but my rugged health proved equal to it, and I was daily thankful for that. We were engaged in a vastly important enterprise, and a momentous general election lay just around the corner. I did not intend to spare any effort to advance the course to which I was committed.

Another heated and at times acrimonious debate took place over the government's bill to continue the Emergency Powers Act for one year to May 31, 1954. The necessary resolution was introduced on February 6; the bill received third reading on March 26. The government contended that Canada still faced a national emergency, which might require them at any moment to take and exercise extraordinary powers at the expense of Parliament and the provinces. They admitted they could if need be invoke the extraordinary powers under the War Measures Act, but they preferred a somewhat less drastic course. We contended that there was little real difference between the two acts and we were stoutly opposed to their renewing the Emergency Powers Act. With Parliament sitting almost constantly there was no need for the government to take special powers. Parliament could act swiftly to cope with any emergency. We did not trust extraordinary powers in the hands of this government. The stage was thus set for a battle royal between government and the defenders of Parliament on issues which had not perished with King Charles I on the scaffold. The measure was in the Prime Minister's name, but he left it to Garson to pilot, and that gentleman tried to be coy and hold back his explanatory statement. Drew, Green, Diefenbaker and Fulton spoke on the first day and made excellent speeches. Unlike previous sessions I was held back to follow Garson whenever he chose to dismount from his high horse. He finally spoke on February 18 and 19, and I moved into the debate on his heels.

In the first year the Emergency Powers Act had been in existence the government had passed nineteen orders-in-council under the powers it conferred, in the second year only five. The great majority were passed while Parliament was actually sitting, and some were not of serious importance. I tore into Garson's defence of the measure and put the government in the accused's dock. Stressing the threat of inflation, I thundered:

> The emergency that does exist in Canada today is to a considerable extent of the Government's own creation. . . . I know the emergency the Government has created in the pockets of the taxpayers. . . . What this Government is interested in is one thing, and one thing only, and that is to possess absolute and untram-

melled legislative powers. Sir, it will be the same thing next year. The Minister of Justice was at pains last night to tell us that this was a continuing emergency, and that it might go on and on. This emergency will go on, you may be sure of it, so long as this Government is in office. . . . Our position in this Official Opposition is crystal clear. We say that it is in Parliament that legislating should be done, not behind closed doors or by secret methods such as has been the case with orders-in-council.

I concluded by stressing three present dangers: taking power away from the provinces, taking power away from Parliament, and the government's impatience over criticism, and closed with these words: "You have present all the elements that are needed to transform Canadian democracy into a dictatorship and Canadian Confederation into a unitary form of government."

I returned to the fray on March 24. The Prime Minister still had not spoken nor had any Liberal private member. Garson was still an inviting target, but at last, two days later, the Prime Minister was forced into the debate. He sought to allay all fears and reassure everyone of the government's innocent intent. In the prevailing state of the world the government had to have "stand-by" powers. The measure was passed. Within a month his assurances were submitted to the test.

On April 20 the Minister of Transport tabled an order-in-council passed on April 17 under the Emergency Powers Act to impose new licensing requirements on all Canadian ships in excess of 500 tons. It was aimed at trade with mainland China, North Korea and in their territorial waters. The Conservatives seized on this as a violation of the rights of Parliament while Parliament was actually sitting and should have dealt with the needs of the situation by amending the Canada Shipping Act. Howe as usual was full of defiance and contempt for Parliament. With his usual tact he announced, "If we have overstepped our powers I make no apology for having done so." I took up the torch on April 22, denouncing the "Star Chamber methods" practised by the government to legislate while Parliament was actually sitting. What had become of the Prime Minister's disarming assurances? What had become of the solemn assurance that the powers under the Act were merely "stand by," to be used only in case of need? I drew attention to the fact that we now had two legislative bodies at Ottawa functioning side by side and each creating law binding on every Canadian. I then delivered this solemn judgment:

Which is the democratic method? The parliamentary method is a method that has been tested down through the centuries and has been found to be the one method that will guarantee the preservation of the rights and liberties of the people. Long ago secret methods were found to be the kind that make it easy for executive bodies to trespass upon the rights of the people. The executive branch of government, historically and in fact, has never been the champion of the rights of the people. It has been Parliament and Parliament alone that has fought the battles for the preservation of the rights and freedoms of the people. Parliament and the people have an opportunity now of seeing under their very eyes Parliament proceeding to legislate in the traditional parliamentary and democratic method, and side by side a cabal consisting of twenty men proceeding to legislate by Star Chamber methods that were found three centuries ago to be so notorious that men were prepared to shed their blood to exterminate them.

The clash did not end there. It was only while checking the report of the debate in the Hansard office at the luncheon adjournment that I became aware that Howe had made a remark to me which I did not hear, but which the Hansard reporter caught and transcribed, "There is no use lying about it." Evidently the Speaker did not hear it either. On my return to the House I rose on a question of privilege, and demanded that Howe withdraw the remark imputing a dishonest statement. Howe responded,

> Mr. Speaker, in reading the transcript I myself noticed it. I knew it was unparliamentary, and I communicated with you, Mr. Speaker, and after that changed the transcript to read "denying it." If my honourable friend would like me to expunge the line I will do that. I am sorry I made the remark. I was a little annoyed at my honourable friend, and I think he was a bit annoyed, too. That is the story. What would my honourable friend like me to do more than that?

I thought Howe had spoken in a manly way, and I replied very briefly, "So far as I am concerned, Mr. Speaker, that is quite sufficient. I am glad the Minister has spoken as he has." The incident ended there.

That evening the House took up Howe's Estimates of the Department of Trade and Commerce. I opened with a full-dress speech containing a comprehensive statement on Canada's trade relations and problems and a declaration of policy. I stressed the importance of Canada's external trade, her dependence upon healthy markets for her exports, our deep concern over the loss of the British market – the traditional market for many of our agricultural products – the need to strengthen our economy by greater processing of our raw materials at home. I expressed further concern over the extent to which our trading eggs were being laid in one basket, namely, the United States, the failure of that country to honour its GATT obligations, and in view of the re-emergence of Japan as a world trader, the need to assure that she would conform to fair trading practices. I set forth a useful list of Canada's trade weaknesses and challenges. I declared Conservative policy, "Our aim is not to restrict trade, but rather to expand it." I urged utmost effort to expand trade and applauded the efforts of our trade commissioners abroad in a manner which earned Howe's thanks. I said we must resist all efforts to divide the free world into two trading blocs, dollar and sterling, and concluded on this note: "Canadians in the years ahead will need to be efficient producers and efficient salesmen. In the export markets of the world we will have to meet competition that will be very keen. No doubt we will be confronted with challenges to keep down costs of production by following a policy of reduced taxation, and the whole Canadian economy will then be geared to a policy of expanding production and expanding sales abroad." It was the most comprehensive and most realistic speech on trade heard in the House since I entered it in 1945.

Broadcasting received much more attention in the 1952-53 session than previously. The Canadian Broadcasting Corporation had completed construction of television broadcasting stations at Montreal and Toronto. To meet the accusation that it was showing favouritism to these two areas the CBC proposed to construct similar facilities in Winnipeg, Vancouver and Halifax. The corporation was in need of enormous funds, and it and the government were still resisting our demand that the regulation and control of both radio and TV broadcasting be vested in an independent tribunal. For years we Conservatives had attacked the annual licence fee of $2.50 on each radio receiving set as a nuisance tax and too difficult and costly to collect.

Normally the motion to appoint the Special Committee on Broadcasting did not become contentious, but this year it was different. Although I had asked for it several times, the government delayed the necessary resolution till January 27, and Dr. McCann made a long speech in introducing it. I followed him with a major speech lasting an hour and a half, in which I set forth in comprehensive form the whole Conservative policy on radio and TV broadcasting. I attacked the government's "monopolistic mania," bad programming, the sterilization and retardation of TV development, the vote of funds to CBC over a period of five years in advance, and the concentration of CBC television stations in the large metropolitan areas. For some strange reason the government did not allow resumption of the debate until March 17; thus fifty days were lost when the committee might have been at work. Moreover, the first speaker on March 17 was Lionel Chevrier, Minister of Transport, who made a bitter partisan speech, absurdly asserting that the Conservative policy would reduce programming in the French language and benefit political friends of our party to the national detriment. I was obliged to describe his assertions as "the most shocking kind of demagogic claptrap." The debate throughout was thus on a very partisan note. The committee fortunately was not handicapped by such tactics. It went about its work earnestly and submitted a unanimous report.

That, however, was not the end of contention and wrangling over broadcasting. There remained the vexed question of CBC revenue. On April 20 the House quickly approved amendment of the Radio Act to eliminate the $2.50 licence fee on the radio receiving sets, as we had predicted they would. On April 21 the government proposed to amend the legislation to give CBC the right to receive the proceeds of the 15 per cent excise or purchase tax on TV sets. It happened that in that particular year the anticipated revenue from the tax approximately equalled the revenue CBC was losing with the end of the licence fee, but CBC's right to this earmarked source of revenue was to be unlimited as to time. Thus CBC, assured of an annual money grant from Parliament year by year for another four years and all the revenue from the 15 per cent tax ad infinitum, was in a position where it was removed from any vestige whatever of parliamentary control for at least four years. This to us was a shocking and reprehensible proposal, and we fought it. It was all very well to argue that CBC needed to do forward planning and required some assurance of revenues for this purpose. Who wouldn't choose assured revenues for years to come without any accounting to the Parliament which was raising the revenues by imposing taxes, then handing over the proceeds to CBC? It was a wicked scheme and another insult to Parliament. Control was being taken right out of the hands of Parliament. In speeches on April 21 and 22 and May 4 I denounced the proposal. I introduced an amendment to make the transfer of the funds to CBC subject to annual vote of Parliament, but this was ruled out. On May 14 on the estimates I made a last and unavailing stand on the issue of parliamentary control of money votes for CBC.

It was usual at the dissolution of a Parliament to honour the Speaker of the House, either by appointment to the Senate or the Privy Council. On the evening of May 12 Mr. St. Laurent announced that in view of the prominent part they would be playing in the Canadian delegation to the coronation, the Chief

Justice of Canada, the Speaker of the Senate, the Speaker of the House of Commons, and the Leader of the Opposition were being sworn members of the Queen's Privy Council for Canada. The announcement was received with loud applause. Ross Macdonald had proven himself a respected and popular Speaker. It was very gracious of the Prime Minister and the government to bestow this merited honour on George Drew.

The termination of a session rarely fails to inspire feelings of profound relief. Members are wont to throw their papers in the air, and even the staid and proper members of the press gallery have been known to send papers floating down from their exalted pinnacle onto the heads of MPs. When prorogation is known to be certain to be followed by dissolution and a general election the mood is bound to be governed or at least affected by the confidence of the individual member in his chances of re-election. Those who lack that confidence are usually counselled to affect it for the sake of the party. I knew but one thing, that after all the toil and the political warfare of the 1952-53 session I was delighted to see the end of it. Likewise I was glad to see Canada's Twenty-First Parliament pass into history. The government's overwhelming majority had predetermined every vote and every issue; there was no exciting possibility of defeating them or even making the outcome close. We Conservatives, hopelessly outnumbered, had put up a gallant fight. We had won significant by-elections in different parts of the country. The future began to glow with hope.

On what day would the general election be held? A journalist had reported the choice of August 10 or 17. I was appalled at the prospect of an election at the very height of the vacation season; it would be impossible to stir electors up to political fervour in the summer. I questioned Mr. St. Laurent in the House about it. I pointed out that in urban areas an August election would have the effect of disfranchising many absent citizens. St. Laurent replied that in deference to the coronation of the Queen on June 2 no date for a general election would be chosen until afterward. If the enumeration of the voters were held in July or August many absentees would be missed from the list. If it were deferred, September 14 would be the earliest date it could commence, and that would defer the election until November. We seemed to be in a cleft stick. An August election I thought was almost assured, and I shuddered at the prospect for Eglinton and many other urban ridings.

CHAPTER TWENTY-TWO

Crushing Defeat

Prorogation made it possible for Alice and me to fly to London on May 23, my forty-eighth birthday, to attend the coronation. It proved to be one of the outstanding privileges of our lives. The program surrounding the event was incomparable. In the three weeks we spent in London we were guests at receptions at Canada House, the Hudson's Bay Company, Mansion House, Blenheim Palace and Clive House, as well as the Royal Garden Party at Buckingham Palace. We attended the running of the Derby, the Trooping of the Colour in the presence of the Queen, the great Naval Review at Spithead, and the Royal Tournament.

The hospitality, both official and personal, extended to us in London made it almost impossible for us to leave that city, but we crowded in visits to Windsor Castle, Stratford and Canterbury. We took full advantage of a glorious season of theatre.

Outstanding was the luncheon tendered by the Commonwealth Parliamentary Association at Westminster Hall in honour of the Queen and addressed by Her Majesty and Winston Churchill. I was deeply conscious of the rare privilege which Alice and I enjoyed as invited guests at the coronation ceremony itself.

But politics pursued us. At the Royal Garden Party George Drew told me that St. Laurent had that afternoon confided in him that the general election would be held on August 10, and the two leaders were curtailing their stay in London to return home to launch their campaigns. Frankly, I was glad that I had no such responsibility. I was very disappointed at the prospect of a summer election. Our return to Toronto on June 17 was followed the next night by my nomination meeting in Eglinton riding. It was well attended, and I received a unanimous nomination for the third consecutive time. I thought I should make a full-dress speech. The evening, however, was very warm, and some of my workers thought my speech was too long for a hot night. This confirmed my fears of a summer election. People were not prepared to forget the heat and exert themselves or become excited as they are wont to do in cooler weather. The difficulty of stirring people continued throughout the campaign.

George Drew launched his campaign with a sixteen-plank platform. It had many commendable features, but his principal issue backfired. Instead of attacking particular extravagances and promising their elimination and restoration to the people in tax reductions of the benefits of these economies, George flatly and initially promised tax reductions of $500 million. The Liberals promptly put him on the defensive by demanding what expenditures he would reduce or eliminate to achieve this impossible goal, and asking if he would reduce the old-age pension or restore the means test. George was kept busy answering these dishonest charges. The Liberals, on the other hand, offered no program and coasted with the aid of a very large campaign fund. Our party funds were meagre. I derived limited assistance from the party, and Ardagh Scythes again raised enough to make ends meet in Eglinton. Nevertheless, we were compelled to budget very carefully.

I was kept very busy on the national campaign. I spoke in all provinces except Newfoundland, but principally in Quebec. I was accorded rousing receptions at our meetings in the French-speaking areas, but interest was lacking in the English-speaking parts. The summer campaign produced some techniques in Quebec that were new to me. Instead of leaving their cars to enter a hot and stuffy hall or to stand at an outdoor meeting those attending would remain in their cars in comfort, listen to the speeches by loudspeaker and express their applause by tooting their horns. The French-language meetings were well attended. I liked the responsiveness of these meetings. I was speaking almost exclusively in French, making full-dress speeches and rousing my audiences. Tributes were being expressed to my "mastery" of the French tongue. It is a more effective vehicle for rousing an audience which understands it than is the English language to those who understand it. I spent some days in Quebec in the early days of the campaign, then after my western and Maritime tours returned to Quebec in the late stages. At this point I found the Liberals seeking to rouse racial and religious prejudice, as they had so often done in the past. This they were directing not only at George, but also at Fiorenza Drew. I denounced their shameful tactics at my meetings in Quebec and back in Ontario.

One event had special personal interest. My friend Raymond

O'Hurley, who later became a colleague of mine in the cabinet, arranged for me to speak in the interests of our candidate Roland Legendre in the riding of Lotbinière at St. Patrice, the place where my grandfather was raised, and from which he had moved to Ontario. There was only one relative left, my second cousin Chrysostome Flamand. Chrys and his wife, after spending long years in Michigan and prospering there, had returned to his ancestral home, bought a small farm and enjoyed ease and comfort in their advanced years. By arrangement about four carloads of Conservative workers accompanied me on August 2 to the home of Chrys, who was highly respected in the community, and enjoyed supper as his guests. He evidently concluded I was genuine, and he thought enough of me to come to our meeting that evening; indeed, he went further and introduced me there as his "petit-cousin." I was welcomed amid a storm of applause and horn-blowing. Our meeting was a rousing success. The introduction by Chrys drew a headline in *L'Action Catholique* published in Quebec City. Many of my listeners in these meetings were dissatisfied farmers. I discussed farm problems in my speeches, particularly the loss of markets.

In all provinces I hammered away at the government's waste, extravagance and contempt of Parliament. In Ontario and the West I urged the electors not to throw away their votes on third parties. The only way to defeat the Liberals was to vote Conservative. All of Howe's tactless and arrogant words were faithfully and often quoted, but some of the issues on which we had been very effective in the House seemed less relevant and effective on the hustings. Mr. St. Laurent went about, exuding amiability and respectability.

I had one misfortune in the West, thanks to a press report of my speech which was either innocently or wilfully mangled. In Winnipeg I had attacked Garson for suppressing the flour milling combine report in breach of the law, and repeated the assertion I had made in the debate in the Commons, that "The Minister of Justice, who should be the nation's principal law enforcement officer, had become Canada's No. 1 lawbreaker." I caught the midnight train out of Winnipeg for Regina. Next morning on reading the first available newspaper I found to my consternation that I was reported to have called Garson "Canada's No. 1 Bandit." I think there is a difference between being a lawbreaker and being a bandit. I jumped off the train at the next station and dispatched a telegram to Canadian Press reporting the error and asking for immediate correction. Their correction did some good, but as usual did not overtake all the damage done to me by what appeared to be vituperation of an opponent. I am not aware that Garson ever sought to make an issue over the misreporting.

Our campaign in Eglinton went reasonably well, although we knew that many of my supporters on vacation in early August would not return to vote; the national campaign, however, did not catch fire. St. Laurent was keeping his effort in low key with just that object in view. The Conservatives seemed to be making all the effort.

On August 10 at breakfast I handed Alice a note bearing my forecast of the vote in Eglinton: Fleming 17,500, Longstaffe (Liberal) 12,500, and McEntee (CCF) 3,000. That night after the counting of the ballots the results were announced as follows: Fleming 17,354, Longstaffe 11,190, and McEntee 2,237. My forecast had been proved astonishingly accurate but, more important, I had again been given the largest majority (6,164) accorded to a Conservative candidate in Canada.

The national results that evening, however, told a very dismal story. We had suffered another disaster, equal to that of 1949. The Liberals had scored another landslide victory, electing 170, plus 2 Independent Liberals and 1 Liberal Labour. We returned only 51, almost unchanged. Fifteen former Liberal seats were picked up by CCF and Social Credit. In the new House of 265 members fewer than one-fifth were ours. In Ontario we picked up half a dozen seats, electing 33 to the Liberals' 50. Outside Ontario we were pathetically thin: Maritimes 5, British Columbia 3, Prairies 6, In Quebec we re-elected Léon Balcer but lost my friends Henri Courtemanche and Paul Spence, and picked up 3, for a total of 4 against the Liberals' 66. Our representation in Newfoundland, always thin but able, was eliminated. The 14 members we elected outside Ontario and Quebec were mostly strong men, who evidently won on their personal merits. Diefenbaker's old constituency of Lake Centre having been eliminated, he had been elected in Prince Albert with a plurality of 3,000 votes, but he was the sole Conservative elected in Saskatchewan. Roly Michener was elected in Toronto – St. Paul's, by a plurality of 515.

The outlook for the party was bleak. All our political ammunition – high taxes, waste and extravagance, the gold-plated piano, inefficiency, overexpenditure, inflation, loss of markets, ministerial arrogance, redistribution, housing, horses on the payroll, legislation by order-in-council, delayed television – had been used up. When we pondered the defiant words of C.D. Howe, "If we wanted to get away with it who would stop us?" it began to appear that he was right. We Conservatives had tried, but had not stopped them; now the sovereign electorate had deliberately chosen not to stop them. The Grits would now be even more arrogant; Howe would be more dictatorial than ever. We did not then realize it, but therein lay the seeds of the government's eventual undoing.

For myself the prospect was appalling. My partners were bound to think their indulgence had been stretched to the limit in a lost cause and that I owed it to them to abandon politics as soon as I could find a convenient excuse. I had worked as few MPs had ever worked before, and all to what purpose? For four years – yes, now for eight – we had fought a bruising uphill battle, only to find that the people of Canada were not with us; we were simply fighting on our own. The future promised nothing better. The party was penniless, debt-ridden, its morale all but destroyed. Yet my own electors in Eglinton had stood by me. On election night in the face of their strong vote of confidence I had declared, "I regard it as a clear mandate to return to Ottawa and give the best service possible." I was committed beyond recall to serve my people. Of the party's grim fate I had on the same occasion testified: "I think George Drew waged an admirable campaign, and the party deserved much better results. I still believe that our party's policies are sound."

Inevitably George Drew's leadership was called into question, and quite seriously. He had proved himself a powerful parliamentarian, a courageous leader, and a hard worker. At no time had he spared himself. And yet the evidence was inescapable that the people for some reason did not like him. During the campaign an over-zealous Grit had maligned George as "the most hated man in Canada," and St. Laurent had won votes for himself by coming to George's rescue and disowning the slanderous attack on him. With St. Laurent riding an enormous wave of public respect and popularity and enjoying excellent health, what possible hope was there for George Drew to turn the tide? Within forty-eight hours of the final election results the press was speculating on the prospect of George resigning or being pushed out, and a successor being found among Diefenbaker, Fleming and Sidney Smith in that order. It was generally agreed that Drew could hardly continue without some expression of confidence from a party assembly, and thought turned at once to a meeting of the Progressive Conservative Association of Canada. It would require some time to call such a meeting.

What position was I to take on the question, perhaps soon to become an issue, of leadership? In the first place I determined to keep my mouth tightly shut. I liked and admired George, and I

felt sorry for him. He was in some respects a victim of circumstances, and I loathed the bitter personal campaign conducted
against him by the Grits. There were questions about Diefenbaker's personal loyalty to George. A number of John's close
friends in the caucus, representing mostly Ontario rural ridings,
had cooled toward George's leadership, and he must have had
qualms about the solidity of his following. I knew that I must not
allow my personal feelings toward George to lead me into a
course out of keeping with the party's best interests. George had
lost three general elections in a row. Only one leader of the party
had lost three consecutive general elections and then achieved
victory at the fourth. That was Sir Robert Borden. If George continued what hope was there, not to mention assurance, that he
could overcome the heavy odds against him and win in 1957?
How many chances was a leader entitled to expect, especially in
the face of the fact that the party had made no perceptible headway in eight years of George's leadership? In the likely event that
Diefenbaker would succeed him would the party be any better
off or would I be happy serving under a man of such tempera-
mental disposition? I left my own ambitions out of the equation.
Loyalty soon prevailed, just as it did in 1963 in an even more
acute crisis. Loyalty was part of my nature. It was a deeply settled part of me. I once heard an eminent preacher contend that
loyalty is not a virtue. I disagree entirely with him. I recognize
that loyalty can be misplaced in any sphere of life, but no
political leader, however talented, can go very far without
loyalty on the part of the party. I determined, as I did in 1963,
that no one would ever be in a position to accuse me of disloyalty
or to say that I had in self-interest raised a hand against the
leader. To deserve loyalty on the part of others a leader must
have proven himself loyal as a follower. If I were ever to become
the leader of the party I wished to present an utterly unblem-
ished record as a loyal follower. I hoped that my loyalty would
never become suspect as Diefenbaker's was in these grim circumstances. With all these thoughts in mind I continued to give
George Drew my full loyalty. We had been drawn closer together. Now that bond became even stronger. George was
openly grateful for my loyalty and support.

Plans for a meeting of the Progressive Conservative Association
of Canada proceeded. Jim Macdonnell, after giving faithful service in the office of president for some years, had been succeeded
by George Nowlan. It was now time for Nowlan also to be stepping down. I was urged to stand, but could not possibly assume
the burden. Plans for the meeting could not wait. I was called in

to participate in some planning for the program. It was decided that Murdo McPherson should make a keynote speech to rouse the audience to support George Drew and that we should seek to give George a standing ovation. I was one of the first on my feet to lead this gesture of enthusiastic support. Even those opposed to George's continuance were too embarrassed to remain in their seats under the direct observation of us who were standing and applauding. The whole audience was on its feet, none daring to appear not to applaud. This was accepted by the press and by the meeting itself as a rousing and unanimous endorsement of George Drew's leadership. Our strategy had succeeded beyond our hopes. To all outward appearances George was securely confirmed in the leadership; at least the known opposition to him had been driven underground for the time being. What would have been the outcome of a secret ballot at the meeting will never be known. It remained for a cruel fate to resolve all questions pertaining to George's leadership after three more years of courageous and untiring effort on his part.

The annual meeting closed the door on the leadership question; it opened the door to the presidency. George Hees was quick to seek it and campaign for it. His ambitions were well known, and he had achieved a certain back-slapping popularity. His abilities were not highly rated by some of his colleagues, and Gordon Churchill was put forward to oppose him. Ellen Fairclough nominated Churchill, and I openly supported him, but Churchill, though able and loyal, was a dour type, and Hees was elected. Many expected him to use the position to advance his own ambitions, but this was tolerable as long as he put the job first. George was interested in organization, and, whatever may have been his uppermost motive, he worked at it, and travelled about the country with enthusiasm.

There is one sad sequel in 1957 which must be told to a happy event recorded in this chapter. Several years after my visit to my second cousin Chrys Flamand tragedy struck, involving both him and his wife, both well past seventy years of age. A robber broke into the farmhouse, beat Chrys unconscious and proceeded to ransack the place in search of money. Chrys revived just enough to drag himself with great courage to a desk in which he kept a revolver. Seeing Chrys reaching for the weapon the robber attacked him again, beating him about the head with the butt. His wife died soon after of shock, and Chrys died later of his injuries. So far as I am aware the murderer was never apprehended.

In a review of leadership material in all parties entitled "The Political Who's Who" the *Monetary Times* in March 1953 had rated me next to George Drew in the party and added that I "can look forward with confidence to the possibility that he may be in line for the leadership of his Party before age rules him out. If a Conservative ministery were to be formed to-morrow Fleming would rate one of the senior portfolios." The year as it unfolded produced neither leadership nor portfolio; rather, I could see ahead only an uphill struggle against an all-powerful government.

CHAPTER TWENTY-THREE

Another Parliament

Canada's Twenty-Second Parliament assembled on November 12, 1953. Although the election had changed the party standings very little, there were nevertheless seventy-five new faces in the House of Commons. These included some who were destined to leave their mark on Parliament. There were now four woman members, three of them Conservatives. Ellen Fairclough, who had proved her formidable abilities in the House, had been joined by Sybil Bennett (Halton) and Margaret Aitken (York-Humber). Sybil was a relative of R.B. Bennett, and Margaret was a niece of Lord Beaverbrook. The fourth woman member was Ann Shipley, a Liberal, from northern Ontario. Western Ontario had sent some new and promising Conservatives to strengthen us: J. Waldo Monteith (Perth), a former mayor of Stratford, who was destined to sit in cabinet; Bob Mitchell (London), a very competent lawyer who would have gone far in politics but chose to leave public life in 1957; Wallace Nesbitt (Oxford), another very able young lawyer. In my home riding of Waterloo South, Howie Meeker had retired, and the seat had gone to Liberal Arthur White, mayor of Galt, over my old friend Bob Barber. Quebec had sent us three new Conservatives: Bill Hamilton (Montreal, Notre Dame de Grâce), who was destined to sit in cabinet, Bob Perron (Dorchester) and Wilfrid Dufresne (Quebec West). In New Brunswick we had lost the gifted Albany Robichaud, but Saint John sent us Tom Bell, a very promising young man.

Once again the Liberals, though receiving only 48 per cent of the popular vote, overflowed the government side of the Chamber, and over forty of them occupied the section nearest to the Speaker on his left. These Liberals in the overflow continued to be known as "Little Chicago" and included some very vociferous individuals. There were nearly as many of them as there were of us Conservatives. With these on our right, the CCF on our left, the Social Credit on their left, and the main body of the Grits in front of us we again seemed to be literally surrounded by adversaries. Two significant changes had been introduced: a sound-amplifying system had been installed; and I had been advanced in the seating. I was now assigned the second seat to the right of the Leader of the Opposition and was desk-mate to Howard Green. I was honoured to be seated as a senior front-bencher. The amplifying system was of some benefit, particularly for those members who did not use their voices adequately. I had no need of it in that respect. It should not be confused with the system of simultaneous translation we introduced later.

A new Clerk sat at the end of the table. Dr. Beauchesne, the greatest authority on the rules and procedures of Parliament since Bourinot, had retired. The urbane Léon J. Raymond, MP for Wright since 1945, had been appointed to succeed him.

The House quickly elected René Beaudoin as Speaker. The nomination was moved by the Prime Minister, and for the first time was seconded by the Leader of the Opposition. I thought this was a very fitting proceeding, and I give Mr. St. Laurent full credit for it. René had already proved himself a very competent Deputy Speaker in the previous Parliament. His knowledge of the rules and his ability to interpret them readily and in judicial language were most impressive. He was the closest friend I had among the Quebec Liberals.

Elected Deputy Speaker was Bill Robinson (Simcoe East), a classmate of mine for four years at Varsity and three years at Osgoode Hall Law School. Bill had distinguished himself first as chairman of the Committee on Broadcasting and then as deputy chairman of the Committee of the Whole. Elected to this latter post was Ted Applewhaite (Skeena). Another change greeted the House: Alphonse Fournier had gone to his reward on the bench, and Walter Harris had become Government House Leader in his place.

There were two new faces on the Treasury benches. Jean Lesage, able and ambitious, had been appointed Minister of Resources and Development. This promotion had been expected. The appointment of the new Secretary of State occasioned some surprise. Mr. St. Laurent, even with his numerous following in the House, had gone outside it to select Jack Pickersgill, Clerk of the Privy Council and Secretary of the Cabinet. I considered it an undesirable practice to appoint men from the civil service; admittedly, in Milton Gregg and Mike Pearson the Prime Minister could point to two successful precedents. Never did a man cast aside the cloak of the non-partisan civil servant and don the cloak of partisan more readily or more swiftly or more whole-heartedly than Jack Pickersgill. From the moment of his elevation to ministerial dignity he out-heroded Herod. He became the most rabid partisan on the Grit benches. It was thought that his preferment was viewed dimly by all the disappointed Liberals in the House who had been passed over. Perhaps this helps to account for his desire to establish his partisan credentials in their eyes. But his zeal did not stop there. Most people on entering the House under these circumstances would have thought it in good taste to remain quiet for a time and modestly leave the infighting to other more seasoned veterans. Not so Jack. He was twittering from the outset with his interruptions and illuminating wise-cracks, points of order and questions of privilege. I labelled him "Jumping Jack."

Pickersgill had some nervous mannerisms. Whenever he spoke he looked around at his Liberal colleagues as if to invite their applause. He is the only member I ever saw applaud his own speech. On two separate occasions after taking his seat he joined the other Grits in applauding the remarks he had just delivered, by vigorously pounding his desk, as they were pounding theirs. Reared in Manitoba, he was strangely given the riding of Bona-vista-Twillingate in Newfoundland to represent. In cartoons he was usually depicted as a seaman garbed in oilskins and dragging a fish by a line. Tom Bell took delight in hailing him, "Every inch a sailor." Of all Grits I ever met the two most extreme partisans were Jimmy Sinclair and Jack Pickersgill.

After electing the Speaker, the House turned to a sad task – to pay tribute to the late Gordon Graydon. The most popular member of the entire opposition and one of my dearest friends, Gordon died soon after being re-elected for Peel on August 10. He had been Conservative House Leader and Leader of the Opposition from 1943 to 1945. Gordon's seniority in the House and in caucus was fully recognized. He was chairman of our caucus organization and spokesman on external affairs. He did not take an active part in the more partisan debates, but contributed his advice on tactics. He was a master of the quip, a most valuable parliamentary device. He had a smile and a jest for everyone. I turned to him for advice often, particularly in my early days in the House. He was trusted implicitly by all. Stories circulated about the friendly relations he went out of his way to establish at the United Nations with the Russians, notably Andrei Gromyko, and the Arabs. The tributes to his memory and service expressed in the House by the leaders were very personal and touching. Everyone had lost a friend.

Gordon's death left two immediate vacancies. Earl Rowe became the desk-mate of the Leader of the Opposition and Acting House Leader in his absence. John Diefenbaker received the coveted appointment as opposition spokesman on external affairs and chairman of the Committee on External Affairs in caucus. This pleased him greatly. Davie Fulton succeeded him as spokesman on justice.

The House sat from November 12 to December 16, then adjourned to January 12, 1954, for the Christmas recess. Two days after the opening of Parliament President Eisenhower paid an official visit. Members of both Houses met to hear from him one of the best addresses ever delivered in Ottawa by a visiting head of state. Ike was in great form, and evidently knew he was among friends and admirers. His principal announcement was of the formation of the Canada–U.S. Joint Economic and Trade Committee, consisting of four ministers from the cabinet of each of the two countries and having as its purpose to meet periodically to discuss in broad terms economic and trade problems and means of solving them equitably. Incidentally, the committee held its first meeting in Washington on March 16. Three years later I was to become Canadian leader on this committee and to breathe fresh life and purpose into it for five years. The President also made an encouraging announcement concerning the St. Lawrence Waterway. He asserted, "Joint development and use of the St. Lawrence–Great Lakes Waterway is inevitable, is sure and certain," and his words were received with loud applause. His third important announcement was that the United States and Canada "can and will devise ways to protect our North America from any surprise attack by air." This was the inception of NORAD.

The five weeks of sitting before Christmas enabled the House to dispose of the debate on the address in reply to the speech from the throne, and to consider some urgent legislation. For many good reasons I was relieved to see the House rise in the late evening of December 16 and to catch the night train for Toronto. The prospect of over three weeks at home was joyous.

As was my annual custom, I attended the Lieutenant-Governor's reception on New Years's Day. It was a great opportunity to see friends by the hundreds. On this particular day I had the good fortune to meet Arthur Meighen. He congratulated me warmly on my work in Parliament and added: "I used to think

Diefenbaker was the man. Now I think you are." This was overwhelming praise from a most respected source. It also called to mind something that Jim Macdonnell had told me previously. He had been talking to Meighen about me. After enumerating what he regarded as my best attributes, Meighen added with very warm approval, "Yes, and he has natural animosity." I never thought of myself as entertaining personal animosity toward anyone, least of all that such was part of my nature. I was, however, always able to register indignation and to base it on moral principles and to take a fighting stance in debate. I think this is what Meighen meant. Margaret Aitken adopted the same theme in her column "Between You and Me" in the *Toronto Telegram* on March 26, 1954, as follows:

> That sparked hot debate, with one of the hottest debaters, Donald Fleming, M.P. for Eglinton. Mr. Fleming adopted one of his favourite debating tricks, which might be called the cloak of natural animosity. Anyone with less natural animosity would be hard to find, but when Mr. Fleming dons his mantle he bristles with animosity.
>
> At one stage Don managed to tie in Rt. Hon. C.D. Howe with a trio of dictators – Cromwell, Hitler and Mussolini. The Speaker demanded a retraction on that one, and we all expected fireworks from our fiery colleague. Not at all.
>
> "Such is my love for you, Mr. Speaker," said Mr. Fleming sweetly, "I will withdraw anything. . . . But if I cannot use the language to which I am accustomed, then I will simply have to resort to Shakespeare:
>
> Upon what meat doth this our Caesar feed,
> That he is grown so great?

The 1954 session resumed on January 12. It had in store for me a heavy load of work and the usual wide range of debating activities. It was to bring tragedy close to me twice.

The subject of redistribution and methods of achieving it again raised its head early in the session, but in a somewhat less bellicose atmosphere than in 1952. This time Chubby Power deliberately chose a period long removed from the decennial census to propose that a committee be instructed to examine methods and principles to be applied. It was a very constructive service. I spoke for the opposition in support of the motion and argued that we must never permit a repetition of the political surgery which was the scandal of the last redistribution. I advocated that the task be performed by an impartial commission, with Parliament making the final decision on the commission's report. The motion was adopted, and the Committee on Privileges and Elections was set to work to carry out the study. The eventual adoption in Canada of the commission method of carrying out the admittedly difficult task of redistribution, adopting the system already established in the United Kingdom and Australia, owes not a little, I believe, to my denunciations in 1952 and 1954 of the highly partisan manner in which the Grits carried out their scandalous gerrymander in 1952.

With the general election behind them the government moved to increase the indemnity of members and the salaries of ministers. This being ever an unpopular project the timing must be delicately weighed. The indemnity of $4,000 per session was set in 1920 and had remained unchanged since. When two sessions were held in a year and two indemnities paid there was strong criticism. An annual expense allowance of $2,000 was created in 1945. Now the government proposed to raise the indemnity to $8,000 per annum, not per session, and to pay it on a monthly basis. It was also proposed to increase the salary paid to ministers and the Leader of the Opposition by $5,000 per annum and that of the Prime Minister by $10,000.

I was fully in accord with these proposals. I considered action was due, the amounts were reasonable and the government was acting responsibly. I had some doubt as to whether the indemnity paid to senators should be doubled likewise, but did not feel strongly over it. The caucus, however, decided to oppose the bill. Drew, Diefenbaker, Green and Fulton took a high-minded, self-denying position. I strongly suspected that there was also present a desire to embarrass the government, and a pretext was welcome for this purpose. George Drew therefore took the position in the House that the need for an increase was admitted, but not the amount and that it should be left to a royal commission to determine what that amount should be. I could not follow the logic of conceding to members the right to determine that $4,000 per session was inadequate, but denying them the right to determine the extent of the admitted inadequacy. I did not need any royal commission to tell me what that inadequacy was; I knew it all too well. Moreover, the amount which a royal commission could be expected to recommend would depend entirely on the personnel selected to compose it. Drew and Diefenbaker may not have needed the overdue increase; I did. The measure was sustained on January 26 by a vote of 130 to 37 and on February 2 by a vote of 155 to 45. I took no part in the debate and deliberately absented myself from the two votes. I accepted the increase, considering myself justly entitled to it. I am not aware that any who for one reason or another placed themselves in the position of appearing to oppose the increase rejected it after it was voted to them over their heroic protests. I am entirely satisfied that if I had retired from public life at that moment and flung myself on the mercies of the cold world I would have improved my income considerably. Moreover, I would rather have quit than play the hypocrite.

For once the constitution escaped debate in the House. I asked the Prime Minister on June 1 if it was the government's intention "to reconvene the Dominion-Provincial Conference with a view to arriving at an agreed method of amending the British North America Act in Canada?" His reply was terse: "No; not at this time." I never understood the Liberal reluctance to seek agreement for this laudable purpose. In the meantime the government was taking the lion's share of the yields from the fields of direct taxation, leaving the provinces in a weakened fiscal position. In this way they were changing the constitution in fact.

The budget gave us an opportunity to enlarge on this theme. Doug Abbott brought it down on April 6. It was to be his last. Not being an election year there were no tax reductions of any significance whatever. The Conservative amendment, besides deploring the government's failure to reduce taxes and expenditure, expressed regret that the government "has failed to reach agreement with the Provinces in regard to a clearly defined reallocation of taxing powers so that the Provincial Governments and Municipal Councils may have adequate financial resources to carry out their rapidly increasing responsibilities." In my speech I pleaded for a Dominion-provincial conference. I reviewed the history of direct taxation in Canada since Confederation, stressing that the provinces in 1942 had agreed to vacate this field and rent it to the federal government only "during the continuation of the present war and for a certain readjustment period thereafter," and now the federal government was exhibiting a marked reluctance to restore the field or even a reasonable share of it to the provinces. I asserted that, "Prior to the war the percentage of the total taxes in Canada collected by the federal government was 39 per cent. Last year that percentage had doubled to 78 per cent. More federal taxation and expenditure mean more federal power at the expense of the Provinces." I accused the Liberals of having poisoned "the wells of Canadian unity" by "bellicose statements exposing the same kind of belligerent truculent attitude that was shown by the Minister of Finance." I charged the federal government with "a determination to beat the Province of Quebec to its knees," to compel "the Quebec Government . . . to come cap in hand and rap on the door of the Minister of Finance." I concluded, "Which course is to be followed, bitterness, disunity and division, or the conference table, the spirit of good will, understanding and accord? The choice rests with the Prime Minister of Canada." Those words were uttered on May 28, 1954. They were equally true in 1980, 1981 and 1982.

My speech drew wide publicity in Quebec. *Le Devoir* the next day ran a front-page article under the headline "M. Donald Fleming Défend la Province de Québec." I had indeed defended the province of Quebec. I had defended all the provinces against the harsh pressures exerted upon them by a centralization-bent and power-hungry federal government.

I had been pleading the cause of the municipalities more constantly than anyone else in the House. I had urged their purchases should be exempt from federal sales and excise taxes. On May 17 on a supply motion George Drew took up this theme and brought in an amendment to ensure exemption in such cases. I believe the speech I made in that debate is the best presentation of the plight of the municipal governments made in my eighteen years in Parliament. I asserted, "While these constitutional formulas have remained virtually unchanged for 87 years, there has been not simply a steady increase in municipal responsibilities but a mounting multiplication of them and the attendant financial burden. . . . In the whole field of education in Canada the burden the municipalities are carrying is one that is entirely disproportionate to their means." Besides education I listed the burden of providing for the unemployable, the employable unemployed, hospitalization and housing – all on basically the same tax base which existed at confederation. "Every sales and excise tax that the Federal Government is today collecting from the municipalities is hidden. That is one of the fundamental curses of these anomalies in the constitutional powers of taxing."

The Prime Minister was absent from the House six weeks at the height of the session on a good-will tour of Western Europe, the Middle East and Far East. He returned on March 18 and made a lengthy report. To me he seemed to be physically and mentally tired. Although he had a Canadian doctor in his party his program made harsh demands upon him. He should either have lengthened it to provide for rest periods or on his return have taken at least several days to rest before returning to the House. In his report to the House Mr. St. Laurent went out of his way to pay me a gracious compliment on my use of French: "I met the Ambassador of Afghanistan to India. He . . . expressed his regrets that I was not visiting his country. He did that in the most perfect French, which I am sure the honourable Member for Eglinton would admire as much as I did."

Unfortunately, the Prime Minister while in the East involved himself in some difficulty by making a statement which was reported around the world and gave rise to controversy. It was to the effect that we must be realistic and recognize the present (Communist) government of China as the government the people of China wanted. On March 25 he entered the annual debate on external affairs for the purpose of explaining away the statement attributed to him. He did not, however, quite deny having made it. Nevertheless, his statement in the House was, of course, accepted and appeared to put an end to the matter. The debate proceeded on other questions, and both Mike Pearson and John Diefenbaker in his new capacity made interesting contributions. I spoke also that day, indicting Russian plans for world revolution. I discussed the proposed European army and returned to the subject of German rearmament. I opposed recognition of the government of China. Having been denounced by the United Nations as an aggressor China could hardly be recognized as eligible for membership in that organization.

What would be the fate of the Emergency Powers Act? Would the government permit it to lapse or would it face a hostile opposition over it as it had in 1953? Hostilities in Korea had been halted by an armistice. Two Liberal members had been won over to vote with us against renewal of the measure in 1953. Would the government risk the certainty of an explosive debate on the issue? The throne speech was totally silent on the issue. On November 18, 1953, I asked the Prime Minister directly, what was the government's intention. Mr. St. Laurent was evasive, "That is a matter of policy about which information will be communicated to the House in due time." We waited for four more months but still the government maintained its silence. We decided to smoke them out, if possible, rather than perhaps be confronted with legislation to renew the powers in the late days of the session. On March 22 on a supply motion George Drew opened up the subject wide. His amendment, "This House desires to record its opinion that the powers granted to the Governor-in-Council under the Emergency Powers Act are repugnant to responsible government," was defeated on division by a vote of 134 to 68. Five weeks later, St. Laurent announced to the House in reply to a question from me that the government had decided not to ask Parliament to extend the act. Had it been able to make up its mind sooner or to be less coy with the House, two days of rather acrimonious debate might have been saved.

254

The Diefenbaker government was evidently not the only cabinet which had difficulty making decisions.

It should not be inferred, however, that the government was now shorn of all its emergency or extraordinary powers. Howe still retained his sweeping powers under the Defence Production Act, and the Export and Import Permits Act gave the government power to prevent either export or import of strategic materials, and these were widely defined. The powers under this measure were due to expire July 31, 1954. The government introduced a measure to extend them to 1957. On March 17 and 18 I delivered a full-dress speech for the party. We urged that the measure be sent to the Banking and Commerce Committee for full study and to limit the period of extension to one year. The government rejected both proposals. Howe's stated reasons for not wishing to limit the extension to one year are interesting: "We dislike to take up the time of Parliament each year in extending this bill; such a procedure is expensive to the Canadian public and annoying to Members of Parliament." What he meant was that it was annoying to C.D. Howe to be accountable to Parliament.

The Estimates of the Department of Defence Production were declining with its procurement tasks. I defined the responsibilities of the opposition, however, as the maintenance of strict scrutiny over its expenditures, which still accounted for almost half of the national budget. As between this department and the Department of National Defence, Howe still followed what I called his "gold-plated piano policy." Whatever DND wanted he bought, and without question. The purchasing policy was to buy Canadian first, then British, then United States, and to spread Canadian purchases as widely as possible. We had no quarrel with the policy thus defined, but we had to maintain watch over its enforcement.

Nineteen fifty-four was the year for the decennial revision of the Bank Act, and I looked forward to participating in this challenging and interesting task in the Banking and Commerce Committee. To my delight the CCF moved to nationalize the banking system. I demolished their proposal in a strong speech on March 9. They had for some time been soft-pedalling socialism. They had now returned to the supreme folly of the Regina Manifesto and its dogma that "control of finance is the first step in the control of the whole economy." I hailed their "self-exposure" and lashed their monopolistic, bureaucratic fallacies.

One startling new proposal submitted by the government was to abandon the age-old prohibition on lending on mortgage security by chartered banks and to allow them to make loans on the security of first mortgage on residential property if the mortgage was insured by Central Mortgage and Housing Corporation. This was accompanied by the introduction of new major legislation on housing. The old National Housing Act was to be repealed, the best of its provisions were to be carried forward into a new National Housing Act, direct lending by CMHC was to give way to a system of insuring first mortgages by CMHC, and chartered banks were to join trust, loan and life insurance companies as approved lenders. Down payments by mortgagors were reduced, and the period of amortization was lengthened from twenty to twenty-five and thirty years. The new legislation gave rise to the leading debate on housing in my eighteen years in Parliament. Some of it was good, and some of it was not.

The government was foolish enough to pretend that the new scheme was the effective solution to Canada's persistent and still serious housing deficiency. As usual they exaggerated grossly the benefits which might be expected to arise from it. Strangely enough, they had held no discussions with the banks to acquaint them with the new role they were expected to play. To the banks, lending on the security of mortgages on residential property was a totally new field; lacking any experience in it they were bound to approach it cautiously. Moreover, they were already lent up to capacity. Were they to reduce their commercial lending, their purchases of bonds issued by federal, provincial and municipal governments in order to free funds for the purchase of mortgages? There were many other questions. One redeeming feature of the government's approach was their announcement at the outset that the bill would be sent after second reading to the Banking and Commerce Committee. This should have helped to reduce the debate up to that stage.

The bill was introduced on the last day before the Christmas recess. It proved to be a major piece of legislation, extending to twenty thousand words, much of it in terms of very involved draftsmanship. I studied it with thorough care and was ready when the debate on second reading opened on January 21. I contended that the assumed benefits from the measure had been exaggerated, that it contributed nothing to the removal of the principal existing bottleneck – namely, the shortage of serviced land – that no one knew what funds would be available for investment in mortgages, that a fundamental change was being introduced into Canadian banking law and practice as it had endured since Confederation, that this was being launched without the slightest consultation with the banks, and that CMHC was being given enormous powers. I was careful, however, not to condemn the bill or the scheme. Time might vindicate the scheme, and the banks would undoubtedly co-operate. I entertained misgivings over what lending on the security of mortgages with twenty-five- or thirty-year maturities might do to impair the essential liquidity of the Canadian banking system, but the bill did embody much that we had supported in the past. Our caucus was divided on the issue of bank lending, but it seemed to me that we could not possibly oppose the motion for second reading of the bill; we would have full opportunity in the committee to probe deeply. Bob Winters, who in my opinion was by far the best minister the government had ever had in charge of housing, complimented me on my speech. He called it a "constructive contribution to the debate," and added, "As usual, the honourable member had done his homework thoroughly."

I had expected our members to observe similar restraint, but I was mistaken. At the first opportunity up jumped George Hees and in a very intemperate outburst labelled the bill "nothing but a gigantic bluff." As so often happened, he was reaching for headlines without pondering the real effect of his words. Doug Harkness, while contributing some useful thoughts to the debate, allowed himself in a moment of vexation to say, "This bill will be an utter failure." The words of Hees and Harkness had so stung the government that Bob Winters in a neat tactical move forced a division on the bill, which carried by a vote of 186 to 2. Doug Harkness was in the House and voted in favour; Hees was nowhere to be seen. The rest of us Conservatives as we voted for the bill had to listen to the jeers from the Liberal benches that he had helped to bring down on our heads.

The Banking and Commerce Committee did a superb piece of work in its hearings on the bill. Between February 2 and March 2 it held no fewer than twenty-three meetings and heard testimony from representatives of all interested national organizations. When the bill was returned to the House I delivered a major speech on March 5 reviewing the evidence taken before the committee. It was done in a non-partisan tone, but my review of the evidence was incisive, fearless and thorough. The evidence exposed the exaggeration attending the bill. Mr. Mansur put existing economic demand at 120,000 houses, and thought the new scheme might add between 5,000 and 15,000 thereto. The banks were very cautious and non-committal. I condemned the folly of all the exaggeration and propaganda in the promotion of the new scheme, and warned of the dangers of centralization, bureaucracy, inflation, the lack of serviced land, the neglect of rural housing and the neglect of the need for slum clearance. Never before or since has housing been the centre of such a major and protracted debate. I take great satisfaction from the constructive role I played throughout. For nine years I had been the party's spokesman on housing, and the most authoritative voice in the House on the subject. I had been critical, but always constructive. I believe I was an effective and beneficial spur in the flanks of the government. From this point on housing would recede as a subject of debate in the House. Measured against the paramount debate of 1954 discussions in later years would seem minor.

My responsibilities as spokesman on trade were very heavy in the 1954 session. I had already criticized the bill to amend the Customs Act and undertaken a monitoring role on the first meeting of the Canada–U.S. Joint Committee on Trade and Economic Affairs. I met Howe on June 10 face to face in debate on his estimates over the government's trade policy and performance. Howe was ever an optimist – as long as he was in charge. I chided him on putting his glass to his blind eye, like Nelson, and failing to see problems and developments which should be giving the government concern. I drew attention to the loss of the British market for Canadian agricultural products – bacon, pork, beef, apples, cheese – and the government's attitude of indifference or resignation. I cited our large deficit in our commodity trade with the United States, and the ever-increasing danger of putting all our trading eggs in that one basket. I chastised the government for not fostering a climate favourable to Canadian producers and allowing taxes and government expenditures to mount. Instead of countenancing these ingredients of a high-cost economy it was time for the government to clean house and contribute to the improvement of the competitive position of the Canadian producer in the markets of the world. It was a thorough and realistic review of Canada's need of a better performance on the part of the government in relation to external trade.

But my principal effort as spokesman on trade was made in the debate on May 12 on ratification of the Trade Agreement with Japan signed at Ottawa on March 31. The Treaty of Peace with Japan had been unanimously approved by the House on June 16, 1952. It was generous in its terms toward a defeated enemy. Japan was increasingly regarded as a major outpost against communism. Russia had vetoed her application for membership in the United Nations. Japan was attaining an impressive economic recovery. She had become Canada's third-largest customer and a most important market for Canadian wheat. The trade agreement extended to Japan Most Favoured Nation (MFN) treatment under our tariff. Our approach to the issue of ratification was beset by difficulties both political and economic. The wounds of war had not fully healed. Japanese wartime atrocities, including maltreatment of the Canadian defenders of Hong Kong, had not been forgotten; neither had the difficulties arising out of Japanese prewar exports of cheap, and often shoddy, manufactured goods to Canada. More urgently, the Canadian textile industry was already in difficulties, in part as the result of imports from Japan. Textile plants were actually closing. Nevertheless, caucus accepted my proposal that we should support ratification. But how should our position be presented? That was left to me without any instruction.

I daresay any critical judge reading my speeches in Parliament would probably single out the speech I delivered on the afternoon of May 12, 1954, as the best I ever made in my twelve years in opposition. It was not a debating speech in the ordinary sense, for I was not answering anything that Howe had said in introducing the motion for approval of ratification. It was rather a frank examination of the arguments on both sides of the issue. To those who contend that parliamentarians should be furnished with research assistance I say most of them should exert themselves to do their own. A great deal of patient and minute research work went into the preparation of that speech; I did every bit of it myself. It was documented and supported by references to history and a wealth of relevant statistics. Indeed, I was well launched into that part of my speech dealing with the economic history and potential of Japan when George Drew turned to Howard Green and said in a voice that was audible to me, "Where on earth does he gather all this information?" I spoke for an hour, pleading for the healing of the old wounds of war, for a new approach based on goodwill, common interest and interdependence. I turned away from none of the difficulties. I uttered no partisan thought. When I took my seat there was a storm of desk-pounding from all parts of the House. I was quite taken aback. Coldwell, who followed me, complimented me on "the exhaustive analysis he gave of both the treaty and matters connected with the formulation of such a treaty." C.D. Howe, who was not given to complimenting members of the opposition, sent me a hand-written note: "Mr. Fleming. Congratulations on an eloquent and excellent speech. C.D.H." I went over to him at the adjournment to thank him for his most generous words. From George Drew I received a hand-written letter: "That magnificent speech is one of which you can always be proud. It has stated our position in words which fully protect the strong reservations we have in regard to this treaty. My warmest congratulations."

Members of Parliament have their triumphs, but they are in no way immune to the mischances and tragedies of life. Two such events brought deep sorrow to members. On April 8 my colleague and friend, Rodney Adamson, MP for York West, and his wife Cynthia, perished in a mid-air collision over Moose Jaw, when an RCAF trainer craft collided with a TCA airliner, causing the deaths of thirty-one passengers and one person on the ground. It was a tragic end to two useful lives. Rodney had represented York West since 1940.

On May 26 death struck again with dramatic suddenness. It was the evening of the annual softball game on the front lawn on Parliament Hill between the teams of the press gallery and the House of Commons. Our infield for years had consisted of Doug Abbott at first base, Lionel Conacher at second, myself at shortstop and Mike Pearson at third, and we batted in that order. Lionel Conacher, thanks to weak fielding by the press gallery and to his own speed, had just stretched a single into a triple. He pulled up on third base, and I came to bat. The first pitch was a called strike. The pitcher was just winding up for his second pitch when suddenly I saw a shadow flash across the left edge of my range of vision. I looked up to see Lionel lying stretched out full length on the ground. Dr. McMillan (Welland) endeavoured to resuscitate Lionel, an ambulance was called, and he was rushed off to the hospital. The crowd, shocked and hushed, dispersed. I feared the worst for my friend Lionel, and for his wife Dot.

The thought would not depart from my harassed mind, "Who is going to tell Dot? If someone doesn't call her soon will she hear from the press or on the radio?" No one else seemed to be undertaking this grievous task. I concluded it was up to me. I went back to my office and called Dot in Toronto. I had determined to break the news in two stages; that would make it easier for her. She answered at once. She was alone, so it was not possible to convey the news through a third party. I asked her to be seated as I had some bad news for her. I explained as well as I could that Lionel had collapsed on the field and had been rushed to the hospital. Plainly agitated, she asked the one question I wished to avoid, "Is he dead?" I suspected that he was, but fortunately at that point I didn't know, so I was able to tell her he was receiving the best available care. I urged her to call in the family, and promised to call her back as soon as I had more news. Within five minutes I had confirmation from Lionel's secretary that he was indeed dead. The oldest daughter Constance was by now at home with her mother and was anxiously awaiting my call. I could only break the sorrowful news to her and ask her to convey my love and sympathy to her mother in this moment of anguish.

I flew back to Toronto the next day and joined many dazed friends on the following day at the funeral service. We said our farewell to one of the greatest athletes Canada ever produced, a true and honourable sportsman and a gentleman. I looked upon him as a genuine friend. As a student at Varsity I had watched him in the late afternoons at the Argonaut rugby workouts practising punting, catching and running. I saw him in the games making fantastic runs through the tacklers for long gains. The admiration I developed toward him then continued through his later career in other sports, in business and in politics. The standards he maintained in life won him respect and acclaim. After serving in the Ontario legislature he was twice elected MP for Trinity. Although we were in opposite parties that fact was entirely irrelevant to our friendship. In the House on May 27 the leaders paid tribute to Lionel. I added mine:

> Mr. Speaker, the leaders have spoken today for all members of this House. May I just add this personal word which comes from the heart.
>
> After a long and quite intimate association with the late Lionel Conacher, in politics, sport and socially, I can say this of our late colleague. Under all circumstances he never failed to be a gentleman. His instinct of fair play and generous concern of others was outstanding. Though the idol of every sport lover in Canada, the outstanding Canadian athlete, a man who attained success also in business and politics, his success had never deprived him of his essential and altogether admirable quality of modesty.
>
> He was essentially a family man, and the hearts of his wife and five children, to whom he was deeply devoted, and who are a great credit to him, are sore and heavy today. His daughter Diane was to have graduated from the University of Toronto today.
>
> It happened that when the tragic moment came, in last night's game, Mr. Speaker, I was at bat, and it was my uncertain hope to bring Lionel Conacher home from third base. A higher power intervened, Mr. Speaker, to bring Lionel Conacher home.

The words were uttered under stress of deep emotion. That emotion returns twenty-nine years later as I pen this recollection of one of the most moving experiences of my life.

The Committee on Procedure was again appointed with unanimous support, its purpose being "to assure the more expeditious dispatch of public business." Brooks, Churchill, Fulton and I remained the four Conservative members on it out of a total of twenty-one. Walter Harris as House Leader began to press for measures to reduce the time spent in debate. We Conservatives as a small minority, having only the right to speak and vote, were bound to be suspicious of any attempt to curtail the right of speech. On June 23 in the House George Drew took issue with any proposal which would curtail debate and urged a better organization of the business of the House, which lay within the responsibility of the government. The most obvious move of the Liberals on the committee was to shorten the forty-minute time allowed to speakers in debate. Harris wanted thirty minutes in the House and twenty minutes in committee. There are times when forty-minute speeches are longer than necessary; at others forty minutes are short enough. I feared any reduction as abridging the opposition freedom to criticize. The committee reported on June 25, but no action was taken on the report at that session. Margaret Aitken wrote in her column in the *Telegram* on June 3:

> There are two schools of thought on these 40-minute speeches. (In the British House of Commons there is no time limit). Some believe the speeches should be curtailed to 30 minutes, even 20 minutes. Others, mostly the more experienced parliamentarians like Donald Fleming, feel there should be no change in the 40-minute limit. His claim is that a speaker needs the time to develop his argument. Personally, I would give Mr. Fleming his 40 minutes any time he wants them. He is a vigorous and skilful debater.

More was to be heard on this subject and on efforts to curtail the rights of the Leader of the Opposition at the 1955 session.

In July 1981 the Canadian Post Office was closed for over a fortnight by a strike of the employees under very aggressive leaders. This outrageous deprivation of their mail service has been inflicted on Canadians and persons doing business by mail with them with painful frequency in recent years. Even when the postal service is in full operation it has declined lamentably in efficiency and promptness. The seeds of this deplorable deterioration were sown years ago. In 1954 the genial and popular Postmaster General, Alcide Côté, introduced a measure to increase the postage on local delivery mail from 3 to 4 cents, and other first-class surface mail from 4 to 5 cents, effective April 1. This was done in anticipation of a deficit on Post Office operations. The measure encountered stiff resistance at the hands of the opposition. Delays in delivery of mail were denounced. The good-natured Alcide parried the attacks with his most engaging smile and disarming gentleness. Any other minister would have been mauled and bruised in such a debate. The government majority carried the measure, but not before I had smitten them on January 14:

> The service in recent years has deteriorated to a shocking degree. . . . The carriers have done and are doing their work well. The fault lies with the management of this Department. . . . Not many years ago the service given by the Canadian Post Office Department was as good as was to be found anywhere in any government service. . . . But that time has gone. The Canadian people take no pride in the kind of service they have been receiving under the management of this Government. . . . They were a tax-reducing government last summer, but come the fall . . . and with the winter setting in they are a rate-raising government. . . . They have not proved their case, and what business have they coming before this House and saying, "We anticipate a deficit," until that situation has arisen? They are altogether too eager. This is a habit born long ago and bred in the members who have grown up in this government, that they think they have a right to increase all rates whether it be for government services or for taxes. It is so easy for them to increase the rates that are imposed on the people. It is a bad habit; it is a vicious habit; and it is to be hoped that the House is not going to tolerate much more of it.

In 1954 I took time to make a number of speeches. One of considerable importance was delivered in Toronto, at the Royal York Hotel, but to the Progressive Conservative Business Men's Club. I entitled it "Distinctive Conservatism." It was intended to answer those who were asking, "What real difference is there between the two old parties?", a question subtly promoted by the CCF. I thought there was a vital difference between the Liberal and Conservative parties, and I said so. I dwelt on the history of the party, its solid achievements and contributions to Canadian development, exposed Liberal attempts to steal credit due our party and set forth essential differences in policy between the two parties. I listed six of these, relating to the Crown, Parliament, the constitution, the Commonwealth, the processing of raw materials, and free enterprise. The theme was timely. The party thought highly enough of the text to have thousands of copies printed in pamphlet form. I believe it proved very useful to party seminars and study groups. Margaret Aitken in her column described the speech, which she heard, as "statesmanlike and patriotic . . . a veritable handbook for any student of Canadian politics."

Prorogation finally arrived on June 26. Seldom had it been so welcome. We had been in session for months, and I had been working to the limit without any relief. Home looked good to me, and I rejoiced in the thought that I would have no occasion to return to Ottawa for five or six months. But I had not been home two days before the phone rang from Ottawa. It was George Drew inviting me to take his place at a government dinner on the evening of June 30 at the Country Club in honour of Sir Winston Churchill and Anthony Eden. Needless to say, I leaped at the opportunity and returned immediately to the capital. There were about thirty-five invited guests at the dinner, and I had opportunity for a chat with both distinguished visitors. Churchill indeed was very affable. He chose to speak particularly about Anthony Eden, and the not mere similarity but virtual identity of the views they entertained. He went so far as to say, "If you took each of us in turn into another room and submitted the same questions to us you would receive the same answers from us both." He praised Eden warmly. St. Laurent was in happy form. As I rode the night train back to Toronto I wished all my visits to Ottawa could be equally pleasant.

Prorogation marked the end of the political road for two very senior ministers, whom I looked upon as friends. Doug Abbott was appointed to the Supreme Court of Canada, and Brooke Claxton returned to private life. Walter Harris, a rising star and regarded as Mr. St. Laurent's choice as his successor, was the new Minister of Finance. The stage was set for the dramatic events of 1956 and 1957. It is interesting to speculate whether if Abbott, Claxton and Chevrier had remained in the government they would have counter-balanced the influence of C.D. Howe in the cabinet and changed the course of those deplorable events. The parliamentary scene was changing. Its centre of gravity was shifting toward C.D. Howe.

CHAPTER TWENTY-FOUR

The Dark Continent

To George Drew and no doubt in part to my own activities as the serving Conservative on the executive committee of the Canadian Branch of the Commonwealth Parliamentary Association I owe one of the most fascinating and instructive experiences of my life. Out of a delegation of seven members from the Canadian Parliament to the Commonwealth Parliamentary Conference held at Nairobi, the capital of Kenya, in what was then known as British East Africa, the Liberals claimed four places, and one each went to the Conservatives, CCF and Social Credit. It was a special honour to be selected as the sole Conservative delegate from Parliament, although I drew encouragement from the selection of Gordon Fairweather as the delegate from the New Brunswick branch of the CPA. However, harmony reigned within the delegation at all times. My friend Dr. Pierre Gauthier was an amiable leader. We all left partisan politics behind us. As usual, the conference itself was preceded and followed by a tour which, combined with the conference, occupied the entire months of August and September. For such a rare opportunity my partners were generous to the point of indulgence.

The conference and the tours had been superbly planned. Once the delegates had gathered in Nairobi we travelled together in chartered aircraft. Short movements were made by bus or car. In South Africa we lived for four days on a luxurious private train. The hospitality, mostly at hotels, but sometimes in private homes, was overwhelming. The program everywhere was designed to give us maximum opportunity to see everything of interest, to talk to well-informed local leaders in politics, business and society, and to study the evolution – economic, political and social – in a strategic area of the world in which the winds of change were beginning to blow. Our opportunities for gathering information and opinions and observing as we moved about

265

could not have been matched. Admittedly the pace was very strenuous. The day commences at an early hour in Africa, and usually mine ended at a very late hour. On my return journey I was in bed two and a quarter hours out of sixty-seven and a half, and many a night on the tours I had less than four hours in bed, but I enjoyed good health, and by maintaining strict precautions escaped all the fevers and ailments so often suffered by travellers. One of the more elderly delegates, Dave Kidd, the popular leader of the New Zealand delegation, collapsed at Kimberley and died within an hour. The pace had been just too heavy for a man of his years.

I spent several days in London on the way over. This afforded me a useful opportunity to visit the Conservative party's research bureau and to confer with the director. I attended a reception given by the British branch of the CPA at Westminster Hall for all the delegates gathering in London. There I saw my friend Derick Heathcote-Amory, who had just been advanced to the cabinet by Churchill and appointed Minister of Agriculture. He advised me to keep an eye at the conference on a promising younger man, Ted Heath, who was one of the British delegates. Among the other delegates I met at the reception were three with whom I was to enjoy closer acquaintance over the next eight weeks: Earl de la Warr, the leader, the Earl of Lucan, the deputy whip of the Labour party in the House of Lords, a career soldier and brother of Lady Alexander, and Derek Walker-Smith, an eminent barrister with a gift of Churchillian eloquence, who might in later years have come close to the top rungs of the British political ladder had he not later differed openly with Prime Minister Harold Macmillan in strongly opposing British entry into the European Common Market.

The five-thousand-mile flight from London to Nairobi took twenty-four hours. I was fortunate enough to be assigned to the Muthaiga Club on the outskirts of Nairobi. I began absorbing information by observation and discussion. The Mau Mau trouble had just passed its peak. This savage cult among the Kikuyu tribe had claimed the lives of some two thousand Africans and a number of Europeans in Kenya in the two previous years, and required the presence of two brigades of the British army as well as support forces. I soon learned, however, that the racial relations in East Africa were less complicated by the presence of Europeans (white) than by the centuries of bloody feuds among the African tribes savagely at war with each other generation after generation, and the presence of East Indians in considerable numbers in the coastal areas all the way from Kenya to Cape

Town. These were the descendants of Indians who had been admitted, often as indentured labourers, to assist in building harbours and roads and cultivating the soil, tasks for which it was considered the Africans were quite unsuited. Some of the Indians had made East Africa their homes for five generations. They had become the commercial class and in some cases the professional class. They were unpopular with the Africans, who looked upon them as foreigners and exploiters.

Our initial short stay in Nairobi afforded me my first acquaintance with African big game and their habits. One of the best things the white man in various African countries has done is to create large parks where game is protected. Just outside Nairobi is the Kenya National Park, where I beheld great herds of wildebeest, zebra, impala, as well as monkeys, baboons, giraffes, and for a long time I watched a lioness stalking a wildebeest. Cars are permitted to drive through the parks. The animals are so accustomed to the cars that they pay little attention to them or their occupants. It is thought also that the smell of petrol overcomes the smell of the human, and the dangerous animals are repelled by it. Passengers, however, are not permitted to step outside their cars.

The pre-conference tour took us to Uganda and to northwestern Kenya for five days each. Uganda is a nation of peasant farmers, growing a wide variety of agricultural products. Race relations were more harmonious than in Kenya. All the land was then owned by native Ugandans. The small white element in the population consisted chiefly of civil servants and persons serving under contract for periods of years, not settlers. A commendable effort was being made to provide education in the mission schools. From Entebbe, overlooking Lake Victoria, we proceeded to Kampala, seat of Makerere College, now a university. There my good friend Father Auguste St. Pierre was waiting to greet me. We had first met at the Vatican in 1948 and had maintained a correspondence in the meantime. It was a joy to see once again this selfless missionary who was devoting his life to bringing the gospel, education and civilization to the people in a whole province.

From Kampala we flew west along the equator to Kasenyi on Lake George, near the border of the Belgian Congo. This is big game country, and we saw numerous elephants, buffalo, waterbuck, and in Lake George innumerable hippopotami. A fish factory has provided employment, a market for fishermen, and support to the economy for miles around. The hippos are herbivorous. They wander about at night, destroying gardens. From there we took several safaris, one of which took us to Kilembe Mines, the manager of which, Mr. Pugley, used to live in Eglinton riding, and the engineer, Mr. Armour, close to it. This mine is a fine example of Canadian enterprise. At Jinja we were back on Lake Victoria, the source of the waters of the White Nile. With the end of tribal warfare the population is exploding.

We re-entered Kenya at Kisumu. Here I had my first experience of African drums. Their throbbing rhythm was wafted over the hills from a mile away. I was told that they were being beaten by the local band of the Salvation Army. They have a stirring, mesmerizing effect. At a dinner I met a couple, Mr. and Mrs. Maurice Strong from Calgary, who were spending two years travelling around the world. Our paths were destined to cross next in Nairobi and often in Canada in future.

At Kericho two of us were the overnight guests of Mr. and Mrs. Oliver Brooke on a large tea-growing estate of Brooke Bond & Company. We toured the estate, observing the benefits brought to this area by Western enterprise and the improved lot of the resident African employees. We were nearing Mau Mau country, and the delegates were being accompanied by soldiers and armed police (Askaris). We made the acquaintance of a custom among the Europeans known as "the sundowner." It is the cocktail party in the early evening under a different name. At Kericho the parents took their children with them to the sundowner and allowed them to sleep in the cars while armed guards protected them.

At Nakuru in the Kenya Highlands and ever closer to Mau Mau country Lord Lucan, Terence O'Neill, the Speaker of the Northern Ireland Parliament, Pierre Gauthier and I were the guests of Lord and Lady Claud Hamilton at their ranch of 28,500 acres. Claud was the younger son of the Duke of Abercorn. He was a relative of Lord Lucan and had served with Terence in the Irish Guards Regiment. Their cattle were being crossed with Jerseys imported from the Bull farm at Brampton, Canada. Here we spent two delightful days. We were less than forty miles from the Aberdare Mountains, the Mau Mau stronghold, surrounded by impenetrable bamboo forest. At police headquarters we were given a briefing on the Mau Mau and their savage raids, and visited a detention camp where I saw and conversed with detainees. The ranch was in territory of the Masai tribe, who traditionally have been herdsmen and enemies of the Kikuyu. Lady Claud said of her Masai, "They are the most lovable people in the world." At her request we met a group of their headmen, and on request I addressed them. On our departure they turned out in numbers and gave us a great send-off. One of them presented me with a bag of eggs as a token of appreciation and goodwill. Ten days later a Mau Mau attack on the ranch was beaten off with casualties.

Our return to Nairobi for a stay of eleven days gave me a pleasant settled feeling. The next day I visited a detention centre where 1,550 Mau Mau of various degrees were incarcerated. I met Moral Rearmament men who were at work among them seeking to reclaim their minds poisoned with hate and lies. Thanks to some of my British friends I alone of all non-U.K. delegates was invited to join them in a tour of army operations. We began with the headquarters of the 39th Infantry Brigade, commanded by Lord Thurlow. From brigade headquarters we were taken in jeeps up the Aberdare Mountains, so that we might witness the problems faced by the army patrols in coming to grips with an elusive enemy in the wet, dark, impenetrable bamboo forests. At one point we stopped on the road and dismounted. Within seconds we were startled by bursts of rifle fire at close hand. This ambush demonstration was very impressive. The fire, which fortunately was of blank rather than live ammunition, came from a patrol of the King's African Rifles invisible to us in thickets eight feet from the road we stood on. We ate a cold box lunch. One of the jeeps broke down and the delegates were obliged to double up. I took one of them on my knee where his full weight reposed while we drove another seventy-five miles over the mountain and back to Nairobi in cold weather. His name was Ted Heath.

The Commonwealth Parliamentary Conference opened on August 21 under the chairmanship of Harold Holt of Australia. We met in the legislative chamber of Kenya, a handsome and brand new building. Fifty parliaments and legislatures were represented. Only India failed to send representatives. Many of the African delegates appeared in native costume. It was a proud day for them. To me was accorded the honour of being the opening speaker in the opening debate. The subject was "The Relationship between Parliament and the Executive." I had thirty minutes to introduce the subject and ten minutes at the conclusion for reply. A week later I was chosen to speak for Canada in the final debate on the theme "Foreign Affairs and Defence." In quality of debate this conference fully measured up to the standard of the two previous Commonwealth parliamentary conferences which I was privileged to attend, in London in 1948 and

Ottawa in 1952 respectively. I look back on all three conferences as a privilege and inspiration. The Nairobi one was the last I was destined to attend.

Thanks to Arthur Henderson, one of the British delegates and former Secretary for Air in the Labour cabinet, I was one of four delegates invited to fly on an RAF sortie over the Aberdares. Unfortunately, the day was cloudy, and we were limited to a height of 7,500 feet. We saw no traces of Mau Mau, but had an excellent view of the ranch country, coffee farms and other properties at the base of the mountains.

On August 29 we bade Nairobi farewell and flew to the coast, passing Mount Kilimanjaro. I beheld the renowned snows reposing on its crest at a height of 19,340 feet. Mombasa, the seaport of Kenya on the Indian Ocean, boasts the largest anchorage on the coast of East Africa, but it had become a bottleneck. On a sidetrip to Melindi, Lord Lucan and I swam in the Indian Ocean and rode the surf on surf-boards. On another sidetrip limited to six delegates we visited Gedi, the ruins of an Arab city, dating from about A.D. 1200 and reconstructed about 1550. No one knows why it was suddenly abandoned. Mombasa also has a long history. Vasco da Gama sailed into its harbour in 1498. In 1698 Fort Jesus, after a siege of thirty-three months, fell to the Arabs, who massacred the Portuguese garrison.

From Mombasa we left Kenya. For me the visit to that troubled country had been a fascinating and profoundly instructive experience. The picture has changed. Jomo Kenyatta, denounced while I was there and jailed for a term of seven years, was released and became Prime Minister. He became a strong stabilizing force in the country. I never met him, but I met his brother a few years later. I was once shown a letter in which Malcolm MacDonald when Governor General had paid tribute to Kenyatta as the strongest moral force in the country. Tom Mboya, who became Kenyatta's right-hand man, visited me in Ottawa once in later days. He was assassinated a couple of years later.

In 1954 British East Africa consisted of three countries, Uganda, Kenya and Tanganyika. The last of these had been a German colony, which was mandated to Great Britain by the League of Nations in 1919 and later administered as a trustee territory by Britain under the United Nations. Lying off the coast was the British protectorate of Zanzibar, consisting of the two islands of Zanzibar and Pembina, rich in resources, ruled by a sultan. We flew to Zanzibar from Mombasa and were graciously entertained by the sultan and the sultana. Zanzibar had for centuries been the centre of the slave trade. It was a fascinating old place with very narrow streets and excellent shopping opportunities.

It was only an eighty-mile hop from Zanzibar to Dar-es-Salaam, the capital and port of Tanganyika. It has a beautiful harbour. At "Dar," as it is popularly known, the Tanganyika branch of the CPA gave us a farewell dinner. Our tour next day entered a new phase.

On leaving Tanganyika and British East Africa we flew overland 1,000 miles to Lusaka, the capital of Northern Rhodesia. The route was dry and flat, rather than scenic. I was fortunate to be one of six delegates chosen for a further flight to Barotseland, a British protectorate three hundred miles west of Lusaka. It proved to be a most interesting overnight trip. Ted Heath and I shared a room in the residence of the district commissioner. At this point the bed of the Zambesi River is very flat. In the wet season the river is twenty miles wide; in the dry season it shrinks to several hundred yards, and the natives hunt the trapped fish with spears. This was the dry season, and the heat, drought and dust were severe. I sank ankle-deep in dust. Here I had my first mishap of the trip. As we drove about the river-flats in a land-rover Pat Lucan knocked the ashes out of his pipe and one live ember lodged in my left eye. I was sent to the local hospital to have it removed. Had it been left till the next morning the British surgeon said it would have ulcerated. I wore a patch over the eye for several days and found it hard on the nerves. I was unable to accompany Ted Heath that evening to an entertainment which had been arranged in our honour.

After a day in Barotseland we flew on to one of the scenic wonders of the world, the Victoria Falls, on the border between Northern and Southern Rhodesia. Here the Zambesi River rushes over a cataract 355 feet high, twice the height of Niagara Falls. It is more than a mile in width. Consequently the volume of the flow at any point is less than Niagara's. We flew back and forth above the falls, absorbing the awesome and fascinating spectacle before landing at the airport and proceeding to the Victoria Falls Hotel, where we were to enjoy a welcome rest for an entire week. I walked about the Falls day by day gazing at them in wonder from every possible angle. One thing I did which was so unspeakably foolish it gives me a fluttering feeling whenever I think of it. Four of us delegates took a small boat above the cataract to an island and at the very brink leaped over four feet

271

of open water onto a rock to see farther down into the gorge. One little slip and a by-election in Eglinton riding would have resulted.

One of the men to whom I was most attracted at the conference was Garfield Todd, Premier of Southern Rhodesia. I was told that the British government looked upon him as the great hope for British Africa. Garfield was born in New Zealand and came to Southern Rhodesia as a missionary. He faced the necessity of adapting to a multi-racial society and accepted the principle of a multi-racial government. We became friends at Nairobi and have remained friends and kept in communication ever since. I left Victoria Falls to spend a day at Salisbury, the capital of the country. There I visited Garfield at his home and met his wife and daughter. I also met the Chief Justice, Sir Robert Tredgold, Acting Governor General, who was a friend of Roland Michener. They had been Rhodes scholars and attended Oxford together. I visited the tobacco market at Salisbury, then the largest in the world.

Many vicissitudes have overtaken Southern Rhodesia since 1954. To me no feature is more tragic than the way in which Garfield Todd was cast aside by his own party and later when Smith seized independent rule he placed Garfield under house arrest for years. It was wicked treatment of a noble gentleman who evidently was ahead of his time. I am relieved that his freedom was restored and that he was consulted in the course of the final negotiations conducted by Lord Soames.

For a fortnight a number of the remaining delegates were next the guests of the South Africa Branch of the CPA. Our tour took us to all four provinces in that picturesque country blessed with an abundance of resources and plagued with deep-seated problems. We were treated everywhere with great kindness and gracious hospitality. South Africa had not yet become a republic and was still a member country of the Commonwealth. We landed at Johannesburg, visited the gold mines in the Welkom area, the Kruger National Park for four great days, the Crocodile Valley, the vast orange plantations at Zebediela, on to Port Elizabeth, Cape Town, Kimberley and Johannesburg. The Kruger is one of the finest game preserves in the world. One morning by going out at an early hour several of us saw lions close in on a herd of gazelles and kill one beside our car. Before the incident ended I saw no fewer than twenty-five lions and took many photographs, including one at a distance of four feet from a lion. We visited the sugar estates near Durban, and were reminded that the growing of sugar and citrus fruit was not indigenous, but was introduced by Europeans. We saw what the government was doing to improve native housing and education. We could sympathize with the government's complaint that no matter what they did for the large black majority they received nothing but criticism from the press of North America and Europe. Apartheid had not yet crystallized into a far-reaching policy, but it was obviously coming. Questions arose in my mind and would not leave me. If you educate people up to a point, how can you deny them the right to further education? If you encourage people to undertake responsibility for local government, how can you deny them any voice in the national government? How can you tell people they can advance thus far and no farther? It is one thing to limit the franchise to people with a basic education; it is another matter to tell them that because of the pigment of their skin they shall never receive the franchise. I could never countenance apartheid. I only hope it will be abandoned without resort to violence.

One of the pleasantest features of the fortnight in South Africa was the privilege of meeting Evan Gill, the Canadian high commissioner, who had recently arrived, and his wife Dot. We became very warm friends. I met and conversed with Dr. Malan, the Prime Minister, and a number of the other ministers at different times.

I turned my footsteps homeward on September 25 from Jan Smuts airport, and was back in London on the 27th for three final, busy days. Derick Heathcote-Amory was leaving town, but insisted that I should occupy his flat, which I greatly enjoyed. I had rounds of conferences, a CPA luncheon where I said good-bye to my delegate colleagues, met officials, friends and relatives, addressed about forty of the senior officers at the Canadian Joint Staff, giving them a review of the political and military aspects of the observations made on my tour. Mike Pearson was in London for the Nine-Power Conference on German rearmament, and we had a half-hour talk together about it. Mike said it was the most important conference he had ever attended.

After my eighth transatlantic crossing I was home on Thursday afternoon, September 30 to be greeted by Alice, Mother and the children. How glad I was to be back! I had covered over thirty thousand miles in sixty days. My life had been permanently enriched by this unique visit to the dark and fascinating continent of Africa.

CHAPTER TWENTY-FIVE

Prelude to the Storm

For the first time since Mr. St. Laurent became Prime Minister there was no fall session of Parliament in 1954, and this departure was received with a sense of relief. We paid for it in the end, however, for while the 1955 session opened on January 7, it extended for nearly seven months. Prorogation was not reached until July 28, halfway through a very hot summer. The sessions were proving so lengthy that the Commons appeared to be left with a choice between sitting in the late autumn and spending half the hot summer in session. The choice was neither pleasant nor reassuring. There appeared to be no hope of shortening the sessions as long as the electorate continued to send four parties to Ottawa, and the CCF and Social Credit talked on every subject. I yearned for the old days of the two-party system.

But if there was no fall session there was an occasion which brought members joyfully returning to Ottawa in the autumn. The Queen Mother paid the national capital a brief visit, and the Speakers of both Houses gave a joint luncheon in her honour in the parliamentary dining room on Saturday, November 13, to which all members of both Houses and their wives were invited. For this privilege MPs and Senators returned in full numbers and with alacrity to Parliament Hill.

The Queen Mother was never more charming. She has played a unique role in the royal family. When one thinks of her and Queen Mary and now our gracious sovereign Queen Elizabeth II one recognizes what the monarchy of today owes to the female members of the royal house.

I was still aglow with the thrills and wonders of my two-month tour of Africa. I was much in demand as a speaker, and my photographs were much admired by friends whom we entertained at a series of Saturday evening travelogues in our home through the winter. I addressed the Canadian Club of Toronto and the Canadian Club of Ottawa at luncheon meetings and received ovations. It was not easy to compress such an experience into thirty minutes, but I did my best. I did not hesitate to pay tribute to the benefits derived by the "darkest continent" from the so-called "colonizing" white nations of the West. The president of the Canadian Club of Ottawa was in the chair for the meeting of his club at the Château Laurier. He was a rather dour person by the name of James Coyne, governor of the Bank of Canada. My friend Tony Lovink, ambassador of the Netherlands, thanked me for what I said about the colonial powers. In an age when the white man has been submitted to endless and bitter criticism for his role in Africa, Tony found it refreshing to hear something of the positive side of colonialism.

The 1955 session did not have the opportunity it deserved to stand out in history. It became too far eclipsed by the momentous events of the unique 1956 session to shine on the pages of political and parliamentary annals; nevertheless, it proved a long and arduous session, and all the seeds of the downfall of Parliament in 1956 can be traced to 1955. The opening scene exposed to view many changes wrought in the six months since prorogation. Gone were Claxton, Abbott and Chevrier. George Marler, Liberal provincial leader in Quebec, had been imported from Montreal and appointed Minister of Transport. He was able and friendly. Unlike Pickersgill, he did not try at the outset to play the partisan zealot. He was stable, polite and down-to-earth. Mr. St. Laurent was still passing over his numerous followers in the House to import new ministers from outside. An exception was the appointment of Roch Pinard, one of my esteemed friends among the 1945 crop of Quebec Liberal MPs, as Secretary of State.

There had been six by-elections in the interval, but no changes in the party standings. Rodney Adamson's seat in York West had gone to John Hamilton, a young lawyer who proved himself one of the most promising new members to enter the House in all my years in the opposition. Lionel Conacher's Liberal seat in Trinity was retained by Don Carrick, another major figure in Canadian sports, a very able lawyer and ever a gentleman. I had a very high regard for Don Carrick. But the most striking change to meet the eye was the absence of George Drew. Without warning, George in November had been stricken with a very serious attack of meningitis. For a long time it appeared doubtful if we would ever see George back in the House of Commons. After a protracted hospitalization he rallied, but was unable to return to the House until February 17. The remarks of the Prime Minister at the opening on January 7 voicing hope for George's recovery and return, and again his words when welcoming George back to the House on his return, were models of generosity and consideration. George's response was most moving. In his absence Earl Rowe was Acting Leader of the Opposition, and in those six weeks filled the position very competently. On his return George took up his duties gallantly, and before long was back in his old vigorous form. The House lost some of its normal interest in his absence. Parliament always depends on the personalities among its members, or at least the more prominent of them, for much of the public interest it generates.

The traditional speech of the Leader of the Opposition on leaders' day, January 10, was ably delivered by Earl Rowe. At its conclusion he introduced a lengthy amendment deploring the failure of the government to deal with a catalogue of problems. I spoke on January 13 and lost no time in attacking the throne speech as "hopelessly lacking in realism." I criticized the government's attempt to minimize the growing unemployment problem and its failure to call a federal-provincial conference to deal with fiscal matters, especially the provinces' taxation rights. Most of the speech, however, was devoted to trade questions: Canada's share of both the British market and the world market was shrinking; farm income in Canada had dropped to the lowest point in seven years; Canada's exports to the United States were largely of raw materials, and a greater effort was needed to process them to a larger degree in Canada; Canada's trading eggs were being "disproportionately and dangerously placed in one basket."

Three debates in the 1955 session deserve to be classified as of major importance. They concerned unemployment, the rearmament of Germany, and the renewal of the powers of the Minister of Defence Production, C.D. Howe. They gave high rank to the debates of what might otherwise have seemed an undistinguished session.

Debates on unemployment later became commonplace, but they were not so in 1955. It was the first time that painful subject had given rise to a sustained debate since the war. Unemployment had been growing, but the figures released by the Dominion Bureau of Statistics on February 23 were startling. The total number of unemployed in January had leaped to 569,000, the highest postwar figure, an increase of 206,900 or 59 per cent in one year. On March 1 on a supply motion the official opposition fastened on these figures and the serious social and economic problem they exposed. Ellen Fairclough's amendment called on

276

the government to "immediately give consideration to the formulation of plans to deal with this emergency, and to the necessary steps to establish a long-term program for expanding employment to be presented to Parliament during the present Session." Her speech was most effective. Howe contributed a lengthy economic survey to the debate, but had little to say about unemployment. This gave rise to charges that he was but little aware of it. He did allow himself to concede that we might be threatened with "the first post-war recession." He claimed to see trade improving. If ministers were unaware of the serious dimensions of the problem the opposition wasn't, and numerous Liberal private members felt constrained to enter the discussion. Despite eight days of discussion the government at no time advanced any proposal to meet the problem. I spoke on March 22, and had some scathing words for the government's denial of responsibility for meeting the problem, their attempt to leave it on the shoulders of the provincial and municipal governments while obdurately refusing to call a Dominion-provincial conference to discuss the serious problem. Our amendment was defeated by a vote of 131 to 71, but the debate had served a most useful purpose.

External affairs were wont to give rise to non-contentious debates. All parties made a serious and commendable effort to keep these discussions on a non-partisan level. Could German rearmament be discussed in such a rarefied atmosphere? The issue of the rearmament of our erstwhile foe could no longer be deferred. On January 20 a government motion to approve the protocol to the North Atlantic Treaty on the accession of the Federal Republic of (West) Germany touched off one of the outstanding debates of the decade of the fifties. The debate continued for five days and maintained a level rarely attained or sustained in the House. Mike Pearson's speech in introducing the resolution was a masterpiece of knowledge and realism and logic. I consider it the best speech I ever heard him make. It contained a forthright and courageous indictment of Communist strategy and Russian deception. Diefenbaker, in the difficult position of directly following Pearson, delivered an eloquent speech in support of the resolution. The CCF were divided right down the middle. Coldwell spoke courageously in support of German rearmament, but most of his followers who took part in the debate opposed it. It must have been profoundly embarrassing to Coldwell. I waited until the fourth day of the debate, then spoke in answer to the CCF opponents of the resolution. No one wished to see Germany rearmed, I said, but the Russians had already rearmed East Germany; admitting the dangers of rearming West Germany it seemed to me much more dangerous to world peace and Western security to keep West Germany in a disarmed condition. I quoted the words of Shakespeare, "Out of this nettle, danger, we pluck this flower, safety." The Communists and those they had duped had mounted an intensive campaign against the resolution and sent numerous and very vocal delegations to Ottawa to lobby the MPs, but in the end they were unavailing. The previous effort to create a European army under EDC (European Defence Community) had foundered on opposition in the French Assembly; the new proposal, which owed much to the initiative and diplomatic skill of Anthony Eden, allowed West Germany to have not more than 500,000 men under arms in not more than twelve divisions and 1,350 defensive fighter aircraft, all under NATO command. Elaborate controls had been attached to the limited measure of rearmament thus permitted. George Pearkes, VC, who had fought the Germans in two world wars, made a most effective and telling speech in favour of rearming West Germany on these terms. The resolution was adopted January 26 by a vote of 213 to 12, only twelve CCF members voting against it. The performance of the House throughout the debate redounded impressively to its lasting credit.

But the principal debate of the 1955 session, and the one which brought the House to its fighting peak, arose over a very short bill containing only two clauses, one of which was quite acceptable to the House. The other purported to remove all time limitations in the Defence Production Act, and thus give permanence not only to the Department of Defence Production but also to the vast powers enjoyed by its minister. There was no opposition to continuing the department, but the government's determination to retain all the minister's extraordinary powers set off a debate which rocked Parliament, kept the parties in battle order, and taught both government and opposition lessons which were to bear their full fruit in May 1956. Parliament was never the same after the latter crisis, which had its birth and prelude in the debate over less than a dozen words in the Department of Defence Production Act Amendment of 1955.

The department had been established in 1951 to meet the emergency in Korea. Mr. St. Laurent then admitted it conferred on the minister some "special" powers "which should not be of a continuing nature." So a five-year limit was placed on the statute creating the department and conferring its wide powers. It was due to expire July 31, 1956. Failing extension of the legislation by

278

that date the department would have come to an abrupt demise that night at midnight. The government, underestimating the determination of the Conservatives, proceeded to paint itself into a corner as the end of the session approached.

The debate well illustrates the reluctance of human beings, and particularly those hungry for authority, to yield up power they have once come to possess. Our system of government, however, at times requires that they should do so. During the war Howe was Minister of Munitions and Supply. As such he had wielded dictatorial powers over the productive and distributive features of the Canadian economy. He continually harked back to the powers he had wielded in wartime. As Minister of Defence Production he enjoyed similar but better defined powers. The program of rearmament instituted in 1951 involved the expenditure of $5 billion, of which by 1955 $4.5 billion had been spent. It seemed to us in the official opposition that that fact alone refuted the government's demand for continuance on a permanent basis of all the extraordinary powers conferred in 1951 strictly for a five-year period. Moreover, they had decided in 1954 not to ask Parliament to continue the Emergency Powers Act. If they could live without the extraordinary powers conferred by that legislation, now deceased, why should they insist on extension of the minister's powers under the Department of Defence Production Act, and these without any time limit whatever?

After three days of exploratory debate the bill was introduced on March 14. For some unaccountable reason the government did not move second reading until June 7. Three precious months were allowed to pass. Perhaps the government was waiting for hot weather to sap Conservative opposition to the bill. I believe they genuinely misapprehended our seriousness and determination.

Howe, who Mr. St. Laurent had said would continue as Minister of Defence Production as well as Minister of Trade and Commerce, opened the momentous debate on second reading on June 7, in a speech of less than fifteen minutes, in the course of which I extracted admissions from him that the department had not found it necessary to invoke or use virtually all the powers which we took objection to renewing. In immediately following Howe I had the benefit of unlimited time, and I took full advantage of it to speak for 101 minutes. It was one of the most important and smiting speeches I ever delivered in Parliament.

I did not mince my words. The atmosphere at times was explosive, and I made it crystal clear that we of the opposition were prepared to fight. I stated the now inescapable issue: "There is as between the Government on the one hand and us of Her Majesty's Loyal Opposition on the other a deep issue, a clear-cut issue, an issue as to the status and the authority as well as the prestige of the Parliament of Canada; and on that issue, that clear-cut, deep issue we are prepared to fight." I pronounced these latter words deliberately and emphatically, then continued: "We are not unmindful of the fact that this is an advanced stage of this Session, that we have had a taste within the past two days of a temperature of 90 degrees, but here is a case that we consider to be of the highest importance, one that lays on every Member of the House the highest kind of responsibility; and on this issue we now join battle." I added: "Under this legislation the Government, and particularly the Minister of Defence Production, hold the Canadian economy in the palms of their hands. The Government can override any other legal obligation howsoever created." I turned on Howe, "The Minister talks about the rule of law, and then admits he does not understand very much about it. It was unnecessary for him to make that open admission. If Parliament is to go on conferring the right of delegated legislation, then we have in fact torn the rule of law to shreds and tatters. Make no mistake about that. Some honourable members may not realize that tonight, but the day well may come when they will realize it." That day was to come sooner than I thought. I challenged the majority in the House, and I quoted the words of Henrik Ibsen, "The most dangerous enemy to truth and freedom amongst us is the compact majority." I closed with ringing declarations, "We will have nothing to do with the grant of powers vastly in excess of need. . . . Supreme over any all-powerful executive, in our view, must stand the authority of a free, sovereign and independent Parliament."

I had thrown the gage of battle to the government. Would our members support it by remaining at their posts in June and July, sacrificing their summer vacation hopes, to do battle for a principle? The government evidently thought not. They were wrong. That was June 7. The battle continued all day on the 8th, then all day on the 9th with general participation by our members, front-benchers and back-benchers alike. On the 13th Howe rose to offer conditional opportunity for debate on any orders which might be made under the legislation. We spurned his offer. The debate continued all that day. By government decision it was not resumed for a week. George Drew had spoken for an hour before the adjournment on the 13th; on the 20th he continued for two more hours, much of it through a barrage of interruptions. He fully demonstrated that he had recovered all his normal health and vigour. Ministers were not taking part in the debate, but Liberal private members could not resist the temptation to speak. By this means, regardless of what they said, they helped us to extend the debate.

By now the importance of time was obvious. The Liberals were accusing us of "filibuster." The government skipped another eight days; the debate resumed June 28 for its sixth day. The Liberals may have thought we were running out of reserves. Alf Brooks then moved an amendment. This gave all of us who had already spoken on the main motion the right to speak again on the amendment. Notwithstanding the summer heat we all plunged again into the debate. The government decreed another interval of a week before resuming debate on July 4. That day the Prime Minister intervened. He refused to place any time limit on the bill. If he hoped to daunt us with this show of naked power he failed. The debate continued all that day, all day on July 5, all day on July 6. On the 7th Howe muttered, "I was never so bored in my life." I think that was probably an understatement. The CCF had been steadily supporting the government throughout the debate. Coldwell now rose to urge the goverment to agree to put a time limit on the bill. That afternoon we ran out of speakers. The vote was taken on our amendment, and it was defeated 120 to 43. Up jumped Walter Harris, Leader of the House, and moved that the question be now put. Drew and I denounced this move as "a gag" and "guillotine." The motion prevented us from introducing other amendments, but it was debatable, so we proceeded to stage a debate on it.

The debate continued all that day, and the government did not call the bill on Friday, the 9th. On Monday morning, July 11, St. Laurent rose in his place and quietly and dramatically announced that he had held private discussions with George Drew over the weekend and had agreed to writing a three-year time limit into the bill. It would accordingly expire July 31, 1959. We had won the battle. The government had capitulated and accepted what it had steadfastly refused to countenance. Our struggle, which had exacted sacrifices of us, had been successful. Howe was not present when the announcement was made. He spared himself that humiliation. Prorogation was delayed until July 28. The measure had occupied fifteen full days in the House. Those precious days might all have been saved if the government had not chosen a course so rigid and autocratic. The official opposition had learned how to carry on and win a struggle which initially had appeared hopeless. The government, resentful over losing face, showed in the next session that it would not yield again. The defeat rankled.

C.D. Howe was a very resilient person. Three days after he had suffered political defeat over the extension of the Defence Production Act he was back in the House as jaunty and defiant as ever seeking approval of the Estimates of the Department of Trade and Commerce. He had made only one speech on trade earlier in the session, and that took the form of an economic review in the debate on unemployment on March 1. His Estimates provided the occasion for the first general debate on trade in over a year. After a setback in 1954 the trade figures for the most recent five months showed improvement. Howe exuded irrepressible optimism. "The Canadian economy is booming as never before. Our exports are at record levels; capital investment will undoubtedly reach the highest figure on record, and production is also at a very high level," quoth he. He based his assertions on figures for only those five months. He conceded that exports of wheat were disappointing, as was our trade with South America. It was typical of him to be selective, rather than balanced, in his treatment of facts and figures and to leap to desired conclusions.

My speech in reply to Howe was a comprehensive and thorough review of Canada's external trade relations. It examined masses of statistics and carefully analysed the current developments. The research done in the course of preparation was extensive; it was all done by myself.

Howe managed to keep himself under control for most of my speech, but later when Howard Green, for whom he always exhibited a personal dislike savouring of enmity, entered the debate the exchanges became bitter and Howe's temper quite unmanageable. When I intervened later in the discussion of some individual items and to ask questions Howe became civil again. I spoke, as I had in 1954, in praise of the men serving in the Trade Commissioner Service. I added, "The Department of Trade and Commerce, I believe, is one of the most fortunate of all Departments in the senior officials it has. . . . The Trade Commissioner Service is one of the government services . . . manned by the best Canadians we have anywhere in our public service." Howe thanked me for the tribute and joined in it.

Howe had faced a very trying time that spring and summer. After fifteen days on his bill to amend the Defence Production Department, the two days of rugged review of his Estimates probably tested his patience to the limit. When I spoke to Bob Winters about the need for him and other ministers to stand up to Howe in cabinet and curb his growing dictatorial attitude,

Bob replied, "But we're just the rookies in cabinet. You can't expect us to thwart Howe." It had become tragically clear that the march to dictatorship would not be arrested within the cabinet; it would require blood-letting in Parliament.

Walter Harris introduced his first budget on April 5. He reported a deficit for 1954-55, and budgeted for another deficit for 1955-56. Although he professed to see improvement in the economy he budgeted for slight reductions in the personal income and corporation taxes and the excise tax. He forecast the appointment of a royal commission to examine Canada's economic prospects. Out of this proposal later emerged the royal commission headed by Walter Gordon.

In speaking on it on May 3, I was highly critical of this budget: "After the closest examination of the budget and of the minister's comments upon it, one can only conclude that this budget is the product of muddled thinking, confusion, indecision and fear on the part of the government to admit the existence of problems with which the taxpayers and the people of this country are all too familiar. . . . So this budget has no pattern and it has no principle; indeed, it is neither flesh nor fowl nor good red herring." I was not impressed by the tax reductions. I pointed out that taxes were eating up an ever higher percentage of the GNP, that the budget made no pretence of grappling with excessive expenditure or the fiscal problems of the provinces or unemployment or taxes which have an inflationary impact. I listed fifteen serious fiscal problems which the budget had simply ignored.

After a lapse of two years the Committee on Broadcasting was appointed on March 10 following a two-day debate. I chose this occasion to set forth fully our policy and to review the history of the subject for the first time in the Twenty-Second Parliament. I advocated the appointment of an independent regulatory body to regulate all broadcasting, whether by the CBC or privately owned stations, and whether of radio or TV. I said the CBC should no longer be permitted to be policeman, competitor, lawyer, judge, jury and executioner simultaneously, as its function was described in *Le Matin*. I declared our firm belief that competition was good for the CBC in its operations. I criticized the corporation for making inadequate use of Canadian talent notwithstanding a large vote of funds to enable it to do so; and I accused it in its programs in the realms of economics and politics of being "too much left of centre" and in its talk programs in the political realm of being too "pro Liberal Government." I reserved my stiffest attacks for the government for holding back the development of TV by privately owned stations, and for its "hare-brained financial policy" in giving CBC funds, in some cases for five years in advance and in others in perpetuity, without an annual vote by Parliament. Our party was given five places on the committee. One of these was wasted on Diefenbaker, who as in other years insisted on being a member of the committee, but spent very little time attending its meetings. I played the leading role of party spokesman in the committee, and remained constantly in attendance. Its report was tabled on June 17. We Conservatives had endeavoured unsuccessfully to amend the report, then voted against it. The Estimates provided an opportunity on July 26 to debate the report, and although we were then within less than forty-eight hours of prorogation and the pressure to accelerate was very strong I spoke at some length and put on record the full text of our amendment to the report. It was a particularized declaration of party policy.

If at first you don't succeed try, try again. This axiom was drilled into me in my youth, and persistence has always been a deep-seated element in my nature. A friend after watching me doggedly return the ball from innumerable angles and wear out an opponent in a tennis match once said, "I know now how you won Alice. After every time she said no you just kept on coming back until you wore down her resistance." After years of advocating in the House and caucus the appointment of a Committee on Estimates I was gratified beyond measure when on February 8 the government at long last proposed the creation of such a committee. I spoke strongly in favour of the proposal, drawing on information I had gleaned as to the practice of the British Parliament at the Commonwealth Parliamentary Conference at Nairobi the previous August. The proposal received general support as promising greater efficiency, better organization and more effective opportunity for studying estimates. A committee of twenty-five members resulted, with five places going to Conservatives. Inevitably I was appointed a member. The other four were Jim Macdonnell, Gordon Churchill, Roly Michener and Monte Monteith. The Grits were half-hearted about appointing such a committee, fearing loss of control over it. They therefore created it only experimentally for one session. Not being a standing committee of the House it had no power to call witnesses or send for papers. The government selected the departments whose estimates it was permitted to review. Nevertheless, the committee functioned as well as might be expected under these tight restrictions. It reviewed the estimates of four departments and saved the House work and precious time.

While one new committee was thus born another completed

its task and passed honourably into history. For the sixth consecutive session the Committee on Procedure was appointed. It had been enlarged to twenty members, of whom four were Conservatives. I was one of eight members who sat on the committee from its first appointment in 1951. This time the committee wrote a final and unanimous report. In many respects its recommendations were a compromise. There were differences, and these were thoroughly discussed. Some of the recommendations I did not support, but I accepted the total report on balance. Speaker Beaudoin contributed much to making agreement finally possible. He tabled the report on June 14. After an interesting two days' debate on July 1 and 12 the House unanimously adopted it. Emphasis was placed on more dispatch and better use of the time of the House. The set debates on the throne speech and the budget were restricted. Speeches in committee were reduced from forty to thirty minutes, but the forty-minute limit on speeches in the House remained, largely due, I think, to my stubborn defence of it. Numerous other changes in the rules were included. The government had sought further curtailments, not least in the rights accorded by the rules to the Leader of the Opposition. He, like the Prime Minister, was exempt from time restrictions in debate. I fought stubbornly against any restriction of the rights of the Leader of the Opposition. At one point Walter Harris, leading the Liberals on the committee, told "Cass," our whip, "We'll never get anywhere with Fleming on the committee." I said to Cass, "He's probably right." No one else knew that I had a direct line of communication to George Drew on this issue and I was acting in accordance with his instructions. In the end we were successful. The rights of the Leader of the Opposition emerged unscathed. These proved absolutely vital to us in 1956 in the pipeline debate. We would have been severely handicapped in that struggle had the rights of the Leader of the Opposition been trimmed in 1955. However, I resisted with equal firmness any recognition of special rights or position to the leaders of the minor parties, which were sought on their behalf. In this effort we succeeded. My principle was, "There is only one Leader of the Opposition."

Against the prevailing trend toward less rugged expression in debate I expressed the belief that

> A great deal will be lost if there is any further trend toward making debates of a namby-pamby nature in this House. Vigorous disagreements should characterize a vigorous House of Commons. There is no reason why, within proper limitations, vigorous disagreement should not be expressed in vigorous terms. For my

part . . . much will be done to revive the vigour of the House of Commons, as it has been revived in recent days, by vigorous cut and thrust of debate . . . . With all its shortcomings, nevertheless this House is and must continue to be the embodiment of the highest function of the democratic system.

Thus ended the first revision of the rules of the House since 1927. It had demanded much patience, understanding and cooperation among members and among political parties. It is fortunate that the committee reported in 1955, for a year later no such inter-party agreement and cooperation would have been possible. The authority of the Speaker and his personal prestige were at their zenith in mid-1955; a year later they were a shambles.

Another committee was about to be added to my responsibilities, but not by vote of the House. One day George Drew called me in for a chat about research, and told me I was the recognized authority on and exponent of research in the party. He said some money had been raised to provide the caucus with research facilities on a limited scale and asked me to be chairman and to direct the effort. I could only agree to accept this challenge. George left the selection of a committee to me, and I promptly chose Jim Macdonnell and Roly Michener, harking back to the work we did together in 1942 before the Port Hope Conference. A regrettably strong Toronto flavour was thus imparted to the committee, but I chose Jim and Roly for what they could contribute. We three functioned as the research committee until after the change of government in 1957. We met together over or after dinner on Wednesday evenings. We engaged the services of Donald Eldon as director of research and later Ruth Rolph as assistant. The quality of work produced was excellent. Our only problem was to channel and select the requests for research studies. To conduct the business of our little research bureau in an orderly manner it was arranged that individual requests would come to me through chairmen of the respective caucus committees. I made the selections and determined the priority, giving precedence to the leader's requests. It was a brave effort and produced excellent results. George Drew was well pleased and gave us full support. I arranged for Donald Eldon to go to London and study the research facilities and organization of both the Conservative and Labour parties, for I thought we were building a permanent party research bureau in Ottawa.

John A. Stevenson, a very senior journalist and writer of "Ottawa Letter" in *Saturday Night*, conferred two titles on me. On

March 26, 1955, he described me as the Progressive Conservative party's "Most militant practitioner of the technique of attack," and on July 9 as "the opposition's best master of aggressive oratory." I was not displeased with the descriptions. On the subject of oratory Margaret Aitken wrote in her column in the *Telegram*: "If I had to find one word to describe Donald Fleming's oratory, it would be the word courageous. He goes in fighting and comes out fighting. Mr. Fleming bristles with belligerency. As someone said recently, after a Fleming flourish, 'I never knew anyone who looks as angry as Don does and isn't angry at all'."

Men in public life are asked some very searching and highly personal questions. Once the answers are published the subject is supposed to become less personal. In Holy Week one layman from each of six major denominations was asked by the *Toronto Telegram* to answer the question, "What religion means to me." I was chosen by the *Telegram* to represent the United Church. My reply was published on April 9 as follows:

> Religion is the most vital and intimate factor in life. It embraces every relationship. It gives life meaning, perspective, and proportion.
>
> *Religion sustains my belief that*:
> God is my Creator, and I am his child.
> His other children are my brothers.
> Love is the law of life, and peace is its path, for all men are my neighbours.
> God's grace is sufficient for my needs, however unworthy I prove.
> My soul is eternal. God did not create it to let it die.
> Life's values are to be measured in spiritual, not material terms.
> The life lived in faith is a life of victory.
>
> *Religion calls me to*:
> Righteousness as the attribute of God and His demand upon his creatures.
> Penitence and repentance.
> Prayer, as the blessed communion by direct access with my Father, who hears and answers.
> Service as a duty and opportunity to express my gratitude to God and my love for my fellow-man.
> Membership and worship in the Church and the giving to her of service, time and talents.
> Search the Scriptures.
>
> *Religion offers me*:
> Light in the midst of the darkness of this world.

> Hope in place of the world's despair.
> Confidence and faith instead of groping and fear.
> Comfort in sorrow and distress, for I am never alone.
>
> Religion to me means Jesus Christ, Son of the Living God,
> my Saviour.

I would not change a word of this statement in 1984, but would add that all my life I have been sustained and upgirded by faith.

On June 12, 1955, one of the staunchest bulwarks of my life was taken from me. To this day I am conscious of the remaining void. For the last year of her life my mother's health had declined somewhat, but I had no reason to think it had been seriously impaired. She continued to spend every Sunday with us, but enjoyed the independence of her own home. When her very limited and tightly budgeted income became insufficient and she dreaded giving up her apartment I was privileged, with Alice's full concurrence, to pay her rent for the last couple of years. She joined us at dinner on my fiftieth birthday, May 23, 1955. When I told her after dinner that I considered I was most fortunate to have my mother with me on my fiftieth birthday she replied, "I won't be here for the next one." I chided her gently over such a thought, but three weeks later she was dead. On Thursday, June 9, she characteristically walked unaided to the Eglinton polling station to cast her vote for the Conservative candidate, Dr. Dunlop, in the provincial general election. In the afternoon she walked to the hairdresser's where she sustained a paralysing stroke. She was brought to our house where she quietly passed away on Sunday afternoon, June 12, not having appeared to regain consciousness except once to squeeze my hand. She was laid to rest in the family plot in Mountview Cemetery in Galt between my father and my brother Bob. She was eighty-one years of age and had outlived my father by more than fifteen years.

No mother ever exerted a more powerful or a more uplifting influence over a son than my mother cast over me. She lived for her family. She was uniquely strong physically, mentally and spiritually, and she devoted all her strength to serve God and her family. I wish she might have lived till June 1957, or, better still, till I was in a position to make life easier for her. May God grant her peace and eternal rest.

Among the letters of sympathy which I received was one from Arthur Meighen which I shall always treasure. In it he wrote, "None can take the place of a mother, as I learned in all its verities 24 years ago. The thrill life's successes have had for you will now be less, but the memory of her must still urge you on. Never, never, let the incentives diminish. My sympathy is very real and I earnestly want you to succeed." How true I have found his words to be!

CHAPTER TWENTY-SIX

Eve of Disaster

Some conspicuous changes had occurred in the House when it assembled for the new session on January 10, 1956. Death had overtaken my esteemed friend, the gentle and genial Postmaster-General Alcide Côté, and two other Liberal members. Three more, all very prominent men – Chubby Power, Dave Croll and Jean François Pouliot – had been appointed to the Senate along with Darcy Leonard and the Conservative John Hackett, and were bound to be greatly missed in the House. We had won two seats from the Liberals, Spadina and Restigouche-Madawaska. Charles E. Rea had redeemed the Liberal stronghold of Spadina and was to become a very popular addition to our ranks. Charles Van Horne, an eloquent debater in either French or English and a powerful platform personality, had broken the tight Liberal hold on the Acadian seat of Restigouche-Madawaska. We were gathering strength.

The speech from the throne was full of optimism. The Liberals looked upon the national scene through rose-coloured glasses. This was especially true of the budget, introduced by Walter Harris on March 20, which contained the most optimistic of all his reviews of economic conditions in Canada. Everything was pictured as being almost perfect. However, he reported a deficit of $52 million, and offered no tax reductions. He forecast a surplus of $113 million for the year 1956-57. He introduced a new 20 per cent tax on editorial material in Canadian editions of foreign magazines, a controversial proposal which was destined to be debated for years. In an obvious example of oratorical carpentry he tacked onto the end of his budget speech a lengthy defence of his tax-sharing proposals to the provincial governments, then closed with a too obvious tribute to the Prime Minister. In my reply on March 27 I did not spare either the budget or its author. I raked it for the absence of any measures to cope with inflation or the revenue problems of the provinces and municipalities. It was another example of "cyclical budgeting," with the election cycle determining that needed tax reductions must await the general election of 1957. In the meantime the government was following the simple policy of "soak the people and ignore their problems." I denounced the magazine tax as a "dangerous innovation." My closing peroration proceeded:

> This is a cynical Budget, and I say to you in my final words, sir, that this Budget, with sickening features about it, . . . reveals the sickness and the infirmity and decrepitude of this Government. This Government is suffering in expenditure from elephantiasis; where action is needed it is suffering, and with it the Canadian people in consequence, from paralysis; to the voice of the Canadian people it is deaf; to its own responsibility to the Canadian people it is blind; and it suffers from a psychosis springing from its own delusions of grandeur, omniscience and infallibility.

That would have been my final utterance as a budget critic had I not chosen on July 3 on the second reading of the bill to amend the Income Tax Act to make another major speech on the budget concentrating on the way it had ignored the need for many reforms of our income tax legislation. I stressed the need for Canadian savings and Canadian capital, and discussed ten subjects urgently calling for redress by amendment of the Act. It was a very constructive and analytical speech.

The magazine tax legislation was held back for five months. On August 7 I again opposed it. The promised new Succession Duty Act was not introduced in 1956 nor in 1957. It was left on my doorstep by Harris at his departure.

The Bank of Canada interest rate became very unsettled in 1956, and we were not slow to exploit the government's embarrassment. The rate was raised five times in one year, something then unheard of. On June 1, I extracted from the Minister of Finance an admission that he was informed of the action before it was taken. In introducing his estimates on August 11 he defended the condition of "tight money" and acquiesced in rising interest rates. Mr. St. Laurent on August 10 declared that, "The Prime Minister will not undertake to have Parliament or the Members of the Opposition act as a court of appeal from the decision made by the Governor of the Bank of Canada." The chartered banks had curtailed commercial loans at the governor's request and undeniably money was "tight." In my speech on August 11 I taunted the minister to say whether he approved the actions taken by the Bank of Canada, but he evaded the issue. I told the Prime Minister that when people disapprove such actions they must not be denied the right to bring their complaints to their forum, namely, Parliament. I called upon the government to clarify their own thinking, and added, "Let them stop applying conflicting and contradictory policies." Looking at inflation I uttered these words which are as true in 1984 as they were twenty-eight years earlier:

> . . . Inflationary factors oftentimes have the subtle support of and exercise a siren attraction upon Ministers of Finance because the Government always shares through the tax impositions in the benefits of inflation, through swollen returns of income tax, corporation tax, sales tax and other impositions. The effect of these repeated increases in interest rates, five in a period of one year, has been a tremendous increase in the burdens cast upon provincial governments with respect to their borrowings and upon municipal governments with respect to their borrowings, and upon business, and punishing losses upon the holders of Canada's obligations. What the Government should be directing its efforts toward in facing the threat of inflation is to seek an increase in productivity.

On January 24 I was pleading for widening of the policy of paying municipal grants equivalent to municipal taxes on federal property enjoying municipal services and for removal of federal sales and excise taxes on goods purchased by municipal councils and boards of education. On March 27 I was complaining strongly that the budget totally ignored the municipalities. At one point the Toronto Board of Control threatened to withdraw municipal services from federally owned property. The Minister of Finance met their representatives. The only result was more federal silence.

But what about the provinces? The Minister of Finance was moving on the fiscal front slowly and rigidly. The tax rental agreements, whereby the provincial governments leased the personal income tax, corporation income tax, corporation tax and succession duty fields to the federal government, were due to expire March 31, 1957. On July 16 Walter Harris introduced his much-heralded Federal-Provincial Financial Arrangements legislation. The purpose was to authorize the federal government to enter into "fiscal arrangements" (i.e., agreements) with the provinces to rent their tax fields for a further period of five years.

I spoke in the debate on second reading. I derided the attitude of a government which would ask Parliament to pass such enabling legislation when no provincial government had yet given its approval to these proposals and in the knowledge that there had been widespread disapproval of its proposals. I pointed to the ever-mounting financial burdens of the provinces and municipalities, urged the immediate calling of a federal-provincial conference with a view to reaching agreement, and suggested that Parliament be called thereafter to approve the agreement. But Harris had no intention of meeting with the provincial governments. He had made his proposals, and there would be no change. I denounced his "take it or leave it" position. This was, I believe, the origin of this expression, which was later employed with devastating effect against the government in the 1957 general election campaign.

I drew attention to the unsoundness of having one government levying taxes for another government to spend. I recalled the words of Laurier, uttered in 1887, "It is an absolutely false principle which claims that one government can collect revenue while another one spends it," and to the words of Mackenzie King, "the governments that spend public moneys must be the governments which through the agency of taxation raise what is to be spent." The formula, by which federal taxpayers in provinces opting out of the scheme would be allowed deductions of 10 per cent personal income tax, 9 percentage points for provincial corporation taxes, and 50 per cent of succession duty, I described as "at best a makeshift; it is no solution of the problem." I flatly declared, "There is no use . . . asking us to approve a form of dominion-provincial fiscal arrangement which has not received the approval of a single provincial government." I concluded constructively by setting forth our policy:

> If honourable members opposite ask me what our position is I can say to them that we would do more for the provinces than the federal government has shown it is willing to do in this measure. We believe the federal government can do more and can afford to do more. Let there be no question about our position in reference to other features of this matter of federal-provincial fiscal relations. We recognize completely the principle of equalization grants, sharing the revenues which if the federal government were not in this field would accrue simply to the provinces. We recognize the claim of the provinces in a weaker financial position; we certainly do. So far as we are concerned that recognition is axiomatic, basic and fundamental in our approach to this subject.

The bill was given second reading by a vote of 128 to 45. In his budget speech on March 14, 1957, Walter Harris announced that eight provinces had rented all the tax fields, Quebec none, while Ontario had rented only the personal income tax. This patchwork, which satisfied none of the provinces, became part of my inheritance in 1957.

The government moved for a two-year extension of the

Emergency Gold Mining Assistance Act. The subsidy had now been in effect for eight years. Since 1941 the number of producing mines in Canada had been reduced by half. Development work had been curtailed, and no new mines had been opened. The subsidy had just kept the survivors alive as they were ground between rising costs of production and a fixed price for their product. In speaking on the measure on June 12 I condemned the government for being "apathetic, lackadaisical and silent" when they ought to have been urging the United States and the IMF to allow the price for newly mined gold to rise. I told the government it had shirked its duty and ignored its responsibility. This was another unsolved problem I inherited in June 1957.

The development of Canada's natural resources for the benefit of Canadians has always been a subject dear to the hearts of Conservatives. On a supply motion on July 9 George Drew at the conclusion of a statesmanlike and comprehensive address moved an amendment which I had drafted along the lines of Sir John A. Macdonald's historic introduction of the famous National Policy by way of amendment to a supply motion in 1876. My version updated it to read as follows:

> This House is of opinion that the welfare of the Canadian people requires the adoption now of a national development policy which will develop our natural resources for the maximum benefit of all parts of Canada, encourage the processing of those resources in Canada, correct the present serious unfavourable trade balances, foster wider financial participation by Canadians in the development of our resources, and promote greater opportunity and employment for a steadily increasing population.

The government held back, and no Liberal had spoken ahead of me. I made a major speech concerning Canada's resources, her trade and her need of capital. By way of emphasis I said, "We do not advocate waving any big stick at our friends in the United States, but we do assert that it is not the destiny of Canada to be the trade satellite or the dumping ground of any country in all the world. We think much can be done to shake our United States neighbours out of their complacent attitude toward Canada and toward Canada's economic interests." I concluded my speech by saying, ". . . the destiny of Canada as a good neighbour, as a staunch ally, as a helpful friend, as the unwavering supporter of the free way of life will best be served by the policy of national development," which was enunciated in our amendment.

There had not been a debate on housing since 1954. A government bill to amend various sections of the National Housing Act and to increase the sums of money provided thereunder gave rise to a very good discussion on April 23, 26 and May 16. The bill won the support of all parties, but the performance of CMHC was subjected to close examination and some criticism. On the resolution stage I made a lengthy speech. I devoted much of it to a description of the Regent Park North project in Toronto, in which I had played a large personal role, and the lessons to be drawn from it in relation to slum clearance and redevelopment. I was critical of the rigid attitude demonstrated by CMHC in relation to the new Regent Park South and Lawrence Heights projects, and the consequent delays. My speech was listened to with unusual interest by the House, not least by the CCF members. I criticized the increase in the interest rate on CMHC mortgages, due to the action of the Bank of Canada in raising its interest rate. I stressed that our purpose must be to meet a social need, not merely to balance books. In conclusion I warned, ". . . we can see the results of too much rigidity, too much bureaucracy, too much of the ivory tower complex, too much of the feeling that the experts in the ivory tower know more than the citizens who are on the spot and face the situation firsthand." In the debate on second reading on April 26 I made another major speech, answering Bob Winters. I contended that the government was claiming credit to which it was not entitled, since half of the houses being built were in fact created outside the terms of the legislation altogether. I also asserted that the government was not doing enough to make use of the legislation which Parliament had enacted, and that they were sitting back waiting for the municipalities to take the initiative in relation to the urgent need of urban redevelopment which the municipalities lacked the financial means to undertake. Again I stressed the social aspect of the purpose of the legislation. My final sentence was, "What is required on the part of all levels of government, and not least of all on the part of the Federal Government, as we must make it our business to remind them, is a dynamic approach to a challenging national problem." It was my last pronouncement in the House of Commons on the subject of housing.

The throne speech announced the appointment of a royal commission "to consider and report upon the development and financing of television and sound broadcasting." My friend Bob Fowler was appointed chairman, and the commission came to bear his name. There was one matter which urgently needed to be inquired into, namely, the cancellation of a program scheduled for December 20, 1955, on the controversial volume entitled *The Mackenzie King Era* by Professors Ostry and Ferns, two young Canadian political scientists who were teaching in England. The book was highly critical of Mackenzie King and the Liberal government, and it was widely believed that the program was cancelled at the urgent request or behest of the government or with its partisan interests in mind. I took up the case on a supply motion on February 7. I charged government interference, however subtle, with CBC programming or a failure by CBC to exercise its freedom in such matters in view of the government's interests. The government did not reply. Both it and the CBC became very coy about the whole matter. Neither of them ever made a straightforward statement in regard to it.

There had been little in these opening weeks to indicate the impending disaster that would strike parliamentary democracy in Canada later in the session. Although the House was often fractious and the air filled with stormy debate, much worse lay ahead.

CHAPTER TWENTY-SEVEN

Pipeline to Humiliation

When government financing for the Trans-Canada pipeline was announced in the speech from the throne that company already had a parliamentary history extending over five years. Legislation to incorporate the company had been enacted in 1951 on its undertaking to build a pipeline by an all-Canadian route and to market in Canada all of the natural gas thereby transported. The undertaking had not been carried out in those precious five years, and the five controlling companies, four of them owned and controlled in the United States, and possessed of enormous assets, were now saying the project could not be financed without government assistance.

Alberta was anxiously seeking markets for its natural gas. There was a very receptive market waiting for it in Ontario and Quebec. There was also a closer and more populous and more profitable market for it in the United States. The best means of transportation was a pipeline or pipelines, but by what route or routes? There was little market through northern Ontario, and construction was bound to be expensive in bridging the long distance between the Manitoba boundary and the centres of Ontario's population south of the lakehead. It was the same problem which had been encountered in the era of railway-building in Macdonald's day. The Canadian route was imperative on national grounds, but it would be costly. The expenditures required in Alberta to initiate the project were estimated at $250 million. The cost of constructing the pipeline to a point near Montreal was estimated at $375 million. Other expenditures would bring the total to a figure in excess of a billion dollars. It would be the longest single pipeline in the world.

This was the background for the bitterest struggle in all my eighteen years in the House of Commons. In ferocity and casualties no other battle came close to equalling it. Between May 8 and June 7, 1956, C.D. Howe brought the Canadian Parliament to its knees. No man ever did so much to humiliate that supreme institution and symbol of Canadian independence and democracy as Clarence Decatur Howe.

Who was this figure unique in the political history of his time? He was about my own build – short and stocky. Born in 1886 in Massachusetts and educated in the United States he came to Canada in 1908 as a young professor at Dalhousie University. Later he moved to Port Arthur and established an engineering practice. He designed a number of grain elevators on the prairies. I am told that he accepted a considerable volume of engineering business from the Bennett government. He was lured into politics by Mackenzie King in 1935, was elected in Port Arthur and with the change of government immediately became Minister of Railways. He had sat continuously as member for Port Arthur and as a minister for twenty-one years. No other minister, including the Prime Minister, had been a minister so long. Howe was very conscious of his seniority among his colleagues. During the war he was Minister of Munitions and Supply, and for his efforts in that portfolio he was rewarded with an Imperial Privy Councillorship in 1946 and the undoubted confidence of Canadian business. No man has ever held such a grasp over Canadian business and industry, and no man up to that time had ever spent so much money of the Canadian government. The men who served under him as controllers during the war were greatly in demand later for senior executive positions throughout Canada. I first met him as a member of a delegation representing Canada's railways in 1936. He gave us an excellent hearing.

Howe had two monumental weaknesses. He had never sat in Parliament as a private member or as a member of the opposition. He was a businessman, an executive. He prided himself on "getting things done." He was impatient of Parliament and its processes. He seemed to regard Parliament as an obstacle to action. Jim Macdonnell once said that Howe did not belong in Parliament, that he was really a Fascist who for some unaccountable reason had by chance wandered into Parliament.

His other great flaw was that he had a violent temper. I have never seen a man who allowed his temper to rage uncontrolled in public as Howe did. At times he would flush with rage, at times throw his papers down on his desk, at times walk out when under criticism. Worst of all, he would quickly descend to vituperation and personal abuse of his critics. No man ever indulged in such insults and name-calling in the House as he did. The rules of the

House failed to restrain him. He relied on intimidating the chairman to overcome the problem of rules. At seventy years of age, far from mellowing he had become more intolerant of obstacles to his will and volcanically short-tempered. He had a special dislike for George Drew, Howard Green and John Diefenbaker, and he found it hard to tolerate me. I will never know whether it was a blessing or a misfortune that I was appointed opposition critic to Howe's two departments of Trade and Commerce, and Defence Production. No man could have enjoyed such a task. It meant constant in-fighting and being the target for endless abuse, but I never took a step back when facing Howe.

The defeat he had suffered in 1955 at the hands of an embattled Conservative opposition over the continuance of his wide powers under the Defence Production Act rankled with him. He had resolved never again to accept such a reverse at the hands of an official opposition which was outnumbered by the Liberals by almost four to one. Were not all those Liberals elected to Parliament to support the government in whatever it chose to do? At the beginning of the 1956 session he bluntly told the Liberal MPs to "toe the line."

It was tragically inopportune that Howe's determination to brook neither opposition nor delay, whether from his political adversaries or the Liberal members in the House, coincided with a visible decline on the part of Mr. St. Laurent. He was taking less and less interest in the business of the House and contributing little to its discussions. Howe appeared to be assuming rule of the cabinet more and more by default.

On March 15 in an elaborate and lengthy presentation Howe introduced what he called the government's "unique solution" of the pipeline problem. The governments would build the link through northern Ontario. He accepted as a fact that private enterprise alone could not profitably build it; he was prepared to release the giant companies promoting the pipeline from their five-year-old undertaking to build it; and he was unwilling to open the project up to bidding by other private and Canadian interests. Moreover, claiming that eastern Canada could not take all the natural gas available he would allow Trans-Canada Pipe Lines (TCPL) to divert part of the flow at Emerson, Manitoba, to the large U.S. market. Already contracts had been signed for the export of large quantities of gas to the United States. The government's scheme was to form a crown corporation to be known as Northern Ontario Pipe Line Crown Corporation (NOPLCC) to which the Ontario government had somewhat reluctantly become a party. The Ontario legislature had unanimously passed a bill to lend up to $35 million to the new company, which would build and own the 675-mile link from the Manitoba border to Kapuskasing and to rent this section to TCPL for a maximum of twenty-five years. The lessee, Trans-Canada, agreed to rent the link and to purchase it as soon as it as lessee could raise the necessary finance, so that NOPLCC would recover its full outlay and investment with interest at the rate of 4.5 per cent per annum. To the five-man board of directors of NOPLCC the Ontario government would appoint two and the federal government three directors. After the financing by the two governments was completed Trans-Canada would offer 51 per cent of its voting shares to the Canadian public, though there was no guarantee that Canadians would buy the stock or that Canadian control would thereby be achieved. Public ownership admittedly would have guaranteed Canadian control, but it was rejected by Howe as second best.

In a masterly speech, lengthy and strongly expressed, George Drew opposed the resolution. He demanded an all-Canadian route for a pipeline under Canadian control. The diversion of gas to the United States made the line dependent on the decision of the Federal Power Commission in Washington, and this was quite unacceptable. The government scheme offered no assurance of Canadian control. Its claim that the pipeline could not be financed privately was spurious, for the government would not allow any other private group to bid. The failure of Trans-Canada to honour its undertaking should have led to its elimination from consideration. The government was largely responsible for the delay of five years which had already occurred. In essence Parliament was being asked to set up a crown corporation which would use public funds to assist financial interests in the United States to establish effective control over one of Canada's major resources. The sponsors were large enough to finance the project themselves, and they should be compelled to carry out their undertaking to do so. The government would create a monopoly; it should not be for the benefit of U.S. interests. George was full of fight. The battle lines had been drawn. The CCF supported him, but wanted the pipeline built under public ownership. The Social Credit MPs, most of whom came from Alberta, heartily supported the government proposal.

Then a strange, uneasy silence of seven weeks settled over the battlefield. It was broken only by Howe's denial that he was in possession of certain letters from Canadian interests, whereas later it came to light that they were in his possession, having been marked "private and confidential."

On May 8 after a Liberal caucus the previous day Howe filed notice of a new and expanded resolution. It embraced all the contents of the already pending resolution and added provision for the construction of the western section of the pipeline in 1956, with the federal government lending Trans-Canada at 5 per cent interest no less than 90 per cent of the cost of constructing this easiest portion of the entire pipeline. Drew demanded, Why not let Canadians have this opportunity? Coldwell denounced the proposal as a "sell-out to U.S. interests." We, of course, contended that the second resolution was out of order, but unsuccessfully. Thus began four weeks of incessant arguments on points of order and questions of privilege. The burden of carrying on these highly technical arguments with the Speaker, the chairman and the deputy chairman fell on the shoulders of Stanley Knowles of the CCF and Davie Fulton and myself for the official opposition. The Speaker on May 10 allowed the second resolution. That was the signal for a series of appeals from rulings, motions to adjourn and long drawn-out divisions which continued with great frequency until the small hours of June 6, for by now the opposition (not including the Social Credit) was fighting with every procedural weapon at its command.

When the resolution was next called by the government on May 14 Howe spoke and gave notice of closure, amidst angry cries of "Guillotine! Dictatorship!" This shortened the time allowed for each speaker with the exceptions of the Prime Minister, who was maintaining silence, and George Drew. It cast a very heavy burden on George to speak at utmost possible length. On the 15th Howe's closure motion was put and carried by a solid Liberal and Socred vote. This was the pattern of every vote from that point to the end. Closure compelled the House to sit without adjournment. We kept the debate alive until 4.42 a.m. when the resolution was finally carried and the bill received first reading. The moving of closure had been resorted to only half a dozen times since confederation. When last applied in 1932, Mackenzie King had described it as "the most coercive and arbitrary act of which a government is capable." Taking my time to speak, I said:

> But here this despotic government announces closure in the opening speech. . . . This debate started yesterday and closure was announced before the debate was even begun. . . . This is a light-hearted assassination of free institutions, and it is perpetrated now by those who call themselves Liberals. . . . No Cromwell could more swiftly and devastatingly have showed his complete antipathy to parliamentary institutions than the Prime Minister and

his Government have done. . . . But it is not only the Minister of Trade and Commerce, for others share the responsibility with him and principally the Prime Minister who sits silent in this House in the face of a major issue, who voted for closure today, who has retired in all but name, who is not doing his duty in this House in sitting silent and allowing measures like this to be perpetrated upon the Canadian Parliament, who is hiding behind a reckless Minister of Trade and Commerce. Behold the wantonness of power!

Howe had had the effrontery to call his project "another declaration of independence by Canada." I was at pains to tell him that there never had been a declaration of independence in the history of Canada, though I acknowledged that there had been one in the history of the United States. I said he was confused as to what country he was supposed to be serving. Later Jimmy Gardiner accused me of playing on the fact that Howe was born, raised and educated in the United States. I replied, "I have never yet judged any man on the place of his birth, because the man is not born yet who has any control over the place of his birth. . . . I . . . judge the Minister . . . not on where he was born, but on his actions, his attitudes and his policies."

The government chose to call other business on May 16 and thus shorten the time for debate. The next stage was second reading; debate on it opened on May 17 and 18. On Monday, May 21, Walter Harris announced closure on that debate; his motion was voted on and carried on the 22nd. On that day Mr. St. Laurent at last spoke, stating that delay would defeat the project and that the majority was entitled to make a decision. Conservatives and CCF protested the imposition of a time limit on Parliament to accommodate the interests of U.S. promoters. We were fighting against that kind of dictation. We kept the debate going until 3.17 a.m., when second reading carried.

The third stage was consideration of the bill in committee. We fought off this stage the next day with a series of procedural objections and arguments, which were overruled. On May 24 the House resolved itself into Committee of the Whole to consider the seven sections of the bill. Bill Robinson was in the chair.

When the first section was called Howe leaped to his feet, was recognized by the chair, and proceeded to say in a couple of sentences that no consideration of the section was necessary and moved that further consideration of section 1 be postponed. The chairman ruled that the motion was not debatable or amendable. The effect of the motion was thus to impose immediate closure. The opposition could take only procedural objection and could not discuss either section 1 or the merits of Howe's motion. It was adopted.

When section 2 was called Howe and Drew both leaped to their feet and Howe was recognized by the chair. The opposition entered strenuous objection to the recognition again of the spokesman from the government side. The chairman persisted, however, in giving the floor to Howe. Fulton moved that Drew be given the floor, but the big Liberal majority, swollen by Social Credit support, voted the motion down. Given the floor, Howe in a couple of sentences asserted that no consideration of section 2 of the bill was necessary, and again moved that consideration of the section be postponed. Again the opposition was not permitted to discuss or amend the motion or section 2 of the bill. Again Howe's motion was adopted with Liberal and Social Credit support, thus applying immediate closure on section 2.

When section 3 was called the same farce was re-enacted. The teamwork between the chair and Howe could not have been smoother or more shameful. Howe's three throttling motions were greeted with cries of "Shame!" from the opposition and tense silence from the Liberal benches. It was a bare-faced sellout of the integrity of the chair. Our protests were unavailing.

On Thursday evening Stanley Knowles took the floor on a point of order, contending that Howe's motion was out of order. He had not completed his argument at the 10 o'clock adjournment.

May 25 was an unforgettable day in my life. As it fell on a Friday the hours of sitting were 11 a.m. to 1 p.m., and 2.30 to 6.00 p.m. In the morning after other business was disposed of Knowles completed his argument, and at 12.20 p.m. I commenced a carefully prepared argument in which I supported him on the point of order. Under the new rule speeches in the Committee of the Whole were limited to thirty minutes. At ten minutes to one o'clock Chairman Robinson rose to inform me that my thirty minutes had expired. I took the ground that the thirty-minute rule did not apply to discussion on points of order in committee. The chairman, however, brushed this opinion aside and gave the floor to Walter Harris, who wished to reply to the point of order. Harris spoke until the adjournment for lunch at one o'clock. As soon as the committee adjourned, however, Robinson immediately came over to my desk. He was very angry. The previous day he had been very suave and pleasant in the chair, but this time he was thoroughly incensed. He chided me with my contention that the thirty-minute rule did not apply to discussion of points of order. I had never previously seen him showing such anger as on this occasion.

The House resumed its afternoon sitting at 2.30 p.m. Walter Harris completed his submission on the point of order in about five minutes. As soon as he had completed his submission the chairman rose. I jumped to my feet and stated that I wished briefly to complete my submission to him on the point of order. Actually, I needed about five minutes to complete it. I spoke first. I got as far as saying "Mr. Chairman, on the same point of order –" when the chairman abruptly stopped me with the words: "Order. I have already seen the hon. gentleman and I am now in a position to make a decision." Drew interjected: "Is this closure? Does Your Honour say that you will hear no more speakers?" The chairman was standing, and said: "May I remind hon. members of the fact when the Chairman is standing other hon. members should resume their seats." I asked: "Are you not going to hear us on the point of order before you make your ruling?" He replied: "I have now heard, in my opinion, sufficient to enable me to decide the point and I should like to do it at this moment." I asked: "Mr. Chairman, will you permit an observation?" To this he returned a flat no.

At this point Stanley Knowles rose on a question of privilege. After some hesitation the chairman said he would hear the question of privilege. He then sat down and heard Knowles at some length. When Knowles had completed his statement I rose and said: "Mr. Chairman, I wish to speak on a question of privilege." The chairman was on his feet, and replied: "Order. That is not a direct question of privilege," evidently referring to the point raised by Stanley Knowles. I repeated my statement that I wished to speak on a question of privilege. The chairman refused and added: "When I am on my feet and about to give a ruling I say it is impossible for members to raise a question of privilege." This was an interesting statement from him since he had just heard Knowles state a question of privilege after rising to his feet to give his ruling. At this juncture Jim Macdonnell rose and said: "Mr. Chairman, I rise on a question of privilege." The chairman replied: "As a courtesy I am going to hear the hon. member," but asked Mr. Macdonnell to resume his seat while he quoted from one of the textbooks. At the conclusion of the reading Robinson announced that he intended to make his ruling on the original point of order. I rose again on a question of privilege, and pointed out that I wished to do so before he made his ruling, as otherwise it would be too late. Then followed about a dozen exchanges on each side between the chairman and myself. I insisted that I had a right to raise a question of privilege, and that the only time I could raise it was before he made his ruling, and the chairman insisted that he would not hear the question of privilege and that as he was on his feet to deliver his ruling I must take my seat and be silent.

In that anguished moment I had to make a decision, without consulting anyone, either to submit to an improper and discriminatory gagging by the chairman or stand my ground in protest against the improper conduct of the chair. I chose to stand my ground. I never had an opportunity even so much as to state my question of privilege, let alone explain it or argue it.

The chairman in deep anger stated that because I had refused to resume my seat he must report the matter to the House. The record shows clearly that I had not refused to take my seat. On the contrary it shows that I persisted in asserting my right to raise a question of privilege. The chairman left the chair to read his report on the incident to the Speaker. In doing so he ignored Fulton's request that the report be read to the committee before he made it to the House. His report read as follows:

> Mr. Speaker, in committee of the whole when it was considering clause 3 of Bill No. 298, an act to establish the Northern Ontario Pipe Line Crown Corporation, I was addressing the committee when Mr. Fleming rose on a question of privilege. I stated that a question of privilege could not be raised while I was addressing the committee and directed Mr. Fleming to resume his seat. This, Mr. Fleming refused to do.

The Speaker resumed the chair, and the mace was placed on the table by the Sergeant-at-Arms to mark the fact that the committee had risen and the House had resumed its sitting. I then addressed the Speaker in words which fell upon a hushed House – in marked contrast to the hubbub in the committee which had accompanied the exchange between the chairman and myself. I spoke in a quiet voice, for I fully appreciated the gravity of the situation. I think my voice rose as I proceeded firmly and out of deep conviction to my concluding remarks. Hansard records those remarks as follows:

> Mr. Speaker, may I be heard? I submit to you, sir, that that report is not a true and accurate report of the proceedings in committee. These are the facts, sir. A point of order was under discussion. The discussion had commenced last night on a point that was raised by the hon. member for Winnipeg North Centre, and I followed this morning on the point of order, supporting it. When I rose the chairman of the committee said that he, at some point,

wished to hear argument as to whether he, as chairman, should hear more than the member raising or introducing the point of order. He did say, however, when I undertook to discuss that subject, that he did not wish the discussion at that point, but that he would reserve that as a separate point for later discussion. I proceeded then to discuss the original point and the second point has not yet been raised.

After I was heard in part, I may say that the chairman ruled that my time was up in the committee about ten minutes to one although I had not quite completed, then he heard the Minister of Finance (Mr. Harris) on the same point of order. After the noon adjournment the committee resumed at 2.30 and the floor was given to the Minister of Finance to complete his observations and representations on the point of order. He was heard to the end, and then the chairman of the committee rose and stated that he was about to make his ruling. I rose and indicated that I wished to complete briefly some remarks on the point of order. Now, if he had given me an opportunity, Mr. Speaker, I would have said that another member of my own party who was going to make a submission on the same point of order had decided to withhold those remarks and let me complete my remarks instead of having a second speaker from my party on that point. I was not permitted even to say that.

At that point the hon. member for Winnipeg North Centre (Mr. Knowles) rose on a question of privilege. Will you bear in mind, Mr. Speaker, that the hon. member for Winnipeg North Centre was at that point heard on a question of privilege. The chairman of the committee had already said he was on his feet and was about to give his decision on the point of order, but even then, even having risen to his feet with that declared purpose, he heard the hon. member for Winnipeg North Centre on a question of privilege. I said I wished then to be heard on a question of privilege. My question of privilege was similar to his, but I was entitled, I think, to state it. The chairman of the committee did not hear me.

Then, the hon. member to my right, my colleague the hon. member for Greenwood (Mr. Macdonnell), rose to his feet and said he wished to address the chair on a question of privilege. Still the chairman of the committee was on his feet and still purporting to make his ruling on a question of order, and without having heard all the discussion on that point, but he said, if you please, that he would hear the hon. member for Greenwood on his question of privilege. I then asked that I be heard on a question of privilege. I had already tried several times, even before, to be heard on a question of privilege, and although the chairman of the committee had heard the hon. member for Winnipeg North Centre on a question of privilege and although he said he was going to hear my colleague the hon. member for Greenwood on a question of privilege, he refused to hear me on a question of privilege. I asserted, Mr. Speaker, my right to be heard on a question of privilege and not be debarred by a decision of the chair from being heard on an important question of privilege on an issue that is as important as any that will ever come before the Canadian House of Commons.

When others enjoy the right – it is not a privilege, it is a right to be heard on a question of privilege – under the same circumstances and while the same chairman was on his feet and engaged in delivering his decision on the same point of order, by what right does he accord to some members of the house the right to rise on a question of privilege and deny it to me? Therefore, Mr. Speaker, I stood my ground.

[Some hon. Members: Hear, hear.]

And I did so, Mr. Speaker, without departing one inch from the respect which, in the 11 years I have been in this house, I have always given to the Chair. But there comes a time when a higher duty is owed, and it is a duty to parliament itself, to the long centuries of tradition of parliamentary freedom. And, sir, the right that I assert here today I assert not for myself alone. I assert it for all members of this House of Commons, not just today, but in days to come, to stand up against discriminatory decisions, in fact, abuse of the rules of this house and denial to members of their clear and proper and constitutional rights to discharge their responsibilities to those who sent them here, their responsibilities to all Canadians, their responsibilities not only today but to generations yet unborn, and I abide by the consequences.

I recollect hearing a storm of applause from Conservative and CCF benches as I took my seat. At that point Stanley Knowles rose to address the Speaker on a question of privilege. He reviewed what had happened in the committee, pointing out the position in which I had been placed as a result of the impression that Bill Robinson had given at the opening of the morning sitting that he would hear argument on the question as to whether he was obliged to hear discussion on a point of order. He concluded by saying that he thought there had been "a serious misunderstanding between the Chairman and the Committee." The Speaker made a lengthy statement concluding with the observation that it was not his duty to decide on the point raised as to whether I had the right to be heard in the committee on the question of privilege. His final words were: "I have nothing whatever to do with what has taken place in Committee-of-the-Whole. All that I have to deal with is the report I have received, and my duty consists merely of presenting that report to the House and this is what I have done. The matter is now entirely in the hands of the House and not in mine."

Walter Harris then rose and introduced the following motion: "That the hon. member for Eglinton be suspended from the service of the House for the remainder of this day's sitting." His motion drew a chorus of cries of "Shame" from opposition benches.

I took no further part in the proceedings in the House. Following the course of the Honourable Dr. Bruce in 1944 I remained silent in my seat throughout the argument which followed, and did not participate in the two votes which ensued.

First Davie Fulton moved the following amendment to Harris's motion:

> That the motion be amended by deleting all the words after "that" and substituting therefor the following:
> "This house record its support of the hon. member for Eglinton in his assertion of the historic and inalienable right of hon. members to rise and speak on a question of privilege in committee of the whole."

Harris sent me over a note expressing his regret at being obliged to take such an action against "an old friend." I said and wrote nothing, but my thought was, "Then why are you doing it?"

The Speaker indicated that the motion was not debatable and not amendable. Discussion on the point of order followed and the Speaker ruled the amendment out of order. An appeal was taken from his ruling and it was sustained on division by a vote of 133 to 54. All Liberal, Social Credit and Independent members in the House voted to sustain the ruling, while all Conservatives and CCF members voted against it.

Thereupon the House divided on the motion of Harris to suspend me for the remainder of the day's sitting. The Speaker called for the usual voice vote. Remarkable as it may seem, the Yeas of some 133 members were drowned out by the Nays of some 54 members, and the Speaker declared that in his opinion "the Nays have it." Had the government been seriously wishing merely to indicate its support of the chair in principle one might have thought that it could have allowed the matter to rest there. They did not do so. They had obviously determined to press the motion to its ultimate conclusion. Five members in such a case can by rising in their places force a division. Those who rose to force the division were the Prime Minister, Howe, Harris and several of the parliamentary assistants who sat just behind them. The result was inevitable then when the government put its whips on the division and made it a matter of confidence in the government. The first member to cast his vote for the motion was the Prime Minister. I eyed him intently as he rose to vote. His glance met mine, and with a Pilate-like gesture he shrugged his shoulders and sat down and turned his gaze away.

The motion was supported by every Liberal and every Social Credit member present. I was later informed of one Social Credit member who deliberately absented himself from the House rather than participate in the action which the government was taking. All Conservative and CCF members voted against the motion and this time the Independent members divided, Thatcher voting for the suspension, and Gagnon against it.

It was not pleasant to watch members on the government side, some of whom had professed to be close friends of mine for years, rising at the behest of the government to vote for this "purge." Party discipline admitted of no exception among them. The Clerk announced the result: "Yeas – 131; Nays – 55." The Speaker rose and uttered words which I have heard hundreds of times, but on this occasion sounded in my ears like the voice of doom; "I declare the motion carried." There may be some question as to whether I was obliged actually to withdraw from the House, since I was not "named" by the Speaker, or "expelled," but only suspended. I had told the Speaker that I would quietly withdraw by the south door of the Chamber the moment the motion was adopted. This appeared to carry his approval as being a proper and dignified course for me to follow. Accordingly, when he declared the motion carried I rose in my place, bowed to him, and then moved deliberately from my seat along the middle of the floor to the far end of the Chamber. It was a moment of indescribable tension. I have been told since that there were tears in the eyes of some of our Conservative members. I was not tempted to flinch or wince, but the thought kept revolving through my mind as I walked toward the end of the Chamber that my political career might then have reached its end. Never for one second, however, did I doubt the rightness of my course in relation to the wider issues involved. As I passed John Diefenbaker's desk he spoke out, "Farewell, John Hampden."

I had not taken more than several paces from my seat when my colleagues burst into thunderous applause. I shall always be grateful to them for their support in that climactic moment. I turned my head neither to the right nor to the left, but I was aware that the CCF members had joined in the applause. When I reached the bar of the Chamber I turned and bowed deeply to the Speaker. It was then that for the first time I observed that all of the Conservative and CCF members were on their feet. I had never heard such applause in my eleven years in the House. It sounded like music in my ears as I suddenly realized I stood alone.

The big clock at the south end showed 4.40 p.m. as I walked out of the Chamber and through the outer lobby to be greeted at the door by a battery of newspaper photographers and members of the press gallery. I answered their questions and made a firm statement to the effect that in the issue which had arisen what happened to me mattered little, but what happened to the right of free speech in Parliament mattered much. I expressed my sincere regret that the incident had arisen, but I again asserted my belief that I had taken the right and proper course.

I knew nothing about the flag with which Ellen Fairclough covered my desk after my departure. I learned the next week that it had been sent for after Harris made his motion.

I then hurried to my office to telephone Alice to break the news to her before she heard it on the 6 o'clock news. The dominating thought in my mind was to go home to Toronto as quickly as possible, but when I got to the airport I found that there was no seat available on the 6.05 flight. At the airport I met Paul Hellyer, who was extremely curt with me. There was no place to go but back to my office. I returned to the Parliament Buildings with an anxious mind. What was the general reaction? How did the journalists in the press gallery react? Had their sense of fairness been offended by the treatment I had received, or were they disposed to take a lighter view of the event? The House had risen for the day by the time I reached the Parliament Buildings. I passed Ted Applewhaite, deputy chairman, in the hall. He walked past without speaking. I saw George Drew, Davie Fulton, and John Diefenbaker briefly, and they brought me words of consolation and support which meant much to me at that moment. From John Diefenbaker I heard of my desk-mate Howard Green's collapse in the restaurant following the gripping tension of the afternoon's proceedings. He was then under the doctor's care. Having been suspended I did not feel at liberty to dine in the parliamentary restaurant, and made my way alone over to a nearby cafe to eat in solitude a meal for which I had little appetite.

The evening passed more quickly than I had expected. George Nowlan, whose office was next to mine, came in and told me things that cheered me greatly. He conveyed to me a report that the reaction throughout the House and the press gallery was sympathetic and that by taking a courageous, if costly, stand I had performed a service for the lasting good of the Canadian Parliament. Derek Bedson, Drew's secretary, telephoned to say that a few friends would be meeting me on my arrival at Toronto airport.

The flight from Ottawa to Malton was uneventful. King Clancy sat across from me. Before the plane had taxied to its appointed place I was startled to hear cheering. At first I thought it must be some group meeting King Clancy. I looked through the window and to my amazement could see a crowd which must have numbered a couple of hundred people with banners and flags. As I stepped out of the plane the crowd broke into cheers. I realized then they had come to meet me. What a homecoming it was! In all my life I have never known anything like it. It took me totally by surprise. Alice and sixteen-year-old Mary were there with a host of loyal friends with flags and banners led by two pipers. Never did the pipes sound more musical.

The CBC was present ready to film the scene and record my remarks for television. I spoke briefly saying that I had endeavoured to uphold the honour and the integrity of Parliament. I thanked all present for their support, which meant much to me in a dark hour. It was after midnight and it was on a weekend when many people would normally have gone away and would be little interested in driving to Malton. Many of them had come considerable distances to be present. My heart was filled with gratitude to every one of them. It had not once occurred to me that I deserved or would receive a hero's welcome. I was vastly relieved that Alice did not seem downcast.

After some more photographs had been taken we drove home where the press conducted further interviews and took more photographs. After they left I had some work to do for the office. By the time I had finished it and retired it was 3 o'clock.

I did not sleep a wink the rest of the night. The telephone began ringing early in the morning and it rang constantly both at the office and at the house the rest of the weekend. Soon the telegrams began to arrive and within the next several days letters in large numbers. The communications numbered in the hundreds. The majority were from persons who described themselves as Liberals who were shocked and infuriated at the course taken by the government. All saw in it a challenge to the democratic rights that so many Canadians had simply taken for granted. We had said: "It can't happen here," and yet it had happened before our very eyes.

My fifty-first birthday fell on Wednesday, May 23. A little family birthday party had been planned for me at the weekend. It was the most disturbed birthday I have ever observed. The telephone did not stop ringing. All through Saturday some familiar words kept haunting me: "This time, Louis, you have gone too far." For a long time, try as I might, I could not remember the source of the words. Then suddenly it came to me. They were the famous words uttered by the Duke of Wellington when he arrived just too late to save the gallant Marshal Ney from execution before the muskets of the firing squad of King Louis Philippe. I took courage to hope that the government's attempt to "purge" the House of Commons of my presence for a mere one hour and twenty minutes might help to draw attention to the degree to which a "Liberal" government had carried the country along the path of dictatorship.

I returned to Ottawa on the Sunday night train and resumed my seat at Monday's sitting. Under the acute nervous strain I had almost completely lost my voice and was obliged to sit silent for the next three days.

The political aftermath of my suspension was, unfortunately, typical. The public reaction had been so strongly condemnatory of the government that Liberal and Social Credit spokesmen and writers sought to excuse the government for the partisan course that it had taken by concocting the story that I had courted suspension, had deliberately "baited" the chairman, provoked the government to bring in its motion, and had pre-arranged the draping of the flag, the presence of the press photographers at the door of the Chamber, and the welcoming crowd at Malton airport. This concoction was, of course, a wicked collection of falsehoods in every particular.

The personal aftermath was equally unforeseen. I was only partly aware that Friday afternoon in the Chamber of the emotional strain. I was destined before long, however, to realize how severe it had been. In the House my place was between Howard Green and Jim Macdonnell. Howard Green had collapsed about six o'clock Friday evening. Jim Macdonnell was taken ill at the weekend and on Tuesday went to the hospital for two weeks. My feelings during the following week I can only compare in my previous experience with a bereavement in the immediate family. The emotional strain resulted in a feeling of utter exhaustion. Some Liberal MPs and senators ceased to speak to me. A couple of Liberal members came to me to apologize for voting for the government's motion and to say that the government put all their whips to work to force members to come to the House to vote, and that but for the whipping numerous members would have chosen to absent themselves.

CHAPTER TWENTY-EIGHT

Twilight of Parliament

On Monday, May 28, the Prime Minister, as if bestowing a privilege on the House, announced that the week would be available to complete the "remaining stages" of the bill. "The retreat from Moscow," commented John Diefenbaker. George Drew introduced a motion, which I had drafted, to adjourn the House "for the purpose of discussing a definite matter of urgent public importance, namely, the subordination by the Government of the office of Chairman of the Committee of the Whole to serve the partisan interests of the Government." The Speaker rejected the motion. After some further discussion of points of order Davie Fulton rose to introduce a motion. Chairman Applewhaite ignored him and proceeded to put Howe's motion to the vote. Davie ignored the chairman and continued to speak. The counting of the vote proceeded, and Davie being on his feet throughout the roll-call was recorded as voting both for and against. Howe's motion that further consideration of section 3 be postponed was declared adopted by a vote of 124 to 53. Although Davie had not taken his seat, precisely as I had done on the previous Friday, this time his defiance of the chair was not reported to the Speaker by the chairman. Evidently the government had for the time lost its appetite for suspensions, and the chairman was ready to turn a blind eye to any such occasion in order to spare the government embarrassment.

The debate on section 4 proceeded Monday and Tuesday. Great speeches were made by Drew and Coldwell, and on Tuesday Diefenbaker made a slashing attack on the Prime Minister. On Wednesday St. Laurent set the next Monday, June 4, for completion of all stages of the bill. The deadline, vital to the government's schedule, was close at hand. The Prime Minister's offer of extra sittings at the end of the week was flatly rejected by Coldwell. The Prime Minister gave notice of motion to apply

313

closure on all clauses of the bill. On Thursday the motion was adopted by a vote of 151 to 61, with St. Laurent speaking in defence of closure. The balance of the day was spent in introducing points of order, rulings by the chair, appeals from rulings, and motions to adjourn. When closure had made the situation look utterly hopeless and the end seemed at hand Colin Cameron of the CCF, a very adroit debater, rose at 9.15 p.m. to call the attention of the Speaker to breaches of the privileges of the House contained in two letters published in the *Ottawa Journal*. They had been written by Eugene Forsey and Marjorie Le Lacheur, charging "the systematic garroting of the Opposition by Mr. Speaker." The speaker allowed discussion on the question whether these words constituted a breach of the privileges of the House. George Drew supported Cameron on the question, contending that they were a breach. After the letters had been read twice, first by Colin Cameron, then by the Clerk of the House, the Speaker painstakingly advised Cameron as to the form his motion should take. Thereupon following the Speaker's instruction Cameron moved "that the statements in the *Ottawa Journal* of May 30 and 31, as just read by the Clerk, are derogatory of the dignity of Parliament and deserve the censure of this House." The motion was debatable and George Drew was on his feet arguing the question of privilege at 10 p.m., the hour of automatic adjournment. The government was powerless at that moment to do anything but adjourn the debate.

Conservative elation at this unexpected turn of events knew no bounds. It had thrown the government's schedule out by a day. Their arbitrary deadline could not now be achieved. In high spirits Conservative members repaired to the caucus room to enjoy sandwiches, which had been ordered in preparation for a late sitting, and to share a great occasion for exultation, of which we had had all too few. A great victory had been won, or so we thought. We were not aware that it was reported that Walter Harris had been seen after the adjournment going to the Speaker's chambers, just as we were blissfully unaware until the next afternoon that Jack Pickersgill's car was reported to have been seen about breakfast time outside the Speaker's residence. I am not able to confirm these two reports, but we assumed there had been communication from the government to the Speaker and that it was in compelling terms.

June 1 was a Friday. The House therefore convened at 11 a.m. As George Drew took his seat he laid a handful of volumes on his desk. He was prepared to continue his speech on the Cameron motion. Considering the circumstances he seemed very fresh in physical appearance, although he must have been up most of the night preparing his speech. He had barely uttered the words "Mr. Speaker," when that protector of the rights and privileges of Parliament stopped him and without calling for or allowing any discussion ruled that no question of privilege was presented by the two letters mentioned in the Cameron motion. He refused to hear any discussion and flatly made his ruling which was, of course, sustained on appeal. He followed this with an even more astounding ruling. On the startled and unbelieving ears of the opposition fell the Speaker's statement that he had made a very serious mistake at 5.15 p.m. Thursday in allowing a point of order and then dilatory motions. It was therefore his intention to submit that the House should revert to the position it was in at 5.15 p.m. Thursday. He called this a ruling and asked the House to sustain it without permitting any discussion on it or on any point of order or question of privilege.

Immediately pandemonium broke loose. Hansard records that I was the first to speak. I managed to say two words, "Mr. Speaker." George Drew said, "I am rising on a question of privilege." Coldwell asked, "What are you doing, Mr. Speaker?" I said, "On a point of order – ." George Drew said, "On a question of privilege, Mr. Speaker – ." Bedlam drowned out everything else. Coldwell, Drew and I were all on our feet. Coldwell, usually mild in manner and strict in decorum, left his place in the House and walked briskly to the end of the table of the House and pointed to the mace, the symbol of the authority of the House. He was noticeably angry and appeared to some to be about to lay his hand on it. Actually he did not touch the mace, but all eyes were on him wondering what he was about to do. George Drew and I remained on our feet and stepped out on to the floor, followed by a dozen other members who were equally stunned by the Speaker's abject somersault. While they walked about the floor below the table I strode across the floor to the desk shared by the Prime Minister and Howe. Dr. McCann, misreading my innocent intent, made a gesture with his ample frame as if to shield them. I said to St. Laurent and Howe, "You are responsible for this." They did not move a muscle or utter a word. Having delivered my message I returned to join George Drew on the opposition side of the floor. At no time did John Diefenbaker leave his seat.

After a time Drew, Coldwell and the others returned to their places and the business of the House was resumed in a very disturbed and almost feverish atmosphere. George Drew was swiftly on his feet to move "That in view of the unprecedented action of Mr. Speaker in improperly reversing his own decision without notice and without giving any opportunity for discussion, this House resolves that it no longer has any confidence in its presiding officer." The Speaker ruled that the motion would require forty-eight hours' notice before it could be debated. The remainder of the morning sitting was taken up with procedural battles in a continuing din. At one point I was able to say, or rather shout, this much: "Mr. Speaker, it should be placed on record that when an hon. member rose on a question of privilege you sat down and refused to hear him and the Liberals instigated such an outburst of disorder that no one could be heard. That ought to be on the record. This is the lowest moment in Canadian parliamentary history; the lowest moment. There has never been anything like it." Tom Bell called out, "This is black Friday." Thus that dreadful day was given the fitting name by which it has ever since been known.

Evidently in the hope of drowning me out the Liberals burst into a well-rehearsed choral rendition of a song entitled "There'll always be a pipeline, The pipeline shall be free" to the tune of "There'll Always Be an England." At the end of one line, "The pipeline shall be free," I with the aid of my stentorian voice am credited on the record with the words, "Not Parliament," and again after a repetition of the same line of the chorus, "Free to American investors."

The Speaker put to the House this question without any motion, "Shall the course of action submitted by Mr. Speaker be followed?" One hundred and forty-two Liberal and Social Credit Members answered "Yea." There were no "Nays." George Drew stated, "We are not voting because there is no question properly before the House." Coldwell added, "I share that opinion."

When the House reassembled at 2.30 p.m. the Speaker simply shut his eyes and ears to the efforts of Fulton, Knowles and myself to address him on points of order. At one point I reminded him that at the morning sitting he had promised to hear me on the point of order. He now stated that he refused to hear me on it. George Drew called out, "You have no right to sit in that chair." The closure motion was affirmed. The bill was returned to the committee where the wrangling on procedural questions and rulings continued. At one point I succeeded in speaking for more than twenty minutes on a point of order. The sitting continued without any dinner adjournment until 1.47 a.m. In the late stages the various clauses were carried on separate divisions, and the bill was reported. Weary members dispersed for what remained of another disturbed weekend. The government's program was back once more on schedule; the Conservatives and CCF had fought a courageous, tenacious, but unavailing battle, and the Speaker yielding to the behest of the government had destroyed himself. More important and worse still he had destroyed the integrity of the high office he held in trust. Beaudoin's capitulation affected me deeply. Among all the Liberals in the House I had no closer friend. Possessed of very great talents his career in the chair had seemed so full of promise. Now that was at an end. Our personal relations were never the same afterward. He appeared to have lost even the respect of his own party. The government certainly did nothing for him as a reward for service either to them or to the country. Later years found him living in the United States, his marriage and his professional career both at an end.

What followed on the first days of the next week seemed almost an anti-climax. On Monday, June 4, George Drew proceeded with his motion to censure the Speaker. He made a lengthy, fair and unanswerable presentation. Coldwell spoke in strong support and called for dissolution so that a new Parliament might wipe out the stains upon the honour of the present one. The Prime Minister moved the adjournment of the debate on the motion to censure the Speaker, and, of course, the majority supported him. He then gave notice of closure. The struggle had entered its final stage as the House debated third reading. George Drew made a final and masterly speech reviewing the course that had been followed from the outset. He said that with the government supplying the finance it would be better to place the project under public ownership than to allow the promoters to take the profit. He had telephoned me that morning to ask if I had any objection to his taking this position as a last resort, and I concurred on that basis. His amendment was aimed to assure Canadian ownership and control.

The St. Laurent closure motion carried by a vote of 150 to 61. I led off in the continuing debate on George Drew's amendment: "We are approaching the final stage in a momentous but sad debate. We in the opposition, make no mistake about it, will fight to the end, to the last minute of debate." This promise was fulfilled to the letter. I pointed out that there had been eight closure motions in sixteen days, compared with a total of only six previously since Confederation. I promised that the debate before the people of Canada would not end that night. I charged Harris with seeking to mislead the people. At a late hour George Drew's amendment was defeated by a vote of 153 to 36. There were more divisions before the bill was finally passed at 3.20 a.m. That was the end as far as the weary Commons was concerned. The bill swept through the Senate and received royal assent on June 7 just in time to meet the deadline agreed by Howe and the promoters.

An hour after the House convened on June 6 it was announced that one of the members, John Macdougall, had died suddenly. The House immediately adjourned out of respect. It was believed that his death was due to the strain of the pipeline debate. His wife was seated in the gallery of the House when he was stricken.

There was a sequel to the sordid tale of the pipeline debacle. In giving all of Parliament's time to that debate the government had inexcusably neglected other business, some of it quite urgent. It needed a vote of interim supply to meet its mid-June bills, including salaries. Stanley Knowles of the CCF came to me to propose that Conservatives and CCF together should oppose such a vote and force a delay. By forcing a default we would greatly embarrass the government and teach them a lesson. From the point of view of tactics and giving the government a punishment they deserved there was much to be said in favour of Stanley's proposal. I was not willing, however, to make the civil service suffer for the sins of the government. Moreover, there was a real possibility that the scheme might backfire. George Drew agreed with me, and I so informed Stanley. When the government asked the House for a vote of interim supply on June 11 both Drew and Knowles asked for dissolution and a general election, but did not withhold supply. St. Laurent said the government would continue with the business of the session.

And so the Parliament of Canada was bent, broken, coerced, dishonoured and put to shame to comply with the demand of one man and by the submission of his colleagues to the dictate laid down by him and the powerful American interests involved. It is a vindication of the wisdom and integrity of thought and purpose of the Canadian people that in so doing most of the perpetrators dug their own political graves. I have written this record at length because the Canadian Parliament was subjected to the greatest crisis of all my years in public life and to bitter humiliation. Let any who are ever tempted to follow such a reprehensible example take heed of the consequences.

The consideration of the Estimates of the Department of Defence Production set off what proved to be another donnybrook. Five years had passed since the department was created and its program launched. Howe conceded that the initial build-up of the defence program had been completed. Now the department's task was the re-equipment of the armed forces and the maintenance of the defence production base. It was a declining program. An aircraft industry had been developed in Canada, and over $100 million had been spent in assisting it. In leading off for the opposition I observed that no other man in Canadian history had had $20 billion to spend as he had since 1939. Of thirty crown corporations in existence fourteen were responsible to Howe. On June 14 I had exposed the fact that Howe was one of the executors of the estate of the late Sir James Dunn, which was then settling with the Department of National Revenue the largest liability for succession duty in Canadian history. The principal asset of the estate consisted of stockholdings in Algoma Steel Corporation, while the Department of Defence Production was placing orders involving the purchase of steel. I said that Howe was in a double position, and he must resign either as minister or as executor. This had thrown Howe into a rage, and he had become very abusive of me outside the House. On his Estimates I gave him the opportunity to take back what he had said, but he declined. Thereupon Howe's conflict of interest became the subject of debate and continued for some time. Davie Fulton took up the issue and discussed it very skilfully. To Howe's claim that so far as the estate was concerned he would confine his participation to property disposal and that he had a legal opinion that there was no conflict of interest in his so acting, Davie pointed out that one cannot have a split personality as an executor, and that in law an executor cannot accept merely a limited executorship. Gordon Churchill referred to principles enunciated in the British House of Commons by Winston Churchill on February 25, 1952:

1. It is a principle of public life that ministers must so order their affairs that no conflict arises, or appears to arise, between their private interests and their public duties.
2. Such a conflict may arise if a minister takes an active part in any undertaking which may have contractual or other relations with a government department, more particularly with his own department. It may arise, not only if the minister has a financial interest in such an undertaking, but also if he is actively associated with any body, even of a philanthropic character, which might have negotiations or other dealings with the government or be involved in disputes with it. Furthermore ministers should be free to give full attention to their official duties, and they should not engage in other activities

which might be thought to distract their attention from those duties.

Diefenbaker was the next to take up the issue. He deplored the abusive remarks made about me by Howe. The conflict of interest was a fact. That Howe sought counsel's advice indicated he had on his mind some grave doubt as to the compatibility of the two interests he was serving simultaneously. Howe's rage was rising. When Bill Hamilton was discussing the issue Howe jumped up and snarled, "If every little twerp – excuse me, some one who is just out of kindergarten can get up and slander me as he likes, I do not like it." Bill was not saying anything slanderous or improper; Howe had slandered me viciously, but that apparently he considered his right. When Bill continued, Howe snarled, "Don't worry about that, smart boy."

When discussion of the department's Estimates was resumed on July 25 interest turned to a payment of $2,880,000 made by the department to Sorel Industries Limited. Howe was very sensitive about the payment to Sorel and as usual resorted to personal abuse to defend it. For minutes he defied the rules of the House, and in the midst of my remarks shouted, "Who was it that was thrown out of this House?" This he repeated a moment later. Ten minutes later he supplied the answer to his own question, "You are the honourable member who was thrown out of the House for butting in." In this he had his facts confused. I retorted, "And you are the man who should be thrown out today." And so it went on. The chair was either helpless or unwilling to enforce order. Chairman Applewhaite simply sat in silence. Jimmy Sinclair, not to be outdone in vituperation by Howe, took his turn at shouting personal abuse. I think it was without doubt the most disgraceful sitting of the House I ever witnessed outside the pipeline debate.

Where was the Prime Minister throughout this travesty of Parliament? He was nowhere to be seen. If he ever had any control over Howe – which is doubtful – it is obvious that he had lost it entirely. How he could tolerate Howe's obvious conflict of interest will ever remain an unanswered question. In this grim situation St. Laurent looked lamentably weak.

Before the donnybrook came to a belated end on July 26 I had extracted one interesting admission from Howe: no orders in the past year had been made under the Defence Production Act. After the battle fought by the government in 1955 to retain all its powers under that statute it was interesting to find that in the intervening twelve months those powers had not been needed or used.

Such a Parliament could not long continue. Personal relationships had so far deteriorated as to make it almost impossible to maintain the normal and necessary amenities on which the functioning of the institution depends. Mr. St. Laurent seemed at least for the time to have lost his grip and perhaps even his interest. Parliament had entered a twilight – a new Götterdämmerung. Minor or cosmetic improvement would no longer suffice. There must be a transformed Parliament if the institution was to recover the respect, not to mention the confidence, of the Canadian people. The 1957 general election had become one of the most urgent necessities ever felt by the nation.

CHAPTER TWENTY-NINE

Candidate for the Leadership, 1956

George Drew had carried a herculean burden throughout the 1956 session. The stresses were almost beyond human endurance. Robust man as he was, the constant strain exhausted his reserves, and before the session reached its end his health collapsed. He made his last appearance in the House on August 2. Before that day passed he was seriously ill. Earl Rowe resumed the role of Acting Leader of the Opposition for the twelve days which remained until prorogation.

Surprise in the ranks of caucus was followed by uncertainty and confusion. George had recovered from a serious attack of meningitis the year before. Would he do it again and return to lead the party in the 1957 session? Even if he did, would he be equal to facing the rigorous demands of a 1957 general election? In the circumstances how long could a decision on George's future wait? A successor would need every possible day to prepare for the election. If the situation were left to simmer very long would not George's hold on the leadership inevitably weaken? Neither he nor the party could afford that prospect. Hope and sombre misgivings struggled in every breast as we dispersed following prorogation.

That summer on the highest medical advice and with utmost reluctance George was persuaded by his physician, his wife and some of his closest friends to resign the leadership. I became aware of his resignation only from the media; I was thunderstruck. George had fought a courageous struggle in Parliament, and public favour was swinging strongly to our cause. He was winning increasing respect and support both in Parliament and outside. The public had come to recognize him as a leader of integrity and conviction. Just at this hopeful moment fate struck him down.

I had committed myself totally to George as leader and given him my unreserved loyalty and dedicated effort. My hopes for my own future and the party's future depended, I thought, on him. A year before in a heart-to-heart talk I had told him of the increasing impatience of my partners with my political involvement and my anxiety over my family's insecurity. George was sympathetic, but said, "Have you ever thought of who will take over here if anything should happen to me?" I replied that I had not chosen to contemplate the possibility of anything happening to remove him from the leadership. He continued, "You are the only one around here I see capable of taking over the leadership of the party." Now what had been seen as only a faint possibility had suddenly arrived.

It came at a most inopportune time. Every personal consideration was opposed to my becoming a candidate for the leadership. Apart from my home I had been unable to build up any capital even though we lived very carefully. I was deeply concerned over my absences from home and the unfair burden this condition was throwing upon Alice in raising our three children. My partners considered that they had been very tolerant of my divided pursuits and that instead of enlarging my political responsibilities and efforts I should be curbing them. Some important clients were impatiently asking, "When is Don going to cut out this political nonsense? When is he going to settle down?" Moreover, I was carrying the heaviest load of work in the House, far more, indeed, than my share.

On the other hand, I had received many expressions of unstinted gratitude from the leader and the people about him whom I most respected, and I had emerged from the party wars in the Commons, and particularly the pipeline debate, as a national figure in the party's front rank. Now, whether I liked it or not, I must decide to be or not to be a candidate for the leadership.

It was obvious that Diefenbaker would be the front runner. His ambition had long been obvious. He did not have family responsibilities comparable with mine. He was not faced with the gnawing problem of insecurity. He had no partners clamouring for his return to full-time professional duty and reminding him of the career opportunities which he was squandering. He exercised enough freedom even during sessions of Parliament to accept speaking engagements in different parts of the country, which I felt obliged to forgo. I knew that he had made himself widely known in this way, and that he would enjoy a base of unchallengeable political strength in western Canada in any contest for the national leadership of the party. He was a brilliant parliamentarian, and his whole life was committed to his political career.

But there was one major weakness in Diefenbaker's political armour – Quebec. Somehow he had incurred the hostility of French Canadians. That was like an Achilles' heel to a national leader. I was not convinced that the Quebec attitude was entirely justified, but I knew that it was real and very strong. Therefore, while I was not sure whether it would defeat Diefenbaker at a national convention, I feared that it would prevent him as leader from strengthening the bonds of Canadian unity, and would probably alienate Quebec from the party. I, on the other hand, was constantly assured that I was "très, très populaire dans la province de Québec." In these circumstances, in the absence of anyone better qualified to cement national unity and party unity, it appeared to be my duty to stand for election. I knew the Quebec members of the party would be disappointed and might even feel resentful if I did not offer myself. Many others regarded Diefenbaker as too unstable to be national leader. Some questioned whether his health would be equal to the strains of office.

The national executive called a national convention to be held in Ottawa and chose December 14 for the vote. I was quietly invited to attend a very private meeting the same evening at the Château Laurier at which were present Léon Balcer, the national president, George Nowlan and Jim Macdonnell, past presidents, Earl Rowe, Acting House Leader, Grattan O'Leary and Dick Bell, the national director. They informed me that they had given thought to the possibility of my being a candidate and they were of opinion that I could not succeed against Diefenbaker, and they asked me to stand aside in favour of Sidney Smith, whom they intended to approach. I said I had great respect for Sidney and had supported him in 1948. I doubted if he would now stand, but if he did do so I would stand aside on two conditions: first, that an immediate answer would be sought from Sid, and second, that if Sid declined they would commit themselves to support me. They all agreed to these conditions.

I had to know without delay whether I was free to stand or not. The approach to Sid was promptly made. After a few days' deliberation he declined to stand. Personally, I think he was right in concluding that it was too late in life for him to attempt to seek the leadership without political experience or position. My embarrassment, however, was increasing with each passing day. I simply had to make and announce a decision. Diefenbaker had announced his candidature, and his campaign had swiftly moved into high gear. After Sid's refusal rumours surfaced that George

Nowlan was about to announce his candidature. I was astonished. For a week I endeavoured to reach him by telephone. He did not reply. Then came a report that Balcer might be a candidate. These developments had a very upsetting effect. George Nowlan later explained that he was attempting to restrain Nova Scotia's delegates from committing themselves to Diefenbaker. In the midst of this confusion I concluded I must announce my candidature if I were ever to do so, and I acted accordingly.

I had no ready-made organization. We put together a small but very capable committee headed by Arthur Pattillo, QC, and including Alan Cockeram, MP, John Trimble and Jim Macdonnell. Of necessity it had to be concentrated in Toronto. Our first endeavour was to enlist Al Grosart as organizer, but to my keen disappointment he informed me that he had already promised to organize John Diefenbaker's campaign. Grattan O'Leary, from whom I had been led to expect active assistance, took off for Europe and returned only at the end of the campaign. I had hoped for open support from Earl Rowe; he attended one meeting. Approaches to several other leading Ontario MPs produced no results. It became obvious that even those who were not ready to support Diefenbaker were reluctant to show their colours openly against him. This was based in some cases on the belief that he was bound to win, in others on fear of his reputed vindictiveness. I doubt if they gained anything from their abstention. Roly Michener did not support him, and incurred Diefenbaker's lasting animosity. Dick Bell and Harry Willis were neutralized by their positions in the party. Harry on request met with my committee once and candidly stated that, "The Fleming campaign has not got off the ground in Ontario." All the available evidence supported his conclusion. At this point Davie Fulton announced his candidature.

One Ontario friend thought perhaps I had been too combative in the House. Considering how often I had been literally thrust into debates, often on short notice, to withstand the government juggernaut and urged by our own members to "Give them hell, Don," this verdict left me disappointed and cynical, if anything could have at that point. The support of George Drew and John Bracken was of little or no assistance, as they were compelled to remain silent. Some of George Drew's staunchest supporters, such as Gordon Churchill, rallied swiftly to the support of Diefenbaker. Doug Harkness came to tell me that pro-Diefenbaker support was so strong among the Alberta Conservatives that he was obliged to go with them, but that he did not think Diefenbaker would last long as leader. Again I learned by bitter experience, as in 1948, that the retiring leader was powerless to transfer his supporters to the successor of his choice.

In the face of this monotonous series of disappointments I found that the Diefenbaker supporters were branding me as the candidate put forward by "the establishment." I never quite knew who composed this mysterious group. Whoever they were, and if they existed, they did not come to my support. Lamentably my campaign was of a personal nature. It was so perforce; outside Quebec there was no organized basis of support. The English-language press was climbing on the bandwagon. My effort was pictured as forlorn, and "anti-Diefenbaker," which was a grossly unfair interpretation.

Two strong allies rallied to my cause – the Maloney brothers. Jim had been a classmate of mine at the Osgoode Hall Law School. He was a minister in the Ontario government of Leslie Frost. He was political to his fingertips. His younger brother Arthur was a rising star in politics and the legal profession in Toronto. The Maloney family, staunchly Roman Catholic, was widely known and highly respected in their native Renfrew and throughout the Ottawa Valley. It was hoped that their support, which they expressed actively and openly, would win support within the Ontario cabinet and the Ontario delegation.

In Nova Scotia George Nowlan was working hard to hold the delegation together and to support me. It was in Quebec, of course, that my campaign really flourished. The efforts of Pierre Sevigny to rally support there for Diefenbaker were making no headway whatever. Many times I wished that the rest of Canada could know the strength and enthusiasm of my support there, but the news of it was ignored by the English-language press, and most of the delegates from the other nine provinces arrived at the convention utterly unaware of it. My Quebec supporters were chilled on arrival at the convention to learn that my popularity in Quebec was a fact quite unknown to most of the delegates from other provinces. I had a good organization in Quebec headed by my friends Guillaume Piette and Lucien Boucher. They and a large group of respected and intelligent Conservatives took full charge of my campaign. It was a joy to work with them.

Funds were very limited. My dear friend Ardagh Scythes worked hard to raise funds, and the expenses of our campaign in Quebec were met by Quebec sources. Our national effort of necessity was conducted on a very modest scale. I toured all parts of the country, but alone. I had no executive assistant or public relations counsel to accompany me and help in making contacts with the media. I was dependent on voluntary local assistance wherever I went.

The final blow came in the autumn, and was precipitated by the Suez crisis. In the storm of controversy which followed the Anglo-French invasion and the denunciation of British armed action at the United Nations, Parliament was recalled on November 26. It could not have come at a worse time for me. My Manitoba supporters, led by Charlie Spence of Winnipeg, had arranged an excellent program of meetings with delegates, press interviews, and radio interviews for me for almost the entire week. The program could not be postponed. I badly needed to make an impression in Manitoba. On the other hand, to absent myself from Parliament in the midst of a crisis which had stirred the whole world and not least Canada, would have exposed me to very strong criticism by an English-language press which was ready to find further cause to support Diefenbaker. Moreover, both Fulton and Diefenbaker planned to attend the session. That settled the question. I tried to do both things, and did not succeed very well. I attended the session the first two days, spoke on the second afternoon, November 27, and then flew to Winnipeg to pick up the mangled remnants of my Manitoba program. By the time I arrived there everyone had lost interest in the national convention and was interested only in the debate in Parliament. In addition, Diefenbaker astutely delayed his speech until near the last day of the debate. The caucus was divided over many aspects of the Suez issue. By waiting till the late stages of the debate he was able to appear as the shining light who avoided smaller issues and idealistically rallied support to the United Nations. His speech was described by the press as a tour de force. It reinforced his support with the media and the delegates. I took it as the final handwriting on the wall as far as the leadership contest was concerned.

The convention was held in the Ottawa Coliseum in frosty December. My committee decided that we should ask Grattan O'Leary to nominate me. He declined on the ground that it would hurt rather than help my cause for him to nominate me. The committee was of opinion that if Grattan was a member of "the establishment" which was reputed to be supporting me we might at least endeavour to extract some benefit from the connection instead of blame only. Grattan on his return to Ottawa declined to take any outward part in my campaign. This keenly disappointed our men and myself, too. John Trimble was outspoken. "We have been led down the garden path," said he to Grattan's face.

All speeches were scheduled for the evening of December 13 and voting for the 14th. Jim Maloney in the end nominated me and made an excellent speech. I did not make Diefenbaker's mistake of ignoring Quebec. My nomination was seconded by Henri Courtemanche, ex-MP. Moreover, we were not going to repeat the mistake made at the 1948 national convention. This time a rousing entry into the Coliseum was planned for Alice and myself. We had a small band which played "When the Saints Come Marching In," leading a goodly number of supporters carrying Fleming banners. As we advanced along the perimeter aisle a number of young men bearing Diefenbaker signs mounted on poles endeavoured to surround our procession and blot out the TV viewers' and delegates' view of the Fleming signs, to make it appear as another Diefenbaker demonstration. I do not know who was responsible for this shabby, contemptible trick, but somebody had obviously planned it. Jim Maloney was so angry over it that he threatened to punch the young men if they didn't go away, but was persuaded not to carry out his threat. I roared at them above the din, "Is this your idea of fair play?" Happily, violence was averted.

The speeches that evening all went well. Nothing untoward was said by any of the candidates or their sponsors. Mine was balanced, realistic and rousing. I dwelt on the themes of restoring the integrity of Parliament, of enlarging Canadian resource development and our party's unequalled record in that regard, of building wider opportunity for Canadians, and concluded with an appeal in French and English for a national unity based upon tolerance, understanding and mutual respect.

Unfortunately, the tricks were not yet ended. That night the editor of a newspaper published in the West who had always declared himself a friend of mine, and at the same time a fanatical supporter of Diefenbaker, printed a news sheet and circulated it among delegates, picturing the Quebec delegation as lining up solidly for the one purpose of preventing Diefenbaker from becoming leader. It was an unblushing attempt to create a backlash at the last minute among English-speaking delegates. Regrettably it did succeed in drawing numerous votes of Ontario and other delegates away from me on the last day. Even some of my friends told me on the morning of December 14 that after reading the sheet they had decided to vote for Diefenbaker "to teach Quebec a lesson." The stratagem and its execution were thoroughly shameful. Unity and mutual respect within the party are not to be built by such unworthy canards.

The vote was taken on the afternoon of December 14. The result was no surprise. Only one ballot was required. Diefenbaker gathered 774 votes, I, 393, and Fulton, 117. Immediately on the announcement I moved to where Diefenbaker was seated, took him by the right hand, led him to the podium, while Fulton supported him on the left. It was then that the celebrated photograph was taken of which large use was made then and later and which adorns Dief's memoirs. This gesture of unity and support, which I followed by my motion that his election be made unanimous and a brief but earnest appeal to all to close ranks behind the new leader, was loudly cheered, but it fell on deaf ears in one large section of the vast auditorium. Large numbers of Quebec delegates rose at that moment and walked out.

Strained and unconvincing efforts have been made to portray this demonstration as something of no significance. It has been said that the afternoon train was about to leave for Montreal, and that the facts that scores of delegates rose as one man and that they did so at the moment Diefenbaker was declared elected, and that they all made straightway for the nearest exit were pure coincidence. No one should be misled by such far-fetched and transparent bluff. The Quebec delegation did what they did in order to demonstrate for all to see that they totally disapproved the choice of Diefenbaker. I regretted that they went to such lengths. I would have endeavoured to dissuade them from following such a course if I had been in a position to do so. But what they did and why they did it, however unfortunate, admit of no doubt whatever. But for Diefenbaker's callous disregard of Quebec at and prior to the national convention of 1956 we might possibly have won a majority in the 1957 general election. In that case the course of subsequent history might have been very different.

Diefenbaker's acceptance speech, even if not his best, was very good. It was rather too long, and it was delivered to a somewhat jaded audience, undoubtedly still disturbed over the withdrawal of the Quebec delegates. I sat back and listened intently. He assured his audience that "we have an appointment with destiny." The "we" obviously referred to himself, and not the party, as some might have thought. He was impressing upon his audience that he was confident he would become prime minister. He also promised that while he might sometimes be wrong he would never be found on the side of wrong.

Late that afternoon after thanking my supporters I paid a visit to the Diefenbaker suite at the Château Laurier, where his gleeful supporters were celebrating their victory. I was accorded a very warm welcome. Dief hailed my visit as the proof of party unity behind his election. I recognized many of my friends in caucus in the excited throng. Thus the leader's crown passed to the brow of John Diefenbaker. He had achieved a high goal, one that he had long and ardently and openly pursued. Having succeeded, he turned on those who had denied it to him sooner. He may have been the first man to be elected leader of the party who then openly arraigned elements within the party. Sadly I did not detect any overwhelming dedication to the necessary and urgent task of cementing unity within the party.

One alleged element within the party which he attacked he called "Bay Street." This, of course, meant Bay Street, Toronto. It was supposed to connote the seats of Canadian high finance. No doubt such attacks were received with vociferous approval in the West. Whether the fact that I came from Toronto had any bearing on this favourite theme I know not. As a matter of fact, I have never quite succeeded in identifying "Bay Street" except in a geographical sense. I have come to know captains of finance and captains of industry who have their offices in or near Bay Street, Toronto, but I have never found unity of opinion among them on political subjects. In 1956 I would have said that the preponderant opinion among them was still favourable to the Liberal government, in large measure due to the confidence they reposed in C.D. Howe. I wish to make it clear as crystal that I received no support at the convention from Bay Street, so-called. On the contrary, such support as I observed coming from Bay Street went solidly to Diefenbaker. Harry Jackman, ex-MP, for example, was a delegate whose support for many reasons I thought I had reason to expect. He openly supported Diefenbaker. I suspect that Bay Street, if it took any serious interest in the convention, was indulging in that very human predeliction for "picking the winner," and it was not hard to conclude in advance that Dief would win. In any event, anyone professing never to be found on the side of wrong should not pretend that Bay Street openly resisted the election of John Diefenbaker as national leader at the national convention of 1956.

I was at peace. I went home to Toronto to spend a happy Christmas. I had no regrets over having contested the leadership again. I had fought a clean fight. I was not surprised in the least at the outcome. True, I would have liked to win more votes, but considering the odds against me I had done surprisingly well to gather 393 of them, mostly from Quebec and Nova Scotia. I had done my duty to my party and my genuine supporters. Some professed to be concerned as to how I would be treated after opposing the unforgiving Dief. I had not the slightest fear on that issue. I was bold enough to believe that he needed me as much as I needed him.

CHAPTER THIRTY

Victory

John Diefenbaker lost no time in entering upon his duties. Everyone expected a general election in the spring of 1957; the time for preparation was short. Parliament assembled on January 8, and battle was joined immediately in the Commons. Great things were expected of Diefenbaker in the House. He could now speak for the party with complete authority. Interest in his performance rose to a very high pitch.

Actually his entry into the House on the opening day to take his new seat was marked by an untoward incident. Earl Rowe had been George Drew's desk-mate. After George's departure in August Earl was Acting Leader of the Opposition. He was personally popular with most of the members of caucus, but for reasons unknown to me he had long before incurred the displeasure and open hostility of John Diefenbaker. The new leader had authority to arrange the seating in the House as he chose, but he had made no change, and he had not communicated with Earl. When Dief made his triumphal entry into the Chamber to a salvo of desk-thumping Earl was already present and was in his old seat. As Dief took his own seat Earl stood up and moved aside. After what seemed like an age Dief motioned to Earl to resume his old seat, which Earl then did. This embarrassing moment could easily have been avoided with a little forethought or magnanimity. It was impressed upon all witnesses that the old breach remained unhealed.

The session was bound to be brief. The government's legislative program was appropriately thin. Dief conducted himself effectively in the House, but he did not spend any more time there than was necessary. He kept his eye trained at all times on the approaching election, and he was devoting as much time as possible to organizing for it. He did not attempt any reorganization of caucus, and he retained the staff of the office of the Leader of the Opposition. He persuaded Al Grosart, who had so successfully organized his leadership campaign, to accept the position of national organizer for the party. This was a master stroke. Al went straight to work. Party funds were low. Dief's election as leader had not opened up the purses of party supporters; perhaps this is why he spoke in hostile tones of Bay Street. Within the caucus there was a prevailing spirit of hope.

Personally I was experiencing a reaction after the exciting events of 1956, and I was anything but happy. I was surprised at the ease and rapidity with which some members of caucus had switched allegiance and support from Drew to Diefenbaker. I felt a little uncomfortable with some who climbed the new bandwagon with impressive alacrity. In defending the work of our research office in caucus I noted some aggressiveness and a trace of hostility on the part of several leading supporters of the Diefenbaker candidature. I was acutely disappointed that Dief made no effort to heal known old breaches, and that his displeasure toward Jim Macdonnell, Roly Michener, Dick Bell, Léon Balcer and others remained all too obvious. He showed no trace of displeasure toward me, however, and this surprised some of those who had actively supported me.

Soon after the convention I was asked by a Newfoundland stalwart to make a political tour of that province. The request did not come through Diefenbaker, and I promptly declined it. I was not going to give anyone reason to think that I was resuming or continuing my 1956 campaign. When the gentleman said there would be great interest in a visit to the province by "the runner-up" I told him that the contest was over, that there was now a leader, but there was no longer a runner-up; we were all followers of the leader.

As a matter of fact, under our party system the runner-up at a convention is not thereafter necessarily the number-two man in the party. That depends on the leader himself. There are many instances to support this conclusion. I was a defeated candidate, and I had no intention of presuming to be number two in the party. Indeed, I resolved to maintain a very low profile in the House, in caucus and in public. This accorded with my own feelings. I had worked like a beaver in the House and in the committees. I was the acknowledged workhorse of the party. I had worked harder than any member of caucus, and my recompense was defeat. These feelings coincided with renewed pressure from my partners to have done with politics and my ever-present concern for my family. My partners admittedly had been very tolerant and very patient, and they had every reason to feel that they should not be asked for any further indulgence.

For the first month of the session apart from a couple of questions I maintained silence in the House. Never since entering it twelve years before had more than several days passed without my saying something on the record. Friends in the press gallery were beginning to observe my silence and conjecture as to the reason. Never in that period was I asked by Diefenbaker or the whip to enter a debate. Finally I pulled myself together and resumed my wonted active role in the House. I made my first major speech of the session on February 12.

One day Dief called me on the telephone and asked if he could come up to see me. This was a generous gesture coming from the leader. I of course insisted that I come down to his office. He had less to talk about specifically than I had hoped, so I assured him of my loyalty, and frankly disclosed to him that in the light of the attitude of my partners and my concern for my family I might not be able to be a candidate at the approaching general election. I assured him this would not be my own wish, that I realized that having been a candidate for the leadership my withdrawal might be misinterpreted as disaffection, but I might nevertheless find myself face to face with stern necessity. He assured me that my loyalty was unquestioned and he hoped I would find it possible to carry on. This discussion helped to clear the air. I felt partly relieved after acquainting him with my predicament.

The weakness of his position in Quebec began to be realized. I had surmised that I would be asked to undertake the formidable task of setting things aright for him there, and, sure enough, that was asked of me. I replied that only he could do that, and that neither I nor anyone else but himself could break down the feeling that had developed against him there. I said flatly that he must go into the province and that sending me in his place might even have the contrary effect. This advice evidently was heeded. A party mass meeting was arranged in Montreal with Pierre Sevigny as chairman. Diefenbaker, Olive, Fulton and I attended en masse. I spoke strongly in French, urging that all close ranks behind the leader. The response was excellent. I felt we were making headway.

Diefenbaker actually took his place in the House as Leader of the Opposition on the last day of the fourth session of the Twenty-Second Parliament. That session, one of the shortest on record, had opened November 26, 1956, and after only four days had adjourned on the 29th to January 8. It met for only a few minutes on the morning of the 8th, then was prorogued, to make way for the formal opening of the fifth session that afternoon.

On February 11 on a supply motion Diefenbaker introduced an amendment in terms identical with one introduced by George Drew in 1956:

> This House is of the opinion that the welfare of the Canadian people requires the adoption now of a national development policy which will develop our natural resources for the maximum benefit of all parts of Canada, encourage more processing of those resources in Canada, correct the present serious unfavourable trade balances, foster wider financial participation by Canadians in the development of our resources, and promote greater opportunity for employment for a steadily increasing population.

I had been the author of this amendment in 1956, and I modelled it on the historic amendment introduced by Sir John A. Macdonald setting forth the National Policy on a supply motion in 1876. By reintroducing the same amendment in 1957 we reasserted our policy and drew public attention to what was to become one of the principal planks in our election program. On this issue I made my first major speech of the 1957 session on February 12. At one point I indulged in prophecy: "We think a Commonwealth Trade and Economic Conference should be called as soon as possible, and there is no good reason why Canada should not take steps to initiate the calling of that conference; and if the government declines to do so the Conservative government which will be formed later this year by the present Leader of the Opposition will do it." That promise was fulfilled to the letter.

Parliament enacted the necessary legislation to create the Canada Council and to endow it with $50 million for the encouragement of the arts, humanities and social sciences, and another $50 million to aid universities with construction projects. St. Laurent, with a great flourish of innocence, assured the House that "no considerations of partisan politics . . . will influence us in the choice of those who will make up the Council." I pressed him on this assurance on February 5, whereupon he added, "My idea of making appointments irrespective of political partisanship does not mean that anyone who has belonged to the Party of the Government should be excluded." He might have said that Grit governments appoint Grits, but that is not to be regarded as political partisanship. I wonder then what it is. A rose by any other name would smell as sweet.

The long-awaited report of the Fowler Royal Commission on Broadcasting was tabled on March 28. Principally it recommended the establishment of an independent board of governors, responsible to Parliament, with jurisdiction over both private and public broadcasting, whether of radio or television. This was precisely what we had been advocating in the eleven years I had been the party's spokesman. No action was taken by the government on the report at the 1957 session.

On the very day the Fowler report was published an issue over government interference with CBC programming, unrelated to the report, arose in the House and quickly cast Mr. St. Laurent onto an irritated and rather peevish defensive. In reply to a question he admitted that he had written a letter to Davidson Dunton, chairman of CBC, criticizing a program in which a young university professor had expressed views on international affairs and criticized the alleged timidity of Canadian policy. St. Laurent had expressed the view that funds appropriated by Parliament should not be used for such a purpose. He did not recall whether the letter had been written on his official letterhead or on plain paper, but he claimed to have written the letter, "not as Prime Minister, but as a Canadian citizen." Dunton had replied, defending the right of CBC to conduct such a program, whereupon the Prime Minister wrote him a second letter. Diefenbaker was quick to comment, "This is a very serious interference with CBC." An interim supply motion the next day offered full scope for discussion of the whole matter, and it was thrashed over for nearly three hours. That the Prime Minister could pretend to be writing to the chairman of CBC merely as a private citizen I described as "the most extraordinary fiction that this House has heard, I am sure, for many a year." Diefenbaker accused the Prime Minister of applying censorship to CBC, which could destroy the independence of that institution. Mr. St. Laurent looked strangely inept throughout this incident.

At long last after repeated exhortations over the years the government chose the eve of a general election to introduce on March 25 a bill to provide insured hospital and diagnostic services in a joint scheme with a minimum of six participating provinces containing at least half the population of Canada. Only five provinces at that time had indicated concurrence. I was critical of the government for rigidly insisting on such harsh conditions that the five other provinces were not yet ready to join the scheme. I was most critical of the exclusion of tuberculosis hospitals and sanatoria and hospitals and institutions for the mentally ill and on behalf of the official opposition introduced an amendment to eliminate these exclusions. It was defeated by a vote of 111 to 54.

Walter Harris introduced his final budget on March 14. It earned him the title of "Six-Bit Harris" and greatly assisted his enforced departure from public life three months later. He painted a rosy picture of the economy, aided by a 4 per cent rise in the external value of the Canadian dollar, but admitted that money was "tight" as the result of action taken by both the Bank of Canada and the government. He reported a surplus of $282 million for 1956-57, but deliberately refrained from recommending any major reductions in the general level of taxation. He proposed slight increases in the scale of family allowances and veterans' pensions. His most famous proposal was an increase of $6 per month from $40 to $46 in the old-age pension and old-age assistance and pensions to the blind and disabled. His final forecast of the surplus for 1957-58 after all tax changes was $152 million.

In presentability this budget hardly compared with the winners introduced by Doug Abbott in 1949 and 1953. In any event it proved a liability to the government rather than an asset in the election campaign. Public attention was focused on the meagre increase in the old-age pension to the exclusion of the other elements in the budget.

On March 21 in my last speech as a budget critic I lashed Walter Harris's effort. I gave it six descriptions and elaborated on each: "full of pretence," "delusive," "cynical," "opiate," "transparent" and "illusory." I said it was the product of a hit-and-miss approach; there was no long-range policy or forward planning or thinking ahead. The horizon was set on a day in June; therefore, it was circumscribed by expediency. It ignored the dangers of inflation; it was unfair to the provinces and municipalities. I made this fateful assertion: "We wish to see a balanced budget because we believe in balanced budgets." Did I thereby give hostages to fortune in a future not clearly foreseen? I closed my speech with an arraignment of the government for the ills it had brought upon Canada and Parliament:

> I ask the house to look at the facts, the true record of this government. Parliament degraded and humiliated, bent to the will of the government and its promoter friends; the people of Canada bearing a crushing tax burden, condemned to pay a record tax total this year; Canada with a record trading deficit last year of $848 million; a record deficit of $1,400 million on international current account; its trading eggs increasingly placed in one basket, the United States; a record trading deficit with that country in 1956 of $1,298 million; agriculture, the basic industry of this country, excluded from the vaunted national prosperity; the provinces and

municipalities denied the revenues necessary to meet their heavy and important constitutional responsibilities and obliged to increase taxes while the federal coffers are filled to overflowing; federal-provincial relations in probably their most difficult condition in our history, with more sand in the constitutional machinery poured there by this federal government than ever before; monopoly thriving under government protection whether in air transport, television broadcasting or a good many other things; confusion on the part of the government in not knowing whether it supports free competitive enterprise or whether it regards socialists still as merely "Liberals in a hurry"; a stealthy weakening of our institutions under this government; a government stooping to divisive appeals to maintain itself in office; a government publicly affronting and denouncing the best friends this country has overseas; the ownership of our resources passing to a hitherto unparalleled degree into foreign hands; a government floundering in the welter of its own incompetence, error, contradictions and arrogance! These are the fruits of this government; and in the words of Holy Writ, ye shall know them by their fruits.

To make way for the election it was necessary to vote supply. It was not possible to review all the estimates for the fiscal year in time for a June vote. All parties favoured June. Therefore approximately one-half of the year's estimates was voted by way of interim supply, but only after a strongly expressed protest from John Diefenbaker. This cleared the decks for the general election. The vote of interim supply was intended to provide for all of the government's foreseeable needs to September 30.

Parliament was dissolved on April 12, and the election was called for June 10. The campaign developed into a great struggle. On the TV screen both St. Laurent and Howe looked very old. It became evident that the public had not forgotten the pipeline debate nor forgiven the Liberal perpetrators. I was confident that with Dief leading we would draw increased support from Ontario and the West, and it was at last within the bounds of possibility that we would succeed in unseating the entrenched government. I exacted a pact from my partners and my most intimate confidants in our Eglinton organization that I should be allowed to run as a candidate on condition that if our party sustained another defeat I would be allowed after one year to retire and return to serve the firm full-time. It was agreed that if the party won it was very unlikely that I would have occasion to return to the practice of law. With this assurance I hurled myself into the campaign with every ounce of energy I could muster. I travelled the length of Canada, delivering many speeches, including one in Dief's own riding of Prince Albert, where I was accorded a very warm reception. I was employed extensively in Quebec, making numerous speeches, mostly in French. We badly needed the support of Duplessis and his powerful organization. He was anxious enough to smite the Liberals, but he hesitated to commit himself openly to a party headed by Diefenbaker, especially since its success elsewhere was not assured. In the end he gave limited support, selecting about fifteen candidates to whom he quietly gave organized assistance. These were reliable men who were thought to have an even chance of winning. Even this limited support was vital to our cause. In the end it made the difference between a national victory and falling short of it.

My own campaign in Eglinton went very smoothly. We mustered a strong organization. This time two of the young men who had come up from the ranks of the Young Progressive Conservative Association undertook the chief responsibility. Warren Armstrong was organizer and Bill Allan my official agent, handling the financial side of our campaign. They proved to be a strong and dedicated team. What they may initially have lacked in experience they more than made up in spirit and unflagging effort. The party was low in funds, and I was left to raise our limited budget almost entirely without assistance from party sources. Ardagh Scythes again set out to raise funds on behalf of my personal campaign. I do not know what I would have done but for the efforts of this dear friend. In the end we covered our budget, but there were no frills.

As June 10 drew near hopes were rising. No one was so bold as to predict a clear victory, but after the disappointing campaigns of 1949 and 1953 it was exhilarating to sniff the scent of success for a change. That evening I stayed as usual at our committee rooms long enough to learn that we had won a resounding victory in Eglinton, then I dashed home to await the arrival of our supporters for whom we always held open house. They soon arrived in unprecedented numbers. The weather was perfect. Again the crowd trampled my flowerbeds, but who cared? The early returns from the Atlantic provinces brought Conservative gains, Quebec gave us 9 seats, Ontario 61. The CCF and Social Credit remained strong in the four western provinces, but we made some gains there. In the four general elections in which I had been a candidate there had never been such excitement as we experienced that night. It rose steadily and never abated. As the results were reported by radio we soon realized that it had become a contest to decide whether Liberals or Conservatives would have the larger total of seats. The Liberals led at the outset on the strength of taking 63 Quebec seats, but after the Ontario results were announced the Conservative total passed the Liberal, and never fell behind. From that point it became a question whether our margin would be sufficiently large that the government would be obliged to resign. In the delirium of that night the final results were: Conservatives 112, Liberals 105, CCF 25, Social Credit 19, others 4. Knowing St. Laurent as a man of strict rectitude I knew he would not attempt to cling to office, as Mackenzie King would have done in the same circumstances, but would follow the honourable course of resigning without delay. Nine of his ministers went down to defeat, including C.D. Howe, Walter Harris, Bob Winters, Hugues Lapointe, Paul Hellyer. Without them St. Laurent would have found it very difficult to reconstruct his cabinet and carry on even had we not won a margin of seven seats. Of all results in individual ridings the defeat of C.D. Howe in Port Arthur brought more joy to our stunned and ecstatic supporters than the result in any other riding with the single exception of Eglinton. The results in Eglinton were Fleming 25,046, Grube (CCF) 2,782, Rolland (Ind.) 252, Wilson (Liberal) 8,337. My majority was the largest accorded to any Conservative candidate in Canada. Such support from the good people of Eglinton riding gave me a strong sense of mandate and a deep sense of gratitude. My hard work and total commitment to parliamentary duty for twelve long years had won vindication. After seventeen sessions my days in the opposition had forever come to an end.

CHAPTER THIRTY-ONE

Minister of Finance

To become a minister of the crown is not far from the hopes of many, perhaps most, parliamentarians. To be summoned to membership in Her Majesty's Privy Council for Canada and sworn in as a minister is for MPs both a dazzling reward and a legitimate ambition. It was so in my case. All through the struggles, defeats and disappointments of those twelve long years in opposition I was sustained in part by the hope that one day I would hold a place on the Treasury benches and have an opportunity to serve my country in the cabinet. I did not talk about this hope; I never admitted to such an ambition; but I was well aware of its place in my thoughts, and I was not displeased when others spoke or wrote of it. Long before our victory in June 1957, the press had speculated confidently that in any Conservative administration I would be given "a major portfolio."

After the electors had spoken on June 10, the dust of conflict had scarcely settled before speculation began to run riot over cabinet selections. The excitement in the press was more than matched by the state of feeling of Conservative hopefuls, both among those who had borne the heat and burden of the day in the twenty-two years in opposition and newcomers to the Commons savouring the heady wine of victory for the first time.

I awaited a call from John Diefenbaker which I was entirely confident would come. I remained in Toronto where I could be easily reached by telephone. The call came within a couple of days of election day. We exchanged congratulations warmly, and he asked me to come to Ottawa for a talk. I promptly presented myself at his office the next morning. Dave Walker was also on the early flight from Toronto, and several other MPs were also gathered outside Diefenbaker's office when I arrived there. I was warmly greeted by Dief, who looked happy, but serious. He showed no sign of fatigue after the rigours of the campaign.

What portfolio would he offer me? Which portfolio would I wish? I had narrowed down the selection in my own mind to four, assuming I had any element of choice. They were External Affairs, Finance, Justice, Trade and Commerce in that order. I had been active in all the debates and discussions on external affairs, had travelled widely, and had proven at three Commonwealth parliamentary conferences that I could hold my own at any international meeting. That portfolio had an aura of glamour about it. No one knew this better than Dief himself, for he had openly sought the role of opposition spokesman on external affairs. Finance I recognized as the most important of all portfolios, the heaviest and the most difficult. I had not given it much thought because I expected it to come to rest on the capable shoulders of Jim Macdonnell, a leading figure in the financial life of Canada, commanding wide respect from coast to coast, and official financial critic for the preceding twelve years. Justice was a portfolio to which very high prestige attached. It related to my own profession, but lacked the excitement of External Affairs and Finance. Trade and Commerce was one of the two portfolios to which I had been opposition critic for six years. I was well acquainted with its functions. Would it not seem the natural portfolio for me? John lost no time in coming to the point. He asked me what portfolio I would like. I commented on the four I had in mind. When I told him I had eliminated Finance in expectation that it would go to Jim Macdonnell, Dief shook his head firmly. Only when he had made it very clear that Jim would not be considered for it did I express any interest in it. Nothing final was said, but I came away from the meeting with the firm impression that Dief wished me in the Finance portfolio. He asked me to remain in Ottawa for the time being. I was dazed at the prospect of filling what I regarded as the most important and most challenging of all portfolios, albeit the most exacting.

I saw him again two days later. Nothing new was said about my portfolio, and I concluded the selection was settled in his mind. He asked my opinion about certain other selections. I expressed full approval of his proposals. We dwelt on one in particular – Minister of Labour. Should he appoint Mike Starr or Dr. Percy Vivian, who had just been elected in Durham? Perce had been Minister of Health in George Drew's first cabinet in Ontario, and had proved highly competent in that role. He and I were old friends from Varsity days. Nevertheless, I recommended Mike, because I thought his appointment would be a very significant gesture, not merely to persons of Ukrainian ancestry, but also to all New Canadians. Dief agreed. The choice went to Mike, and it was a good one.

I could see no advantage in remaining in Ottawa since the swearing-in would not take place until the next week, so I returned to Toronto to break the news to the family and my partners. They were by this time mentally conditioned for the big break which was impending. It was hard to settle down, particularly to any work at the office, as I did not expect to be there more than several days at most. On Sunday evening I received a telephone call from Dief to tell me that Bill Blair had that day died suddenly. Bill was one of my closest friends in the House and had been chosen by Dief to be his Minister of National Health and Welfare. The shock of his death was succeeded by a crushing feeling of disappointment that Bill would not after all be a colleague in the new cabinet. Two days later Dief called to say the new cabinet would be sworn in on Friday morning, June 21. I said I would arrive in Ottawa on Thursday. That afternoon I attended a party at the home of our old friends Ewart and Jorie Fockler, and left early to catch my flight with a salvo of good wishes from the guests. No one knew which portfolio was to be mine. I had said not a word to anyone outside the family and my partners, but much shrewd speculation was proceeding. At lunch at the National Club I had met my friend Bert Ashforth, chairman of the Toronto-Dominion Bank. He was naturally anxious to know who the new Minister of Finance would be. I couldn't tell him that he was talking to the very man.

Jim Macdonnell's great hope was to become Minister of Finance, and he had unanswerable claims to the position. Time, however, was unkind to him. He was already seventy-two years of age. During the campaign while flying with Senator Tom Crerar east from Winnipeg in the midst of discussing the election prospects the senator asked me this pointed question, "Whom have you got for Minister of Finance?" I was surprised that a friend of Jim's and a wise and experienced man would ask a question to which the answer was so obvious, but I replied, "Jim Macdonnell, of course." He shook his head and commented, "That job will kill Jim in six months." But Jim wanted the job. He posted himself in his office in the Parliament Buildings awaiting a call from Dief. When it did not come and it became clear that it was not coming Jim said to me, "I'll take this to caucus." I had to say to him, "Jim, there is no caucus, and there won't be one for several months. Besides, it will be a very different caucus from the one you and I have known for twelve years where we

343

could raise any question. Diefenbaker is to be the Prime Minister, and he can choose whom he wishes." Jim was crushed. Dief disliked Jim and did not wish him in the cabinet. In the end Olive Diefenbaker and Bill Brunt with no little difficulty succeeded in persuading Dief that he could not pass over Jim entirely, and Jim was included in the cabinet at the very last minute as Minister without Portfolio. He never hid his disappointment. It showed even in the photographs. Dief continued to show his hostility to Jim at various times and treated his views with little respect. He resigned when he reached seventy-five. I would have quit sooner if I had been treated as he was.

Thursday, June 20, was a very hot evening in Ottawa. Mrs. Campbell had moved to her cottage for the summer, so I could not return to 196 Clemow Avenue, where I had made my home away from home for twelve years. I had been staying at the Château Laurier. For some reason I decided to try the Beacon Arms, right downtown. There was absolutely no air-conditioning in the building in those days, and the heat was sweltering. I opened the doors onto the balcony for air, and found myself listening to an all-night succession of heavy trucks stopping at the traffic light just below. I wanted a good night's sleep in preparation for the momentous day on the morrow, but between the heat and the noise not a wink was I able to snatch. At the first sign of dawn I was up. What a preparation for what was to be one of the most important and memorable days of my life!

On June 21, 1928, at 11 a.m. I was called to the bar; on June 21, 1945, at 11 a.m. my brother Bob died in Detroit; and on June 21, 1957, at 11 a.m. I was sworn into ministerial office at Government House. As ministers-designate light-heartedly arrived at the front door under the watchful eyes of the press we were handed sheets bearing the roster of portfolios. It began, "John G. Diefenbaker, Prime Minister and Secretary of State for External Affairs; Howard C. Green, Minister of Public Works; Donald M. Fleming, Minister of Finance and Receiver General of Canada. . . ." It meant that after Howard Green I had been given precedence. My eye lit on those words, "Receiver General of Canada." I had not stopped previously to realize that that office went along with that of Minister of Finance. As I often described it afterward, my reaction was, "That's that miserable creature in whose favour I've been writing tax cheques all these years. Every time I wrote one I hated him; and now I'm it!"

We proceeded to the library where we were received by the Governor General, Vincent Massey. No guests, observers, photographers, press or family were permitted to be present or witness the ceremony. I was sorry that Alice and the family could not be with me at this high moment of my career. The Secretary of the Cabinet and Clerk of the Privy Council, Bob Bryce, administered the oaths. They were three in number and were administered individually in order of precedence. First was the oath of allegiance to the Queen, then the oath as a privy councillor, then the oath as minister. The oath of the privy councillor forbids the deponent to disclose outside the council what is done or said within it. It protects freedom of expression at all cabinet meetings. Whatever be the vagaries of political fortune the privy councillor holds office as such for life. When I emerged from the library I was the Honourable Donald M. Fleming, PC, for life. After I completed my third oath I turned to Dief, thanked him for the great honour, and assured him he would never have cause to regret it.

When all ministers had taken their oaths we proceeded to the south patio where group photographs were taken. I think we all looked rather pale and gaunt after the rigours of the campaign and the strains in the interval. We were bidden to assemble in the Council Chamber in the East Block at 3.30 p.m. for our first cabinet meeting, but, strangely, as it seemed to me, we were given no direction or instruction as to where to report in our respective departments. I did not even know precisely where my office was to be found. Nobody came from the department to take me by the hand. As a matter of fact, the officers were probably pondering the news they had just received as to who their new minister was to be.

In any event, instead of proceeding to the Confederation Building, where I would probably have found the officers out to lunch, I went off on a fruitless house-hunting expedition up the Gatineau with my friend Lester Randall. We succeeded only in becoming lost and hot and gathering a layer of dust on our shoes. I was back at the Council Chamber at 3.30 p.m. for our first cabinet meeting, dust and all. In the next six years cabinet was to hold 826 recorded meetings in addition to numerous unrecorded conferences. I felt uncomfortable at that first meeting after my hot and dusty foray up the Gatineau, but I can say with respect to all those 826 meetings that I never went to one of them unprepared. Regardless of the hour I never took to my bed until every document and every memorandum pertinent to all the items on the agenda for the cabinet meeting the next morning had been thoroughly studied.

The first meeting was held to an hour, but it afforded an opportunity for learning the rules, if we were not already acquainted with them. There would be no votes, frank discussion would lead to a consensus of opinion, and then a decision by which all members must abide. The agenda for every regular meeting must be circulated the previous day with supporting memoranda contributed by ministers sponsoring items of business. The memoranda must be distributed in time to allow for review thereof by officials of the Department of Finance and the Treasury Board. This meant that I must be briefed by the latter on all matters having any financial implications.

Following the practice in the United Kingdom it was agreed and ruled that ministers would not have access to the minutes and recorded conclusions of the previous government. To this day I have never seen any record of any meeting of the St. Laurent government, and I hope no one not a member of it has ever seen any record of any meeting of the Diefenbaker government.

The Council Chamber is a simple room with windows looking out toward the east and north. In six years facing the maple trees outside I think I could have counted every leaf. The cabinet table was a very large oval just long enough to accommodate all ministers and the ample armchairs on which they sat. Initially Diefenbaker sat at the end of the table, but later moved around to the middle of the west side for better acoustics. Howard Green sat next to Dief on his right, and I on his left. Other ministers were seated in order of precedence. George Hees was on my left followed by Davie Fulton, George Pearkes and Doug Harkness.

In Dief's absence Howard was to be acting prime minister, and in the absence of both of them myself. As a matter of fact over the years I had occasion to be Acting Prime Minister and to preside at cabinet meetings not a few times.

As her new government we despatched at once to Her Majesty a beautifully expressed message of loyalty, duty and good wishes. Overnight we received Her most gracious reply.

Within less than twenty-four hours of our swearing in we also received from President Eisenhower a message of congratulations and good wishes delivered by the U.S. ambassador, Livingstone Merchant, a delightful person who soon became a good friend of mine. Of all the American presidents since the Second World War, General Eisenhower was the most friendly to Canada and the best informed about us.

The first appointment made by the new government was to designate George Drew as Canadian high commissioner to Great Britain. George was the ideal person for this post, the most important in Canada's external service. At the time I expressed the hope that all our appointments might be as good as the first. George served with great dedication in London for seven years. His experience and forthrightness in representing Canada's interests won him and his country the highest respect.

The Treasury Board was set up at that first meeting by cabinet. It is the statutory finance committee of cabinet, charged with responsibility for supervising all expenditures and all programs of the various departments. It consisted of myself as chairman and five other ministers. It never attempted to function as an "inner cabinet." It sat every Thursday afternoon, and the meetings seldom lasted less than five hours. The chairmanship proved a very heavy burden, but it was an invaluable vehicle for investigating and controlling expenditure. Nowadays Treasury Board functions under a separate minister. It must be more difficult in consequence for the Minister of Finance to hold control of government fiscal policy. On taking over the chairmanship I found three hundred recommendations to the board by ministers of the previous administration pending. I ordered them all to be returned to the departments which submitted them and required specific review thereof by the new minister in every case. The Treasury Board had an outstandingly capable staff at all times. Dave Waters, Bob McNeill, Ernie Steele and John Macdonald won the full confidence of the ministers serving on the board.

The annual review of the estimates of all departments each year by the Treasury Board was an enormous task. I made a point of presiding over every meeting of this exacting exercise. I made it my personal responsibility to inquire into every item and every program of every department which involved the outlay of public funds. The officials told me at the outset that of all the departments the worst administered was the Department of External Affairs, and this was due to the fact that of all the ministers in the St. Laurent government Mike Pearson was the worst administrator of his department. I saw to it that this department was sharply curbed in its loose spending habits. They also informed me that of all ministers Paul Martin was by far the most prolific source of Christmas cards at public expense. His mailing list was over ten thousand, as many as the Governor General. I put a stop to the issuance of Christmas cards by ministers at public expense.

One inheritance from our predecessors as reported to us at that first meeting of cabinet was most welcome. St. Laurent had invited Her Majesty to open the first session of the new Parliament on October 14, which was Thanksgiving Day. As a new government we wished to call the new Parliament to meet in September, but back in 1952 the government had promised the use of the Parliament Buildings to the Universal Postal Union from August 14 to September 27. Her Majesty was most accommodating, but in the end we confirmed the original plan, and set about preparations for a great event, the first time a reigning sovereign had opened a session of the Parliament of Canada.

For one meeting, and that an inaugural one, we touched on some subjects of high import, and all within the space of one hour. I then betook myself to the Confederation Building to meet the senior officials of the Department of Finance, and to find my office. Word was sent from the cabinet office that I was on my way, and the deputy minister, Ken Taylor, was waiting in the hall to greet me. In the five years of our close association together we became close friends, and I had a high regard for his sense of duty, but I never knew precisely how glad he was to see me as his minister on that afternoon. I told him I considered myself fortunate to be appointed minister of a department with such eminent and capable senior officers as Finance. He managed to say, "We consider ourselves reasonably fortunate in the choice of our minister." Later I roasted Ken unmercifully for the heavy and not very flattering emphasis he placed upon the word "reasonably."

We proceeded to the minister's suite of offices where I met my personal staff. Apart from one messenger they were all females. Miss Doris Bentley was the private secretary, Miss Edith Shephard receptionist, Miss Ida Proctor in charge of filing, and three excellent stenographers, Miss Ruby Bumstead, Mrs. Audrey Ironmonger and Miss Eleanor Farman, all of whom remained with me for several years. Miss Shephard and Miss Proctor served throughout the entire period I was minister. Miss Bentley managed the office, and did it very competently. She had been brought to Ottawa by Colonel Ralston as private secretary and had served succeeding ministers of Finance. This spoke very favourably for her ability and loyalty.

I then passed into my personal office, a room in which in the next five years I was destined to spend long and trying hours. It was very spacious, but rather austere. It boasted one single air-conditioning unit. The walls were ringed by the imposing photographs of my eighteen predecessors in the portfolio since Confederation. For those five years they gazed down on me rather grimly, I thought, and unsympathetically. Only two of them, Tupper and Bennett, ever became prime minister. W.S. Fielding was undoubtedly the most distinguished and long-lasting of all the Liberal ministers of Finance, and probably Sir George Foster the most eminent of the Conservatives. I thought of the time when as a young university student I heard the eloquent Sir George deliver a noonday address at Hart House in which he exhorted his student listeners as young men to "catch a vision."

The only piece of furniture in the room of historical interest was a large table with green baize top, which had adorned the office of Sir John A. Macdonald. It adjoined a large plain desk and gave me an abundance of table surface. The rug was not in the best condition. Beside the telephone stand it was worn through. I concluded that previous ministers must have stood on the rug at that point while nervously engaging in frustrating telephone conversations with their colleagues. The rug at this spot was an eyesore, but I never replaced it. In the five years I occupied the office the hole grew and became uglier, but as a matter of principle I chose to make no change. That hole in the rug was worth thousands of dollars to me in my efforts to economize. I used it to ward off many raiders in search of rugs and furniture. As an example it was unanswerable. Had I ever replaced it I would have opened up the floodgates to demands of all kinds.

Into these, to me, novel surroundings Ken Taylor led about a dozen of the senior officers of the department, with several of whom, such as Ken Eaton and Wynne Plumptre, I was already personally acquainted. After I had greeted each individually they stood around in a circle, and I addressed a few unprepared remarks to them. I said that I would be seeking their advice on a multitude of matters in the responsibilities which we would be sharing: the advice I sought was honest advice, their best, but their own, and never did I wish them simply on that account to advise the course of action which they might think I desired to take. Never in my six years as a minister did I encounter a case where an adviser coloured his advice to me in the hope of gaining favour by supporting a point of view which I was known to entertain. I always received honest advice.

The desk had been thoroughly cleaned out. Walter Harris left only one thing on or in it – an invitation of the Canadian Bankers Association to join them at dinner that very evening at their half-yearly meeting at Montebello. I had been told of the event earlier that day, so was not taken by surprise. The association then consisted of the general managers of the chartered banks. Now with the proliferation of general managers and vice-presidents in the Canadian banking system, membership tends to go to the chief operating officer of each member bank. The presidency rotated among the banks on an annual or semi-annual basis. Bill Nicks of the Bank of Nova Scotia was then president, and he drove me to and from the Seigniory Club that evening, and made the trip most pleasant for me. We had met when he represented the CBA before the Banking and Commerce Committee previously. Our paths were destined to cross in the future, and he to influence the course of my life in later years. The upshot of that encounter was that I received a visit the next week from the manager of the principal branch of the Bank of Nova Scotia, opened an account with him and did all my personal banking in Ottawa with the Nova Scotia for the six years I remained in the capital.

It had been a day of exciting new events. My arrival at the Seigniory Club was to add one more. The first person I met at the club was Mary McCulloch, now Mrs. Blair Gordon, my boyhood sweetheart in the old days in Galt. We had not seen each other for at least twenty years, but she was well aware of what had happened to me that day and threw her arms around me in the most affectionate greeting I had ever received from her. It was a heart-warming meeting on a day of unforgettable events.

The group I was joining consisted of about twenty-five senior bankers and James Coyne, governor of the Bank of Canada, who was also a guest. I was given a most cordial welcome and treated with great deference. I had to pinch myself from time to time to remind myself that they were receiving the Minister of Finance. They expressed appreciation of my joining them on such short notice on my very first day in office. After dinner I addressed them. It had to be an unprepared speech, but I took advantage of the occasion to praise the Canadian banking system as the best in the world, to pay my compliments to Canadian bankers, and to assure them that at all times I would aim to work sympathetically with them in strengthening and improving the system. I think my visit made a good impression. I made a point of attending their semi-annual dinner in future whenever possible. Most of my official meetings later with the banks were attended by the chairmen among whom I made some very good friends.

Coyne spoke briefly after me at the dinner. I realized that he and I were likely to be closely associated in the days to follow. I had met him only once or twice before. He told me privately that he was leaving Ottawa next morning for Winnipeg to be married, and that he would like to call on me to pay his respects before leaving if I could find time to receive him before my cabinet meeting at 9.30 a.m. I gladly agreed to be at my office at 8.30 even though no staff would be on duty. I tried to avoid making the arrangement sound formal.

Arriving back in Ottawa after midnight I concluded that I had had a great day and that if the other days were like the first I was going to enjoy being Minister of Finance. My slumbers were disturbed in the middle of the night by the house detective entering and turning on the light. What he wanted at that hour I did not take the trouble to ascertain. I bade him depart in haste. This disturbance was prophetic of my new life.

The meeting with Coyne next morning was pleasant, though the atmosphere was rather more formal than I was accustomed to under the circumstances. I had not yet come to realize that having become a minister I must expect that people would treat me more formally than was my wont or inclination. I soon learned. I avoided any discussion of policy with Coyne at that initial meeting and particularly the subject of "tight money." I knew there would be later occasions for that theme. So we made it all very brief. I extended best wishes to him on his marriage. As he had his car and I had none he kindly drove me up the hill to the East Block, but strangely asked me if I would mind being deposited a block away. I readily acquiesced and proceeded on foot. I concluded that he did not wish to be seen driving me up to the main door of the East Block. Whatever his reasons were I did not understand them. It was an odd way of emphasizing the independence of the Bank of Canada. We agreed that we would plan another meeting after his return from his honeymoon. I learned later that his bride was a very beautiful widow with two young sons.

Dief was leaving on Sunday for London to attend the Commonwealth Prime Ministers' Conference, so our meeting on Saturday morning was conducted under pressure, but he carried with him to London a mandate to sponsor a Commonwealth Trade and Economic Conference. No particular thought had been given to holding it in Canada, and it appears to have been assumed at that stage that it would be attended by prime ministers. We had for years urged such a conference when in opposition; the Liberals had always received it coldly and ignored it. Now we had our opportunity and we would spare no effort to bring about our precious Commonwealth Trade and Ecomonic Conference. George Pearkes, Minister of National Defence, accompanied the Prime Minister to the conference and planned also to visit our NATO forces in Europe.

Dief early laid down a rule which I applauded. Ministers were to relinquish all directorships they held, whether in public or private companies. This was in contrast with that of Mackenzie King and St. Laurent, who told their ministers in such circumstances to "let their conscience be their guide." We would not be faced with such improprieties as Dr. McCann being director of a trust company doing frequent business with his Department of

National Revenue, and C.D. Howe acting as executor of Sir James Dunn's estate while his department was buying steel supplied by Algoma Steel Company, controlled by the estate. There was never any trespass upon this salutary rule laid down at the outset by Dief.

At noon that Saturday Ken Taylor and Wynne Plumptre, Assistant Deputy Minister of Finance, took me to lunch at the Rideau Club, and we had our first down-to-earth chat. They were particularly interested to learn in what form I wished to receive submissions from sources within the department. I laid down a simple formula: I wished a full presentation of the relevant facts, an outline of the possible alternative courses of action or decision, and the officials' recommended choice between them, so that if possible I could simply endorse it "Approved" with my initials and the date. This method proved so satisfactory that we applied it without any deviation all the years I remained Minister of Finance. After lunch we walked past one government building. Ken Taylor pointed to its basement and shook me with the comment: "In that basement there are two billion dollars' worth of securities, and you're responsible for every cent of them." However, I did not offer to count them.

Wynne Plumptre was to become a very close associate and adviser to me. He came from Toronto, where he had been a professor of economics at Varsity. He was short, prim, and his manner savoured of the school teacher. He was a man of outstanding ability, and he could write. He headed the international section in the department, including trade, tariffs, loans abroad, aid, the International Monetary Fund, the International Bank for Reconstruction and Development, and many other related subjects. I knew his parents. His father was Canon Plumptre, rector of St. James's Cathedral, when I did the legal work for the rector and churchwardens. I sat with his mother, the eminent Adelaide Plumptre, on the Toronto City Council.

Wynne did me a great kindness that day. He and his wife Beryl, an economist in her own right, were leaving on a month's vacation, and Wynne offered to rent to me furnished his fine new home in Rockcliffe. I jumped at the opportunity. This would be an immediate and happy, though temporary, solution to my housing problems, deliver me from confinement to a hotel bedroom at the Château, give me a pleasant place to work at nights, and a home for Alice to share with me whenever she found it possible to leave Toronto. To cap it all, there was a swimming pond a short distance away, and I revelled in the delightful use of it. Alice was able to join me for part of that month, and I had the benefit of home life in the capital for the first time in the twelve years I had spent in Ottawa.

I went back to Toronto Saturday afternoon for a short weekend. I was deluged with congratulations. We attended church as usual on Sunday morning, but the minister, Reverend Ernest Marshall Howse, made no mention of the new government or the new Minister of Finance sitting in front of him. He might at least have prayed for them. After the service he told me that I should have insisted on being appointed Secretary of State for External Affairs, and that my appointment as Minister of Finance was no good. This was so encouraging.

If there was to be a Commonwealth Trade and Economic Conference it was necessary to begin preparations for it without delay. Gordon Churchill, Minister of Trade and Commerce, and I met with senior officials of our departments and the Department of External Affairs. We soon agreed that if a conference were to be called its scope should not be confined to trade; it should moreover be expedited in the hope of slowing down British interest in the European Free Trade Area, the group of countries scattered about the perimeter of the six European Common Market countries.

The annual meetings of the governors of the International Bank and the International Monetary Fund were to be held in Washington in late September, and would be attended by the Ministers of Finance of the various Commonwealth countries. It was their custom to meet each year in London as guests of the British government just prior to the Washington meetings. We put forward the idea that Canada should take the lead and invite the meeting to be held in our country after, not before, the Washington meetings and to include the Ministers of Trade. This would be preliminary to the full Commonwealth Trade and Economic Conference we had promised. Time would be required to organize the latter, and we must not risk failure. Cabinet readily approved this proposal; Howard Green relayed it to Dief in London, and he made effective use of it at the Prime Ministers' Conference. I was confident that some positive steps could be taken at this early stage. I was struck by the lack of consultation which had prevailed before our arrival on the scene. The Canada–U.K. Continuing Committee was composed only of officials and had not met actively. It was all too apparent that the St. Laurent government had taken no interest whatever in the idea of a Commonwealth Trade and Economic Conference. It was our idea, and we would succeed or fail on our own efforts.

With cabinet meetings Friday, Saturday, Monday, Tuesday

and two on Thursday it was small wonder that ministers began to complain that the meetings were so frequent and so lengthy that they had little time to attend to their own departmental responsibilities.There was a heavy accumulation of cabinet business, partly due to the change of government and partly to the usual neglect during a long election campaign. On the other hand, ministers were needed in their own departments to grapple with a large backlog of business there, much of it urgently requiring decisions.

On June 27 I was appointed a governor of the International Monetary Fund and a governor of the International Bank. These interesting responsibilities were to continue for six years. The practice was to hold the annual meetings of the two organizations together, for two years in Washington, then one abroad. In my six years, four of the annual meetings were held in Washington, one in India in 1958 and one in Vienna in 1961. All six meetings proved of intense interest to me.

Responsibility for housing went to Howard Green as Minister of Public Works, and George Nowlan was made minister responsible for reporting for Canadian Broadcasting Corporation. These two areas of government had been major responsibilities of mine throughout my twelve years in opposition. I knew all too well that my duties as Minister of Finance would keep me totally occupied wiithout housing and broadcasting. I never again made a speech on either of these subjects. There was some regret in my mind about dropping them, but under the circumstances the sense of relief prevailed.

Messages of congratulations and good wishes on my appointment poured in by the hundreds. Many of them came from ministers of the gospel. It was thrilling to find that old friends and new friends and some very notable people were taking such satisfaction from seeing me become Minister of Finance. Peter Thorneycroft, Chancellor of the Exchequer, sent a very kind message. To every person kind enough to send such a message went a personal letter of thanks signed by me personally. Photographs were sought. Karsh telephoned that he would like to take my photograph. I made the mistake of thinking I was too busy to bother. I was always sorry later that I did not have a photograph by this master of the art. I did, however, pose for Gaby, an eminent Montreal photographer, who came to take photos of all the new ministers. He did extraordinarily well with the available material.

It was not long before the deluge of congratulatory messages was followed by another deluge, this time from persons and organizations seeking interviews to present a case for some purpose. I did my utmost to organize these, but the avalanche continued. It seemed that everyone whose case had been rejected in the course of twenty-two years of Liberal government wished to try his hand again with the new Minister of Finance. It seemed also that they nearly all feared that if they were not heard immediately all would be lost. I received many delegations and listened to many presentations. No matter what the pressure on my time I never curtailed such a presentation. These people were citizens and taxpayers, and I took the position that they were entitled to present their case as they saw fit without interference. I listened patiently. I endeavoured to treat every member of every delegation with the utmost courtesy.

One episode caused me no little trouble and irritation. Harold Morrison, a well-known member of the press gallery, sought an interview with me, and I took the trouble to fit him in one evening while Diefenbaker was still in London. I answered most of his questions by referring to the statements made by the Prime Minister in the election campaign. That might not have much fresh news value, but I considered I would be on safe ground. When he asked about expenditure I said we were committed to the reduction of unnecessary expenditure: Dief had said so. When he asked about tax reductions I pointed to Dief's promise of tax reductions, and added that he was a man of his word. He asked if I as Minister of Finance would be responsible for carrying out these promised tax reductions. I replied that tax changes were the responsibility of the Minister of Finance. He asked if that would necessitate a budget. Without committing myself to any date I said that tax changes would require a budget. That was all.

News stories must have been scarce that night, and Harold must have thought it necessary to make it appear he had a scoop. His news report that night created big headlines on the front page of the early edition of the *Globe and Mail*: the Minister of Finance had promised a budget with tax reductions. By 10 p.m. I began to receive telephone calls from the press gallery, the first from Bob Needham of the *London Free Press*. I endeavoured to play the story down, pointing out that I had said nothing which had not been said during the campaign weeks before by the Prime Minister. But the story attracted a wide press, and to some it was made to appear as an indiscretion on the part of a new Minister of Finance. Dief heard about it in London and was furious. On his return he took me to task over it. I became rather annoyed that he did not appear to recognize the quotation of his own promises. Weeks later when I proposed to bring down a budget in December, Dief, backed by Hees, strenuously opposed the idea and would have none of it. What might have been a major financial presentation was played down to my great annoyance and disappointment. Dief said he didn't want a budget debate under the rules of the House. I still believe he was trying to clip my wings and humiliate me for my answer to Nicholson's question.

The episode had another consequence. It made me very cautious in talking to the press, and journalists do not like reticence. It was carried to the point where in a cartoon I was accosted by a polite citizen wishing me a good morning, to which I was pictured as cautiously replying, "I will take that as notice and reply to-morrow." It all did not make for the best relations between the press and the minister.

I still had to give thought to my legal practice and my responsibilities to both my clients and my partners. The national holiday, July 1, fell on a Monday. I needed a holiday. Instead, I spent two long days that weekend at the office with my secretary Audrey Hanna, writing letters to clients thanking them for the privilege of serving them in the past, explaining that because of entering the government I must give up practice and adding that other members of the firm would be pleased to be of assistance to them in future. When the task was completed and the letters all deposited in the mailbox I had a sinking feeling. I realized that in just two days I had liquidated a practice which it had taken me twenty-nine years of hard labour to build. We were but a minority government, we had not yet even faced the new House of Commons. Suppose we were defeated in the House and then at the polls, where would I be? Had I not done something that was foolish, irresponsible and unfair to my family?

My final business session with my partners was disappointing. I had thought that they would at least be pleased with my appointment as minister and perhaps even take a little pride in it. After all, the firm had been founded in 1850 by a politician, Adam Crooks. One partner expressed himself as "hurt" that I had not referred certain clients to him personally; one wished to charge me personally for Audrey's salary for the two days I was writing letters trying to retain clients for the firm; and one expressed the view that I had no right to take Audrey away from the firm. I was able to tell him that she had told me she would be leaving the firm in any event when I left. So the parting fell far short of my hopes. My withdrawal from the firm was dated back to May 1; I was paid a salary of $500 for my services beyond that date – and had to wait some time for payment – and out of the considerable assets of the firm was graciously allowed to take with me my desk and chair – nothing more. With my approval my name was removed from the letterhead and several years later from the firm name. So the law partnership of Kingsmill, Mills, Price and Fleming passed into history. I had entrusted my fortunes and those of my family to the uncertainties of political favour and the whims of John Diefenbaker.

On my personal staff at Ottawa I retained all the survivors of the personal staff of Walter Harris. I saw no reason, even though they were not civil servants, to dispense with their services merely because they had served him or had been recruited by him. They all served me loyally. There were vacancies to be filled. Audrey Hanna, who was the best secretary I ever had, joined my staff as deputy private secretary, and a year later succeeded Doris Bentley as private secretary when Doris married. Bill Allan joined me as executive secretary and handled all political relations, both in Eglinton and farther afield. The appointment of my long-time friend and barber Emil Simonsen as a messenger came about unexpectedly. He worked in the barbershop at the Royal York Hotel. When he was cutting my hair there a few days after my appointment he startled me by asking, "Have you got a job for me?" I replied that the only position I was entitled to fill without recourse to the Civil Service Commission was that of messenger, and I did not think either the salary or the duties would interest him. That appeared to end the matter.

Two days later Miss Bentley came in to tell me that there was a man outside who said he had come to start work. It was Emil. He wished to work for me, and though very surprised I was as happy about it as he was. Apart from being a most willing and industrious messenger he continued to cut and wash my hair after hours. We had a most companionable relationship. He drove a little Volkswagen car, which with my permission he parked in front of the Confederation Building in the space marked "Reserved for the Minister of Finance." If I were too much delayed to walk to cabinet meetings he would drive me up to the East Block in the little Volkswagen, as ministers in those days were not provided with cars and chauffeurs. This unusual relationship ended suddenly one morning three years later with a paralysing stroke. After that I used to visit him at his home in Toronto until death settled the account finally. He was succeeded on my staff by James Moir, who was kind enough to tell me I was the best boss he ever worked for. I have always appreciated such compliments from those who have worked for me personally. I never allowed my staff to become as large as my predecessor's.

I have mentioned my surprise at being appointed Receiver General of Canada. I was similarly surprised to find that I was also Minister of Insurance. At one time insurance had been in the Department of Finance. It was now a separate department, and its head, the superintendent, held the rank of deputy minister. Ken Macgregor was the superintendent. He was an actuary and a most capable official, and I developed a very high regard and respect for him. After I left Ottawa he was appointed president of the Mutual Life Assurance Company of Canada. I joined him later on the board of directors of the company.

Bob Bryce, secretary of the cabinet, and as such in effect a deputy minister to the Prime Minister, was an outstanding civil servant. He had been trained as both an engineer and an economist. Brilliant, urbane and pleasant, he gave inestimable service to both cabinet and the Prime Minister. He remained, however, always under the cloud of Dief's suspicion of senior civil servants. To me his loyalty was beyond question.

CHAPTER THIRTY-TWO

Taking Hold of the Department

Even with the reputation I had earned for hard work I had never experienced a summer like that of 1957, and difficult as later summers were, they never quite matched the rigours of 1957. All ministers were tired before they even began, for they had just emerged from an exhausting campaign. In my case I had been travelling and speaking constantly for seven weeks. Then I had to close my law practice. I had to make new living arrangements in Ottawa. I had to face a long line-up of hopeful delegations from almost every part of Canada. Dief had no departmental responsibilities after he shed External Affairs and he kept calling cabinet meetings without regard for the demands made on ministers by their inescapable departmental responsibilities. I had to make staff adjustments. I had to become acquainted with the senior officials of a department which, with the Treasury, numbered five thousand employees. I had to deal with a mass of paperwork coming ceaselessly and in volume from the department. In addition I was given the senior responsibility for preparing for the major international conferences in the offing.

Cabinet meetings meant special work in preparation for the Minister of Finance. Not only must he study the agenda and the submissions and memoranda accompanying the agenda, but in all cases involving expenditure, and most of them did that, he had to confer with officials of the department and principally the Treasury Board in regard thereto. This all took time. I advanced the working portion of my day, commencing work at my office at 8.15 a.m. before most of the staff arrived, yet my conferences with Treasury Board officers sometimes continued while I walked down the hall and stairs on my way to cabinet meetings at the last minute. Yet I never was late for a cabinet meeting.

In addition to Treasury Board I served on a number of committees of cabinet, the most important and interesting being the one on defence. Time was so elusive. The hours simply sped by. The phone calls came incessantly, and often I could not return them for hours. Jim Macdonnell kept exhorting me to delegate responsibility. He did not realize that the Minister of Finance had very limited scope for delegation. He has available excellent assistance and competent advice, but he must personally make innumerable decisions. This is required of him; this is expected of him; sometimes it is prescribed by statute. I was carrying home bags of work every evening. In innumerable matters officials needed the minister's decision or direction in order to proceed.

Never had I worked such long hours. Sports and even minimum recreation simply vanished. For the first six weeks I was working regularly until 2 a.m. I knew this could not be expected to last; I expectantly looked for the time when I would surmount the hump, overtake all arrears, and establish a more sensible and humane routine. One night in the middle of the summer I finished my day's labour by midnight and went to bed happy in the thought that I was at last on top of the job. The mirage was brief; the next night my work kept me till 2.30 a.m.; the next week the preparations for the international conferences intensified, and I was obliged to stay at my desk until 3 a.m. night after night. People asked me, "Can you sleep when you finally go to bed?" I answered, "My only problem is in staying awake till I go there." I took no stimulant whatever to keep awake. Had I not strictly avoided tea and coffee I would soon have become dependent upon them and addicted to them. One Saturday evening when the family were with us I was simply overcome, and flopped into bed in a stupor at 9.30. At one point I developed a gnawing headache, probably neuralgia. It lasted for three weeks. I knew the cause and the remedy, but I simply could not ease up. I never told anyone about it. It would only upset Alice to know.

And so the pace continued, week after week, month after month. Then as the session of Parliament drew near the labours on the legislative program multiplied. Davie Fulton, as chairman of the committee on the program, did a most competent job on the legislative proposals and bills, but I was vice-chairman of the committee and expected to attend all meetings and pass on every item of legislative business. Sunday mornings I did not work; we attended church with unfailing regularity. But as soon as Sunday dinner was over I headed for my desk and files, and spent the balance of the day at them. My working day reached seventeen hours, and my working week a full one hundred hours. This pace continued without let-up.

I was not a slow worker; the long hours were not due to a slow

360

pace. I organized my program of work day by day, and evening by evening. A hit-and-miss approach would have defeated my effort. Fortunately, over the years I had developed an unusual power of concentration, and I employed it now to the limit. Years later a senior banking associate likened my receptivity to blotting paper. But the power to retain is just as important as the power to absorb. I was blest with what the experienced journalist Clarke Davey, writing in the *Globe and Mail*, once described as "Mr. Fleming's prodigious memory." Both memory and the faculty of apprehension must be cultivated. They require concentrated effort. Diefenbaker had both. He could read faster than anyone I ever met. Often we had to read a page together; in such cases he would always outdistance me. With his phenomenal speed he would read the page in about 80 per cent of the time I required for the purpose. He also possessed a remarkable memory. Sometimes it was too good. He would have done better to forget some things, such as the hurts, real or fancied, that he had received from others, and his resentments. I gave more attention to detail than he, and it is important for a Minister of Finance to be a master of detail as long as he does not clutter his brain with useless information. I endeavoured to feed into my inborn computer only useful facts, but there were so many of them that I desired to retain.

How did I maintain this pace? How did I escape a physical and mental collapse? I suppose I did not escape the effects altogether. I badly needed sleep. This lack was bound to tell on the nervous system. I took special pains to control my tongue and my temper lest want of sleep result in irascibility. Mental fatigue can result in mistakes, and these I had to avoid at all costs. In the Normandy campaign General Crerar required all unit commanders to be in bed by 10 p.m. lest they make mistakes of judgment in battle. Had I been so commanded in the summer of 1957 I would have been in great fettle, but the backlog of work arrears would have swamped me. The press could not understand why I did not look merry or act in a thoroughly light-hearted fashion. I found some of them quite lacking in understanding of the elementary facts of the situation. However, I kept Diefenbaker informed, and I never complained about the workload. My colleagues seemed to think I was enjoying it.

My constitution was rugged, and I had paid strict attention to the laws of health. I began with that advantage. I had always avoided alcohol in any form, tobacco, tea, coffee. I was careful of what I ate, both in quality and quantity. I walked when I was not obliged by time or distance to ride. I daily practised the calisthenics that I had learned as a boy at the YMCA in Galt. But all these factors, important as they were, could not alone have sustained me in maintaining a killing pace of work. There were, I think, three overriding elements which carried me through.

First, I found an enormous sense of challenge in my tasks, undoubtedly the greatest and most exacting challenge I had ever faced. That sense fortunately did not diminish; it grew. I was serving Canada and the Queen. I was not devoting my efforts to benefit myself or a few others; rather, I was serving twenty million Canadians. It was a sobering and inspiring thought. I did not flatter or delude myself into thinking they would be intensely grateful for my service, but I still had the undoubted privilege of serving them. Moreover, it soon became evident to me that my position in importance and influence was second only to that of the Prime Minister. That of itself was challenging enough to keep me at my tasks day and night. And with the sense of challenge went a sense of satisfaction in filling such a role and discharging the responsibilities that it imposed. My success in that role was vital to the success of the new government, and I was determined that it should not fall short through any failure or lack on my part.

Secondly, it helped me greatly that Alice was able to join me for most of the summer. After the month in Wynne Plumptre's home in Rockcliffe we were privileged to occupy the residence of Clayton Elderkin, Inspector-General of Banks in my department, alongside the Rideau Canal for five weeks while he and Mrs. Elderkin were away on vacation. David and Mary had summer jobs, he as a labourer on a farm and she as a waitress in the hotel at Windermere. Donald was in camp for part of the summer and for part with us. But for Alice's sustaining help and unselfish commitment to sharing my burdens the load might well have proved beyond endurance. If I had to work every night to a late hour at least I was delivered from having to eat my solitary dinner in some restaurant and confine myself in a hotel room. Both in those two summer months and throughout the next year Alice carried the burden of maintaining two homes and caring for a scattered family, but at no time did she complain or make my tasks more difficult. Moreover, for the first time I was relieved of the trip by train to Toronto every weekend and the nightmare of trying to do a week's work each Saturday at my law office. By spending most of the weekends in Ottawa I saved valuable time and was spared much physical wear and tear. Concentration was also assisted.

Thirdly, I was sustained by faith. Often when the load seemed too heavy to bear I was thankful to call on the inner resources which God in his mercy imparts to those who turn to Him for strength. One verse of Holy Scripture came to me many times in the heat and burden of that first summer, "They that wait upon the Lord shall renew their strength." I never turned to that unfailing source in vain. I do not blush to say that I was upheld by prayer and the answer to prayer. I feel sorry for those who have not discovered this source of understanding and strength and who try to "go it alone." I cheerfully confess that, strong man though I was, I could never "go it alone."

Lunch downtown was a problem. I had no time or disposition for eating in public places. The parliamentary dining room and cafeteria were closed till Parliament opened in mid-October. I needed a place that would provide privacy, a place to entertain and a nearby location. I joined the Rideau Club and for six years made good use of its luncheon service between sessions of Parliament. I also joined the Country Club in the futile hope of swimming there occasionally in the summer. It proved useful as a place for entertaining officially, for the government had absolutely no facilities of its own when Parliament was not sitting. The trouble was that no other minister joined the Country Club and only one or two the Rideau Club. When some of my colleagues chose to entertain officially they found it very convenient to use my membership in these clubs. I paid the membership fees out of my own pocket.

The return of the Elderkins at the end of August sent me house-hunting again. Through the kindness of George and Blytha Pearkes I occupied their suite at the Château Laurier for two weeks, then was cast adrift again. In September a more lasting solution was found. The widow of Dr. Clifford Clark, former Deputy Minister of Finance, was remarrying, and her furnished residence on Maple Lane in Rockcliffe became available, and I was very happy to rent it for a year. David was returning to the Ontario Agricultural College at Guelph. Mary followed in her father's footsteps, registering at Varsity in University College in the honours course in English. She had graduated from Lawrence Park Collegiate with the top scholarships and awards of the school and a Varsity scholarship. Had Alice been continuing to reside in Toronto, Mary might have lived at home; to free Alice to join me in Ottawa, Mary entered the University College women's residence (Whitney Hall) and spent her four years there. We enrolled Donald as a boarder at Ashbury College in Rockcliffe under the benign eye of my old friend and classmate in Varsity days, Ron Perry, the headmaster. Suddenly Alice and I were reunited, but the family was scattered, as never before. In future they were reunited only at holiday times and special weekends. We decided we must keep our home in Toronto open. While we remained a minority government my hold on my portfolio was too tenuous to allow of any disposal, even renting, of 259 Glencairn Avenue. Alice divided her time between Rockcliffe and Toronto, coping with the problems of running two homes, not to mention the expense I bore. It was the most unsettled year we ever experienced.

I have not yet mentioned political problems. I adjusted quickly to my role in cabinet. As Minister of Finance I had to pass judgment on proposals emanating from all departments where expenditure or staff complements were involved. This duty singles out relations between the Minister of Finance and his colleagues as being different from those subsisting between them and any other minister. I quickly became very conscious of this. Looking at our budget commitments and election promises I was constantly opposing programs, some of them good, put forward by other ministers. Alf Brooks soon dubbed me "the bulldog of the Treasury." I think he meant "the watchdog." I acquired the reputation of saying no to almost every proposal. I was sorry on personal grounds to be cast constantly in the role of opposing the ideas of my colleagues. No doubt some departments were testing out the strength and determination of the Minister of Finance and the influence he could exert in cabinet. One colleague in particular, George Hees, complained that I was always taking a position on proposals of other departments. I explained that that was the system we operated under, and whether he disliked it and whether I found it irksome only cabinet could override it. I think some of my colleagues sympathized with me, particularly those who sat on the Treasury Board; others wearied of the predictable no from the Minister of Finance, whom they chose to dub "The Leader of the Opposition in Cabinet." One day when patience was wearing thin I asked, "With all the intelligence we have ranged around this table can't someone sometime bring forward a program which doesn't cost money?" There were few takers.

My relations with my senior officials gave me much more happiness. I was coming to know them personally and appreciate their capabilities. A healthy mutual confidence was growing. I remained for a time uncertain as to how much formality ought to be permitted to be observed between us. It seemed unfair that senior officers should address me as "Mr. Minister," or "Sir," while I took liberties with their names. For a time in the interests of fair play and reciprocity I addressed most of them as "Mr." with their surnames. This, however, seemed intolerably stiff and formal and might even be interpreted as unfriendly. From that point I called them all by their first names. They continued to address me as "Mr. Minister," and I am sure they preferred it that way.

Other ministers were less fortunate in their staff relations. Some were inclined to be rather suspicious of officers who had served Liberal ministers for years, and questioned the loyalty of some. The example of former civil servants like Mike Pearson, Milton Gregg and Jack Pickersgill in jumping the traces and emerging as committed Liberal partisans was not lost on some of my colleagues. Then there was a fear that strong-minded senior civil servants would take advantage of the inexperience of some ministers and dominate them. This will always be a possibility, as will the reverse position where a timid senior civil servant will give up too easily endeavouring to convince his minister when the latter most needs advice and restraint. Diefenbaker was suspicious by nature, and a couple of ministers emulated his attitude. This was bound to lead to frictions in their departments. A good example was the Department of Trade and Commerce. In February the highly respected Fred Bull had been appointed ambassador to Japan, and he was succeeded as deputy minister of that department by Mitchell Sharp, whom I knew and whose abilities I recognized. On February 21 I wrote Mitch a letter of congratulations on his appointment and good wishes for the future. He responded on March 4 with a very warm expression of appreciation. Friction and a kind of distrust soon developed between him and his minister, Gordon Churchill. I supported Mitch until he resigned and left the public service to join big business. For my intervention in his support I received my reward: Sharp ran against me as the Liberal candidate in Eglinton in the 1962 general election. Dief frequently chided me for being, as he said, too trustful of others. I will concede that my trust was abused and betrayed in the end by some people who at convenient junctures openly donned the robes of the Liberal party, but I could not go through life with a chronic distrust of others.

Another consequence of distrust of some senior civil servants by several ministers is that when I too vociferously defended the loyalty of civil servants I came under suspicion of Dief and others as being too much under the influence of the senior civil servants in the Department of Finance. It was necessary to walk warily. I am convinced that some of my senior officers were aware of the suspicions entertained by Dief and a couple of other ministers. I could never have asked for more loyal officers, just as devoted to the public good as any minister.

My relations with the Liberal opposition were developing interest as well. It was reported to me in rather ominous tones that the Liberals were out to "get" me, that they had taken such heavy punishment from me in debate for so many years that they were planning savage attacks against me once Parliament met and that they were preparing themselves by reviewing with a fine-tooth comb everything that I had said in the House or outside on fiscal subjects for the last twelve years. I treated the information, which was undoubtedly authentic, with amusement. I said I thought it would do these Liberal spokesmen much good to read all my speeches; they could not fail to derive enlightenment from them, and I was not planning to change views which I had firmly held and consistently expressed since entering the House in 1945. However, I did take the precaution of having Donald Eldon, head of the party research bureau, collect my utterances on fiscal subjects in the House. He prepared a tidy volume of them. I found nothing in them that I would wish to withdraw or modify. I remained quite unworried about the threatened Liberal offensive and rather flattered and gratified that I had really smitten them to the point where they chose to single me out for retaliation.

Liberal journalists suddenly took an interest in the views I had previously expressed on fiscal issues. Grant Dexter, former editor of the *Winnipeg Free Press*, and now Ottawa representative of that biased Liberal organization, wrote a series of four articles entitled "Mr. Fleming's views." Naturally, they were not intended to put my views in the most favourable light; those views, however, emerged in almost unrecognizable form. Grant did not interview or communicate with me. He purported to base his articles on the record; in fact, he based them chiefly on the flights of his own prejudiced imagination. He began by asserting that in the recent general election campaign I "did comparatively little travelling in the campaign outside of Metropolitan Toronto and received relatively little public attention." Considering that I had travelled between twenty and twenty-five thousand miles and delivered approximately seventy campaign speeches I could only conclude that geographically he thought that Metropolitan Toronto embraced all of Canada from coast to coast. Moreover, he grossly misrepresented my views on such topics as equalization payments for the smaller provinces and planned debt reduction. I wrote him two letters that July to give him the facts, but he totally ignored them. I concluded that he was not interested in facts, and that he had other things to write about. I came to a somewhat similar conclusion with respect to some other journalists representing Liberal newspapers. I could have forgiven their prejudices if only they would tell the truth. They were disposed to write from an idea and to mould the facts to support the idea. When I read back today some of the speculative articles published in that period and later by these Liberal writers I can only call them trash.

Blair Fraser was regarded as one of the more respectable of the Liberals in the press gallery, where he represented *Maclean's* magazine. That publication blotted its copybook by publishing just after the election what purported to be a news article announcing the return of the Liberal government. The post-election issue evidently faced a pre-election deadline, so Fraser and the editors evidently took the risk not merely of making a prophecy but of stating as fact what was proven false by the electorate. This gem of journalistic irresponsibility was followed in the August 31 issue by an article by Fraser which matched the June monstrosity. Without even a shred of truth he announced that in our early weeks in office I had said to friends: "If I had known we were going to win I would have been a lot more careful of what I said." I wrote him to deny categorically ever having made such a statement, but once again I never received so much as even an acknowledgement.

In the view of foreign governments the Canadian Minister of Finance is regarded as the linch-pin of the Canadian government and therefore a vital contact. Numerous high commissioners and ambassadors called on me from time to time, sometimes formally to pay their respects, sometimes to establish a contact for future reference, sometimes to obtain information or the views of the government. I enjoyed these important meetings and gradually developed pleasant personal relationships with many members of the Ottawa diplomatic corps. They were on the whole a distinguished group. For most of them Ottawa was regarded as a very desirable posting. Life in the Canadian capital was pleasant, problems were not too serious, relations were friendly, and while the winters to some seemed long and severe there was always good skiing at Camp Fortune, and the Gatineau country offered relief from the heat of summer. Dinners and receptions under diplomatic auspices were very frequent. Some of my colleagues did not attempt to attend these functions; I did. I considered them very important to Canada's international relations. Of course, an hour spent at a reception or an evening at a dinner did nothing to liquidate my paperwork; it meant rather working later with less sleep. Nevertheless, I never discounted the importance of these diplomatic contacts. Sometimes they proved to be the means of furthering high enterprises.

Life on the ministerial level is not removed from the local, the personal, and the simpler things of life. One of the first contacts I made as Minister of Finance was with a blind man, George Blake by name, who sold newspapers at the door of the Confederation Building under some arrangement with the Canadian National Institute for the Blind. George was always cheerful and bright. Every morning as I entered the building I paused to chat with George. He was a staunch and outspoken Conservative. It is small wonder that we became good friends. He knew me by my voice. If I had had his handicap I wonder if I would have been able to maintain his cheerful and friendly attitude. He, probably without being aware of it, set me a daily example.

A single incident from this period lives in my memory. It concerns the disappointment of a boy. On Friday, August 2, I was invited to present diplomas or certificates at Ryerson Institute of Technology in Toronto to those who had graduated from a technical course under a federal-provincial cost-sharing plan. It was designed to help meet the need for qualified technicians, rather than engineers. The graduates were not all young, and some had come a long distance to take the course. One of them I observed as he crossed the platform to receive his diploma at my hands. He was middle-aged. I could read a story of the effort of an ethnic immigrant, perhaps a refugee, to improve his family's lot in a new land of promise. As he crossed the platform I observed a teen-age boy near the front stand up to take his father's photograph at a moment that would climax the family's pride and expectation. The line of graduates moved a little faster, and the boy missed his picture. Following the presentation I addressed the graduates and their assembled families and friends, but I could not dismiss from my mind the disappointment of that boy. At the close Alice and I took our leave and had driven half a block on our way to meet our family for lunch when I said to Alice, "I must go back and find that boy." Back we went. Fortunately, I found the boy and his father. I re-enacted the presentation and posed for other photographs. The boy had his pictures. He was happy, and I, too, went away supremely happy.

In the midst of my pressing and hectic program a close friend called me one day and asked me to see a well-known Canadian developer. I explained how beset I was, asked for the reason and inquired if it could be deferred. My friend sympathized, but nonetheless urged me to meet with this man, so I did so on a

368

Saturday afternoon. He had nothing of immediate moment to discuss with me, but he did wish to meet me. There was something prophetic about the incident as I meditated upon it afterward. Was I allowing myself to give so much time to individual matters that I was failing to reserve enough time to think and ponder on the large and far-reaching issues? It seemed hopeless to find time just to think, as Mackenzie King used to do at Kingsmere, but it was essential.

That season would not have been complete without the agony of a threatened national rail strike. I gave up a party given by close friends in Toronto in honour of Alice and me to sit all through Saturday night in the Privy Council Office while the parties negotiated in an adjoining room. Dief was able to sleep on the chesterfield in his office. I tried to remain awake chatting with my friend Buck Crump, chairman of the CPR. Ministers accomplished nothing by their intervention. I was sorry then and afterward that I hadn't gone to Toronto for the party. I had to learn to live with frustrations.

CHAPTER THIRTY-THREE

The Tale of the Empty Till

When John Diefenbaker left for London on June 23 he had not completed his cabinet selections, but in the short time at his disposal he had made quite remarkable progress. The principal unfilled vacancies were External Affairs, Agriculture, Mines and Technical Surveys, and National Health and Welfare. He did not know the new Quebec members and needed time to estimate their qualifications for office. In August and September he completed the cabinet. Doug Harkness was appointed Minister of Agriculture and relinquished Northern Affairs and Natural Resources; Paul Comtois was named to Mines and Technical Surveys; Waldo Monteith was named to National Health and Welfare; Alvin Hamilton to Northern Affairs and Natural Resources. Dief consulted me on all these appointments, and I concurred in them. If I were facing the question again I think I would have left Doug Harkness in Northern Affairs, where he was happy, and named Alvin to Agriculture, to which he succeeded a couple of years later and where in my judgment he proved successful. John Charlton had been chairman of our caucus committee on agriculture for twelve years, but he was from Ontario, and Dief was determined that that senior and very important portfolio should go to the Prairies. John Charlton had expected to receive the appointment. He was a friend and supporter of Diefenbaker, and he was acutely disappointed. I saw him sadly coming out of Dief's office just after the Chief had broken the news to him.

External Affairs remained. One day Dief called me in and asked me what I would think of Jules Leger, the undersecretary of that department. I voiced my admiration of my friend Jules, my belief that he was not by nature suited to a political role and my disapproval of appointing civil servants. That was the last I heard of that idea. I think I did Jules a service under the circumstances. Weeks later Dief called me in to ask me what I would think of the appointment of Sidney Smith. I immediately replied, "That would be a ten-strike." The wide respect in which he was held throughout Canada and his academic eminence would win strong acceptance even though he bore the handicap of having no experience in Parliament. His appointment followed, and George White's seat of Hastings-Peterborough was opened for him. Senator Haig was later appointed Government Leader in the Senate and Minister without Portfolio. The cabinet was now complete, and it was a strong one. We needed more representation from Quebec and from eastern Ontario. Dick Bell was the man who could have given us what we needed in eastern Ontario, but Dief was very hostile to Dick – most unfairly so. The parliamentary secretaries were appointed on August 19. I prevailed upon Dief to appoint Dick and assign him to the Minister of Finance. He proved of invaluable assistance to me in that capacity in the next five years, as I knew he would.

It was time to confront problems which were already developing, problems with serious fiscal implications, problems of a kind which would dog us all our days in office. Merely four days after we took office we learned that the forecast of unemployment for the coming winter was alarming. Immigration was at record levels and was becoming difficult to absorb. The St. Laurent government had evidently made no preparation whatever to meet the problem of unemployment. This was a sad failure. Cabinet took the threat very seriously. I had already told Coyne that he could expect no support from the new government for his tight-money policies. He contended that there was no such policy in effect. I was asked to talk to him again and to the chartered banks, and Howard Green was to talk to the president of Central Mortgage and Housing Corporation with a view to stimulating house construction. If the new government was unprepared for the problem of unemployment at least it was willing to take swift action to reduce the volume of unemployment over the period of the next eight or nine months. A fortnight later cabinet restricted immigration. By July 23 cabinet had approved a plan to launch 15,000 additional new housing starts in the autumn to provide 45,000 on-site jobs and 65,000 off-site jobs. Financing of the program still remained to be discussed, but $150 million would be needed, and the Treasury was empty. Our predecessors had bequeathed to us an empty till. The money market was weak, and I said we must not then turn to it. Nevertheless, cabinet decided in favour of lending $150 million of government funds under the National Housing Act to home-owner applicants, builders and rental investors through approved lenders operating as agents of CMHC. I assured my colleagues that they had the legal power to lend these funds, but they had no funds. Our predecessors had walked out of a bare cupboard and handed us the keys.

The next claim on an empty Treasury was for salary increases for the civil service. The increases, costing $120 million per annum and effective from May 1, had been approved by our predecessors. They evidently were determined to take full credit in the eyes of the civil service for conferring the increase; they just overlooked the problem of providing needed funds. In order to pay the increases we would require a vote of interim supply by October 23, and that would necessitate interrupting the throne speech debate, a practice which we had criticized in the past and were anxious to avoid. It would become necessary also to provide similar increases for the armed forces and the RCMP, which would cost another $110 million per annum.

No appropriation had been provided to meet the cost of caring for Hungarian refugees beyond mid-August. The previous government had made the commitment but provided no funds to pay the cost. No Governor General's warrant had been issued since 1949, and we were the last people to wish to resort to this non-parliamentary device. Reluctantly we were compelled to issue a warrant for $2 million for this purpose. Otherwise the refugees would have gone hungry.

By July 26 the Canadian dollar was being quoted at a premium of 5 per cent, and the premium was widening. The Bank of Canada was intervening to purchase U.S. dollars to keep the premium from rising. At April 1, Canada's holdings in the Exchange Control Fund were $1,155 million of gold and $796 million of U.S. dollars. An advance in the price of gold would have been very helpful at that juncture. The South African high commissioner had visited me that day in that connection and had brought the disappointing news that the United Kingdom was not supporting an increase in the price. It seemed that South Africa and Canada would have to go it alone in the IMF.

The New Brunswick government needed funds to complete the highly desirable Beechwood Power Project. At one time the St. Laurent government had rejected the request of the province for a federal guarantee of its bonds to cover the cost of the hydro-electric plant, and we in opposition had criticized them for refusing this modest aid. In the campaign Dief had promised federal assistance. Now the provincial government had complicated the situation by changing its mind: it no longer wanted the federal guarantee. This touched off protracted discussions and delays.

On October 31 a federal loan to the province was authorized to finance the cost of building the plant, with interest at the federal borrowing rate plus the usual service charge of one-eighth of 1 per cent.

For the fiscal year ending March 31, 1958, Walter Harris had forecast a budget surplus of $152 million. The Supplementary Estimates which we inherited amounted to $95 million and the salary increases for the civil service would wipe out the Harris surplus in its entirety. We could expect that the Liberals would endeavour to deceive the public into believing that we were responsible for its disappearance. I was determined that we should report a balanced budget. I was left with no hope of a surplus unless of merely nominal proportions, but I fought to avoid a deficit even within the restricted area left for manoeuvre.

The Estimates introduced by Harris had died at the end of the session in April. Estimates must be introduced by the new government and voted by the new Parliament. After inquiry through the Treasury Board it became incontrovertibly clear that with Parliament meeting in October we simply did not have time to prepare fresh Estimates of our own. In the face of this unpleasant fact cabinet adopted my plan that we reintroduce the main Estimates in the same form as presented by our predecessors, and that individual ministers should endeavour to effect reductions wherever practicable beginning immediately, so that they would be in a position to move reductions or elimination of items when the Estimates of their departments were before the House in Committee of Supply. For the first two months of the fiscal year (April and May) both revenue and expenditure were higher than budgeted for by Harris. I reported that some substantial savings in expenditure must be made if we were to avoid a deficit, and I thought the departments of National Defence and Public Works offered the best hope of material reductions. George Pearkes for the Department of National Defence reported that we faced a need to re-equip our NATO component. The brigade needed more armour, and the air division must be re-equipped because our present-day fighter had passed the term of its usefulness. Later he proposed, in order to effect economies, that the erection of the Naval Reserve building in Charlottetown be held in abeyance, but cabinet promptly rejected that idea. I could see that my economy campaign faced a hard road.

Then there was the increase in the old-age pension. The electorate had clearly rejected Walter Harris's increase from $40 to $46 per month as inadequate. We had promised to increase his $46, but we had never officially said by how much. Of all our election promises this one called most urgently for legislative fulfilment. An increase of each $1 per month in the pension would cost the Treasury over $10 million per annum. This set cabinet to work on all kinds of permutations and combinations. The discussion continued for days.

There was financial trouble in the air. On September 19 there was a run on sterling. The Bank of England raised its bank rate from 4.5 to 7 per cent. That unsettlement was not calculated to lend stability to the Canadian market.

We were faced with the necessity of borrowing money in a market which in July was showing signs of weakness, but we had to pay our bills. The CNR had been allowed by our predecessors to borrow $360 million from the Treasury and had made no plan to recover it by means of a public borrowing. Recently an Ontario government bond issue with a very high 5 per cent coupon had encountered difficulty in its marketing. I was anxious not to go to the market with a bond offering, and I hoped that a good response to a Canada Savings Bond issue in October would tide us over. But could we hold out till then? With the approval of cabinet I exercised my right to direct crown companies to deposit their excess cash balances with the Minister of Finance. They were not deprived of their working capital, and they were paid a rate of interest one-half of 1 per cent below the average for the month of the weekly Treasury Bill tender rates. We increased our Treasury Bill offering in mid-summer, and closely examined the terms of the forthcoming CSB offering. We needed an enthusiastic response. An increase in the interest rate over the 1956 issue was unavoidable. Cabinet would not agree to making the late coupons 5 per cent to induce retention to maturity. On August 20 the terms were settled – a thirteen-year savings bond, the first two years to yield 3.25 per cent, the next eleven years 4.75 per cent, with an average rate to maturity of 4.46 per cent. We had read the market accurately. Sales totalled $1,217 million. It was a most gratifying result.

But we were not able to wait for the returns from the CSB issue. Our cash needs, together with a maturity of $700 million on October 1, forced us to go to the market that day with our first bond issue. We offered a one-year maturity with a 3 per cent coupon priced at 98.25 to yield 4.81 per cent and a two-year maturity with a 3 per cent coupon priced at 96.30 to yield 4.97 per cent. Within half an hour of opening the books the issue was oversubscribed. We proceeded to allot among subscribers. This first test on the open market was a resounding success and a strong vote of confidence in our handling.

374

On these two ventures into the market I had full opportunity to test the method followed then and for years before. The Bank of Canada accepted responsibility for advising the Minister of Finance with respect to debt management. Two of their deputy governors, Bob Beattie and Ralph McKibbin, were in charge of such matters. After conferring with the senior officers of the department as to the needs, the condition and estimated receptivity of the market, the interest return needed to attract subscriptions, the precise timing, the precise pricing and all other questions, Bob and Ralph submitted their recommendations to the minister. I grilled them thoroughly. I had to be thoroughly convinced before I was prepared to take the proposal to cabinet for approval. Once approved, Bob and Ralph handled everything along with an advertising firm selected by the government. As time passed and experience grew I developed strong confidence in the method used and also in the judgment and competence of Bob and Ralph. In later years we introduced the system now in effect of announcing the issue several days in advance, in order to alert all investment dealers, withholding the pricing terms and yield to the morning of opening the books. It is an excellent system.

The coupon rate and the pricing always gave my colleagues deep concern. They were very tight-fisted about the terms, often times failing to appreciate that we were going to the market, not making it, and that interest rates are a result – a result of the operation and counter-operation of many factors and the decisions of many people who are borrowing and lending according to their circumstances and the inducements offered to them. I had to attempt to show them that the more they had to borrow the more they were strengthening the forces of demand, while the less they needed to borrow the more they were helping to reduce interest rates. Diefenbaker was the most difficult of all. He had the western farmer's inveterate hatred of interest if he had to pay it. He thought that somehow he could curb and control interest rates without curbing expenditure and the need to borrow. The terms of bond offerings remained a source of contention all the years I served as Minister of Finance. Sometimes they created unpleasantness between Diefenbaker and myself. But his mortal fear of interest rates did not deter him from spending. He never showed that he understood the connection between the two. He never was at home with economics. It was a very weak spot in his array of talents.

We were planning an attractive package of fiscal measures and tax reductions to be introduced in December. I had already said that these would require a budget to be introduced. As I mentioned above, Diefenbaker vehemently opposed the introduction of a budget as part of the sessional program. He wished to avoid a formal budget debate, which would occupy many days, and he seemed too uncertain of our overall fiscal policies to submit them to the scrutiny of such a debate. He thereby threw away an opportunity to give a much more effective presentation of our package and laid us open to the charge that we were being unfair to Parliament and to the country in not giving a proper accounting of the nation's financial position. This decision, taken on July 8, vexed and troubled me deeply. I hoped light would prevail before December.

CHAPTER THIRTY-FOUR

Mont Tremblant and Other Conferences

If many Canadian interests were insistently seeking interviews with ministers and bringing delegations to Ottawa in the wake of the change of government it was equally true that some other countries were interested to meet and take stock of the new ministers. Above all, the hopes of the new government were set on bringing about the holding of a trade and economic conference to be attended by all Commonwealth countries. It is small wonder that I still think of the summer of 1957 as the season and heyday of international conferences, climaxed by the one we hosted at Mont Tremblant. There never was a season quite equal to that one. It convinced me that I had a special aptitude for and interest in international affairs and contacts. It headed me into a more active role in the international scene than any previous Canadian Minister of Finance had ever been called upon to play. In that role my portfolio, my long experience in trade matters in the years in opposition, my command of French, my extensive travels and my own intrinsic interest in relations between Canada and other nations all found scope and useful expression.

When cabinet on June 27 appointed me the Canadian governor to the International Monetary Fund and the International Bank at Washington I learned the annual meetings would occupy nearly a week in that city in the fourth week of September and that I would be leading a powerful delegation of officials to it. That would require extensive briefing and intensive preparation on my part. This leading event unexpectedly became the turning point in our efforts to secure the holding of the Commonwealth conference.

When John Diefenbaker left for London on June 23, he carried from cabinet a strong mandate to persuade the Conference of Prime Ministers which he was about to attend to seek a quick decision to hold a trade and economic conference. He had inade-

377

quate time to develop the theme and to create plans; that was done by me in his absence in intensive meetings attended by Gordon Churchill and the senior officials of the three interested departments of Finance, Trade and Commerce, and External Affairs. I doubt if it had seriously occurred to us Conservatives that other member countries of the Commonwealth would be less than enthusiastic for such a major meeting. Hopes become built up on such gatherings, as we have seen with "summit conferences" in more recent years; those taking part carry very heavy responsibilities and run great political risks; the objectives are not always sufficiently limited or defined; and the peril of failure is very serious and can indeed prove critical. I am sure John Diefenbaker did his eloquent best to convince his colleagues at the Prime Ministers' Conference, but the reports he sent back to us were rather gloomy. He probably thought of it as another Prime Ministers' Conference. It would no doubt have been easier to win support for a conference to be attended by ministers of finance and trade ministers. In any event the going proved unexpectedly difficult. Prime Minister Harold Macmillan gave his vitally important support to the proposal, but Australia and New Zealand surprisingly were cool to the idea, and South Africa was cold. India and Pakistan gave modest support. At this point Dief fell back on the proposal which we were developing at Ottawa in his absence.

For some years the ministers of Finance of the Commonwealth nations had met annually in conference just prior to the annual meetings of the governors of the IMF and IBRD to discuss matters of mutual interest. The meetings had always been held in London, always presided over by the Chancellor of the Exchequer, and always held prior to the Fund and Bank meetings. The ministers travelling from the Eastern countries to attend these meetings as governors found it convenient to stop at London en route to Washington; for Canada it meant going in the wrong direction. Gordon Churchill was new to Trade and Commerce, but he gave stout-hearted support to anything which would strengthen the Commonwealth, and he had unusual influence with Dief. The officials quickly convinced me that the meeting of finance ministers was the key to our hopes, and Churchill gave his support. The plan was to transfer the annual meeting of ministers of finance to Canada and to hold it after the Washington meetings. That would give us a little more time for preparation and the great advantage of having the meeting on our home grounds. Dief advanced the invitation in London and reported some headway, but was less hopeful of an early meeting of Commonwealth Prime Ministers to discuss trade and economic problems. Moreover, the indications pointed definitely toward British entry into the European Free Trade Area ("the Outer Seven"). When Dief returned to Ottawa on July 6 he gave a rather gloomy report on the project. It was left to me to follow up.

Fortunately Robert Menzies, the Prime Minister of Australia, was planning to return home via Ottawa. It was rumoured in the press that he and Dief had not gotten along too well at London, and that as an old hand at Commonwealth meetings he looked with no great favour on Dief as the new boy trying to steal the show at London. But there could be no jealousy where I was involved. Perhaps fortunately Menzies fell ill in London and was obliged to delay his visit to Canada to the end of July. Dief had to be away the first two days, so he asked me to initiate the discussions with Menzies. I gladly assumed this responsibility. It was by this time clear to me that we would make more progress if we avoided treating the conference of finance ministers in Canada as a commitment to a full-scale Commonwealth trade and economic conference and allow it to become one item on an agreed agenda. Menzies's support was vital to our hopes. I liked him at once. He was blunt and straightforward. I gave a luncheon in his honour and he came to my office for discussions. The Australian high commissioner gave a dinner. We agreed that the September meeting should be exploratory and not for the purpose of making specific arrangements for a full Commonwealth Prime Ministers' trade and economic conference in 1958. Our purpose now must be to lay foundations for the 1957 conference as a meeting of Commonwealth finance and trade ministers.

Meanwhile we were proceeding with our preparations. By July 26 we had gained Menzies's support and had the acceptance of the Chancellor of the Exchequer, Peter Thorneycroft. This was vastly encouraging. By August 16 we had received acceptances from all the Commonwealth countries, and the 1957 conference was assured. Cabinet gave approval to my message and memorandum to all Commonwealth finance ministers defining the scope, purpose and agenda. We had cleared the first hurdle. More, however, awaited us.

Menzies had intimated that one reason for his hesitancy in London to support the Canadian proposal was that he feared that the Americans might be concerned about the damage which a Commonwealth conference could do or plan to do to U.S. trading interests. I had already been at pains to assure the U.S. government through their ambassador, Livy Merchant, that the projected conference was not aimed against them. However, on

August 19 we received from the U.S. government a request for a meeting of the Canada–U.S. Joint Committee on Trade and Economic Affairs. I would have preferred one meeting at a time. Moreover, the joint committee had not met since September 1955, and preparations for a meeting were bound to be onerous. I did not need another conference at that moment. However, in the end I think the meeting proved timely. It was necessary for us under all the circumstances to welcome the American proposal warmly, and we did so. It was agreed that the meeting be held in Washington on October 8 and 9. Diefenbaker was still Secretary of State for External Affairs, but he could not attend the meeting. The ministers selected to represent Canada were Finance, Trade and Commerce, and Agriculture. The leadership of the Canadian delegation fell to me, as well as the drive to prepare for what was bound to be a highly important meeting with representatives of our closest neighbour.

In this developing strait-jacket I was greatly aided by two decisions of cabinet. The first was that Parliament should meet on October 14. That gave us opportunity to complete the full round of conferences before the opening and before House duties would commence. The other decision was of less immediate bearing, but it had a place. On August 20 cabinet decided not to apply for membership in the Organization of American States (OAS), but to continue to be represented at its meetings by an observer. Thus I was relieved of what would have been a burden of preparing instructions for a Canadian delegation and participating in extensive preparations for the deliberations of yet another important international gathering. Ahead of us lay NATO meetings in Paris in December, and the need to call a federal-provincial conference. My officials were spread thin in all the preparatory tasks, and I had my hands full. To add to my labours the important cabinet Defence Committee, consisting of the Prime Minister and the ministers of National Defence, Finance, and Defence Production, was already examining problems which would soon enough require serious decisions, and John Foster Dulles, the U.S. Secretary of State, was planning a visit to Ottawa on July 27 and 28 for some very important discussions.

It was my first meeting with John Foster Dulles. The dominating urge of this far-sighted American was to check communism and contain the Russian expansionist drive throughout the world. The Western world owes him a very large debt. The visit was over a weekend. At the Sunday meeting the Prime Minister, Fulton and I met with Dulles and Livy Merchant to discuss the vital question of air and ground inspection on both sides of the

Iron Curtain. We were agreed that inspection was essential if there were to be more than a pretence of disarmament or reduction of nuclear weapons. Russian inspection in the West could prove irksome, but it was of vital importance that the West should have the right of inspection behind the Iron Curtain. Dulles was enormously well informed, firm, realistic, down-to-earth and straightforward. There was no trace of condescension or sense of superiority in his manner or words. I quickly came to understand how he exercised the principal influence within the Eisenhower administration. He was strong and direct without dominating.

By September 5 agreement had been reached to hold a federal-provincial conference on November 25 and 26. Preparation was launched at once. It was clear from the outset that the provincial governments were hungry for fiscal benefits and that their interest and purpose were to discuss a better financial deal for them. The burden of carrying the conference was bound to be borne by the Prime Minister and the Minister of Finance, and the burden of preparation would be borne by the latter. Fortunately, in Ron Burns I had a very able director of the division of federal-provincial relations in my department. With other senior officers of the department participating the preparation was carried out very ably and very thoroughly.

Preparations for the meeting of Commonwealth finance ministers claimed a high priority throughout the balance of the summer. The inclusion of trade ministers was bound to assist our purpose. Gorden Churchill took a full part in the meetings in preparation. The officials were a formidable company. From the Department of Finance we had Ken Taylor, Wynne Plumptre and Simon Reisman, from Trade and Commerce, Mitchell Sharp and Claud Isbister, and from the Bank of Canada, Louis Rasminsky. Diefenbaker was still Secretary of State for External Affairs, but did not attend our meetings. I kept him informed of our progress. The officials of his department were very helpful. Jules Leger and Klaus Goldschlag attended. We received invaluable assistance from Norman Robertson, who, after years of service as Canadian high commissioner to the United Kingdom, had recently taken up his post as Canadian ambassador to Washington and attended our meetings. His experience was profoundly helpful to us. Bob Bryce, secretary of the cabinet, was a tower of strength to us. It was necessary to hold the meetings in the evenings. It was simply impossible to draw so many senior men away from their other pressing duties and interruptions during the daytime, so we gathered in the Privy Council chamber around the big oval table in the evenings till after 11 o'clock. The senior civil servants were at first disposed to speak with some caution and circumspection, but their ideas were very instructive. I felt the challenge of a major responsibility. When Sidney Smith became Secretary of State for External Affairs in September the preparations and arrangements were already advanced. This being primarily a conference of finance ministers, Dief confirmed that I would lead the Canadian delegation and preside at the conference.

After exploring all other possibilities we chose Mont Tremblant as the location for the conference, which has naturally become known to history as the "Mont Tremblant Conference." It was an ideal choice. Situated in the Laurentians within driving distance of Montreal and Ottawa, the Mont Tremblant Lodge offered comfortable accommodation for delegates in private lodges, excellent central facilities with dining-room and suitable meeting rooms in the Chalet des Voyageurs, an atmosphere conducive to relaxation, and privacy from all the world. No one who was not an accredited delegate or a member of the hotel staff would be permitted within half a mile of the secluded spot. The timing also was to prove ideal. The forests nearby would be a blaze of autumn colour. The selection of the site made it possible for the detailed planning to go forward smoothly. The World Bank and IMF meetings were due to end at noon on Friday, September 27. We arranged to have a government plane ready to bring all delegates from Washington that afternoon to Montreal and to drive them from there to Mont Tremblant, where we would spend the next four days in earnest consultation. Cabinet endorsed our position papers, our plans and program. And then a cloud crossed our bright and promising horizon.

At the airport on his return from London John Diefenbaker, in urging the calling of a Commonwealth trade and economic conference, had said by way of example that if 15 per cent of Canada's purchases from the United States could be transferred to the United Kingdom we would have gone a long way to strengthening Canada's trading position. Some sections of the press promptly interpreted this as a declared policy of effecting a transfer of 15 per cent of Canada's imports from the United States to Britain. Diefenbaker always denied to me that he had said or meant this. He was stating an objective rather than a policy, and illustrating it with an example, but it was an unfortunate and ill-considered remark and it haunted us for years. It was difficult, however, for him to take up the subject negatively in public or appear to retreat from a position at the moment he was pressing for a Commonwealth conference on the subject. It was embarrassing enough to cope with misinterpretation in Canada, but much greater embarrassment rose from another source. On September 3 Sir Saville (Joe) Garner, the British high commissioner, requested a meeting for Derick Heathcote-Amory, Minister of Agriculture, and Sir Frank Lee with Dief and me "to give some advance indication of the general lines of the U.K. government's thinking about certain ways in which trade between Canada and the U.K. could be expanded." This was the only warning we were given of what soon proved to be a bomb-shell. To us it appeared that our friends were coming for talks preliminary to the Mont Tremblant Conference, and we welcomed the opportunity. Derick, of course, was my esteemed personal friend, and Sir Frank Lee was already known to me. He was Joint Permanent Secretary to the Treasury. Until his retirement from the public service on his appointment as Master of Corpus Christi College, Oxford, in 1962, he played a leading role on behalf of the British government in all trade negotiations, including later those respecting British entry into the European Common Market, and he and I became warm friends.

The meeting on September 9 proceeded pleasantly. We talked in Dief's office about all the plans for the Mont Tremblant Conference and explored the agenda. We gave a luncheon for our visitors at the Rideau Club. At its conclusion I excused myself to attend another meeting. Derick followed me out and as we stood said there was one thing he wished to lay before me personally. The British government had taken note of the desire expressed by Diefenbaker to transfer part of Canada's trade with other countries to the United Kingdom, welcomed the proposal and had authorized him to propose that Canada and the United Kingdom enter a free trade area; Britain would reduce as soon as possible its present quotas on Canadian products and manufactured goods, and in exchange British manufacturers would have free entry into the Canadian market.

This was an astonishing proposal submitted under most unusual circumstances. I called Dief and went into conference with our officials to examine the British proposal carefully. Before his return to London I informed Derick that it was too radical and one-sided to be acceptable. It was obvious that the benefits to Britain would greatly outweigh the benefits to Canada. The proposal also would be complicated by GATT. I reported fully and carefully to my cabinet colleagues and expressed the hope that our reply would not affect the attitude of the British government toward the Mont Tremblant Conference, for we needed their support. Even before the free trade area was proposed the British had asked for bilateral talks with Canada during the conference. In reply I had suggested that we defer such talks until after the conference to avoid giving other Commonwealth countries any impression that special arrangements were being entered into between the United Kingdom and Canada, lest such an impression impair the possibility of holding the larger Commonwealth conference which we sought. It wasn't long before news of the British proposal of the free trade area hit the headlines. It did not come from Canadian sources. Other officials were angry and candid in expressing their opinion that the manner in which the British offer was submitted was outrageous and that the British government sources had deliberately leaked to the press what should at that early stage have been treated in strictest confidence. The British had been especially shrewd, and it began to appear that hard bargaining with them could be expected at both Mont Tremblant and Ottawa.

If the British had hoped to embarrass us with an offer known to be unacceptable, they succeeded. Perhaps they were testing out Dief's 15 per cent declaration to see how far the Canadian government really meant to go. Perhaps they were seeking to impress the British voter. In any event, it jarred Dief and me and, I think, our colleagues. Dief undoubtedly was sorely embarrassed by the attempt by the Liberal press to make political capital out of his injudicious comment. If he was dismayed by this onslaught he kept quiet, but I was in charge of the trade negotiations and as such it would not be possible for me to remain silent and ignore the issue which was being openly exploited by a hostile press. Perhaps the British had outsmarted us, but we still needed their support for our declared goal of a Commonwealth trade and economic conference. We would need to treat the whole issue with the utmost restraint and caution lest we create new embarrassments for ourselves. I realized that I would be fortunate to emerge unscathed.

Embarrassment from another source developed the week before the Washington meetings. I had been bombarded with representations concerning the plight of the Canadian textile industry. It was a decentralized sector of the national economy, and numerous communities in eastern Canada relied on textile mills for local employment. Most imported woollen and worsted fabrics came from the United Kingdom, while cottons came largely from the United States. Any action we took with respect to woollens would hurt the British at a time when they could ill afford to lose any part of their Canadian market. Action was needed in Canada to prevent the closing of further textile mills in Canada; some one hundred thousand jobs were involved. In the face of this dilemma I recommended a reference of certain items related to textiles and fluorspar to the Tariff Board for a report and recommendations, and cabinet approved. We suspected that the British were well aware that some such action was bound to come. In any event, for our part it seemed better to announce it before the Mont Tremblant Conference than to hold back the formal reference to the Tariff Board until after the conference and be accused at that point of bad faith. However, we had not heard the last of this troublesome headache.

The meetings in Washington proceeded from September 23 to 27. I led a strong Canadian delegation, including James Coyne, Louis Rasminsky, Wynne Plumptre and others. I soon learned that the annual meetings of the International Bank and the International Monetary Fund draw most of the ministers of finance and governors of central banks in the free world. Together they formed a world parliament of finance. For me it was a great opportunity to meet persons in positions of similar responsibility in many other countries. In addition, the chairmen of nearly all the Canadian commercial banks attended, as did the heads of many large Canadian life insurance companies and other financial institutions. The Canadian ambassador held a reception in my honour to which he invited all the visiting Canadian financiers. I conferred with Eugene Black, head of the International Bank, Per Jacobssen, Swedish head of the IMF, Peter Thorneycroft, Chancellor of the Exchequer, Bob Anderson, U.S. Secretary of the Treasury, and many others. Seating in the plenary meetings was arranged alphabetically, so I found myself seated beside the delegate from Cuba. I was warned that he distributed boxes of the most beautiful cigars. His first question to me was, "Do you smoke?" I could not in all honesty say yes, so I received no cigars. Several years later the triumph of the Castro revolution in Cuba put an end to the cigars.

I spoke at the meetings of both institutions. My speeches, to which Lou Rasminsky contributed both ideas and expression, were brief. I declared the policy of the new Canadian government to support both institutions. I made a point of meeting all the Commonwealth finance ministers to whom I was to be host at Mont Tremblant and assuring them of a very warm welcome. Our wives accompanied us to Washington and enjoyed the delightful social program which had been arranged. Coyne was accompanied by his beautiful bride. One evening after we had all attended a delightful dinner party at the Canadian embassy I proposed a business meeting of the men at our hotel. It was evident that Coyne wanted no such meeting at that late hour. He affected a yawn, so I called off the meeting. I could not fail to be impressed by the high regard expressed on every hand for Lou Rasminsky. He was widely known and highly respected among the other delegations. This added to my own confidence in this brilliant Canadian authority on international finance.

On Friday afternoon our flight took off for Montreal with nearly one hundred of the leading finance and trade brains of the Commonwealth. I knew that everything must run smoothly from the outset. Canadian efficiency, as well as Canadian hospitality, was being tested. I was well aware of how much depended on me as the principal host, and did everything I could think of to be a good host. Away from the public all could begin to relax at once. On arrival at Mont Tremblant, all were ushered to their respective lodges, had time to settle, then dine informally. Then they had the balance of the evening off to rest and prepare. I spent most of the dinner period moving from table to table making certain that all our guests were being made happy. I was beginning to sense a rising response to our friendly welcome and outgoing hospitality.

Such a conference might expect under any circumstances to be useful. The finance ministers always found their annual meetings valuable occasions for exchange of ideas and experience, for discussion of those subjects which haunt finance ministers, such as budgets, prosperity, employment, interest rates, the flow of capital, currency, borrowing, taxation, and the like, and for invaluable personal contact. The importance of this last factor in international meetings must never be underestimated. This particular conference would accomplish these goals, but it had to be different. It had to impress all the delegates and all the countries represented.

There was, of course, other business to be done, but by far the most important objective for the Canadian government was to secure agreement to hold a Commonwealth trade and economic conference later at a generally convenient time, presumably in 1958. We could not too openly or persistently disclose or declare this overriding purpose, but we must pursue it by soft sell methods. By and large the Canadian press failed to grasp our purpose clearly. Those who were hostile to us were much more interested in the British free trade area proposal and entertained the idea that that was or should be the principal topic on the agenda, little realizing that it was one that I was determined to keep off the Mont Tremblant agenda.

I held a press conference in my office about ten days ahead of Mont Tremblant. It was my first official and general meeting with the press. Its purpose was to acquaint the press gallery with all the arrangements and outline the program. In my caution I decided to make it all off the record. The journalists were thus informed and prepared for what was to come, but they were precluded from writing stories for their papers. Their job is to write stories of interest to the public and to the satisfaction of their news editors. I think I made a mistake in so limiting the use of their notes on my remarks. They would have been much better pleased to be using them in writing stories.

To protect the delegations and our meetings from the intrusions of the press we isolated the conference. This was appreciated by the delegates, but not by the press. They were accommodated in another hotel half a mile away, and the precincts of the Mont Tremblant Lodge were beyond limits to them except at certain stipulated hours. The press writers were consequently idle much of the time. This was unfortunate, and I paid a grievous price for this mistake.

The Commonwealth was fully represented. Nine countries and two new federations sent delegations. The personnel were most impressive. Australia sent Sir Arthur Fadden, Minister of Finance; Ceylon, Stanley de Zoysa, the Minister of Finance; the Federation of Malaya, Sir Henry Lee, the Minister of Finance; the Federation of Rhodesia and Nyasaland my old friend from the 1952 Commonwealth parliamentary conference in Canada, Donald Macintyre, Minister of Finance; Ghana, K.A. Gbedemah, Minister of Finance; India, T.T. Krishnamachari, Minister of Finance; New Zealand, T.L. Macdonald, Minister of External Affairs; Pakistan, Amjad Ali, Minister of Finance, and the high commissioner; South Africa, J.F. Naudé, Minister of Finance, whom I had met at the Commonwealth Parliamentary Conference at Nairobi in 1954, and the high commissioner. The British government sent a most impressive delegation in both quality and numbers. This alone gave us great encouragement as indicating the importance they attached to the conference. They sent no fewer than three ministers, all holding senior portfolios: Peter Thorneycroft, Chancellor of the Exchequer, Sir David Eccles, President of the Board of Trade, and Reginald Maudling, Paymaster General. They were supported by four top British civil servants, Sir Roger Makins, Sir Frank Lee, Sir Leslie Rowan, Sir Henry Lintott, and the high commissioner, Sir Saville Garner. For Canada the Minister of Finance and the Minister of Trade and Commerce were powerfully supported by twelve officials: Ken Taylor, Wynne Plumptre, Simon Reisman, Lou Couillard, Maurice Schwarzman from the Department of Finance, Bob Bryce and Ross Martin from the Privy Council Office, Lou Rasminsky from the Bank of Canada, Mitchell Sharp and Claud Isbister from Trade and Commerce, Klaus Goldschlag from External Affairs, and my executive assistant, Bill Allan.

We gathered Saturday morning at 10 o'clock in the Chalet des Voyageurs. Ministers sat at a hollow oblong table with their staffs behind them. I addressed words of welcome to all the delegates, spoke of the importance attached to the Commonwealth by the Canadian government, expressed the hope and belief that more could be done to expand trade within the Commonwealth and the economic interests of member nations, thereby contributing to the causes of freedom, peace and prosperity in the world. Thereupon, on motion of the Chancellor I was elected chairman of the conference. By agreement the remainder of the meeting was closed to the press.

The morning was devoted to discussion of exchange problems and developments within the sterling area, with the Chancellor leading. Canada, as the only country represented outside the sterling area, took no part. The afternoon subject was the European Common Market (ECM) and the European Free Trade Area (EFTA), led by Reginald Maudling, whose function as Paymaster General and thus deputy to the Chancellor was to conduct negotiations for his government for an industrial free trade area. The discussion revealed concern over the trend of the negotiations and the fear that the ECM countries might not follow outward-looking policies. Gordon Churchill spoke for Canada, stressing our concern for our markets for wheat. The only reference to the British proposal for a free trade area with Canada came from the Chancellor who briefly described it as one of various means of achieving an increase in British sales to Canada. He admitted the suggestion presented difficulties on the Canadian side.

The day had gone well, but it had not ended. At 6 p.m. I gave a reception to which all representatives of the press were invited. This would give them an opportunity to meet the ministers and other delegates. They all came. Drinks were free and in some cases became rather frequent. A request had been made for a press conference with Peter Thorneycroft and myself, and we had agreed. It was to take place at the press hotel at 8 p.m. The reception continued right up till then. Peter and I deferred dinner and dashed to the press hotel.

What awaited us there shocked me. I do not expect others

necessarily to share my strictly abstemious habits, but I do expect leading Canadian journalists to conduct themselves with some measure of propriety when meeting the Chancellor of the Exchequer. Peter and I were ushered into a room in which were gathered about thirty newsmen, mostly from the press gallery at Ottawa. It was at once obvious that a deplorably large number of them had been drinking to excess, and not slightly, either. I made an opening statement and introduced the Chancellor. He also made a statement, followed by questions to us both. These quickly showed only a mild interest in the Mont Tremblant Conference, but an active interest in the British proposal of a free trade area. The questions became more and more rude. Peter explained the proposal at some length, and I avoided condemning it, although saying it presented formidable difficulties. I indicated it was being studied and it was not on the agenda of the conference. Some of the journalists were dozing, others loudly raising their voices. I regret to say that several friends of mine were among the most uncontrolled. Peter and I finally withdrew. I apologized to him for the outrageous way he had been treated. "My word!" he replied, "I must say they are persistent."

Press relations are very important to any minister. I learned at Mont Tremblant that one should never stage a two-hour reception for the press with free drinks before a press conference, and the press should not be left idle for a weekend away from home with nothing to do. As Peter and I returned to the Lodge I shuddered to think what stories would adorn Canada's newspapers on Monday morning. I realized that the Canadian public would draw its impressions of the conference, not from what had actually happened or what was actually said, but from the stories which some quite disabled journalists would send out. It all seemed so grievously unfair.

The weather was gorgeous. Sunday the sun shone gloriously out of a clear sky, and the riotous autumn colours of the woods surrounding Mont Tremblant, particularly the maples, were dazzling. That morning Peter Thorneycroft and I attended public worship at a little United Church not far away. He and I were developing a real sense of companionship. We had arranged for a small plane to take the delegates in parties of twos and threes aloft to behold the beauties of the woods and hills. I went up with Mr. Krishnamachari, the Indian Minister of Finance. It was a day of rest and relaxation for most delegates. I telephoned a report to the Prime Minister in Ottawa. He was appalled at the news of the press conference.

The item on the agenda Monday was our precious Canadian

proposal. The speech which I made to the conference that morning was undoubtedly one of the most important in its content and consequences I ever delivered. I was careful not to make merely a plea for the holding of a Commonwealth trade and economic conference. That would have been too obvious and limited. I advanced rather a case for expanding Commonwealth trade and promoting economic relations among Commonwealth countries. The proposed conference thus became a means, not an end. I put forward a long list of subjects which required the concerted, prepared examination which only a plenary conference could impart. They included improved methods of consultation, better communications, direct aid, technical assistance, investment, gold, uranium, ocean freight rates, tariffs, quotas and import restrictions, marketing of wheat and other agricultural products, tourism, procurement and government purchasing, our interest in ECM and EFTA, and a collective approach to freer trade and payments. In conclusion I invited all delegations to share Canada's belief in the need for a comprehensive effort by the Commonwealth, and said Canada would be honoured to be host to such a conference in 1958. I stressed the need for consummate preparation and urged meetings of officials for the purpose.

Sir David Eccles for the United Kingdom welcomed "the broad survey" which I had put forward "with such deep sincerity." The leaders of all delegations spoke in similar supportive vein. The comprehensiveness of my approach won special commendation from India, Rhodesia, Malaya and the support of South Africa. Peter Thorneycroft concluded the discussion with a very practical endorsement. He and I agreed that London would be the best place for the officials to meet, but not for the Commonwealth conference. Canada's hospitality and the efficiency of our organization for Mont Tremblant had won very strong support for holding the Commonwealth conference in Canada. When I telephoned the good news to Dief he was beside himself with joy.

We concluded the conference the next morning by adopting a communiqué drafted by a group of officials headed by Sir Frank Lee. We had won unanimous support of all delegations for holding a Commonwealth conference in 1958, and had taken practical steps toward it by agreeing that a committee of officials should meet in London early in 1958 to begin the work of preparation. In the parting addresses I was overwhelmed with compliments on the manner in which I had conducted the conference. Artie Fadden said it had been easily the happiest and the most successful and most fraternal conference he had ever attended in his long career. Stanley de Zoysa of Ceylon said I had laid the foundations for closer association within the Commonwealth. Every delegation head spoke in similar congratulatory terms. It was one of the great days of my life. In closing the conference I reminded delegates that we were meeting on the soil of Quebec, and I brought the conference to a close with a few remarks in French. At the conclusion a man rushed over to me to offer his congratulations with extraordinary warmth. He added, "I didn't think you could do it." His name was Mitchell Sharp. The generous commendations I heard that day did not find their way into the newspapers, but they were a tonic to me.

Dief reported to our colleagues that day that I had succeeded in obtaining unanimous agreement for holding the conference next year without making any bargains with the British or others to gain their support. He considered that I had staged "a splendid performance." On my return he kindly paid tribute to what he called my "able and persuasive presentation" which had convinced the doubters and won unanimous support.

The Canadian public was never given the truth about the Mont Tremblant Conference by the press. All the attention of the press was concentrated on the British free trade area proposal as though that were the main theme and purpose of the conference. I was pictured as having fumbled this principal business. The Liberals took great comfort from this gross distortion and pursued me with it for years. The fact is that the conference was called for a very different purpose, namely, to promote the Canadian proposal for a Commonwealth trade and economic conference, and that the British free trade area scheme was irrelevant and for that and other good reasons was firmly excluded from the deliberations.

The British ministers and their party returned to Ottawa to continue with us the discussions of their proposal for the free trade area. On October 4 we issued a lengthy statement on our talks. Both sides agreed that the expansion of Anglo-Canadian trade was a primary object of policy of both governments. The communiqué added this significant comment:

> Among proposals discussed with this aim in view was the proposal of the United Kingdom Ministers for a free trade area with Canada. It was emphasized by the United Kingdom Ministers that this proposal involved not only the progressive removal of tariffs, but also a speedier reduction in the quantitative restrictions now applied by the United Kingdom against imports from Canada. It was also emphasized by the United Kingdom Ministers that their proposal was a long-term one and not designed to come into full effect

save over a period of twelve to fifteen years. The United Kingdom Ministers recognized that this proposal raised serious and complex problems and difficulties. In view of the long-term nature of the proposal the United Kingdom Ministers did not ask the Canadian Ministers for an expression of their views on the proposal. The Ministers for both countries therefore addressed themselves to the immediate problem of expanding the beneficial two-way flow of trade between Canada and the United Kingdom.

Thus the political barb was removed from a proposal which in the bare terms in which it was first couched was impracticable, unacceptable and embarrassing to the Canadian government. We committed ourselves, on the other hand, to three courses of action which we hoped would be productive of a material increase in Canadian purchases of British goods: a review of government purchasing, including that of crown corporations; an increase in the customs duty exemption of tourist purchases by Canadians in the United Kingdom; and a visit by a high-level trade delegation from Canada to Britain. These undertakings were all carried out in due course.

The communiqué reaffirmed the support of both governments for the decision taken at Mont Tremblant and their anticipation of fruitful benefits for all Commonwealth countries from the holding in 1958 of a "Commonwealth Trade and Economic Conference." It was the first time that expression had been spelled out in capitals. It was now the proper name of an assured event. Mont Tremblant had accomplished its high purpose. It had been an unqualified success.

The story of the role played in my life and political career by the Mont Tremblant Conference and its successor the Commonwealth Trade and Economic Conference 1958 cannot be fully told without mention of the personal, high-level friendships forged at Tremblant. The arrangements had been made to give ample opportunity for maximum personal contact, removed from the public gaze and press intrusion. This had produced healthy results which were to continue long after the delegates had left the delightful setting of Mont Tremblant. I was privileged to enjoy the friendships of and personal contacts with Peter Thorneycroft, David Eccles, Reggie Maudling and the other ministers. Amjad Ali of Pakistan and Stanley de Zoysa of Ceylon became particularly warm friends of mine. Artie Fadden and I found each other especially congenial company. He and I had occasion to sign an agreement between Australia and Canada, so we arranged a televised little ceremony, in the course of which each of us made a few remarks. Artie chose to pay me a glowing tribute. At its conclusion the TV cameraman confessed he had run out of film and missed all of Artie's speech. Artie was understandably annoyed and disgusted, and addressed a few remarks in plain Australian dialect to the blushing cameraman.

Trade delegations usually have for their purpose the selling of their country's products. Our trade mission to the United Kingdom in the autumn of 1957 was for a very different purpose, to stimulate purchases from British sources of goods then being imported from non-Commonwealth countries. It was a large delegation, headed by our Minister of Trade and Commerce, Gordon Churchill, and including leading representatives of business, industry, labour, agriculture and other primary production from all parts of Canada. It is hard to isolate and reckon the extent of purchases of British goods attributable to our sending this trade mission, but they must have totalled a considerable figure. Cooperation on both sides was complete, and the tour engendered much goodwill and the interest of the business communities of both countries.

The first meeting of the Joint Canada–U.S. Continuing Committee on Trade and Economic Affairs in two years was held in Washington on October 8 and 9. Of a number of meetings of the committee which I was destined to attend it no doubt proved to be the least productive from the Canadian point of view. The advance preparation was carefully carried out by the Ministers of Finance, Trade and Commerce, Agriculture and their officials and the officials of External Affairs. When Sidney Smith became Secretary of State for External Affairs in mid-September some eager beaver in the press and information section of his department rushed out a release announcing that the Secretary of State for External Affairs would lead a delegation of ministers to Washington for the meeting. I drew this to Dief's attention and requested clarification. He lost no time in having cabinet designate me formally as the chairman of the Canadian delegation.

The meetings were held in the State Department at Washington in an atmosphere that was much too businesslike. The four ministers from the two countries confronted each other on either side of a table. The blunt John Foster Dulles presided and kept his three colleagues under a tight leash. It was the first time most of the eight ministers had met each other. In fact, probably Dulles and Bob Anderson and I were the only ones who had met before. Fortunately, long strides were made toward improving the atmosphere and the conditions of later meetings of this important committee.

Nevertheless, the meetings served a useful purpose. All present became better acquainted, and the exchange of views and information could not fail to be beneficial. I reviewed the Canadian trade scene, stressing our large import surplus in Canada–U.S. commodity trade. Dulles commented: "We need that surplus in order to provide aid to other countries." I also gave a report on the Mont Tremblant Conference and the plans for the Commonwealth Trade and Economic Conference the following year. Doug Harkness registered Canada's strong complaint over the American surplus disposal program and the disorder it was causing in our traditional overseas markets. The U.S. ministers assured us that the program would not be so harmful to us that year as in the past, but we Canadians said we were not satisfied with this very limited assurance and would continue to watch the operation of the program very carefully. After one of our meetings one of the U.S. ministers, the Secretary of Commerce, Mr. Weeks, indiscreetly announced to the press, "We fixed 'em." We did not become aware of this diplomatic faux pas until our return to Canada. At once it caused resentment and was given wide publicity by the press. When Dief met with Eisenhower in Washington on October 18 the President apologized for the offensive remark, and assured Dief that he was most anxious to remove all causes of division between Canada and the United States. Mr. Weeks himself issued a full and disarming statement, which I read to the House on October 23, but the damage had been done.

Numerous articles appeared in Canadian newspapers expressing scepticism as to the value of the committee and questioning the usefulness of the conference. But the best meetings of the committee lay ahead.

Parliament was called to meet the next week. After all the meetings of that summer and the preparations for them and others to follow I was not sorry to put away my travelling bags for a while and to give thought to legislative duty and the visit of the Queen.

CHAPTER THIRTY-FIVE

The Queen and Parliament

On July 9, 1957, a proclamation was issued summoning Parliament to meet on Monday, October 14. That meant a long wait for eager MPs. In my opinion it proved a blessing that we could not begin in September as Dief had hoped, for we needed the extra time for preparation of important legislative measures which we purposed introducing. In my case, carrying as I was the burden of numerous important international conferences, the session opened quite early enough.

The visit of the Queen and Prince Philip for the opening of Parliament quickly put an end to any criticism over the delay. Never before had a session of the Canadian Parliament been opened by a reigning monarch. The preparations were bound to be much more elaborate and detailed than usual.

The preparation of the legislative program fell to a committee, of which Davie Fulton as Minister of Justice was chairman and I vice-chairman. Dief originally planned a short session confined to the autumn, then a new session commencing in January 1958. Therefore the legislative program should not be lengthy. How he ever expected a new Parliament not meeting till October 14 to pass any serious volume of legislation before Christmas I never did understand. As a new government our legislative program was bursting at the seams. The measures we had promised were bound to engage Parliament for months. To call a second session in January would also have meant two speeches from the throne and two debates thereon within the space of three months. The ability of Parliament to pass legislation would be reduced accordingly. In the new Parliament many new MPs would naturally be anxious to make speeches. And since we were a minority government, liable to be defeated at any moment, it was essential that we place our legislative wares on display in a convincing profusion. I therefore put little stock in Dief's plan of a short fall session and a short legislative program. Circumstances soon settled any such question: the session would continue into 1958. Only one thing could stop it.

The choice of Speaker of the House was not easy. Stanley Knowles of the CCF was a recognized authority on the rules of the House, and as long as he remained a private member he was bound to be a thorn in the side of any government. The idea quickly won favour: why not elect Stanley as Speaker? I liked the idea. He would be honest, fair, impartial and correct. The choice would demonstrate our respect for Parliament and our sincerity in seeking to restore the integrity of the Speaker's office. So Dief offered the Speakership to Stanley, who after consulting Coldwell, his party leader, as I think he was bound to do, declined the post. I think he made a mistake in so doing. Dief became very annoyed with Stanley over it all, blaming him for letting the cat out of the bag, and for a long time scarcely spoke to him. Before the end of August we knew Stanley had rejected the offer, preferring the role of the thorn in the side of the government. The choice then was bound to fall to a Conservative. The man with by far the highest qualifications for the post was undoubtedly Roly Michener. Roly, however, had incurred Dief's strong displeasure by supporting me for the party leadership in 1956. That mortal sin could never be forgiven. Only very slowly and reluctantly did Dief come around to accepting Roly. The final decision was not taken until close to the opening of Parliament. Dief was never happy afterwards with the choice and always blamed me for it. In the eyes of others Roly was an excellent choice. He was erudite, urbane and scrupulously fair. He understood Parliament, and he had a good knowledge of French. It was necessary to choose a French Canadian for the post of Deputy Speaker. We had so few to choose from, and we needed them in debate. The choice fell to Henri Courtemanche.

The Conservative members were called to meet in caucus at Ottawa September 9 and 10. The meeting allowed the new members to become acquainted with their colleagues and vice versa, and also with their duties. It helped also to reduce the long period of waiting for Parliament to meet. Howard Green was named government House Leader and also chairman of caucus. He filled both roles admirably. Some thought that caucus should be free to choose its own chairman and that he ought to be a private member. The time for such a method of choice had not yet come. Howard amply held the confidence of caucus.

A few days before the opening of Parliament Dief showed me his seating arrangement for ministers in the House. I felt greatly honoured when he told me that I was to be his desk-mate. Howard Green as House Leader would sit on his left, and Gordon Churchill would be on my right. It is a great advantage to share a desk with the Prime Minister. Apart from the prestige it carried it enabled us to discuss many subjects in confidence and to exchange a multitude of comments. This unique privilege continued for six years.

A question was bound to arise over party representation on the committees of the House. If representation was to be proportional we would be in a minority position on every committee. If three opposition groups combined forces at any time they could easily defeat us in committee. That would not be equivalent constitutionally to defeating the government in the House, but it could be politically embarrassing and might also thwart important elements of our legislative program. Should we on the other hand take the position that as a government, and therefore enjoying the confidence of the House until defeated, we were entitled to a majority of the places on each committee? We knew this was likely to be sternly resisted by the opposition. Was it an issue on which we would wish to risk defeat in the House? We decided it was not. We accepted the principle of proportional representation on all committees, and therefore assumed all the risks of being in a minority position in them. This had one clear implication: Conservative members appointed to committees must be prepared to be punctual, constant and regular in their attendance at meetings. This would not preclude, but it would reduce, the danger of defeat.

Such questions inevitably turned our thoughts to the subject of strategy in the House. Were we seeking defeat or survival in the House? That was one of the easiest questions to answer. Survival is the first law of any politician's nature: we very seriously wished to survive. We were far from ready to court defeat, either openly or by stratagem. If then we aimed to survive how were we to shape our course to avoid defeat? We never deviated from our purpose to keep faith strictly with the electorate and to submit our legislative program to Parliament. We would not be unnecessarily provocative, but we would not retreat in face of the foe. If faced with defeat we would do our best to select the issue upon which to incur our defeat and draw utmost benefit from it in the inevitable ensuing general election. Meanwhile a state of readiness throughout caucus and the party was enjoined. The party had no war-chest, and it would take time to build financial resources to meet the demands of another general election coming so soon after the last. Time appeared to be on our side, but in the uncertain circumstances we must be wise as serpents and harmless as doves. The manner in which the government conducted itself would determine the outcome in almost any circumstances, or so we thought. The fact is that in the end the issue as to our survival depended less on us than on the opposition.

The session had not progressed far before it became patently clear that the last thing the opposition wanted at that time was another general election. As a government we could probably survive any division with the support of even one of the three opposition groups in the House. It was most unlikely, therefore, that they would unite on any vote against the government. They would, of course, bluster and pretend that they wished to administer to us the worst beating that any government ever suffered, but they would stop short of making good their professed intention when the division bells rang. Their bark would be worse than their bite. Solon Low, leader of the Social Credit party, one day in conversation strangely chose to give me reasons why an election would be unthinkable. I told him that must depend upon the will of the House. He satisfied me only that he feared a general election, and well he might. With such encouragement the government became more confident and ready to face risks. "The Lord hath delivered them into our hands," said Cromwell as the Scots moved down from the hills at Preston. Their own internal problems, fears and mistakes were delivering the three opposition groups into our hands. I was not the only minister to observe this and to be emboldened by it to do battle with the Liberals.

Into this developing scene stepped Her Majesty Queen Elizabeth II, accompanied by His Royal Highness Prince Philip. Her presence at the opening of Parliament imparted an air of romance, joy and excitement to the parliamentary scene such as it had never experienced before. From every point of view the visit was an historic event.

After the welcoming ceremonies at Uplands Airport on October 12, the royal party drove to Government House, to the joyous accompaniment of church bells and the peeling of the Carillon in the Peace Tower.

Sunday, October 13, was a clear, sunny, warm day. Her Majesty and His Royal Highness laid a wreath at the War Memorial on Sussex Drive in a brief and solemn ceremony, attended by groups of veterans and disabled veterans. The royal couple then proceeded to Christ Church Cathedral for divine service, at which Prince Philip read the second lesson. At 9 p.m. the Queen broadcast a message by television to the children of Canada. It was actually the Queen's first television broadcast, and it came through beautifully.

Monday, October 14, began with a cabinet meeting at 10 a.m. in the dining-room of Government House. It is the only time in my experience when a cabinet meeting was ever held at Government House in Ottawa. But of much greater historic importance was the fact that it was attended by the Queen. Her father, King George VI, had attended a meeting of the Canadian cabinet in Ottawa in 1939 during the course of the royal visit of that spring. Ministers were attired in morning dress for this great occasion. Her Majesty sat at the head of the long table with Mr. Diefenbaker on her right and I next to him. It had been arranged that after formal presentation of the ministers one item of business would be transacted. I was given the unique honour of presenting it to Her Majesty. It involved only giving approval to some new regulations relating to old-age pensions. In addressing the Queen, I explained briefly the statutory authority for the regulations and the effect they would have when brought into force. I then said that I had the honour on behalf of cabinet to advise that they be approved. She listened very attentively to the explanation. What she was about to do might be a unique historic act; she did not, however, treat it as a mere formality, but a serious exercise of royal power on the advice of her constitutional advisers, and she applied her mind and attention to every word. The Prime Minister then requested her to sign the order-in-council. In a gentle voice she replied, "I usually just initial these orders-in-council." She then proceeded to pen the initials "E.R." to this simple but unique document which thereupon found its permanent place in the records of Her Majesty's Privy Council for Canada.

The cabinet had desired to pay Prince Philip some Canadian honour. That morning on the advice of the cabinet conveyed through the Prime Minister he was sworn in as a member of Her Majesty's Privy Council for Canada. He took the oath of allegiance to his royal wife as Queen of Canada, then the Privy Council oath, in the same form as my colleagues and I had taken it on June 21. The initials P.C. have followed His Royal Highness's name and honours since.

The formal meeting of cabinet was brief. I was surprised in September 1981, in reviewing cabinet minutes in the Privy Council Office, to find that no minutes of this historic occasion were kept in the Minute Books. Once the formalities were concluded we posed for an official photograph, with Prince Philip and the Governor General participating. The Queen shared the end of the table with Prince Philip, with the Governor General on his left. On the Queen's right was the Prime Minister, and I on his immediate right. The ministers had been ranged along the two sides of the long table in order of seniority. This presented difficulties for the photographer as the Queen's position would have been too distant from the camera. Nine of the Ministers therefore left the lower end of the table to take up positions standing behind Her Majesty.

Once the photographer had taken the last shot we moved out of the dining-room and down the hall. I had the honour of walking out with Her Majesty, who was in a happy mood. I congratulated her on the excellence of her broadcast the previous evening. She beamed, thanked me and in a gentle voice which nevertheless could not disguise a wife's pride she answered, "My husband is my producer." Ministers then retired, and Her Majesty proceeded to receive high commissioners from Commonwealth countries and their wives, followed by heads of foreign missions and their wives. Ministers proceeded to the House of Commons where the Gentleman Usher of the Black Rod enacted the traditional ceremony of informing the Commons that the Queen could not meet with them until they had elected a Speaker. Thereupon on nomination by the Prime Minister, seconded by Mr. St. Laurent, Roland Michener was elected Speaker and placed in the Chair. On the conclusion of certain formalities the House adjourned to the afternoon.

Her Majesty and Prince Philip arrived at the Parliament Buildings at 2.55 p.m., and were greeted by the Prime Minister and the government leader in the Senate, Senator Haig. They stood at the top of the steps in front of the Peace Tower to receive the royal salute, then proceeded by way of the Hall of Fame and East Corridor to the Senate Chamber. The Commons was summoned to the Chamber. At the bar of the Senate, Speaker Michener took up his station, while as many MPs as could find standing room ranged themselves about him. It was a colourful scene. The Queen, seated on the elevated Throne Chair, wore a pale evening gown flashing with brilliants and the royal crown; Prince Philip was in uniform; the ministers, senators and many MPs in morning dress with decorations; the ladies in evening gowns. Never has the stately and imposing Senate Chamber witnessed such a colourful scene.

The Queen read the speech from the throne, on which the cabinet had laboured long. Her voice was high-pitched and her diction clear. After the reading in English she read the French version in flawless French, the tongue which the royal family is

400

taught to speak as its second language. The audience listened with rapt attention. The entire ceremony was televised. It would have been a loss to history had it not been both instantaneously transmitted and also recorded for the future. The reading of the speech occupied half an hour. The Commons then returned to its chamber, and the Queen and the Prince returned to Government House in an open vehicle, surrounded by an escort from the Royal Canadian Mounted Police, the pennants on the tips of their lances fluttering in the breeze of a perfect October day.

I thought the closing words of the speech from the throne, which were highly personal, were a gem. I think it was Bob Bryce who located the words of the first Queen Elizabeth. They imparted a magnificent and touching finale to the speech:

> As I now address you here for the first time, I will call to your minds the words of the earlier Elizabeth when, more than three centuries ago, she spoke from her heart to the Speaker and members of her last Parliament and said, "Though God hath raised me high, yet this I count the glory of my crown, that I have reigned with your loves." Now here in the new world I say to you that it is my wish that in the years before me I may so reign in Canada and be so remembered.
>
> On this happy day when we give thanks to God for all that He has bestowed on us, I ask that He may bless and guide you.

The Commons took up its legislative duties. In the age-old tradition it asserted its independent right to take up legislation outside the speech from the throne as the Prime Minister introduced the bill Respecting the Oaths of Office, a bill which is never heard of again after being given first reading on the day of the opening. Even after rallying to hear the throne speech read by the sovereign the Commons was mindful of its ancient prerogatives.

That evening the Queen gave a state dinner at Government House. The occasion, of course, was entirely formal: the ladies wore evening dress with decorations, the men white tie or uniform, with decorations. Her Majesty wore a golden-coloured gown slashed with maple leaves in dark colours and a diamond tiara, Prince Philip white tie and decorations. The dinner was followed by a state reception. The presentations went by precedence. Her Majesty received each one of the 285 guests most graciously, with the Governor General on her right and Prince Philip on her left. Alice and I have a much prized photograph of our presentations to the royal couple.

By the time the guests had been received the Ball Room had been cleared of the dinner-tables, the guests gathered there, and the royal couple returned to mingle with their guests. On presentation Alice did a proper curtsey, and I caught myself just as I was about to follow her example. I substituted a bow in the nick of time. The *Ottawa Journal* the next day recorded our chat with Her Majesty:

> She had a long conversation with Finance Minister Fleming and Mrs. Fleming. It was learned that with Mr. Fleming and other members of the Conservative ministry she spoke with knowledge of the matters covered by the Speech from the Throne she had read in the Senate Chamber. Her interest ranged to Canadian pension rates, the qualifications for pensions and the methods of financing them.

The report remarked that "The Queen became grave when discussing such affairs of government, but most of the time she was relaxed and smiling." It must have been a long and tiring day for her.

Two days later, after a glittering state dinner and numerous official functions, the royal couple left Ottawa for the United States. The visit had been a dazzling success. Official Ottawa had responded with warmth and loyalty to a beloved queen and prince, and Parliament as an institution had recovered the self-respect which it had forfeited seventeen months before. The visit had had a profound impact on Canadian public life. In all the intervening years I never lost the feeling that there was a highly personal bond between my sovereign and myself and that it was my exalted privilege to serve her and my country.

Her Majesty did something very gracious to John Diefenbaker. When she travels abroad she is accompanied by a minister. Her ensuing visit to Williamsburg, Virginia, had been arranged by the British government, so for it she was accompanied by a minister of that government, but for her visit to Washington to follow she chose to invite Dief to accompany her. With the hearty approval of the Canadian cabinet he of course was delighted to accept. It was a significant gesture that in making an official visit to Washington Her Majesty saw fit to be accompanied by her Canadian prime minister. The visit to Washington also gave Dief opportunity to meet President Eisenhower and to engage in some useful talks with him.

The captains and the kings had departed. Cabinet the next week received the annual pre-session deputations from the Canadian Congress of Labour, the Canadian and Catholic Confederation of Labour as well as several unions. The legislative grind was on, and both in Parliament and outside it a very busy autumn awaited me.

The Queen's visit was followed by a popular announcement on November 18. The term of office of the Governor General, Vincent Massey, was extended for a year beyond its expiry in February 1958. He had admirably served the demands of the highest office. There was no criticism. He held the crown in veneration. To him as to me it has a most beneficent and vital role to play in our democracy.

CHAPTER THIRTY-SIX

The Twenty-Fourth Parliament

The Twenty-Fourth Parliament was very different in tone, appearance and orientation from the Twenty-Third. Of all the six Parliaments in which I sat the Twenty-Third was undoubtedly the worst. The Twenty-Fourth, on the other hand, was one of the best. Stanley Knowles used to praise it as a fine example of the merits of minority government. Naturally, the CCF liked minority government, for it gave third parties and minority groups in the House much more influence than would be tolerable under conditions of majority government. They had their finest – and happiest – hour a few years later when they actually held the balance of power in the House, and David Lewis held sway over the minority government of Mr. Trudeau.

To the right of the Speaker sat 111 Conservatives. There were empty seats in the far right corner. In the opposition were ranged 107 Liberals, including a couple of alleged Independent Liberals, 25 CCF, and 19 Social Credit. The government side was greatly outnumbered, and looked it. Howe and numerous other leading Liberal ex-ministers were gone. Mr. St. Laurent seemed lost without Howe at his side. The mood of the Liberals was mixed. Some were chastened by defeat, others were impatient to let loose their bitterest attack on the government, and particularly, I was told, on me. Who, they wrathfully pondered, were these usurpers who dared to occupy the Treasury benches, which the Liberals had long ago come to regard as their private and permanent property, theirs, indeed, by some kind of divine right? Rumours were already circulating that Mr. St. Laurent would step down. He had never sat in opposition, and he had no stomach for the often thankless and always difficult role of Leader of the Opposition. He never seemed at home in it.

But what of the twenty men and one lady who occupied the

Treasury benches? If hardly any of the Liberal members had ever before sat in the opposition, none of those twenty-one new ministers had ever sat anywhere else in Parliament. After the twenty-two years the Conservative Party had spent in the wilderness not one of the ministers, including the Prime Minister, had ever before sat in the government. Earl Rowe was the only Conservative in that Parliament who had ever served as a minister, and then only for a couple of months in 1935 as Minister without Portfolio; and Diefenbaker entertained such animus toward Earl that he had no intention of inviting him to be a member of the government. Most of the new ministers were skilled parliamentarians of long experience, but could they adapt themselves to a totally new role in the House of Commons? Having been trained for years in the arts of attack and opposition could they now suddenly be transformed into new creatures in Parliament? Only time would tell. For my part I was resolved to be courteous and dignified, respectful toward the House, and as patient as my nature would permit, but I had no intention of giving ground to the Grits, particularly if they chose to direct their assaults at me. Of all the ministers the one who underwent the greatest outward change was Davie Fulton. He appeared to have risen above partisan skirmishes. "What's come over Fulton?" Dief asked me repeatedly in utter astonishment. "All the fight has gone out of him. He put up such a good fight in the pipeline debate, but you wouldn't recognize him now." I was as puzzled as Dief. Whatever his reasons, Davie in the role of Minister of Justice deliberately stood aside from the struggles in the House and left these to others to conduct. There were times when we needed his formidable fighting qualities in the debates which ensued. Dief was a fighter and he liked a fighter.

Dief was very concerned about cabinet leaks. As early as July 11 he professed to find evidence of leaks. On the eve of the opening of Parliament he again complained and threatened that any minister found responsible would be asked for his resignation. He stopped the circulation of cabinet minutes among ministers lest copies should be carelessly exposed to unauthorized eyes. I regretted this. I had made a practice of reading these voluminous records. Now all was left to memory, and ministers could conduct no check on the record written.

The CBC was permitted to televise the opening of Parliament, but Dief made no secret of the fact that in principle he was strongly opposed to broadcasts or telecasts of events in the House. In later sessions he accepted television broadcasts of the opening, but no more. He looked on TV as an interference with the functioning of the House. He could not tolerate the play-acting and simpering of politicians on the TV screen.

British Prime Minister Harold Macmillan and Selwyn Lloyd, Secretary of State for Foreign Affairs, visited Canada on October 25 and 26 following their meetings in Washington with President Eisenhower. They conferred the first evening with the Prime Minister and the Secretary of State for External Affairs, then the next morning met the entire cabinet. On both occasions Macmillan assured us that the United Kingdom would not become a full member of the European Common Market and that British interest was limited to the proposed European Industrial Market. In a very cordial Ottawa atmosphere the British leaders reviewed the international situation, particularly in the Middle East, and the dangers arising from Russian infiltration of Syria. They thought that since the days of Suez the eyes of the United States were opening. I had spoken to John Foster Dulles in Washington a fortnight before on that very same question. He still expressed himself strongly over Anthony Eden's failure to consult with Washington before launching hostilities over Suez, and commented to me, "You can't make an alliance work without mutual consultation."

Prior to the opening of the session Dief admonished ministers during the next two months to refrain from accepting a large number of invitations outside Ottawa. He stated that it was imperative that all ministers attend cabinet meetings regularly and that they be present as often as possible in the House of Commons. This was timely exhortation, because I for one was being inundated with speaking invitations. I was declining more than I was accepting, yet there were many which appeared to be too important to miss.

On September 17, three of my Toronto friends, Henry Langford, Dent Smith and Bev Matthews, organized a dinner in my honour at the York Club. I told the story of my involvement in political life and my political philosophy. I became specific as to what I hoped to accomplish in the Ministry of Finance – the elimination of waste, extravagance and inefficiency in government, the reduction of taxes, the maintenance of the free enterprise system and national unity.

On November 1, I addressed the eminent Canadian Society of New York. Many Canadians, including numerous friends, attended. I stressed the basic principles of our economic and political creed and invited responsible foreign investment in the development of Canada's natural resources.

406

Considering the number of flights I was taking to Toronto, especially at weekends, it would have been a wonder if a mishap had not overtaken me at some time. On November 15 I was invited to lay the cornerstone of a new building for Union Carbide Company in my riding. The plane was late arriving in Toronto, but we might have come close to reaching the site in time had the driver sent by the company to meet me not taken the wrong turn and involved us in traffic trouble. I never did arrive for the ceremony, so my old friend Nathan Phillips, the mayor, substituted for me. A few months later the tower of the building came crashing down. I told Nate that the misfortune was obviously due to some faulty workmanship on his part, and that I would have laid the cornerstone more carefully had I been there.

On the invitation of the Investment Bankers Association of the United States I enjoyed my first trip to Florida at the beginning of December for the purpose of addressing their annual meeting at Hollywood. In my speech I stressed the government's dedication to free enterprise and our welcome to foreign investment, while reminding them of the responsibilities of investors.

At the beginning of December Gordon Churchill returned from the United Kingdom with our trade purchase mission bringing a glowing report. The mission had been an unqualified success. Apart from those actually visited, no fewer than seven hundred other British firms had asked for the opportunity to meet the Canadian mission. British industrial recovery since the war had impressed the members of the mission. The cooperation received from the Board of Trade and Sir David Eccles, the president, and from the Dollar Exports Council and its chairman, Sir William Rootes, had been enthusiastic. My colleague now thought that diversion of 15 per cent of Canadian imports from U.S. to U.K. sources could be regarded as a goal ultimately capable of achievement. It was a brave hope.

On November 28 we announced one of the best appointments we ever had occasion to make, when we designated my friend the Honourable Mr. Justice J. Keiller Mackay Lieutenant-Governor of Ontario. Never was there a more popular incumbent of the office than Keiller. He retained it till February 1963.

In our years in office we appointed numerous royal commissions. All were composed of able men, and in each case they filled the need for a serious inquiry and report. I had to take issue in the end with parts of only two reports. The first commission we appointed was the Royal Commission on the Sources of Energy, chaired by Henry Borden, QC. Appointed October 15, it made a monumental report on the control of development and marketing of sources of energy, particularly oil and natural gas. The second was the Royal Commission on Price Spreads in Food Products, appointed in December.

The prosperity of agriculture and the liquidation on advantageous terms of the huge wheat surplus we inherited from C.D. Howe were always accorded high priority by Diefenbaker. Gordon Churchill was given the responsibility of unloading the wheat surplus. He never lost an opportunity to sell or give away a bushel of wheat. Sales on credit, gifts of wheat as part of Colombo Plan aid, and every other means imaginable were all employed. We took strong exception to the American program for disposing of its wheat surplus, for it was interfering seriously with orderly marketing and our traditional markets. The competition between the United States and Canada was very keen. Much of our selling was to countries behind the Iron Curtain and on credit. Cabinet was so anxious to dispose of wheat that it extended credit rather freely to facilitate such sales.

A policy of agricultural protection was for me quite another matter. In my absence in Washington on September 27 the cabinet approved a policy of comprehensive protection for our agricultural products against competing imports and sent it to the Interdepartmental Committee on External Trade Policy for recommendations as to how the policy could best be implemented. This was linked with a new plan of price support for agricultural products. I was disturbed at the implications of such a policy.

Legislation to provide cash advances on farm-stored grain was easier to support in principle, as we had consistently done in opposition, than to elaborate into sound, detailed legislation. Cabinet devoted lengthy study to the measure, which inevitably proved very complicated. In my absence in Washington a decision was taken that interest costs should be borne by the Treasury. There was too much of a pattern for my liking about these costly decisions taken when I was known to be absent on government business.

The contribution of the Department of Finance to the sessional legislative program was to centre around my tax proposals to be introduced in early December. I obtained approval of my proposal to introduce as part of the package the new Estate Tax Act, which would in time replace the Dominion Succession Duty Act. It was not my intention to proceed with the new measure at this session, but to reintroduce it at the next following session. This would allow all parties concerned ample time to study the bill and make any representations they chose. Meanwhile I obtained cabinet approval to amend the Succession Duty Act to provide a basic $50,000 exemption for all estates. Before this time, only estates of a total value of not more than $50,000 were exempt.

My sponsorship of what I regarded as important and urgent legislation to amend the British and Canadian Insurance Companies Act readily won cabinet approval. Its purpose was to prevent loss of Canadian control of Canadian life insurance companies. There was in force at that time $30 billion of life insurance in Canada. Most of it had been written by twenty-eight companies, of which six were mutual and twenty-two joint stock companies. The paid-up capital of the twenty-two was only $14 million, which was extraordinarily low in comparison with their total assets, aggregating nearly $6 billion. They were therefore very attractive to American speculators and investors. Already in the last two years six of the twenty-two had passed under U.S. control. I looked upon our life insurance companies as national institutions, whose policies and investments affected many Canadians. To preserve Canadian control I proposed legislation to encourage the mutualization of joint stock companies, and to impose restrictions on the transfer of shares of joint stock companies. No objection to my amending legislation was offered by any of the life insurance companies. I informed my colleagues that I would be prepared to introduce similar legislation with respect to chartered banks if necessary to prevent loss of Canadian control thereof.

I had studied the possibility of introducing similar legislation with respect to the ownership of casualty and fire insurance companies, but concluded it was too late to be feasible. Less than 30 per cent of that type of insurance was written through Canadian companies.

The introduction of a system of simultaneous translation in the House was considered. It was thought that it would encourage more Quebec MPs to speak in French, knowing that their remarks would not be lost on members who did not comprehend French, and therefore such a measure would be popular in Quebec. We proceeded cautiously, announcing in the House in late November that the matter was under consideration by the Commissioners of Internal Economy. In February 1958 we committed ourselves to the new system. It involved the use of earphones by members, and these I thought were ungainly in appearance, but undoubtedly extensive use of them was made by English-speaking members, and more French was spoken in the House in consequence. For my part I never used my earphones. I preferred to obtain the benefit of listening to the original French. The acoustics of the House had been greatly improved by the sound-amplification system which had been introduced previously and allowed the activation of panels affecting different parts of the House. If the amplification system failed, earphones could be used to hear the speech either as delivered or in translation. There was no longer any excuse for anyone not hearing a speech, even if the member delivering it failed to use his voice adequately.

It seemed like a mockery that the new government should be asked to come to the aid of Trans-Canada Pipe Lines Limited to fulfil an undertaking given by C.D. Howe without any authority, but less than a year and a half after the pipeline debate that indeed happened. In typical fashion, without reference to either government or Parliament, Howe, when minister, had written two letters to Midwestern Gas Transmission Company to be sent on to its parent, Tennessee Gas Transmission Company, agreeing to grant a permit to allow export of gas at Emerson and Niagara respectively. It was reported to us that the export of gas to the United States at Emerson had been planned from the very outset, that the pipe into Manitoba was for that reason 34 inches in diameter and only 30 inches east from there, that construction of the line had been undertaken and securities sold and large investments made by Canadian and U.S. individuals and companies in the expectation of exports. The Alberta government supported the export of gas, and our refusal to recognize Howe's unauthorized commitment would be looked upon in the United States as an act of repudiation on our part. We proceeded slowly, taking legal advice from the Department of Justice. It went strongly against the grain with us that we should be called upon to pull Howe's chestnuts out of the fire when he had exceeded the powers conferred by Parliament. We decided to await the report of the Borden Royal Commission on the export of natural gas.

We also faced developing problems with imports and loss of Canadian production and employment. One of these arose out of the flooding of the Canadian market with imports of rubber and canvas footwear from the Orient. Cabinet approved my proposal to direct a reference to the Tariff Board on the relevant tariff items, while the imports of these commodities became an ever-increasing problem for us. They and other imports raised a question as to what our policy was to be toward GATT. The twelfth session was due to open at Geneva on October 17 and the tariff negotiations on October 1. I recommended that we agree in general to the binding of the Canadian tariff schedules for three years from January 1, 1958, subject to subsequent discussions on

410

rubber footwear and textiles. To this proposal cabinet gave general approval. By the end of November the Tariff Board recommended increases in Canadian duties on fruits and vegetables. Action of this nature was bound to give rise to problems with the United States and GATT; after thinking the matter over for a fortnight cabinet approved my recommendation that we negotiate at GATT and with the United States to implement the increases recommended by the board.

It was becoming all too clear that if we were to hold the line on the numbers of civil servants it would not happen of its own accord, but rather as the result of someone's persistence, and it was all too apparent who that someone had to be. On September 20 I expressed to my colleagues my sense of shock at the overall results of the annual review of personnel establishments in departments. The review had just been completed, and the officials of the Treasury Board had reported to me that departments were requesting a total increase of two thousand positions for the next fiscal year. I hit the roof. To make matters worse, in several departments the figures had been considered by officials only, and not by ministers personally. This was not the kind of cooperation I had been led to expect. It appeared to me that the civil service was still testing out the new government and was not yet aware that our intentions to hold the line were serious. With the concurrence of cabinet I returned all of the departmental establishment reports for the personal consideration of each minister to make all possible reductions in order to eliminate this increase. Frankly, I was appalled at the evidence that some ministers were not involving themselves in responsibility for holding down expenditure, and not realizing that to control a burgeoning civil service was where our efforts must begin. I was quite prepared to be unyielding, uncompromising and relentless in resisting unnecessary expenditure, but I hoped I would not be waging a one-man crusade. There would be no hope of retaining a shred of popularity with my colleagues if that proved to be the case.

The prospect of widespread unemployment haunted Diefenbaker. At every report he affected to see us going the way Bennett went in 1935. Such jitters were usually the prelude to asking cabinet to embark on some half-baked job-creation program without adequate consideration of the cost or the dangers of the precedents we were creating. The Treasury had been left in a depleted condition by the St. Laurent government, and they had done nothing whatever to prepare for unemployment. For lack of well-prepared programs we were constantly agonizing over appeals for aid in individual situations. The closing of Britannia

Mines in British Columbia was an example. Though it was put to us as a matter of life and death for the mine, the provincial government, though much closer to the scene and the economic loss, initially declined to contribute a cent to the needed subsidy. After discussion extending over a period of three weeks cabinet, disregarding my solemn warning, approved a subsidy of $20,000 per month, 20 per cent of it to be paid by the province, and 80 per cent out of an empty federal Treasury. The federal government in my opinion had no business involving itself in local situations of this kind; what was needed was a sensible national program beginning, not ending, with the provinces. It was all too evident that I was going to be living with a terrified John Diefenbaker as long as unemployment continued or threatened.

Our housing program, on the other hand, was progressing very satisfactorily. New housing was being constructed at a record pace. CMHC was administering the plan efficiently and fairly. It was operating from coast to coast, and producing benefits in increased employment and the creation of needed homes. On November 19 cabinet decided to ask Parliament to reduce the down-payment on NHA-financed houses from 30 per cent to 10 per cent. This also was a sensible move in the circumstances.

But the housing program cost money, lots of it. Where was that money to be found? I was asked to talk to James Coyne. I did so. I asked him to do what he could to ease credit and help meet unemployment. In particular I asked him to relax the requirement that the banks hold liquid assets to the extent of 15 per cent of their deposit liabilities, and reduce this minimum to 13 per cent. Coyne asked for two weeks to consider the economic situation. This did not exactly please my colleagues and precipitated lengthy discussion. I was directed to have further talks with Coyne and impress upon him the necessity of taking measures to relax the present tight money policy and to remove credit restrictions. Six days later reports appeared in the press that I was to have a meeting with Coyne and that the government would not tolerate a refusal by him to ease monetary restrictions. This embarrassed me acutely and made further discussion of the subject most difficult. Coyne was naturally perturbed. He told me that he had been informed that the news report was based on a statement from a cabinet source. I never learned who was the unthinking source of this perverted cabinet leak, but I have my suspicions. Coyne pointed out that the banks' liquid assets now amounted to 17 to 18 per cent of their deposit liabilities and that they were already in a position to lend more freely if they wished. This episode followed within a week of a loan of $100 million made by the Central Bank to the Minister of Finance to replenish for the time being our empty till.

Of what does "tight money" consist, and what are the evidences of such a condition? It can take various forms, but two of these are unavailability of bank loans to credit-worthy customers and high interest rates. At that time the banks were not fully loaned, and interest rates were declining.

At the end of November we announced a new bond issue in two maturities: $250 million due in twenty-one and a half months with a 3 per cent coupon at 98.60 to yield 3.81 per cent and $400 million due in three years with a 3 per cent coupon at 97.60 to yield 3.85 per cent. The offering was heavily oversubscribed, and the books were closed within half an hour of opening. Further, Canada Savings Bonds were producing record sales. In view of the drop in interest rates we decided in mid-December to close sales on December 31.

The previous government had delayed for a long time going to the market with a CNR issue, evidently preferring to continue lending to CNR itself. By December the railway owed the Treasury no less than $500 million. I obtained authority from cabinet to offer a CNR issue of $300 million, with a government guarantee, maturing in 1981, with a 4 per cent coupon, priced at $97 to yield 4.2 per cent. It was immediately oversubscribed.

All our public borrowings had achieved striking successes. I was naturally pleased, or, more accurately, relieved. Perhaps success gave my colleagues an excess of confidence about what we might always expect of the market. Perhaps less spectacular success in borrowing might have given rise to a stronger reluctance to borrow and a compelling desire to conduct our financial course so as to reduce our borrowing needs as much as possible. That would have been helpful to me later. In any event, by the beginning of 1958 the Treasury was in a far healthier condition than when we took office six and a half months before.

National defence was to play a larger part in my responsibilities than I had previously supposed. I found myself at once a member of the cabinet Defence Committee and a member of the NATO Ministerial Committee along with the Minister of National Defence and the Secretary of State for External Affairs. As such I would be expected to attend the annual meeting of the Ministerial Committee in Paris each December. Later when the Canada–U.S. Joint Ministerial Committee on Defence was established I found myself a member of it along with the same colleagues and also the Minister of Defence Production. National defence forms a major portion of the national budget, and it has a role of such over-riding importance in national policy that I quickly concluded that there are sound reasons for involving the Finance Minister deeply in defence. Be that as it may, I responded to the role and took an active part in all deliberations and activities associated with national defence.

On July 31 Air Marshal C.R. Slemon was appointed Deputy Commander in Chief of Canada–U.S. Air Defence Command (NORAD), and Hugh Campbell was appointed Chief of Air Staff with the rank of Air Marshal, with effect September 1. Both were excellent appointments. The meetings of the cabinet Defence Committee were attended by General Charles Foulkes, chairman of the Chiefs of Staff, and the Chief of Staff of each of the three armed services. I saw these officers frequently, and never had the slightest reason to doubt their fitness for the high positions they held. I never understood why, but Diefenbaker in his dealings with these senior officers in the Defence Committee meetings and outside always acted as though he had a chip on his shoulder. In my opinion, they showed him proper respect; equally, in my opinion, he did not show them proper respect, and this I regarded as unnecessary and lamentable. When I learned that Charles Foulkes after his retirement had sought the Liberal nomination in his riding at the general election I could only regard the fact as deplorable. I cling to the belief that his decision was a reaction and an expression of want of confidence in Dief and some resentment toward him. I always found these officers most friendly, forthcoming and courteous. All were men of ability and a high sense of duty.

By late September future events were already casting long shadows on the defence scene. The committee reviewed defence activities with a view to determining those which could be cut back so that essential priorities could be met without increasing the budget. Naturally, this concerned me deeply. It was accepted that in the event of nuclear war reliance must be placed on forces-in-being. The role of the reserve forces was being studied in the light of this concept and the need which would be certain to arise for them in case of a nuclear attack on the North American continent. A gradual reduction in officer training in universities was proposed, but much more important, the committee recommended cancellation of the CF-100 Mark VI program and that part of the Sparrow missile program related to it. No interference with the CF-105 Arrow was contemplated, and the Sparrow was retained for the CF-105. The defence advisers offered no resistance to this recommendation, which would have achieved a saving of $66 million in the next year. This was duly reported to cabinet.

414

A month later it was reported that the subsidiaries of the A.V. Roe Company were already laying off large numbers of workers in consequence of the cancellation of construction of the CF-100 Mark VI, and by July 1, 1958, no fewer than 1,750 men would be laid off at the Avro Aircraft plant and 1,200 at the Orenda Engines plant. Our MPs for the constituencies affected by the prospect of this massive layoff were appealing for reconsideration of the cancellation. Such urgency was attached to the situation that a conference was called for that very evening between the four ministers, including myself, and officials of the company, who were to hold up further layoffs in the meantime. I attended the conference that evening. We faced a very unpleasant situation.

Avro officials reported they were employing 9,600 men, and by next April this number would be reduced gradually by 2,100. Of these 800 would be laid off as a direct result of the cancellation of the CF-100 Mark VI program, and 1,300 for other reasons. The Orenda officials reported they then employed 5,300 men and would be laying off immediately 1,120, of whom 400 could be attributed to the cancellation, but there would be no further layoffs until the next March. Both companies were almost entirely dependent on defence contracts to stay in business. If the CF-105 program were also cancelled both would be forced into liquidation. Another meeting was arranged for the next week. A program was arrived at to reduce the layoffs. It was, of course, a compromise. An additional twenty CF-100 Mark V aircraft were ordered with cabinet approval. The RCAF had no need for them, but they might be acceptable as mutual aid for some NATO countries. Some other work would be transferred also. The overall result would be a reduction in layoffs by next June from 1,370 to 450 at Orenda and from 2,100 to 1,075 at Avro. These forecasts depended on the continuation of the CF-105 (Arrow) program, and it was carefully examined. The Arrow was a supersonic, all-weather fighter designed for defence against the anticipated Russian bomber threat in the 1960s. By March 31, 1958, the sum of $226,260,000 would have been spent on its development. It had not yet flown, and further development and testing would be required before any decision could be taken to go into production for squadron service. In the next fiscal year an estimated additional $172,612,000 would be required for the Arrow and related equipment, including the Sparrow II missile. Production would not commence until the year following that. The pre-production program contemplated construction of twenty-nine aircraft. The Arrow had been reassessed, and it was thought to be superior to any known contemporary fighter. The work on the Arrow could be stopped at any time. Cabinet agreed to its continuation for another twelve months, as recommended by the Chiefs of Staff.

Thus a decision of enormous importance was made. It was interim, it was costly, and it was influenced by employment conditions as much as conditions of national defence. In the end it came to nought. In the light of hindsight it might have been better to have terminated the program then and there, thus saving $200 million. As an unemployment measure it must be one of the most costly on record, at least up till that time. But who can say, given the knowledge and the expert advice and the responsibility for the nation's safety on which the decision to continue was based, that it was wrong?

The Emergency Measures Organization (EMO) was to be often heard of in later years. The first reference to it that I recall was on November 14, when cabinet approved in principle the inclusion of an item in the main Estimates for 1958-59, to provide for preparatory work, not within fields of particular departments, on emergency measures to be ready in the event of war. As it was concerned with the continued functioning of the government under conditions of attack, EMO was attached to the Privy Council Office and not to the Department of National Defence.

On November 13 and 14 Ottawa was favoured with a visit by General Lauris Norstad, Supreme Allied Commander in Europe. The government gave a dinner in honour of this impressive, vital man the first evening. He talked frankly to us of NATO's responsibilities and the means at its disposal. The next morning he addressed MPs and senators. His visit did much good, giving Canadian parliamentarians much information and realistic assessment and strengthening support for the North Atlantic Treaty Organization.

As General Norstad departed by one door one of the heroes of the Battle of Britain in 1940, Viscount Portal, RAF, entered by another. The government gave a luncheon in his honour at the Rideau Club. He called on me at my office in the afternoon. It was a high privilege to meet this man whose orders to the RAF fighter squadrons turned the course of history and won immortality for "the few" whom he commanded.

CHAPTER THIRTY-SEVEN

The Dominion-Provincial Fiscal Conference, 1957

The long-awaited Dominion-Provincial Fiscal Conference was held on November 25 and 26. It was the first time such a conference had been held with a Conservative government representing the federal authority since such conferences had begun during the Second World War. The timing was not perfect. Some of the provincial governments, hungry for a larger share of revenues, wished the conference to be held much earlier. Actually, it was held as soon as it could be arranged, considering all the other conferences that were held that summer and autumn, that Parliament was sitting, and that with eleven governments involved it was not easy to find a date suitable to all. In the end the conference was attended by all premiers and all provincial treasurers, supported by powerful delegations. It was to be the first of a number of Canadian fiscal conferences called by our government.

There was no legal compulsion to hold the conference. The provinces had all made their decisions under the Federal-Provincial Financial Arrangements Act of 1956 with respect to the shared fields of taxation. For the five years commencing April 1, 1957, eight provinces had rented all the tax fields to the federal government. Ontario had rented the personal income tax, but retained the corporation tax and the succession duty. Quebec rented none to Ottawa. Federal taxpayers in provinces opting out might deduct 10 per cent of their personal income tax, 9 percentage points of the corporation taxes and 50 per cent of succession duty (10-9-50). I called this condition a "patchwork, which satisfied none of the provinces," but it was a patchwork which was legally binding until March 31, 1962. It was, moreover, not a settlement which could be rewritten on short notice. The Prairie and Atlantic provinces had no desire to re-enter the rented fields, which they had been renting to the federal government for the past fifteen years. There was no machinery left for collecting such taxes, it would have taken time to recreate it, and it would have proved very expensive.

On the other hand, we Conservatives had denounced the inadequacy of the provision made for the provinces under the 1956 legislation. In my major speech in the debate on the subject on July 23, 1956, I had asserted flatly, "We would do more for the provinces than the Federal Government has shown it is willing to do in this measure. We believe the Federal Government can do more and can afford to do more." Diefenbaker had echoed the same theme during the election campaign. Our commitment was crystal clear. It was small wonder that the provinces were impatient to meet with the new Conservative government and were hungry for better fiscal terms than they had received from our predecessors. After all, we had helped to create or at least encourage that hunger. Provincial governments were anxious also to explore the attitude of a new government which had denounced the high-handed, dictatorial, "take it or leave it" attitude of its predecessors.

Besides the joint fields of direct taxation there were various cost-sharing programs in effect between the federal and provincial governments. The federal government had made many of them irresistibly attractive to the provinces, but the provincial treasurers were known to be chafing over the cost of meeting the provincial share of these programs. The latest one was the provision of insured hospital and diagnostic services. The program was so expensive and the conditions imposed by the federal government so harsh that some of the provinces had hesitated to join the scheme. Moreover, I had been more critical than anyone else of the exclusion of tuberculosis hospitals and sanatoria and hospitals and institutions for the mentally ill from the coverage in the scheme. Indeed, I had unsuccessfully sought to amend the legislation to eliminate these exclusions.

Another aspect of federal-provincial fiscal relations which had been callously ignored by the St. Laurent government, but which had won no little sympathy and vocal attention from us, was the weak fiscal position of the Atlantic provinces in comparison with the others. They did not possess the resources enjoyed by the other provinces nor the revenues yielded therefrom. New Brunswick was in a particularly weak fiscal position, and its able and highly respected Premier Hugh John Flemming had raised this issue with impressive effect. While the principle of equalization payments was accepted by all and was intended to reduce the disparities in the fiscal position of various provinces, it

418

failed to meet the fiscal needs of the small provinces. No attempt had been made at the federal level to recognize the problem or to devise a formula to meet it. It would be only fair to seek the concurrence of all provinces in a new type of fiscal provision limited to the Atlantic provinces and also necessary to obtain agreement among the four Atlantic provinces themselves on the distribution.

These were the conditions which faced us in the autumn of 1957. There was one other. No financial provision had been made by our predecessors for augmenting payments to the provinces. Had they been re-elected the division written into the 1956 legislation and agreement subsequently entered into under its provisions would have remained in effect until March 31, 1962. Any attempt on our part to augment the payments to the provinces in the 1957-58 fiscal year would of a certainty produce a deficit. Was this a fiscally acceptable course under the circumstances? I wanted no deficit, but could we risk delay in aiding the provinces? Would even delay not appear to be a default on our part? In our weak political position dared we risk a confrontation with ten provinces?

The municipalities must also be considered. I had championed their fiscal cause for years, though I had never advocated subsidies for them out of the federal Treasury. I wanted the municipalities to be paid grants equivalent to the taxes they would have been able to impose on federal property had it not been owned by the federal government and to be exempted from federal sales and excise taxes on purchases. As early as September 25 we received a request from the Association of Ontario Mayors and Reeves for representation at any federal-provincial conference which might be called and the right to submit representations. It would, of course, have been unprecedented to include municipalities in such a conference and to give them independent status at it. How was the basis of representation of thousands of municipalities in ten provinces to be determined? I proposed that the association be told that they would be welcomed as part of provincial delegations, if their province so decided, and that they should make their request to their provincial government. Dief discussed the problem with Leslie Frost, the Premier of Ontario.

It was essential that cabinet decide its strategy for the conference so that I might proceed with the formidable preparatory work. Here Dief and I differed. He began with the idea that we would at the opening of the conference submit some proposal of benefit to the provinces and spend two days bargaining over it.

There was nothing that we desired from the provinces. The exercise was merely to give them something in the hope that they, or as many as possible of them, would say they were satisfied. I did not consider it realistic to expect many of them to admit they were satisfied, least of all that they were grateful. Moreover, I thought it hopeless to attempt to arrive at agreement among eleven governments in two days. If we were to entertain such a purpose we should be submitting our proposal to them in precise form well in advance of the conference.

I proposed an entirely different approach. I argued that if we advanced any proposition it would be said by the Grits that we had done so in a "take it or leave it" attitude. Our attacks on them for adopting such an attitude in 1956 had damaged them severely, and they would be seeking any opportunity to turn the tables on us and use our own weapon to smite us. Even if we proposed a handout of millions to the provinces the Grits would contend the offer was final. Therefore, I recommended that we make no offer at all. Let us, I said, throw the conference wide open to every one of the eleven governments to bring forward its ideas and proposals on fiscal terms and responsibilities. Let us seek basic understanding. Let us make this meeting exploratory, and after a free exchange of points of view let us adjourn the conference to a date in early 1958 at which we might hope to come to grips with problems discussed during this first phase of the conference. To this end we should at it appoint a committee of officials, with each government represented on it, to digest the ideas, seek common statistics and prepare thoroughly for the second phase to make it fully productive. My proposal was adopted in its entirety by cabinet in just two meetings. To give full effect to it a committee of cabinet and also an interdepartmental committee of officials were appointed to assist in the preparation. My recommendations on the positions to be taken at the conference were approved. The federal delegation would consist of the Prime Minister, myself, Balcer, Nowlan and Monteith.

The meeting went incredibly smoothly. After the Prime Minister made the opening address in general terms we went around the table hearing what each province had to say. Nobody was told he was wrong. There was no slashing debate. Rather, ideas were exchanged by Canadians interested in finding a solution to a problem shared by all. It fell to me then to go into detail. I discussed the three percentages in the tax-sharing formula, and noted the cost of various adjustments thereof; I asked the views of the provinces as to where among the three shared fields they preferred to see any adjustment made in their favour. Secondly, I referred to the Unemployment Assistance Act and the threshold clause (0.45 per cent) before federal participation in the cost commenced and noted that the provinces had long found it objectionable; I gave them the reckoned cost of removing the threshold. Thirdly, I said we were still in favour of including tuberculosis hospitals and sanatoria and hospitals and institutions for the mentally ill in the cost-sharing formula for insured hospital and diagnostic services. This would cost $68 million, a sum so large that it must be taken into account in tax-sharing. Our problem was to find funds. There was no possibility of meeting the cost of all proposals the provinces might bring forward. Therefore, we asked their help in stating their priorities. The principle of the equalization grants was accepted by all. Could we improve the governing formula, and, if so, how? Then I made a strong plea for recognition of the special fiscal needs of our four Atlantic provinces, and asked the other provinces as to their attitude. I then asked the four provinces how they would propose to distribute a bulk grant among the four of them. Finally, I proposed the appointment of the committee of officials, under the chairmanship of the Deputy Minister of Finance, to continue study and discussion with a view to resuming the plenary conference about February.

The conference was very nearly all sweetness and light. The atmosphere, calm and friendly, was so unlike that of previous conferences that press and ministers openly commented to that effect. The discussion ranged widely over a variety of subjects. Our hospitality helped to engender harmony and better acquaintance. As the Prime Minister reported to the House, the representatives of the provinces expressed their satisfaction at being able to put their views before the conference, both in open session and in committee.

In the House on November 27 the Prime Minister read a statement on the conference. Agreement had been reached on four subjects. The government had undertaken to remove the threshold clause in the Unemployment Assistance Act, and legislation was being drafted for that purpose. The date on which the Hospital Insurance and Diagnostic Services Act would come into force would be advanced. Most important of all, it was generally agreed that the overall position of the Atlantic provinces justified some special grants in aid. The federal government would examine the statements of the provinces on tax-sharing, and the conference would reconvene as soon as possible in the new year. The resumption of the conference in early 1958 was thwarted by the dissolution of Parliament and the calling of a general election, but the committee of officials remained in existence and continued the preparation and exchange of essential information. The federal government had the benefit of the direct expression of the ideas of the ten provincial governments in its further approach to existing fiscal problems. It was clear they all wanted more money, they wanted cash, and the income tax was the source which interested them most. The conference was of particular assistance to me in providing me with future guidance.

I benefited also from the opportunity to meet the premiers and provincial treasurers. Some of them held both portfolios. Leslie Frost, Maurice Duplessis, Tommy Douglas, Bob Stanfield, Hugh John Flemming, and Ernest Manning, I had met before. A.W. Matheson of Prince Edward Island, W.A.C. Bennett of British Columbia, Donald Campbell of Manitoba and Joey Smallwood of Newfoundland I met for the first time. I was much attracted to Ernest Manning, the long-time Social Credit Premier of Alberta. His total sincerity was impressive. He engaged in less asking than the others. Donald Campbell, the Liberal Premier of Manitoba, and I hit if off from the outset. His ideas and mine on the subject of fiscal responsibility were close to being identical. He was a down-to-earth Scot. I met him again most recently at a Scottish Rite meeting in Winnipeg in 1980. We met as old friends. The future was to bring me into close contact at times with Cec Bennett, and Joey Smallwood of Newfoundland. Matheson was the only one with whom unpleasantness developed early. For some reason or other which I never fully understood he did his utmost to pick a partisan quarrel with me a year or so later.

I was delighted to have the opportunity of sitting in conference with my old friend Maurice Duplessis. After our meetings in 1948 I regretted that our paths directly crossed rarely. He scored his last general election triumph in June 1956. I wrote him a letter then to convey my congratulations – in French, of course. With great courtesy he replied to me in English.

> Dear Mr. Fleming,
>
> It is very thoughtful of you to send me the delicate letter of congratulations dated June 28th.
>
> I appreciate your friendly courtesy and your remarkable knowledge of the French language.
>
> Personal and official regards,
> M.L. Duplessis

His padlock law and some other measures attracted strong criticism outside Quebec, but under his leadership La Belle Province made great strides. The development of resources, highways and communications in that period set records. He had strong convictions and maintained them. I always knew where he stood on relations between the federal and provincial levels of government. He treated the constitution with the utmost respect. Unlike some other provinces, Quebec under him never ran to the federal government seeking favours or aid. Quebec had its rights and he defended them; Quebec also had its responsibilities and he discharged them. All he asked of Ottawa was "Respect the constitution and leave us alone to manage our own responsibilities." I honoured him for it.

It seemed for a time that the conference had taken the pressure of the provinces off us. But there was one wise old political owl who did not intend to be put off. Even while pressures arising out of the Liberal national convention were driving us toward a new general election he decided to strike. On January 17 I received a visit from George Gathercole, economist of the Ontario government, and sent by Premier Leslie Frost, to press for a change in the existing 10-9-50 formula progressively over the next four years to 15-15-50. As an interim measure for the fiscal year 1958-59 he demanded a move to either 11-10-50 or 13-9-50, preferably the latter. Either formula would cost the federal Treasury $60 to $65 million. Frost was firmly opposed to the federal government becoming involved in direct dealings with the municipalities. Then came the sting: if his proposal were not met he would find it difficult to assist in a general election campaign as he had in 1957. He added that a statement of intent on the part of the federal government would not suffice. If this was not political blackmail it was at least a very cold-blooded ultimatum of a political ally at a critical point of time. With a general election looming closer every day, cabinet yielded. On January 24 a telegram was dispatched to all provincial premiers explaining that it had become impossible to reconvene the conference in January, but to assist them in preparing their budgets for 1958-59 the federal government would commit itself to a 13-9-50 formula – that is, an increase of three points in the provincial share of the personal income tax. This concession cost the Treasury $62 million for the one year.

At my request cabinet approved grants-in-aid to the four Atlantic provinces totalling $25 million per annum for the next four years, to be distributed among them as they should decide. At a meeting in Halifax in January they agreed on the proportions – $3.5 million to Prince Edward Island and $7.5 million to each of the other three provinces per annum for the four remaining years of the period covered by the agreements under the Federal-Provincial Tax-Sharing Arrangements Act. I fathered this measure of fiscal aid to the Atlantic provinces, and I have always been proud of my paternity of it. It was an act of justice, and it won us wide support in the Maritimes.

It is fair to add that Diefenbaker considered he needed Leslie Frost's open support in Ontario in the forthcoming general election, and he received it. In particular we welcomed the opportunity to present a united party front and to enjoy the assistance of those incomparable Conservative organizers, Hugh Latimer and Dorothy Downing.

CHAPTER THIRTY-EIGHT

Mini-Budget

Two highly important announcements coincided with the opening of Parliament. Mike Pearson was awarded the Nobel Prize for Peace, and Louis St. Laurent resigned as leader of the Liberal party. Everyone was pleased over the recognition accorded to the popular Mike for his services to the cause of peace. Mr. St. Laurent's decision brought many a regret and a new complexion to federal politics. St. Laurent was seventy-five years of age. He had been leader of the Liberal party for nine years, and a minister for sixteen. It was thought that he was at first willing to continue as leader after his party's defeat, but it was reported that some of the younger men about him, including Jimmy Sinclair, thought it was time for a new and younger leader. St. Laurent was not the type to cling to office. His resignation occasioned many sincere expressions of regret. I had differed often and strongly with him, but I respected him highly. Had he retired at the end of 1955 he would have escaped the stain of the pipeline disaster as well as the defeat of his government and party. A Liberal convention was called in Ottawa for January 16, 1958, to select his successor.

Finance played a major role in the debates of the 1957 fall session. I felt thoroughly at home in my new character in the House. I well knew that the Grits were gunning for me, but I think this only added to my interest. On October 17 Jimmy Sinclair announced to the House that he had been chosen as Liberal financial critic. There is no doubt that he was pleased with his selection. The most surly and partisan member of the House, he had at one time been parliamentary assistant to the Minister of Finance, and latterly had been Minister of Fisheries. He evinced a strong personal dislike for John Diefenbaker, myself, and anything Conservative.

On the second day of the session I tabled the Estimates, explaining that there had not been time for us to write new Estimates. As the programs provided for were well advanced I was simply retabling the Estimates tabled by the previous government in the pre-election session. I reserved the right to withhold support for any of the programs and said we would bring to Parliament's attention such changes as we proposed when the individual items affected were being considered in Committee of Supply. The opposition did not like this approach. They kept demanding a list in advance. I left it to each minister on his own estimates to announce the changes affecting his department. To have issued a complete list in advance would have provoked a lengthy and acrimonious debate. In any event, the review was continuing, and no final figure had yet been arrived at.

The debate on the throne speech had scarcely begun when it was interrupted by my supply motion to provide funds to meet expenditure to the end of November. We would have run out of funds in October. Ostensibly for the benefit of the new members of the House I set forth a full explanation of the role of Parliament in voting supply and controlling expenditure and the procedure in Committee of Supply, then Committee of Ways and Means, then in the House on the Appropriation bill. Solon Low, leader of the Social Credit group, was good enough to commend my effort. He said, "I thought he gave a very lucid explanation of the reason for interim supply, perhaps the best I have heard at any time since I have been a Member of the House. It certainly did provide for the new Members, and perhaps a good many of the older ones who have not yet been fully immersed in financial affairs, the kind of explanation they require to be able to understand the complicated system that is used." Speaking of the legacy bequeathed to us by the Liberals he concluded, "they certainly left things in a mell of a hess."

I drew a kind word also from the Rev. Dan McIvor, Liberal for Fort William, the elderly coach of the House of Commons baseball team: "I remember how he started as the shortstop on our baseball team. He was there on the job, and if he does as good a job on the team of which he is now a member I can tell you he will be No. 1." That was the last kind word to fall on my ears for a few days.

Sinclair was bitterly critical and full of jibes. He ridiculed our procedure on the old Estimates and demanded a budget. He and Paul Martin and other Grits treated us to a sample of the distortions to which we were destined to become accustomed from them. They just fired blindly. The debate occupied the entire

426

day. They did their utmost to bait the Minister of Finance, but without success. I announced that we would call for a recorded vote on each motion and would observe how these Liberals with all their bravado would actually vote. In Committee of Supply the vote was 147-0, and on second reading of the bill, 194-1. Sinclair and Martin voted for the government bill. They were hooted as they rose to vote.

On October 23 I made a full report to the House on the conferences – Mont Tremblant, the bilateral discussions with the United Kingdom at Ottawa on the Free Trade Area proposal, and the Joint U.S.–Canada Committee on Trade and Economic Matters at Washington. The questions which followed were numerous, but ineffective.

However, questions as to whether there was to be a budget became more frequent and for me more embarrassing. The Liberals were raising the question at every opportunity, but Diefenbaker was not weakening in his determination to prevent a budget and avoid a budget debate. I was convinced that the House and the country were entitled to a full budget accounting.

The throne speech debate on Coldwell's amendment dragged on to November 14. I was chosen by my colleagues to deliver the government's answer. I examined the government's record of action and achievement in less than five months against the backdrop of the problems we inherited:

First, the heaviest tax burden on the Canadian people in all their history; second, expenditures running at the highest rate in all Canadian history; third, waste and extravagance in government; fourth, a record wheat surplus . . . to inherit at the hands of a Government which had neglected the problem; fifth, the highest trade deficit in Canada's history; sixth, a record deficit of astronomical proportions in our commodity trade with the United States; seventh, the continued loss of the traditional market of the Canadian primary producers in the United Kingdom; . . . eighth, our Canadian trade eggs . . . placed to a dangerous degree in one basket; ninth, a cost of living that had been rising . . . not just for months, but for years; tenth, the highest interest rates in a generation; eleventh, the tightest credit conditions; twelfth, a substantial measure of unemployment, substantially larger than a year before at the same time; thirteenth, Dominion-Provincial relations in a very disturbed condition with provinces and municipalities up and down this country, ten provinces and 4500 municipalities, all complaining about injustices received at the hands of the Dominion Government; fourteenth, pensions inadequate for our aged persons, for disabled persons, the blind and the veterans; fifteenth, . . . a public till that was practically empty; sixteenth, . . . the

$100 million to be provided for the Canada Council in this year's accounts instead of taking care of it last year; seventeenth, heavy maturities of Dominion Government bonds falling due . . .; eighteenth, a capital shortage that was causing financial embarrassment for provinces and municipalities and businesses.

I challengingly asserted, "No previous Government in Canada's history has accomplished as much in five months for the good of Canada as has this Government," and reviewed in detail what we had accomplished. It was the kind of speech that built up the morale of our supporters to fighting pitch. The Coldwell amendment was defeated by 152 to 25, with the Liberals supporting the government to a man.

On November 15 Diefenbaker endeavoured in the House to justify our failure to introduce a budget. That was clear indication there would not be one. On November 18 I was back with a supply motion. Mr. St. Laurent waived his right to seek a redress of grievances, but the CCF stepped into the resulting vacuum with an amendment to bring hospital insurance into immediate effect. It was defeated next day by a vote of 142-32, with the Liberals again lining up to support the government.

On December 2 in my absence Diefenbaker formally and finally ruled out a budget. In 1873, 1919, 1930 and 1947 there had been a second session but no budget thereat. He concluded, "We feel that a formal budget is not necessary at this time." That settled the question beyond any doubt whatever. Paul Martin turned around and succeeded on a motion to adjourn the House to discuss a matter of urgent public importance, namely, the closing of auto plants in Windsor because the car dealers were no longer taking delivery in anticipation of our reducing or eliminating the 10 per cent excise tax on motor vehicles.

On December 4 I moved for interim supply for December. Normally it would have required only a few minutes to dispose of it. Sinclair made a short speech with another attack and announced support. Stanley Knowles solemnly announced that "it is not our intention to prolong the debate," but "two or three of my colleagues will have something to say." They proceeded to talk all morning and all afternoon, with ten of the CCF making speeches and other Liberals joining in. Jean Lesage delivered a highly protectionist speech in support of the textile industry in Quebec. I think I was justified in losing my patience.

The evening of December 6 was set for delivery of my financial statement on the opening of consideration of the Estimates of the Department of Finance. That morning I faced a barrage of anticipatory questions. It would have been so much simpler to deliver a budget. Dief was absent, and Howard Green was too timid to allow me to give copies of my statement to the press at noon in confidence behind locked doors. Every stupid thing possible was done to give the mini-budget the worst possible reception and of course the press blamed me for denying them the usual courtesy and trust. Statements by the Minister of Finance involving tax changes must always be delivered in the evening when the markets are closed, but who ever heard of choosing a Friday evening when half the members had gone home for the weekend? I should have just given copies to the press on the usual terms without consulting cabinet. I felt pressed to the limit and came very close to resigning. I had become so irritated over the way I was being treated and over the inability of cabinet to make up its mind to approve my tax proposals that at one point I snapped at Dief so sharply he said angrily, "Don't talk to me like that!" Had I quit at that moment I might have spared myself half a dozen later experiences which also drove me to the verge of resignation. Relations between us in early December 1957 were quite strained.

At eight o'clock on that Friday evening, in the absence of the Prime Minister and of many other members, and under the eyes of a press gallery displeased over not receiving advance copies, I introduced proposals to fulfil some of our major election promises – to reduce taxes. Normally the presentation of a budget is a highlight of any session and attracts enormous interest on the part of the public, the press and Parliament. Yet here we were, not trumpeting our program of tax reductions, but playing down the whole presentation by every possible means. The drama was squeezed right out of it to the last drop. But the loss of the dramatic possibilities was far from being my major preoccupation.

I began by reviewing the year's accounts, reckoning up the reductions in expenditure and the additions to the Harris budget, and concluding that these left us with a surplus of $106 million. I asserted, "I am not proposing now nor do I intend to propose at any time in this Session any increases of any kind in taxation," and I added with as much grace as I could muster, "That made it quite unnecessary to submit to the House anything resembling a budget." I proposed the following tax reductions: –

– *in the corporation tax*: increase from $20,000 to $25,000 the income attracting the low tax rate of 20 per cent;
– *in the personal income tax*: increase by $100 the allowance for dependents, reduce the tax rate on the first $1,000 of taxable income from 13 to 11 per cent; and reduce the tax rate on the second $1,000 of taxable income from 15 to 14 per cent;

– *in the succession duty*: repeal in 1958 the Succession Duty Act and replace it with the Estate Tax Act, a tax reduction measure;
– reduce the excise tax on motor cars from 10 to $7^{1}/_{2}$ per cent.

Part way through my review of the proposed reductions my precious thirty minutes expired; I was permitted to continue only by unanimous consent of the House. It was a demeaning and stupid position to be placed in.

I reckoned that after the tax changes for the balance of the year a surplus of $80 million would remain. I stressed that we were seeking to create more incentive, particularly for those in the low income brackets, and that in the first few months in office it had not been possible to achieve all the measures of tax reform which the government would like to put into effect. I closed with a paragraph which I now quote in full because it was ridiculed by Sinclair in his reply and by that exalted Liberal journalist Charles Lynch. I thought it was a humble expression of dedication to the service of Canada:

> In these arduous five and a half months since taking office on the 21st of June the members of the Government have been sustained by the example and the leadership of the Prime Minister. Those who have seen Finance Ministers come and go have informed me that none has faced as heavy a volume of work in the space of five and a half months as has faced this incumbent during the past five and a half months. But, Mr. Chairman, may I say very humbly that 17 to 18 hours' work per day and 100 hours' work per week are an insignificant price to pay for the high privilege of serving Canada.

Sinclair, Coldwell and Low followed on behalf of their parties with very bitter attacks. Sinclair as usual was very personal. They did not dare to attack my proposed tax reductions; indeed, they avoided mention of them, but they did attack, and attack ferociously, the government's failure to bring down a budget. Of course, I was blamed for this deadly sin, and I had to listen to denunciations of myself and the route I had followed. Even at adjournment time an argument broke out as to the propriety of my course, with Stanley Knowles arguing that any taxation changes must be made in Committee of Ways and Means. It was one of the most humiliating experiences of my political career. Diefenbaker was not even present to witness what he had created and imposed upon his Minister of Finance.

The further consideration of the Estimates of the Department of Finance was adjourned and not resumed. Two days later, on December 9, I introduced bills to amend the Excise Tax Act and the Income Tax Act to carry our tax reductions into effect. Stanley Knowles repeated his argument, but the Speaker ruled definitely that as the purpose of the amending bills was to reduce taxes it was unnecessary to have a resolution of either the Committee of Supply or the Committee of Ways and Means. The bills were therefore properly introduced. However, they were not yet passed. The Liberal members from Windsor, Martin and Brown, wanted the excise tax on motor cars abolished entirely, even though Martin had been a member of the government that had applied it, and neither he nor Brown had ever said a word about it in all their years in the House. After Martin's endless talking, the bill was passed on December 12 by a vote of 175 to zero. Coldwell, Knowles, St. Laurent, Pickersgill and Chevrier all voted for it. Martin escaped that embarrassment by fleeing Ottawa to Windsor in his campaign for the leadership. In committee Knowles introduced an amendment to reduce the excise tax on motor cars further to 5 per cent. To the astonishment of the government the chairman, Ted Rea, ruled the amendment in order. It was promptly defeated by a vote of 30 to 70. It embarrassed the Liberals, but the ruling created a bad and dangerous precedent.

The bill to amend the Income Tax Act was debated December 12, 13 and 14. In committee the CCF, exploiting Ted Rea's ruling, moved to increase the exemptions for dependents beyond my proposal. Rea was bound by his ruling, so this time we appealed it. Our appeal was upheld 72 to 60. The sitting on that Friday the 13th opened with St. Laurent, Coldwell and Low on behalf of their parties extending to the Prime Minister, George Pearkes and myself good wishes on our departure that afternoon for Paris to attend the extraordinary meeting of the NATO Ministerial Council. It ended for me at 10 p.m. still listening to CCF and Liberal orators flogging dead issues. They carried on their delaying struggle till noon on Saturday, taking their revenge on me for the absence of a budget and our overturning of Ted Rea's ruling.

That was the end of the budget that never was a budget. I have always thought of it since as a kind of mini-budget. The tax reductions which it contained were undoubtedly of great benefit to the government's cause in the general election which followed, but those advantages could have been gained with much greater effect and at small cost in time if Diefenbaker had been willing to proceed without bypassing a budget debate in Parliament. He succeeded in 1957, at my cost. He did not succeed in 1962.

That episode introduced a pattern which was to be duplicated on numerous occasions in future. I was left to defend decisions which I not merely disapproved, but had strenuously opposed in cabinet discussions. In the House I took most of the punishment which ought to have been borne by others and most of all by Diefenbaker himself. His 15 per cent trade diversion was another example. He did not consult me before announcing it, but left it to me to explain, defend and implement if possible. It remained an albatross of his making but draped about my shoulders. The Liberal press as well as the Liberal party in the House were always pleased to place the blame in such situations on my personal shoulders. Perhaps I was too loyal a defender.

It was bound to be only a matter of time till the CCF precipitated another debate over the trans-Canada pipeline. My supply motion on December 9 gave them their opportunity to air this grievance. Their amendment sought to bring the pipeline under public ownership. The situation had radically changed in the last year and a half, and stock ownership had passed into the hands of new investors. The question as to export of gas to the United States had been referred to the Borden royal commission for study. Coldwell, in submitting the amendment, made a strong speech, but chose to spoil it by charging that the government had sold out to those whom Diefenbaker had denounced in 1956 as "buccaneers." He proceeded to cast miserable aspersions on Henry Borden. The Liberals remained silent throughout. Howard Green made a very effective reply to Coldwell. The amendment was trounced by a vote of 172 to 22.

But December was not all bad. I had the pleasure of piloting my bill to amend the Canadian and British Insurance Companies Act smoothly through the House and the Banking and Commerce Committee. I am satisfied that it was responsible for arresting the loss of Canadian ownership and control of Canadian life insurance companies to foreign interests.

The House adjourned on December 21 for the Christmas recess. By that time the new government had been in office for six months. But it was a short recess. The session resumed on Friday, January 3, 1958.

CHAPTER THIRTY-NINE

NATO Initiation

To the formation and the support of the North Atlantic Treaty Organization Canada had made a formidable contribution. One of St. Laurent's outstanding services to Canada was the part he played in fashioning this defensive alliance and giving it firm support. Mike Pearson similarly played a constructive role in developing and applying the broad policies of the alliance. Canada's support was vital to NATO for numerous reasons, and in opposition we Conservatives had given strong and undeviating loyalty to the alliance. Now in the role of government we were determined to play a positive and helpful part.

One of the institutions forming part of the structure of the alliance is the Ministerial Council, composed of three ministers from each member country. The choice of ministers as laid down was wise: they were to be those of Foreign Affairs, Defence and Finance. The inclusion of the Ministers of Finance I came to respect as far-sighted. Having regard to their responsibilities they were needed, and many benefits followed their meeting and conferring together. The Ministerial Council met annually in mid-December at Paris at the Palais de Chaillot, headquarters of the organization.

In the history of NATO, 1957 was a very special year. The regular annual meeting of the Ministerial Council was to be also the occasion of a Heads of Government Conference. This was to bring President Eisenhower, Prime Minister Macmillan, Chancellor Adenauer of Germany, Premier Gaillard of France and the heads of government of the other member countries together. John Diefenbaker, of course, was to attend for Canada, along with Sidney Smith, George Pearkes and myself and a strong official delegation augmented from our posts at Paris and London. As a government plane was flying the party to Paris the wives of the four ministers were included. We were to be away a week altogether, including a stop for business in London after the NATO meeting in Paris. The departure was set for Friday afternoon, December 13. Cabinet met both early in the morning and at 1 p.m. to dispatch its business before the departure of four of its senior members. But "the best laid schemes o'mice and men gang aft a-gley." The CCF were aware that I was due to depart that afternoon with my colleagues and that our mission was of the highest importance. Out of sheer perversity they prolonged the debate on my tax resolutions on Friday. As long as the debate continued I was obliged to remain at my post in the House. Our time schedule called for their adoption before Christmas, and I would not be back in the House before it rose for the Christmas recess. So the government plane took off on schedule without me. I was disgusted and angry with those CCF nuisances who were talking as usual to hear themselves, evidently to spite my travelling plans. The tiresome debate continued till Saturday afternoon. A well-earned early political demise awaited most of these CCF orators.

With the help of a lift by government plane to Montreal I succeeded in catching an Air France flight to Paris. Arriving there early on Sunday morning I looked about in vain for someone to meet me and concluded that my message had not been received. After a while an official of the French government arrived, and then George Drew as soon as he had received my message. We proceeded to the Plaza Athénée, a delightful hotel, where I joined Alice and later the rest of the Canadian party. I learned that I had missed an evening at the Folies Bergère the night before. In all my numerous visits to Paris I have never been to the Folies or the Lido. I hold the CCF responsible for this grievous deprivation.

The NATO meetings were opening next morning, so the afternoon was spent in preparation under the able guidance of Dana Wilgress, Canadian ambassador to NATO. That evening we four ministers and our wives, Jules Leger and Bob Bryce were all entertained by my old friends Jean Désy, now Canadian ambassador to France, and his charming wife Corinne. Among the other guests were leading figures in the government of France – Félix Gaillard, the Premier, M.C. Delmas, the Minister of Defence, P. Pfimlin, the Minister of Finance, M. Faure, Secretary of State for Foreign Affairs and L. Joxe, Secretary-General for Foreign Affairs. They were a most distinguished group, including several men destined to be premiers of France. I found the evening very stimulating and instructive. Our French opposite numbers were a joy to meet, and Jean and Corinne Désy were as always gracious hosts.

The assembly areas of the Palais de Chaillot next morning were overrun with newsmen and photographers. Of the delegations from European countries that of the United Kingdom attracted maximum interest, but the rush of cameramen to the American delegation easily surpassed all others. I observed that politicians of every country appear to look with benign favour upon those who ply the photographic art.

Then the hall was cleared, and after listening to Paul Henri Spaak's report we heard spokesmen of the Military Committee give some top secret information on armed strengths. The meeting proceeded on that basis to the end a couple of days later. The heads of government were listened to with close attention. Diefenbaker made a good speech, but cut his text somewhat and, as I thought, unnecessarily. Two impressions stood out in my mind: the reliance of the other countries on the United States, and the concern of the United States that the European countries should pull their weight in the common cause.

I confess that there were moments in the first afternoon session when the five-hour jet-lag coming on top of a sleepless night on my flight from Montreal caused my head to nod. That was no fit behaviour for a delegate to a conference of world importance, but the flesh was weak. The European delegations enjoyed a great advantage in this regard over those coming from North America. In the years to follow I learned to arrive whenever possible at least twenty-four hours before the commencement of international meetings in Paris or London.

In the evening we were the guests of President Coty at a magnificent banquet at the Palais Élysée. It was my first experience eating from gold plates and wielding gold-plated cutlery. The food was superb. I thought of how the kings of France and their dinner guests used to fare on French cooking. I also wondered how the gold plates and cutlery were kept out of reach of Hitler's invading forces in 1940. The food, needless to say, was matched by the service.

President Eisenhower was the featured visitor. Warm tributes were paid to him as leader of the military forces which liberated Europe. The generosity of the United States in providing Marshall Plan aid, which supported and made possible European postwar recovery, also drew praise. I searched out my friend Bob Anderson and told him I would like to meet President Eisenhower. He obliged me immediately. The President was at his friendly best. He greeted me very warmly, and we chatted about the conference and what we hoped might come out of it in knitting the alliance more closely. Attempts have been made to reduce the accomplishments and the stature attained by President Eisenhower in war and peace. In my opinion, he was one of the great leaders of our time. As with vast numbers of ex-servicemen my first meeting with Dwight Eisenhower was on French soil. The future was to give further opportunities to meet him in both Canada and the United States.

Wynne Plumptre had lived some years in Paris and knew the city well. While the ladies were shopping we did some on our own. He took me to an upstairs shop where men's ties were made by hand. This interesting discovery was perfectly timed, coming ten days before Christmas. Though I dislike shopping, in succeeding years I visited this shop regularly before Christmas.

Our several days in London were delightful. Alice and I were entertained at luncheon at his official residence, 11 Downing Street, next door to the Prime Minister's residence, by the Chancellor of the Exchequer and Mrs. Thorneycroft. He again spoke in warm praise of what had been accomplished at Mont Tremblant and later at Ottawa and of the manner in which I had conducted the conference. We agreed that we would do everything in our power to achieve a major success at the Commonwealth Trade and Economic Conference.

George and Fiorenza Drew gave a great dinner for us at the high commissioner's residence at 12 Upper Brook Street with a dazzling list of British guests, including the Lord Chancellor and Lady Kilmuir, the Lord Chamberlain and Lady Scarborough, the Secretary of State for Commonwealth Relations and Lady Hume, Admiral of the Fleet Lord Mountbatten, Lord Alexander (former Governor General of Canada), Lord Kindersley and his Toronto-born wife, the Chancellor of the Exchequer and Mrs. Thorneycroft, the President of the Board of Trade Sir David Eccles, the Queen's Private Secretary, Sir Michael Adeane and Lady Adeane, and the Dowager Lady Bessborough, widow of the former Governor General of Canada. That remarkable gathering at dinner was, I thought, a great tribute to the mark George Drew had already made in London and the courtesies which British leaders always seem ready to extend to Canadians.

An event in London brought great satisfaction to us all. Following an announcement made on September 17, the Queen conferred an Imperial Privy Councillorship (Rt. Hon.) on the Prime Minister in a private ceremony at Buckingham Palace. We were all delighted to see John receive this distinction.

436

But the London visit was not all social. There were important discussions with George Drew and others. These were of great mutual value. And one highly important piece of business was done one chilly morning while we stood on the northwest corner of Trafalgar Square.

Canada House was a far-sighted acquisition for which all credit is due to the late Peter Larkin, when he was Canadian high commissioner. Located on the western side of Trafalgar Square it gave Canada one of the most strategic locations in London. The building itself was durable and impressively proportioned. The lofty ceilings, stone pillars and handsomely designed curving staircase could not fail to impress the visitor on entering by the massive front door. It had a basement and three floors served by an elevator. The housekeeping was efficient, and the building had been maintained in excellent condition. It housed the high commissioner's offices and the Department of External Affairs in London, but the Joint Staff and other Canadian government departments were housed elsewhere, and mostly in scattered locations. The pressure on space was increasing. The St. Laurent government had recently acquired a new site on Pall Mall with a view to locating government offices there. At George Drew's request Sid Smith and I inspected it and quickly concluded that it was too expensive and was unsuitable in any event. We agreed that it should be disposed of.

To the north of Canada House stood the building which housed the Royal College of Physicians and Surgeons. From the exterior it and Canada House appeared to be one building. The architectural design was identical for both, and the two combined occupied one short city block. George had learned that the property might become available for acquisition. He and Sid and I inspected the location and conferred on the street corner. There under the protecting shadow of Nelson's Column we made our decision to acquire the building and physically unite it with Canada House. As chairman of the Treasury Board I authorized George to take all necessary steps to facilitate the acquisition. On February 3, 1958, cabinet formally approved the deal. It was of immense advantage to Canada. It would have been a tragedy had the Royal College building been disposed of to some other interest and Canada had lost the opportunity to enlarge Canada House. Had we not done so the growing pressure on the limited accommodation afforded by Canada House might in the end have compelled the government to relinquish this unsurpassed location in the very heart of London. It was incredibly opportune that I was in London at the critical moment when decision was necessary. C.D. Howe never acted more swiftly or decisively than I did in the situation then arising. To this day I take pride in the vital, timely, constructive and decisive role I played in grasping an opportunity of critical importance to Canada.

The return flight across the Atlantic at the end of an epic week was worth remembering. We had a government plane, slow and a little antiquated, but the rear cabin had two pullout double beds. The Diefenbakers occupied one and the Flemings the other. We all had a laugh about camping in the sky. George and Blytha Pearkes were in the forward cabin with the other members of the delegation. Seniority gave me the benefit of a prone position and a comfortable mattress, but I did not sleep well. I envied John his remarkable and valuable ability to snatch sleep in any position and at any time. I think it preserved his health and lengthened his life. The sun shone brightly as we came within sight of Canada, already wearing a blanket of snow in Labrador. John was in great spirits. The four of us took turns dressing in the cramped washroom and laughed off any little embarrassments. We enjoyed a good breakfast and were back in Ottawa at midday. After a rather dismal beginning the trip had proven to be a delight for me.

Parliament had already recessed, so there was nothing to do but wade into a formidable accumulation of work in my office and enjoy Christmas with the family in Toronto. They were all home and we were complete once more for a few precious days. Thank God for Christmas! How would we ever weather the rest of the year without the unique joy of the Holy Season! It was our nineteenth and last Christmas at 259 Glencairn Avenue.

Mercifully Dief did not call any cabinet meetings until the new year. Alice and I returned to Ottawa for its arrival. Doug and Fran Harkness had a little party at their apartment on New Year's Eve, and there they and the Diefenbakers, the Macdonnells and the Flemings at midnight bade farewell to the old year and hailed the new. We all embraced and wished each other a Happy New Year. Nineteen fifty-seven had been a remarkable year. It had wrought a far-reaching change in my life. Indeed, life would never be the same again. What would 1958 bring? I think I faced it with a confidence born of a sense of challenge and a zest tempered by a sober realization that it would bring a weight of responsibility.

The Governor General held his traditional levée on New Year's morning. It was the first one I had ever attended. Always I had been in Toronto and for many years had attended the Lieutenant-Governor's reception at Queen's Park. I had invariably derived enjoyment from paying respects and extending greetings to the sovereign's personal representative in Ontario and from meeting many friends gathered there. Now New Year's Day would be spent in an Ottawa setting. As we waited to be marshalled in order of precedence I had opportunity to greet the high commissioners and ambassadors. I was deriving increasing satisfaction from the closer relations which existed between us. They were not merely formal and official; happily they were becoming more and more personal.

The Governor General, Vincent Massey, received his guests in the Senate chamber. After exchanging a multitude of greetings I proceeded to the Rideau Club to enjoy the annual New Year's Day buffet luncheon. It was all such a happy and friendly and carefree way to launch the fateful year 1958.

CHAPTER FORTY

His Finest Hour

The House commenced its 1958 sittings on January 3 on a very serious note, and it involved me deeply. It may to some appear strange that the Minister of Finance should play the leading role in policy questions affecting exports of Canadian crude oil to the United States, but I found myself inescapably in that position.

In 1950 at the height of the war in Korea the U.S. and Canadian governments had together adopted a "Statement of Principles for Economic Co-operation," in which they declared without any limitation of time or circumstances that "It is agreed . . . that our two Governments shall co-operate in all respects practicable, and to the extent of their respective executive powers, to the end that the economic efforts of the two countries be co-ordinated for the common defence and that the production and resources of both countries be used for the best combined results." Dean Acheson, the U.S. Secretary of State, may not have fully foreseen the circumstances in which seven years later I invoked his "Principles of Co-operation," but the agreement undeniably was still in full force and effect.

The communiqué issued in Paris in December at the conclusion of the NATO ministerial meeting contained these two significant clauses:

> – We will co-operate among ourselves and with other free governments to further the achievement of economic stability, a steady rate of economic growth, and the expansion of international trade through a further reduction of exchange and trade barriers.
> – We recognize the interdependence of the economies of the members of NATO and of the other countries of the free world.

These principles were to be put to an immediate test, of which President Eisenhower may not have been aware when he subscribed to the communiqué.

440

A year earlier as the result of the blocking of the Suez Canal the United States had been faced with an acute threat of a shortage of oil. By late 1957 the threat had passed and U.S. producers were exerting maximum pressure on Congress and the administration to restrict oil imports. For such purposes the United States was divided into five districts, No. 5 consisting of the three states on the Pacific – Washington, Oregon and California. It was the district which was of vital importance in the marketing of Canadian crude oil. The Canadian product moved to the United States by pipeline instead of the more hazardous ocean transportation, which was vital to the United States in wartime. Under existing legislation the President had power to curtail imports of any article or commodity which was being imported into the United States in such quantities as to threaten to impair the national security. Exercising this power, he had already restricted imports of crude oil into districts 1 to 4, but without hurt to Canadian exports. Now under pressure from domestic producers the U.S. government was about to restrict imports into District 5. This was bound to hurt Canadian producers, and in broader terms it called into question American good faith in relation to its commitments to Canada by solemn agreement.

The subject had been discussed at the meeting of the Canada–U.S. Joint Committee on Trade and Economic Matters at Washington in November, but the situation had not then fully developed. We were then urgently pressing the administration not to restrict imports of Canadian lead and zinc. But throughout December the pressure on Washington from the oil producers intensified, and Canada's concern and opposition were being conveyed to Washington almost daily. When in Paris I seized the opportunity to discuss this growingly urgent problem with my friend Bob Anderson, U.S. Secretary of the Treasury, and later with him and Douglas Dillon, U.S. Deputy Undersecretary of State. The problems I was destined to share with these two men were constant and of the highest importance, and it was a blessing that we became warm personal friends. I greatly admired them both. They were men of the highest integrity and broad understanding. I was able to discuss the oil import problem with them with complete candour.

On December 24 the U.S. administration yielded to the pressure and extended the restrictions to include District 5. They had kept us closely informed at all points, and as soon as their decision was announced I issued the same day a statement, concluding with a paragraph couched in language which by diplomatic standards was strong: "The Canadian Government cannot accept the view that there is any justification for U.S. limitations on oil coming from Canada, either on economic or defence grounds. The Canadian Government will continue to press its objections."

Cabinet, in the absence of the Prime Minister, on January 2 reviewed the situation and decided that I should make a statement to the House at its opening the next morning. My statement covered the subject fully. It was followed by a salvo of questions and expressions bordering on hostility toward the United States. On that and later occasions I firmly rejected invitations to retaliate against our neighbour. I pointed out that the Trade Agreements Extension Act (U.S.), under which the President derived the power which he had exercised to enter into trade agreements with Canada and other countries, would expire in 1958, and we did not wish to jeopardize its chances of extension by Congress. On January 15 the Canadian ambassador presented a formal note from the Canadian government to the U.S. administration protesting the restrictions. Questions relating to Canadian exports of crude oil to the United States were to engage me for a long time. I was in the oil business, whether I liked it or not, and I was in it to stay.

Vitally important conferences loomed ahead. It seemed to me that no year could match 1957 in the number and importance of the conferences it produced, but time proved me wrong. There were as many in 1958, but fortunately they were better spaced. I was facing the resumption of the Dominion-Provincial Conference, the Commonwealth Trade and Economic Conference, probably another meeting of the Canada–U.S. Committee on Trade and Economic Matters and possibly a meeting of the Canada–U.S. Committee on Defence, the annual meeting of the International Bank and the International Monetary Fund, which this year were to be held in India in September, and the annual meeting of the NATO Ministerial Council in Paris in December. The calendar was filling rapidly.

By early January nine of the eleven Commonwealth countries had accepted the Canadian government's invitation to hold the Trade and Econonic Conference in Canada. Arrangements had been completed to hold a meeting of officials in London in February and probably another in May to complete the agenda. These plans had been greatly facilitated by my meeting with Peter Thorneycroft, the Chancellor of the Exchequer, in London in December. We were stunned by the announcement of his resignation on January 6, but reassured by the appointment of Derick Heathcote-Amory as the new Chancellor. I knew that he would give the conference enterprise his strong support. On February 7 cabinet approved my recommendation that Sydney Pierce, a senior Canadian diplomat of ambassadorial rank with Montreal business connections, be appointed secretary general of the conference and that he be released from all other duties for the purpose. It was a happy choice. Sydney in his quiet and competent way rendered a brilliant service both in the preparations for the conference and in the conduct of its meetings. I came to lean heavily upon him; never once did he fail me.

Some of the western provinces began pressing for resumption of the Dominion-Provincial Conference. Naturally they wished to have a date set before they called their legislatures into session. In the disturbed political atmosphere prevailing in Ottawa it was quite impossible for the federal government to commit itself to a date. The subsequent dissolution of Parliament compelled a lengthy postponement in any event. However, we lost no time in pressing ahead with the legislation required to put into effect those measures on which agreement had been reached at the November conference. The "threshold" provision limiting federal participation in unemployment assistance was quickly abolished, with benefit to both the provinces and the unemployed. On January 27 I presented the legislation to provide the Atlantic Provinces Adjustment Grants and to raise the provincial share of the personal income tax from 10 to 13 per cent. All the opposition parties declared their support for the measure, then proceeded for three days to detain the House while they engaged in a make-believe performance. Martin and Lesage roamed widely and engaged in distortions of our position. Lesage already had his eye on the leadership of the Liberal party in Quebec. He was, of course, joined in hurling personal abuse at the Minister of Finance by Jimmy Sinclair. The tempers of Liberal members had not yet calmed down after the disaster they had suffered in debate earlier in the week. The bill brought timely financial aid to the provinces, it fulfilled our pre-election promises, and it earned us widespread support in the forthcoming general election now looming directly ahead.

I was able to introduce another measure of economic aid to the Maritimes – legislation to allow the federal government to make loans not exceeding $30 million to New Brunswick for the development of hydro-electric power at Beechwood on the Saint John River. This plan was the outcome of lengthy discussions with the province, which opted in favour of the loan rather than the earlier proposal of a federal guarantee of provincial bonds which we had supported when in opposition. The interest rate was the same as that charged on advances to crown companies, that is, our own borrowing cost plus one-eighth of 1 per cent. The loan was repayable in eight equal annual instalments.

The legislation was accompanied by a sister measure, introduced by the Minister of Northern Affairs and Natural Resources, to authorize the federal government to enter into agreements with any of the Atlantic provinces to provide assistance in the generation of electric energy by thermal electric power projects and in the control and transmission of electric energy, and including provisions for the payment of a subvention on coal used in the production of electric energy. It took four days to obtain enactment after interminable speeches by the Liberals led by Pickersgill.

My supply motion on January 7 found the Liberals silent prior to their national convention, and Coldwell seized the opportunity to introduce an amendment calling on the federal government to take steps to relieve "the financial crisis in education" by granting financial assistance to the provinces. It brought Sid Smith into the debate with a most enlightening speech. The amendment was defeated by a vote of 163 to 27. Pearson then delivered a warm-up speech on trade, unemployment and other subjects on which he had not been heard in the House previously. The speech was obviously directed less to the House than to the Liberal delegates soon to assemble. Evidently he was seeking to prove that he was not merely a specialist in external affairs and that he could be more versatile.

On January 15 I tabled the Public Accounts and the Auditor General's report. It was a new experience for one who had torn holes in government accounts in the past. But I gave the House full assurance that all departments had been instructed to take under scrutiny the portions of the Auditor General's report which affected them and that they would do whatever was required to remove irregularities that existed under the former government.

The House spent considerable time in committee on the Estimates of the Department of National Defence, but the Prime Minister found it necessary in the House on January 11 to give assurance that no U.S. aircraft carrying atomic or nuclear weapons were crossing into Canadian airspace without first obtaining specific permission from the Canadian authorities and that in this respect there had been no change from the policy applied by the previous government.

The Liberal leadership convention was to open on Thursday, January 16, and to continue for the remainder of the week. On

444

the 11th Dief moved that the House not sit on the evening of the 15th or at all on the 16th, and his motion was adopted without discussion. Coming at such a busy stage of the session his motion was generous, but who could say that the positions of the two parties might not be reversed some day in the future?

There were three possible candidates for the leadership – Pearson, Gardiner and Paul Martin. The doughty Jimmy Gardiner was only one year younger than St. Laurent, by whom he had been defeated at the last Liberal convention in 1948. There was little likelihood that the party would select a seventy-three-year-old, so Jimmy did not become a candidate. Paul Martin was an abler parliamentarian and a more astute politician than Mike Pearson, but did not rank as high in popular esteem. The award of the Nobel Prize became a very effective boost to Mike's hopes in the forthcoming contest. We Conservatives watched it more closely than we cared to show.

In the voting at the end of the week Mike Pearson was elected, defeating Paul Martin by a comfortable margin. He concluded his acceptance speech to a wildly cheering convention with the shout, "A nous la victoire!" It was a bold claim to victory, and he no doubt meant, and his audience understood he meant, immediate victory. It was the plainest intimation that with a new leader at the helm the Liberals in the House would transform their tactics from seeking to avoid defeating the minority government to openly challenging it to mortal combat. Moreover, Pearson had employed fighting words to clothe his grim challenge. Was he capable of vindicating it in battle in the House of Commons? Could this ex-diplomat, accustomed over many years to seek agreement by compromise in international meetings, who spoke with a lisp and with one hand in his coat pocket, who was not an orator or a hard-shelled debater, somehow muster the decisiveness, the boldness and the command of a wide variety of issues, political and economic, to lead the Liberals to victory against a government which commanded a wealth of experienced debating power and which had been busy compiling the most impressive record of keeping election promises in Canadian political history? The answer would not be long delayed.

On Monday, January 20, the galleries were filled and people stood in line outside. Like good drama the sitting opened quietly and with little hint of the clash to come. As Leader of the Opposition, Pearson had exchanged seats with St. Laurent. The Prime Minister at the opening of the sitting at 2.30 p.m. paid a gracious tribute to Mr. St. Laurent, voicing a sincere admiration for him, and followed with a tribute to Pearson, congratulations on his election and good wishes in his new role. Coldwell and Low on behalf of their groups followed in similar vein. Mr. St. Laurent then expressed his thanks in a moving short speech. Mike followed with a pleasant little speech in which he joined in the tributes to Mr. St. Laurent, spoke of the importance of the role of Leader of the Opposition and promised to do his best to live up to his new responsibilities. Everything was very proper and in the best of taste. The House proceeded with its business as if the day was just an ordinary one like any other. After an hour of preliminaries I introduced a supply motion, in accordance with previous announcement. This gave Pearson full opportunity to introduce a want-of-confidence amendment and to select the issue. He was not compelled to do so save by his own choice and his ambitious rallying of his followers at the convention. It would have been hard for him in the face of the opportunity presented by the supply motion to back away in the hope of fighting on another day.

There was no doubt in Diefenbaker's mind as to the course which Mike would follow. At the opening he brought in with him and laid on the desk we shared a very thick folder of papers of assorted sizes and only loosely arranged. One slip over the edge of the desk and they would have fallen in a hopelessly scrambled heap. His small hands and thin fingers betrayed a fidgety nervousness. Something was afoot.

Pearson had scarcely completed the introductory paragraph of his speech before he began to assail "the sins of omission and commission of the Government in the handling of current business." The battle had begun. For a few minutes he encountered interruptions and comments from the Treasury benches. Toward the end of his long speech he announced that the present Parliament should continue, but in view of the government's failures and the policies espoused by the Liberal convention, it should have a Liberal government. When he made the astounding statement, ". . . our motion . . . is to ask the government to make way in this Parliament for a Government pledged to implement Liberal policies," I commented, "Mike, it is sad to see you come to this." When at the end of his speech, Mike repeated that we should make way for a Liberal government his proposal was so ludicrous to his own knowledge that he could not maintain a straight face. He concluded by introducing a lengthy amendment calling upon the government to submit its resignation forthwith. This was an extraordinary proposal. Clearly he did not wish an election because he feared it; he did not wish us to advise the Governor General to dissolve Parliament; he simply wished us to give up our places on the Treasury benches in favour of "a government pledged to implement Liberal policies." This hare-brained manoeuvre has been attributed to Pickersgill, and this seems a likely explanation. It was inconceivable that it could be the brain child of any other Liberal front-bencher.

Diefenbaker spoke in reply for two and a half hours, divided into two parts by the dinner recess. He faced continual heckling from the Liberal benches, but drew fresh vigour from the interruptions. He chided Pearson for his fear of an election and the ridiculous tactic into which terror had driven him; he dissected the amendment and poured withering scorn over each element in it, destroying the convention resolutions by pointing to Liberal inaction on such matters when they were in office; he then reviewed his government's record of action and fulfilment of promises, stressing what had been done for housing, old age and other pensions. Then he launched into the subject of unemployment, and began to quote from the report *Canadian Economic Outlook* by the Economics Branch of the Department of Trade and Commerce in March 1957. It contained numerous and serious warnings of a deterioration in the economy and of unemployment to follow. These should have put the Liberal government on guard, but they ignored all the warnings, pretended to the public that Canada would enjoy a boom, based their policies on boom conditions, and made no preparations against recession and unemployment, even though all Liberal ministers had had access to the report. Dief scored point after point on Pearson and the Liberals to the thundering applause of his supporters. Pearson looked at first merry, then serious, then uncomfortable, then disturbed, and finally sick. His followers knew all too well that he was destroyed. Some of them, like Sinclair, endeavoured to come to his rescue with senseless interruptions, but these proved ineffective. The Prime Minister threaded his way through his multitude of sheets, pieces and scraps of paper without ever losing them or the coherence of his remarks. It was his finest hour. Of all his debating speeches I rate this as the greatest. It simply overwhelmed Pearson and crushed him. If Pearson and his ill-chosen adviser had any hope of winning CCF support it was quickly dashed. It did not take Coldwell two minutes to disclaim "anything as unintelliegent" as to support the Liberal amendment. Solon Low for the Social Credit also announced that "we could not possibly vote for the amendment." Pearson's discomfiture was complete. He walked out of the House alone, his files under his arm, the picture of dejection and embarrassment. The crowds in the galleries had melted an hour before. The Liberal members left the Chamber quietly and without the normal trace of mirth or relaxation. What was to have been their day of triumph had given way to the night of despair. Diefenbaker was cheered to the echo by his excited and jubilant followers. An election had been made virtually certain, and its outcome was now assured.

The debate continued the next day, but it was an anticlimax. Chevrier made an unsuccessful effort to renew the attack, but the fight had gone out of the Grits. Even Paul Martin was dragged in to rescue the Pearson amendment. I was chosen to answer for the government. I pictured the shambles in which the Liberals found themselves, and likened Pearson to Humpty-Dumpty:

"All of Chev's horses
And all of Paul's men
Won't put Mike
Together again"

I scorned the Liberals for their fear of the ballot box, and added, ". . . if we ever get them to the ballot boxes it will only be by dint of dragging them, kicking and screaming, to the polls." The Pearson amendment was defeated 150 to 95.

The entry of Paul Martin, the defeated candidate, into the House, was in quiet contrast to the vociferous organized demonstration attending Pearson's entry. Paul took his place wearing an unmistakable expression of deep disappointment. I sent him across the floor of the House a note of sympathy and encouragement, assuring him that of all the members of the House, I more than anyone could understand his feelings. He replied gratefully.

On January 30 the government announced a program of technical assistance to the Federation of the West Indies and Ghana. This was the inauguration of what was to become a program of growing magnitude and importance, in which I was deeply involved.

The adoption of a bilingual form for cheques and other negotiable instruments issued by the federal government had been under consideration for a long time. Cabinet was not yet ready to make the change. A bill to adopt the bilingual form was introduced by a private member on December 3, 1957, and talked out. Rather unexpectedly it reappeared on January 31 when the government least wanted to face the issue. In the ensuing division ministers supported the bill, and it was adopted by a vote of 167 to 9. Those opposed were Conservatives. However, the bill was then talked out in committee.

With the threat of dissolution hanging over the House it was inevitable that, as supply for the year had not been fully voted, a question would arise as to how expenditure would be met if Parliament were not sitting. The Financial Administration Act makes provision for the issuance in such circumstances of Governor General's warrants. The practice had been authorized by statute since 1878. We were obliged to resort to them in the summer of 1957, and I tabled a statement thereof at the beginning of the 1957 session. On February 1, I made a clarifying statement to the House on the use of warrants. It was my last speech in the Twenty-Third Parliament.

February 1 was a Saturday. The House met at 11 a.m. in an air of apprehension. That morning cabinet approved an approach to the Governor General for dissolution of Parliament. Dief made a secret flight to Quebec City to present the request. Mr. Massey readily approved. The only question that remained was when to sign the order and how it should be communicated to the House. As the afternoon wore on the House was engaged in Committee of Supply on the Estimates of the Department of Citizenship and Immigration. Jimmy Gardiner was one of the speakers, and I had a feeling that the Commons was hearing from the redoubtable Jimmy for the last time. It made me a little sad. Dief and Howard Green sat in Dief's office, and I doubled between there and the House as we three sought to choose the precise timing for the announcement. I drafted the statement. The Prime Minister, Howard and I entered the House just before the six o'clock hour of adjournment. The Prime Minister read the statement outlining the problems encountered over the minority position of the government and the need to fortify its position by a direct and unquestioned mandate from the people. Accordingly Parliament was dissolved by proclamation under the Great Seal of Canada, and writs had been issued for a general election to be held March 31. It was all over.

Parliament had indeed heard from Jimmy Gardiner for the last time. It had also heard from Jimmy Sinclair, M.J. Coldwell and many others for the last time. The voice of Stanley Knowles, most talkative member of the House, would not be heard in the Twenty-Fourth Parliament. The Canadian House of Commons was about to undergo a drastic housecleaning.

CHAPTER FORTY-ONE

Political Revolution, 1958

The general election of March 31, 1958, was different. In my experience there had never been one quite like it. In the first place, we called it; that of itself was new and different. Next, it was a winter election. The campaign was carried on through two rugged months of a severe Canadian winter, marked by unusually heavy snowfall. Everyone, forgetting that general elections had been held in winter in 1874, 1887, 1891 and 1940, had always said that it would be impossible to hold a general election in Canada at that season, that the roads would be impassable, the farmers would be isolated and the electorate would be angry. Television, radio, snowploughs and automobiles changed much of that. But marking the 1958 general election out from all others was the fact that everything went well for us. It was incredible the way all our plans worked out smoothly and successfully. All the breaks went to the Conservatives. The electorate was aroused and interested everywhere. Audiences were receptive; notwithstanding inclement weather, meetings were well attended. Campaigns would be an undiluted pleasure if they all went the way the 1958 one went – that is, for us. The national organization was efficient, the publicity effective and timely, the campaign was adequately, but not lavishly, financed. The reports from all parts of the country were encouraging throughout. No blunders were made, and no setbacks of consequence occurred. The tide did not ebb and flow; the swing throughout continued in one direction.

It was the same in Eglinton. Our organization, which had functioned so effectively in the spring of 1957, was still intact, and morale was at an all-time high. We had all our workers ready, and they really worked. Campaign funds were adequate to the need. We had the best campaign quarters we ever had on Yonge Street in the heart of the riding. The two-storey building of the Consumers' Gas Company became available at the right time in the perfect location and at a reasonable rent. It gave us commodious accommodation on the street floor on a corner and a large room upstairs suitable for public meetings in the evenings at any time. My friend John Jory was in charge. We used the label "Canada's Minister of Finance" with my name on all our campaign material, and the response was excellent. In giving my occupation on the ballot paper I showed "Minister of Finance." The Liberal candidate took exception to this, contending I should have shown it as "barrister." I replied that I was no longer practising law, that my occupation was indeed Minister of Finance, and it was proving to be a full-time job and more. We found that C.D. Howe had described himself previously as minister on the ballot paper. The commotion which the Liberals endeavoured to create proved to be a dud. Our Eglinton workers redoubled their efforts because of my absences on the national campaign. I was left with relatively little time for participation in my own campaign.

The national campaign took me from coast to coast. I could hardly have been busier. My life was a constant round of speeches, meetings, press interviews, TV and radio programs, photographs and travelling. But it was pleasant because it all went well. My major contribution to the national campaign was, of course, delivered in Quebec. This time the press of Ontario paid some attention to what was happening there. In a review article published on February 25 the *Globe and Mail* said: "Mr. Fleming, who spoke yesterday at St. Hyacinthe for Theo Ricard, will assume the lion's share of the work being assigned in Quebec to out-of-province ministers." It was indeed a lion's share with over thirty speeches entirely in French. I was received everywhere with enthusiasm and the warmest welcome. I really loved campaigning in La Belle Province. The audiences were so responsive, vital and ardent, and always so ready for humour and a bit of wit. Judith Robinson of the *Toronto Telegram* surprised me by appearing in the front row of a big rally I addressed in Quebec City on a Sunday afternoon in mid-March. After a most amusing account of our motorcade in which the large shiny car bearing the Hon. Doe-nald Flem-mang had a contraption in the exhaust set to go off like a rifle-shot every half-minute, and loudspeakers, between martial airs, bellowing invitations to one and all to come and hear Monsieur Flem-mang, she gave an illuminating description of my reception and speech:

> By the time the orator of the day arrived applause in St. Charles School was hair-triggered. It went off in a double round that

wafted Mr. Fleming onto the platform where he was assured in full chorus that he had gained his epaulettes.

All this was courtesy. The real applause came with the realization that the orator of the day was speaking French. Not declaiming a set piece by rote and not reading lamely a text prepared by someone else; but speaking with ease and effect the native tongue of the electors of Quebec South.

Talking in French with an accent so pleasant and with such effortless earnestness it is probable that the hon. member for Eglinton Toronto could have recited a table of weights and measures and been acclaimed for it in St. Charles School, Sillery, but the courtesy of his auditors was not put to the test.

Donald Fleming's speech was a lucid and closely reasoned statement of the Conservative position, and of Conservative Government policy. It included a series of neatly phrased comparisons between past Liberal performances and present Liberal pretensions. It ended with an appeal to the voters of Quebec which may be translated thus:

"Canada has now had for eight months a Conservative Government. The people of Quebec have now had full occasion to judge it by what it has done and to compare the reality with the multitude of false accusations which the Liberals have launched against the Conservatives in the Province of Quebec during many years.

"Our Prime Minister has given proof of the most exact respect for the guarantees contained in the Constitution as they concern the French language and culture and provincial rights. We are not like the Liberals, centralizers; we are respecters of the constitution.

"The Conservative Government is certain of being returned to power on March 31 . . . I appeal therefore to the Province of Quebec to contribute to strengthening the Government. It would be good neither for Canada nor for Quebec that this Province should leave its parliamentary representation isolated in opposition".

The audience in St. Charles School hall cheered and cheered. Revert to Chicoutimi, and a Liberal election meeting.

"Bilingualism", the Liberal leader (Pearson) said there, "is not set by decree nor can it be a law. It is a state of mind". He said it in French, reading but not with élan from a script prepared.

Judging by the two performances the Tory member for Eglinton's state of mind is considerably more bilingual than that of the Leader of the Liberal Party.

Although Judith did not think it possible we did win the seat. My friend Jacques Flynn redeemed the Liberal stronghold of Quebec South from the forty-year grip of the Power family and the Liberal party.

One Sunday in the campaign in Quebec remains fresh in my

memory. I left Toronto early on Sunday morning by plane for Quebec City. I was taken ill en route with stomach flu. I was the guest of my friends Mr. and Mrs. Gerry Martineau at lunch, but became so ill I had to leave the table. I could not disappoint our people, so, although I was by this time running a temperature, I pulled myself together and addressed a big rally in one riding at 2.00 p.m. By 4.00 p.m. I was in another riding addressing another rally of working people. How I came through and delivered my speeches with my wonted vigour and conviction I shall never understand. Instead of attempting to eat dinner I rested in my hotel. At 7.30 p.m. I was addressing a meeting of farmers in Dorchester, and rushed twenty miles away from there to address another meeting at 8.45 p.m. We were driving through canyons of snow piled fifteen feet high on either side of the highway. It was growing colder. On leaving the second meeting of the evening I could think of nothing but to drive back to Quebec City and crawl into a warm bed. I was told, however, that there was a large crowd waiting for me at Beauce, fifty miles away, that my expected appearance there had been widely advertised, and there would be keen disappointment if I failed to come. "Tell them if they'll wait I'll come," I replied as my driver and I sped off on a rather icy highway. Those good people did wait. I arrived at 11 p.m. to receive a tumultuous welcome and made a stirring forty-five minute speech. It was 2 a.m. before I was back in my hotel in Quebec City. Strangely, by that time I was beginning to feel a little better. Next morning I was off on the campaign trail at an early hour.

A politician must be capable of quick adaptation and not least of all during an election campaign. In Windsor amid photographers I proclaimed my confidence in the city's future and visited my brother Gordon at his home, then was presented with the key to victory by our candidates in the local ridings. In Renfrew, along with the Conservative candidate Jim Baskin, I was photographed with a big Indian bow drawing a bead on some target, presumably an apple resting on the head of a Liberal, while Chief Big Flower, Prince Running Deer and Chief White Eagle, in full Indian dress, looked on with satisfaction. Back in Eglinton for the last weekend I was photographed in the midst of young winners of plaques for swimming proficiency at the North Toronto YMCA.

In the course of the campaign I had covered over twenty thousand miles and had addressed seventy-one meetings, thirty of them in French. At a homecoming reception on the last Saturday evening in our committee rooms six hundred citizens turned out to wish me well. In my speech I said that the greatest danger facing our party on election day was over-confidence, and I concluded with these words: "What Canada needs now above all else is a strong, stable government with sufficient strength to enable it to go forward with a long-range program for developing our natural resources. That situation can't be achieved unless the government has an absolute majority and strong backing in Parliament."

The "Follow John" slogan introduced in the campaign was skilfully exploited, particularly in the West. Cards bearing the slogan and two black footprints adorned many cars. The Northern Vision, developing a theme of Richard Rohmer, caught fire. We were basically, however, running on our record, and for a government which had been in office only a few months it was an impressive one.

– Old-age pensions increased to $55 per month;
– Old-age assistance payments increased;
– Payments to disabled persons extended;
– Pensions for the blind increased;
– War veterans allowance benefits increased for 60,000 veterans, widows and orphans;
– Supplementary benefit period for unemployment insurance extended from 16 to 24 weeks;
– Home building loans increased by $300 million resulting in an all-time record winter home construction;
– Income tax reduced for four and a half million people by $146 million, taking 100,000 off the tax rolls;
– Financial assistance to the provinces increased by $87 million;
– Cash advances provided for farm-stored grain;
– Increased salaries for civil service and pay for armed forces;
– Legislation to stabilize farm prices and assure a fair relationship to costs of production;
– Action to remedy trade imbalances and restore overseas markets;
– Development of domestic and foreign markets for Canadian products;
– Federal assistance for power development in the Atlantic provinces;
– Projects commenced to aid development of natural resources;
– Nationwide program of construction projects to provide jobs;
– Hospital insurance scheme advanced six months;
– Federal grants for hospital construction doubled;
– The integrity of Parliament restored.

We had carried out the promises made to the electorate in 1957. Now we asked a mandate to continue the same policies.

Early one morning at Toronto airport I met Mike Pearson sitting on a bench reading mail while he waited for a plane. He was all alone, and I thought he looked forlorn. Surely the Liberal party might have had some supporters present to welcome him and cheer him on.

One incident in mid-March threatened trouble. It was the practice of the Governor of the Bank of Canada to submit his annual report to the Minister of Finance and for the minister to authorize its immediate release. Ken Taylor warned me that I might expect the report and that it would be necessary for me at the height of the campaign to pass judgment on it and determine whether it should be released. During the 1957 campaign there were repeated accusations that the Bank of Canada was maintaining a policy of tight money, which was strangling credit, and that this was causing hardship to business, especially small business. I conveyed these criticisms personally to Coyne, who denied the existence of "tight money" and declined to ease money terms even to assist cabinet's house-building policy. The annual report was delivered to me in Toronto one afternoon in March, and I was asked to authorize its immediate release to the press, as Parliament was not in session. I spent several hours reading it through. My worst fears were quickly justified: in his most tactless style Coyne flatly denied that there was or ever had been a tight money policy. I was all too well aware that the press were or would be apprised of the existence of the report and would be instantly clamouring for copies. If I delayed the release until after March 31 I was sure to be accused of suppressing information to which the voting public was entitled. I knew equally well that the moment it was released the Liberals would use the report as election ammunition against the government. Nevertheless I directed its immediate release. Pearson leaped upon it at once and claimed that the governor had effectively contradicted what the government had been saying. I was asked at once by the press for comment. I said very briefly that the report was the governor's, not mine, that I did not share his views on the subject of tight money, and that the public, having already experienced tight credit, would know and decide whether Canada had had tight money or not. Pearson did his utmost to make an election issue out of the report, but the results at the polls did not indicate that he had been very successful. When Coyne wrote his report he must have been well aware that Pearson would hope to turn it to Liberal partisan advantage. The incident served to embitter my colleagues further against Coyne. Dief was convinced that Coyne was doing his utmost to sabotage us. He never deviated from that opinion. One week before the end of the campaign while I was in Vancouver I was asked by the press if I intended to fire Coyne or seek his resignation. I replied, "No. I shall respect the independence of the Central Bank."

On my visit to Prince Edward Island on March 5 I encountered a savage blizzard which compelled us to cancel our meeting at Souris. The provincial Liberal government called out all the snowploughs that evening to open the roads to a Liberal meeting, but allowed the snow to close the roads to our meeting. Alf Brooks and I spent the evening in the agreeable shelter of our hotel rooms.

Notwithstanding March weather the voters flocked to the polls on the 31st. That evening a large throng of workers gathered early at my committee rooms in a state of high excitement. Well they might. From the early polls the trend was unmistakable. The opposition was wiped out in Nova Scotia and Prince Edward Island. The Quebec results were fantastic; it had elected twenty-five Liberals and fifty Conservatives. Ontario returned sixty-seven Conservatives and fourteen Liberals. Not one Liberal was elected west of Ontario. The three Prairie provinces were solidly Conservative apart from one lone CCF seat (Hazen Argue) in Saskatchewan. Social Credit was wiped out completely. In a House of 265 seats the Conservatives held 208, a record since Confederation, while forty-nine Liberals and eight CCF had survived the deluge to form an opposition of fifty-seven. Veteran CCF leaders M.J. Coldwell and Stanley Knowles had gone down to defeat, and they would be missed in the House. Only four Liberal ex-ministers survived, Pearson, Chevrier, Martin and Pickersgill, to become known later as "The Four Horsemen." Jimmy Sinclair and other well-known ex-ministers had met their end. The opposition was left weak in debating power.

Quebec presented a fascinating study. I doubt if anyone, however optimistic, had expected the province to elect fifty Conservatives; the largest number elected previously had been forty-eight out of sixty-five in 1882, and forty-five in 1867 and 1878. The Union Nationale had supported us openly. People like Gordon Churchill were quick to point out that even without the Quebec members the government had a clear majority. I did not share his satisfaction that the government could govern without the aid of Quebec. This idea and the expression of it grated on my ear. I was happy that Quebec had fully shared in the public opinion that had been expressed right across Canada, and I looked for a rebirth of national unity.

Eglinton gave me the greatest victory at the polls in my entire life. The vote was:

Fleming	28,565
Wilson (Liberal)	9,468
Grube (CCF)	2,646

My plurality (19,097) was unprecedented in the history of the riding. It was the second largest ever given to a Conservative in the history of Canada.

Surveying the national results that night in Ottawa, Grattan O'Leary commented: "This is not just an election victory. This is not merely a landslide victory. It is a political revolution." The crowd gathered in our committee rooms was elated; it was also dazed by the extent of the sweep. All the uncertainty attaching to the government's position in Parliament was now gone. Minority government had been transformed into government with the most powerful majority in Canada's history. Everything now lay within the power of the government and its following in the House. It had a clear and ringing mandate from the Canadian people. There could be no excuses now for failing to take needed and corrective action in any circumstances. The honeymoon was over.

There was no lingering in Toronto to savour the fruits of victory. Back I went to Ottawa the next day to begin ten weeks' work on the budget. Cabinet met Thursday morning, and the old routine resumed its sway.

Dief had again proven himself the most effective campaigner on the scene in English-speaking Canada. He revelled in campaigning, at least in the circumstances of 1958. What Conservative wouldn't have in that contest? Pearson was not in the same league with him. What effect did this unprecedented triumph have on Diefenbaker the man? I observed two principal effects. He had been ready to accept the complete credit for our success at the polls in June 1957. In the autumn on one occasion when Davie Fulton and I were stubbornly differing with him he said very testily to us, "You forget how you come to be here in these senior portfolios." I thought Davie and I had pulled our own weight and more in the 1957 contest. The government's sensational success in 1958 undoubtedly confirmed Dief's opinion that we all owed our advancement to him. There were, of course, many persons who were all too ready to flatter him and add to his own conviction in this regard. One of these was Howard Green. I once heard him say, "The Prime Minister has more political sense in his little finger than all the rest of us put together." This was nonsense, but, more still, it was mischievous. Dief regrettably just lapped it up.

The other effect was that Dief continued to act and think as though he were running a general election campaign. He could not bear the thought of losing ground. Any government with 208 out of 265 seats was bound to lose ground and bound to lose some seats in by-elections. The electorate would wish to correct some of the distortion of party strength in the Commons. What he should have done was to select all the unpopular measures which were needed and put them into effect at once, then in later years before the next general election reap the benefits from these and add the popular measures at that point. Dief was not guided by any such long-term strategy. His dominating purpose was to maintain his proven popularity at the polls as demonstrated on March 31, 1958. One way to do so, thought he, was to spend money and issue hand-outs. This was understandable, but it was regrettable. It added enormously to the burdens of my portfolio.

CHAPTER FORTY-TWO

The Twenty-Fifth Parliament

The political scene in Canada was changing rapidly. The West, long hostile to our cause, was now almost solidly Conservative. Quebec, long a secure Liberal domain, had shifted its allegiance overwhelmingly to us. Mr. St. Laurent had disappeared from the political scene. On Febrary 17 he had announced his retirement. Indeed, he took no part in the election campaign, choosing to spend the time in Florida. He recorded one radio speech in support of Pearson, but this was interpreted as weak support and did the Liberal cause little good. He was acutely missed in the Liberal campaign in Quebec. The Social Credit cause was totally submerged in the West. How permanent were these drastic changes in the Canadian political scene to be? That was a major question in my mind as we surveyed the aftermath of the March 31 political revolution. Was this all a flash in the pan, an ephemeral phase of Canadian politics, or had we seen some abiding shifts of political power and sympathy, with permanent consequences? Was this a genuine triumph of the Conservative party or was it a wave of Diefenbaker support, attaching to him personally? Only time would supply the answers to these vital questions, and the answer was to be one more illustration of the ancient truth, so often repeated in history, that the truth is not long to be found in extremes. In medio veritas.

It was refreshing to fill some speaking engagements under non-political auspices. On February 13 I addressed the Empire Club of Canada in Toronto on the business outlook, choosing as title "Dollars and Sense." I urged businessmen to stand on their own feet and not to rush to government for a quick, ready-made and painless solution of their problems. This exhortation drew editorial applause.

That evening I had the delightful experience of returning to my home city Galt as the guest of honour at the annual meeting

459

of the Galt Board of Trade. It was a memorable homecoming. Many friends of boyhood days turned out to greet me. In the chair was the President of the Board, George Dando, now a druggist, one of the playmates of my childhood; we had begun public school together in 1910.

On February 20 during Brotherhood Week I addressed a luncheon meeting of the Congregation Shaar Hashomayim in Montreal, where I was warmly welcomed by Rabbi Wilfred Shuchat. In my speech I said:

> We are all brothers. The concept of the brotherhood of man rests on a single philosophical basis, the belief that God is our common father. Brotherhood is not negated by differences between people, but overrides them. Before all the world we Canadians have a unique opportunity to set an example in mutual tolerance and goodwill. Much of the prejudice of the world is inherited, and much of the hatred we encounter today has been taught to childen. If I could I would place a 100 per cent inheritance tax on prejudice.

This last remark caught the fancy of some editorial writers and was widely applauded.

Problems do not normally suspend or resolve themselves during election campaigns even though action on them may for the time be suspended. The Board of Transport Commissioners had deposited two major problems on cabinet's doorstep in January. The board authorized a general increase in railway freight rates, effective January 15. All provinces except Ontario and Quebec petitioned cabinet to exercise its power to rescind the increase. The board also issued an order authorizing an increase in telephone rates. We met the two problems by suspending the increases, first to March 1, then by further suspensions. At least this deferred difficult decisions until after the general election.

The civil service was beginning to seek the right of collective bargaining. The Civil Service Federation, a major group, demanded full collective bargaining, but without the right to strike. The attitude of the other associations was not as clear. This headache became my responsibility. With the support of a cabinet committee I recommended quiet discussions by our officials with the staff associations, without any prior commitment, on a trial basis, of a plan for collective discussions, not yet called bargaining, between representatives of the associations and the Treasury Board, with the Civil Service Commission acting in the role of conciliator. Later Arnold Heeney, as chairman of the commission, was to take up this subject seriously and put drive behind it.

Till Parliament met we functioned financially by the use of Governor General's warrants. The first, on February 7, was for by far the largest amount in Canadian history, $544,290,332.32. We still had to borrow money, and it was fortunate for us that interest rates were falling. Facing maturity of $600 million of bonds on May 1st we floated an issue of $800 million in three tranches, a fourteen-month issue with $2\frac{1}{2}$ per cent coupon at 99.5 to yield 2.94 percent; a three-year issue with a 3 per cent coupon at 99. to yield 3.35 per cent; a twelve-year issue with a $3\frac{3}{4}$ per cent coupon at 96.5 to yield 4.01 per cent. Cabinet weighed every cent of the rates and prices before approving the terms. However, I was becoming accustomed to this. All the issues were oversubscribed, the two shorter overwhelmingly. When later questioned as to why I didn't accept all the subscriptions I had to explain that many brokers subscribed for more than they really wanted in anticipation of aggregate oversubscription and a consequent allotment; it would be bad psychology and sharp practice to take up more than we had announced as our goals. We would be returning to the market every three months this year and wished it to be receptive, and the Bank of Canada required a considerable portion of each tranche in order to be in a position to manage the market after the issue. I was delighted that the market had supported this large offering so strongly; some of my colleagues thought we must have made the terms too attractive. I invariably found cabinet difficult to deal with on bond offerings. They acted like about fifteen different ministers of finance, each with his own ideas.

Treasury Board under my chairmanship pursued its labours on the estimates for the year 1958-59. On April 3, I presented these to cabinet, amounting to $5,179,343,555, an increase of $200 million over the year 1957-58. Treasury Board had been tough in its approach, but the new programs, including the increases in the old-age pensions, increases in the payments to the provinces, and increases in salaries to the civil service, armed forces and RCMP, had made the overall increase inescapable. Obviously, these were our own estimates, unlike those of the previous year, which we inherited from our predecessors, and we must be prepared to justify them. I expressed my disappointment that we had been unable to reduce the total. Continuing my financial report, I thought it probable that we would escape a deficit for the year 1957-58, but that taking into account our tax reductions, the cost of new programs and additions to old ones, a mammoth deficit of as much as $850 million could be expected for 1958-59. This dismal forecast shook cabinet. The election was past; the carefree mood of 1957-58 in voting new expenditures and reducing taxes must now give way to the sober reckoning which I had foretold from the beginning. Coming just three days after our election triumph it was like "the morning after the night before." The chickens were coming home to roost. Why must they come quite so soon? From that time on they never quite left us. For the next four years they never ceased flapping their wings about my ears.

Two of the new programs were commendable enough, but they still cost money. On February 18 in my absence cabinet approved increased assistance to university education under a five-fold plan worked out by Sid Smith, most knowledgable in such matters. The scheme would:

– increase the per capita grant to the universities from $1 to $1.50;
– provide federal scholarships for university students;
– amend the National Housing Act to allow loans to universities, on the same terms as loans under the act to limited dividend corporations, to finance the construction of residential housing accommodation for students and staff;
– make no federal loans available to students, as that responsibility should be left to the provinces;
– work out arrangements, if possible, with Quebec, by which grants for universities in that province would be paid over to the provincial government to be used by it for the purpose of university education.

I regarded the decision against student loans as sound; in my opinion, that was clearly a provincial responsibility. The last point I could only regard as naive. Well I knew that as long as le Chef, Maurice Duplessis, was Premier of Quebec the government of that province would have nothing to do with federal university grants.

On March 4 cabinet decided to ask Parliament to provide another gift to the Federation of the West Indies, this time a ship to be used in the inter-island shipping service. This was announced at once, but the necessary discussions were deferred to take place at the Commonwealth Trade and Economic Conference later in the year with representatives of the Federation. It was thought that this was the type of gift which would help to hold the Federation together, and this goal was much sought by the British government.

But unemployment remained the besetting problem facing cabinet. It dominated all our meetings. Not even after the general election did it yield the leading place in our deliberations. It simply terrorized Diefenbaker. Even in early January we were given a forecast that unemployment during that winter would reach a postwar record. Our predecessors had not made even the slightest preparation for such an eventuality. Rejecting the warnings in the report of the economics section of the Department of Trade and Commerce, Walter Harris had based his 1957 budget on the maintenance of high economic activity. The public and Parliament were misled by this folly. When unemployment began to rise we searched for a shelf of public works which we fully expected the St. Laurent government would have prepared against such a day, but none was to be found, not even a trace of one. Howe and Harris, if they ever gave unemployment a thought, evidently considered that a few more empty boasts of "Liberal prosperity" would solve the problem, or at least take the minds of the people off it. In such circumstances there was great danger that cabinet, in seeking to assemble an immediate "crash" program, would do something hasty and ill-considered. I was obliged to oppose some well-meant suggestions for this reason. Undoubtedly the municipalities were in the best position to undertake works programs that would provide immediate employment, but they did not have the funds. Premier Les Frost proposed the employment of one thousand men in the municipal parks of Metropolitan Toronto, with the federal government paying half the cost, the province 30 per cent and the municipality 20 per cent. Cabinet rejected this proposal. My friend Fred Gardiner, chairman of Metro Toronto, telephoned me on May 15 to request a federal contribution toward the cost of the planned $200 million east-west subway because it would provide employment. I was in favour of the construction of the subway, but I could not justify a federal contribution to the cost, and cabinet agreed with me. It was difficult enough dealing with ten provinces; how could we even begin to deal with forty-five hundred municipalities? Besides, Toronto politically was the last place, not the first, for a Conservative government to commence direct aid to municipalities.

By late May the situation had improved sufficiently for us to begin to question its duration. The figure of persons "without a job and seeking work" had dropped in April by 74,000 to 516,000, but was still 8.6 per cent of the labour force. (These figures compare with 1,658,000 and 12.6 per cent in March 1983.) Immigration, which had reached a high volume in 1957, was not now being encouraged, and was expected to drop by one-half in 1958.

There were pitfalls in making individual deals with companies, as well as municipalities, to maintain or proceed with programs which would provide local employment. The Dominion Coal Company in Nova Scotia had requested financial aid to avoid layoffs in the face of excessive inventory accumulation. The Prime Minister turned over this problem to me. I conducted discussions with the officers of the company and with Bob Stanfield, Premier of Nova Scotia. The company was controlled by the A.V. Roe Company and McIntyre Mines. It had excellent banking connections and had not exhausted its credit with the Bank of Montreal. In the face of my opposition cabinet authorized aid, with the province contributing 20 per cent. We had opened the gates, creating a precedent of which others would seek to take advantage. Among them was one John Diefenbaker.

Time was marching on in other quarters. My friend Jean Désy had passed sixty-five years of age and was under medical care. He retired as our ambassador to France, and Pierre Dupuy was appointed to succeed him. We were fortunate to have such gifted and experienced diplomats to fill this very important post abroad, second in importance only to London and Washington.

The problems of defence were almost as persistent as those of unemployment. Canada had a frontier in Europe to defend along with her NATO allies. She also had a frontier of her own in the Arctic to defend from possible Russian attack by the manned bomber and later from intercontinental ballistic missiles (ICBMs). The United States had an equal interest in defending that frontier. This was the origin of the North American Air Defence (NORAD), the alliance between Canada and the United States for air defence of North America. It was a new concept in Canadian history. As a government we had entered into NORAD wholeheartedly in 1957; we must meet the implications as they developed later. A series of defence lines was established in northern Canada, for the purpose of detecting the approach of hostile aircraft and setting in action defensive measures. The Supreme Norad Command was located at Sulphur Springs, Colorado; a Canadian, Air Marshal Roy Slemon, was Deputy Commander-in-Chief. To that extent the Royal Canadian Air Force in peacetime was placed under American command, and the U.S. Air Force under Canadian command. This unified command was not an easy concept to accept, but Canada had to learn it in 1957 just as Lloyd George had to learn it at Doullens amid heaps of British dead in 1918. After a two-day debate on June 10 and 11 the House approved the agreement respecting the organization and structure of the North American Air Defence Command signed at Washington May 12, 1958. The vote was 200 to 8. Only the CCF opposed approval. The Prime Minister stressed that while U.S. bombers were flying over Canadian territory carrying nuclear weapons they must obtain specific Canadian permission in every case in advance. Bombers of the U.S. Strategic Air Command (SAC) continuously patrolled the skies over northern Canada. They had available to them in the United States atomic weapons. Should they be allowed to carry them while patrolling the skies over Canada? Should they be permitted to store atomic bombs in Canada for use in the joint defence of Canada and the United States? These were problems which dogged us throughout all our years in office and helped to destroy us in the end. The Americans were asking for agreement. Cabinet met at the end of April to consider the American request for the right to stockpile atomic weapons in Canada to be used in retaliatory attacks by SAC and also by the U.S. and Canadian navies against enemy submarines. Cabinet did not reach a decision, but it was agreed that if the stockpiling were permitted, the use and deployment of the weapons must be subject to the approval of the Canadian government. This was a reasonable condition. It would have been far better, both defensively and politically, if we had made our decision then and there. The issues were clear enough in my mind. If Canada was attacked we would be compelled to use every weapon at our disposal to defend ourselves and our shores. We were fortunate to have the United States sharing in our defence to the utmost. We had been glad enough to accept a promise by President Roosevelt in the Second World War that the United States would come to our aid if our shores were ever attacked. Surely we wished our joint defence to be successful, and this required preparation. What was the moral distinction between having bombs stored a mile outside our frontiers and storing them inside when we knew that in either case they were intended to be used for the defence of Canada? Had we made an affirmative decision in April 1958, the opposition and criticism which would undoubtedly have arisen would have spent themselves long before 1963. No good resulted from the delay, and our defences were to that extent weakened. We would moreover have proven that we were capable as a government of making difficult and serious decisions. Diefenbaker did not like making difficult decisions, so we deferred action. Storage of atomic weapons under strict control would not have abated our efforts for peace in the great international forums; it might even have lent urgency to our pursuit of peace. The subject was bound to arise in Parliament and in public discussion from time to time.

A related question arose from our discussions. Should Pearson as Leader of the Opposition be consulted concerning the U.S. request? No decision was reached on this question either. We had enough self-respect not to consult him until we had made some decision ourselves. At least we were definite that there should be no consultation with the CCF. Would the consultation, had it occurred, have been for the purpose of seeking concurrence or of merely informing the Leader of the Opposition? In my opinion, it could only have been for the latter purpose, if indeed at all. In the past Mr. St. Laurent had consulted George Drew from time to time, but had not asked him to commit his party. George had, however, been asked what he himself thought about certain matters. It must be very embarrassing for the Leader of the Opposition in such circumstances to be given important information on a basis so confidential that he cannot share it with any of his colleagues, and yet while denied access to their thoughts to be expected to state his own to the Prime Minister.

Parliament was called to convene on May 12. To meet our need of funds proceedings would be compressed. The mover and seconder of the Address would speak on the opening day, the leaders on the 13th, and I would move for interim supply on the 14th. Under the influence of the extraordinary success achieved in televising the Queen's opening of the 1957 session it was agreed that once again the opening proceedings should be televised, but this was not to open the door to the broadcasting of the sittings. On this point the Prime Minister was adamant.

What was to be the position of the eight CCF members? Were they to be recognized as a group in the debates in the House? It was a ticklish question. Coldwell had always been given the floor after the Leader of the Opposition in debate. There was also the question whether places in the debating order should alternate equally between government and opposition, or be apportioned in accordance with their numerical strength. This was a question which could not be decided by the Speaker. In the end both questions largely solved themselves. The CCF kept their collective recognition.

A suggestion was put forward that Coldwell, following his defeat and later resignation as CCF leader, should be made a privy councillor. No action was ever taken by the Prime Minister on the suggestion. What would in my opinion have been a more appropriate course would have been to appoint him to the Senate, where his debating talents would still have been at the service of Parliament, but there were no vacancies, there were many eligible and worthy Conservatives, and something had to be done to reduce the top-heavy and lobsided Liberal majority in the Red Chamber.

A reorganization of the cabinet was necessary, particularly to give Quebec more representation. Ellen Fairclough was shifted from Secretary of State to Citizenship and Immigration. The veteran Senator Haig retired from the cabinet and from the post of Government Leader in the Senate. Raymond O'Hurley was sworn in as Minister of Defence Production and Henri Courte-manche as Secretary of State. Senator Walter M. Aseltine was appointed Government Leader in the Senate, but was not made a member of the cabinet. We were now ready to meet the House.

The selection of the Speaker was given very deliberate con-sideration – much more deliberate than I should have thought necessary. Roly Michener had been Speaker for just four months in the Twenty-Fourth Parliament, and although not firm enough in the opinion of the Prime Minsiter in putting down the opposi-tion when they exceeded their rights, had won distinction and acceptance. He was obviously the best qualified member of the House for the position. Dief raised the question as to whether re-election of Roly might give rise to pressures for a permanent Speaker and give offence to Quebec. The French-Canadian ministers made short work of that fear. So Roly was chosen and the usual compliments were paid him. The Prime Minister's nomination was seconded by Pearson, and was warmly received by the House. The two leaders conducted him to his chair.

Regrettably, that was not the end of the matter. Diefenbaker was never happy over Roly's re-election, and his feelings became stronger and more evident as time passed. I had supported the re-election strongly, so I was given the blame. Time and again throughout the Twenty-Fifth Parliament when Roly appeared to be giving the opposition, and particularly Paul Martin, too much latitude, Dief would turn to me and say most unpleasantly, "There's that man again you imposed on me as Speaker. He just lets the Grits push him around." Roly undoubtedly was generous in his treatment of the Liberal leading spokesmen, and Paul Mar-tin was quick to take advantage of the opportunities thus pro-vided, but with such a preponderance of government strength the Speaker may be pardoned for leniency in dealing with a weak opposition. Pierre Sevigny was elected Deputy Speaker and Ted Rea re-elected Deputy Chairman of Committees.

The seating plan for the new Parliament was very fair to the opposition, but their numbers looked very shrunken. The gov-ernment supporters occupied all the places to the right of the

Speaker and the farther half to his left. The CCF occupied the first section to his left, and the Liberals beyond. This placed Pearson and Chevrier opposite the Prime Minister and me, and Martin and Pickersgill on either side of them. In the Twenty-Second and Twenty-Third Parliaments the overflow of government supporters was seated immediately to the Speaker's left. In the Twenty-Fifth our overflow was located farthest from the Speaker. Our new members were placed in the overflow section.

The day before the opening A.C. Casselman, MP for Grenville-Dundas, died, and tributes were paid to him at the opening. Cass was Dean of the House. He was first elected in 1921, then gave up his seat to create an opening for Arthur Meighen. He returned to Parliament in 1925 and sat continuously for thirty-three years, until his death. He was Conservative Whip until 1955. In the resulting by-election on September 29 he was succeeded by his widow Jean, daughter of Earl Rowe.

The throne speech contained some matters of importance. First, it announced that all Commonwealth countries had accepted the Canadian government's proposal that the Commonwealth Trade and Economic Conference be held in Montreal in September. To meet the problem of unemployment the speech promised an acceleration of useful public works and steps to encourage the development and processing of natural resources in Canada. An amendment to the Unemployment Insurance Act would extend special seasonal benefits by a further six weeks. In addition to the house-building program it was announced that the government was ready to cooperate in further projects for slum clearance and urban redevelopment. Public works would also be undertaken to relieve unemployment. The speech proposed a new regulatory agency for TV and radio, both public and private, and the installation of a system of simultaneous translation in the Commons. It proposed also the appointment of a special select Committee on Broadcasting, a Standing Committee on Estimates and a Standing Committee on Veterans' Affairs, all to have power to send for persons and papers. I was very pleased with what the speech contained about inflation:

> The easing of the stringency in the capital markets of Canada during the past eight months encourages confidence in the expectation that large programs of public investment can be successfully financed not only by Government and its agencies, but also by provincial governments and municipalities. My ministers remain mindful of the importance of financing their large program of expenditures in such a manner as will best safeguard against a recur-

rence of inflationary pressures in future. They wish to urge upon all groups in our society a recognition of the dangers and inequities of inflation and the need to restrain demands which will give rise to increases in prices and the cost of production.

The next day I tabled the Main Estimates for 1958-59 and reported on the Governor General's warrants. I announced that we had cut $73.6 million off the 1957-58 estimates of the Liberal government.

On May 14 I moved for interim supply, giving all the usual undertakings to preserve the rights of members. At the conclusion of my introductory statement Bill Benidickson rose, having been chosen as opposition finance critic. I congratulated him and placed the services of the Department of Finance at his disposal to supply any factual information he might require at any time in the discharge of his responsibilities. My motion carried that afternoon. Benidickson suffered from the handicap of never having sat in the government, but he had been a parliamentary assistant. I had thought one of the Four Horsemen would have assumed the finance responsibility. Perhaps they feared it.

The first division in the new House occurred on my birthday, May 23, on the CCF amendment in the debate on the throne speech. It was defeated 194 to 8, attracting the support of only the eight CCF members, who had chosen Hazen Argue as their House Leader. He was vocal, but was not in the same league with Coldwell as a debater. The CCF also felt the loss of Stanley Knowles on procedure. The Liberal amendment was defeated 181 to 52.

The decks were thus cleared for the business of the session. What was happening outside the legislative mill? One appointment made early in 1958 gave me special satisfaction. On January 30 the Honourable Onesime Gagnon was appointed Lieutenant-Governor of Quebec. This distinguished French Canadian had sat in Parliament from 1930 to 1935, and served for a time as Minister without Portfolio in the Bennett cabinet. He had been a member of the Quebec legislature since 1936 and in the Duplessis governments for seventeen years, the last fourteen as Minister of Finance. I was honoured to enjoy his friendship. He and I campaigned together in Quebec at various times. The appointment was, of course, made in consultation with and bore full approval of Premier Duplessis. Gagnon was succeeded as Minister of Finance by the Honourable John S. Bourque.

On May 27 final authorization was given to the purchase of the Royal College of Physicians Building in London at a price of £375,000. We proceeded to have it united structurally with

Canada House. My personal part in the acquisition of this valuable property on advantageous terms gave me great personal satisfaction.

Mackenzie King has always been given great credit for launching the National Capital Plan. We did much to advance the cause of planning and beautification of Ottawa. I considered that money spent for this purpose was well spent for highly constructive ends. In June we took a major step in authorizing the acquisition of the greenbelt around the Ottawa area. It was not a simple matter, and it gave rise to numerous problems, but the wisdom of our action cannot be questioned.

An appointment which may have had unforeseen consequences was made in June. Mitchell Sharp had been appointed Deputy Minister of Trade and Commerce by the previous government to succeed Fred Bull when Fred was appointed ambassador to Japan. Sharp was regarded as a protégé of C.D. Howe. He was known to maintain a tight rein in the department and to insist that all communications to the minister pass through his hands. Gordon Churchill desired more business experience at the senior level of his department than Sharp possessed at that time. Accordingly, on June 24 James A. Roberts, a man who had had wide business experience and a distinguished military career, was appointed Associate Deputy Minister. It was an excellent appointment. How Sharp felt about it I never learned, but he lived with it for three years before resigning to enter the business world and later to plunge into politics in opposition to us. I never had reason to believe that relationships between Churchill and Sharp were particularly cordial.

Some other appointments awaited action on the part of the Prime Minister. Parliamentary assistants to the ministers had been appointed in August 1957, and I was fortunate enough to have Dick Bell, MP for Carleton, as mine. The appointments ended with dissolution in February 1958. Diefenbaker wrestled with the question of such appointments in the first session of the Twenty-Fifth Parliament, but took no action. I was thus deprived of Dick's valued assistance throughout the 1958 and 1959 sessions.

However, help arrived in a different quarter. After my Mont Tremblant experience with the press Alistair Grosart convinced Diefenbaker that I should have an assistant in charge of press relations. It took some time to convince me that I stood in need of such an addition to my staff. However, after consulting two friends in the press gallery I accepted the idea, and Grey Hamilton was appointed. Grey was young and very capable. He

470

had been on the staff of the *Globe and Mail*'s Ottawa bureau, and George Drew and I agreed that he wrote the best series of reports on the pipeline debate in 1956 to come out of the parliamentary press gallery. His father was a well-known Toronto barrister and a friend of mine. Grey joined me in the summer of 1958 and continued to handle my press relations till April 30, 1962. His services proved of great assistance to me. I was relieved of all direct calls from the press when he took over. Moreover, he was often able to obtain information which might not otherwise have reached my ears or as soon. He accompanied me on many of my travels and proved a very useful, as well as congenial, companion.

The first anniversary of our swearing-in as a government was celebrated on June 21 by a dinner at the Château Laurier, attended by some hundreds of jubilant supporters. Unfortunately, it was felt necessary to call on all the ministers for speeches. It reminded me of the banquets in honour of the Toronto Board of Education in 1938. I chose to make the shortest speech for that reason. I had been acquiring the reputation of being tough and of always answering my colleagues with a firm no, so I told them I would make my favourite speech. I said "No" and sat down. Subsequent anniversaries were not officially celebrated. Ministers were usually too busy to find the time.

I had long been concerned about the inadequacy of the pensions of retired civil servants, members of the armed forces and the Royal Canadian Mounted Police, as well as the widows and children of deceased members of these groups. Many had retired when salaries, and consequently pensions, were much lower than in the case of those retiring in 1958. The rise in the cost of living had further exposed the recipients to a reduction in the purchasing power of their pensions. The problem was complicated, and I studied it a long time. On July 18 the cabinet approved my plans to augment the pensions. This was handled in 1958 by an item in the Estimates. Before 1959, however, the problem had become recognized as permanent; so, with the benefit of the 1958 legislative experiment, a statute was enacted to deal with the problem. This was a necessary and advisable course of action. It brought a fair solution to the problem.

There were times when I fell heir to responsibilities outside the scope of the Department of Finance. In capital cases I was not usually disposed to interfere with the judgment of and the sentence imposed by the courts unless the reasons for commuting sentence were strong. Such cases went to the Governor General personally with the advice of cabinet. Vincent Massey was very conscientious about reviewing them and read all the papers. On one occasion, in the absence of Davie Fulton and Léon Balcer, I spent a Sunday afternoon at the Prime Minister's request with Mr. Massey personally reviewing and discussing all aspects of one case. It was an illustration of the extreme care expended on capital cases in administering the exercise of the royal prerogative of mercy.

I have already mentioned the first requests from civil service sources for collective bargaining. I spent a long time with the aid of Ken Macgregor, Superintendent of Insurance, in developing a medical-surgical benefit plan for civil servants. The cost to the Treasury would be $6.5 million per annum with the government paying half the premium. I presented the plan in late July, but cabinet deferred action on it. Participation by the government as employer was not approved by cabinet until December 22.

On July 17 cabinet decided generously to offer the chairmanship of the Public Accounts Committee to the official opposition. I should have thought that the Liberals would leap at this opportunity, but Pearson, for reasons known only to him, decided to be very coy. He declined to nominate any of his followers for the position. We decided therefore that we would nominate a Liberal of our choosing, and if he declined the nomination, to elect a Conservative. On July 24 it was reported to us that the Liberals would not accept the chairmanship, but would not instruct one of their members to refuse the post if nominated. It was a strange game they were playing. In the end Alan Macnaughton was nominated and accepted. He proved to be a very acceptable and fair-minded chairman. I believe that it was because of his conduct in the office that years later he was chosen as Speaker.

Simultaneous translation of speeches in the House was accepted in the end by the House on August 11 without any opposition. Diefenbaker paid a warm tribute to the French language and delivered one short sentence in French. The time had come to move a step further. On June 24 cabinet finally approved the issuance of bilingual cheques. A few of our Ontario supporters found this hard to accept and no action was taken at the 1958 session.

The position of Comptroller of the Treasury is one of the most important in the Department of Finance, indeed in the whole government service. B.J. McIntyre, the highly respected incumbent, retired in September after a long and distinguished career. To succeed him we appointed Herbert Balls, an exemplary public servant whom I greatly admired.

CHAPTER FORTY-THREE

Visiting Season

During the spring and summer of 1958 the national capital was honoured by a series of visits of very distinguished leaders from other countries. Ottawa welcomed them and the Twenty-Fifth Parliament in its first session paid tribute to the political leaders among them.

Ottawa enjoyed a close and friendly relationship with the royal family of the Netherlands. The street on which I resided during most of my years as a minister was named after Queen Juliana, and the Princess Beatrix took refuge in Ottawa during the German occupation of her country. One of the first visitors to Ottawa that year was the popular Prince Bernhard of the Netherlands. In keeping with protocol he was accompanied by the Canadian ambassador to the Netherlands, Tommy Stone, known to be a close friend of Mike Pearson. The government tendered a dinner in honour of the Prince at the Country Club. The occasion gave rise to a most unfortunate incident. It was an illustration of the sound axiom that diplomats should not mix alcohol and diplomacy.

Mike and Maryon Pearson were guests at the dinner, seated across the table from the Prime Minister and the Prince. Stone was seated beside them. I was seated on the opposite side of the table, as was George Hees several places away. Early in the dinner I observed that Tommy Stone was speaking in a loud voice. I realized that he had chosen to argue with the Prime Minister, who did not continue the argument, and that Hees had intervened to put Tommy in his place. At this point Tommy turned to the Pearsons, put his arm around Maryon and said, "Come on, Maryon and Mike, let us go," in a manner which breathed loyalty to the Pearsons and hostility to the ministers. The incident must have been embarrassing to the Prince, but most of all to Mike Pearson, who blushed deeply and endeavoured to ignore

473

the excited Tommy. Everyone else very properly affected to be unaware of the incident, but a painful moment of deathly silence ensued before the conversations were resumed around the table.

It was the first time I had met Tommy Stone. Wisely he left the diplomatic service a few months later and joined the International Nickel Company. Strange as it may seem, he and I later became good friends. Diefenbaker treated the incident as further proof that Canada's diplomatic representatives were all Pearson partisans.

In mid-May, Field Marshal Lord Montgomery, hero of the battle of El Alamein, visited Ottawa, and I found myself seated beside him at a government luncheon. It was the first, but not the last time, that I was to have the honour of meeting and conversing with the famous Monty. He had a curious way of saying everything twice in a high-pitched voice. Drawing on his experience at El Alamein he expounded to me three military lessons, which I presume apply as well in the political realm: never enter a battle unless you are sure you can win it; battles are won by preparation; and in every great battle there is a crisis: anticipate it and be prepared to meet it.

On May 29 Paul Henri Spaak, Secretary-General of NATO, addressed both Houses informally at noon in the big Railway Committee Room. He also conferred with the cabinet. He gave a very useful exposition of the role of NATO, its resources, its goals and its responsibilities.

On June 2 Dr. Theodor Heuss, President of the Federal Republic of Germany, paid Ottawa an official visit and addressed both Houses formally in the Commons chamber. He spoke in German, and his words were translated. It was a goodwill visit, the first by a German head of state since the war, and it had favourable results. It could not have been an easy experience for him.

Prime Minister Harold Macmillan visited Ottawa following his meetings in Washington with President Eisenhower and John Foster Dulles. On June 13 he addressed a joint session of both Houses. He also met with the cabinet, reviewed many subjects and answered questions. He reported that relations between the United Kingdom and the United States were now closer than they had been for many years. He said he looked on Dulles as a man of great character and industry, and the strongest figure in the United States. He commented that President Eisenhower enjoyed great goodwill, but he had not the physical power to take daily control of events. He thought some limited progress was being made along the road to a summit meeting, the objects of which must be to achieve agreement on "anti-surprise" measures, including tests and inspection of armaments. In relation to Suez he said he had told the press in the United States that if Eden had been better supported in 1956 the world would be better off. He told us frankly that the Canadian government of that time had behaved better than the U.S. government and had helped Britain in its difficulties, but had not helped at the time the government most needed it. He believed that Ike and Dulles now knew that a great error had been made in not supporting Eden and that they were now trying to remedy the situation resulting from it. Later he conferred with Gordon Churchill and myself on trade and economic questions. I sat beside him at dinner that evening, and he became very personal and friendly. He opened by saying, "I understand that you and John pretty well run things here." I replied that I was only endeavouring to do my job as well as I could. Knowing that I was to bring down my budget the next week he spoke of his own experience as Chancellor of the Exchequer, and made this interesting observation: "Every budget should have a theme. That will distinguish it."

At that moment I feared that the feature of my forthcoming budget was likely to be a massive deficit. From that conversation I drew the thought that I should make the theme of my budget realism and confidence, two positive and related concepts. I questioned him as to the sudden resignation of Peter Thorneycroft as Chancellor of the Exchequer in January. He replied very directly, "He wanted to get me out. He wanted to be Prime Minister." I was sorry to hear this said of Peter. It is a hard world, and I daresay politics is at times the roughest part of it, but it is always sad to see friends part company.

Among the subjects discussed by Macmillan with Canadian ministers it was inevitable that his government's current negotiations to enter the European Free Trade Area should arise. He gave us solemn assurance that the United Kingdom would continue to pay close attention to the interests of Canadian agricultural producers in the British market and would ensure that their interests would not be adversely affected. He said firmly that if it should prove necessary to make some concessions concerning agriculture, these would have to be borne by domestic producers in Britain. He made the clear statement that no agreement would be entered into which would worsen in any way the competitive position of Canada's agricultural exports in the British market.

These were powerfully reassuring declarations coming from

the British Prime Minister. But these were not all. In his first conference with Diefenbaker and Sid Smith he stated that in the negotiations his government would also bear in mind that in the past Canada had shipped to Britain a wider range of agricultural commodities than it was shipping at present, including particularly cheese and pork products, and that it was the wish of the Canadian government that Canadian producers should have an opportunity in future to export such commodities to the British market if Canadian prices were competitive. Macmillan later repeated this assurance to me. I accepted it with a profound sense of relief.

On July 21 Dr. Kwame Nkrumah, Prime Minister of Ghana, visited Ottawa and on invitation addressed the members. It is a pity that this promising leader later allowed himself to fall under Russian influence and adopted dictatorial methods in ruling his country. In 1958, however, he was hailed as a leader truly devoted to democracy.

The most important of the political visits was that paid by President Eisenhower for several days in July. He was accompanied by Secretary of State Dulles. He addressed a special session of both Houses on July 9. He was in good speaking form and received a rousing welcome, but his speech, while it contained many gratifying assurances, disappointed those who were looking for a better balance in commodity trade between Canada and the United States. He defended the American role as a dependable supplier as well as his administration's wheat disposal policies and its restrictions on imports of Canadian oil. He stood very firm, however, in resisting the menace of Communist imperialism and praised the agreed plan for joint air defence for North America.

Following his address to Parliament he, Dulles and ambassador Livy Merchant met with the cabinet. The President was in fine fettle, warmly commending face-to-face meetings and down-to-earth discussions. He talked frankly about the U.S. Trading with the Enemy Act and the problems it created for subsidiaries in Canada and other countries of American parent corporations. Ike could not have been friendlier. He seemed to be enjoying his visit to Canada thoroughly. Mr. Dulles spoke of the difficulties of holding alliances together. He said he had told President De Gaulle that he had never known an international task as difficult as the one of holding a peacetime alliance (NATO) together. Dief voiced praise for Ambassador Merchant. It was evident that Dief and Ike had established very cordial personal relations. Dief later showed me a note from the President, signed

476

"Ike," with no little satisfaction and told me the President had asked Dief to address him that way. Great good is bound to result when the head of state of the United States and the head of government in Canada are on such friendly and personal terms. I found great benefit in the similar relations which I enjoyed with several members of the U.S. cabinet. Very friendly feelings also existed between Dief and Harold Macmillan.

One concrete accomplishment arose from the direct discussions between the President and the Prime Minister. Looking at the useful purpose served by the Canada–U.S. Joint Committee on Trade and Economic Matters they decided to set up a similar Joint Committee on Defence, with three ministers on each side. The Canadians were to be the ministers of National Defence, External Affairs and Finance. Cabinet on July 7 had given approval in advance. I was gratified to find myself appointed to this new, vitally important, small and intimate committee. It was a long jump for the lieutenant in the Queen's Own Rifles to plunge into defence planning at the highest level. Some of the most fascinating experiences of my public career were associated with this new responsibility. Besides contributing to the coordination of defence planning, the committee was intended to aid in maintaining civilian control over the military. I called to mind the firm instructions given by Sir Robert Borden to Colonel Walter Gow in the First World War: "Remember, Gow, the civilian authority must always be paramount over the military." It is a principle which many governments in many countries in this century failed to learn until it was too late. I was to be an eyewitness in Peru in 1969 to the familiar pattern of the consequences.

The visits of Eisenhower and Macmillan were of the highest political importance. The visit of Her Royal Highness Princess Margaret was the most delightful. She had never been to Canada before. The tour commenced in British Columbia for a change and moved east from there. A minister was assigned to be in attendance on her at all times, and these honours were rotated by provinces. I had the happy assignment of her visit to Ottawa. Cabinet decided that a mountain in Alberta and a bridge in New Brunswick should be named for her in honour of her visit.

The Princess arrived in Ottawa at noon on Saturday, August 2, and departed at noon on the following Tuesday. The inside reports from the West had described her as "hard to talk to." The fears which were naturally engendered by these reports proved to be groundless. I found her vivacious, witty, down-to-earth, very outspoken and delightfully interesting.

Her busy program commenced immediately on arrival with a luncheon at the Prime Minister's residence, and Alice and I were presented to her there. Following lunch she and I drove in an open car along Sussex Street first to the new City Hall, which she officially opened, and then on to the Château Laurier where a large reception was to be held. The weather was beautiful. The route was lined with crowds, and it seemed that every second or third person was armed with a camera. The Princess was on the right-hand side of the car. Because we drove closer to the right side of the road the people there with cameras had a better opportunity for photographs than those on the left curb. Some of the latter to attract her attention so that she would turn in their direction for their precious photographs called out, "Margie! Margie!" Instantaneously the Princess turned sharply away from them. I expressed my regret at the rudeness shown; she told me it wasn't the first time it had happened. She added that she didn't like being called "Margie" (pronounced with a hard "g").

At the reception she stood in line with the Prime Minister and Mrs. Diefenbaker and shook hands with four hundred people. Her kid glove, white at the beginning, was black in the palm at the end. How could she avoid a sore hand with so much handshaking? This question was discussed, unfortunately after, and not before the reception. Dief demonstrated to her how to avoid a sore hand: in the handshake extend the right hand with the back of the hand on top, not sideways with the thumb on top. The Princess absorbed the instruction gratefully. I observed that the Prime Minister was showing a fatherly solicitude for her well-being. She and he and I had a very friendly and very informal time together. On her return to Government House my duties for the day were at an end. The Governor General gave a dance in her honour that evening and sensibly invited only young people to it.

Sunday morning the Governor General drove the Princess to the cathedral for the service of public worship. The church was packed, and the heat stifling. The Dean and I met her on the doorstep and escorted her to the front pew. The beautiful service proceeded. In the middle of the last hymn "City of God, how broad and far" the Dean came down to her pew and led her and me to the vestry where she signed the register. With the conclusion of the service we made a procession down the aisle to waiting cars which were to take us by a long route, the purpose of which was to allow as many people as possible an opportunity to see her, up the Ottawa River, across the Champlain Bridge, down into Hull for a civic reception, then back across the river to

Government House. The route was too long, and it had the effect of thinning the crowds. The day was hot, and we were again in the open car. She was still very annoyed with the Dean for having deprived her of the singing of the entire last hymn, which happened to be one of her favourites. In the heat and under the weight of his vestments the Dean's face was dripping with perspiration, but this earned him no sympathy.

On the long route we had ample time to chat. The Princess told me that the party at Government House had continued until 3.00 a.m. and she had spent the next hour sitting on the edge of her bed chatting with her lady-in-waiting. The heat consequently was now making her very drowsy. To keep awake she had the driver turn on the radio, but the volume had to be kept low so that the people standing at the side of the road would not hear it. This proving insufficient, she donned coloured glasses. Her private secretary and I endeavoured to provide interesting conversation. Knowing her interest in the theatre I talked of various theatricals then current, particularly my favourite, *My Fair Lady*. I told her of my recent experience taking the family to New York and paying scalpers $25 for $8 seats, the best in the house, to see the original production with Rex Harrison, Julie Andrews and Stanley Holloway. The Princess was shocked at this robbery, and added that she did not like *My Fair Lady*, anyway.

As we approached Hull and the crowds lining the route became more dense I thought it time to prepare for the approaching reception at the Hull City Hall. I told Princess Margaret that in presenting the mayor to her I would address these words to her, "Votre Altesse Royale, j'ai l'honneur de vous présenter le maire de Hull, Monsieur Mongrain," and then, "Madame Mongrain." Then I added, "I must confess that I have never met the Mayor of Hull, and don't know if I will be able to identify him correctly at the City Hall. I hope I find the right man." The Princess put me immediately at my ease, saying, "Don't you worry. I can smell a mayor a mile away." I laughed all the remainder of the journey to the City Hall. No difficulty ensued. Mr. and Mrs. Mongrain stood alone in front of the Hotel de Ville and were easily identified.

That afternoon I escorted the Princess and her party to their waiting aircraft. Before parting I told her that I would always look back on the two days spent in attendance on her as one of the great privileges of my life. She seemed genuinely pleased by this compliment and thanked me warmly, then took off for a day's rest in a remote location. Fortunately, we were to meet again at Brussells several months later.

Princess Margaret has had her ups and downs since those days. I remember her as a very human and genuine person playing a difficult role.

Rarely has Ottawa played host to so many different world figures in a period of ten weeks. They added immense interest to the national scene.

CHAPTER FORTY-FOUR

Budget, 1958 Model

No other event in Parliament stirs up so much interest both in and outside the House as the annual budget. Some issues giving rise to debate will for the time being arouse equal interest and generate as much excitement. For example, the debate on conscription in 1944, the pipeline debate in 1956 and the controversy over James Coyne in 1961 all stirred enormous public interest and the House played to full galleries, but these were special and unique events never to be repeated. But the budget is an annual event. It owes nothing to being unexpected in the excitement it provokes; on the contrary, it is so completely expected that only the date of its introduction is unknown long beforehand and members busy themselves often for weeks in advance questioning the Minister of Finance on that aspect. If no budget is forthcoming, as in the autumn session of 1957, the House vents its displeasure on the Minister of Finance. Members of all parties await the budget with impatience. Government supporters look to it for solutions of many current problems and answers to many criticisms which they have been obliged to endure; opposition members hail it as their principal opportunity to indict the government and unburden themselves of ammunition which they have been accumulating, often for months. The budget debate is the most uninhibited of all debates. Everything is relevant to the budget; members can speak without any fear of being chided by the Speaker for trespassing on subjects outside the realm of relevance. The budget presents the press gallery with its greatest challenge. Swift and understanding reporting invariably taxes the resources of the gallery to the utmost. Reports and articles are to be written by the news writers, and no self-respecting editorial page can ignore the budget.

The timing of the budget is highly important. In Westminster the budget is normally introduced on the same day in the first week of April each year. This system possesses some advantages, but suffers from rigidity. It has not been followed in Canada. My annual budgets in five years spanned a period of three months, from March 31 in 1960 to June 20 in 1961. Circumstances, economic and political, influenced the choice of dates. The fiscal year ends March 31, and theoretically a budget should not be long delayed into the new fiscal year. On the other hand, the accounts for the previous year cannot possibly be completed until some weeks after its conclusion; a budget early in the new fiscal year must therefore result in a large element of estimating, instead of actual verifiable figures, in reporting both revenue and expenditure of the previous year, and this is not very satisfactory. I brought down two mini-budgets in December, but for special reasons in each case.

The provincial treasurers are assisted in their tasks by an early federal budget, as it is more difficult for them to compose their budgets if they do not know the thrust of the federal budget. The exigencies of business must also be considered. No one watches for the budget or examines it more closely than businessmen, particularly those leading our financial institutions. The precise text of the speech is scrutinized by lawyers and accountants with a fine-tooth comb. Business is always looking for a budget, because in planning it needs to know the policies of the government on as up-to-date a basis as possible.

Suggestions were offered from time to time during my years in office that an annual budget is too infrequent. It is argued that economic conditions change too rapidly nowadays to accommodate themselves to an annual review. This is often true; certainly it was of my experience in 1960. However, budgetary accounting must be constructed on the basis of uniform periods, and for governments and business institutions the year or twelve-month period has long proven acceptable. The trouble, of course, is that government budgets must serve numerous purposes. They must provide an accounting of revenues and the disposition thereof; they must examine the tax structure and propose needed changes therein; and they must examine economic conditions and endeavour to read the economic signs and influence the discernible direction and trends so far as may be deemed desirable or possible.

This last purpose, of course, brings us to the subject of Keynesian economic theory. I studied the works of John Maynard Keynes when I was a student of political economy at university. He had at that time not yet attained the pontifical authority which he gained later with his idea of cyclical budgeting. This theory was to come in full flower in the postwar period. Keynes, however, in his latest days expressed some doubts about his earlier views. Even then it was said that if six leading economists were locked up in a room and the same question was submitted to each, seven different answers would emerge, and two of them would be supplied by Keynes. In our days in opposition we had found that the cycle which guided Liberal budgets was not the economic, but the political, cycle. I detected strong traces of Keynesian thinking among economic advisers in the Department of Finance; I never adopted the Keynesian thinking altogether. To apply that thinking at the national level successfully one would need to wield dictatorial powers, be reviewing and modifying policy constantly, serve an electorate which was totally submissive and cooperative, and be entirely independent of the next general election. I did not possess these advantages, so Keynes and his ideas were obliged often to yield to harsh reality. However, in examining the economy and the trends at work in it each year, I could not escape Keynes.

The preparation of the budget was a mammoth exercise. It extended over a period of about ten weeks of as intensive effort as my duties in the House, in cabinet, and in the Treasury Board would permit. It began on completion of the review of the Estimates by the Treasury Board, and that challenging and laborious exercise itself lasted about two months. For the budget preparation the public were invited to submit briefs and ideas. The submissions from the large national organizations, such as the Canadian Chamber of Commerce, the Canadian Labour Congress, the Canadian Manufacturers' Association, usually involved meetings with the entire cabinet, and covered more ground than just the budget. They were helpful, as were the submissions of professional organizations and individuals. At some point in January or February I would announce in the House that we were about to begin intensive review of all submissions and therefore that only those received by a particular stated day would be considered. When that day came it was the duty of my officials to analyse, study and catalogue all submissions. After that we were ready to begin our sittings on them.

The selection of the officials, particularly those from the Department of National Revenue, in attendance depended on the subjects under consideration – for example, income tax, sales tax, excise tax, tariff, trade, international finance. Anywhere from a dozen to twenty officials sat around my desk in a semicircle, and we went through all proposals. These were catalogued in what I called "the black books" and numbered usually several hundred. Each was considered fully and either approved, rejected or held for further study. This exercise occupied weeks. However, it was only concerned with the minutiae; we still had the problems associated with the balance of ways and means, tax changes and broad economic policy. Finally there remained the writing of the budget speech. Fortunately, among my officials were some very competent scribes. We discussed together in a smaller group our ideas, and they went to work to write the drafts of their respective portions of the speech. These were then unified. I redrafted all parts, both as to content and style, for, as the officials reminded me, "This is *your* speech." After various drafts those who participated in the final review were Ken Taylor, Wynne Plumptre, Simon Reisman, Ken Eaton at first and later Claud Isbister, Lou Rasminsky, Dick Bell, Grey Hamilton, and myself. We sat around a lovely old octagonal table in the office of Ken Taylor when we were so engaged. All ministers of finance did not pursue the same method or apply the same degree of meticulous care. Ken Taylor told me that one year Doug Abbott spent the week prior to the delivery of his budget at a curling bonspiel. The officials wrote the speech and Doug returned just in time to read it to the House.

Secrecy was imperative. The slightest leak would have had irreparable consequences. Ken Taylor took charge of all copies and copying. The papers which I was obliged to take home at nights I actually took into the bed with me. No one could have laid hands on them without rousing me. The final copying was carried out under the capable supervision of Ken's secretary by a group of trusted senior secretaries, no one of whom was permitted to type two consecutive pages of the text. Ken kept all sheets, even the carbons, in the safe. The final photocopying and distribution by air to offices of the Bank of Canada in various cities of Canada was carried out by the Bank. My reading copy was typed double space in a loose-leaf black binder. I still retain the reading copies of all my budget speeches.

My budgets were all delivered on a Tuesday or Thursday evening. There was no superstition in this; it is traditional and prudent to deliver the speech after the close of the markets. The House does not normally sit on Wednesday evening, and the attendance of members on Monday and Friday evenings is reduced by weekend travel. That left Tuesdays and Thursdays.

At noon on the great day copies of the speech are delivered to such members of the press gallery as present themselves in the Railway Committee Room, take a pledge of secrecy, and submit to being locked up until 8.00 p.m. Departmental officials usually

484

join them in the late afternoon to answer questions and supply information. There has never been a violation of secrecy by the gentlemen of the press. At 8.00 p.m. they are free to enter the House. As the minister in his reading comes to the beginning of each section of the speech it is released. In the House as soon as the minister commences reading a copy of the speech is handed to the Leader of the Opposition, the financial critic, and the leaders of the other recognized parties.

In all my years there never was a budget leak. The speculation in advance as to the contents of the speech is universal and impossible to control. Sometimes it proves correct. One year correct speculation by one journalist led to an accusation by another that there must have been a leak. I thought otherwise, but to be certain I had a swift and thorough investigation made and was completely satisfied that there had been none.

It is customary for the Minister of Finance to announce the date of the budget about eight to ten days in advance. The customary announcement is guaranteed to empty the press gallery immediately as its members rush to the telephones with the news. Members of the opposition thereafter frequently put loaded questions to the minister, which he turns aside without too much difficulty. Photographs of the minister are taken by the press with increasing frequency, posed either in his office or out of doors carrying a briefcase. With each succeeding budget it becomes more difficult to devise some new pose. I was party to a considerable number of them, but once, to the disappointment of Grey Hamilton, who was handling press relations for me, I declined to pose with my shirt-sleeves rolled up, because I never worked that way in my office. I thought I had to be honest with the public even in a pose for a press photograph.

The presentation of the budget really commences the previous day with the tabling by the minister of the white paper containing the budget papers. The search by the press for intimate details about the minister on the day of the budget is insatiable. Always I was expected to disclose precisely what I ate for breakfast and for lunch. I endeavoured to leave my office in the afternoon after Question Period and to go home to enjoy some peace and quiet, and look over the text for the last time, making a point of walking a good part of the distance. Alice served dinner early, and digestion was well advanced before we left home about 7.15 p.m. I didn't wish to have too many minutes to spend in my office before 8.00 p.m. However, there were always last-minute press photographs of us climbing up the stair to my office and of Alice pinning a carnation on my lapel – always, of course, a Conservative blue one. I had never thought of myself as being unduly concerned about my clothes, but it was on such occasions that reference regularly appeared in the news articles to the "dapper" Minister of Finance and statements which greatly surprised me to the effect that "The Minister is always one of the best-dressed Members of the House of Commons." If there was any truth in this last comment I can thank Alice for it. In the United Kingdom the Chancellor of the Exchequer traditionally wears a new pair of shoes and sips a drink spiked with rum. I was never tempted to follow this example in either respect.

The air is filled with excitement and expectation on the night of nights. The crowds begin lining up at dinner-time, and the corridor is filled with a column of those hoping to find a seat in the galleries. By eight o'clock every seat in the galleries is occupied and also almost every seat on the floor of the House. The minister does not enter at eight; he waits another couple of minutes till everyone is seated, then makes a dramatic entry to a salvo of thunderous applause from the government benches, and takes his seat. I was fortunate to be cheered also beforehand on entering the lobby by my good friends the Conservative members from Quebec, gathered there en masse for the purpose. The minister rises in his place, bows to the Speaker and makes this traditional motion, "That Mr. Speaker do now leave the chair for the House to go into Committee of Ways and Means." Then he's off! The reading of the fateful text proceeds.

I have not yet mentioned the most difficult feature of the preparation, or what was so for me, namely, obtaining the approval of cabinet. In England the Chancellor of the Exchequer enjoys more freedom at the hands of his colleagues. The night before the delivery of the budget the cabinet meets with the chief government whip present. At a signal the whip locks the door and the Chancellor of the Exchequer reveals to his colleagues the contents of his budget. Before my first budget was too far advanced I went to see the Prime Minister to give him a preview of my intentions. As it still had to be submitted to cabinet for approval I accomplished little by giving the Prime Minister the preview, and I abandoned it in later years. I do not know what practice the Liberal cabinet followed, whether they gave the Minister of Finance a free hand or insisted on passing judgment on every feature of the budget. The insistence of my colleagues on sitting in judgment on all my proposals created difficulties for me which are obvious enough, but it added a special problem: at just what stage should I seek cabinet's approval? Should I consult them early before the budget and the speech had taken advanced

486

form, or should I wait till they were virtually complete? The former would have been an open invitation to cabinet to write a different budget, or, more probably, about fifteen different budgets; the latter ran the risk of having my budget upset when time was too short to effect the repairs. I presented my 1958 budget to my colleagues on the morning of the day before its announced delivery. Adopting Harold Macmillan's advice of the previous week, I told them its theme would be realism and confidence. My budget, as outlined to them at a meeting which lasted all morning and part of the afternoon, won their approval, but numerous suggestions were made which I was asked to consider. Better late than never!

The 1958 budget was brought down on June 17. I was in no position to distribute any big plums. In the important matter of tax reductions I had largely shot my bolt the previous December, though the reductions I made had served us well during the election campaign. We were faced with an enormous deficit, so I had no room left to manoeuvre. As if that were not trouble enough, several developments in the spring set me back further.

On April 3 I had told cabinet I still thought it probable that we would escape a deficit for the year 1957-58. On April 18, with the figures at March 31 available, I was obliged to report that we would indeed have a small deficit. Revenues had dropped, while expenditures continued at the expected level. A large number of substantial income tax refunds had been issued by the Department of National Revenue in late March. Had these been held back till April we would have escaped the deficit, although our deficit in 1958-59 would have been that much greater. Dief was convinced that there were people in the Department of National Revenue who had expedited the refunds simply in order to show us in as bad a light as possible. The result was very disappointing to me. Even a very small surplus under the circumstances would have had positive psychological consequences for the government and particularly for me.

On May 27 I informed cabinet that the Tariff Board had submitted its report on woollens and worsteds. The board recommended no changes in the MFN (Most Favoured Nation) tariff rate on wool and only slight upward revisions in the BP (British Preference) rate on certain woollen fabrics. The latter recommendation was bound to be acutely disappointing to Canadian manufacturers. I warned that, in the plight of the Canadian textile industry, and with growing unemployment, I foresaw a need to restore the provisions of the old section 35 of the Customs Act to prevent dumping of goods in Canada at prices below the cost of production. The provision had been repealed by the Grits in 1948, but before that had been in effect since 1930. On June 5 cabinet approved my proposal to include in my budget the restoration of this reasonable safeguard against an advanced form of dumping.

Moreover, we were faced with the necessity for substantial borrowing. Although with the recession interest rates were declining and our bond offering at May 1 had been impressively successful, we still faced a maturity of $400 million on October 1 and another $950 million on January 1, 1959. In addition, we would require to raise from $300 million to $450 million of new money on each of these dates and also in July 1958 and April 1959. Such a large volume of borrowing might easily set interest rates rising again and create competition with the provinces and municipalities. To obtain the best advice on marketing our issues my colleagues advanced ideas which usually involved advance consultations with those who would be purchasing our bonds or making deals with financial institutions upon whom we were also depending to finance our ambitious home-building program. I never found a better method of marketing our bonds than the one in use then and still in use in 1984. It gave rise to very little criticism from the market. Equally, I never found a better source of advice on the terms of new issues than Bob Beattie and Ralph McKibbin, deputy governors of the Bank of Canada. At all times during my years in office the Bank of Canada discharged its task of debt management for the Ministry of Finance admirably. Nevertheless, I was faced with the necessity of raising $3.75 billion in a period of twelve months. The responsibility for this bleak task rested almost entirely on the shoulders of our Liberal predecessors. I was tempted at times to believe that they must have been relieved to escape the task of shouldering the consequences of their want of foresight.

Then in May the country was threatened with a rail strike as the result of the imminent layoff of diesel firemen. I wondered what more could go wrong. Although unemployment declined materially in the spring it was evident that a recession had descended on Canada as on the United States and countries of Western Europe, and that no preparation had been made by our predecessors to meet it. It was anything but a happy background for my budget. I resolved to give the country a frank review of economic conditions and the economic outlook and to state the grounds of my confidence. I think I chose the right theme for the budget – realism and confidence. And if I was not in a position to propose any major tax reductions I could propose a dazzling number of tax reforms and minor reductions. I could also attempt a comprehensive statement of government policy in all fiscal-related fields. All this I proceeded to do.

My budget speech on June 17, 1958, was the longest and most comprehensive one I had up to that time heard delivered in the House of Commons. I spoke for over two hours and finished as strongly as I began. I did not take even one sip of water throughout. At the conclusion our members accorded me an ovation. Paul Martin told Alice it was the best-delivered budget speech he had ever heard in his twenty-two years in the House. He stopped short of saying it was the best budget speech he had heard.

I scored one historical first, and I did it deliberately. A careful review of all the budget speeches delivered in the Canadian Parliament since Confederation disclosed that in no case had any portion of any budget speech been delivered in French, and this had surprised me. On three occasions – December 7, 1867, April 28, 1868, and May 7, 1869, in the days before the Hansard reports of debates, the scrapbooks on the proceedings showed that following the budget presentation by the Honourable John Rose, Sir George Etienne Cartier followed in French with an explanation or abstract of the statements of the Minister of Finance. I made history by delivering two passages of my speech in French. Needless to say, these were very carefully chosen.

I proceeded to deliver a warm tribute to the officials who had assisted me in preparing the budget, and particularly to Ken Eaton, Assistant Deputy Minister and Director of the Tax Division of the Department of Finance, who was retiring to enter practice as a consultant after having played a leading role in the shaping of every budget in the last twenty-five years. I thanked him for continuing beyond the intended date of his retirement to assist me in the completion of my first budget. Of all the officials in the department Ken was the one I had known longest and best. He had planned his retirement before I became minister.

The speech was divided into twelve sections, the principal ones being economic review, government accounts for the year 1957-58, international trade and economic relations, the Emergency Gold Mining Assistance Act, government accounts for the year 1958-59, and tax policy and tax changes. I examined every aspect of the national economy, and concluded we were in "a fairly mild recession" and that we were coming through it better than the United States and other comparable countries. The labour force had experienced a record increase. Between June 1957 and May 1958 the Consumer Price Index had risen from

121.6 to 125.1, or 3 per cent. Wholesale prices dropped for ten months of 1957. The value of the Canadian dollar had risen to $1.06 U.S. in August 1957, then declined to a low of $1.01 U.S. in January 1958, and stood at 103.75. I gave a balance sheet of the advantages and disadvantages of a premium dollar and the functions of our Exchange Fund, both of which are, I believe, as valid in 1984 as in 1958. I delivered a solemn warning against the dangers of inflation. I reported that our desire for a balanced budget would not take precedence over the necessity to provide jobs for the unemployed.

I gave a very comprehensive review of developments in our international trade and economic relations and of government policy. I examined our trade relations with the European Common Market ("the Six") and the European Free Trade Area, and expressed our concern that they pursue outward-looking, rather than protectionist, policies. I reported on our progress with the planning for the Commonwealth Trade and Economic Conference to be held in Montreal in September, warned that we were not proposing a new system of Commonwealth preferences, and stated our objectives.

On gold production I announced an increase of 25 per cent in the scale of assistance for the years 1958, 1959 and 1960 in the hope of maintaining the level of gold production in Canada and promoting the well-being of our northern gold-mining communities.

I reported a deficit of $39 million for the year 1957-58. I reckoned our budgetary expenditures for 1958-59 at $5,300 million, an increase of $215 million over the previous year, due to increased pensions, the cost of hospital insurance and expenditures for national development. I based my forecasts on a gross national product of $32 billion, a 2 per cent increase over 1957, mainly in price levels. After tax reductions I estimated revenue at $4,652 million, with a deficit of $648 million.

As to tax policy I examined the merits of proposals for general tax reductions, public investment, and income maintenance as a means of combatting the recession. It is interesting to note that the debate on such alternative policies in similar circumstances is being actively continued in Ottawa and Washington in 1984. I commented, "My own view is that just as there is no single remedy for the problems of inflation, so there is no one way to meet the problems of recession. We need to use all the means available to us. The essence of sound policy lies in using the right balance or the best 'mix' of the various means, and to apply them in a timely fashion."

I recommended many individual tax reductions. Prescribed drugs, eyeglasses, ambulance outlays were to be included in medical expense deductible from income, charitable gifts by corporations were to be exempt up to 10 per cent of income, and with this I coupled a strong plea for assistance from corporations to universities in a period of expansion, gifts of homes by spouses and gifts of farms from parents to children were exempted from gift tax within limits, and many others. I reintroduced the Estate Tax Act and pointed out that it was a tax-reduction measure, particularly for estates in the lower brackets. I announced repeal of the magazine tax introduced by Walter Harris. I added that we were not unaware of the difficulties faced by the Canadian magazines and stated that we were prepared to examine any serious proposal to assist them provided it infringed on neither the freedom of the press nor the reading preferences of the public.

I had much to say about the tariff changes, both those recommended by the Tariff Board and others. I announced the intended restoration of section 35 of the Customs Act to prevent dumping of imported goods at a price below the cost of production. This was of major concern to the beleaguered textile industry, and because of the number of mills in Quebec I delivered part of my remarks on that subject in French. I increased the exemption on goods purchased abroad by Canadian tourists to $300 in cases where the tourist had been outside Canada at least fourteen days.

On my concluding summation I said, ". . . a Minister who is faced with a deficit of $648 million is severely circumscribed in writing the kind of budget he would have wished. But we live in a world of realities." I expressed my concern over costs of production and prices in Canada. I said, "We are in danger of becoming a high-cost economy. Such a prospect is particularly perilous in the case of a country like Canada which must sell so much of its production in markets abroad." I warned that "increases in incomes can be justified by increased productivity and by increased productivity alone." I declared the purpose of the government in the budget "to encourage the enterprise, industry and self-reliance of the Canadian people."

My final paragraph in French was translated thus:

> As debtors to the sacrifices of the generations which have gone before us and heirs to the fruits of their labours, we Canadians take pride in the unyielding march of this nation to her great destiny. The advances of these ninety-one years have surpassed the dreams of our forefathers; yet today we know that we stand but on

491

the threshold of the true greatness of this favoured land. There remains for us a sacred duty, that of contributing to the realization of the hopes and aims of the Fathers of Confederation.

I closed in English with this affirmation:

> This budget has been born of confidence in Canada's future, not blind wishful thinking, but unshrinking realism. We have sought to face our difficulties squarely and to prescribe bold courses to meet them. We have not veered and shall not veer from our unshaken belief in the shining future of Canada. Providence has blessed this land with vast resources. Our people are vigorous and enterprising. The advance of this nation to greatness has derived its strength and inspiration from the courage, the industry, the self-reliance and the thrift of God-fearing pioneers. We stake our unwavering belief in Canada's destiny on these Canadian virtues, and as God gives us wisdom and this House gives us its support, we shall strive to meet the challenge of our responsibilities.

In the painful circumstances of 1982 and 1983 it all sounds so idealistic. I sat down to a storm of applause.

The Liberal amendment regretted that "the government, in its budget proposals, has failed to cope satisfactorily with the problems of recession in spite of the largest peacetime deficit in Canadian history and that it is moving towards greater trade restrictions at a time when other countries in the western world are moving in the opposite direction." The CCF supported the Liberal amendment and by their own sought to add to it the following: "This House further regrets that the Government contemplates no action at this Session to recognize the loss of purchasing power to the majority of Canadian citizens because of the lowered value of the dollar as related to consumer goods and prices, by amending the Income Tax Act so as to raise the amount of permissible income to single and married persons without taxation." In the face of Mr. Benidickson's rantings about the record deficit, Dick Bell in his very effective speech on June 20 pointed out that in 1909 W.S. Fielding, greatest of Liberal Ministers of Finance, had no concern over a deficit which represented 35 per cent of total annual expenditure; Mr. Dunning was unworried when in 1930 he budgeted for a deficit equal to 19 per cent of expenditure, and in 1935 a deficit of 14.6 per cent.

The CCF amendment was defeated by 146 to 43. It was supported by the Liberals. Before the Liberal amendment was defeated on July 2 by 161 to 47 I closed the debate on it. I attacked the Grits for their distortions, their inconsistencies and their self-contradictions. Not one of them had had the courage even to mention the magazine tax. Not one of them had offered a suggestion to reduce the deficit by so much as a dollar; on the contrary, all the Liberals, including Pearson, had voted for the CCF amendment which, if carried, would have increased the deficit by a very large amount. Pearson finally spoke just at the close of the debate on July 3. After all we had heard from his supporters about the horrendous deficit I was astonished to hear him say: "It is not the deficit as such that we are criticizing, because deficits are required in the kind of situation we have in this country at the present time." My motion was carried by a vote of 146 to 47.

But that merely moved all my budget resolutions into Committee of Ways and Means. There they were threshed over in detail. Then the bills were introduced, and they each passed through three readings and committee stage. The process lasted for weeks. In the end the required legislation was all passed. I spent a busy summer piloting through the House a heavy volume of legislation, including the new Estate Tax Act, bills to amend the Excise Act, the Excise Tax Act, the Income Tax Act, the Financial Administration Act, the Canadian Farm Loan Act, the Customs Tariff, the Trust Companies Act, and the annual bill to authorize the capital expenditures of Canadian National Railways. Most of these measures arose out of the budget.

It remains only to add that the budget was well received by the press. It was not to be expected that dyed-in-the-wool Grit newspapers like the *Winnipeg Free Press*, the *Ottawa Citizen*, the *Toronto Daily Star*, the *Saskatoon Star-Phoenix* would see much good in it. However, even Charles Lynch, writing in the *Citizen*, reluctantly conceded that on the strength of the budget and my presentation of it the Minister of Finance had risen in his estimation. My tribute to Ken Eaton was warmly commended in an editorial in the *Ottawa Journal*. The French-language press praised me for employing that tongue in a budget speech for the first time in Canada's history, and hailed me as "Un vrai Canadien."

Ken Eaton left the department on July 15. How was I to fill such a critical vacancy? His excellent assistant Ray Irwin was thought to need more experience. At that moment the name of Claud Isbister was put before me by Ken Taylor. I knew Claud. He was Assistant Deputy Minister of Trade and Commerce. He had taken a leading part in trade negotiations at Geneva. "What does he know about our tax structure and its detailed provisions?" I asked. "Give him the chance, and I'll guarantee that in six months he'll know it all," replied Ken. But there was a more serious difficulty in the path. Claud had come under suspicion by Gordon Churchill and consequently by Diefenbaker as a Liberal sympathizer and therefore a saboteur of our government. Claud and I discussed this charge in my office one day. The suspicion rested on remarks alleged to have been overheard in an adjoining room in a London hotel. Claud denied having any part in this alleged conversation in which senior government officials were said to have expressed hostility to ministers. I was completely satisfied with Claud's denial. He had already decided to leave the Department of Trade and Commerce to escape the pall of his minister's suspicion and to seek a university appointment if I chose not to offer him the post in the Department of Finance. I determined to face the wrath and suspicion of Diefenbaker and Churchill and to appoint Claud. The inevitable result was that some of the suspicion rubbed off on me as I well knew it would. It added weight to their belief that I was under the influence of senior civil servants.

The appointment was made and Claud became Assistant Deputy Minister of Finance and Director of the Taxation Division. He was happy in his new position removed from baneful suspicion and proved a most valuable addition to the senior ranks of the staff of the department. He completely fulfilled Ken Taylor's prophecy. I never found him wanting in knowledge of our tax structure and its multifarious and multitudinous details, and he was under all circumstances loyal to his responsibilities and highly capable in the discharge of them. I take strong satisfaction in retaining him in the public service of Canada and in that way contributing to his subsequent distinguished career as a deputy minister and international official.

CHAPTER FORTY-FIVE

The Conversion Loan

A few days after the presentation of the budget James Coyne came to see me. He never called me directly on the telephone, choosing to make appointments with me through Ken Taylor, who was always present at our meetings. Coyne always left matters pertaining to bond issues to his deputies, Bob Beattie and Ralph McKibbin. This time, however, he came alone. I had no prior intimation as to the purpose of his coming. Ken had been made fully aware of the project to be laid before me and had concurred in it, but thought it best to allow its author to present it from the outset without any introduction by anyone else. Coyne proceeded to lay before me one of the biggest financial proposals in Canadian history and to expound a brilliant plan to resolve a present and future problem of immense magnitude. The problem sprang out of Canada's wartime financing.

During the Second World War Canada had of necessity floated numerous bond issues, called Victory Loans. The first four of these had already matured, but numbers 5 to 9 inclusive, all bearing a 3 per cent interest coupon, were outstanding and overhanging the market. They aggregated $6.4 billion, which was more than 60 per cent of the outstanding national funded debt, excluding Canada Savings Bonds and Treasury Bills. Every cent of this enormous sum would have matured by 1966: the Fifth Victory Loan, $947 million on January 1, 1959; the Sixth, $1,165 million on June 1, 1960, the Seventh, $1,315 million on February 1, 1962; the Eighth, $1,295 million on October 1, 1963; and the Ninth, $1,691 million on September 1, 1966. This $6.4 billion was only part of approximately $10 billion of government securities which would fall due for payment before September 1966. All five Victory issues were callable before September 1, 1961, and this added to their overhanging weight on the market. It was necessary in the interests of orderly debt management to plan to meet this rapid succession of maturities and not to allow them to take us unprepared. It was not a problem to be approached on a piecemeal basis; it was necessary to have a comprehensive plan. Of necessity it must be a plan of unprecedented magnitude. The effect of the overhang was to contribute greatly to the general feeling of uncertainty in Canada's bond markets over the previous four years; its continuance would exert an increasingly grave pressure on the market not only for federal, but also for provincial, municipal and good corporate bonds, and would virtually inhibit long-term borrowing. The average length to maturity of the Canadian public debt was down to five to six years. Apart from the holdings of corporations and financial institutions, the Victory Loan bonds were held by two million private individual holders.

The solution Coyne proposed was to offer new and longer-term bonds in exchange for the Victory Loan holdings and to diversify the maturities into four tranches: $3\frac{1}{4}$ years with a 3 per cent coupon; 7 years at $3\frac{3}{4}$ per cent; 14 years at $4\frac{1}{4}$ per cent and 25 years at $4\frac{1}{2}$ per cent. The owners of the fifth and sixth Victory Loans could convert into any of the four new issues; holders of the seventh into any of the three longest new maturities (1965, 1972 and 1983); holders of the eighth and ninth into either of the two longest new maturities (1972 and 1983). To adjust equitably the current market prices and yields of the old bonds to the new offerings it would be necessary to make appropriate cash adjustments on conversion, and these would range from nil to $1.99 per $100 par depending on the old issue surrendered and the new maturity selected.

There had been numerous previous conversion loans against maturities of Victory Loans of both the First and Second World Wars, but none had been on as comprehensive a scale as that now proposed. It would require a promotional program bigger than any assembled for a Victory Loan sale during the war. For this purpose it was proposed to assemble in Ottawa a sales organization patterned on that employed in the Second World War and pending public announcement to swear all the persons involved to secrecy. They would be drawn from investment houses, banks and other financial institutions.

I studied the proposal in detail. I could find nothing wrong with it. I was impressed with its comprehensiveness and completeness down to the last detail. Coyne and Taylor answered my many questions to my complete satisfaction. In the end I congratulated Coyne, and told him that I liked the boldness of the plan.

But I still had to deal with my colleagues. I went to the Prime Minister, and laid the whole plan before him. Before I left him he had approved it. We timed its submission to cabinet with utmost care to avoid leaks. Approval had to be obtained not later than Saturday, July 12. Dief called cabinet to meet the day before at 5.00 p.m. after the markets were closed and warned there must be no market transactions by ministers. I presented the plan carefully and completely. It was immediately pounced upon by several western ministers, alarmed at the prospect of higher interest rates and the cash adjustments. The opposition was so outspoken that Dief began to wilt and weaken. Instead of lending the plan his support he withdrew to the neutral sidelines. I was appalled at the situation, because with Diefenbaker's full approval we had commenced calling in the organizers to meet in Ottawa. I was irretrievably committed to the plan, as Diefenbaker had committed himself, but I could not withdraw my support as he appeared to be about to do. At the end of the meeting a committee consisting of Green and Fulton was appointed to meet first with Coyne and later with representatives of the financial leaders and report back to a meeting of cabinet at 9.30 the next morning (Saturday).

I hurried back to my office, communicated with Coyne and Taylor, arranged the first meeting in my office for 8.00 a.m., and asked them to arrange the second with the financial men later, and confided in them that my personal position was becoming untenable.

For the only time in my six years as a minister I did not sleep that night. Coyne made a reasonable presentation of the plan to Green and Fulton and answered all their questions. Somehow I did not feel he was winning them over. At the conclusion, as the ministers were compelled to leave for the meeting with the three representatives of the financial leaders who had been called in, Coyne, apparently sensing failure, said to Green and Fulton, "I must see the Prime Minister." He was perfectly right as to his duty in these ultimate circumstances, but his tactlessness in expressing himself and his rather high-handed manner gave offence to my two colleagues, as I knew they would. The meeting ended rather abruptly on that sour note. I purposely did not accompany my colleagues to or at their meeting with the committee of bond experts.

As I walked up the hill to the East Block I was faced starkly with the question of my resignation. I had burnt my bridges behind me in my law firm; I had no right to return to it or to recover my clients. My personal staff, Audrey Hanna, Bill Allan,

Grey Hamilton, would lose their positions after giving up secure situations in order to join me. I had an intense feeling of loyalty to my colleagues in cabinet, and to all those 208 Conservative members of the House. The last thing I wished was to cause a disruption which would be bound to have grievous effects. Yet I did not see any glimmer of possibility of continuing in the cabinet if the plan to which, with the Prime Minister's full and total approval, I had committed myself was rejected.

To my surprise and profound relief Howard and Davie in reporting on the meeting gave the plan strong support, and cabinet had no alternative but to approve it. The committee of bond experts had convinced my colleagues. I rushed from the meeting to join Coyne in meeting a distinguished group of 137 of Canada's most eminent investment dealers and heads of financial institutions, to whom we expounded the plan. Nothing, of course, was said about cabinet's hesitation to endorse the Conversion Loan. In following me on the program Coyne was kind enough to say, "Canada will never know how much it owes to Donald Fleming." It was a generous statement. It was also true, and it was prophetic. The press remained in total ignorance of what had happened and what was happening over that weekend. The whole episode inevitably shook my confidence in the reliability of Diefenbaker's promises of support. I never fully accepted them after that.

It remains only to add, as we shall see later, that Diefenbaker later seemed to think he had done me a great favour by joining in cabinet approval of the Conversion Loan in the end. For his own reasons he adopted the attitude that all the benefits of the plan would flow to eastern Canada at the expense of western Canada, and that the prairie farmers because of that and the tariff were entitled to some compensation out of the federal Treasury. This was utter nonsense. One of his schemes was being hatched. It was not long before my suspicions were confirmed.

The financial organizations reacted positively and enthusiastically to the plan, and evinced their willingness to go to work at once. Till I could make an announcement of it in the House on Monday, July 14, strict secrecy must be maintained, and this would be supremely difficult with so many well-known investment dealers in Ottawa and in the hotels there. I was pleased to see among them my esteemed friend General Bruce Matthews, president of the Liberal Federation of Canada. I thought his support augured well for our project.

In the midst of all this I received a long distance telephone call from James Muir, president of the Royal Bank of Canada, Canada's largest commercial bank. After I had taken office in 1957 he came to see me in my office on a get-acquainted mission. He was known to me as a powerful, able, aggressive leader who could be domineering when it suited his purposes. He informed me that I had called in one of his bank's officers, Mr. Case, and sworn him to secrecy, that he (Muir) was entitled to receive any information given to any officer or employee of the Royal Bank, whether received by that officer under oath of secrecy or otherwise, that he would compel Case to break his oath and reveal all the information communicated by me or under my authority to him. If Jim Muir thought he was about to stage one of his domineering triumphs he had chosen the wrong man. He had spoken with some heat as though he had been aggrieved. My anger rose somewhat as in the course of a long conversation (and I was pleased that he was paying for it) I assured him that confidential information had indeed been communicated under my authority to Mr. Case, that it was serious and important in nature, that I would not share that information with Mr. Muir, that I would not authorize Mr. Case or anyone else to communicate it to Mr. Muir, that Mr. Case had taken a solemn oath not to disclose that information to anyone, that I would not release Mr. Case from his oath, and that if Mr. Muir tampered with that oath or endeavoured to force Mr. Case to break it I would see that the full rigour of the law was invoked against Mr. Muir personally. On that clear note the conversation finally ended. Mr. Muir so far as I am aware exerted no more pressure on Mr. Case to break his oath. Whenever I met him after that episode he was invariably friendly: we were Jim and Don to each other. It appeared that neither of us betrayed any lingering resentment over the episode, but I had learned the necessity of not giving ground to him.

On Monday, July 14, I made a full announcement to the House. I opened it by saying, "Today we are embarking upon the largest and I believe the most constructive financial operation in the history of Canada, of the successful outcome of which I am fully confident." After outlining the terms I reported: "I have received from all quarters pledges of enthusiastic and vigorous support in carrying this enterprise to a successful conclusion." The offer to convert would remain open up to and including September 15. I pointedly observed that the plan would not provide us with any new cash, and that to cover our cash requirements until December 15, when our cash receipts from the Canada Savings Bond campaign would be complete, we had arranged to sell an issue of $400 million of five-month bonds bearing interest at the rate of $2\frac{1}{2}$ per cent per annum, to the Bank of Canada and the chartered banks. In conclusion I made two statements: first, I expressed confidence "that this great conversion loan will lay foundations for a new, healthy and confident tone to our whole bond market, and that the beneficial results of this will extend well beyond the market for Canada bonds and into the market for provincial, municipal and corporate bonds"; second, in view of the extent to which loss of confidence in the future value of the dollar had prevented governments, both in Canada and even more severely in the United States, from borrowing in the long end of the market, I added, "I wish to emphasize that this Government attaches great importance and a high priority to the preservation of a sound currency and stability in the purchasing power of our dollar."

Pearson and Argue followed with statements of approval on behalf of their parties, and endorsed my appeal to the public to support the loan. Pearson expressed the hope that I would receive the cooperation of everyone concerned "and all Canadians must hope that this operation will be a success." Even the *Toronto Daily Star* at first allowed itself to commend the Conversion Loan and to bespeak support for it. On later thought the paper turned against it. Its reasons for this reversal or the influence responsible were never adequately explained. Its new attitude was based upon gross misrepresentation.

The campaign swung smoothly into high gear. That same afternoon Coyne and I featured in a closed-circuit TV program that was used extensively for the instruction of sales personnel. The press hailed the plan with headlines, "Biggest Ever Financial Program," "Bold, Courageous," "Investment Houses Give a Roaring Welcome to the Government's Announcement." Diefenbaker and I launched the loan with a half-hour program on the national television network that evening. He did one half in English; I did the other half in French. It was preceded by a crisis at the studio. The film unravelled all over the floor. Diefenbaker, ever ready to suspect sabotage by the CBC or the civil service, was furious. Fortunately, CBC president Alphonse Ouimet was present. He apologized profusely. The film was gathered up and rewound. The Prime Minister composed himself and delivered his address without a trace of his anger. At the conclusion Alphonse commented to him, "You didn't seem to be angry," to which Dief snapped in reply, "I'm not angry at the people of Canada." He left no doubt, however, that he was still very angry with the CBC.

The campaign achieved a success surpassing all expectations.

The greater its success the more the Liberals sought to undermine and attack it. On September 4 on my Estimates when the conversions had already reached $5 billion and the campaign had just another eleven days to run they spent most of a day in the House on the attack. They achieved nothing except, perhaps, to please the *Winnipeg Free Press*, which was hostile to the Conversion Loan. After spending over an hour refuting their misdirected criticisms I concluded my remarks with a prophecy: "Succeeding Ministers of Finance whether they be Liberal or whether they be Conservative will have reason to be thankful in the days ahead that the Government in 1958 had the vision and the courage and the realism to undertake this, the greatest financial operation in Canada's history." At the time of maturity of the ninth Victory Loan in 1966 a Liberal government was having difficulty in marketing its bonds. Had the Conversion Loan not absorbed most of that maturity ($1,447 million out of $1,691 million) the government would have been swamped by the Victory Bonds then maturing. Of course I received no credit or thanks from them for preserving them from such a calamity. I expected neither.

The Conversion Loan achieved the conversion of over 90 per cent of the Victory Loan bonds, and well over 60 per cent of the new bonds taken were in the two long maturities, as follows:

3% – $3^{1}/_{4}$-year issue – $1,020.7 million
$3^{3}/_{4}\%$ – 7-year issue – $1,266.7 million
$4^{1}/_{4}\%$ – 14-year issue – $1,366.6 million
$4^{1}/_{2}\%$ – 25-year issue – $2,151.5 million

The average interest rate on the total of $5,805.5 million was 4 per cent. The amounts of the five Victory Loans surrendered were:

5th Victory Loan	– $ 905,248,450
6th Victory Loan	– $1,118,711,700
7th Victory Loan	– $1,262,166,050
8th Victory Loan	– $1,072,799,150
9th Victory Loan	– $1,446,594,500
Total	– $5,805,519,850

The Liberals maintained their niggling criticisms. We had attempted too large a conversion of debt; we were paying too high interest; the campaign had been too costly; the cash payments were a handout to the big financial institutions. They wasted a protracted and struggling effort in a lost cause. The Conversion Loan was not only the largest financial operation in Canada's history, but the greatest success. That success attracted interest and inquiries from departments of finance and central banks around the world, and drew many admiring messages from them. When I attended the annual meetings of the International Bank and the International Monetary Fund in New Delhi in late September I met many inquiries and numerous expressions of envy from the representatives of other countries there. Washington watched the success of our campaign with close attention. When I visited Japan in November our Conversion Loan was one of the first subjects on which the Minister of Finance and his officials sought full information and expressed their admiration. Our bold effort gave a lead to other countries, including the United States. A prophet is not without honour save in his own country and among his own people.

The conversion of all five Victory Loan issues in one mammoth operation was more equitable, more efficient and less costly than any piecemeal approach could possibly have been. No other operation could have been even nearly as successful in removing from the market the overhang which was making it virtually impossible to market long-term new issues. As a matter of fact, the only criticism I ever heard from an informed source was that we had been so successful in marketing our long issues maturing in 1972 and 1983 that we had fully occupied that area. This, however, was not a generally held view.

By the success of the Conversion Loan we achieved a notable and most desirable reduction in the proportion of the public debt of Canada held by the banking system and a relatively substantial increase in the proportion held by the public outside the banking system. We also effected a very beneficial lengthening of Canada's debt. Before conversion only 17 per cent thereof, other than savings bonds, was in maturities over ten years. The conversion raised this figure to 43 per cent. Before conversion 39 per cent of the debt, other than savings bonds, was in market issues with maturities of less than two years; conversion reduced this figure to 25 per cent. The overall average maturity was lengthened from six and a half to ten and a half years, double the comparable average maturity in the United States.

Just before I introduced my budget on June 17, 1958, a major break in the bond market in the United States occurred. It had the effect of raising interest rates. This trend continued almost without a break into 1959. It had a similar influence in Canada. Our success with the Conversion Loan was all the more noteworthy in view of these adverse conditions with which it had to contend and which by its success it greatly helped to overcome. As I said on April 28, 1959, we could not at that time have

502

achieved success in marketing the new bonds at an overall average interest cost as low as 4 per cent. The operation was completed none too soon. Interest rates were still rising in late 1959.

The last stupid Liberal criticism, that the effects of the Conversion Loan were inflationary, was answered by the Governor of the Bank of Canada in his 1958 report:

> It must be remembered that important and valuable benefits were achieved by the success of the Conversion Loan campaign through the lengthening of the term of the debt. The reform of the structure of the Government debt, and the contribution it made to improving conditions for the sale of future issues of government bonds to non-bank investors, were important elements in monetary policy in the broadest sense and an essential anti-inflationary achievement.

Finally, the Conversion Loan saved hundreds of millions of dollars in interest charges over the years. The Liberals gleefully pointed to our increase in interest charges in 1958. The rates which Canada was obliged to pay for money borrowed at the dates of maturity of the five Victory Loans were in aggregate considerably higher than the the rates on either the Victory Loans or the Conversion Loan. The latter, apart from the other benefits it conferred, achieved economies in Canada's burden of debt charges.

I have never wavered in my belief that James Coyne did Canada a monumental service in proposing the Conversion Loan of 1958. I likewise derived the utmost satisfaction from my part in it.

The maturity of the last of the Conversion bonds, "the four halfs of 83," on September 1, 1983, did not escape the attention of the press. The investment fraternity saw in it the disappearance of an issue which had for years been the market bellwether. Not all of the press articles were accurate. In this respect they relied excessively on a book, *The Bond Market in Canada*, by Douglas H. Fullerton. He contends that the objectives of the loan did not accord with the "the expansionist policies" outlined in my budget a month earlier. This is utter nonsense. That budget was no expression of "expansionist policies." They had to wait for three more years to find expression in my budget of June 1961. Fullerton also makes the claim, "Events in 1961 and 1962 suggest that the Government itself changed its mind about the Conversion Loan, in spite of protestations to the contrary." This likewise is sheer nonsense. I heard not one such change of mind

expressed by a cabinet colleague at any time after the fantastic-
ally successful loan campaign of 1958. Some investment activists
have begrudged the sheer success of that enterprise. Nothing preceding it and nothing in the twenty-five years following it has
ever rivalled or challenged the constructive achievement of the
Conversion Loan of 1958. It yielded enormous benefits to
Canada in the management of the public debt and in preserving
the strength and stability of our currency.

The summer of 1958 had scarcely arrived before reports of
drought conditions on the prairies, particularly in Manitoba and
Saskatchewan, began to reach cabinet. No other subject except
unemployment could so quickly rouse John Diefenbaker. The
Saskatchewan Wheat Pool was urging "deficiency payments" to
assure the western farmer of a fair return over his cost of production. Our forty-seven Conservative MPs from the three Prairie
provinces supported some form of payment. On July 24 cabinet
approved payment of half of the cost of shipping haying equipment, fodder and livestock from July 1. But the condition did not
improve. On August 8 the Prime Minister first openly proposed
payment of a subsidy to western farmers in the form of acreage
payments. In my absence a committee recommended against a
two-price system for wheat and in favour of acreage payments to
cost $50 million. The two-price system would have meant charg-
ing a higher price for wheat used for domestic consumption than
Canadian-produced wheat would fetch on the world market. I
would have resisted any effort to penalize the Canadian consumer in this fashion. Its rejection, however, increased the
pressure for acreage payments.

The clash came during August. We were already doing much
to help the western wheat farmer at a cost of nearly $200 million
for 1958. Storage charges would cost us $40 million, surplus dis-
posal to non-commercial markets $75 million, Prairie Farm As-
sistance Act payments $24 million, and $50 million for expenses
in connection with other proposed measures. The acreage payments were said to have the advantage of helping the small
farmer. I flatly opposed acreage payments. I considered them
unsound and calculated to strengthen irresponsible leadership in
the West. The statistics did not support the proposal to single out
the western wheat farmer for a reward or to make a raid on his
behalf on a thin and hard-pressed treasury. Between 1948 and
1957 the average earned income from operations of farmers in all
of Canada was $2,446, on the prairies $2,895, and in the rest of
Canada $2,102. Actually, the average earned income in Canada

of persons with jobs was $2,771. I deplored the haste in assembling a scheme in the dying days of the current session. It had all the earmarks of hurried thinking and would create a dangerous precedent. The payments would increase an already large deficit, for which I was made to take the blame. I warned solemnly that if there were any more demands I must consider an increase in taxation. Of course, an increase in taxation was the last thing I wished to sponsor or ever have my name associated with, and I suppose cabinet was aware of that fact. Because of previous discussions in my absence the battle was half over before I could enter it. Diefenbaker pointedly reminded me that he had reluctantly agreed to the Conversion Loan with the benefits it provided to bondholders in eastern Canada, and of the burdens borne by the western farmer in favour of eastern manufacturers under the tariff.

On August 22 cabinet authorized a Supplementary Estimate of $40 million to provide payments to western grain producers of $1 per specified acre up to a maximum of two hundred acres per farm, to be distributed through the Canadian Wheat Board. It was a day of deep gloom for me. Cabinet was authorizing a handout from a declining Treasury. Should I resign? Only a month before I had faced the same critical question over the Conversion Loan. We were only days away from the opening of the Commonwealth Trade and Economic Conference in Montreal, which was my special responsibility. How could I walk out on the eve of a meeting I regarded as of supreme importance? Something told me it would always be so. Whenever I faced the question of resignation there would always be some factor of overriding importance to outweigh my reasons for refusing to be a party to a cabinet decision from which I vigorously dissented.

On August 29 cabinet went further and gave the Prime Minister a free hand to announce a broader and more supportable program by approving another item in the Supplementary Estimates of $75 million for loans to foreign governments to assist them in the purchase of Canadian wheat and flour.

While in the mood cabinet authorized inclusion of another item in the Supplementary Estimates to increase the federal university grants from $1.00 to $1.50 per capita, notwithstanding what I considered two very grave objections. In the first place, Duplessis when approached by Léon Balcer and others had again declined to allow universities in Quebec to accept the grants. In the second place, the basis of distribution perpetuated a wide disparity between the provinces as related to university student registration. In Nova Scotia the grant was equivalent to

$140 per student, in Newfoundland $421. Cabinet decided that these two problems could await solution. The increase in grants served to aggravate the problems.

While cabinet was indulging its generous instincts I faced financing problems as usual. It would be necessary for us to raise $2.1 billion before March 31, 1959. The bond market in the United States was deteriorating, and long-term issues there were selling as much as ten points below their prices of the previous spring. The market in Canada, thanks to the Conversion Loan, had been stabilized in spite of the U.S. decline. Cabinet approved a new Canada Savings Bond issue, not to be announced until September 16, just after the close of the Conversion Loan campaign. It was to be a fifteen-year bond with a $3\frac{1}{2}$ per cent interest coupon for the first year and $4\frac{1}{4}$ per cent coupons for the remaining fourteen years, with an overall yield of 4.19 per cent to maturity. The loan proved highly successful. The payroll savings plan yielded $207 million in sales, and the public sales $717 million, for a handsome and most welcome total of $924 million.

The terms of the Union with Newfoundland in 1949 contained an Article 29 which was now destined to become famous. It provided for the appointment of a royal commission within eight years to determine what further federal subsidy should be paid to the province to bring its services up to the standard prevailing in the Maritime provinces. The St. Laurent government appointed a royal commission, consisting of Chief Justice McNair of New Brunswick, Chief Justice Sir Albert Walsh of Newfoundland and Professor John Deutsch of Queen's University pursuant to Article 29. Their report, received on August 8, recommended the payment of additional sums annually for four years, then for the fifth year and thereafter $8 million per annum. Premier Smallwood publicly denounced the work of the commission as "a dead loss." Newfoundland was already receiving from us $7.5 million per annum as its share of the Atlantic Provinces Adjustment Grant, so cabinet wisely decided not to take precipitate action on the report in the dying days of the 1958 session. The Newfoundland Liberal members pressed hard for an interim payment of $8 million in 1958. It was left to me to explain that the report would require more study before action could be expected. The royal commission had presented us with a hot potato of which more, much more, would be heard in future.

The coming into force of the Ontario Hospital Insurance Plan presented a question which cabinet resolved on August 26. On my recommendation cabinet decided in favour of the compulsory deduction of the premium from the salaries of all civil servants

506

and employees of crown corporations resident in Ontario. We also included at their option the Governor General, the Lieutenant-Governor, the Speakers, ministers and judges resident in the province.

The subjects chosen by the Liberal opposition for debate in cases where under the rules of the House this right was open to them followed an interesting course. One arose out of the threat of the A.V. Roe Co., controlling Dominion Steel and Coal Company, to shut down its coal mines in Cape Breton and the mainland of Nova Scotia for five weeks because of lack of markets. On June 30 and July 1 the Liberals strove to make a grievance out of our handling of this issue. Their amendment to my supply motion was defeated by 137 to 42. On July 7 on my next supply motion Mike Pearson moved the following amendment: "This House is of opinion that, in present circumstances of declining private investment, a balanced policy of national development requires consideration by the Government of active measures to meet the urgent needs of social capital especially in the form of transportation facilities, municipal improvements, and other facilities to stimulate economic development and to promote social well-being in the settled areas of Canada." This could mean socialism or merely a program of public works. The CCF hailed it as the former. The CCF moved to add long-term loans to small businesses. The Liberals and CCF supported each other. Both amendments were defeated by a wide margin.

My final supply motion of the session on August 4 was an echo of the debate in January, which had proved so disastrous for Pearson in his maiden speech as leader. The Prime Minister's effective use of the report, *Canadian Economic Outlook* written in 1957 had exposed the warnings to the St. Laurent government to prepare for recession and unemployment which the government rejected in favour of a rosy pre-election picture of the economy. Diefenbaker, at the insistence of the opposition, had tabled the report, but without a cover. The Liberals contended that the cover had been marked "Confidential." I had been sitting beside him in the House as he handled the report and read excerpts from it, but I had seen no such word on any cover. The Liberals now contended that the government ought to table the 1958 report, and at the same time accused the Prime Minister of violating the confidentiality of the 1957 report. Their attempt to exchange the roles they and we had played in the January debate failed pathetically, as did their attempt to re-open and reverse the January debate. An angry debate ensued in which "The Four Horsemen," Pearson, Chevrier, Martin and Pickersgill, the sole survivors of the St. Laurent government in the House, all took part, and I answered for the government. The Pearson amendment was crushed in the vote. I know that senior civil servants were disturbed over the Prime Minister's use in the House of a report which they regarded as written for the confidential use of ministers, and not for publication. Ken Taylor at the time had voiced his concern to me, and said Mitchell Sharp, as deputy minister of the department involved, was very upset. It may be that this incident influenced Sharp to enter politics. I considered that the government as recipient of the report had the right to determine what use should be made of it. I am aware that the circle of intended readers of the report may influence the form of the report at the hands of its writer, but ultimately the decision as to how far the report is to be circulated must rest with ministers, and not with the writer. I question whether civil servants have the right to tie the hands of the government thus. Having regard to the nature and timing of the report in question I would defend Diefanbaker's use of it in January 1958. Furthermore, his publication of the report by tabling it at the demand of the opposition in the course of the debate does not oblige the government to make public any other report. As to the assertion in Pearson's amendment that the Prime Minister by tabling the report had "seriously weakened the value of confidential advice from civil servants," I would reply that nothing in my lifetime has so weakened the value attached to the advice tendered to ministers by civil servants as the repeated recruitment by the Liberal hierarchy of senior civil servants for partisan warfare: for example, Pearson, Pickersgill, Sharp, Drury, Francis, Foulkes and others. It was that reprehensible practice which compelled Conservative ministers to look over their shoulders constantly and filled some of them with distrust in their relations with their advisers. No one had more to answer for in this respect than the same Mike Pearson.

CHAPTER FORTY-SIX

The Commonwealth Trade and Economic Conference

Mention of a Commonwealth Trade and Economic Conference was apt to conjure up in the minds of Canadians memories of the famous Commonwealth Conference in Ottawa called by Prime Minister R.B. Bennett in 1932. It was concerned exclusively with trade. Heroic efforts were made to enlarge Commonwealth preferences by tariff action, including the raising of tariffs against imports from non-Commonwealth countries. In the face of the reluctance of the Labour government in Britain to raise tariffs the conference achieved only part of Bennett's objectives, but its results were of invaluable benefit for Canada.

The scene in 1958 was very different. The Commonwealth had become larger and embraced more diverse interests. We were not proposing a new system of Commonwealth trade preferences. Indeed, as subscribing members of GATT we were precluded from enlarging any existing preference. But we did purpose to maintain the existing system of preferences. Moreover, the scope of the conference was to be much broader than that of 1932. In addition to trade, great emphasis was laid on other economic goals. In my budget speech on June 17 I stated our objectives:

> In the first place we aim to expand the opportunities for mutually profitable trade between Canada and the other countries of the Commonwealth. We hope that progress can be made in removing restrictions and discriminations which are imposed against us.
> Second, we would like to explore with our Commonwealth partners ways and means of making more rapid progress towards currency convertibility and a freer system of world trade and payments. We appreciate that this poses a complex of difficult problems. We would like to see steps taken to increase world liquidity in the means of international payments. We shall support constructive steps to promote appropriate trade and financial policies on the part of the principal creditor nations, and the

509

development of sound relationships with the new trade groupings now being set up in Europe. All of this cannot be accomplished by the Commonwealth acting alone. But we should concert our Commonwealth efforts and in this way encourage other countries to move along parallel lines.

Third, it is desirable to promote measures which will assist in the economic development of Commonwealth countries, particularly the new members which are less industrially advanced, and to improve their standards of living. Finally, we wish to extend and deepen our Commonwealth institutions so that they can contribute more effectively to our joint economic and political strength and in all these ways, by our example and by our achievements, defeat the threatening inroads of communism.

The conference required careful and intensive preparation. The Canadian government had been the leader in pressing for it and was its host. Consequently we had more interest at stake than any other country. We were deeply committed to achieving a more active and vital role for the Commonwealth. That role had languished as the result of the indifference and neglect of the St. Laurent government over the years. Our task was one of revival and challenge. We had learned, principally at the Prime Ministers' Conference in London in June 1957, that we could not expect all other Commonwealth nations to be as enthusiastic for a broad economic program under Commonwealth auspices as we were.

Responsibility for the success of the conference was laid on my shoulders. I did not shrink from this added responsibility; I welcomed the challenge. In addition to the budget and other current burdens, the work of preparation continued throughout the entire summer of 1958. I gave it the highest priority. Gordon Churchill and Jim Macdonnell shared in the labours, and we had the invaluable aid of a strong group of senior civil servants drawn from the Privy Council Office, the departments of Finance, Trade and Commerce, External Affairs, and the Bank of Canada. Between April 29 and September 8 we held fifteen preparatory meetings, thirteen of them in evenings. Norman Robertson, Canadian ambassador to Washington until his appointment as Undersecretary of State for External Affairs on October 15, came up to attend some of these meetings and gave us valuable assistance. Above all, Sydney D. Pierce proved his quite remarkable competence in the planning for the conference. It was indeed a masterpiece of detailed preparation. Nothing was overlooked.

The Queen Elizabeth Hotel at Montreal was a very happy

choice as the venue. Although newly opened it afforded superb accommodation and excellent service. Don Mumford, the general manager, took a keen personal interest in the conference and in our guests. I did not encounter a single complaint from anyone concerned.

The conference opened on September 15. The Canadian delegation consisted of myself as chairman, Churchill, Macdonnell and Raymond O'Hurley. We were joined for part of the conference by Sidney Smith, who played a significant role on certain items on the agenda pertaining to scholarships. The last-minute preparations were intensive. The Chancellor of the Exchequer, Derick Heathcote-Amory, and I dined together privately the evening before the opening and had a very useful discussion. I well remember his wrestling with the sealed windows of the totally air-conditioned hotel, endeavouring in typical English fashion to admit some fresh air. In the end he was obliged to accept a measure of claustrophobia.

The importance of the conference was emphasized by the eminence of the delegations, both ministerial and official. The United Kingdom sent four ministers – Derick Heathcote-Amory, the Earl of Home, Secretary of State for Commonwealth Relations, Sir David Eccles, President of the Board of Trade, and Reginald Maudling, Paymaster General. Australia sent John McEwen, Deputy Prime Minister and Minister for Trade, New Zealand A.H. Nordmeyer, Minister of Finance, South Africa A.J.R. Van Rhijn, Minister of Finance, and Dr. J.E. Holloway, India Morarji Desai, Minister of Finance, and Manubhai Shah, Minister of Industry, Pakistan Syed Amjad Ali, Minister of Finance, and Sardar Abdul Rashid, Minister of Commerce and Industries, Ceylon Stanley de Zoysa, Minister of Finance, Ghana K.A. Gbedemah, Minister of Finance, Malaya Sir Henry Lee, Minister of Finance, and Tan Siew Sin, Minister of Commerce and Industry, and the Federation of Rhodesia and Nyasaland Donald Macintyre, Minister of Finance, and Frank Owen, Minister of Commerce and Industry. In addition to these eleven self-governing nations, the colonies, or, to speak more politely, the "emerging nations," were well represented. The Earl of Perth, Minister of State for Colonial Affairs, led them and six countries were separately represented: Nigeria by Chief Festus Okotie-Eboh, Minister of Finance, the Federation of the West Indies by Dr. C.G.D. La Corbiniere, Federal Minister of Trade and Industry, Kenya by E.A. Vasey, Minister of Finance and Development, Tanganyika by C.E. Tilney, Minister of Finance and Economics, Uganda by C.G.F.F. Melmoth, Minister of

Finance, and Sierra Leone by M.S. Mustapha, Minister of Finance. Practically every delegation included its high commissioner to Canada and a dazzling array of experts in the fields of government finance, trade, economics, and education. The total number exceeded 160. Many of the delegates I was able to greet as old friends. By the time we had spent two weeks together in daily sessions we were all personal friends. The atmosphere remained cordial and thoroughly pleasant throughout. Many of those attending later attained very high office. Alex Douglas-Hume (after giving up his title, Earl of Home) became Prime Minister of the United Kingdom; Morarji Desai became Prime Minister of India. I had the good fortune to establish lasting friendships with them and a number of the other ministers and officials.

At the opening of the conference I was elected its chairman. Statements were then delivered by all heads of delegations and representatives of the colonies. I led off, speaking in both English and French. I offered a slogan to summarize the objective of the conference, "An Expanding Commonwealth in an Expanding World Economy." I enlarged the theme in these words:

> We seek to expand trade, to advance development of resources, to strengthen the economic and cultural and spiritual links among the countries of the Commonwealth. We seek to improve communications and methods of consultation among us. In a word, we aim to make our economic relations serve our freedom and our prosperity for each of our countries. . . . We represent 660 million people who are doing one-quarter of the world's trade. . . . The mere fact of our meeting is of itself a matter of world significance. It is a challenging and sobering thought that, for those 660 million people, what we do here may well affect, for better or for worse, the food they eat, the clothes they wear, the houses they live in, and their way of life.

I was careful to stress, "This conference is aimed against no country. We do not seek solutions for our problems at the expense of others."

The Chancellor had penned virtually the same slogan as I to define the objective of the conference. There had been no connivance between us in doing so. I liked his better – "An expanding Commonwealth as a dynamic partnership in an expanding world community." Morarji Desai uttered in arresting terms a thought shared by all: "The Commonwealth is, if I may say so, the world in miniature. It is multi-racial, multi-lingual and multi-national. Its parts have an individuality of their own, and they are free in every way to shape their own policies. Yet, they are held together by certain common bonds, the most important of which is loyalty to the democratic ideal. It is our duty, jointly and severally, to do everything in our power to strengthen this common bond." He called urgently for economic development of the underdeveloped countries of the Commonwealth. The speeches, sixteen in number, were all marked by eloquence, inspiration and unity of purpose. The conference was launched in public session under the happiest of auspices.

Thereafter the conference proceeded in closed session. The meetings became less formal as we proceeded, set speeches gave way to more and more discussion, and the order in which delegations spoke was varied. The seating was arranged in the form of a hollow oblong. The Canadian and British delegations occupied the two ends, facing each other, with the other delegations ranged along the two sides. The officials sat behind their ministers. The Canadian Privy Council Office provided the secretariat with some reinforcement from other departments. Except on the night before the final day there was no evening session. It became possible in this way for delegates to survive two weeks of meetings without undue exhaustion and for delegations to conduct their own consultations among themselves day by day so that the conference might proceed without impediment or delay. We broke for coffee each morning and for tea each afternoon at the half-way mark. This contributed to a relaxed atmosphere and avoided tension.

The press arrangements were excellent. Ample accommodation was provided in the hotel for the nearly one hundred representatives of the press, who came from all parts of the world. Bob Farquharson briefed the press twice daily, once after each session, having orally first outlined to the conference the statement he planned to give the press. As an old and senior newspaperman himself Bob handled our press relations in a masterly manner. Some problems which arose out of erroneous newspaper reports were no fault of his.

The heads of delegations constituted the steering committee. Its labours were greatly aided by the admirable work done in advance by the officials who had met in London in February and June and again in Montreal for several days prior to the conference. The economic papers which they had prepared for the assistance of all delegations proved to be a mine of information. No problems arose over the agenda. The officials had planned it thoroughly. Their work drew high praise from all ministers.

I presided at all sixteen sessions, and I found there were many matters for the chairman to attend to when not presiding and many individual little discussions to take part in. For the first three days of the conference I did not once set foot outside the hotel. After that I tried to leave the hotel for three-quarters of an hour each day. Some of these recesses I spent in attendance at services at a nearby Catholic Church. Otherwise I was cut off from the outside world.

On Thursday evening the Canadian government was host at a formal dinner addressed by the Prime Minister. Dief made a very good speech, which impressed the delegates. Senator Sarto Fournier, mayor of Montreal, also delivered a welcoming speech at the dinner, and on another occasion gave a reception at the city hall for all delegates. We deliberately avoided overdoing the social entertainment, believing that the delegates needed some freedom.

We did not sit at the weekend. I spent it back in Ottawa, attending a Sunday cabinet meeting called for the purpose of hearing my detailed report on the progress of the conference and other pressing business. Cabinet was on the whole pleased with the interim report I presented.

The conference was an event of world significance, and it attracted widespread attention in the press of Commonwealth countries. I was interviewed on one occasion by transatlantic radio, my questioner being in London. The hookup produced very clear reception. I also held press conferences as the conference proceeded.

Even to sit through the plenary sessions of the conference would have been an education in economics. To hear first-hand presentations of the trade and economic problems of countries at such widely varied stages of development and scattered over the face of the earth was as instructive an experience as could possibly be crowded into a span of two weeks. The discussions embraced a world economic spectrum: international liquidity, world recession, convertibility of currency, non-discrimination, exchange reserves and their inadequacy, shortage of capital for development, low prices of agricultural products, import restrictions, agricultural protectionism, surplus disposal by the United States, export of textile products by developing countries, expansion of world trade, technical training and education, employment of human and material resources, stabilization of commodity prices, the harm of wide fluctuations in prices of exports of primary products, the price and role of gold, competition both economic and uneconomic from Communist countries and state trading, the role of international institutions, such as the International Monetary Fund, the International Bank for Reconstruction and Development, the International Development Agency, the Food and Agricultural Organization, the General Agreement on Tariffs and Trade, relations with the European Common Market and the European Free Trade Area, the proposed establishment of a Commonwealth Development Bank, the strengthening of the Commonwealth Economic Secretariat, technical training, university scholarships, means of consultation, and a host of other subjects. Every presentation received a sympathetic hearing. Every speaker was encouraged to believe that his contribution was regarded as important, and one or two of the representatives of colonies needed that encouragement in their first interventions. The entire proceedings with a summary of every contribution to the discussions were printed afterwards in a massive volume. The time has come to liberate this volume from the restriction of confidentiality under which it has been smothered for the last twenty-five years.

The highlights were many. It was the first time Morarji Desai, though about sixty years of age, had ever set foot outside India. He was a strict vegetarian, eschewing meat, fish and even eggs. He wore the dress of the Congress Party and the white Gandhi cap. Mr. Gbebemah of Ghana brought as his economic adviser Professor W.A. Lewis from the West Indies, who was destined to reach the highest positions in the financial institutions of the Caribbean, and whom I met there in later years. The South African delegation played an active part in all the deliberations. The contribution of their Dr. J.E. Holloway on the subject of the price of gold and the relationship of that subject to trade, inflation, competition with Russia, and exchange resources was in my opinion one of the most erudite and effective heard in the conference. Chief Festus Okotie-Eboh, Minister of Finance of Nigeria, soon became a favourite with all delegations. He was a big black man with a delightful sense of humour. When he laughed his ample frame shook. When he was about to say something humorous he would begin to laugh before he even uttered it. This set the delegation laughing before they heard the joke. Festus and I became especially good friends. Our paths were destined to cross from time to time until he was murdered some years later in a revolutionary uprising which proved a prelude to the tragic civil war in Nigeria.

Each country had special problems and interests. This tremendous variety added to the complexity of the tasks facing the conference. Canada, for example, was keenly interested in the convertibility of sterling and the removal of restrictions imposed by the United Kingdom against dollar imports in order to safeguard exchange reserves. During the course of the meetings the British obliged us by announcing removal of restrictions on a number of products of interest to Canadian exporters. Overseas markets for our agricultural exports were of paramount importance to us. The Canadian delegation contributed numerous initiatives. I made a number of the presentations on behalf of the Canadian delegation, but Gordon Churchill and Jim Macdonnelll also spoke from time to time. Sid Smith came up from a United Nations Assembly session at New York to make an impressive presentation on the new Canadian program of Commonwealth scholarships for university education.

The Commonwealth covered an area of 12 million square miles. It did one-quarter of the world's trade. Half of the total trade done by Commonwealth countries was exchanged within the Commonwealth. The per capita income in India and Pakistan stood at $60 per annum, that of Tanganyika at $46. They preferred to earn by trade, rather than receive aid, yet markets for their limited range of products, including young textile manufactures, were hard to find and difficult to enlarge. The need of development capital was enormous. Of all the countries of the Commonwealth the United Kingdom has been the only one with a surplus of savings for investment abroad. Economically the Commonwealth is thus very lopsided. The developing countries had derived valued assistance from the International Bank and other international organizations. President Eisenhower's bold proposal to increase the resources of both the IMF and the IBRD was strongly supported by all in anticipation of action at the forthcoming annual meetings of the governors of those two beneficent institutions at New Delhi three weeks later.

The pending negotiations of the United Kingdom with the six countries of the European Common Market (ECM) and for the creation of a European Free Trade Area in which the export markets of Canada, Australia, New Zealand and other producers for "food, drink and tobacco," as their agricultural exports were described, were of intense interest. Reginald Maudling gave an illuminating report on the state of negotiations in which he declared that the United Kingdom was not prepared to join the Free Trade Area at any price and Commonwealth trade preferences were not negotiable. This assurance was received with appreciation by the other delegations. It was vital to their interests that "the Six" (ECM) should pursue outward-looking trade policies rather than restrictionist programs.

There was no bargaining at the conference, indeed not even a semblance of it. Nevertheless, what the press wrongly called concessions or benefits were announced. I have already referred to the freeing by the British of certain commodities of interest to Canadian exporters from exchange conservation restrictions. Lord Home announced a generous contribution to the Commonwealth Scholarship program, and more loans for development of the underdeveloped countries of the Commonwealth. These were parallelled by the Canadian announcements of the binding of certain Canadian tariff rates on commodities of interest to British exporters, the increase from $35 million to $50 million in our annual contribution to the Colombo Plan over the next three years, an increase to $10 million of the Canadian aid program to the Federation of the West Indies, our contribution to the Commonwealth Scholarship Program, and increased technical assistance and increased loans and grants to less-developed countries for purchase of Canadian wheat and flour.

The discussions ended on September 24. The next day was spent with the officials on the tremendous task of writing the report. In the end this important responsibility was placed in the hands of three brilliant officials – Henry Lintott of the United Kingdom, Douglas Le Pan of Canada and L.K. Jha of India. They worked non-stop all through Thursday and right through that night to complete the writing. All delegations expressed their approval, and the report was adopted unanimously at a closed session. At 11.00 a.m. on Friday, September 26, the conference held its final sitting in public. All heads of delegations delivered closing statements, and I gave the final address as head of the Canadian delegation. Several followed my example in delivering part of their remarks in French.

The report is a voluminous document, extending to 86 numbered paragraphs and nine thousand words. It breathes the spirit of achievement, responsibility and confidence. I single out paragraph 19:

> The objectives we have outlined, under our general theme of an expanding Commonwealth in an expanding world, require the cooperation of other countries and especially that of the United States with its great economic power. As we collaborate amongst ourselves we must also work together with others, in the international organizations and elsewhere, to further our efforts to foster economic growth, to expand world trade, to strengthen the international financial machinery, and to accelerate the economic development of less-developed countries. But as a family of free nations in all parts of the world we have a crucial part to play; we

have a unique responsibility to help in fostering the progress of human society and in solving its problems. That is a duty which we are determined to discharge to the utmost of our ability.

The report announced the Commonwealth Scholarship Project, to enable one thousand Commonwealth scholars and fellows to study in other Commonwealth countries at any one time, with the United Kingdom paying half the cost and Canada a quarter. The report also recorded the agreement in principle to construct a Commonwealth coaxial cable which would provide the first round-the-world telephone service, to be completed in stages over a ten-year period. Finally, in the interests of continuing Commonwealth consultation the conference agreed to coordinate all existing organizations and channels, including the annual meeting of Commonwealth finance ministers in a new Commonwealth Economic Consultative Council. It was contemplated that this would, like the conference itself, meet probably annually prior to the annual meetings of the governors of the International Bank and the International Monetary Fund. The British offer of Lancaster House in London as a home for the Commonwealth organization was gratefully accepted.

The report was unanimously adopted by a group drawn from heterogeneous sources, but united in purpose and idealism by the Commonwealth family bond. That link is surely without parallel in the world. It is so valuable and so necessary that it deserves to be nurtured with the utmost care. Indeed, the entire conference was a remarkable event and an outstanding achievement. In my closing address I was able to say:

> The spirit of this conference has been almost a unique creation. Out of it have emerged decisions and accomplishments which we survey with the deepest satisfaction. Only those who have attended the sessions of this Conference can have any conception of the spirit of this conference. There has been a complete absence of the spirit of controversy. Not one cross word has been spoken in our deliberations, and never has a single unsympathetic word been uttered in our discussions. No misunderstanding has arisen at any time. The spirit of understanding, sympathy and mutual helpfulness has prevailed here. At no time has the spirit of bargaining entered into any of our discussions. None of us knew in advance of those announcements which were made from time to time throughout the conference of benefit to other members of it. What have been described in some quarters outside this conference as "concessions" were voluntary declarations of policy made in the spirit of the Conference. Our meetings must surely have been almost unique in international gatherings . . .

. . . We have laid the groundwork for the expansion of trade, for the advancement of the development of resources. We have taken measures which will contribute materially to strengthening the economic and cultural and spiritual links among the countries of the Commonwealth. We have taken effective measures to improve communications and methods of consultation among us. We have recommended courses of action which will make the economic relations within this Commonwealth serve our freedom and our prosperity for each of our countries . . .

. . . It is perhaps too early to assess the full value of this Conference or the full extent of its accomplishments. I express my conviction that it will prove to have been an historic conference; that it will hold an enduring place in the history of the Commonwealth. I believe we have added something lasting to the value of membership in the Commonwealth. Our report may well prove to be of itself a historic document, a guide-post to economic co-operation and an example to the world.

We are independent and diverse nations, but we have given a new meaning to interdependence and co-operation. . . . We have borne our witness to our own countries, to the other countries which will one day join this family as full members of it, and to the world, of our devotion to common and worthy ideals and the fruitful and beneficent destiny of this family of nations which measures its greatness and grandeur in terms of freedom and service to the high causes of mankind. This Conference has, I think, served the things of the spirit.

These sentiments were echoed by the other heads of delegations in their speeches. We had met for what many would regard as material ends; we had ended by measuring the achievements of the conference in spiritual terms.

Lord Home uttered these words, which I consider memorable and have often quoted since:

At this conference we have been talking of one aspect of our common interests, that is finance and trade, but under the cold statistics, not far from the surface, have always been the moral and the human values, the rights of the individual, impartial justice under the law, and liberty and tolerance for all men. For us around this table these values transcend the differences, the wide differences in the world of colour, race and creed. Is it too much to hope that we around this table at this conference have shown, if only in a small way, that these great ideals may point mankind to the way of unity, and therefore, that what we do to-day may win or help to win this great prize for our grandchildren of to-morrow?

Glowing tributes were paid by all heads of delegations to the invaluable service rendered by the officials, the secretariat and particularly Sydney D. Pierce, who took over his duties as the newly appointed Canadian ambassador to Brussels soon after concluding the work of the conference.

The officials supporting the ministers in the seventeen delegations fully deserved the compliments and tributes bestowed upon them. Rarely has such an imposing array of senior government officials gathered in one place for one purpose. The United Kingdom brought no fewer than twenty-five, and among them were a number who had earned world fame. The importance attached to the conference by the governments of the various countries is reflected not only in the numbers of officials but in their recognized seniority, experience and brilliance. Canada fielded a very distinguished and talented team of experts. I cannot speak in too high praise of them. If the British civil service is still rated the best in the world I think the British team would have rated the Canadian team as of quite comparable calibre. I was proud of them all.

Tributes to the conduct of the chair were most generous. I was particularly grateful to Sir Saville (Joe) Garner, British high commissioner to Canada, who was one of the British delegates to the conference, for a letter he sent me on his return to Ottawa, from which I quote,

> . . . I feel I must say to you what an outstanding success the Conference was and how much of that success was due to your efforts. . . . The harmony and good feeling between Delegations had to be seen to be believed. We have produced an agreed report which will, I believe, act as a beacon to guide the future policies of all our Governments. These are tremendous achievements, but they could not have been won without leadership from the Chairman, who, if I may say so, demonstrated a very remarkable combination of ability to make us concentrate and finish the job and of perpetual good humour and tolerance. It has been a great Conference, and you have done a great job.

I took quiet satisfaction from the undoubted strengthening of the Commonwealth as a result of the conference, and from the personal contribution I had made to that goal. I had been exceedingly fortunate to establish warm friendships with some of the most influential leaders in other Commonwealth countries around the globe. Years later, indeed after I had left public life, on a visit to Ghana in June 1963, a senior government official, whom I had not met previously, said to me, "You are a legend throughout the Commonwealth."

CHAPTER FORTY-SEVEN

Around the World in Forty-Eight Days

As I sped back to Ottawa on that Friday afternoon of September 26, it seemed as though I was moving into, or returning to, another world. For two weeks I had been virtually immured within the Queen Elizabeth Hotel, living among delegations, concentrating on Commonwealth problems. Now I was suddenly returning to the world of Ottawa with its unceasing problems of meeting bills, counteracting recession, unemployment, drought on the prairies, reckoning deficits, choosing defence equipment and a hundred other matters. I might have been pardoned for wishing the Montreal conference had continued longer. While in the Queen Elizabeth Hotel I had been spared cabinet meetings, telephone calls, correspondence, and urgent interviews. But all the problems at Ottawa remained. Absence did not solve them. Of this grim fact further experience was about to provide ample additional proof.

Exactly three days remained after my return to Ottawa before I was due to leave on a trip around the world. That might have seemed like a sufficient respite, but a by-election in the Quebec riding of Montmagny-L'Islet was coming to the vote on Monday, September 29, and our organization and candidate had pleaded for my entry into the campaign. I had agreed to speak on Sunday evening at what was to be a monster Conservative rally the night before the election. That required the preparation of a speech in French with a typed text and copies for the press. It also meant a trip into eastern Quebec and a return at an awkward hour to Ottawa. But everything turned out happily. We had an excellent candidate, Louis Fortin, a young lawyer who had served with the RCAF from 1939 to 1945 and had for five years been president of the Young Progressive Conservatives of the province. Jean Lesage had represented the riding since 1945, but had held it at the general election on March 31 by a majority of only 726 votes, his lowest in five such contests. He had resigned the seat on his election as Liberal provincial leader. We therefore had every reason to make a supreme fight to win. A large crowd attended our meeting, and I was in happy form. I received a heart-warming welcome, and my speech drew an ardent response. Not far away is the community of St. Jean-Port Joli, the location of Quebec's best-known woodcarvers. After my speech a ceremony was conducted on the platform. The leading sculptor, Jean Julien Bourgault, presented me with one of his artistic carvings. It is entitled "Donation," and depicts an old couple in the act of conveying the farm to their son in the presence of the notary, while the hired man peeks in at the kitchen door. It is a masterpiece and has hung ever since in my home. Following the meeting Mr. Bourgault invited me to his studio, where I had an opportunity to admire his work and become acquainted with his techniques. My visit to Montmagny has ever since been a very pleasant memory.

The rally provided the last push needed for a Conservative triumph. Louis Fortin was elected with a majority of one thousand. On the same day Jean Casselman retained Grenville-Dundas by a large majority in the other by-election. These victories brought Conservative strength in the House of Commons to an all-time peak, 209 out of 265 seats, and our strength in the Quebec seats in the House to 51 out of 75, also a Conservative record, until 1984. From that lofty pinnacle and thrilling triumph there was no place to go but down. The disconcerting question was bound to be, how fast and how far?

When I was a boy one of the most imaginative novels on the market was Jules Verne's *Around the World in Eighty Days*. It was an exciting piece of fiction, in which a London gentleman on a bet with the aid of a balloon circles the globe in eighty days just in time to win his wager after some very thrilling episodes. A movie based on the book, starring David Niven, was made some years ago, and I enjoyed seeing it. Since boyhood I had dreamt of one day circling the earth. My opportunity came in 1958, somewhat unexpectedly.

Every third year the annual meetings of the International Bank and the International Monetary Fund were held abroad. In 1958 they were held in New Delhi, India, in early October. The World Fair was being held at Brussels, and I was urged by officials to visit the Canadian Pavilion, on which substantial expenditures had been made under the supervision of the Treasury Board. Knowing that I was coming to India the government of Pakistan extended to me an invitation to visit their country. The government of Ceylon followed with a similar invitation. This opened the way for me to visit Canadian Colombo Plan projects in South and Southeast Asia. Should I return via London or cross the Pacific? I had for some time been strongly urged by the Japanese ambassador to visit Japan for talks with his government and with textile, plywood and shoe manufacturers concerning the quotas on their exports to Canada. The circle was completed when I was advised to visit Singapore, Malaya, Thailand and Hong Kong. The entire world-girdling tour as planned would occupy seven weeks, and I wondered how I could possibly be absent from Ottawa for so long a time, particularly after spending two weeks in Montreal. Diefenbaker thought the trip offered too many advantages to be missed. Parliament was not sitting, and he himself was planning a similar tour of the Commonwealth countries of the world. Alice was included in all the invitations. Thus it was that she and I set forth on September 29 on a tour around the world. It proved to be one of the most instructive experiences of my life. Indeed, in itself it was a comprehensive education. What is more important, Canada undoubtedly derived benefit from it.

All of our visits to the various countries in Europe and Asia were of an official character. The local arrangements and the local program in each case were in the hands of the government of the country and the Canadian diplomatic representatives. This greatly facilitated every feature of our plans. Virtually everywhere we were guests, usually of the local government. We were accompanied by Grey Hamilton throughout. It was our first long trip together, and he proved himself enormously helpful. A Canadian minister simply cannot make an official visit abroad without the aid of an accompanying executive officer. Wynne Plumptre and Lou Rasminsky, accompanied by their wives, were with us for the annual meetings of the IMF and IBRD in India. Wynne joined me later as well for the trade discussions in Japan.

Our first visit was to Brussels, where we were the guests of the Canadian ambassador and Mrs. Charles Hébert. The World Fair had been open there for nearly six months and had but three more weeks to run before closing. Glen Bannerman, a classmate of mine at Varsity, was the commissioner in charge of the Canadian Pavilion. I had the honour of welcoming Princess Margaret on her visit to the Pavilion. She was in good spirits and was keenly interested in our exhibits.

Amid the round of dinners, luncheons, talks with notables, tours of the Fair, one other event stands out. It was a formal luncheon at the British Embassy attended by the Queen of the Belgians, Princess Margaret, Prime Minister Eystens and other eminent persons. Queen Elizabeth was the widow of the late King Albert, King of the Belgians, leader of the heroic Belgian resistance to the German invasion in 1914. I had the privilege of a conversation with her and Princess Margaret after the luncheon. I spoke feelingly to her of the debt the whole world owed to her late husband and the precious days that Belgian resistance had won for France and Britain in the month of August 1914, which I remember vividly. She seemed very pleased. She asked me if I knew Dr. Charles Best, the co-discoverer of insulin, and when I said he was a personal friend of mine she asked me to convey her message of greeting to him. That royal mission I was, of course, honoured to fulfil.

The next three days we spent in London as the guests of George and Fiorenza Drew. We were guests of honour at a reception given by my good friend Jim Armstrong, Ontario Agent-General, and Mrs. Armstrong, attended by a number of visiting Canadians, including Senator Salter Hayden. Doug and Fran Harkness were also present.

Next morning at Canada House I faced a press conference with about a dozen British correspondents. Their questions revolved mostly around the forthcoming New Delhi meetings, convertibility of sterling, trade between Canada and the United Kingdom, and the economic outlook. At noon the Lord Chancellor, Lord Kilmuir, gave a luncheon at the Dorchester on behalf of the British government in honour of Doug Harkness and myself. Among the very distinguished guests present was Kim (later Lord) Cobbold, Governor of the Bank of England, with whom I had an appointment for the afternoon. He conducted me on a tour of the Bank, including the vaults, where I was able to inspect the stock of gold bars. We reviewed the Montreal conference, the proposals for a Commonwealth Development Bank, Canada's recovery from the recession, the outlook for increased trade between Canada and the United Kingdom, export credit and the Conversion Loan. The Governor was very complimentary about the success of the loan operation. Indeed, I found the loan and the conference were well known in London, and I received many compliments on the success of both.

While at New Delhi for the IMF meetings we were the guests of Mr. and Mrs. Chester Ronning at the high commissioner's residence. The house was constructed in the form of a hollow square, and with the office building was enclosed in a compound. The garden was one of the most charming I have ever seen. It was flat, surrounded by tall trees and adorned with tropical flowers and singing birds.

The meetings of the Bank and Fund began on October 2 at the Vigyan Bhavan, a large air-conditioned building resembling the United Nations Assembly Hall in New York. Prime Minister Nehru opened the meeting with a welcoming speech. At noon I was a luncheon guest of the British high commissioner, Mr. Malcolm MacDonald, lately British high commissioner in Ottawa, and Mrs. MacDonald, whose home had been in Ottawa. I enjoyed a good visit with them. In the garden I saw my first mongoose, the enemy of snakes. The Chancellor of the Exchequer, Derick Heathcote-Amory, and the President of the International Bank, Eugene Black, were also guests. Eugene and I were destined to become very good friends. I developed a very high regard for him, as I did also for Per Jacobsson, managing director of the IMF.

Throughout the week of the meetings there was a very pleasant round of luncheons, receptions and dinners. The functions included a dinner given by the governor of the Reserve Bank of India in the sumptuous palace built by the Nizam of Hyderabad and expropriated by the government. Next day Alice and I were the guests of Mr. Nehru at a small luncheon at the official residence of the Prime Minister, which in the days of the British Raj had been the residence of the Commander-in-Chief. It is a handsome building with a large and beautiful garden. Twelve of us sat down to lunch. Mr. Nehru was assisted by his daughter, Mrs. Gandhi, who was later to succeed her father in the office of Prime Minister. They were charming hosts. Mr. Nehru was not a vegetarian, but we were introduced to some new and interesting Indian dishes. I sought information from Mr. Nehru concerning his work habits and learned that he gave his dictation in the evenings to relays of secretaries. His letters were typed and signed before breakfast. He slept regularly six hours per night. He previously had been accustomed to work until 2 a.m., but Mrs. Gandhi told me he was then making a practice of retiring at midnight. He looked very fit.

Mr. and Mrs. Ronning gave a reception and dinner in our honour. Among the political figures who came was Mr. Jain, the Minister of Food and Agriculture. I plied him with questions as to how agricultural production was being increased to feed India's growing population. I learned that after much effort production had been increased by 2 per cent over the previous year. He expressed profound gratitude for Canadian wheat provided by means of a loan from the Canadian government.

Morarji Desai, Minister of Finance, entertained us at lunch one day at his official residence. It was an imposing home with a beautiful garden. All ministers were provided with official residences. Another evening we were guests of Mr. Gbedmah, the Minister of Finance of Ghana, at a reception, and on another evening attended a farewell dinner given by Per Jacobsson in honour of my good friend Sir Arthur Fadden, Minister of Finance of Australia. Artie retired the following year. That was my last meeting with him.

The meetings went well. I delivered a short speech on the second day. I supported the proposal to increase the reserves of both the Bank and the Fund and said the increase ought to be not less than 50 per cent. Nobody else, even among those supporting an increase in principle, had ventured to name a figure.

I had a long conference with my good friend Bob Anderson, U.S. Secretary of the Treasury. He was much in demand, but we found we had so many things of mutual interest to discuss that what was to have been a twenty-minute meeting grew to forty-five minutes. I dashed off a report to Diefenbaker on this meeting.

The All-India 1958 Fair was officially opened in the middle of the week. It was the first exhibition of its kind organized in the eleven years since independence, and was the responsibility of the Minister of Finance. Morarji Desai made the opening speech, followed by Nehru, who opened his remarks in Hindi, then switched to English for most of his speech. Speaking before a mammoth crowd, and without notes, he reviewed India's progress since independence. I did not find him a rousing orator.

Mr. Sato, the Minister of Finance of Japan, discussed plans for my forthcoming visit to Japan. We quickly became friends and continued as such over many years. He was a man of destiny, later becoming Prime Minister of Japan. During the week I received an invitation from Mr. Fujiyama, the Japanese Minister of Foreign Affairs, for Alice and me to be his guests while in Japan. After consulting Fred Bull, the Canadian ambassador to Japan, we gratefully accepted. This did not affect the arrangements that we would stay at the Canadian embassy with Fred and Marjorie Bull as their guests, but it would give us the status of official guests of the government while we were in the country, and this would be of great advantage to us.

Plans in another direction underwent an abrupt shaking-up.

We had accepted the invitation to visit Pakistan as guests of the government, and were looking forward to going there the next week. On Wednesday we were dazed by the news of a political coup in Pakistan. President Iskander Mirza had abrogated the constitution, cancelled the pending elections and dismissed the cabinet with severe denunciations of ministers alleged to be guilty of intrigue, treachery and corruption. I saw Amjad Ali, who confirmed that he was no longer Minister of Finance, but was still a governor of the Bank and Fund and said he would remain at New Delhi until the conclusion of the meetings. He assured me that the coup should not be permitted to affect our plans to visit Pakistan. However, we soon became aware that a censorship had been imposed on outgoing news and messages from Karachi, the capital. The high commissioner for Pakistan to India also kept urging me to carry out our plans without change. All doubt was removed on Friday when he showed me a telegram from the president personally renewing the invitation. I was thus convinced that we should make the official visit as planned, and I so advised Ottawa by wire. The fact that the coup had been carried out by the head of state removed the diplomatic problem; had it been engineered by a revolutionary I could not have gone to Pakistan until the new regime had been formally recognized by the Canadian government.

The premier social event was a reception given that afternoon by the President of India, Dr. Rajendra Prasad, at his official residence, which had been the Viceroy's palace in the days of the British Raj. The Marquess of Curzon, Lord Willingdon and Lord Mountbatten had all lived there while serving as viceroy. It is a huge and imposing building, constructed around 1928 and designed by Sir Edwin Lutyens, who designed all the other government buildings and planned the new capital. The grounds, including the lawns, gardens and pools, are laid out after the fashion of the Mogul emperors of several centuries before.

There were two more receptions and a dinner in store for us the same evening. The first was held by the high commissioner of Ceylon in the garden of his residence. The trees were illuminated with coloured electric lights, and the scene resembled fairyland. For the reception by the Punjab National Bank the whole front of the Imperial Hotel and the trees to their tops were festooned with lights in varied colours. We received a very warm greeting from the chairman, who had visited Canada some months before.

The dinner was at the home of my dear friend Frank Anthony, MP, president of the Anglo-Indian community of the country. We had maintained communication ever since we met at the

Commonwealth Parliamentary Conference at London in 1948. Among many gifts which he and his wife Olive presented to us were two beautiful brass jars, a brass plate handpainted by Frank's cousin and entitled "The Old Birdman," and five small elephants carved in ivory, a token of good luck, one for each member of our family. All these generous and handsome gifts have graced our home ever since.

Our visit to India now entered a new and vastly different phase. We would see no more of the Bank and Fund celebrities, the country's political leaders, the throngs of ministers of finance, governors of Central Banks, senior civil servants, bankers and newsmen to whom we had become so accustomed. We were off to central India, to the city of Ratlam (pronounced "Rutlamm"), to spend the weekend with Dr. Bob McClure, the Canadian medical missionary, and his wife Amy. He had been sponsored in his years as medical missionary to China by Bloor Street United Church in Toronto, of which I was a member, elder, and former general superintendent of the Sunday School. I had driven his children, who lived near to us in North Toronto, to Sunday School every Sunday afternoon throughout the years of the war, while Bob was working to keep the Burma Road open and the Japanese put a price on his head. I had been with his father, Dr. William McClure, when that distinguished medical missionary celebrated his one hundredth birthday on April 9, 1956. We were very intimate friends, and now we were to have the privilege and joy of visiting Bob and Amy in the midst of their new life in India and observing Bob's work at his mission hospital in Ratlam. It seemed incredible.

From Delhi, we rode for thirteen hours in a private compartment in a modern air-conditioned train hauled by a Canadian locomotive, which had been a Colombo Plan gift from Canada. Our route took us across the great plain which lies south of Delhi. We were impressed by the contrasts between old and new, antiquated and modern. A warm welcome awaited us at Ratlam, and we spent two and a half happy days with Bob and Amy at their home in the Mission Hospital Compound. Everywhere we went in India both on the Ratlam visit and later in southern India we were garlanded with floral leis and presented with beautiful bouquets.

The next day was Sunday. In the early morning we listened to an unearthly screeching of birds, monkeys and other animals which abound in the neighbourhood. Church service was held at 8.30. Dress was simple – just slacks and a bush shirt. The service was conducted in Hindi and lasted an hour and a half in the presence of about three hundred people. The singing was hearty. At the conclusion of the service Alice and I were conducted to the front of the church and presented with a series of floral leis by the different organizations in the church as well as bouquets.

Ratlam is a city of 100,000 people. In driving through the main streets we dodged herds of cattle, buffalo and goats, as well as many bicyclists. One imposing building attracted my attention. It was a cattle orphanage donated by a Hindu who combined piety, wealth and philanthropy. It was noteworthy, however, that there was in the city no orphanage for children or home for aged persons. We saw cows walking into the front doors of homes. No one interfered with them. A dead buffalo's carcase was being fought over by vultures and a dog.

Next morning we paid a round of visits to a cotton factory, the Labour Union building, the strawboard factory and the Ratlam Degree College. The college visit was an unforgettable experience. I went there on the invitation of two students to speak on "International Finance" to what was expected to be an audience of about eighty students. To my surprise I was welcomed by several hundred students and their professors gathered out of doors. When I spoke several hundred other persons gathered outside the fence to listen. In the face of this audience I abandoned the announced theme in favour of a heart-to-heart talk to the students on the responsibility attaching to the privilege of education and citizenship and their duty to give leadership in the new India. I closed a speech of half-an-hour with some references to the value of membership in the Commonwealth. I was rewarded with a storm of applause. The students crowded about me seeking autographs or to shake hands. They pressed so tightly I could hardly sign any. We had great difficulty taking our departure. It was a thrilling and somewhat pathetic experience.

The afternoon tour took us to new government housing for the lowly railway sweepers, then to a fruit farm, then to a village. India is a land of villages as well as large cities. This experience I recorded thus in my diary:

> The third stop was at a very old village. We went first of all to see the new well which has been built for irrigation purposes. Water is drawn by means of a pump operated by a diesel motor where formerly bullocks drew it up by plodding around a wheel. The old headman of the village informed me that the headmanship had been in his family for 200 years. He offered us food, consisting of small cakes and chopped fruit. Another man used his jackknife to peel an apple for me. Heeding the admonition I had received against eating fruit which I did not peel myself, I was glad to settle

for a banana. I had not yet seen the village and asked to do so. It proved to be quite a sight. We threaded our way up a path frequented by cows and buffalo, and found a crowded circle of huts. A woman sitting on the patio in front of one with her baby when she saw us coming put down the baby and hurried into the house. I observed that the baby was about six months old and its face was covered with flies. There must have been 200 of them on the little face. We entered the house and found it consisted of two rooms, a small one for the use of the humans and a large one for the use of the cattle. Another door let to a pool of water which was covered with green scum.

I was invited to address the Rotary Club that evening. Bob informed me that it was the one institution in the city in which people of different faiths met and worked together. For the occasion the thirty-odd members had been permitted to bring their wives and friends. It proved to be the largest meeting in the history of the club, with over one hundred present. I addressed them on matters of government and finance of common concern to India and Canada. Bob had warned me that it would be imprudent at the meeting to refer to him as a missionary.

We departed from Ratlam next morning in the darkness on the 5.50 train. At the station we had trouble moving about the platform, which was covered by the forms of homeless persons sleeping on the concrete surface and even on the hand-trucks used in shifting baggage. Notwithstanding the hour and the darkness and the chill a number of Bob's friends turned out to say goodbye to us. We reached Mathura at 4.15 p.m., and there we were met by Chester Ronning with a motor car. It was just an hour's drive to Agra, the seat of government of the Mogul emperors of other days. Here we were the guests of the government and were accommodated at the residence on the government grounds, to which we were officially and warmly welcomed by two magistrates. We had a glimpse of the world-famous Taj Mahal in the twilight, but returned to it early the next morning. It is a dazzling sight, a tomb constructed of white marble, built by the Emperor Shah Jahan for his favourite wife and himself. It was commenced in 1631 and completed in 1648. Jewels and precious stones from various countries were originally inlaid in the marble in the most exquisite designs. We also visited the Red Fort, the famous seat of the Mogul emperors, the mausoleum of Itimad-Ud-Daula and the tomb of Akbar the Great. We had a feast of the beauty and splendour of Mogul architecture. By evening we were back in New Delhi at the high commissioner's residence after an absence of five days during which we had witnessed scenes which remain vividly etched on my memory twenty-five years later. My sleep that night was troubled by a strange dream of the court of the Emperor Shah Jahan. I was astonished to find that his Prime Minister was none other than John Diefenbaker.

On arrival at Karachi, capital of Pakistan, the next day we were greeted by our hosts, the Canadian High Commissioner Herb Moran and his charming wife Fran, three officials of the Foreign Department of the government, and the entire staff of the high commission and their wives. It was a royal welcome indeed. That evening the Morans held a reception in our honour attended by one hundred guests, including my friend Amjad Ali, no longer Minister of Finance, who I found had become very taciturn concerning the overturn of the government, and a former Prime Minister, Mr. Suhrawardy, who was much less circumspect in his comments. This was followed by a delightful dinner given in our honour by Amjad Ali at his home.

Karachi presented a striking contrast to New Delhi. It was very well laid out, with wide streets and relatively few animals. Its pre-Partition population of 300,000 had swelled to two million as the result of the influx of Moslem refugees from India. It is surrounded by an arid plain, and the heat was intense. It had been chosen as the capital of the new country because it was located at a safe distance from the border of India, whereas the attractive city of Lahore, though closer to the centre of the country, was only twelve miles from the Indian frontier.

The next day began with a conference with Mr. Hasnie, Permanent Secretary of the Department of Economic Affairs, discussing Colombo Plan projects, then a call on the President, Major-General Iskander Mirza, at his residence. He extended a warm welcome to me and expressed hearty gratitude for Canada's Colombo Plan aid. He denounced the activities of the politicians which had led him the week before to oust the cabinet. He assured Herb Moran and me that he would follow the same foreign policy as had prevailed previously and might tilt it more to the West.

Next followed a press conference during which I talked chiefly about Canada's Colombo Plan aid to Pakistan. Then ensued a call on General Mohammed Ayub Khan, Commander-in-Chief of the Pakistan army and martial law administrator. He also welcomed me warmly and expressed gratitude for Canada's Colombo Plan aid to Pakistan. In the uniform of a full general he was a striking figure, tall, handsome, with clear blue eyes and a ruddy complexion. Trained at Sandhurst, his vigour and directness were striking. I had been assured that he was a man of fine character. He informed me that he had no wish to take over power, but affairs in Pakistan had fallen into such a mess as a result of the follies of the politicians that, had he not intervened, the country would have fallen into a condition of irreparable misery. He derided the idea of giving the franchise to uneducated people. He demonstrated his determination to cut through red tape by instructing Mr. Hasnie to speed up the decisions on Colombo Plan projects. These had languished before my arrival.

At noon we were the guests of honour of the President and the Begum at lunch at his residence. The twenty guests included General Ayub Khan and half a dozen senior army officers. It was quite clear that they were devoted to the general. The afternoon being a holiday was devoted to relaxation. We drove twenty miles west of Karachi to enjoy a swim and tea with the staff of the Canadian high commission and their wives at a pleasant sandy beach on the Arabian Sea where the surf is heavy and the water has few equals in the world for saltiness. On our route back to the city we passed many new places of fine appearance and one miserable-looking refugee camp which emitted a stench which was almost sickening. The new government had issued an order that such conditions be cleaned up.

That evening we were the guests of General Ayub Khan at the official residence of the Prime Minister, into which he had moved only that day. The evening was warm, and the garden lovely, and he and I discussed the political and economic problems facing Pakistan and questions of defence and arms procurement. We exchanged expressions of goodwill on behalf of our countries.

The next morning, Saturday, October 18, we were off to Lahore, where we were to stay at the residence of the governor of West Pakistan. It was a handsome building of regal appearance, whose beautiful grounds included a fish pond and vast lawns. The first wing of the building was constructed in 1845; the last was added on the occasion of the visit of the Prince of Wales in 1923 and was occupied then by him. The Flemings occupied it in 1958. It included a large drawing room, dining room, bedroom, dressing room and bathroom, all in palatial style and proportions.

The governor, Mr. Akhter Husein, a short, pleasant man of most courteous manner, made us feel at home. We quickly wished we had more time to spend enjoying such comfort, but our program was not made for ease or relaxation. We were conducted on a tour of Lahore, visited the famous Shalimar Gardens built in 1642-43, and the tomb of his father and the fort, all built by Shah Jahan, the same Mogul emperor who built the Taj Mahal. The mosque at Lahore, which we visited, is the largest in the world. The governor personally conducted us on a tour of the grounds of the residence, at first on foot, then in a pony cart. The amenities included a school and hospital for the staff, who numbered nearly one thousand. We then drove five miles to have tea with Lady Noon, wife of the recently dismissed prime minister. Lady Noon had been born in Austria and raised in England. She was a friend of Roly and Norah Michener and had visited Toronto. During our travels in Lahore that day we passed the building of a very well-known newspaper, the *Civil and Military Gazette*. It was there that Rudyard Kipling pursued his journalistic career. We also passed Kim's Cannon, made famous by Kipling's rousing tale.

We left Lahore early the next morning and flew to Peshawar, the city of the north country. It lies in the foothills of the mountains. We were welcomed at the airport by officers of the air force and driven to the governor's residence. It was a handsome and commodious building about half the size of the governor's residence at Lahore. We simply dropped our bags and proceeded on our way on what was to prove a very exciting tour. It was a Sunday morning, and the air was cool. We were accompanied by a military convoy. After driving about the buildings of the University of Peshawar we headed for the Khyber Pass and the Warsak Dam. Little did I think when a boy reading Henty's tales of adventure in the famed Khyber Pass that I would one day be driving through it.

The Khyber Pass was the route of the conquerors from the north. It begins twelve miles from Peshawar and for twenty miles wends its way through low mountains and rocky hills to the border of Afghanistan. Forts and military lookout points at advantageous places are located along the tortuous route. At the first fort an interesting ceremony took place, of which fortunately I had been forewarned. There we found a group of about twenty-five headmen from the Pathan tribes lined up at the side of the road to greet us. They were tall, blue-eyed and wore full beards, some of which had been dyed red to show that the possessor had made a pilgrimage to Mecca. I went down the line shaking hands with each and exchanging greetings. Their spokesman then addressed me at some length in Pushtu, which is the Pathan language and is related to Persian. His words were translated by the commissioner who accompanied us. He expressed thanks for the aid which Canada was giving to the region in constructing the Warsak Dam and expressed the hope that Canada would assist Pakistan to obtain a just settlement with India in their dispute over control of the waters on which this area depends. He then presented to me two of the largest sheep I have ever seen and warmly invited me to visit their village. In replying to his speech I found that the spokesman understood English perfectly. I expressed my thanks to the headmen for their great courtesy in meeting us, for the gift of the sheep and for their invitation to visit their village, my gratification that Canada had been able to undertake provision of the great dam, my hope that it would be of immense benefit in providing electric power and irrigation for that large area, and my deep regret that because of previous plans I would not be able to visit their village. I therefore invited them to take my two sheep and feast on them back at the village. They accepted, and we parted with many handshakes and expressions of goodwill.

We passed other forts and along the way could see tribesmen with rifles standing stiffly at attention on rocky promontories as we passed. They were saluting me. These men, called Khassadars, formed an impressive sight. It is an honour passed on from father to son through many generations. These Pathan tribesmen are proud, self-reliant, brave and fiercely independent, as the long border wars with British troops testify. General Ayub Khan is a Pathan. From time to time we saw carved into the solid rock on the side of the road the coats of arms of famous British and Indian regiments which had fought there for the protection of India. We drove right to the border of Afghanistan, where I inspected the guard supplied by the Khyber Rifles Regiment.

A few miles from the Afghan border we stopped at regimental headquarters, where we were to be guests for lunch at the officers' mess. At Herb Moran's thoughtful request the regimental pipe band in kilts was on hand to play a program of Scottish music. As we entered the compound the band struck up "The Bonnets of Bonnie Dundee." That was the regimental tune of the Galt Kilty Band of my boyhood. Here I had come half way around the world to hear the same stirring air. I was thrilled. It was played again at our departure.

At the fort where we had been welcomed by the Pathan headmen in the morning we were now met by Canadian officials of the Warsak Dam, headed by the project manager, E.L. Miller, and the construction manager, Cory Robbins. The construction of the dam was an enormous undertaking. I had been much involved in it officially and had some conception of its magnitude, but it proved to be a more massive work of man and nature than I had imagined. Located nineteen miles from Peshawar, a vast canyon had been cut through the rocky hills. A force of three hundred Canadians and ten thousand Pakistanis was at work on it. The task had commenced from scratch three years before, and was due to be completed in eighteen months' time. By that time it would irrigate 125,000 acres and generate 240,000 kilowatts of power. I inspected the project from both sides of the canyon, then visited the buildings which had been constructed, including the well-equipped hospital and the club-house, where a reception in our honour was held, thus giving us the opportunity to meet all the Canadians.

We returned to Karachi the next day to find it enveloped in a dust storm which penetrated everywhere. The temperature was 99 degrees, and the humidity was very high. We would experience no more cold air on our trip, for we were about to travel south and east. We were off early next morning, Tuesday, October 21, first to make a formal call on the Chief Minister of the state government of Bombay, then to drive through the teeming city and twelve miles beyond to Trombay, where we were greeted by Canadian officials and inspected the Canada-India Atomic Reactor and the adjacent plant where thorium was being processed from monasite sand. We crossed the harbour and inspected the famous Elephant Caves, which contain a Hindu temple carved out of solid rock thirteen hundred years ago. The heat was the severest we encountered on our entire journey around the world.

We enjoyed our visit to Bombay, while regretting its brevity. It is a great city, and deserves its claim to be called "The Gateway to India." Next to Calcutta it is the greatest commercial metropolis of India, and is the principal port on the west coast. It then had a population of four million people. Its growth was built on cotton in just two hundred years.

We next visited Madras, a well-designed city with broad avenues and many fine buildings, some of which show the Portuguese influence of earlier days. It is the third city of India, with a population of two million. Those who live in the south claim it is "the real India." The people are smaller and darker than those in the north. The weather is much hotter, and the clothing is scantier. I held a press conference and addressed a dinner attended by leaders in the business and financial life of Madras. Our sightseeing was fascinating in this historic city. Sir Robert Clive was governor here, Sir Arthur Wellesley (later the Duke of Wellington) lived here in 1798, as well as Elihu Yale, then a writer, who later founded Yale University. Curiously, it is not the custom in Madras to mix men and women at large dinners. Alice therefore was separately entertained on the evening of my speech.

The language of south India is Tamil, and it is from south India that the Tamil part of the population of Ceylon (now Sri Lanka) is drawn. There is a tradition that St. Thomas visited Madras, and a large hill just outside the city is named after him. The tradition draws support from the fact that when the Portuguese first came to this area they found Nestorian Christians.

Next morning, Friday, October 24, we bade farewell to India after spending a total of fifteen days in that fascinating subcontinent. A large group of friends and government officials were at the airport to see us off. We were twice garlanded with beautiful gilded leis before taking off for Ceylon. Everywhere in India we had been received with kindness, and everywhere we had found the old and the new side by side. I wrote at the time: "India is a land of innumerable contrasts. One sees evidence of new energy at odds with ancient lethargies. India faces tremendous problems. One will be the reconciliation of the democratic idea of equality with the Hindu caste system, which is still very strong. The high birthrate is neutralizing many of the efforts that are being made to improve the standard of living as 5,000,000 new mouths are added to the population each year." I was amazed to learn that I am the first Canadian Minister of the Crown ever to visit south India.

I was not the first Canadian minister to visit Ceylon, but I was the first Canadian Minister of Finance ever to do so. We were welcomed at Colombo airport by the Canadian high commissioner, Nik Cavell and Mrs. Cavell, and the Minister of Finance, my friend Stanley de Zoysa and his wife, and, to our great surprise, by Wynne and Beryl Plumptre, who had been detained as the result of a strike on BOAC. We drove to the residence of the Prime Minister, S.W.R.D. Bandanaraike, where we were to be guests of the government. It is a lovely estate with a beautiful garden, all surrounded by a high wall, located within a mere four-minute walk of the ocean. I called on the Prime Minister and had a long talk followed by tea. We discussed the need of stabilization of markets, prices of agricultural products and the effect of GATT. He was much concerned over the drop in prices of Ceylon's primary products, including tea, rubber and coconut. A tour through Colombo quickly convinced me that the British influence and the use of the English language are much stronger here than in either India or Pakistan. Indeed, Gandhi once referred to the Ceylonese in disgust as "black Englishmen." At a dinner that evening I met a number of political leaders and was happily surprised to meet again Siddiq Ali Khan, whom I had met at the Commomwealth Parliamentary Conference in Nairobi in 1954. He had become high commissioner for Pakistan and dean of the diplomatic corps.

The next morning we left for Kandy, to be the weekend guests of the Governor General, Sir Oliver Goonetellike. Our drive to it took us through the hills, past rice paddies, coconut groves, rubber and tea plantations. During the drive I absorbed a fund of information from Nik Cavell concerning political and economic conditions. It was not all reassuring. The island has resources, a fertile soil and an equable climate, but progress was being slowed down by labour troubles, low prices of exports and rifts in the government coalition.

Sir Oliver gave us a hearty welcome. We found him a very genial and polished host. He had some stories to tell about Lord Mountbatten, who made his headquarters in Ceylon at one period during the Second World War. Government House, where we stayed, was a fine building over one hundred years old, with a beautiful garden of tall trees and bright flowers. We went to see the famous Royal Botanical Gardens at Peradeniya. They are as beautiful as any I have ever seen, and contain many varieties of trees and flowers. Orchids are cultivated in the greenhouse as a specialty. There were 250 varieties and literally thousands of blooms. Kandy is in the midst of the tea-growing country, and we visited tea estates and tea factories before returning to Colombo. The program on Monday was varied, including visits to the offices of the Aerial Survey, with a Canadian in charge, a fish refrigeration plant built with Canadian Colombo Plan aid, a fish market, a luncheon with the cabinet, a meeting with the staff of the Canadian high commission, inspection of a technical school built with Canadian aid, a formal farewell call on the Governor General, and a press conference.

A seven-hour flight brought us to Singapore, where we were the guests of Sir Robert Scott, the United Kingdom Commissioner-General for Southeast Asia, at his residence, and our program was in the able hands of the Canadian trade commissioner, Mr. M.P. Carson. We found Singapore an impressive and thriving city of one and a half million people, of whom 86 per cent were Chinese. It was for this reason that the Malayan population of Malaya would have no political union with Singapore. I held two press conferences. I met and conversed with all the political leaders either at a luncheon at the Raffles Hotel or at a nine-course Chinese dinner at the Adelphi Hotel. At the latter I met Mr. Lee Kuan Yew, who soon after became Prime Minister of Singapore on its attaining independence. He was a graduate of Cambridge and only thirty-four years of age. I found him, as did the other Canadians present, very argumentative, glib and cocksure of himself, but he has given Singapore stable and competent government.

On our arrival at Kuala Lumpur, the capital of Malaya, we were met by Sir Henry Lee, Minister of Finance, and Mr. A.R. Menzies, the Canadian high commissioner. We were guests of the government at the Federal Hotel. Kuala Lumpur is a young city, presenting a western appearance, with a population at that time of just 350,000. Tigers roamed eighty years before where the city stands. In the absence of the Prime Minister I met the Deputy Prime Minister, Dato Abdul Razak, a coming strong man. As Minister of Defence he was responsible for combatting the terrorists, and had been successful in greatly reducing the extent of their operations. We made a formal call on their Majesties Tuanku Abdul Rahman and his consort, who received us very graciously. Under the new constitution of the federation he had been elected king for a five-year term by the other sultans.

Mr. Tan Siew Sin, Minister of Commerce and Industry, who had attended the Montreal conference, entertained us at lunch, and Sir Henry Lee held a dinner in my honour at his home. At both functions I met all the political leaders.

Our next stop was Thailand. We arrived in Bangkok at 11 p.m., but even at that hour were met by Mr. C.V. Narasimhan, the Executive Secretary of the United Nations Commission for Asia and the Far East, and Mr. Grieve of the British embassy. The paths of Mr. Narasimhan and myself were destined to cross significantly in the future. He was a brilliant and charming Indian. Alice and I were made welcome and comfortable at the residence of the British ambassador, Sir Richard Whittington, a descendant of the famous Dick Whittington. I had misgivings about our visit to Thailand, as a revolution, led by Field Marshal Sarit, had taken place just a fortnight before, and there were no ministers left. However, we managed well enough under the circumstances. Perhaps ministers are not so indispensable after all. It was the second coup which had occurred on our trip, fortunately without bloodshed in either case. It was a lesson in political stability.

The next day Alice and I visited the royal palace and nearby the famous Temple of the Emerald Buddha, both of striking Siamese architecture of the late eighteenth century. The temple is one of the most beautiful and ornate of all Buddhist temples in Southeast Asia. I conferred with Mr. Narasimhan and his senior United Nations staff concerning the Mekong River Project, for which Canadian aid was being sought. It involved an aerial survey and development of the river with the cooperation of Thailand, Laos, Cambodia and Vietnam. Alas! war soon destroyed these fair hopes and much more.

I was entertained at lunch by Dr. Serm, the Acting Minister of Finance, and conferred with him and officials of his department and the Central Bank of Thailand. The economy of Thailand was strong. It had no problem of over-population or religious intolerance. Of its twenty million people seventeen million were Thais and principally farmers; the other three million were Chinese, and merchants or traders. The soil is fertile, and the standard of living considerably higher than that of surrounding countries.

We rose a little reluctantly at a very early hour the next day to take a three-hour sightseeing boat trip up the Cambodia River during which we saw the famous "floating market." Many merchants in small boats laden with fresh fruit and vegetables ply the canals stopping at the houses to sell their merchandise. Later I enjoyed an instructive chat with Sir Richard as to the political situation in the country. A dinner that evening given by him and Lady Whittington in our honour at the embassy and attended by senior government officials completed our program, which had been relatively relaxed, thanks in part to the revolution. We were off at a very early hour by Japan Air Lines to Hong Kong. We flew over the Mekong River, mountainous Laos, Vietnam and the South China Sea, arriving at our destination at noon.

What is commonly known as Hong Kong actually consists of the island of Hong Kong and Kowloon, which is the tip of a peninsula and is located on the mainland. The harbour is a bowl surrounded by hills, some of which rise to a height of eighteen hundred feet. The island and Kowloon are linked by a ferry which accomplishes the crossing in six minutes. The population is largely Chinese, and was then growing rapidly as the result of the flood of refugees from Communist China, creating serious housing problems. Otherwise the appearance of the colony was completely Western.

We were met at the airport by C.J. Small, the acting Canadian trade commissioner, and airport officials. We were to stay at the Peninsula Hotel on the Kowloon side.

The next morning (Tuesday, November 4) I performed a solemn act of remembrance at the Sai Wan Military Cemetery on the north side of the island, facing toward Kowloon. There I laid on the war memorial a wreath in the form of a maple leaf in silent tribute to the 281 Canadians who gave their lives in the defence of Hong Kong against the Japanese attack in December 1941 or who died in prison camps later, and who are buried there. The cemetery is located on a hillslope looking down over the harbour in a scene of incredible beauty. We then proceeded to Stanley Military Cemetery, an old military cemetery on the south side of the island, where nineteen Canadian soldiers lie buried. It was a source of great satisfaction to see both these cemeteries kept in immaculate condition. At Sai Wan the Canadian graves are assembled in a group. At Stanley they are scattered among the graves of other soldiers from Commonwealth countries who died in defence of Hong Kong. I identified the graves of Brigadier John K. Lawson and Colonel Patrick Hennessy, the two senior Canadian commanders, and on my return to Ottawa wrote letters to their widows to tell of the wreath-laying and to describe the cemetery. I received touching replies from these ladies. The photograph taken of my laying the wreath was subsequently published on the cover of *Torch*, the publication of the Canadian Legion.

At noon we were guests of the Governor, Sir Robert Black, and Lady Black at luncheon. After a tour of the island I did a TV program for the Canadian Broadcasting Corporation. Later Mr. and Mrs. Small held a reception in our honour at the Hong Kong Club, attended by about one hundred guests, including government officials and representatives of the leading banking and commercial interests in the colony.

The next day we toured the mainland. Of its total area of 391 square miles only 33 are under outright British sovereignty. The remainder constitute what are known as "The New Territories," which in 1898 were leased by the government of China to the British government. We drove through the New Territories along winding roads and over high hills in the most delightful scenery for twenty miles until we entered a closed area adjacent to the Chinese border. There we were provided with a police escort and drove to the border, which at this point was a narrow river crossed by a railway bridge on the line connecting Kowloon and Shanghai. We walked across the bridge to the barricade where we found ourselves being glowered at by a Chinese Red soldier on sentry duty on the other side. He fully reflected the hostility of his government at that time toward the West. On the way back we took the opportunity to observe farming methods and visited a textile plant. There was little time left for shopping in this shoppers' paradise.

Hong Kong is well named "the jewel of the Pacific." It was the most charming place we saw on our world tour. The scenery is beautiful; the harbour will accommodate the largest ships in the world in large numbers; the place is free of insects; the colony is efficiently governed; the police force is one of the best in the world; and our three-day visit coincided with glorious weather. We flew out the next morning to Tokyo.

We were given a most flattering welcome on our arrival at Tokyo Airport. The Canadian ambassador, my esteemed friend Fred Bull, and his wife Marjorie were there, with Mr. Fujiyama, the Minister of Foreign Affairs, and other officials of the Japanese government and the Canadian embassy. The drive between the airport and the Canadian embassy normally occupies one hour, but even in the rush-hour traffic our police escort whisked us there in the record time of twenty minutes. That was a sample of the considerate treatment we received throughout our fabulous five-day visit as guests of the government.

The Canadian embassy was then regarded as the finest in Tokyo and the best of Canada's diplomatic buildings abroad. The residence and the chancery were conveniently contained within the compound. We were made most comfortable in a suite at the residence. But at 8 a.m. Tokyo experienced an earthquake. In the seismic count it registered three. It was my first experience of an earthquake, but it was not to be the last. The trouble is that one never knows how long the quake will continue. I was hopelessly unprepared for this one. In fact, I was sitting on the toilet when the whole building began to sway. I was mortally embarrassed by the grim thought that my body, dead or alive, would be exhumed in these circumstances. However, after several good lurches the swaying ceased. I was able hastily to complete the task and with a great sense of relief to extricate myself from the unpleasant situation.

Alice and I enjoyed breakfast privately in our suite, then I proceeded to the chancery, where I met each member of the staff of thirty-five. Our first call was at the Imperial Palace where we signed the book. The building is actually only the chancery, the Imperial Palace having been destroyed as the result of bombing during the war. Emperor Hirohito unselfishly determined that the palace should not be rebuilt until the people's housing problem had been solved. Tourists were permitted within the palace grounds, where peasants were to be seen at work rendering voluntary service. Fred Bull informed me that there is a waiting list of two years of applicants for this honour.

Meetings followed with the Prime Minister, Mr. Kishi, and Mr. Fujiyama at their respective offices. We discussed political and commercial relations between Canada and Japan. At noon Mr. Sato, Minister of Finance, entertained us at lunch. Here I encountered an interesting Japanese custom. The Japanese were all seated on one side of the table, the Canadian guests on the other. It results in less turning of heads sideways in conversation. The place cards were written on both sides and stood in a vertical position, the name of the guest written in Japanese facing the Japanese hosts, the names of the Japanese hosts written in English facing the Canadian guests. It is an admirable system where two languages are involved. After lunch Mr. Sato and I strolled through the charming garden. He showed great interest in the success of our Conversion Loan.

In the afternoon we met with Mr. Takasaki, Minister of International Trade and Industry. We came to grips with numerous outstanding commercial problems, and our talk was most satisfactory. Mr. Takasaki took a very understanding view of the Canadian position, for while the balance of trade between the two countries was favourable to Canada in aggregate terms, the Japanese exports to Canada were of labour-intensive manufactured goods, whereas Canada was selling Japan primary products such as wheat and coal. Moreover, Japanese exporters were concentrating on a limited range of products, such as textile goods, hardwood plywood, rubber-soled canvas footwear, and these were already having devastating results for our domestic producers. Therefore, we were compelled to insist that the Japanese government apply quotas on exports of such goods to the Canadian market, and these were negotiated each year between the two governments. The system left the Japanese government exposed to pressure from Japanese producers in search of export markets. Mr. Takasaki pressed us for early extension of the facilities in the harbour of Vancouver for bulk loading of ores in order that Japan might increase her direct purchases of ores from Canada. We were also interested in enlarging the sale of Canadian coking coal to Japan.

Later I held a press conference at the embassy. It was attended by no fewer than forty representatives of the press, and was carried on through an interpreter. Inevitably it featured trade relations between the two countries, and I dwelt on the problems I had discussed earlier with the minister and our determination to solve them amicably. A reception in our honour as guests of the Canada-Japan Society and the Canada-Japan Trade Council followed. It was attended by Canadians resident in Tokyo and Japanese members. Prince Tokugawa and Mr. Ito, presidents respectively of the two societies, received with us, and the Prince delivered a very kind address of welcome to which I replied.

We were up at 5.15 the next morning, which was a Saturday, to commence our tour of the Kansai area, the Japanese industrial heartland. Our tour was conducted by Ambassador Yoshida and Prince Tokugawa. We could not have wished for better auspices. We arrived at Nagoya after a ride through a pleasant countryside, past Mount Fuji and a succession of gardens, rice paddies, and tea and orange groves. Nagoya, a city of one and a half million people, had been a munitions centre during the war and had been destroyed by bombs and fire. It was completely rebuilt after the restoration of peace. On arrival I held a press conference, following which we were entertained at a luncheon by Mr. Kuwahara, governor of the prefecture (or province), Mr. Kobayashi, the mayor of the city, and Mr. Sasaki, president of the Nagoya Chamber of Commerce and Industry. It was a delightful function. In the afternoon we visited three industries, Nihon Toki Company, producers of the famous Noritake china, Toyo Plywood Company, manufacturers of hardwood plywood and pianos, and Ando Shippo Shop, makers of cloisonné vases and other artistic creations. I was deeply impressed not only by the invariable courtesy extended to us but by the fact that these industries were operating on Saturday and maintaining a six-day work week not merely for the production line but for the office staff as well. Everybody we happened to see in these factories was really hard at work.

We moved on to Kyoto, the former capital of Japan and centre of the country's ancient culture, and stayed there for the remainder of the weekend. We visited ceramics plants and museums of art, the Katsura Palace, built three hundred years ago, the Kinkakuvi Temple with its beautiful golden pagoda, restored after being destroyed during the war, and took part in the ancient "Urasenke" tea ceremony established four hundred years ago as a sort of cult which claims 200,000 disciples. The ceremony was quaint. It had a tranquilizing effect, and maybe I needed some of that.

One thing happened at noon that day which touched me deeply. Two men arrived unannounced from Kobe, representing

Mr. K. Nozawa, a merchant who was importing asbestos from Canada and had a son studying in Canada. The two men had come to present me on behalf of Mr. Nozawa with an incense-burner, called a Goshoguruma, three hundred years old. It is a beautiful little objet d'art. To me it typifies not only Japanese art but also Japanese earnest desire for friendship with Canada, of which I witnessed so many convincing proofs.

Osaka, Japan's second largest city, with a population then of four million, was the last and most impressive of the Kansai cities included in our tour. It is a great industrial centre and the heart of the textile industry. We first visited the Kanebo Yodogawa cotton mill, impressive in the quality and artistic beauty of its products and the degree of automation in its production. The next meeting was my major engagement of the Kansai tour. It was with the Japan Cotton Spinners Association. It brought me into direct contact with a large assembly of heads of the textile industry who were seeking assurance that their exports to Canada would not be curtailed. I talked very frankly to them and answered their questions through an interpreter.

Our final event in Osaka was the inaugural meeting of the Canada-Japan Society of the Kansai. My arrival was greeted by the playing of "O Canada," and I was given a very warm welcome. I delivered a message of greeting and goodwill to the society.

We returned to Tokyo in the late afternoon for a dinner given in our honour by Fred and Marjorie Bull at the embassy. The guests included the two senior ministers, Mr. Fujiyama and Mr. Sato, and their wives, the ambassadors of Pakistan, Australia and India, and other distinguished Japanese and Canadian guests. Fred Bull had established a leading position in the diplomatic circle in Japan. I had come to feel thoroughly at home among our Japanese friends.

Tuesday, November 11, was our last day in Japan. Alice and I were received in audience at the Imperial Palace by the Emperor and Empress. It was a culminating privilege of our visit to Japan. We dressed informally for the occasion. Their Majesties are charming, natural people, and they received us most cordially. The audience, instead of lasting twenty minutes, as expected, lasted forty. For the first thirty the Emperor talked with me through an interpreter, while the Empress chatted with Alice; for the last ten minutes His Majesty talked with Alice and the Empress with me. His Majesty was very much interested to hear of my impressions of Japan and especially Japanese industry. He was pleased with my reply. He was very interested in moving pictures as a hobby, and I had earlier presented to him two films produced by the National Film Board depicting seasonal scenes in Canada. The Emperor referred to these films, praised them and thanked me for them. The audience was a highlight of the world tour.

Was it a mere coincidence that on Remembrance Day at the hour of 11 a.m. I was the guest of the Emperor of the country whose leaders had treacherously plunged the entire Pacific into war at Pearl Harbor and whose army had inflicted unspeakable cruelties on Canadians and their allies? I think not. For there was an almost sacramental quality in the quiet, earnest and supremely friendly conversation between four of God's children in that room in the palace at Tokyo on the fortieth anniversary of the armistice of 1918, when the bugles blew their ceasefire and quiet descended over the western front and over the heroic dead. Could that thirteen-year-old lad blowing a bugle in the Galt Collegiate Institute Bugle Band in the victory parade on November 11, 1918, ever have dreamt that forty years later to the day he and his wife would share the committed joys of turning swords into plough-shares and spears into pruning hooks in Japan?

The Bulls, the Plumptres, Grey Hamilton, and the Flemings had found great enjoyment in each other's company throughout those five memorable days in Japan. Sharing such an experience was to me a bond among us which has proved an enduring blessing. My diary records our sendoff that afternoon at the Tokyo Airport in these words:

> A beautiful bouquet of flowers was presented to Alice on behalf of the Nisei Society, composed of persons of Japanese race who have lived in Canada. More than twenty persons were on hand to see us off, including Mr. Fujiyama, the Minister of Foreign Affairs, and his wife, Prince Tokugawa, officials of the Japanese Government and of the Canadian Embassy. It was the warmest sendoff imaginable. We have experienced five wonderful days in Japan which could never be forgotten. Everywhere we have been treated with the utmost kindness. Everywhere there have been evidences of anxiety for good relations with Canada. Mr. and Mrs. Bull have obviously rendered notable service in representing Canada in Japan.

After thirty-eight days in Asia we were on our way home. Our first stop was at Wake Island, the scene of one of the major naval battles in the Second World War. Another 2,300 miles brought us to Honolulu for a couple of days' rest. Here we were entirely on our own for the first time since leaving Ottawa – no appointments, no program, no ministers, no ambassadors, no lodging at

Government House or embassy, no servants to unpack us. Grey Hamilton rented a car, and we spent four hours driving about the island of Oahu with him. The second day I visited Pearl Harbor, scene of the infamous Japanese attack on Sunday, December 7, 1941. Two wrecked battleships remain: the USS *Arizona*, which sank in twenty minutes after being hit, and carried 1,102 men to a watery grave, and the USS *Utah*, which went down with 58 men. The other ships that were sunk were later refloated.

We flew overnight from Honolulu to San Francisco, where we were met by Mr. Christopher C. Eberts, Canadian consul general, and Mr. Douglas Hicks, the consul, early on Friday morning, November 14. From our hotel I telephoned my office in Ottawa to arrange for our arrival in the capital on Sunday and a press conference on Monday. At Mr. Eberts' luncheon we met the Canadian television actor Lorne Green.

Saturday we went sightseeing and reading newspapers to catch up with the news. We took off at midnight and were back in Toronto by noon the following day. There to our delight many friends had gathered to welcome us home. David and Mary were there with Alice's father, her sister Margery and husband Don Tow, sister-in-law Aileen Watson, our close friends Ewart and Jorie Fockler, and our future son-in-law Don Wilson. Bill Allan was there with about twenty of our Eglinton faithful. It was the happiest of homecomings. The press were on hand for photographs and an interview.

On November 16 the 28th flight of our world tour brought us to Ottawa and a final welcome home. Donald was there, and Ken Taylor, the Plumptres, who had returned from Tokyo by a more direct route, and Emil Simonsen among others. It was cold. The press and TV were on hand, and the TV interview was conducted out-of-doors. Home looked good to me.

On Monday morning I held a press conference attended by twenty members of the press gallery. One of them amazed me after my strenuous tour, loss of sleep and time-adjustments by describing me as "rested, refreshed and reassured." I devoted an hour to an account of my 35,000-mile journey and answered questions for another forty minutes. I stressed the strategic importance of South and Southeast Asia, and noted the high respect enjoyed by Canada in all countries there. I defended Canada's contribution to Colombo Plan aid on humanitarian, political, practical and business grounds respectively as follows:

- We cannot shut our eyes to starvation on the other side of the world.

- We must do something to offset Communist pressure on Southeast Asia; we just cannot ignore it.
- Much of the money for Colombo Plan aid is spent in Canada, for the goods and equipment we give them.
- These nations of Southeast Asia could provide us with enormously productive markets.

I was proud of Canada's diplomatic representatives in the countries I visited. They were all representing Canada worthily and ably, and were winning ever-increasing goodwill and esteem for Canada. They included some men of outstanding capacity. All of them considered that my visit had done much good in the country to which each was accredited. No mistakes had been made, no diplomatic faux-pas; on the contrary, I had, they assured me, created much goodwill for Canada. In this task Alice had been immensely helpful and quietly effective. Diefenbaker later brought back confirmatory reports from these countries as to the value of the strenuous efforts I had put forth. These had been of significant service to Canada.

I returned to find that my friend Walter Crocker, Australian high commissioner to Canada, had been moved to India as high commissioner there. I wrote him at once. His gracious reply, dated November 26 from New Delhi, contains the following:

> I am much touched by your letter of 18 November. Any good feelings you have about me are more than reciprocated by my good feelings about you. In all countries men in public life who, in addition to political competence, combine intellect and character are rare. You struck me at once not only by your mien of an athlete and your manifest physical stamina but also by something that is not as common in Cabinet Ministers as it should be – both the necessary mental capacity and the necessary self-discipline to master the technical job of your office. You also have the courage of a fighter.
>
> And may I say a word about Mrs. Fleming. There, if ever, is a person who was not to be deceived by the glitter of the world and who would not bow to the powers and principalities.

God bless Walter Crocker!

CHAPTER FORTY-EIGHT

Farewell to 1958

Nineteen fifty-eight was a year of major experiences and extraordinary events: the general election with its landslide victory, my first budget, the Conversion Loan, the Commonwealth Trade and Economic Conference, and my trip around the world. No year in my life surpassed that succession of formidable and unique happenings. Later years lacked the romance of 1958. But even these unforgettable events had less influence on my life from day to day than the saddening change which came over the domestic scene in the middle of the year.

We had made our home at 259 Glencairn Avenue since August 1939. We loved it. The house was well constructed and of excellent appearance. Its location was unsurpassed. Our neighbours were our friends. I loved the garden and particularly its profusion of roses and peonies. It was the only house in which Mary and Donald had ever lived; it was the only one that David remembered. Their playmates were all close neighbours. In nineteen years our roots had gone very deep there. The election victory resulted literally in a severe uprooting. For a year Alice managed two houses, but it was too much for her and too expensive for me. Of necessity we faced a grim decision, to sell the house and move to Ottawa. Parting with our home was the hardest thing I had ever had to do. It filled me with genuine sorrow. I raised the price above the figure proposed by the agent and told him I hoped he would not find a buyer. Within a couple of days he produced an offer from a friend of mine at my figure. In leaving that home in the summer of 1958 I left behind a family life which I have never fully recovered since as the family grew up.

We rented a fine home in Ottawa in Rockcliffe Park on Juliana Road from Commander W.P. Hayes of the Royal Canadian Navy. It was a split-level bungalow, which was to be our home for three years until his return from a tour of duty at sea, and we were very happy there. I had a library on the lower floor where I did my night and weekend work. David was at Guelph, attending the Ontario Agricultural College, Mary in residence while attending University College of the University of Toronto, and Donald at Ashbury College, then at Lisgar Collegiate, and later at school in Montreal. We were together only for parts of the summers and for the principal holidays.

But if the move resolved my housing problem in Ottawa it left me with a major housing problem in Toronto. I had always stayed close to my electors. My residence was always within easy reach of them by telephone or in person. Now that was all changed. By degrees I arrived at a makeshift solution with the aid of the proprietor of the Glenview Terrace Apartments. I could not afford to rent one on a full-time basis, so he agreed to rent me one whenever I was in Toronto and take telephone calls for me on his switchboard during my absences. I thus maintained an answering service in Toronto, but this was not enough. I found my Eglinton executive expecting me to continue to make frequent appearances in the riding, and this became increasingly difficult. I was better able to concentrate on my duties in Ottawa – and these made ever greater demands on me – but I was able to present myself in my riding correspondingly less and less. This worried me and it disturbed my riding workers. In 1958 I went three months, at another time six weeks, without setting foot in Toronto. It became serious enough that a meeting was held to discuss the problem one evening in Eglinton. I had to explain to my well-meaning friends that I was carrying the heaviest and most exacting of all portfolios and that the only way I could increase the time spent in the riding would be by asking the Prime Minister to assign me a lighter portfolio. Bill Allan as my executive secretary provided effective liaison with the riding, but my personal appearances were missed, and I undoubtedly suffered a cooling of political support in consequence. A fundamental change had come over my life.

Another change brought about a break with the past in its own sphere. On July 26 I participated in a cabinet decision to sell the University Avenue Armouries to Metropolitan Toronto as the site of the new courthouse. It was a very appropriate use of the property, but I was sad to see the Armouries demolished. From them thousands of brave Canadians had marched off to face death on battlefields in distant lands. Through its portals General Malcolm Mercer, head of the firm in which I served as an articled law student, had marched at the head of the Queen's Own Rifles, my regiment, in August 1914, later to give his life at the

Battle of Sanctuary Wood. Within those same walls I had trained in the Second World War, and the Queen's Own Rifles officers' mess on the second floor I still loved to frequent when opportunity offered. Only the memory remains.

On my return from my world tour I plunged into an accumulation of problems and labours. None of the financial problems had solved themselves in my absence. The Prime Minister was abroad on his tour of the Commonwealth countries and did not return till December 15. By that time I was in Paris. I did not see him from September 22 until December 20. On November 27 I gave the cabinet a full report on our financial and budgetary position. The success of the Conversion Loan had strengthened our position greatly and just in the nick of time. The bond market on the North American continent had weakened considerably in the meantime. Our Canada Savings Bond campaign had gone remarkably well, but market pressures were closing the long end of the market to new issues. The four categories of the new Conversion Loan bonds had all sold off substantially. The rise in yields was not the result of a tight money policy, for the Bank of Canada had considerably expanded the money supply in the last sixteen months. Holdings of government securities by the chartered banks in the last year had increased by $1,343 million, and the Bank of Canada had been obliged to increase its holdings by $234 million to take up sales by the public. As to the budget, my forecast of the deficit for the current year was likely to prove correct. The outlook for the following year, however, was worse. With estimated revenues of $5 billion, departments had submitted estimates of expenditure totalling $5.9 billion. A deficit of $900 million would alarm the public and shake their confidence in the value of their dollar. It would be a political disaster and would compel an increase in taxation. A reduction in the estimates was essential. The cash needs of the government to the end of April were $800 million, to be followed by a maturity of $400 million on July 1. Cabinet authorized an issue of $400 million in two tranches, both short maturities: (a) 3 per cent due in one year priced at 99¼ to yield 3.77 per cent; and (b) 4 per cent due in four years priced at 98¾ to yield 4.34 per cent.

The market response was the weakest since we had taken office. For the first issue the subscription totalled $401 million, and for the second $111 million. It was evident that the dealers would receive a much larger allotment than they expected, and this would mean a weak after-market. I gave my colleagues a lecture on the growing dangers of inflation and the threat of inflation hysteria. In December I was authorized to increase the Treasury Bill issue.

Cabinet approved larger than proportionate increases for Canada to subscribe to the capital of the IMF and IBRD. These increases were, however, non-budgetary; they involved no borrowing or increase in the public debt. They also increased our borrowing potential.

I referred in an earlier chapter to the cabinet's embarrassment over appeals to it from decisions taken by the Board of Transport Commissioners allowing general increases in railway freight rates and telephone rates. These proceedings had been stalled by a series of orders by cabinet suspending the increases, but the issue had now to be faced. The appeals were both heard in November by a large committee of cabinet. The increase in the telephone rates was allowed. The proposed 17 per cent general increase in freight rates was a more far-reaching problem, and cabinet turned to the idea of paying a subvention to the railways to mitigate the increase. I strenuously resisted this proposed solution and other similar ones as a raid on the Treasury, which had already quite enough claims upon it. In the end cabinet authorized a subvention of $20 million per annum as a temporary measure to reduce the 17 per cent increase to 10 per cent pending a complete review of freight rates. I warned that the subvention was based on no principle and politically could not be withdrawn.

Federal-provincial fiscal relations would not long remain silent. The Liberals were naturally desirous of casting themselves in the role of champions of the provinces after we had succeeded in occupying that position and turning it to our advantage in the general election. If a federal-provincial conference was called the provinces would be sure to come to Ottawa asking, and no doubt expecting, a larger share of the yields from the shared fields of taxation. On the other hand, not to call them together would invite criticism from the Liberals in the House and from the provinces. On one point, I considered that the provinces had enjoyed much the better of the federal government. In those provinces to which the services of the Royal Canadian Mounted Police were supplied under contract the cost was being divided between the two levels of government, 60 per cent borne by the federal and 40 per cent by the provinces. The latter ought to have been paying more like two-thirds of the cost. Admittedly, there were some intangibles to enter the reckoning, and we did not wish to be too abrupt in seeking a more realistic division of cost, but with the support of Treasury Board I persuaded cabinet to seek renewal of the contracts on a 50-50 basis. That was still generous to the provinces.

In my absence on October 23 cabinet considered the calling of a federal-provincial conference for January or February. By December 9 Dief thought it should be delayed as long as possible. This to me made sense because the state of the Treasury would not admit of any increase in the provincial share of the yield from the personal income tax. Les Frost was pressing hard and insistently for more money or a resumption of the 1957 conference. He was supported by the premiers of Newfoundland, Saskatchewan and Manitoba. In the end cabinet decided against reconvening the conference at that time, but agreed instead that the Prime Minister should write the premiers promising that legislation would be introduced to continue for another year the payment to the provinces of the yield from the three additional percentage points of the personal income tax, as in the current year. There the matter stood until I opened up the subject with the provincial treasurers the next spring.

In mid-December I joined George Pearkes and Sid Smith in attending the annual meeting of the NATO Ministerial Council in Paris. This assembly did not have the glamour of the one held a year earlier which had been attended by the heads of government of the member countries, but it produced some highly important results. The Russians had critically aggravated the situation in Berlin, and that acute problem overhung the deliberations of the council. Khrushchev had made proposals that would have turned Berlin into a Russian satellite. These were firmly rejected. It was claimed that the Russians had been kept out of the Middle East; obviously that claim at best was only temporary. To me the most remarkable feature of the entire meeting was a statement made by John Foster Dulles in the course of the discussion of Russian tactics about Berlin. Speaking calmly and very deliberately, and with no notes, Dulles said that if the Russians attacked Berlin it might mean the destruction of Western Europe with nuclear weapons, but the moment the Russians attacked the United States would release its retaliation forces and could and would destroy all of Russia. He thought the Russians knew that. Henri Spaak, Secretary-General of NATO, said that since the Second World War there had been no greater threat to peace than the Berlin situation. It was stated that the German ground forces would soon be the largest in NATO. It was the last NATO meeting attended by John Foster Dulles, and it was the last time I saw him. He died the following May of cancer.

Advantage was taken of the presence of so many ministers in Paris for the NATO meeting to hold a meeting of ministers of the Organization for European Economic Co-operation (OEEC), the structure which had been created to funnel U.S. Marshall Plan Aid to the countries of Western Europe after the war. It had attained growing importance as a channel of economic cooperation among the countries of Western Europe, and the United States and Canada had been admitted as associate members. This was my first personal contact with an organization which was shortly to be transformed into the OECD, the Organization for Economic Co-operation and Development, in which the United States and Canada were to be full members, and in which I was destined to play a leading role. There were some shocks for a newcomer attending his first OEEC meeting. The British and French disagreed so openly and so strongly that threats had been uttered. No solution had been reached, and the meeting had been adjourned to January. The Chancellor of the Exchequer had asked the Canadian delegation if our government would use its influence with the French to persuade them to be more accommodating. This was asking quite a bit of a French government headed by De Gaulle.

Four by-elections were held between the 1958 and 1959 sessions. Three were won by Conservative candidates. The fourth, held in Toronto-Trinity on December 15, was won by a Liberal, Paul Hellyer, a former minister in the St. Laurent government, by a plurality of a mere 751. It was the first seat yielded up by the government since its victory in March, and was bound to happen at some time. The fate of the government was not at stake. A government with 208 seats in the House could hardly claim that it needed another. On the other hand, the need to strengthen the opposition was all too obvious.

The same kind of thinking was emerging in other quarters. More and more the press was showing sympathy for the Liberals in the House. The Grits were so weak in numbers and so lacking in debating strength that it was natural enough for the press to see them as the underdog and wish to give them a helping hand at times or to curb the power or abate the successes of a government possessing overwhelming strength. Diefenbaker in his days in opposition had enjoyed model relations with the press, which were much envied by other members. After our landslide victory in 1958 those relations seemed gradually to weaken and deteriorate. I had no reason to believe the alteration was due to any change of attitude on his part so much as to an understandable shift in sympathy on their part. But it did occur, and I well know that Diefenbaker was aware of it and concerned over it. He had become the constant subject of the cartoons in the press. Indeed, he was said to be the cartoonists' delight, for his features lent themselves to exaggeration. The Liberal prime ministers never were made the butt of cartoons in the way and to the extent that Dief was. I think that subtly the same feeling entered the mind of the Speaker. When Diefenbaker was criticizing him for not being firm with the Liberals I think that, consciously or unconsciously, he was bending over backwards to protect the Liberals against any appearance of oppressive use of its powers by our government. The arbitrary use of its powers by the St. Laurent–Howe government was fresh in his mind.

It is opportune now, as it was natural then, to engage in stocktaking at the end of the year 1958. We had been in office for a year and a half. Though we did not then know it, one-quarter of our ultimate course had been run. The political honeymoon was over. The electorate had given us the strongest mandate ever given to a government; it expected results. We had fulfilled our election promises. We had revived and strengthened Parliament. Diefenbaker's personal stock was very high, and he was concerned at all times to maintain his national popularity, perhaps too concerned. He was quite willing to accept full credit for the government's victory at the polls. The country was contending with recession and unemployment. How long could we continue to place the blame for all these woes on the Liberals? They had made no plans at the governmental level to cope with unemployment, but how long would the man-in-the-street, particularly if unemployed, accept that fact as a sufficient excuse for the continuance of unemployment? Major problems faced us; others were in the offing. Nearly all of them had financial implications and complications.

What of myself? I was aware that my personal prestige stood high, more so perhaps abroad than at home. I had gained experience of extraordinary value, and with it confidence. I had also gained an increased measure of control of fiscal policy, but I was still having difficulty with my colleagues in obtaining their approval and their understanding of the cost of borrowing. I was receiving far less assistance from them and from the Prime Minister than I needed, particularly in resisting expenditure. I found myself constantly at odds with them and far too often playing a lonely role in rejecting expenditures we could not afford. It was impossible for us to make ends meet then, but I never lost sight of that goal or weakened in my determination to achieve it. Diefenbaker was loud in his praises of my loyalty, but these generous encomiums were invariably uttered in the presence of no one but the two of us. My relations with Coyne and the Bank of Canada had steadily improved, and there were glimmerings of a better relationship with the press. Next to Dief himself I drew attention frequently from the cartoonists. In fact I derived great amusement from the cartoons about myself and acquired the original drawings of some of the best of them. Best of all were my relations with the senior civil service. I knew I had won their respect and confidence, and this to me was profoundly gratifying. I had come through as exacting an experience as any minister in Canadian history, and my physical endurance and stamina were unimpaired. They needed to be, for stiff and persistent problems and difficult decisions awaited us.

Index

556

Blenheim Palace, London, 238
Bloor Street United Church,
    Toronto, 42, 64, 193, 528
BNA Act, 115-16, 141, 181, 200-201,
    213, 252
BOAC airline, 536
Board of Trade, Galt, 460
Boddy, Margaret, 59
Bombay, 535
Bonavista-Twillingate riding, Nfld.,
    248
Bond Market in Canada, The, 503
Bonn, 219
Borden Royal Commission, 407-408,
    410, 432
Borden, Henry, 75, 100, 407, 432
Borden, Sir Robert, 9, 33, 73, 74,
    75, 115, 243, 477
Boston, 66, 148
Boucher, Lucien, 326
Boucher, Russ, 170
Bourgault, Julian, 522
Bourinot, Mr., 247
Bourque, John S., 469
Bowles' Lunch, Toronto, 52
Bracken, Mrs., 104, 146
Bracken, John, 94, 97-99, 104, 106,
    124, 128, 129, 135, 136, 137,
    138-39, 140, 146, 169, 171, 174,
    177, 178, 325
Bradford, Dalton, 51
Bradford, Hannah, *see* Wright,
    Hannah
Bradford, Samuel, 51, 52, 53, 54
Bradley, Gordon, 173
Brampton, Ont., 268
Brandon, Man., 203
Brantford, Ont., 178
Brandenburg Gate, Berlin, 165
Bray, Ernie, 84-85
Brebner, Dr. James, 16, 39-40
Breen, Joe, 44
Breules Gold Medal, 48
Bridges, Frank, 125
Britannia Mines, B.C., 411-12
British Insurance Companies Act,
    409, 432
British Columbia, 122, 132, 150,
    222, 241, 412, 422, 477
British East Africa, *see* Kenya
British North America Act, *see* BNA
    Act

British United Press, 217
Broadcasting, Committee on, 247,
    283-84, 468
Broadview riding, Ont., 185
Brooke, Mrs., 268
Brooke, Oliver, 268
Brooke Bond & Co., 268
Brooks, Alf, 262, 281, 364, 456
Brown, Harold, 43
Bruce, Dr. Herbert A., 98, 308
Brunt, Bill, 145-46, 344
Brussels, 164, 520, 522, 523-24
Bryce, Bob, 345, 358, 381, 388, 434
Buckingham Palace, 152, 153-54,
    238, 436
Buffalo, N.Y., 57, 66, 148
Buffs Regiment, 167
Bulgaria, 95, 157, 181
Bull, Fred, 365, 470, 526, 541, 542,
    544, 545
Bull, Marjorie, 526, 541, 544, 545
Bumstead, Ruby, 348
Bundesrat, the, 219
Bundestag, the, 219
Burke, Edmund, 74, 75
Burns, Ron, 381
Burrill, Mr., 103
Business Men's Noonday Bible Club,
    Toronto, 64, 182
Byers, Reeve, 76, 77
Byng, Lord, 75

Cadet Corps, 33, 69
Cahan, C.H., 93
Calcutta, 535
Calgary, 66, 211, 268
California, 441
Callaghan, Morley, 53
Cambodia, 539
Cambodia River, 539
Cambrai, France, 96
Cambridge, 152
Cambridge, Ont., 17
Cambridge University, 152, 538
Cameron, Professor, 42
Cameron, Colin, 314-15
Campbell, Mrs. H.G., 110, 344
Campbell, Hugh, 414
Camp Fortune, Ont., 367
Campney, Ralph, 222-23
Canada Cement Co., 44
Canada Council, 335, 428

Canada House, London, 150, 152,
155, 217, 238, 437, 470, 524
Canada-Japan Society, Osaka, 544
Canada-Japan Society, Tokyo, 543
Canada-Japan Trade Council, 543
Canada Savings Bonds, 374, 413,
428, 495, 499-500, 506, 550
Canada Shipping Act, 233
Canada Southern Railway, 57
Canada-U.K. Continuing
Committee, 353
Canada-U.S. Joint Committee on
Defence, 413, 442
Canada-U.S. Joint Committee on
Trade and Economic Affairs, 258,
380, 385-86, 393
Canada-U.S. Joint Committee on
Trade and Economic Matters, 427,
441, 442, 477
Canada-U.S. Joint Economic and
Trade Committee, 249
Canadian Allied War Relief Fund,
159
Canadian and Catholic
Confederation of Labour, 402
Canadian Army, 224-32 *passim*
Canadian Army Service Corps, 32
Canadian Army Works Service,
224-25, 226
Canadian Bankers Association
(CBA), 141, 349-50
Canadian Bar Association, 66, 202,
212
Canadian Bar Review, 58
Canadian Broadcasting Act, 200, 236
Canadian Broadcasting Corporation,
see CBC
Canadian Canoe Association, 60
Canadian Chamber of Commerce,
483
Canadian Club, Ottawa, 275
Canadian Club, Toronto, 101, 274
Canadian Corps of Signals, 80
Canadian Economic Outlook, 447,
507
Canadian Encyclopaedic Digest, 58
Canadian Farm Loan Act, 493
Canadian Insurance Companies Act,
409, 432
Canadian Labour Congress, 402, 483
*Canadian Law of Motor Vehicles,
The*, 53

Canadian Legion, 540
Canadian Manufacturers'
Association, 483
Canadian Military Mission, Berlin,
165, 166, 219-20
Canadian National Exhibition,
Toronto, 15, 69, 87, 153
Canadian National Institute for the
Blind, 368
Canadian Pacific Express Co., 45
Canadian Pontifical College, Rome,
163-64
Canadian Post Office, 262-63
Canadian Press (CP), 240
Canadian Railway Cases, 58
Canadian Society of New York, 406
Canadian Wheat Board, 505
Canadian Wheat Board Act, 131
Canadian Woman's Army Corps,
223
Canterbury, 166, 238
Caouette, Réal, 118
Cape Breton, 507
Cape Town, 266-67, 272
Cardin, P.J.A., 105, 116-17, 144
Carleton riding, Ont., 170
Carlyle, Thomas, 47
Carrick, Don, 275
Carscadden, Dr. Thomas, 36-37
Carson, M.P., 537
Carter, Janet, 36
Carter scholarship, 37
Cartier, Sir George Etienne, 144,
489
Case, Mr., 499
Case, Garfield, 102
Casselman, A. Clare (Cass), 105,
198, 285, 468
Casselman, Jean, 468, 522
Castro, Fidel, 385
Catherwood, Mr., 214
Caucus, 11, 135, 169-70, 174, 179,
207, 243, 249, 257, 286, 332-33,
343-44
Cavell, Mrs., 536
Cavell, Nik, 536, 537
Cavendish Laboratory, Cambridge,
152
CBC, 112-13, 120, 200, 235-36,
283-84, 296, 311, 336, 354, 405,
500, 540
CCF, 94, 100, 102, 103, 120, 131,

1st Battalion, 69
First World War, 21, 29, 31-33, 57, 62, 96, 171, 224, 477, 528
Fisher, Joe, 140, 215
Fisheries, Department of, 125, 222
Flaherty, Francis, 53
Flamand, Mrs., 240, 244
Flamand, David, *see* Fleming, David
Flamand, Chrysostome, 240, 244
Fleischer, Cyprianna, 12
Fleming, Alice Mildred Watson, 60, 61-64, 67, 69, 70, 77, 82, 101, 106, 140, 146, 147, 148, 150, 174, 184, 191, 210, 238, 241, 273, 284, 288, 310, 311, 345, 352, 360, 362, 363-64, 369, 385, 401, 402, 436, 438, 478, 485-86, 489, 523, 525, 526, 529, 538, 539, 541, 544, 545, 547, 548
Fleming, Barbara, 12
Fleming, Bruce, 49
Fleming, David, 18-19, 25, 73
Fleming, David, Jr., 63, 64, 69, 71, 163, 184, 191, 215, 362, 363, 546, 548, 549
Fleming, Donald, Jr., 63, 64, 71, 184, 191, 215, 362, 363, 546, 548, 549
Fleming, Elizabeth Plews, 18, 25
Fleming, Ethel Phillips, 49
Fleming, Gordon, 19, 22-23, 26-27, 28, 32, 34, 49, 67
Fleming, Gordon, Jr., 49
Fleming, Hilda Lee, 49
Fleming, Jeane, 49
Fleming, Louis Charles, 17, 18, 19, 28, 32, 33, 34, 35, 36, 39, 40, 45, 53, 56, 63-64, 70, 73, 288
Fleming, Margaret, 49
Fleming, Mary, 63, 64, 67, 69, 71, 184, 191, 215, 311, 362, 363, 546, 548, 549
Fleming, Maud Margaret Wright, 15-16, 17, 18, 19, 21, 28, 32, 35, 39, 40, 41, 53, 70, 71, 73, 91, 106, 273, 288-89
Fleming, Paul, 49
Fleming, Robert (Bob), 17, 19, 22, 26, 27, 32-33, 36, 49, 58, 288, 344
Fleming, Robert, Jr., 49
Fleming, Stuart, 50
Fleming family, 24-29, 39-40, 53, 62, 63, 64, 71, 110, 137, 140, 167,

184, 191, 215-16, 273, 288, 334, 345, 356, 360, 362, 363-64, 434
Flemming, Hugh John, 418, 422-23
Florida, 407, 459
Flynn, Jacques, 452
Fockler, Ewart, 43, 61, 63, 343, 546
Fockler, Marjorie, 61-62, 343, 546
Folies Begére, 434
Food and Agricultural Organization, 515
Forbes, Marjorie, *see* Fockler, Marjorie
Foreign Exchange Control Act, 126-28, 133
Forsey, Eugene, 170, 314
Fortin, Louis, 521, 522
Fort Jesus, Kenya, 270
Fort William, Ont., 66, 93, 426
Foster, Sir George, 348-49
Foulkes, General Charles, 414, 508
Fournier, Alphonse, 230, 247
Fournier, Sarto, 209, 514
Fowler, Patricia, 12
Fowler, Robert, 295
Fowler Commission, 295, 335-36
Fox, Charles James, 75
France, 31, 32, 155, 220, 223, 433, 434-36, 464
Fraser, Blair, 136, 367
Fraser, Rev. J. Keir, 53
Fraser, Neil, 53
Fraser, Peter, 151
Frederika, Queen (of Greece), 156-58, 160, 163
Freemasonry, 65-66, 422
Free Press (London), 355
Free Press (Winnipeg), 366, 493, 501
Friedensburg, Dr. F., 165-66
Frost, Cecil, 95
Frost, Leslie, 169, 326, 419, 422, 423, 444, 463, 552
Fujiyama, Mr., 526, 541, 542, 544, 545
Fullerton, Douglas H., 503
Fulton, Davie, 105, 108, 112, 139, 205, 207, 213, 214, 227, 232, 249, 251, 262, 301, 303, 305, 308, 310, 313, 319, 325, 327, 329, 334, 346, 360, 380-81, 395, 405, 457, 472, 497-98

Gaby, Mr., 354
Gagnon, Onesime, 175-76, 309, 469

568

Laver, Bert, 88
Lawrence, Allan, 143, 145
Lawrence Heights, Toronto, 295
Lawrence Park Collegiate, Toronto,
81, 124, 191, 363
Law Society of Upper Canada, 50,
55, 56, 57
Lawson, Mrs., 540
Lawson, General John K., 540
Lawson, Dr. Smirlie, 44
League of Nations, 68, 270
League of Nations Society, 66
Le Devoir, 143-44, 183, 253
Lee, Sir Frank, 383, 387, 390
Lee, Sir Henry, 387, 511, 538
Legendre, Roland, 240
Leger, Jules, 370-71, 381, 434
Leger, Cardinal Paul Emile, 163-64
Legislation Committee (Toronto), 86
Le Lacheur, Marjorie, 314
Le Matin, 283
Lemay, Tracy, 89
Leningrad, 86
Leonard, Darcy, 290
Le Pan, Douglas, 517
Lesage, Jean, 113, 187, 247, 428,
443, 521-22
Lewis, David, 404
Lewis, W.A., 515
Liberals, 18, 62, 73, 76, 92, 94, 103,
113, 120, 143, 144, 171, 172, 173,
177, 178, 186, 196, 205, 206, 214,
230, 241, 254, 291, 299, 301, 303,
308-309, 312, 316, 317, 338,
339-40, 365, 366-67, 373, 384,
391, 404-405, 422, 425, 426, 428,
430, 432, 443, 444-48, 452,
455-56, 457, 459, 463, 467, 468,
469, 472, 488, 492-93, 507, 522,
554
Liberal Federation of Canada, 498
Lido, Paris, 434
Lintott, Sir Henry, 387, 517
Lismer, Arthur, 46
Little France, Scotland, 149
Livingstone, Sir Richard, 152
Lloyd, Harold, 47
Lloyd, Selwyn, 406
Loch Lomond, Scotland, 149
Loch Story, Scotland, 149
Loggia of Raphael, Rome, 164
London, 58, 123, 147, 148, 150-51,
152-53, 155, 166, 167, 168,
217-18, 238, 266, 273, 286, 346,
351, 353, 355, 377, 378, 390, 433,
436-38, 442, 469, 470, 513, 514,
518, 524
London, Ont., 246
Londonderry, Ireland, 149
Longstaffe, Mr., 241
Lorne, Marquis of, 153
Lotbinière riding, Que., 18, 240
Louis Philippe, King (France), 312
Lovink, Tony, 275
Low, Solon, 150, 398, 426, 446, 447
Lowe, Rev. John, 152
Lucan, Earl of, 266, 268, 270
Lusaka, Rhodesia, 271
Lutyens, Sir Edwin, 527
Luxembourg, 70
Lynch, Charles, 430
Lytton Park, Toronto, 193

Macdonald, Mrs., 525
Macdonald, John, 347
Macdonald, Sir John A., 113, 144,
145, 294, 297, 335, 349
MacDonald, Malcolm, 151, 270, 525
Macdonald, Ross, 178, 237
Macdonald, T.L., 387
Macdonnell, Jim, 23, 94, 95-96, 99,
110-11, 127, 130, 136, 143, 178,
185, 210-11, 227, 243, 250, 284,
298, 304, 306, 312, 324, 325, 333,
342, 343-44, 360, 438
Macdonnell, Marjorie, 23-24, 438
Macdougall, Mrs., 318
Macdougall, John, 318
Macgregor, Ken, 358, 472
Macintyre, Donald, 387, 511
Mackay, Colonel J. Keiller, 77, 407
Mackendrick, Dr. Harry, 32
Mackenzie, Ian, 105, 119, 123,
125-26
Mackenzie King Era, The, 295-96
MacLean, Angus, 203
Maclean, Coulter, 92
Maclean's, 136, 367
Macmillan, Harold, 266, 378, 406,
433, 474-76, 477, 487
Macmurchy, Angus, 48
Macnaughton, Alan, 472
Macnicol, John R., 93
Macpherson, Murdo, 92, 95, 97, 98,

South African War, 19
South America, 282
South House, *see* Devonshire House
South Korea, 189-90
South Waterloo riding, Ont., 45
South York riding, Ont., 132, 170, 178, 201
Spadina riding, Toronto, 290
Spaak, Paul Henri, 435, 474, 552
Sparrow II missile, 414-16
Spaulding, Dr., 78
Spearman, Alex, 153
Spence, Charlie, 327
Spence, Paul, 215, 241
Spence, Wishart, 48, 53, 54, 55-56
Spithead, Eng., 238
Spotton, George, 76
Stalingrad, 86
Star-Phoenix (Saskatoon), 493
Sri Lanka, *see* Ceylon
Stanfield, Robert, 177, 422, 464
Stanley Military Cemetery, Hong Kong, 540
Stanstead riding, Que., 114
Starr, Mike, 215, 342-43
Steele, Ernie, 347
Stevens, Harry, 97, 98
Stevenson, John A., 286-87
Stirling, Grote, 132
Stirling, Ont., 77
Stockholm, 164
Stone, Tommy, 473-74
Stratford, Eng., 238
Stratford, Ont., 246
Strong, Mrs., 268
Strong, Maurice, 268
Student Christian Movement, Toronto, 44
Succession Duty Act, 291, 409, 430
Sudan Interior Mission, 192
Suez Canal, 327, 406, 441, 475
Sulphur Springs, Colorado, 464
Supply, Committee of, 228-31, 373, 426-27, 431, 449
Supreme Court of Canada, 53, 56, 58, 179, 264
Supreme Court of New Brunswick, 215
Supreme Court of Ontario, 53
Supreme Norad Command, 464
Surveyer, Dr. Arthur, 200
Sweden, 155

Swift, Jonathan, 166
Syria, 406

Taj Mahal, 530
Takasaki, Mr., 542
Tanganyika, 270, 271, 511, 516
Tariff Board, 129, 385, 411-12, 487-88, 491
Taxation, 119, 127, 129, 173, 194, 201, 223-24, 252-53, 283, 290, 291, 292, 293, 337-38, 355, 408-409, 421, 423, 427, 429-31, 443, 454, 483, 487, 489, 490-91, 505, 550, 552
Taylor, Ken, 348, 349, 352, 381, 388, 455, 484, 493-94, 495, 496, 497, 508, 540
Telegram (Toronto), 48, 107, 140, 215, 250, 262, 287-88, 451
Templehof Airport, W. Germany, 219
Temple of Cerces, Greece, 158
Temple of the Emerald Buddha, Bangkok, 539
Tennessee Gas Transmission Co., 410
Thailand, 523
Thatcher, Ross, 309
39th Infantry Brigade, 269
Thorneycroft, Mrs., 436
Thorneycroft, Peter, 153, 354, 379, 385, 387, 388-89, 390, 392, 436, 442, 475
Thurlow, Lord, 269
Tilley, W.N., 58
Tilney, C.E., 511
Todd, Garfield, 272
Todd family, 272
Tokyo, 541-43, 545, 546
Tokyo Airport, 541
Tokugawa, Prince (Japan), 543, 545
Tolstoy, Leo, 74
Tomb of the Unknown Soldier, Athens, 156, 159
Torch, 540
Toronto, 10, 15-16, 33, 39, 51, 54, 63, 65, 76, 77, 80, 85, 94, 108, 109, 154, 167, 176, 184, 192, 193, 207, 235, 238, 261, 263, 286, 311, 325, 330, 341, 343, 352, 353, 363, 364, 366, 367, 407, 438, 453, 459, 463, 528, 546, 549
Toronto Bible College, 192